LAND, MOBILITY, AND BELONGING
IN WEST AFRICA

D1557760

PLACE IN RETURN BOX to remove this checkout from your record.
TO AVOID FINES return on or before date due.
MAY BE RECALLED with earlier due date if requested.

DATE DUE	DATE DUE	DATE DUE
JUL 2 9 2015		
0 4 15 1 5		
FEB 2 1 2016 111 3 1		
FEB 21 3622019		
0 JUL 12 28 2020		

5/08 K:/Proj/Acc&Pres/CIRC/DateDue.indd

LAND, MOBILITY, AND BELONGING IN WEST AFRICA

Carola Lentz

Indiana University Press

Bloomington and Indianapolis

This book is a publication of

Indiana University Press
Office of Scholarly Publishing
Herman B Wells Library 350
1320 East 10th Street
Bloomington, Indiana 47405 USA

iupress.indiana.edu

Telephone orders   800-842-6796
Fax orders   812-855-7931

Manufactured in the United States of America

Cataloging-in-Publication Data is available
from the Library of Congress.

ISBN: 978-0-253-00953-1 (cloth)
ISBN: 978-0-253-00957-9 (paper)
ISBN: 978-0-253-00961-6 (ebook)

1 2 3 4 5 18 17 16 15 14 13

Contents

Illustrations

Tables

Maps

Preface

Pᴀʀᴛs ᴏғ ᴛʜɪs book were written, or rather rewritten, after I had become increasingly critical of earlier drafts, during a sabbatical year at the W. E. B. Du Bois Institute for African and African American Research at Harvard University in 2008–9. While struggling to reconceptualize the book's central narrative, and how I could make the very rich, but also overly complex and local material from remote corners of Ghana and Burkina Faso more interesting for a broader readership, I often interrupted desk work with a stretch of jogging along the Charles River that traverses Cambridge. Many times had I run past a memorial stone at Sir Richard's Landing and in passing glanced at its inscription, until one day it dawned on me that this stone had everything to do with the stories of African "first-comers" and founders of settlements over which I was musing. The stone had been placed on Cambridge lands by inhabitants of the neighboring city of Watertown, and its inscription read:

> Here at this river's edge, the settlers of Watertown led by Sir Richard Saltonstall landed July 30, 1630. Here, Reverend George Phillips' protest in 1632 against taxation without representation struck the first note of civil liberty heard in this wilderness. All of the territory from Sparks Street to Mount Auburn bridge, originally a part of Watertown, was annexed to Cambridge in 1754. Erected by the Historical Society of Watertown, 1948.

Here, carved in stone, was an American version of a first-comer narrative, invoking arguments to boost territorial claims and assertions of property that resonated very much with my West African interlocutors' contentions. The amateur historians of Watertown wanted to remind all passersby that their ancestors, and not the later Cambridgean occupants, had been the very first persons to discover and set foot on this land. Of course, they failed to mention any Indian inhabitants who might have happened to live in the area prior to Sir Richard's landing—a typical strategy of first-comer narratives that implicitly define who belongs to the potential claimants while completely silencing the claims of others. As if this were not enough, the authors of the inscription added that discovery and occupation were followed by an important political act, namely taming the "wilderness" and thus taking a leading role in preparing the road to American democracy. Almost two hundred years had passed since the land originally owned by Watertownians had been "annexed" by Cambridge—a turn of phrase that insinuates an illegitimate act—and yet some Watertown patriots felt impelled to set the historical record right by erecting a commemorative stone that memorialized their moral right as first-comers to the territory they later lost.

African village elders and earth priests, when they wanted to convince me (and others) of their legitimate property rights or of the injustice they had suffered in being dispossessed of land, presented very similar claims of discovery, first possession, and taming of the wilderness into which their ancestors had moved. And although they did not erect commemorative stones with lengthy inscriptions, my African interlocutors, too, pointed to landmarks, such as rivers, hills, rock outcroppings, or remarkable trees, where specific events were supposed to have taken place and that now served as mnemonic devices, a kind of *aide-mémoire*, to support the stories. In some places, annual communal hunting expeditions to these landmarks and walks along the village boundaries, interspersed with sacrifices, kept the villagers' memory of the settlement history alive and transmitted this knowledge to the younger generation.

In the savanna hinterland of Burkina Faso and Ghana, where the modern state has not yet established any written registers of land titles, the settlement narratives, and the commemorative practices that punctuate them, serve as a kind of oral land registry. For the local population, the question of who owned the land is inextricably tied to the issue of who came first. The often contradictory details of hunter narratives and other stories of founding a settlement that so bewildered me during fieldwork—and that my interlocutors found so important—aim at determining whose ancestors were the first to establish themselves in a place, how those perceived as late-comers were incorporated or excluded, and which rights the purported first-comers had transferred to later immigrants. Violence and coercion certainly were, and sometimes continue to be, important for gaining access to and appropriating land, but they alone cannot ensure long-term, uninterrupted use; the latter needs to be strengthened through building consensus. Convincing narratives of the origins and subsequent transfers of property are central to bringing about this consensus. The validation of first-comer narratives in the face of rival claims, on the other hand, depends on which public authority and which supporting networks the competing parties can rally. Authority and power thus play as decisive a role in property dynamics as persuasive narratives do. And, as the Watertown/Cambridge rivalry reminds us, the politics of property necessarily involve politics of social belonging—that is, struggles over whom to count among the first-comers and how to define the relevant property-holding community and its relations to outsiders.

The present book is the result of many stays in Ghana and Burkina Faso, most of which were organized in the context of the Special Research Area 268 on the "West African Savannah" at Goethe University, Frankfurt/Main, and funded by the German Research Foundation. I greatly benefitted from joint travels and stimulating intellectual exchange with my research team, comprising Richard Kuba, Volker Linz, Michaela Oberhofer, Katja Werthmann, and Andrea Wilhelmi. I owe thanks to the Institute of African Studies at the University of Ghana and to the Département d'histoire et archéologie of the University of Ouagadougou, who kindly acted as host institutions for our team during fieldwork. I am also very grateful to the local research assistants who have worked with me over the years, and who tirelessly accompanied me even to the remotest of the more than seventy Dagara and Sisala villages in which we documented the various lineages' migration-and-settlement narratives: the late Samuel Tigwii Amoah, Simon Hien, Isidore Lobnibe, Sylvain Poda, and Grégoire Somé. Furthermore, I enjoyed the hospitality and support of a great many Ghanaians and Burkinabé, only a few of whom can be mentioned here. First and foremost, I wish to thank my Dagara hosts who took me into their fold and adopted me as early as 1987 into their Kpiele patriclan, the large Bemile-Meda family, and particularly two of my "brothers," the late Bartholemew Bemile and Sebastian Bemile, for their love, friendship and encouragement. Great thanks also go to my "mother's brothers" of the Bekuone patriclan, the family of the late Gaston Hien, who eventually enticed me to build a small house in Ouessa (Burkina Faso), near the Ghanaian border, and thus "root" myself more firmly in the very landscape whose history and current predicaments I was exploring. During research stays on the Ghanaian side of the border, Nandom Naa Dr Charles Imoro was always a most warm and gracious host, as were the late Lambussie Kuoro K. Y. Baloro and his son Tong Baloro, and the late Lawra Naa Abuyifaa Karbo. Last but not least I would like to express my gratitude to several colleagues from Burkina Faso and Ghana, the late Claude Nurukyor Somda as well as to Kojo Amanor, Pierre-Claver Hien, Benjamin Kunbuor, Georges Madiéga, Magloire Somé, Alexis Tengan, and Edward Tengan, who shared my passion for migration narratives, settlement history, and land rights, and who were often willing to discuss my findings and offer their invaluable insights.

The writing of this book has had a long history that was supported by various sabbaticals. The Netherlands Institute for Advanced Study in the Humanities and Social Sciences (NIAS) at Wassenaar offered, during the academic year 2000–2001, a congenial setting for the painstaking analysis of my interviews and field notes, and for exceptionally stimulating discussions of my findings with colleagues from a variety of disciplinary backgrounds. It was during these discussions at NIAS that the idea took hold of rethinking my material in the light of property theories in order to make it speak to an audience beyond the narrow confines of West Africanists. The Max Planck Institute for Social Anthropology, Halle/Saale, and its director, Günther Schlee, kindly awarded me a three-month fellowship in 2003 that allowed me to restart the book after having been caught up in teaching and administrative tasks after my stay at NIAS. Last but not least, the W. E. B. Du Bois Institute for African and African American Research as well as the Committee on African Studies, Harvard University, hosted me in 2008–9 during a sabbatical year that was supported by a Fulbright fellowship and, although actually intended for work on a different project, ended up providing me an opportunity to also rewrite earlier drafts of the book.

During all these research stays and the numerous occasions where I presented chapters of the book in departmental seminar series or at international conferences,

I incurred innumerable debts of gratitude, especially to the following colleagues: Jan Abbink, Erdmute Alber, Nassirou Bako-Arifari, Tom Bassett, Gerd Baumann, Sara Berry, Thomas Bierschenk, Deborah Bryceson, Jean-Pierre Chauveau, Jan-Georg Deutsch, Mamadou Diawara, Julia Eckert, Honorat Edja, the late Georg Elwert, Richard Fardon, Jim Fernandez, Veronika Fuest, Peter Geschiere, Sten Hagberg, Amanda Hammar, Axel Harneit-Sievers, the late Gerti Hesseling, Holger Kirscht, Ben Kunbuor, Murray Last, Pierre-Yves Le Meur, Birgit Meyer, Christian Lund, Valentina Mazzucato, Knut Myrhe, Paul Nugent, Pauline Peters, Martin Rein, Don Robotham, Mahir Saul, Nikolaus Schareika, Parker Shipton, Daniel Jordan Smith, Wayne te Brake, Katherine Verderey, Keebet und Franz van Benda-Beckmann, Han van Dijk, Rijk van Dijk, and Achim von Oppen.

Special thanks also go to those faithful personal friends who have stood by and cheered me on throughout the long years of what seemed like an eternally unfinished book project and who have patiently listened to my despondent thoughts on how to bring this book to a close: Regine Bantzer, Walter Mann, and Parnel Wickham. I also owe thanks to Katja Rieck for her patient commitment and always stimulating editorial input, as well as to Mirco Göpfert and Richard Kuba for their great help with the maps in this book. Finally, I would like to express my gratitude to Emmanuel Akyampong for his tireless and warmhearted encouragement while I was looking for a publisher for the manuscript, to the anonymous reviewers for their extremely helpful comments, and to Dee Mortenson for her cheerful dedication to seeing this book project through.

LAND, MOBILITY, AND BELONGING IN WEST AFRICA

Introduction

"Do you see that hill, right behind our house? It was once a very dangerous place, and that is why this village is called Tantuo, bitter hill," Charles Tantuoyir told me when I visited him in his home village in 1989. I had met Charles a year earlier in Obuasi, at Ashanti Goldfields Corporation, Ghana's largest gold mine, where I was exploring the long history of labor migration from Ghana's Upper West Region. I was fortunate to meet many Dagara mine workers like Charles who were not only willing to share their life stories with me but also introduced me to their families "back home." When Charles visited his home village, as he did every year during his annual vacation, he invited me to his house and introduced me to his parents, brothers, uncles, nephews, and many more. And he took pride in showing me around Tantuo, with its dispersed large adobe homesteads set in a softly undulating savanna landscape of sorghum and millet fields, dotted with huge baobab trees and rocky outcroppings, such as the hill behind the Tantuoyir house.

In Obuasi, Charles and I had talked at length about the dangers of underground labor; his memories of his arrival in Obuasi in 1960 and the excitement about the goods he was able to purchase with his first wages; the history of the Dagara migrant mine workers' associations that he had helped to build; and many related topics. Having worked for many years as bar man at one of Ashanti Goldfields' social clubs, Charles presented himself as an accomplished urbanite, well acquainted with Obuasi's small, but pulsating, fast-paced world of taxi cabs, money that went as quickly as it came, booze, music, dance, women, and swank clothes. I was surprised that back home, where Charles had spent so much less of his life than at the mine, his attention was focused entirely on how to organize the farm labor in his father's house, resolve conflicts over field boundaries with a neighboring farmstead, and similar everyday problems of a peasant family. And I was even more surprised that he obviously felt that the most important thing I should learn about his family and his village was the story of how his ancestors had come to settle in Tantuo—a story in which the "bitter hill" played an important role.

I soon learned that Charles was no exception. For other migrants, too, close relations to their home village were of vital importance. The family farmstead in the North was an economic safe haven in case of unemployment or illness and during old age, but even more important, it was central to the definition of belonging. Despite being fellow Ghanaians, the "natives" of Obuasi and other mining towns would always regard the migrant workers as "strangers," Charles explained. In Ghana, as in many other West African countries, most people believe that in order to be a legitimate citizen of the nation-state, one first needs to be recognized as a "son" or "daughter" of a local community, and that it is only in one's "home" community that one enjoys full rights over landed property and can legitimately partake in local political affairs. And because of such politics of "primary patriotism," as Peter Geschiere and Joseph Gugler have termed this widespread, popular concept of citizenship,[1] migrants like Charles invest much in keeping their home ties in good repair and validating their families' deep historical roots, embodied in the ownership of a piece of land.

A few years after my visits to Tantuo, this importance of belonging, in its double meaning of something one owns and membership in a community, was driven home most forcefully by the eruption of violent conflict in the cocoa-producing forest belt of the Ivory Coast. Clashes between immigrant farmers and local youth, who protested that they were the true "autochthones" but were now disadvantaged because the immigrants had outstayed their welcome and usurped far too great a share of the local resources, resulted in the expulsion of tens of thousands of these "strangers." Among them were many Dagara farmers from villages in Burkina Faso, just across the Black Volta River that runs nearby, west of Tantuo. In Ghana and Burkina Faso, too, zones of rural immigration have often become sites of intense disputes over belonging and property rights that, although much less dramatic, pose serious consequences for local populations and, at times, spill over into national politics. And, every so often, ethnic tensions in the mining towns remind Charles and his colleagues of how important it is to be able to return to a home from which one cannot be driven away. Ultimately, home is where one can call a piece of land one's own, and the strongest claims of ownership are those that can be traced to the deep past.

At the end of my first visit to Tantuo, Charles insisted that I should come back with my tape recorder and properly interview his father. The old Tantuoyir, born around the 1910s, was one of the first mine migrants from Tantuo and had worked as an underground laborer in Obuasi during the 1930s and 1940s. But again, before talking about his own and his colleagues' experiences in the mines—which was the subject I was most interested in at the time—he wanted to educate me on how his grandfather had been able to make Tantuo his home. By the time I had prepared the tape recorder for our interview, an impressive crowd of old and young men and women from the house and neighboring homesteads had assembled, listening attentively to what Tantuoyir had to say. It was a story with which they were obviously familiar, and which one of the elders occasionally amended whenever he thought Tantuoyir had left something out. "It was from Napaal," Tantuoyir began, pointing in the direction of this neighboring village,

> that our grandfather, who was a great hunter, came to Tantuo. He had a friend named Ketuo, actually the earth priest of Ketuo[2] [a neighboring settlement], who invited him to come, but also told him that this hill was not good and that he should instead settle in Ketuo, near him. When our grandfather came, he realized that the hill was indeed a dangerous place, but he insisted that he would settle in this very place [where the interview took place], and he started building the house. When the construction of the house had reached a certain stage, the spirits of the hill [*tang bibiir*, literally, the children of the hill] came and pushed down the building. So my father went to report the incident to Ketuo, and Ketuo reminded him that he had told him not to settle at that place. So my grandfather kept quiet and went back home to Napaal. Then around midnight, he came over to the place where he was building the house and saw the spirits of the hill gathered in his unfinished house. When he saw them, he shouted at them, and they all ran into their hideout, a big tunnel in the hill. When they were all inside, he rolled a very big stone over to cover the tunnel entrance. Then he went back and told his friend Ketuo that he had been able to find the people who pushed down his house, and that with the punishment he had served them, they would not be able to push down his house again. And in fact, the spirits never did manage to escape from their hideout, and my grandfather was then able to continue building his house.
>
> When he built the house, there was nobody in this place. So nobody owned this land, we are the owners of this place, and that is why I am called Tantuoyir [literally, the house of Tantuo]. If anybody says that he is the owner of this place, then the person is telling lies. Every year we sacrifice a cow to the hill, and we, the Birfuole [Tantuoyir's patriclan], are the owners of this village Tantuo.[3]

Later, I discovered that other elders in the village told a slightly different story of how the hill was tamed. Some explained that it was wild animals rather than spirits that had made the place so dangerous. Others asserted that the house had been pulled down by human beings, namely some Sisala-speaking families who had previously lived in the area and were strongly opposed to the Dagara newcomers' settlement. The earth priest of Ketuo, for his part, challenged Tantuoyir's claim to own the land. He declared that his own predecessors had been the first-comers to the entire area; they had given late-comers, like Tantuoyir's ancestor, permission to settle in the surrounding bush, but they had never relinquished their ultimate ownership rights and therefore still needed to be consulted on any major decision concerning the land. In one respect, all these conversations were alike: no matter how old my interlocutors were and whether they had gone to school or worked outside the village, they were all eager to instruct me about the local settlement history and their ancestors' origins, subsequent migrations, and deeds. And no matter what research topic I pursued—labor migration, the history of colonial rule and chieftaincy, or the ethno-regional development associations that the educated elite had established—migration-and-settlement narratives like the story that Charles and his father, Tantuoyir, told me kept coming up.

When I finally decided to explore these settlement histories and related stories more systematically and collected information in numerous Dagara and Sisala villages in North-Western Ghana and the adjoining areas of Burkina Faso, I was soon overwhelmed by the wealth of narratives and baffled by the often contradicting versions of the "same" history that different interlocutors forwarded. It was easy to become addled by all these stories about brave hunters who ventured into the wilderness looking for uninhabited stretches of bush (and claiming that the place was "empty"), but then, as the narrators often eventually conceded, accidentally stumbled upon an unwilling bush spirit, some aggressive animal, or another hunter, and began to argue over who had come first. To me, most stories initially sounded confusingly similar. The variations, however, were obviously of great importance to my interview partners, and they wanted to make sure that I got the "correct" version. I soon discovered that these stories were not only presented to the foreign anthropologist but were also put forward in all manner of local disputes relating to land. In disagreements about the precise course of village or field boundaries, in disputes over competing claims regarding the right to fish in rivers and ponds, to collect firewood or to harvest shea nuts, in arguments over the distribution of gifts that a "stranger" presented in return for the allocation of land, and many similar conflicts, the contestants would always attempt to bolster their position by turning to the settlement history and the events that had taken place during their ancestors' times.

The longer I listened to such stories and the more attention I paid to how they were used in disputes about land rights, the better I understood that these first-settler narratives served as a kind of oral land registry. They are stories of "first possession" that legitimate the origin of property rights and construct a link between the founding ancestors and the storyteller (and his group) through which the rights established by first possession have been transmitted to the current proprietors. In Tantuoyir's and many other stories, this linkage is imagined as straightforward descent; in other cases, property rights are claimed to have been imparted along the lines of friendship, marriage, patron-client relations, or ethnic alliances. In any case, an individual holds rights over land only by being a member of a specific community—ranging from the nuclear or the extended family and the patriclan to the larger ethnic group.[4] Membership in these groups, however, is not a given. It is contested, negotiable, and can change over time.

As the stories of Tantuoyir's ancestor and other village founders reveal, violence and coercion played, and sometimes still play, an important role in gaining access to and appropriating land. However, they alone cannot ensure its long-term, uninterrupted use. A successful farming community and a prosperous settlement need to be strengthened by building consensus and having their property rights acknowledged. "Property is persuasion," as the legal historian Carol Rose has succinctly put it, and convincing narratives of the origins and subsequent transfers of property are central to bringing about this consensus.[5] Stories about "first possession," Rose argues, are a classical and almost universal strategy to legitimate property claims. And in a context of mobility and expanding agricultural frontiers, assertions of first possession are supported by first-comer narratives like Tantuoyir's tale.[6]

This book, then, explores the construction, contestation, and transformation of such first-comer claims, and their significance for rights over land and for membership in the local community. It investigates the dynamics of property rights and the politics of belonging in a West African savanna region where the people have been continually on the move, driven by the imperatives of an economy based on hunting and shifting cultivation, the desire to break away from oppressive family and village conflicts, to escape enslavement, or, more recently, the need to deal with increasing land scarcity. Examining the history of agricultural expansion in the Black Volta region of what is today North-Western Ghana and South-Western Burkina Faso, roughly from the late eighteenth to the late twentieth century, the book discusses the role of ritual, narrative, and persuasion, but also of violence and power in shaping the region's history of mobility, property, and belonging. It looks at how the politics of belonging have influenced mobility and land rights, and, conversely, the ways in which land ownership has become, and continues to be, a symbol of belonging, and how first-comer status and property rights are converted into political authority. And, finally, it addresses the question of how local property rights over, or otherwise stable access to, land resources have been secured, lost, contested, and negotiated in changing political environments—in highly decentralized "stateless" societies, under colonial rule, and under different postcolonial political regimes.

This book therefore contributes to recent debates on customary tenure and autochthony—on which I will comment below—a rich historical case study of the social organization of mobility, the multiple strategies of establishing and contesting property rights in land, and the politics of belonging and identity in segmentary societies of the West African savanna. That history and memory are important resources in conflicts over property and belonging has been asserted by numerous authors. However, by focusing on the instrumental uses to which various actors put historical narratives, many studies remain, to a certain extent, committed to a presentist perspective. They hardly explore the precolonial history of property claims in its own right. Most important, none examines the challenges to property regimes that arise in the kind of context of agrarian mobility that constituted the setting of my research. My book therefore aims at examining mobility, land, and belonging in a broader historical time frame that encompasses the precolonial, colonial, and postcolonial periods. The past is not, as Appadurai has convincingly argued, "a limitless and plastic symbolic resource." Substantial convictions of what constitutes the past are not purely "of the present."[7] More generally, I attempt to show not only how present concerns inform visions of the past, but also how past developments, including those from before the colonial encounter, forcefully shape the present configurations of mobility, property, and belonging. The book thus reconstructs both the regional history of mobility, settlement and property rights, and the politics of memory, that is, how Dagara, Sisala, and others remember, argue over, and reinterpret this history in the light of current concerns. It looks not only at how people invoke history in claim making, but also at how their understanding of land, their rights to it, and their identity in relationship to it are products of the historical unfolding of migration and settlement in the region.

Land Tenure, the State, and First-comer Narratives in Africa

The case that this book explores concerns a small area of the West African savanna, but the story it tells is a much bigger one. The Black Volta region is indeed typical of much of rural Africa, which defies popular Western images of a continent of permanent crises or exotic cultural traditions. The region studied in this book has known periods of drought and of excessive rains as well as many small-scale disputes about land ownership, administrative boundaries, and ethnic relations,[8] but it is not ravaged by extensive ecological disaster and hunger or violent conflicts that would have made international nightly news. Nor does it offer any spectacular natural wonders, wildlife, or archaeological treasures that would make it a candidate for a natural reserve, world heritage site, or other tourist attraction. Apart from some small-scale alluvial gold deposits, the Black Volta region is not rich in minerals or other economically promising raw materials, nor has it become a site of major cash-crop ventures. It is, in many ways, a very rural and very "normal" region whose inhabitants somehow manage to survive, some more comfortably, others certainly much less so. Most have to creatively combine their small-scale subsistence-oriented agriculture with income from labor migration and need the support that better-off, educated relatives are able to send from the cities.[9] Others keep moving into new regions in order to find fresh farming land, although now, unlike in the times of Tantuoyir's ancestors, they can rarely assert themselves as first-comers but usually have to become clients of established groups of landowners with more abundant resources. In any case, agriculture continues to be the most important activity in the local economy, and access to land is vital, both for economic survival and social belonging.

This is representative of much of the African countryside. Population and occupational statistics from the region are notoriously unreliable, but we can assume that from 60 to 80 percent of West Africa's population live in rural areas and depend on agriculture for subsistence, even though cultivation is often complemented by other sources of income.[10] Figures for the rest of Africa are probably similar. The case study discussed in this book contributes to our understanding of how these rural populations have secured, contested, and negotiated access to land; how they have organized and stabilized their communities while on the move as mobile farmers or labor migrants; and how they deal with actions of the state (colonial boundaries, colonial rule through chiefs, postcolonial land policies, etc.) that affect their access to resources, social relations, and political rights.

Since the colonial period, the state has set itself up as the ultimate guarantor and arbiter of property rights, either by declaring land to be national domain or by defining the extent to which "customary" claims to ownership that predate its own establishment will be recognized. In both cases, however, African governments generally did not, and still do not, command the necessary resources to enforce national land legislation in any systematic or comprehensive way. Only 5 percent of all West African land is titled, that is, owned and registered under some state-controlled, formalized cadastral system.[11] The rest is held under some form of customary claim—often enshrined in the kind of narratives that Tantuoyir and many other of my interlocutors told me. There are no comprehensive figures for other African regions, but most likely, the picture is similar. Active state surveillance is thus often restricted to urban lands, zones of intensive cash-cropping, or other areas where the economic value of land has increased. In economically, and often also politically, marginal areas of rural Africa such as the Black Volta region, the management of land issues is usually left largely in the hands of the local population. This does not mean, however, that state legislation and policies have no impact on land matters: state agents do sometimes intervene in their own or the urban elite's interest in local tenure regimes, and state laws do influence people's ideas on land and have diversified the ideological arsenal employed in local struggles over property rights. Furthermore, litigants often attempt to involve state-controlled courts and government authorities in the recognition (or denial) of contested claims to land, particularly when the economic or political stakes rise and access to state institutions becomes affordable. However, indigenous institutions, such as lineage elders, earth priests, and chiefs, continue to play a central role in land disputes. And even in state-mediated forums, local ideas and strategies of constructing, contesting, and enforcing property claims have remained immensely important.

The resilience of customary land tenure and the longevity of legal pluralism[12] typical for much of rural Africa have been long-standing concerns of policy makers. The 1970s and 1980s were a period of great expectations, as Sara Berry has put it, marked by state-managed rural development schemes and attempts to modernize tenure regimes.[13] During these decades and well into the 1990s, the World Bank and many African planners were convinced that secure property rights, preferably in the form of private, individually held titles, were vital to making African agriculture more productive and environmentally sustainable.[14] Some policy makers believed that because traditional tenure systems were too unresponsive to change, individualized rights needed to be instituted and enforced by state institutions. Others were adherents of an "evolutionary theory of land rights"[15] and considered customary rights to be flexible enough to adapt to the demands of the modern economy and develop into an appropriate system of private property rights that would merely need to be formalized and consolidated, not created from scratch. Whichever position governments preferred, however, the ambitious land-titling programs that were instituted in a number of countries failed, partly because they offered ample opportunities for subversion, misuse, and corruption, and partly because the resources necessary to ensure a comprehensive enforcement of the effected land reforms were simply lacking. This forced policy makers to consider the possibility that indigenous tenure systems might not be as inherently dysfunctional as they were first believed to be. The notion therefore began to spread that customary tenure may, in fact, be sufficiently flexible and efficient to adapt to modern economic challenges, without necessarily entailing the development of a property regime based on private, individual titles.[16]

All throughout these reform efforts and policy changes, for a majority of rural Africans customary tenure continued to be of great practical importance for the management of their daily lives. But customary tenure, as this book will show, has never been as static or homogeneous as many policy makers and researchers have assumed.[17] Even in precolonial times, and more so during colonial rule and after independence, indigenous tenure regimes were not coherent and stable systems of rules and beliefs, but contested pastiches of historically grounded arguments about property rights and access to land resources as well as to membership in the local political community. Legal pluralism did not only result when the modern state introduced legislation and the concomitant institutions, but has been characteristic of indigenous tenure regimes from the very beginning.

What the most important lines of conflict and contestation were, and how rural people's ideas about tenure have changed in response to new challenges, depend very much on the particularities of local conditions and historical trajectories. This is why they need to be studied in detail and historical depth: concrete cases, as this book proposes, can hardly be generalized for the entire continent. Nevertheless, the book does make two broader propositions: first, that the dynamics of African tenure regimes can be usefully understood in terms of struggles over property rights, and, second, that first-comer narratives are a particularly widespread and attractive idiom to assert property rights because they are extremely malleable. They therefore allow for significant changes in the nature and scope of claims to land ownership while upholding the basic principle of an order based on precedence. At the same time, they locate the origin and legitimacy of property in man's encounter with nature and the spiritual realm, and thus remove it from the volatility and contingency of human politics. I return to this second proposition below when I sketch the book's major argument. Regarding the first, a few remarks are necessary here because this book's focus on property rights is at odds with some rather romanticist views of (precolonial) African land tenure that are still widely held.

Conceptualizing Property Rights: Theoretical Debates
and Indigenous Perspectives

For a long time, the conventional wisdom has been that land in Africa was a free and plentiful good, and that political control, in Jack Goody's classical formulation, "tended to be over people rather than over land" and "neither individuals nor kin groups bother[ed] to lay specific claims to large tracts of territory."[18] Africans were believed to be indifferent to rootedness in physical space,[19] and the territorialization of identities and the growing interest in control over land not only as an economic asset, but also as a basis of taxation and political control, was largely regarded as the result of colonial rule. Anthropologists like Paul Bohannan or Elizabeth Colson, for instance, argued that notions of property were conspicuously absent from traditional tenure regimes, and that African villages were descent-based, mobile communities that "did not claim land."[20] Flexible "short term farm tenure," instead of any notion of property, was, in Bohannan's eyes, characteristic of rural Africans' relations to land.[21] Colonial officials developed, often in close cooperation with African chiefs, a slightly different view of African land tenure that still seems to influence some present-day policy makers—namely that Africans imbued land with deep religious meaning and that land was owned communally, held in trusteeship by the chiefs. But like the above-mentioned anthropologists, they were convinced that Africans deemed land to be inalienable and that they traditionally would not fight over access to, or control over, land.

This book argues that the dominant paradigm of precolonial Africa's free surplus land—indifference to territoriality and absence of property, as well as the inalienability of land—needs to be reassessed. A closer study of the history of agricultural expansion in the Black Volta region, but also in other parts of Africa, reveals that competition over resources such as land, water, pasture, and trees, between first-comers and late-comers and between hunters, agriculturalists, and pastoralists, sometimes articulated in the idiom of ethnic difference, is a phenomenon of the *longue durée*. Both images of the precolonial past—the colonial idea of inalienable, uncontested communal owner-ship, held in trust by chiefs or earth priests, as well as Bohannan's and Colson's concept of ritual territories with flexible farm tenure, but without property rights (and hence similarly inalienable)—seem to be misleading, or, at the very least, grossly simplified. A number of studies have shown that at least since the early nineteenth century, land in agricultural frontier zones with emerging cash-crop economies became more and more highly valued, and that land markets developed.[22] But even in "backwater" areas with less economic potential, such as the Black Volta region, the pioneers attached great importance to the material and ritual control of the new territories into which they moved, and there is evidence of a long history of contestation over whether earth shrines, which invest the most comprehensive rights over land, can be transferred to newcomers or are the inalienable property of first-comers.[23]

In order to understand these claims, debates, and conflicts, it is useful to employ the notion of property—but, of course, one that does not limit "property" only to things that can be alienated and acquired in a market situation, as Duran Bell has recently proposed.[24] The broad concept of property underlying this book's argument emphasizes the social and political embeddedness of ownership and allows for a continuum of rights, ranging from mere access to the right to alienate land, as well as a continuum of right holders, ranging from individuals to extended families and larger communities.[25] A useful starting point is Hobhouse's early elucidation of the minimal conditions under which control over an object—in our case, land—may be understood as property: this control "must in some sort [sic] be recognized, in some sort independent of immediate physical enjoyment, and at some point exclusive of control of other persons."[26] Property thus implies social recognition, long-term control, and some kind of exclusion, both of people who are not granted free access and of certain kinds of uses that are considered inappropriate. And although most African languages do not make the distinctions that, for instance, English common law does, between allodial title (the most comprehensive and historically "deepest" property rights), freehold, leasehold, and lesser rights, there are indeed elaborate local discourses on these different and sometimes competing layers of rights.[27] Working with a broad notion of property allows us to explore the history of indigenous concepts of land tenure as well as their interaction with colonial and postcolonial understandings of ownership. We can thus capture both continuities and transformations without having to posit a dramatic rupture between "African" and "Western" concepts. And we can avoid the African exceptionalism that has often hindered useful comparisons of African land tenure with, for instance, cases from Asia, the Americas, or European history where researchers have rarely hesitated to speak of conflicts over property.[28]

At the same time, African histories of contested concepts of land ownership constitute very rich case material that allows us us to gain a deeper understanding of important tensions entailed in all property rights regimes. The question of whether property was created through a social (or ultimately divine) contract or through the appropriation of nature by human labor, for instance, has been discussed since early modern times,[29] and the African narratives discussed in this book provide an insightful perspective on these debates. More generally, an analysis of the dynamics of property, authority, and belonging in Africa throws some of the basic tenets as well as challenges of property rights into sharp relief.

For one, African histories of land ownership are usually set in a sociohistorical context of pronounced mobility. Establishing control over immobile resources, namely land, in a region where the people, including the agriculturalists, have been continually on the move, constituted a particular challenge. Exploring the strategies that Africans have developed vis-à-vis these challenges can shed light, for instance, on the ambiguities of the politics of persuasion that are part and parcel of stories of first possession. Carol Rose has characterized these stories as "moral narratives" that aim at communicating and legitimating property.[30] In the African context of mobility, however, which makes the question of who came and appropriated land first extremely difficult, the contested and political nature of these stories becomes particularly evident. Obviously, the politics of persuasion must also mobilize some kind of authority to validate the stories' claims as well as delimit and strengthen the solidarity of the group whose rights the stories are supposed to legitimate.

Second, the absence of strong states that has characterized much of African history has meant that property orders have had to be negotiated, and conflicts solved, at the local level, without an overarching authority that could have imposed clear, definitive rules. This, too, brings the tensions inherent in property regimes to the fore. Because claimants often did not, and still do not, agree on the rules of what constitutes legitimate property, the competing ideas had to be made rather explicit. Africans often argued, and continue to argue, about how far back in time one has to trace an attachment to a specific piece of land in order to successfully claim the most comprehensive rights. They differ on the question of what precisely constitutes the "pivotal event"[31] that defines first-comer status—merely discovering the site of the new village, actually clearing the bush or forest and cultivating the land, or "civilizing" the land and its inhabitants by instituting a new political order. They tend to disagree about whether it is possible for later-comers to an area to acquire these rights through conquest, exchange, or the continuous investment of agricultural labor. They are at variance about the social boundaries of the property-holding groups, that is, the question of who "belongs" to the relevant community or the "bundle of owners," as Geisler and Daneker have aptly put it.[32] They argue about the spatial boundaries of the territories to which a group lays claim. They debate about the precise content and order of the multiple layers of rights to natural resources, or the characteristic "bundle of rights," as Meek once called it.[33] And, finally, they tend to disagree about who has the legitimate authority to settle such disputes over competing claims, property narratives, and boundaries.

Studying the history of such struggles, and analyzing the strategies with which Africans have claimed, contested, and redefined property rights over land, can thus contribute to broader debates on property rights and elucidate the nexus between ideology and consensus, on the one hand, and power and authority, on the other. Studying these questions in a region that is not characterized by far-reaching violent conflict, such as the one discussed in this book, has an added advantage. It allows us to understand not only the ample opportunities for competition and conflict that the local concepts of first-comer status and property rights provide, but also the ways in which people manage to contain such potential for controversy and to farm and live their daily lives more or less peacefully. The widely shared moral principle that everybody should have the right to the fruits of his or her labor and, even more important, that it is immoral not to grant access to land for subsistence, is one of the factors that allows for the containment of conflict. Another is that the property claims are enshrined in an oral "land registry" that consists of narratives that can constantly be refashioned.

Debates on Customary Tenure

Customary tenure has been a central theme not only in policy, but also scholarly debates about land in Africa. During the late colonial period and the 1960s, colonial officials as well as scholars interested in applied research produced a number of highly nuanced studies of indigenous tenure regimes. While attesting to the complex bundles of ownership and use rights, however, these works tended to overemphasize the stability, coherence, and orderliness of indigenous tenure regimes.[34] Since the late 1970s, anthropologists, sociologists, and historians began to focus more on the consequences that the incorporation of traditional land tenure into modern market economies and (post)colonial political systems had for small-scale agriculturalists. They argued that state and elite intervention in land rights contributed to the emergence of a class society in rural areas.[35] Customary tenure was now considered to be a product of political interests and alliances, an "invention" of African elites, particularly chiefs, and colonial officials.[36] Much like with the discussion of the "colonial invention of tribes,"[37] however, there was little sensitivity regarding the complexity and flexibility of the colonial codification of "custom."

This flexibility and the malleability of indigenous concepts of land ownership, as well as the capacity (or lack thereof) of customary tenure to respond to economic changes, regained the attention of researchers in the 1990s. This was partly in response to the concerns of policy makers who were coming to terms with the failure of state-led reforms of land rights and, who, on the basis of a rather simplistic understanding of "traditional" tenure regimes, began to advocate the "communal fix."[38] Sara Berry, in particular, has examined the changing meanings of "custom," and it is from her work that this book draws much inspiration. She has shown, for instance, how disputes over property claims multiplied as land values rose, due to urban growth and to the expansion of commercial agriculture as well as the mining and timber industries. Contrary to Chanock's and others' earlier assertions of the reification of custom invented by colonial officials and chiefs, Berry has insisted that custom entails continuous struggle and negotiation, and that the colonial regime, far from simplifying customary tenure, has rather created further opportunities for competing interpretations of indigenous land rights. Most important, Berry has emphasized the political dimensions of land ownership and argued that "struggles over land in postcolonial Africa have been as much about power and the legitimacy of competing claims to authority, as about control of property per se."[39] In a context of legal and institutional pluralism, the sustained investment in social networks and political alliances is therefore crucial for the securitization of property claims and use rights.[40]

That conflicts over land rights invariably entail disputes not only about the contents of "custom" but also about which institutions are competent to arbitrate between competing claims has been a central concern of Christian Lund's work on land in Niger, Burkina Faso, and Ghana.[41] In his study of Ghana's Upper East Region, for instance, he has shown how a group of earth priests formed a political association in order to gain more leverage in bargaining for the restitution of property, or at least for adequate compensation for land once expropriated by the state. And he has forcefully demonstrated how new political conjunctures—here, Ghana's 1979 constitutional restitution of Northern lands formerly vested in the state to their "original owners"—can provoke appeals to customary rights, including extended debates on first-comer narratives and settlement histories.[42]

However, the recent emphasis on the flexibility of customary tenure and the inconclusiveness of land disputes has also provoked criticism. Henry Bernstein, for instance, has asserted that at the heart of the increased contestation of property and use rights, whether couched in the idiom of "traditionalist" claims or modern entitlements, lie growing inequality and "intrinsic class dynamics."[43] Similarly, Pauline Peters argues that instead of "privileging contingency, flexibility and negotiability," we should pay more attention to the "processes of exclusion, deepening social divisions and class formation . . . that limit or end negotiation and flexibility for certain social groups and categories."[44] And Kojo Amanor, echoing the 1980s "invention of custom" discussions, insists that "[c]ontrary to many assumptions, customary land law is essentially formulated from above. Its origins lie in colonial domination and the desire of colonial authority . . . to facilitate the integration of rural African producers into the markets of empire. . . . [It] enabled European concessionaires and settler farmers . . . to gain land on suitable terms for their ventures."[45] In a recent volume on contestations of "land and custom" in Ghana, Janine Ubink and Kojo Amanor forcefully criticize contemporary state projects to further devolve land administration to local and customary-based institutions.[46] They warn that, far from promoting the equitable distribution of land and securing use rights for the general population, this policy will most likely only provide even more opportunities for local and state elites to manipulate notions of custom to further their own interests.

As important as such warnings against too rosy a view of customary tenure are, these approaches, in my view, overemphasize the one-sided instrumentalization of indigenous concepts of property and use rights. Whether the colonial and postcolonial transformations of customary tenure increased flexibility or rigidity, privileged local elites, or empowered previously disadvantaged groups very much depends on the particular historical circumstances. To move forward, we need a revision of the revisionist approach, much like the one Thomas Spear achieved in his critique of the "invention of ethnicity" approaches.[47] The *longue durée* perspective that this book adopts works toward such a revision. A broader historical time frame helps to avoid overestimating the impact of colonial rule on ongoing struggles over property and belonging, in which colonial officials (and later postcolonial authorities and development aid donors) sometimes intervened only to find themselves caught up in local power dynamics that they neither fully understood nor were able to change in predictable ways.

Land Rights and Ideologies of Autochthony

That land rights are closely connected with issues of belonging, politics, and power—
"the property-sovereignty nexus," to use Metzer and Engerman's term[48]—has long
since been regarded as self-evident in general debates on landed property in Europe
and the Americas. Almost nowhere have property rights in land been universally
accessible to everyone; rather, they were and continue to be closely tied to notions of
citizenship, ranging from membership in local communities to the nation-state. Moreover, the reverse is the case as well: land ownership serves as a signifier of belonging to
the relevant people, and in the early phases of modern political representative regimes,
it was even the prerequisite for the right to vote.[49] However, these political implications
of land did not elicit much research in the African context. It was not until the recent
violent conflicts over property rights and citizenship in the Ivory Coast and similar
struggles elsewhere that the links between "property and constitutional order, land
tenure reform and the future of the African state," as Catherine Boone has put it, have
begun to figure more prominently on the research agenda.[50]

In many of these recent conflicts, discourses on autochthony have played an important role. Ideologies of autochthony argue, for instance, that comprehensive rights to
property and political representation should be reserved for the "sons of the soil."[51]
Autochthony's allure is, as Geschiere and Nyamnjoh argue, the result of its "combination of staggering plasticity and celebration of seemingly self-evident 'natural givens.'"[52]
It appears to offer primordial security to those who belong, who define themselves as
having been there before others came. At the same time, it creates considerable latitude
to redefine the boundaries of the relevant community— ranging from local villages to
entire ethnic groups or even nations—according to changing contexts and interests.
The relative "emptiness" of what it means to be an "autochthon" permits redefining the
"other," the "stranger," by drawing ever-narrower circles, thus creating "a basic insecurity." In fact, many conflicts, as Geschiere and Jackson point out, reveal a "somewhat
surprising 'nervousness' of discourses on autochthony . . . : there is always the danger of
being unmasked as 'not really belonging,' or even being a 'fake' autochthon."[53]

The recent upsurge of discourses and policies regarding "autochthony" in Africa
owes much to the specific "conjuncture" of belonging in an increasingly globalized
world.[54] As Ceuppens and Geschiere argue convincingly, "notions such as autochthony or indigenous appear to defend a return to the local, but in practice are more
about access to the global . . . [and] excluding others from access to new avenues to
riches and power."[55] A number of studies have demonstrated how democratization
and decentralization have intensified conflicts over belonging, and how both local
and national political elites have manipulated idioms of autochthony in order to
stay in, or gain access to, power.[56] These studies have been less concerned, however,
with an exploration of the "limits of invention" and with the ways in which current
idioms of autochthony are anchored in and rework long-standing local ideas about

first-comers, property rights, and belonging. It is this historical perspective, along with an exploration of the connections between mobility, belonging, and property rights, that this book brings to bear on the current debate on customary tenure and autochthony.

In the remainder of this introduction, I sketch out the two main concerns on which the argument of the book centers. The first pertains to the changing significance of landed property in the Black Volta region, the second to the role of first-comer claims in this history of agricultural expansion and struggles over property and belonging. I then explain the research approach and methodology and give an overview of the chapters that follow.

The History of Property Rights in the Black Volta Region

In the Black Volta region, as in many other parts of West Africa, first-comers, be they individuals or, more commonly, a group of relatives, are believed to have established a special relationship with the spirits of the land and thus played a crucial role in "opening up" the uncultivated bush for human settlement and agriculture.[57] First-comers established shrines at which regular sacrifices were, and continue to be, offered to the earth god in order to ensure the fertility of the land and the well-being of the community. The office of the earth priest, the custodian of the shrine, was usually vested in the lineage of the first-comers, at least according to widespread norms. Where the office was appropriated by powerful late-comers, the latter still often presented their claims in the idiom of first-comership by reinterpreting the settlement history such that they could assert that they were the true first-comers. While in some areas, the earth priests' authority was more or less confined to the spiritual domain, in other regions, as in the one under study in this book, first-comers and their descendants also assumed, and continue to do so, more extensive roles that touch on many aspects of everyday life.[58] Thus, they regard themselves as the "allodial" owners of the land, that is, the group with the historically deepest and most comprehensive property rights,[59] who claim control over all nonagricultural resources connected to hunting, fishing, and gathering; allocate land to later immigrants; grant the right to build houses and bury the dead; and mediate conflicts over land boundaries and land use. What their allodial rights mean in practical terms if, over the years, all land has been shared out, is highly controversial. Tantuoyir's story and his disagreement with the earth priest of Ketuo give us a glimpse of such conflicting interpretations. People challenge, for instance, an earth priest's insistence that he must be consulted before they can give land to "strangers" or his claim to have the right to reallocate to new immigrants the land of a lineage whose members fled one colonial regime and went to settle in the neighboring colony. Nevertheless, earth shrines remain powerful embodiments of original property claims, and even where the authority of earth-priestly lineages is less extensive than it once was, they may, when circumstances change, still exert their ritual authority to secure economic and political privileges.[60]

In the early phases of expansion into the frontiers of the Black Volta region, property rights were geared both at organizing agricultural activities as well as securing large hunting territories. In the vicinity of settlement areas, households would clear land, establish farms, and thus by the exertion of labor secure some form of enduring rights over their fields. Boundaries of land farther afield, that is, beyond the homesteads and their cultivated fields, over which the first-comers to an area claimed control, on the other hand, were defined only vaguely, marked by ritually charged landmarks, such as rocks or rivers, beyond which wounded game would no longer be pursued and within which the earth-priestly lineages demanded a share of the hunt as well as other "products" of the bush. These two modes of land tenure, the one regulating hunting and gathering activities and the other related to agriculture, were associated with different conceptions of space. As Tim Ingold has convincingly argued, hunters establish control over specific sites and routes, whereas agriculturalists control plots of land, imagined as a two-dimensional mental map.[61] However, since in the Black Volta region hunting and farming were exercised by members of the same group, or even by the same persons, these mental maps coexisted and interlocked.

With increasing population densities, and as more and more bush was brought under cultivation, agricultural property rights had to be defined more precisely. For instance, questions of who held which rights over fallow land and hitherto "unclaimed" land in an earth-shrine parish needed to be resolved, and boundaries with neighboring settlements delineated more exactly. Furthermore, since the boundaries of agricultural land were circumscribed only laterally, extending indefinitely outward into the bush, farmers eventually started to cultivate land outside the reach of their own group's earth shrine. At the same time, newly immigrating frontiersmen established their own settlements on any shred of unclaimed land they could find, that is, at the interstices of all these already claimed lands. In any case, the property rights related to hunting and similar activities did not completely disappear, but were overlaid by more narrowly defined agricultural property rights. This created a situation of long-standing "legal pluralism," with ample opportunity for competition and debate. First-comers who considered themselves the owners of large hunting territories, for instance, would attempt to translate hunting boundaries, based on routes and landmarks, into the new dominant idiom of agricultural mental maps and to claim prerogatives and privileges over the "late-coming" agriculturalists.

Furthermore, people created a variety of shrines for spiritual protection, venerating not only the earth god, but also bush spirits and lineage ancestors. Changes in the scope of property rights were often accompanied, and even initiated, by establishing new or manipulating existing shrines. Hunting shrines or lineage-owned field shrines, for instance, could be redefined as village earth shrines. Similarly, prominent earth priests could attempt to extend their spheres of influence by offering their spiritual services in neighboring settlements and later interpreting these services as proof of their allodial title. Ritual politics and property dynamics thus went hand in hand. Late-comers, on the other hand, sometimes used the competition between various earth priests to strengthen their own entitlements, or resorted to violence to forcefully turn themselves into "first-comers" by driving inhabitants off the land.

Colonial rule, and its introduction of chieftaincy, created further challenges to this palimpsest of rights and claims because it connected land ownership, belonging, and political office in new ways, while at the same time limiting opportunities to use violence in the appropriation of land. French and British colonial officers tended to regard being a "native" as a prerequisite for legitimate chiefly status, and the identities of natives were, by and large, defined by their association with landed property. While precolonial strategies of expansion among the Dagara and neighboring segmentary societies were not aimed at political conquest, some lineages now used the multilayered nature of property rights to support claims to an allodial title and chiefly office.

The reinterpretation and transposition of different layers of spiritual, economic, social, and political meanings of land continued after independence. They have gained momentum as land has become scarcer and acquired new value for the cultivation of cash crops or as building land, and as allodial property rights continue to be regarded as an important foundation of local and, by extension, national citizenship. And while the economic and political stakes of land rise, the ideological arsenal employed in the struggles is further diversified as supralocal actors such as government officials, lawyers, or youth associations become engaged and bring European notions of ownership to bear on local conflicts. Some parties now attempt to translate the multifarious indigenous concepts of property in simplified terms of more exclusive tenure, while others, particularly in Ghana, draw on ideas about customary tenure from the southern parts of the country, namely the notion of "stool lands" controlled by the chiefs.

These potentially conflict-ridden processes of extending, challenging, and reinterpreting property rights, and the concomitant redefinitions of the boundaries of the property-holding groups were, and continue to be, connected with ethnicity, but this is not necessarily the case. They could, and still can, occur within any ethnic group, pitting neighboring earth priests against each other, earth-priestly families against "late-comer" lineages within a settlement, and late-comers against latest-comers. However, when the distinctions between first-comers and late-comers have coincided with linguistic and ethnic difference, conflicts over land rights have often intensified. In the Black Volta region, such conflicts have become particularly acute between Sisala first-comers and Dagara frontiersmen as the competition over land increased and exit options gradually closed. How the transmission of property rights between these groups, often symbolized in the exchange of earth-shrine stones, has changed over time, what role violence and its subsequent suppression through the *pax colonia* played in these changes, and how people have debated the alienability of the allodial title are central themes that this book explores.

The Politics of First-Comer Claims

Because property depends not only on the de facto appropriation of land, but also on some sort of consent, or at least temporary acquiescence, all these struggles over land rights and their transmission were punctuated by competing narratives of migration, settlement, and first possession. Even Dagara who settled on Sisala-owned land during the colonial period and were unable to acquire full property rights would insist, in typical first-comer fashion, that they were actually the ones who had opened the bush. First-comer narratives rest on the conviction that some sort of pact with the earth god and the spirits of the land, embodied in an earth shrine, is necessary in order to ensure the fertility of the land and the people. First-comer narratives constitute a common social and cultural grammar that was, and continues to be, shared by all groups in the region, across cultural and linguistic differences. It provided the framework in which mobility and encounter, competition and complementarity, assimilation and separation could be negotiated and justified.

What made first-comer narratives so attractive that to this present day they figure prominently in conflicts over land rights as well as more generally in the historical memory of villagers and their educated migrants alike? To begin with, these narratives reflect important aspects of the frontier process and the ways in which first possession was established. Despite the fact that they usually conceal the collective nature of land appropriation and the role of violence, they constitute "invented traditions" that make, as John Peel has expressed it, "a genuine contact with people's actual experience, that is with history that happened" and therefore are particularly effective.[62] First-comer narratives are, in many ways, intellectually and emotionally attractive.

Second, defining first-comers, imbued with some form of control over landed resources and with ritual authority as earth priests, helped to order the social reproduction of frontier communities. Once the pioneers and their immediate followers, who stood to gain from their close association with the former, had established this ordering principle, it became self-reproducing and self-legitimating. Late-comers had little choice but to either accept this basic order, choose an exit option, or overthrow it by force. If they opted for the latter, this was only to impose themselves as first-comers vis-à-vis subsequent newcomers. And once this earth-shrine-centered order was in place, there was no way to return to a concept of "unowned," open-access space.

Third, first-comer justifications of property were flexible enough to allow for significant changes in the nature and scope of property rights while upholding the basic principles of an order based on precedence. First-comer claims were, and continue to be, widely accepted as the basis of rights to land, but they are extremely malleable and thus can be adapted to the changing meanings of property. First-comer narratives can define the decisive event or activity that marks first-comer status in very different ways—for instance, by making this event the discovery of the site of the new village in the course of a hunting expedition, or by asserting the definitive event to have been the actual clearing of the bush and cultivation of the land. Further, the narratives may also delineate the territorial and social reach of the group that is claiming first-comer status in more or less inclusive ways.

Finally, first-comer narratives locate the origin of legitimate property not in any social contract, but in the encounter between man and nature, or, to be precise, man and the earth deities or bush spirits. Sally Falk Moore's succinct formula that property is "not about things . . . but about relationships between and among persons with regard to things"[63] thus needs to be complemented. At least some societies' representations of property insist that property is not social, if not exactly about things, then about nature and the spiritual realm. This lends property claims, on the one hand, a sense of absoluteness and power. On the other hand, since the ways of the gods often defy the limits of human comprehension, and since the relevant events took place in the distant past, there is ample room for debating and interpreting what the gods actually intended. Casting property and the origins of earth-priestly authority in naturalized, or rather sacralized, terms was particularly suited to segmentary societies that recognized no centralized political authority. As kin groups were regarded to be a kind of natural community, the allodial title could be legitimately transferred only by inheritance. The question of whether it could also be purchased, as Dagara late-comers tended to argue, was a matter of considerable debate. In any case, legitimate claims to the allodial title had to, and still have to, relate back to an act of first possession in a chain of transmission, which tends to systematically downplay the role of violence and social convention. First-comer narratives thus remove the origin of property from the volatility and contingency of human power and prowess.

That violent conflicts over land rights occur despite the persuasive power of first-comer narratives goes almost without saying. First-comer claims are inherently contradictory because they combine notions of mobility (having come "first" implies having immigrated from somewhere) with the apparently natural legitimacy of being autochthonous (having been there before the arrival of others). First-comer claims thus reflect the tension that exists between the imperatives of mobility, which characterize the livelihood strategies of many West African agriculturalists, and the need for stable access to the immobile resource—land. The recognition of mobility and claims to autochthony are always copresent in first-comer claims. Over the course of time, however, their respective weight may shift in response to new challenges and interests. Increasing pressure on land and new concepts of territorial politics introduced by the colonial and postcolonial state are the most important of these challenges. Over the past decades, the agenda of first-comer claims has shifted, from organizing mobility so as to allow the gradual inclusion of late-comers in existing settlements, to privileging sedentariness that justifies the exclusion of late-comers from full control over land. In conflicts over land or political authority on the "frontier" between Sisala and Dagara communities, for instance, first-comer claims have often been extended from founding lineages to entire "tribes." First-comer narratives have thus been converted into an ideology of autochthony and are increasingly used to legitimate the exclusion of immigrants and ethnic strangers, who can no longer acquire an allodial title, from local citizenship and full political participation. In some cases, such as that of the Ivory Coast, this ethnicization and politicization of land rights has resulted in violent conflict between "autochthones" and "strangers." In the case of the Black Volta region, however, conflicts over property rights and belonging have not hardened into such clear-cut fronts, and late-comers continue to struggle, and with some degree of success, to extend their entitlements to land and avoid exclusion from full citizenship.

Reconsidering the Local Impact of Francophone and Anglophone Property Regimes

In an area like the Black Volta region, where the effective implementation of colonial rule came rather late and state boundaries remained porous, a "nationalist" perspective on the phenomena of mobility, property rights, and belonging would be highly unsatisfactory. When I began to investigate the historical development of the Dagara-Sisala frontier and retraced the migration histories of various patrilineages along the different "stops" that my interlocutors' ancestors had reportedly made, I often had to cross the state border more than once. I therefore decided to delimit the area of research along the contours of these migration-and-settlement dynamics that defied later politico-administrative boundaries. Even during the colonial and postcolonial periods, movements across the border remained central to the social dynamics of the area, and one cannot properly understand either by focusing on Ghana or Burkina Faso alone. At the same time, because colonial rule and postcolonial land legislation in Ghana and Burkina Faso have followed a somewhat different trajectory, this cross-border research design also afforded comparative opportunities and promised to yield insights into the resilience of indigenous institutions and narrative strategies.

There is a "striking unevenness in real patterns of centralization and decentralization of state power," Catherine Boone argues in her comparative study of state building in rural West Africa; "some zones were governed intensively, through tight, top-down control, while others were left to their own devices, granted extensive autonomy, or simply neglected and not incorporated into the national space."[64] The Black Volta region studied in this book certainly belongs to the latter type, at least most of the time. Its population stayed on the margins of precolonial state formation and was never conquered by any of the neighboring Mossi, Dagomba, and Wala kingdoms. Economically, the area had little more to offer than manpower—first slaves, later labor migrants—and thus remained, in comparison with the agricultural frontiers of cash-crop production in the forest belt of West Africa, in many respects a marginalized hinterland.

Both colonial powers were intent on suppressing violence, establishing a somewhat more centralized and manageable political order through the introduction of chieftaincy, and facilitating the exportation of labor. British and French colonial officials, after having spent the first decade trying to consolidate control over the region by alternating between peaceful tours of inspection and violent punitive expeditions, came to rely on administering the area in an "indirect rule" fashion through local chiefs.[65] However, when it seemed that law and order were threatened, neither administration hesitated to wield a firmer hand by resorting to intermittent bouts of more or less despotic "direct rule." French officials attempted to impose a head tax and forced labor from the very start, and tended to support despotic chiefs, if these appeared particularly effective in controlling the population. But because increasing numbers of French subjects fled across the border to join their relatives in the British protectorate, there were limits to the intensity with which *mise-en-valeur* (development and improvement) policies could be implemented. Thus, on the whole, the colonial state remained a "minimalist" project on both sides of the border. And despite some intermittent attempts to enforce more rigid controls, the international border remained permeable, and continues to be so until today; in any case, it hardly put a halt to the ongoing agricultural expansion and rural-rural migration.

Firmin-Sellers's and Boone's observations[66] that the British and French colonial regimes differed considerably in their treatment of chieftaincy and land tenure do not quite apply to the region considered in this book. Colonial recognition of "stool lands" administered by the chiefs was limited to the Gold Coast Colony and the Ashanti Protectorate. In the Northern Territories, the British placed all lands under the control of the governor.[67] Indeed, up until 1979 all Northern Ghanaian land remained vested in the government, much like under the "national domain" principle of French colonial and later postcolonial land legislation across the border. However, on both sides of the border, the day-to-day management of land remained largely in the hands of local lineages, earth priests, and, in some cases, chiefs. In the British protectorate, the "native authorities," that is, the chiefs, were officially charged with granting permission to and imposing taxes on "non-natives" who wanted to settle in their areas, but earth priests were not as systematically sidelined as Lund asserts has been the case in North-Eastern Ghana.[68] Nevertheless, the ambition of chiefs to intervene in land affairs, and more generally their political influence, is perhaps the most important colonial legacy that distinguishes North-Western Ghana from South-Western Burkina Faso, where chiefs have all but disappeared, while earth priests have regained a greater role. Yet, the similarities in the settlement dynamics and micropolitics of land tenure, past and present, are striking. This is particularly remarkable since the current legal framework of land tenure—after brief periods of "revolutionary" user-rights supportive regimes in both countries, under Rawlings and Sankara respectively—is distinct, with the allodial title vested in the "original owners" in Ghana and in the state in Burkina Faso.

Research Approach and Methodology

The major focus of this book's case study lies on an area east of the Black Volta where Dagara agriculturalists began to move into what had once been Sisala territory,

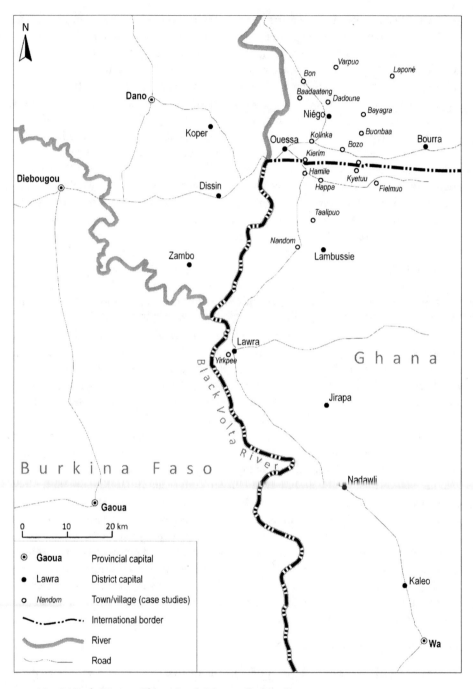

Map I. North-Western Ghana, South-Western Burkina Faso

probably in the early or mid-nineteenth century, and where until today they continue to establish new settlements farther eastward. Because the age of the various settlements differs considerably, the interaction between older, more permanent settlements and mobile frontiersmen can be observed *in nuce*, permitting us to gain a more nuanced understanding of the interplay between mobility and sedentariness that characterizes all migratory processes. The definite advantage of working on a relatively "young" frontier is that the changing strategies of how land was appropriated are still vividly remembered by the local population. Many developments discussed in this book took place only two, three, or four generations ago. Furthermore, thanks to colonial pacification, the Sisala first-comers, whom the Dagara frontiersmen had forced out of their villages toward the end of the nineteenth century, were not driven very far from their original settlements, unlike in older frontier regions, where populations escaped to distant areas or disappeared completely from the historical map. On the younger frontier east of the Volta, we can therefore usually reconstruct both perspectives, that of the former first-comers and that of the new frontiersmen. And finally, since the Dagara continue to establish new settlements, albeit under changing circumstances regarding land rights, the case-study region provides opportunities to observe a frontier still in the making, allowing insights that may partially apply to older frontiers as well.

Despite these unique research opportunities, however, the reconstruction of the precolonial history of migration and settlement in the area also entails thorny methodological problems.[69] Contemporary written sources are entirely absent for the period prior to the arrival of the French and the British in 1897. Neither do there seem to be Arabic manuscripts from the nearest Islamic centers, Kong, Sya (Bobo-Dioulasso), Ouahabou, or Wa, pertaining to this area, which did not fall along any major trade route. In the 1930s, British district commissioners carried out some historical research because they wanted to base their administrative reform projects of "indirect rule" on historical arguments and debated which local traditions could serve as the basis for the political centralization of previously stateless societies. However, they mostly relied on narratives from a limited number of informants, mainly from the families of the newly created chiefs, who used settlement history, if at all, to substantiate their claims to office.[70] French colonial officials seem to have been much less interested in history, at least with regard to the stateless societies west and east of the Black Volta. Furthermore, the relevant colonial files are scattered between the archives of Abidjan, Bamako, Dakar, Aix-en-Provence, Ouagadougou, Diébougou, and Léo, and they contain no information on precolonial Dagara expansion. The writings of the administrator-ethnographer Henri Labouret on the "tribes" of the "rameau lobi"—that is, Lobi, Birifor, Dyan, Phuo, etc.—paid more attention to the Samorian and French conquests of the Volta region than to regional settlement history, and did not deal with the Dagara.[71]

Oral traditions thus remain the most important source. However, they hardly go deeper than four or five generations. They consist of numerous and contradictory accounts by the different patrilineages of their respective migrations and establishment in new settlements. There are no indigenous professional historians, like the *griots*, and no official village histories. People in general are reluctant to talk about history beyond that of their own forebearers and patriclan. Women, in particular, do not feel authorized to speak about their ancestors' migration and settlement history, despite the fact that their husbands' or fathers' stories sometimes reveal the important role that enterprising women could play in establishing new villages. One is saddled, then, with history, or rather fragmented histories, as narrated by male lineage elders, and can only indirectly reconstruct a more comprehensive account and appreciate the importance of young men and women for the frontier process. The earth priests, ostensibly the descendants of the founders of the settlement, may give a more comprehensive account. However, in many cases their claims to first-comer status and their historical narratives are contested. More generally, since competing oral traditions play an important role in supporting claims to land and positions of authority, they can obviously not be taken at face value.

The local actors themselves, however, claim not to disagree on how some established historical events should be interpreted, but rather on the narrated "facts."[72] My Dagara and Sisala interview partners sometimes emphatically confirmed the truth of their statements by pointing to the reliable and respected authority of the source from which they had received their version of local history. For instance, in one of my interviews with the chief of Bu, a Sisala village in Ghana, my interlocutor concluded his narrative by asserting, "This is what we know. This is what our ancestor told us," and proceeded to narrate graphically how he and other elders would establish the truth if somebody dared to contradict them: "We testify this by the use of three fowl. When you go out with the fowl, you will say to the person against you: 'If it was your ancestor who settled there first, then collect his fowl and kill it. If you told a lie and killed the fowl, you are dead.'"[73] A credible story is thus supported not only by the authority of the ancestors, but also by the spiritual powers of the land. But this socially sanctioned "truth" is conveyed in poetic images and stories that often concentrate diffuse historical developments and extended series of events into easily memorized and immediately comprehensible single episodes.[74] Therefore, in order to reconstruct the history of regional migrations and expanding settlement frontiers, it is necessary to explore the micropolitics and poetics of oral traditions—their relationship with present interests and conflicts, as well as their use of regionally dominant tropes and images.

To be able to do so, it is necessary to systematically collect a substantial corpus of stories from a wider area. In order to reconstruct the history of the eastern frontier of Dagara expansion, I conducted almost two hundred interviews in more than seventy Dagara and Sisala villages, covering settlements in both Ghana and Burkina Faso. This survey-type material was complemented by detailed case studies of selected villages that were established during different periods.[75] This rich, multifaceted corpus of oral accounts of the migration and settlement of individuals, lineages, and patriclans allows us to identify which stories and episodes deviate from regionally dominant tropes, thus providing particularly valuable information about historical events.[76] Moreover, as the Sisala were often displaced from their former settlement areas by incoming Dagara groups, there are also "winner" and "loser" versions of the struggles over land rights. Convergence and disagreement between these versions and the different ways in which they draw on a limited pool of images provide further clues as to how these struggles developed and were resolved.

In addition to a careful analysis of oral traditions and oral history, it is important to take non-narrative sources into account that may corroborate or contradict the narrative material. Trees, and more specifically the spatial distribution of "agricultural parks," that is, park-like stands of trees near settlements, can help to evaluate settlement narratives and assess the relative age of settlements.[77] Village names often indicate how a settlement was founded. An analysis of the spatial distribution of lineage segments can reveal information about migration patterns, and the present-day observable relationships between lineages and clans (exogamy, alliance, joking relationships, or other ritual ties) often reflect earlier connections. Finally, the ritual hierarchies that in many cases currently exist between earth shrines of different villages can often be interpreted as sedimented settlement history.[78]

Much of this non-narrative material was accessible because I had been doing fieldwork in the area for more than twenty years and had gained insight through many informal conversations with the Dagara family who "adopted" me, and with Dagara and Sisala friends and assistants. I learned much about current property rights when I acquired a plot of land and constructed a house of my own on the family lands of my "mother's brothers" in Ouessa. I have been invited to assist at sacrifices at ancestor shrines and earth shrines, and I learned a great deal about people's mental maps when listening to the stories they associate with certain landmarks as I walked with them through the fields or traveled to neighboring villages. All of these narrative and non-narrative sources have been used in my reconstruction of the regional history of mobility, property, and belonging.

The Structure of the Book

This book explores the changing ways in which Dagara-speaking groups have expanded, and continue to expand, the territory over which they exercise some kind of enduring claim. In more specific terms, it looks at the various problems the Dagara (and other agricultural people) encountered as they moved into new regions: how to migrate while remaining connected to their places of origin; how to establish and exercise claims to land; how to organize and stabilize their communities; how to define themselves in relation to others whom they encounter in their travels; and how to deal with actions of the state (colonial boundaries, colonial rule through chiefs, postcolonial land policies, etc.) that affect their access to resources, social relations, and political rights. The book discusses the changing strategies with which the Dagara (and others) have dealt with these problems. It also looks at their interaction, sometimes peaceful and sometimes violent, with Sisala-speaking groups who claim to have been first-comers to the areas on which my fieldwork has concentrated. The book analyzes recent conflicts over belonging and land, both within Dagara communities and between Sisala and Dagara, in a historical and comparative perspective. It explores the changing significance of earth shrines, the ritual embodiment of first-comer claims, as sources of social control in an era when claims to land are increasingly subject to supralocal economic and political pressures. And it discusses how, with the construction of modern nation-states, local property disputes and politics of belonging have become increasingly interwoven with ideologies of autochthony and ethnicity.

Although the book takes a historical approach, the five chapters are not organized to produce a linear chronology. Instead, each highlights one of the key facets of the frontier process and first-comer claims referred to in the title of this volume—mobility, land, and belonging. Each chapter provides accounts of historical contexts, and each may be read as a self-contained unit, the sum of the chapters providing the basis for a holistic understanding of the case material on contemporary land conflicts discussed in the final chapter.

The first chapter reconstructs the strategies of territorial expansion and the relationships between the Dagara frontiersmen and the Phuo and Sisala "first-comers" whom they encountered in the areas east of the Black Volta. It discusses the dynamics of peaceful cohabitation and violence in the precolonial settlement process and analyzes the impressive ability of the Dagara to mobilize broad, flexible networks of patri- and matrikin, joking relationships, allied clans, and friends that made, and continue to make, it possible for the pioneers to recruit and integrate a relatively large number of new settlers within a short period of time. This was an important asset that protected newly founded settlements and allowed the Dagara to encroach on their neighbors' territories. While initially Dagara expansion seems to have been mainly driven by the quest for autonomy, during the colonial and postcolonial periods the search for fertile land has become ever more important, particularly as population densities have increased. However, even today an ethos of frontiersmanship is typical of Dagara young men, whereas other groups, like the Sisala, value local stability, the cohesion of the "big house," and long-term residence in one place. The first chapter discusses how Dagara strategies of mobility, and Sisala resistance to Dagara encroachment, changed under colonial rule and after independence, and shows how the new political contexts affected the local balance of power.

The second and third chapters analyze how a stable ritual order and property rights over immobile resources were established, and contested, in a sociohistorical context of mobility. Dagara earth shrines were surprisingly mobile and flexible institutions that could either be derived from the shrines in the migrants' original villages or purchased from Sisala already living in, or near, the new habitat. In both cases, control over shrines promoted the "autochthonization" of newcomers, who thus established themselves as landowners with full ritual authority. Under the *pax colonia*, this flexible landscape of allodial property rights was reified, at least to a certain extent, and the creation of new earth shrines ceased. However, this did not put an end to the contestation and reinterpretation of claims to ownership, on the contrary. The chapters show how the ambiguities of the spatial boundaries of earth-shrine territories, as well as the typical fuzziness of the composition of the "bundle of rights" that newcomers acquired, provided, and continue to provide potential for debate and sometimes conflict. These chapters analyze indigenous theories of property, as well as their interaction with colonial policies that eventually privileged the notion of the inalienable "allodial" property rights of first-comers.[79] But colonial and postcolonial reinterpretations of indigenous notions of property did not eliminate their ambiguity, which continues to offer considerable latitude for negotiation and the adaptation of property rights to new challenges.

The fourth chapter explores how belonging was, and is, constructed in the context of agrarian mobility and how membership in a community (lineage, patriclan, village, ethnic group, etc.) is translated into rights over land. It discusses how the distinct patterns of mobility and settlement of the groups who eventually came to see themselves as Dagara and Sisala gave rise to complementary forms of imagining "ethnic" unity, even before colonial rule, and shows how the colonial ideology of "tribes" eventually privileged more sedentary forms of belonging. With the colonial establishment of chiefdoms and new administrative boundaries, older idioms of host-stranger relations were reinterpreted as configurations of autochthones and immigrants. Under colonial rule, control over land and allodial property rights became the basis for claims to local citizenship and political participation—a development that tended to exclude late-comers, immigrants, and ethnic strangers.

Analyzing three contemporary cases of conflicts over land, the final chapter elucidates how the developments analyzed in the preceding chapters, namely the changing strategies of mobility, the negotiation of property rights and the politics of belonging, interconnect. This chapter shows how these conflicts were shaped by the history of agricultural expansion, land rights, and political authority, and how, in turn, people used first-comer narratives to bolster their claims. It discusses the conflicts' processual dynamics, how and where the struggles evolved, which allies were mobilized, and which institutions became involved, and it explores how first-comer histories were reworked as the conflicts moved through different arenas. The chapter concludes with a general reflection, beyond the Black Volta region, on the conditions that have shown themselves to be conducive to perpetuating such conflicts and the concomitant debates about first-comer claims.

1 Pushing Frontiers

The Social Organization of Mobility

"Mobility in its ubiquity is fundamental to any understanding of African social life," write Mirjam de Bruijn, Rijk van Dijk, and Dick Foeken in their introduction to a volume aptly entitled *Mobile Africa*.[1] They prefer to speak of mobility rather than migration because, they argue, the latter usually implies notions of linear and unidirectional movement, a more or less definitive change of residence, and such dichotomies as home and abroad, the rural and the urban, and so forth. Ultimately, the term "migration" often carries with it an idea of rupture in society, while, in reality, in many African societies, "not being mobile may be the anomaly." As De Bruijn, van Dijk, and Foeken suggest, we should regard mobility, in its manifold forms, not as a result of "social disarray," but rather as integral, vital "part of life and of making a livelihood."[2]

In a similar vein, Igor Kopytoff's earlier work presents a model of the "internal African frontier" that is premised on the assumption that African populations are continually on the move. Criticizing colonial (as well as postcolonial) stereotypes of Africa as "a continent mired in timeless immobility," Kopytoff argues that African societies were usually rather recent creations, forged by frontiersmen of various origins who met in open, less densely populated spaces between, or on the peripheries of, existing "metropolitan societies," as he calls established and often more hierarchically organized polities. Attracting followers from among kin, friends, clients, as well as occasionally slaves, and building on cultural traditions from their places of origin, the frontiersmen would construct new social orders "in the midst of an effective institutional vacuum." African histories, Kopytoff asserts, were "filled with the movement of the disgruntled, the victimized, the exiled, the refugees, the losers in internecine struggles, the adventurous, and the ambitious." In brief, Africa was a "frontier continent," characterized by population movements of various kinds and dimensions, ranging from long-distance displacements triggered by famines, civil wars, or other disasters to less dramatic mobility on a smaller scale due to family quarrels or lack of fertile farmland.[3] It is for this reason that studying the internal dynamics and strategies of mobility as well as how the dynamics and strategies of different groups affect each other—the themes of this chapter—is so important.

One may question whether Kopytoff's model fits the entire continent and whether its assumption of a self-sustaining perpetual cycle of fission and fusion of "metropolitan" and "frontier" societies does not ignore long-term historical shifts in population densities and the availability of land as well as major political developments connected, for instance, to the slave trade. However, the model of the "interstitial frontier" and a focus on mobility certainly help to understand the social dynamics of the Black Volta region. This region's inhabitants indeed were, and still are, continually on the move. Partly, mobility was driven by the imperatives of an economy based on hunting and shifting cultivation, which made the continuous opening of fresh land a necessity. Partly, people moved in order to break away from pressing family conflicts or quarrels in the village, or to escape the expansionist desires of neighboring chiefdoms or the attacks of slave raiders. Further, some people were adventurous and keen to explore farther afield, to improve their livelihood as well as their social position, becoming household heads and leaders of new settlements. During the colonial period, movements were often motivated by the desire to cross the international border in order to escape the exigencies of forced labor, or punishments meted out by harsh chiefs. More recently, the need to deal with increasing land scarcity has become ever more pressing.

Forms and strategies of mobility in the Black Volta region, as in other parts of Africa, have been manifold, in precolonial times as well as today, ranging from long-distance journeys "without return" to circular migration and small-scale movements in the vicinity, when, for instance, farmers create new villages out of what were initially bush fields and thus gradually push the settlement frontier into the surrounding bush. Furthermore, these larger movements involving changes of residence have always been complemented by (sometimes preceded, and sometimes followed by) mobility on a smaller scale connected with visiting near and distant markets, marrying men or women from farther afield, pilgrimage to powerful shrines or healers, and so forth.[4] What is fascinating, however, are the notable differences in the patterns of movement and strategies of migration between the various groups inhabiting the Black Volta region. From the eighteenth and nineteenth centuries onward, Dagara-speaking lineages were generally highly mobile and expansionist, while Sisala-speaking groups were far more sedentary. According to the latter's migration narratives, they seem to have moved over long distances due to traumatic disruptions, but once established in their new abode, they entrenched themselves without much interest in moving farther afield. Dagara-speaking groups, on the other hand, seem to have developed a pronounced ethos of frontiersmanship, and privilege mobility over sedentariness. One important reason for these different attitudes toward and patterns of mobility probably lies in the historical circumstances under which each group arrived in the region—the Sisala came first, which gave them the opportunity to chose the best ecological niches that allowed for more sedentary settlements, while many Dagara groups had to establish themselves in less favorable environments as well as continue to move into new areas.

In any case, the Black Volta region has witnessed, since the mid-eighteenth century and possibly even earlier, an impressive agricultural expansion of Dagara-speaking groups. Dagara frontiersmen occupied unpopulated bush as well as sparsely settled areas where Sisala-speaking groups, but also Phuo, Yeri, and Dyan, lived. In many cases, the expansion was peaceful and saw the linguistic and cultural assimilation of immigrants and previous inhabitants. However, there was also violence, and previous settlers were driven out by immigrating Dagara, particularly in the second half of the nineteenth century, as the incursions of Muslim slave raiders rendered large stretches of land in the Black Volta region insecure, and competition over land suitable for settlement thus intensified. Unlike the frontiersmen of expansionist centralized polities, the Dagara pioneers, belonging to a segmentary, stateless group, were not interested in establishing political control over the previous inhabitants of the territories into which they moved. They were, however, seeking to gain control over the land, materially and ritually. Following an initial phase of relatively peaceful cohabitation, this aim often involved the displacement of the previous inhabitants. In some cases, the latter were driven away under the threat of being killed; in other cases, they opted to move away "voluntarily" and sometimes even handed over the earth shrine—in which the communication with the spirits of the land crystallizes and which marks legitimate land ownership—to the Dagara immigrants. In any case, the Dagara's quest for land was more successful than the claims of these earlier inhabitants, at least until the early years of the twentieth century. And even after the circumstances of expansion changed during colonial times and the Dagara immigrants were no longer able to take control of earth shrines and thus establish themselves as full-fledged landowners, Dagara families continued, and still continue, to extend the area where they settled and farmed.

Though problematic, estimates of the size of language groups can give at least a rough idea of the demographic impact of Dagara expansion. Currently, there are well over 1 million Dagara speakers[5] in Ghana and Burkina Faso, while the number of speakers of the various Sisala dialects is estimated at approximately 140,000, and that of Phuo and Dyan at roughly 14,000 each.[6] Dagara settlements occupy an area of about 3,500 square kilometers in Burkina Faso and roughly the same area in Ghana. Differences in population densities, too, bear the mark of past and ongoing processes of expansion. In Ghana's Lawra District, which constitutes, so to speak, traditional Dagara heartland, population densities reach 93 persons per square kilometer, while they drop to 31 per square kilometer in Sisala West District, one of the zones into which Dagara migrants moved only more recently. In Burkina Faso's Ioba Province, where Dagara have settled since the eighteenth century, the average population density is 49 persons per square kilometer, while Sisili Province, Sisala-owned territory that currently attracts Dagara migrants, has only 21 inhabitants per square kilometer.[7]

It would be misleading, however, to think of Dagara expansion in terms of a deliberate and collectively planned endeavor on the part of the ethnic group to conquer new territories. Dagara mobility was, and continues to be, made up of a myriad of piecemeal migrations of small groups of kin and allied patriclans. There was no overall ethno-political organization that could have mobilized large-scale collective action. And yet, the continuous colonization of new frontiers does seem to have been more than just the accidental by-product of the fission of domestic groups and individual mobility. Dagara migration-and-settlement narratives invariably emphasize the pioneer spirit of the ancestors and a more or less aggressively asserted feeling of superiority of the Dagara over the earlier inhabitants. There was a strongly developed sense of pushing the "frontier . . . on the margin of the inhabited world," setting out from the "hinterland" and moving into "outlying areas which [were] both a source of danger and a coveted prize," as Ladis Kristof has characterized frontier processes.[8] Furthermore, the Dagara frontiersmen aimed at securing larger territories not only for themselves and their immediate relatives, but for their entire patriclan.[9] In this sense, the history of Dagara mobility can indeed be characterized as a history of expansion.

The success of expansionist stateless societies in Africa and elsewhere has been attributed to their effective sociopolitical and, by implication, military organization. Marshall Sahlins, for instance, considered the segmentary lineage system to be an "organization of predatory expansion." He attributed the "fantastic predatory encroachment" of societies like the Tiv or the Nuer on their neighbors to the ability of their flexible political system, based on the principle of "segmentary opposition," to make different lineage segments temporarily combine forces.[10] However, as other authors have shown, the territorial expansion of segmentary societies was usually a gradual process that involved temporary skirmishes and raids along the settlement frontier, but no full-fledged wars.[11] In the Black Volta region, small-scale armed conflicts between Dagara patriclans and settlements were as frequent as conflicts along ethnic boundaries on the frontiers, and violence was used only intermittently. However, the psychological and social effects of occasional strategic acts of violence on the population of a larger area should not be underestimated.

Some authors have explained expansionist movements by using a wave model of invasions and expulsions. According to this model, several societies move in the same direction, following each other, exerting pressure on the one in front while each is itself pushed by the one following.[12] It is not only historians explaining early European history who use this kind of chain-reaction model of *Völkerwanderungen*; the population in the Black Volta region sometimes views its history in similar terms.[13] The "wave" model is popular because it has the advantage of explaining a number of multifaceted phenomena within a single causal frame, but it does not do justice to the complexity of population movements and offers a rather mechanistic ex post facto rationalization.[14]

We may still want to ask whether, in the case of the Dagara, "external" events—and if so, which ones—set the expansion in motion. Generally the motif of slave raiding or other violent conflicts as reasons for migration is much less prevalent in Dagara narratives than in stories told by Sisala and Phuo. Dagara accounts usually put more emphasis on the lack of cultivable land or on small-scale internal conflicts. However, the absence of contemporary and explicit sources does not allow a definite answer.[15] In the settlement narratives that local Sisala and Dagara elders present today, episodes of violent expulsions, akin to the wave model, coexist with accounts of peaceful cohabitation of different groups or of the voluntary departure of the previous inhabitants. In order to understand these apparent contradictions, we need to know more about how the expansionist movement operated, how it was organized internally, and how the relations between Dagara immigrants and earlier inhabitants developed. Historical developments in the wider region may have propelled migration here and there, although they are rarely remembered, but they cannot account for the extraordinary strength of the Dagara expansion.

This chapter therefore examines the internal dynamics and strategies of territorial expansion, and the relationships between the Dagara frontiersmen and the Sisala first-comers whom they encountered in the areas east of the Black Volta. It focuses on the forces and factors that encouraged, or inhibited, mobility, and compares Dagara and Sisala cultural ideals as well as practices of migration and settlement. Why and how did they move, and how did they appropriate the unknown territories into which they moved? Under what conditions did the initially peaceful cohabitation of Dagara immigrants and earlier settlers turn into the forcible expulsion of the latter by the former? And how did Dagara strategies of mobility, and Sisala resistance to Dagara encroachment, change under colonial rule and after independence? After some general considerations on the expansion of segmentary societies and the challenges of the frontier, I explore these questions in three chronologically arranged case studies. The first traces the movements of a particular kin group and analyzes the long series of precolonial migrations of the Kusiele patriclan. The second focuses on the gradual colonization of a specific area, namely the region of Ouessa, by Dagara immigrants in the course of the nineteenth century. Finally, the third analyzes a case of recent and still ongoing peaceful immigration of Dagara hoe-farmers into Sisala territory, and looks at the making of a migrant community under conditions of restricted access to land. In all three cases, politics of memory are central to the creation of a sense of belonging and the construction of community in a context of mobility. The chapter therefore also examines how the expansion process is reflected in, and aided by, narratives of migration and settlement that propagate certain ideals of masculinity and frontier spirit, and that support the creation of new ties of neighborhood.

Pioneers and Followers: Coping with the Challenges of the Frontier

In the settlement process, Dagara and Sisala encountered similar challenges and had similar cultural ideals with respect to finding adequate solutions to these challenges. They shared the idea that first-comership entailed specific rights over the land (and its inhabitants); that attracting many followers to a newly founded settlement was desirable; and that settlements needed the spiritual protection of an earth shrine. However, depending on the different contexts in which their respective migrations took place, the strategies that the Dagara and Sisala actually employed on the settlement frontier differed. Most important, they valued (and continue to value today) mobility in different ways. Before turning to the common challenges of the frontier, therefore, a few remarks on their different attitudes toward mobility and sedentariness are in order. At this point, I limit myself to briefly sketching out a phenomenology of these different ideals; later, I discuss the different historical experiences that they embody.[16]

Ideologies of Mobility versus Sedentariness

Among the Sisala, we encounter an explicit ideology of local stability, the cohesion of the "big house" and long standing occupation of one place. The separation of a group of kin from its original home is usually explained in terms of traumatic conflict, and in most cases links with the former settlement are severed. Many of my Sisala interlocutors insisted that still today they could not return to, or even visit, their ancestors' original village, lest they be afflicted with illness, misfortune, or even death. Sisala present their migration as an affair of the past; they became mobile not by their own choice, but because circumstances beyond their control—including conflicts among close kin—forced them to move. Neither the ideal of autonomy nor an ethos of "go forth, young man" are as prominent as among the Dagara.[17] As reasons for migration, some Sisala narratives refer to conflicts between brothers, for instance, over not fairly sharing the spoils of a joint hunting expedition;[18] others invoke a dispute about the sex of an unborn child that resulted in the death of the woman (and the embryo) because one party cut her open in order to determine who was right.[19] Migration-and-settlement stories of villages, which were established not until the second half of the nineteenth century, often explain that the founders of the village fled from the incursions of Muslim warlords or the aggressions of neighboring Dagara settlements, but usually combine such historical realism with the conventional, more metaphorical motifs of the conflict between greedy brothers or the pregnant-woman-slit-open story.[20]

Significantly, and in keeping with their distinct ethos of mobility, Dagara narratives hardly ever resort to the greedy-brothers or pregnant-woman motifs in order to explain their own migrations.[21] They proudly report that they have continued up to the present day to found new farmsteads and village wards on the settlement frontier. They seem to find it neither astonishing nor problematic that many nuclear families move several times in the course of an adult life, and that in most domestic groups some members have moved out and settled elsewhere. More generally, the ideal of autonomy, that is, of becoming the head of a house (*yirsob*), is rated highly and may account for the relatively easy and frequent fission of Dagara patrilineages.

Tensions and conflicts between siblings are given as one of the reasons for leaving the father's compound, but another is the lack of available land. However, when Dagara informants reported that their ancestors migrated because of "hunger" and "in search of food," or simply because "they were too many," this usually does not refer to any objectively measurable scarcity of land, but culturally defined ideals of sufficient space and autonomy.[22] Jack Goody has argued that the norms of matrilinear inheritance of moveable goods among the "LoDagaba," as he has called the speakers of the northern Dagara dialects around Nandom and Ouessa, provided a particularly strong motif for the early independence of sons from their fathers.[23] The fruits of the labor that sons had invested in their fathers' fields, namely the contents of the granary, cattle, tools, money, and other assets, would eventually be carried away by their mother's brothers' sons, and thus it was advantageous to separate from one's father's farmstead as early as possible. However, early mobility was, and continues to be, also pronounced among Dagara groups with a strictly patrilinear system of inheritance, as for instance the Dagara-Wiile, who rapidly colonized the frontier west of the Black Volta. All these Dagara groups view mobility not as rupture or anomaly, but rather as part and parcel of the normal course of life. Just as he did in the past, an enterprising Dagara young man with little hope of inheriting his father's position as lineage head often continues to migrate in search of farming lands over an extended period of time. He attaches himself to various relatives for a number of years until he finally encounters a frontier zone where he is the first-comer, relatively speaking, with enough surplus land to allow him to accommodate later Dagara arrivals. Often, this migration takes place with the explicit consent of the elders of the domestic group in the original settlement.[24]

The Lonely Hunter and His Supporters

While the reasons for and attitudes toward mobility differ among Sisala and Dagara, the problems that needed to be solved in the settlement process were similar. Going into the bush and opening up new land for human settlement was a risky undertaking. Beyond the known and cultivated territory protected by the earth shrine and the ancestors lay potentially dangerous encounters with wild animals, hitherto unknown neighbors, and capricious bush spirits. It is therefore no surprise that the founders of new settlements are usually described as strong hunters who knew how to cover long distances, orient themselves in unknown territories (usually by following water courses and locating conspicuous trees), and, most important, defend themselves physically and spiritually.[25] Even today, establishing bush farms and eventually new villages in the frontier zone is regarded as an arduous and dangerous task, although it no longer requires the skills of a hunter. Oral traditions leave no doubt that the foundation of a new settlement was a gradual, risky, and, up to a certain point, reversible process, starting with the hunter's erection of a simple temporary shelter, followed by the establishment of a more permanent mud hut, and culminating in the construction of a regular adobe house, to which the hunter's family then moved.

Many Sisala and Dagara migration-and-settlement narratives are centered on the figure of the wandering hunter who is compelled to leave home for some reason; discovers a suitable site with sufficient water, shadow trees, and wildlife for a new settlement; clears the bush; and starts to build his hut and, eventually, a house. A typical example of such a narrative is the account given by the Sisala chief of Bozo, a village just a little southeast of Bakoteng:

> Our ancestor, with the name of Guo, came from Tokuri.[26] . . . How it went, there was a debate between two men over a pregnant woman. One said she would give birth to a baby boy and the other said she would give birth to a baby girl. The debate went so high that they got up, caught the pregnant woman, killed and operated on her and saw a baby boy. Do you think the owner of the woman would allow us to settle together? This was the cause why we scattered. . . . Our ancestor Guo who ran away was a hunter. This place [Bozo] was a big, thick forest; there was nobody around here. Guo killed many animals. He sat and had many animals roaming in his direction without even noticing because of the thick forest. He cleared under a tree, sat there and killed many animals. He smoked them, but he had nobody. He sat and later dug a hole and crossed it with sticks and put all the smoked meat on top of the sticks, cut some sticks again, crossed them on top of the meat and covered that with mud. After this he went back to Tokuri. Those who had run away, leaving few of them, he begged and they came and carried the meat home for him and he gave that to the children to eat. After that he came back. He said: "As I am seated here, in this thick bush infested with mosquitoes [*buse*] . . . , under this tree, where I am settling, should be called Bozo." . . . Since we came in from Tokuri, we never went back there. . . . If we want to perform any sacrifice, we will only mention Guo. It is Guo who will draw the attention of the ancestors in Tokuri.[27]

The lonely-hunter story of the foundation of a new village is an expression of the cultural ideal of the importance of the first-comer and his original pact with the spirits of the land. In many Sisala narratives, the hunter motif is simply added to an episode of flight before conflict, and the narrators apparently see no contradiction in emphasizing, on the one hand, the extraordinary circumstances that led to the departure of their ancestors, and claiming, on the other, that the location for the new settlement was discovered in the course of a regular hunting expedition. Dagara stories, too, focus on the hunter roaming in the uninhabited bush as the archetypical frontiersman, although additional episodes eventually acknowledge the presence of previous inhabitants. Interestingly, Dagara narrators have recourse to the lonely-hunter motif even for villages founded during the colonial period, on land controlled by Sisala earth priests. The Dagara founder of Fielmuo, for instance, a Dagara settlement established around 1918 on Sisala land, in what was then the British protectorate, is said to have been a famous hunter. My Dagara informants in Fielmuo narrated how, setting out from Niégo in the French colony, this hunter roamed in the bush as far as the future site of Fielmuo, where he met fellow Sisala hunters and eventually asked them for some of their fertile land in order to resettle his family and invite his friends to join him.[28]

While in the case of settlements founded after the turn of the century, the lonely hunter is quite obviously a metaphorical figure, it would be misleading even for earlier periods if we were to take the motif at face value. Migrants and settlers in precolonial times had to cope with an environment of overwhelming insecurity, and many of my interlocutors insisted that traveling could indeed be extremely dangerous. Extended networks of kinship and friendship served like a password in encounters with unknown strangers in the bush. In addition, a new settlement could survive only if a critical mass of people could be recruited to come and live there. Such a critical mass was necessary for defense purposes as well as for clearing the thick bush and fending off wild animals. Furthermore, only a sufficiently large area of open farmland could keep endemic sicknesses like trypanosomiasis and onchocercosis in check.[29] According to censuses from the early colonial period, the average settlement in the region had between 200 and 450 inhabitants. Settlements that had only a few dozen inhabitants in the early twentieth century usually disappeared in the following decades.[30] My interlocutors often mentioned sicknesses as the reason why a settlement was abandoned, as well as attacks by unfriendly neighbors or mounted warlords.

The foundation of a new village was therefore a collective enterprise that usually involved the founder's patri- and matrilineal kin as well as allied clans or befriended individuals who quickly attached themselves to the nucleus of the new village. They were attracted by the unexploited resources such as fertile farming land and plentiful game in the vicinity of the new settlement. To enhance security, the founder sometimes invited relatives or friends who were known as capable warriors to join his group. Significantly, while the Sisala often recruited additional settlers and allies among other ethnic groups, the Dagara usually invited only fellow Dagara—a phenomenon that I discuss in more detail in chapter 4. In either case, the recruitment of relations and allies was crucial in stabilizing a new settlement, but it also posed dangers. Later immigrants would usually first build their houses near the first-comers' compounds, but later would move farther away and form new sections as tensions or even open conflicts grew between the different kin groups. Such late-comers could, and in many cases did, challenge the status of the first-comers as ritual overlords and allodial landowners—a phenomenon that Kopytoff has discussed in terms of the indispensable social and political "entrepreneurship" of the frontiersmen who needed to both recruit and control adherents and allies.[31]

Recruiting Followers: The Role of Patriclans

The comparison of the ways in which the Dagara and the Sisala dealt with the challenge of recruiting followers gives us some clues as to why Dagara expansion was so successful. Among the Sisala, the ideology of local stability goes hand in hand with the absence of a developed patriclan system and of the far-ranging supralocal ties that such a system can support. Sisala narratives usually mention only the actual settlement and the place of origin, but no intermediate stops. In contrast to the Dagara expansion, where the settlement frontier in general expanded gradually through interlinked small-scale migrations, Sisala migration is remembered as having been disjunctive. Even where Sisala pioneers are reported to have recruited a few additional settlers among their families in their original villages, they purportedly severed these ties once their new abode was firmly established. Sisala villages tended to remain rather small, and if the founding lineages wanted to expand their settlements, they seem to have accommodated strangers from different ethno-linguistic backgrounds who happened to come through the area, rather than actively enlisting people from their own hinterland.[32] Neighboring Sisala villages sometimes point to shared geographical origins of their founding ancestors and explain their current relations in terms of the joint migration of senior and junior brothers. However, the resulting mental map is less geared toward supporting mobility than toward reinforcing sedentariness and local ties in the new habitat.

Dagara frontiersmen, on the other hand, drew on a much wider range of networks, including patriclans, matriclans, clan alliances, and institutionalized friendships, in order to mobilize followers and stabilize settlements on the frontier. The Dagara patriclan system in particular was, and continues to be, a crucial mechanism in recruiting new settlers because it created, and continues to create, complex supralocal networks of wide geographical reach. As in most African languages, there are no separate Dagara words for what anthropologists usually distinguish as patrilineage (a corporate group of agnatic kin tracing common descent back over two to four generations to a named ancestor) or patriclan (a larger agnatic descent group without a named ancestor at the apex). The word *yir* can refer to the house (in a material sense), the residents of the house, and, more generally, patrikin.[33] The precise meaning depends on the context and the interests of the actors who are invoking the concept. However, the Dagara do have specific names for their more than two dozen exogamous patriclans,[34] which can have several thousand members, or more. Specific clan taboos are often used to establish (fictive) kinship with clans among Dagara speaking different dialects or among the neighboring Sisala, Phuo, or Nuni. Patriclans—and even the smaller patrilineages—constitute potentially translocal communities, defined by ties forged in the past. The concept of *yir* thus provides a flexible idiom of cohesion, both in local kin groups and in the context of mobility.

The process of Dagara territorial expansion took place—and continues to take place—through the fission of domestic groups.[35] The patriclan system made it possible for the newly created kin units to maintain bonds of solidarity with one another, even when precise genealogical ties were difficult to establish. This system worked extremely well in a context of mobility and rapid expansion, as the example of the Kusiele and the Gane patriclans discussed in the remaining sections of this chapter shows. Fission also worked at the level of entire clans, and there are numerous aetiological narratives that explain how a particular clan, in the course of migration, split into distinctive subsections, which would take on different names (often referring to the specific circumstances of the division), mix their own arrow poisons, perform important ritual roles for one another, and eventually marry each other.[36]

The patriclan system not only helps to occupy a large new territory, but also to maintain vital relations with the original home—usually the father's or even father's father's house. These relations are important if an exit option is needed in case local conditions on the frontier turn out to be unsuitable for permanent settlement. Furthermore, Dagara frontiersmen believed that only the maintenance of the ritual umbilical cord to the original patrilineage could guarantee the spiritual well-being of their group on new land. This bond was (and still is) often symbolized by a power object that the father or another family elder gave to the man who wanted to found a new compound. The next step to building a proper house entailed the transfer of the ancestral shrine(s) (*kpiin daar*), and usually the shrine room was the first room of the house to be built.[37] The transition from the temporary hut to the proper house was ritually marked by the presence of the ancestor shrines, and it was consolidated when the house's founder died and was buried at the new house, not in his original village. Even today, these are the symbolic actions that distinguish a new house from a seasonal farm settlement, as I show below in the case study of Laponé.

Dagara migration stories always mention several places where the ancestors had settled for a while before they arrived at their final destination. This reflects the importance of retaining vital links to one's father's or grandfather's house, but also to one's maternal relatives as well as to the wider social networks in which all of these relations have become involved during their travels and that can support the frontier process. On certain family occasions, or when divination demands it, the settlers in the new villages will retrace their own or their forefathers' migration route and perform sacrifices at the old ancestral shrines if the original house is still inhabited. Sacrifices may also have to be performed at the ruins of the patrilineage's old houses, or at certain rocks, rivers, or trees along the migration route that the ancestors had appealed to for protection. The migratory route of the settlement's founding patrilineage is recollected at certain ritual occasions at the village earth shrine and, at least in some clans, during the initiation ceremony (*bagr*), as the example of the Kusiele below shows. The migration of the forefathers is thus always present in the collective memory.

The clans that arrived later in a new settlement tend to remember and present migration routes that are similar to, or even identical with, the route of the founding clan. This may be due to the obliteration of deviating migration routes, but it can also reflect the joint migration of allied clans. Indeed, there seem to be many cases when two or three patriclans moved together over long periods of time. Such alliances are explained in terms of friendship, joking relationships, or relationships between a "maternal uncle" and a "nephew" (*madeb-arbile*), as the case of Ouessa illustrates.[38]

All in all, the founding of new Dagara settlements was, and continues to be, firmly embedded in a dense network of alliances between specific patriclans. Listening to the settlement accounts, one is left with the impression of a landscape covered by patriclan networks, spun around nodal places that are interconnected in multiple ways by routes of patriclan migration.[39] Some central places figure prominently in many accounts of the migratory routes of different patriclans, others are of ritual importance only to specific clans, but all join to form a mental map, a ritual and kinship topography of Dagara country (*Dagara teng*). Its full extent and details were not known by any single individual, but all Dagara firmly believed that they would be able to find relatives in every corner of "Dagara land." Indeed, today a Dagara can travel well over a hundred kilometers from one end of *Dagara teng* to the other, meet people whom he or she has never met before, and immediately establish a more or less close relationship of kinship. It is likely that this was not very different during the nineteenth century, or even prior to that.

The Dynamics of Cohabitation and Conflict

In order to better understand the case studies of Kusiele migrations and the colonization of Ouessa and Laponé that are presented in the remainder of this chapter, a few general remarks on ethnic conversion, cohabitation, and conflict between Sisala first-comers and Dagara late-comers are necessary here. A thorough analysis of the Dagara stories of the foundation of new villages—beyond the obvious hunter motif—reveals that many of the present Dagara settlements were originally founded by other groups and were only later taken over by Dagara. In a number of cases there is debate—which I explore in more detail in the next chapter—concerning whether the Dagara installed their own independent earth shrine or acquired the shrine from the previous population. Where the latter is claimed, the trope of the peaceful transfer of the earth shrine often contrasts with accounts of the forced expulsion of the Sisala. This contradiction must be interpreted as an expression of two different phases of the settlement process. These phases—of peaceful cohabitation and conflict—recurred as the frontier of Dagara expansion moved into land occupied by other groups.

In the areas east of the Black Volta, the first Dagara pioneers often asked for land to farm, and settled close to—or even in the middle of—existing Sisala villages.[40] The security of an established community and favorable ecological conditions, especially the availability of water throughout the year, were probably crucial factors that determined where the first Dagara immigrants chose to settle. In addition, hoe-farmers often prefer second-growth land, that is, bush growing on old fallows, to "virgin" territory, because the former is as fertile as the latter, but much easier to work.[41] What followed was a phase of more or less peaceful cohabitation. Stories of the friendship between a Dagara frontiersman and his Sisala host, as well as the identification of Dagara patriclans and Sisala lineages who have the same taboos and established a joking relationship, may have their roots in this kind of situation. The further development of these "multiethnic" settlements seems to have taken two different directions: either the Dagara late-comers were gradually absorbed into the first-comer community by processes of clan conversion and linguistic-cultural assimilation, or else the Dagara immigrants maintained their distinct identity and eventually established a separate settlement.

Where the cohabitation of Dagara immigrants and earlier settlers did not result in processes of ethnic conversion (and thus deemphasis of Dagara identity), the immigrants would eventually build their own settlements, spatially separate from their former hosts. Separation—and maintenance of a distinct identity rather than assimilation—seems to have occurred when the Dagara pioneers were able to recruit a sufficient number of followers from their own ethno-linguistic group in the hinterland. There are even some indications that assimilated Dagara pioneers, or their descendants, sometimes reemphasized their Dagara identity when new groups of Dagara-speaking immigrants arrived and established themselves in the vicinity of the Sisala settlements.[42] In any case, the establishment of these early Dagara villages seems usually to have occurred with the consent of their Sisala neighbors.

Generally, ethnic conversion tended to operate in only one direction: Dagara became Sisala, but rarely vice versa. As mentioned above, the Sisala seem to represent a kind of community of refugees that incorporated strangers of various ethnic origins. There seems to be a paradox here concerning the regional demographic development. Sisala recruited people from outside and should therefore have grown in numbers, but in fact they became regional minorities, both in Ghana and Burkina Faso, and their territory shrank under the encroachment of the Dagara. The Dagara, on the other hand, were less inclusive, but were still able to expand their settlement frontier, apparently without depopulating their hinterland. Both Sisala and Dagara occasionally integrated slaves into their houses, at least during the latter part of the nineteenth century, but in neither case does this seem to have played a major role in the recruitment of followers on the frontier.[43] One may speculate whether differential rates of fertility and population growth allowed one group to expand in space while the other stagnated. Unfortunately, there are no reliable data on this. Alternatively, even similar growth rates would produce an increasing difference in absolute numbers if one group was significantly bigger from the outset.[44] In any case, it is likely that particular external events such as the incursions of slave raiders had different effects on the different groups and seem to have worked in favor of Dagara demographic strength.

Where the small communities of the first Dagara settlers gradually grew in size, as more and more patri- and matrikin joined them, Sisala (and Phuo) communities often "voluntarily" opted to move away and sometimes handed over the earth shrine to the

Dagara settlers. However, the Sisala's exit options, toward the north and the east of the Dagara frontier, were severely restricted when the Zaberma slave raiders established their headquarters in the region of Leo during the latter part of the nineteenth century and attempted to bring the surrounding villages under their control. During the same period, the Phuo, on the western frontier of Dagara expansion, suffered the incursions of warlords from Ouahabou, in the north, especially during the reign of Moktar Karantao. The Dagara, on the other hand, seem to have been much less affected by the attacks of Muslim warriors because the Phuo and Sisala settlements served as a kind of buffer zone between them and these mounted raiders. This confluence of historical circumstances may, at least in part, account for the demographic advantage the Dagara enjoyed on the agricultural frontier.[45]

Where an exit option did not exist or was not chosen, tensions between the Dagara, the Phuo, and the Sisala increased. Narratives from both sides report numerous instances of stealing of livestock and even of murder, and conflicts could lead to armed hostilities along hardening ethnic boundaries. Most probably, it was often not the first generation of Dagara immigrants that was responsible for the escalation of conflicts, but rather groups newly arriving from Dagara settlements in the hinterland. This period of ethnic conflict is reflected in Sisala village names with meanings such as "finding a refuge" (Hamile) or "lift up and see . . ." (". . . whether you are stronger" [Pina]), and their Dagara counterpart Navrikpe, "we enter against all odds," or Dadoune, "to bring about enmity." In some restricted areas, small-scale feuds seem to have developed into full-fledged warfare, usually ending with the retreat of the Sisala. Armed conflict was sometimes ended by a peacemaking ceremony, which involved the sacrifice of a dog and the burying of weapons at the spot that indicated the new boundary between Sisala and Dagara territory, thus symbolically confirming the territorial gains of the Dagara. In most cases, the Dagara had either already acquired a shrine stone from their Sisala neighbors before open conflict broke out, or they placed the newly conquered territories under the protection of existing Dagara earth shrines.

This advance, however, came to a halt under the colonial regime, which had a profound impact on mobility and ethnic relations. The colonial administration aimed to restrict the residential mobility of their subjects in order to have better control over labor resources, military recruitment, and poll-tax collection. Furthermore, the imposition of the *pax colonia*, which only really became effective in most parts of the research area from the 1910s onward, largely removed the opportunities to use violence in the appropriation of new territories. This changed the balance of power in favor of the Sisala, halting the expansion of Dagara earth-shrine areas. Much of the current pattern of ritual ownership of territory is due to the colonial freezing of a previously highly dynamic situation. At the same time, the options for the Sisala to leave were considerably reduced. Open, uninhabited spaces, without "owners," were no longer available, and Sisala settlements therefore put up more resistance to being displaced.

Although no additional land came under Dagara ritual control after the 1920s, the Dagara continued to found new settlements, now on territory owned and ritually controlled by the Sisala. Since independence, the expansion of the Dagara has continued at an impressive rate. New Dagara compounds and hamlets are being founded not only along the former northwestern and northeastern frontiers but also toward the south, in the Ivory Coast and the Gonja and Brong regions in Ghana.[46] Significantly, the Dagara acceptance of the ritual overlordship of their host communities is something hardly imaginable for Sisala. They prefer to promote the idea of a stable, permanent community on their own land, and to solve any problem of scarce resources by turning to more intensive methods of farming and to labor migration (in which the Dagara also engage). These cultural ideals, however, have a material base, because the land resources of the Sisala are quantitatively and qualitatively superior to those of the Dagara—one of the effects of the colonial freezing of their status as first-comers to the region.[47]

Precolonial Strategies of Expansion and the Politics of Memory of a Dagara Patriclan

The Kusiele are one of the largest Dagara patriclans, currently numbering in the tens of thousands of members, if not more. Kusiele men and women live in numerous villages, both in Ghana and Burkina Faso, straddling boundaries of dialect and cultural practice.[48] They furnish the earth priests of many settlements along the banks of the Black Volta, from the area around Nadawli up to Kokoligu, just south of Ouessa. Even in villages where the Kusiele did not assume the office of the earth priest, they were often able to found large and influential sections, not least because of the strong supralocal ties among clan mates whom they were able to mobilize.

The history of Kusiele migrations is a typical example of the role of the patriclan in Dagara expansion. It shows how the clan's movement took place through the fission of domestic groups and the decentralized migrations of small groups of patrikin, and how male elders, young men, and women of all ages assumed different responsibilities in the group's travels and the foundation of new settlements. At the same time, it illustrates how the effective cooperation between these smaller groups, who often specialized as hunters, hoe-farmers, or warriors, allowed the entire clan to expand and claim new territories. And finally, it demonstrates how various practices of remembrance—ranging from aetiological legends and regularly recounted migration narratives to sacrifices along the various subgroups' routes and stopovers—created a sense of commonality among patriclan members that supported, and continues to support, intraclan solidarity.

While the strategies of intraclan cooperation and politics of memory can also be found among other Dagara patriclans, Kusiele in general, and particularly those residing in and around Lawra, seem to have sustained an unusually rich repertoire of narratives about their ancestors' wanderings. One of the reasons for this may be the early encouragement that local historical interest received from British colonial officers. The British chose Lawra, one of the populous Kusiele settlements near the Black Volta, as the site for the headquarters of a large administrative district, and appointed a member of the Lawra earth-priestly family to serve as paramount chief ("head chief") of the surrounding villages. In the course of time, this chiefly house came to play an important role in local and regional politics, due to its proximity to the district headquarters and an astute management of power by some of the Lawra Naas, as the paramount chiefs are called.[49] As early as 1907, a history of Kusiele migrations and of the foundation of Lawra by Kontol, one of the Kusiele frontiersmen, was recorded in the district record book. This version, that was later included in a schoolbook collection of legends from Northern Ghana and thus widely read (and then orally recirculated), obviously aimed at legitimating the political authority of the new chief and extending its territorial reach.[50] At the same time, however, competing versions of local and clan history continued, and still continue, to exist, not least because the lesson that history may help to boost one's claims was also learned outside the chiefly house.

Another factor that contributed to the time depth and richness of detail of Kusiele historical narratives is their inclusion in the corpus of stories recited during the Kusiele *bagr*, the initiation rites that all Dagara patriclans used to organize, and that those who have not converted to the Catholic faith continue to celebrate up until today.[51] The *bagr* ceremonies in the Lawra chiefs' house were, and still are, extraordinarily well attended by clan members from far and near, and the Lawra version of Kusiele history is thus relatively well known by many other Kusiele lineages. Furthermore, the recital in verse, typical of all traditions presented in the *bagr* context, serves as an *aide-mémoire* and helps to transmit the migration-and-settlement story in more detail than is usually the case in more profane settings. Finally, regular sacrifices offered during the *bagr,* as well as during annual communal hunts at all landmarks in the vicinity of Lawra that are mentioned in the Kontol narrative, also support the collective memory. Many Kusiele trace their forefathers' migration back to Lawra and Babile, and the Kusiele elders in Lawra have become a kind of repository of the early history of the clan.[52] Thus, both the influence of modern chieftaincy politics and particularly elaborate traditional practices of commemoration contribute to an unusually well-developed historical consciousness among the Kusiele of Lawra and surrounding villages.

I first learned about Kusiele history and Lawra's founding ancestor, Kontol, from the late Lawra Naa Abeyifaa Karbo, with whom I often conversed during my research on the political history of North-Western Ghana. Karbo had been trained as a teacher and entered politics in the 1950s, and after serving as member of parliament for the Lawra-Nandom constituency for many years, he held various high-ranking political offices until he retired in the 1990s.[53] He was an indefatigable informant not only on the local history of chieftaincy and party politics, but also on Kusiele and Lawra traditions. However, although he was an initiate of the *bagr* and had often listened to the Kusiele *bagr* recitations about Kontol, he insisted that I should also record a version at the "source," as he put it, namely from the elders of the house in Yirkpee, where Kontol is said to have settled first.

In Yirkpee I was met by the late Yobo Kiebang, then a man of eighty or more years and a *bagr* "mother"—an experienced *bagr* initiate who sponsors initiation ceremonies in his house.[54] Without much prompting, Kiebang spoke for more than two hours, only occasionally interrupted by his elder brother Kuuzin, who corrected a name or complemented some detail—a seamless flow of prose on lineage and clan history such as I rarely encountered in interviews with members of other patriclans.

Kiebang's Narrative of Kontol's Wanderings

It is not possible here to present Kiebang's story in full, but even excerpts from his narrative convey its flavor and, although exceptional in their richness of detail, give a good idea of Dagara stories about their ancestors' expeditions. Kiebang began his story with Gangnaa, the earliest Kusiele ancestor whom he remembered by name, and with Gangnaa's sons Zegnaa, Gmaada, and Dasor. He related how they set out from Ture, in what is today the northern Ivory Coast, and, fleeing from unspecified "enemies," eventually crossed the Black Volta and reached Kusele. In Kusele, the three brothers parted company.[55] Zegnaa moved northward to Nadawli,[56] Gmaada went northeastward toward Jirapa, while Dasor ventured northwestward to Babile. This image of the dispersal of three sons aims at creating a sense of unity between spatially and genealogically rather distant Kusiele lineages—a sense that was reinforced by occasional sacrifices at the ruins of the "original" house in Kusele, which many Kusiele attended, at least according to Lawra Naa Karbo's recollections. Kiebang's account then focused on the movements of Dasor, whose son Kontol later eventually founded Lawra. Somewhat confusing for a first-time listener like myself, Kiebang first introduced Kontol as one of Dasor's brothers, but later explained that Kontol was in fact Dasor's son. This may have been a narrative device to attribute to Kontol not only the foundation of Lawra, but also earlier important discoveries and thus turn him into an even more impressive culture hero.

Interestingly, Kiebang did not attempt to trace a direct line of descent from Kontol to his own immediate ancestors. We can assume that intermediate generations, between Kontol and Kiebang's grandfather, have been forgotten, and that in the course of time, Kusiele lineages diversified to such an extent that it would be difficult to trace such connections with any certainty. This also makes it difficult to put any definite dates to Dasor's and Kontol's migrations. Calculating on the basis of the genealogies of founders of Kusiele settlements that were established later than Lawra and whose migration-and-settlement narratives claim descent from Kontol and his people, we may tentatively assume that Yirkpee and Lawra must have been in existence by the late eighteenth century. But they could also be older, and since there are no archeological data, such dates will remain speculative.

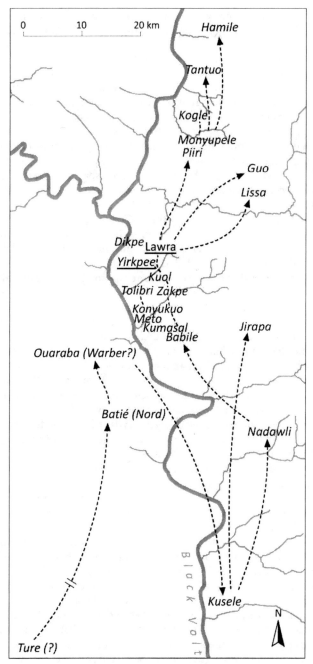

Map 1.1. Kusiele migrations according to Kiebang

"Yirkpee was founded not by our generation. Those of our ancestors who founded this place are dead and gone," Kiebang opened his account, going on to explain:

Our ancestors came from a faraway place called Ture. It was the shooting of the arrow that made our ancestors evacuate Ture. The whole of their generation was in danger of being wiped out by enemies who persistently shot arrows at them. So they decided to move away to another place called Benpo. At Benpo the enemies still followed them with the arrow. They left Benpo again to Furesi, but the enemies again got there. From Furesi they left and went all the way to Yilo. When they settled at Yilo, the enemies looked for them for a very long time before they found them. But again, the danger of the arrow was not yet over. They decided to leave Yilo for Gyani. Even at Gyani, the enemies did not spare them, and they left Gyani for Wuli. All was not well at Wuli, and they continued to Bakyibaga. At Bakyibaga they noticed that they were still not far off from the enemies [Kiebang consulted his brother Kuuzin] . . . , so they left there again to Gyilo. From Gyilo they went to Batié. When peace again eluded them at Batié, there was an understanding between Gangnaa's sons, namely Zegnaa, Gmaada, and Dasor, to leave Batié for Warber. By then, their father had died.

It was at Warber that our ancestors were able to evade their enemies for a long time. During one dry season, the young men went out for a hunting expedition, and discovered that they had been living not far from the river [*man*, i.e. the Black Volta]. Meanwhile, their elder brothers Kontol, Zegnaa, and Gmadaa, who had stayed home became worried about the long stay of their younger brothers in the bush. Kontol, who was the eldest and a hunter, was particularly worried . . . and decided to look for the young men. To Kontol's amazement, however, the young men had a very successful hunting expedition. The meat they got was so much that they had difficulties carrying it to the house. The young men then broke the news to Kontol that they had come across the river, which was not far away. They led Kontol to the river. Kontol was so happy with the young men's discovery that he hurriedly took them to the house where their father [Dasor?] and other brothers were still waiting. When the news was broken, the father exclaimed that it was God who was still leading them and who was about to show them the best place to settle where peace and comfort was no longer going to be ephemeral.

The father took Kontol with him for further exploration. While at the shore of the river they looked around and saw that there was sand somewhere in the middle of the water. The old man asked Kontol to use a stick to determine how much sand was in that part of the river. Fortunately, it was a bed of sand which could help them to cross the river. The old man further asked Kontol to wade through the water and, if possible, attempt crossing over to the Nadawli side [*nadolgang*]. . . . Back at the house, Kontol said that the young men's discovery . . . averted the complete annihilation by their enemies. For without the discovery of the Black Volta [and the ford], it would have been quite possible that they were going to flee in that direction, in the face of attacks by their enemies, only to be trapped. It was then decided that the whole family should move across the river to settle on the other side. During the night, the children were asked to ensure that all the cattle, poultry, sheep, and goats were properly housed. The women were asked to carry all their pots, basins, and other belongings down to the riverside for safekeeping. At dawn the cattle were chased into the river amid mooing and bleating. All lambs and calves were successfully carried over to the other side of the river, and so were all the belongings of the women.

On the other side of the river, they found a vast, flat area that was not only good for settlement, but also a land far away from the enemies. Kusele was this first site that attracted the attention of our ancestors. After they settled for some time at Kusele and found peace and prosperity there, Zegnaa, Gmadaa, Dogfuu, and Dasor, who was the most senior, all decided to move in different directions to found new settlements. Zegnaa wanted to found his settlement in an easterly direction, at Nadawli, from where the sun usually rises. Gmadaa also said he was moving east of Kusele. Dogfu and others all left Kusele in different directions with their families to found new settlements.

The story of Dasor's and Kontol and his brothers' wanderings clearly illustrates the Dagara ideology of mobility discussed above. Although Kiebang explained his ancestors' early moves as attempts to evade the violent attacks of unnamed foreign enemies and Dasor's nephews, meager harvests and a sense of lack of space were just as important motives for moving, as shall become clear in Kiebang's account of Kontol's further movements. More generally, Kiebang regarded it as perfectly normal that the Kusiele apparently did not stay very long in any particular place and continued to spread out and found new villages.

Dasor told Kontol and Kaal that now that the family was splitting, he thought the best place for them to go was to move to a place where the sun usually sets, for without settlement the sun cannot set [*teng be woi, mwintong ku kyen to kpei*]. They also then moved to Babile. However, the enemies were still able to sniff and trace their footsteps up to Babile. Among their enemies were their own *arbili* [sisters' sons] who harassed them. They used to pay a visit to our ancestors in the daytime, but went home very late in the night. . . . They would feign to have gone home, hide themselves in the bush, and watch until the able young men went to sleep. They would then select one of them, and after he was fast asleep unleash a poisonous arrow right into his body. Several young men at Dasor's house were killed in this way by his own *arbili*. But anytime there was a funeral they came around to shed crocodile tears. . . . Dasor called Kontol, the eldest son, and his brothers and told them that he had come to realize that the deaths that were still plaguing the house even after their long journey from the enemies' land to Babile were not the work of distant enemies but his own *arbili*. He charged Kontol with the task of looking for a new settlement site since he was a hunter.

. . . Kontol first made a stop at a place now called Kumasal where he made a mark on a tree which could help him to find his way back home. He made several marks on trees until he got to [Kiebang consulted Kuuzin] . . . Konyukuo. He made another mark there and was satisfied that from Konyukuo he could find his way back home. He advanced into where is now Tuma and made another mark on a tree. He continued his journey to Zakpe, then to Meto, where he made another mark on a tree. During all this time he had not set eyes on a single settlement. Tolibri was another place where he stopped. At Tolibri there was a plateau that overlooked the whole area. He climbed the plateau and looked at the landscape with satisfaction. Fulo was the next stop from Tolibri, and the whole area was uninhabited. From Fulo he went to Kuol, near Lawra, where he saw paths that must have been created by human beings. He also saw the remains of the houses of the Dyani, who, because they cannot bear the sight [*nyuu*, literally, smell] of we the Blacks [*nisele*], must have run away with all their cowries when our ancestors arrived at Babile. At this point, Kontol was overwhelmed by fear, but thanks to his bravery [*deblu*] continued to advance into the old settlement of the Dyani. He saw several dilapidated houses, climbed on one of them and looked at the old settlement with amazement and content. Unfortunately, the sun was setting, and he was compelled to retrace all the tree marks he had made right to the house at Babile.

In these and further episodes, Kiebang's narrative describes vividly how young and old, men and women, and hunters and hoe-farmers cooperated in organizing the movement. The physically stronger young men were sent by their fathers as scouts to explore the route and discover new sites for settlement. Kiebang explained the techniques of orientation, typical of a hunter (for example, marking the trees), but also emphasized the importance of the scout's *deblu*, his manliness, courage, and spiritual power. The scout's discoveries were then assessed by the seniors back home with respect to the needs of the entire group. A suitable location had to provide extended "empty" bush for hunting, and some protection against external aggression. It had to offer sufficient drinking water and readily available housing—the ruins of the houses of previous inhabitants and the hollow tree were preferred to the virgin forest. And it needed fertile soil for agriculture as well as other resources necessary for establishing a household, such as rocks suitable for fashioning mortar and pestle for the women, as we shall see when Kiebang narrates how Kontol discovered the site of the future settlement of Lawra.

In Babile, Kiebang continued, Kontol informed his father about his discoveries at Kuol.

After having heard all about Kontol's long journey, the father gave the go-ahead to move with his two younger brothers Bure and Kaal, who had married, and to occupy the old settlement of the Dyani. The father instructed him to take along with them some seeds of pumpkin, groundnuts, and beans, all of which could be the source of vegetables for the family. They were also to repair the dilapidated houses of the Dyani at Kuol, not only clearing them but also setting some small fires into them which could drive away dangerous reptiles. They were also expected to take along some cereal seeds, such as millet and maize. However, after a year's stay in Kuol, they were disappointed with the farm's produce. Kontol's younger brothers advised that they return to Babile, but Kontol cautioned them to exercise some restraint and wait for him to go around the area once more....

Kontol set out for another journey and got to a hill called Sobaaltang. It was on Sobaaltang that Kontol sat and surveyed all the area stretching out to Ambor and Dikpe and found that the whole area was really uninhabited. He continued his search for a better settlement site and got to this shrub at Yirkpee.

Kiebang pointed to a wooded area about a half kilometer away from the site where our interview took place. "When Kontol reached this shrub," Kiebang explained, he saw a lot of bush cows [*wenii*, buffalos] resting there. He removed an arrow from his quiver and was tempted to shoot at them. But it occurred to him that if he shot at them and they got wild, he was going to get lost, even if he was able to escape from them. He therefore advised himself not to disturb the bush cows, hid himself somewhere, and followed them when they went out of the shrubs. To his surprise, the bush cows took him to the river [Black Volta]. What a pleasant surprise and blessing it was for Kontol! That was what he had been looking for. He immediately saw a stone in the middle of the river [*garakuur*], which he mistook for a crocodile. It is because of this stone that we, the Kusiele children [*Kusiele biir*], are sometimes referred to as the *garakuur kutuo kye* as one of our praise names. . . . When Kontol was sure that it was not a crocodile, he stepped into the water, sat on the stone, and drank water. . . . When he came out of the river, he saw another path of the bush cows which he followed, leading to a well. The well was called Vil.

At this point, Kuuzin wanted to add some information, but Kiebang stopped him, explaining that he wanted "to shorten things" for me, since he supposed that I was "in a hurry." Kuuzin protested, but Kiebang went on with his story:

There is a big stone . . . on which one can find a grinding stone and the grinder which is suitable for grinding all sorts of soup ingredients. Kontol had also discovered this big stone when he continued to follow the footsteps of the bush cows. . . . Meanwhile the bush cows which he had been following had also disappeared into a thicket that he dared not enter. At any rate, he saw a big baobab tree whose stem had been covered with *ura* branches.

These are fibrous twigs of a tree that Sisala and Dagara use for roofing, and the name Lawra, originally Lura, is supposedly derived from these *ura* branches.

Kontol was amazed at the way the *uri* had been naturally arranged around the tree. With their help he climbed to the top of the baobab tree only to notice that the whole stem had a big hole, with an opening at the lower part. He ventured peeping into the hole, but was greeted by many black bats. But as a man, he picked up courage and looked deep into the hole. . . . To him, this was the realization of his father's prophecy that God was going to give him a better settlement place in the near future. Quietly he said to himself: "Is this hole not a *yirkpee* [literally, big house; name of Kiebang's village] that God has made for me to live in?" That is why this place is also called *tengyog*. It was at this point that Kontol returned home [to Kuol] for a final movement to settle at this place.

Kiebang continued that Kontol and his brothers finally moved to the new place, together with their wives, and

lived a normal life in the baobab tree for three good years. It was from that hole that they all decided to build a real house. . . .When the family size increased, the need arose again for them to move out into the vast area, with their individual families . . . and through these scattered buildings the whole place came to be opened up. Our joking partners, the Bilbogbe, also arrived later. . . . It was from here in Yirkpee that some of us left to Guo, Lissa, Monyupele, Piiri, Tantuo, Hamile and Kogle. It was individuals who left this place with their families to settle in all these places. Some of our people even went across the river [Black Volta]; . . . others made a backward migration toward Babile; and some of us are in Duori, Zambo, Eremon.

Kiebang went on to enumerate the many places where Kusiele have settled, and then explained how his forefathers built a house near the original baobab tree in which Kontol established his first dwelling. Kiebang's narrative finally ended with an account of how Kontol, during his further explorations in the vicinity of Lawra, acquired an earth-shrine stone and established the boundaries of the area under its control.

Obviously, Kuuzin had wanted to go into more detail concerning the spiritual dimensions of mobility at which Kiebang had only hinted. These aspects are more explicit in the *bagr* version of Kontol's migrations, namely that it was Kontol's supernatural alliance with the bush cows that guided him to a suitable dwelling place, that he had to take care to properly transport the ancestor shrines, and that he needed to recruit joking partners among other patriclans in order to be able perform the *bagr* initiation. In any case, Kiebang left no doubt that the movement was a collective task and the establishment of a new settlement a gradual process. It began with the discovery of a potential site, was followed by a period of a minimum of one agricultural cycle during which the site's suitability was tested, and ended with the construction of socially and spiritually fully equipped houses under the protection of ancestor and earth shrines.

The Kusiele as Frontiersmen and Late-comers

Through his narrative, Kiebang obviously wanted to establish that Kontol and his people were first-comers, not only to Lawra, but also to many neighboring settlements, and therefore repeatedly insisted that the area that Kontol surveyed from his various lookouts was "really uninhabited." At the same time, however, Kiebang's account revealed that in many places along the route Kontol and other Kusiele were in fact late-comers, relatively speaking, and had to come to terms with previous inhabitants. In order to understand these apparent contradictions, it is useful to complement and compare Kiebang's story with information from other Kusiele (and non-Kusiele) interlocutors.

To begin with, unlike Kiebang, other informants did not portray Kontol and his forefathers as victims of violence, but rather as fearsome warriors whose services were occasionally enlisted by other Dagara groups that needed support against some enemies. As Lawra Naa Karbo explained, this was how Kontol's group became embroiled in local feuds and why they had to flee. Karbo even believed that, in the early phases of their migration, his Kusiele ancestors did not farm, but earned their living as mercenaries of sorts, and that it was only when they arrived in Lawra that Kontol and his people buried the war arrows and started farming.[57] Other informants would not support this strong claim, but were also proud of the warlike qualities of the Kusiele and readily admitted that they were sometimes invited by earlier Dagara settlers to help defend their new villages. By definition, this implies that the warrior factions of the Kusiele clan were not the first-comers to the area in question.

A case in point is Babile, on whose foundation Kiebang was rather silent. As Nalukuu, the Kusiele earth priest of Babile, explained, when his ancestors arrived in the area, they met members of the Kpagnyaane patriclan who had already established themselves as earth priests and claimed control over a vast territory. In the beginning, Nalukuu's forefathers accepted the Kpagnyaane earth priests' authority, but eventually relations grew tense. Disputes about what the Kusiele were obliged to give to the earth shrine developed into armed conflict, and ended with the establishment of an independent Kusiele earth shrine for Babile.[58] As Nalukuu related, Kontol's father Dasor and his group, who were clan mates of the Kusiele of Babile but did not belong to the same lineage, must have arrived during the conflict and were invited to help fight the Kpagnyaane. Most likely it was the Kpagnyaane *arbili* who later took their revenge on the young men of Dasor's house and thus motivated the latter's further migration.[59] But Dasor's people also felt that Babile was "too crowded," as Nalukuu put it, and therefore soon moved on.

Taken together, these data suggest that different Kusiele lineages—and sometimes different persons within one lineage—specialized in different activities, namely warfare, hunting, and farming, and that it was their cooperation that supported the rapid successful expansion of the group as a whole. Cros and Dory, who studied the similarly expansionist Lobi west of the Black Volta, conjectured that the Lobi were first hunters who resorted to violence in order to secure exclusive rights over vast hunting territories, before they later became hoe-farmers who attacked their neighbors mainly in order to capture women and thus increase their labor force.[60] This evolutionist hypothesis does not apply to the Kusiele case, and the Dagara in general, who combined warfare, hunting, and farming from very early on, albeit over time the relative importance of these different activities certainly shifted toward agriculture.

Kiebang's narrative leaves no doubt that Kontol and his people preferred occupying sites that had previously been opened up and then abandoned by the original inhabitants. Such locations offered the advantage of working second-growth bush, which is easier to cultivate than "virgin" territory, as well as the opportunity to stake out unchallenged first-comer claims. In the vicinity of Lawra, as Abeyifaa Karbo reported, the Kusiele settlers discovered ruins of earlier farmsteads, including the remains of ancestor shrines and clay pots, which the previous inhabitants had supposedly left behind when they fled before the Dagara newcomers. Kiebang and Karbo identified these earlier inhabitants as "Dyani" whose descendants are currently living in the area of Diébougou.[61] Kiebang also explained, however, that these previous settlers had run away because they could not tolerate the "sight" or "smell" "of we the Blacks [*nisele*]"— a turn of phrase commonly used in reference to dwarfs and other spirits of the bush (*kontome*). Kiebang thus dehumanized the previous inhabitants—a familiar narrative strategy that aims at strengthening the immigrants' first-comer claims, as Kopytoff has succinctly argued.[62]

More generally, the dehumanization of previous inhabitants is prominent in narratives about Dagara settlements established during the early phases of expansion. In more recently founded villages, however, previous inhabitants are generally portrayed as concrete human beings, particularly if their descendants still live in neighboring settlements and sometimes challenge the Dagara immigrants' claims to land ownership. The development of these villages is characterized by the dynamics of cohabitation and conflict outlined above. The history of Ouessa discussed in the following section is typical for the intertwining of peaceful and violent strategies of Dagara territorial expansion. Further, it provides another example of the important role that some Kusiele lineages played as warriors who helped to push the Dagara settlement frontier into Sisala territory.

Uncles, Nephews, and Friends: Peopling the Frontier (1820s–1900)

During my first visit to Ouessa, my host's son led me to one of the bars, along the busy interprovincial road that runs right through the small district capital, where I should greet the local dignitaries, the earth priest Hien Daniel, the old Ouessa chief Nandi Meda, and Charles Meda, the son of the former *chef de canton*, the French colonial counterpart of the British paramount chiefs.[63] Although in the 1980s, the Sankarist régime of Burkina Faso had all but abolished the chieftaincy, Charles Meda, an *ancien combattant* and very outspoken old man, still regarded himself as the highest traditional ruler of the locality. He proudly declared that he was the most authoritative source on Ouessa history, and insisted that he should always be present when I interviewed other informants because he wanted to make sure that they told me "the truth." The earth priest Hien Daniel, for his part, arranged to later speak to me alone, and told me that the glory days of chieftaincy were fortunately over and local power had reverted to where it always belonged, namely to the earth-priestly family. He explained that his ancestors, who belonged to the Gane patriclan, were the founders of Ouessa, while Charles Meda's grandfather Demaal Naab, of the Dikpiele patriclan, had come much later. And although Naab's group, along with Ouessa chief Nandi Meda's Kusiele ancestors, had certainly helped to effectively occupy the large territory of which the Gane claimed ownership, this did not justify Charles Meda's pretentions concerning Ouessa history.

This first encounter confronted me forcefully with the local politics of memory. Who was authorized to tell which part of the local history, which version was the valid one, and why there were so many conflicting stories were questions that my interlocutors in Ouessa and its environs debated vigorously? "The men who knew the true history are all dead," was one of the standard local explanations for contradictory accounts. But people also pointed to the vested interests that some villagers had in "forgetting" certain events and silencing some genealogical connections, while foregrounding others. Using these comments and pulling the various fragments together, I present a tentative model of how Ouessa and its environs were occupied by Dagara immigrants, and how the settlement developed from modest beginnings to the sizeable village that it was by 1902, when the French administrator Maurice Delafosse visited the area and admired the relative wealth of Ouessa's inhabitants and their many "high and comfortable compounds . . . crowned by numerous towers and flanked by walled-in court-yards."[64] I discuss both the politics of memory and the Gane first-comers' strategies of bringing such a large area, of roughly thirty square kilometers, under the control of their powerful earth shrine.

The Foundation of Ouessa: Contradictory Accounts

Shortly after my first encounter with the Ouessa notables, earth priest Hien Daniel granted me an interview. He talked about his ancestors' migration route and their discovery of Ouessa, their encounters and battles with previous inhabitants of the area, and the succession of earth priests that led up to his own installation as officeholder.

> Our ancestor Kontchire came from Mebar, a village behind Dano. He first settled at Memer, then at Petit Leo, until he finally arrived here in Ouessa. This area was inhabited by Pougouli [Phuo] and Sisala. When Kontchire and his people first arrived, they found a woman and wanted to kill her. But the woman told them that if they were to spare her life, she would show them the earth shrine and all they needed to know. . . . Everybody had fled from the area, leaving this Pougouli woman behind, who was the wife of the earth priest killed in battle. She stayed with our ancestors until her death. . . .
>
> Kontchire discovered this area on one of his hunting expeditions from Petit Leo. He was a great hunter of big game, and this place had abundant wildlife as well as fertile land. So he decided to come. The conquest was in two steps. Our ancestors attacked a first time, and the Pougouli suffered the loss of many lives. Then they attacked a second time, and this is when the Pougouli fled and left the woman behind. . . .
>
> Kontchire was the first *tengansob* [earth priest]. He was followed by Kontchire-Wale, his younger brother. From Wale, one of Kontchire's sons, called Mbaazie, took over. Afterward another son of Kontchire, Sornuor, succeeded. Then a third son, Laazie, followed by Dakpin, Kognele, Benongweb, Dougzie, Tiidem, Gbang, Anwo-kobe, and finally myself, Daniel.[65]

Quite unlike Yobo Kiebang in Yirkpee, Hien Daniel was not a very enthusiastic narrator, preferring to present matters in a nutshell. Many of my questions remained open, and I talked to him as often as I could during the following years, always hoping to fill in the gaps and clarify the incongruities that I perceived. During one of these conversations, Hien Daniel repeated the information about the arrival of his ancestors at Ouessa, but now no longer spoke of Pougouli (Phuo) as the original owners of the land, but of Yeri.[66] I was initially confused, but eventually learned that such a shift in ethnic names is quite common in Dagara narratives about previous inhabitants who were

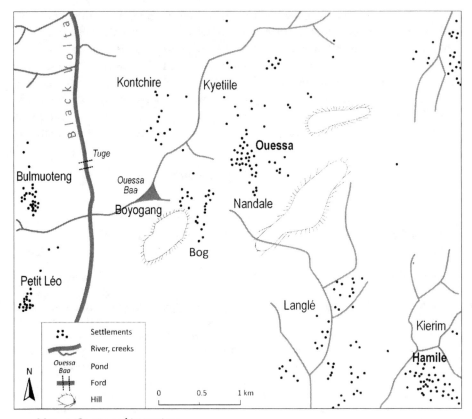

Map 1.2. Ouessa and its sections

killed or displaced.[67] Whenever they describe their ancestors interacting with Sisala who continue to live in the vicinity, on the other hand, the Dagara narrators usually take care to define the earlier inhabitants' identity more precisely because this can be of vital importance in current land conflicts. In any case, Hien Daniel was adamant that when Kontchire arrived, no Sisala lived anywhere nearby—very different from what the *chef de canton*'s son Charles Meda told me when he insisted that Ouessa had received her earth shrine from the neighboring Sisala of Kierim.[68]

However, it was not only members of other patriclans like Charles Meda who presented me with different accounts of how Ouessa was founded. Other members of the Gane clan and the earth-priestly family, too, told different stories. Samson Gompag, for instance, who became the new earth priest after Hien Daniel died in 1999, presented a much less martial story than his predecessor. According to him, before their Gane ancestor Kontchire and his people arrived at Ouessa, there existed a small bush camp that Dyan iron smelters had erected—a group similar to the Phuo, but not to be

Table 1.1. Synopsis of Gane Narratives on the Foundation of Ouessa

	Hien Daniel	Somé Gompag	Meda Casimir
Encounter with previous inhabitants	Gane pioneers kill Pougouli or Yeri	Dyan iron smelters flee before Gane pioneers, no battle	Gane pioneers violently displace Yeri
Origin of Ouessa earth shrine	Wife of Pougouli/Yeri gives earth-shrine stone in exchange for sparing her life	"Lost" wife of Dyan earth priest gives earth-shrine stone in gratitude for hospitality	Gane establish their own shrine with a local stone
Migration route of Gane ancestors	[Cape Coast] → Djikologo → [Mebar] → Memer → Petit Leo → Ouessa	North-Western Ghana → Ouizin (near Dissin) → Petit Leo → Ouessa → Memer	Cape Coast → Daazugri → Pognuu (near Lawra) → Nakon → Petit Leo → Ouessa → Memer
First Ouessa earth priest	Kontchire (Sornuor = Kontchire's son)	Sornuor/ Kontchire (Sornuor = Kontchire's junior brother)	Sornuor (Kontchire = only a place-name)

confused with the Dyan of Diébougou, as Gompag explained.[69] Gompag asserted that his own father had once showed him the ancient slag heaps that these iron smelters had left behind and that testified to the camp's existence. When these Dyan heard shots from the guns, which Gompag's and Hien Daniel's Gane ancestors used for hunting, they fled. During the flight, Gompag continued, one of the Dyan women lost her way, wandered into the bush, and one day appeared at the doorstep of Kontchire's house, where she was received kindly. She stayed for quite a while, learned Dagara, and eventually explained that her people had fled out of fear; her hosts, in turn, assured her that they never had intended to kill anybody. When the woman finally returned to her family, across the Volta, as Gompag surmised, she reported how well she had been treated by Kontchire and made sure that her husband gave him an earth-shrine stone.

Gompag's and Hien Daniel's versions share the motif of the exchange of the earth shrine for the life of a woman. This metaphorical equation is typical of Dagara narratives about the ritual appropriation of new territories that I discuss in more detail in the next chapter. What interests me here, however, is the fact that even members of the same extended family—and in the Ouessa case, consecutive earth priests—can narrate different versions of the settlement history. Casimir Meda, for instance, another member of the Gane patriclan, whose father, Bapele, served as Ouessa earth priest during the 1930s and early 1940s, forwarded yet another version of the origins of the Ouessa earth shrine. He explained that after driving the Yeri away, the Gane pioneers established their own earth shrine autonomously, without any help from these previous inhabitants. First-comers like his Gane ancestors, Casimir explained, could simply pick up a stone and transform it into a shrine stone by sacrificing to it.[70]

The Gane narratives also differed with respect to their ancestors' migration routes and even the identity of the first Ouessa earth priest. Hien Daniel initially related that Kontchire set out from Mebar and migrated to Memer and Petit Leo and from there to Ouessa, but in subsequent interviews he omitted Mebar and added other stops before Memer, such as Cape Coast and Djikologo (near Diébougou).[71] He repeatedly asserted, however, that Kontchire was the first Dagara to arrive in Ouessa, and hence the first earth priest. Gompag also mentioned Petit Leo, where, according to him, the Gane hunters had built some huts and from where they roamed until finally discovering Ouessa. However, Gompag insisted that they came first to Ouessa and then continued to Memer, not the other way around, as Daniel had said.[72] And initially, Gompag told me that the first Ouessa earth priest was actually Sornuor, succeeded by his son Kontchire. Only later did he identify Kontchire as the first-comer and Sornuor as his junior brother.[73] For Casimir Meda, on the other hand, Kontchire was merely a place-name—derived from the Gane's hunting activities, literally *kone e jile*, "to shout and encircle"—not the name of a person, and he let the history of Ouessa begin with the establishment of an earth shrine by Sornuor. Like Hien Daniel, Casimir believed that the Gane started from Cape Coast and passed through Petit Leo, but he agreed with Gompag that they came to Ouessa before discovering Memer.[74] Interestingly, when I went across the Black Volta to Memer in order to find out what the Gane earth priests of that village said about their ancestors' migration, they supported the first-Ouessa-then-Memer version and agreed that Sornuor was Ouessa's first earth priest. However, they established their own seniority by insisting that Sornuor was a junior brother of Nabog and Bojaga who continued across the river and founded Memer.[75] In short, almost every interview added another version of Ouessa's history that was not quite compatible with what I had recorded so far, and the stories became even more diverse when I talked to members of different patriclans.

Different Lineages, Multiple Stories, and Colonial Discontinuities of Oral Tradition

To a certain extent, such contradictions between different historical narratives are a research artifact. Some incompatibilities between different migration-and-settlement narratives or even within a single account may only become evident when they are fixed in writing but otherwise escape the narrators' attention. Furthermore, the researcher's questions may prompt informants to creatively bridge gaps in their own historical knowledge by borrowing from stories that they have heard about neighboring

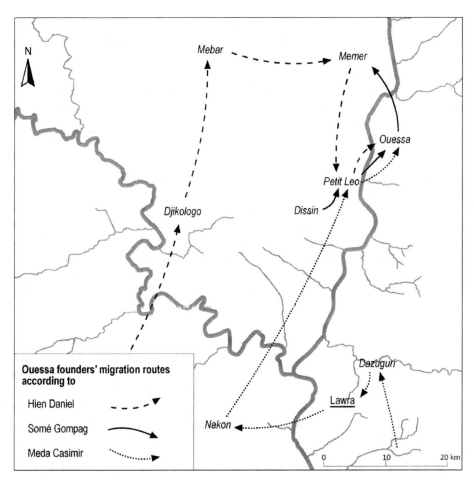

Map 1.3. Ouessa founders' migration routes

settlements. And, of course, some interlocutors may wish to protect certain family secrets from the stranger's gaze and therefore suppress crucial details.

However, the contradictions also reflect general characteristics inherent to oral traditions that are independent of the research process. Laura Bohannan observed that Tiv genealogies are usually learned "casually and in scraps," only to the extent that they are needed in daily social interaction and to support the group's political interests.[76] This also applies to Dagara historical memory. Moreover, all performances of oral tradition rely on mnemonic devices, such as clustering complex information in particularly vivid metaphors and episodes, telescoping genealogies, and using place-names or images of spatial progression.[77] Most important, we have to abandon, as Jack Goody convincingly argues, the idea that there exists a single original template,[78] a "true" eyewitness report that we could reconstruct by carefully scrutinizing the more or less corrupted "copies." Rather, we have to assume that from the very beginning the various lineages and patriclans narrated different accounts that were subsequently expanded and embellished or abridged and simplified.

In the case of Ouessa, it is possible that the Gane did not come in a single group, but in various waves, from different locations, under different leaders, constituting themselves as a united clan only at their point of arrival in Ouessa—a development that could account for some of the contradictions discussed above. Past conflicts over the succession to the earth-priestly office may be another factor that resulted in contradictory versions. And finally, the effects of colonial rule produced significant discontinuities in the web of historical memory. The wealth in people and animals that Ouessa had attained by the beginning of colonial rule—the French administrator Louis Tauxier counted nearly one thousand inhabitants and a large number of cattle[79]—was not to last. Ouessa's prosperity and its strategic location near an important ford through the Black Volta attracted colonial attention and made the demands of taxation and forced labor more exacting here than in other, remoter places. Particularly when the French decided to build a bridge near the ford in the early 1930s, the requisitions of labor became unbearable. Entire families decided to flee to the nearby British protectorate, whose regime was generally considered to be gentler than French colonial rule. The situation was compounded by a series of vicious epidemics that struck Ouessa severely, not least because fewer adult men in the village meant that less bush—potential breeding grounds for the tsetse fly that transmits sleeping sickness—could be cleared. Outlying sections of the village were completely deserted, and even in the central parts few houses remained.[80] Ouessa recovered its former size only gradually, partly through the refugees' or their descendants' return, partly through the arrival of land-seeking Gourounsi and Mossi immigrants.[81]

Among the refugees and victims of epidemics were also many Gane. When Ouessa earth priest Dougzie lay on his deathbed sometime in the 1940s, his sons were still very young, and there was no suitable successor. Dougzie had to call on Deboru, a man from a distantly related Gane lineage who had fled to the British protectorate. Deboru agreed to come back to Ouessa and take up the office,[82] but his itinerant life had never permitted him to learn the details of the family and village history that were normally transmitted in the course of growing up in the earth-priestly house and regularly participating in sacrifices. Hien Daniel, too, had stayed away from Ouessa for many years, working as a labor migrant in Kumasi. Furthermore, he had grown up with his Bekuone relatives, not in his father's house. When he finally assumed the earth-priestly office, the knowledgeable Gane elders had died, and he had to fill the gaps in his fragmented knowledge of the family history on his own by borrowing from common topoi and using what his Bekuone relations had told him. This may be one of the reasons why Memer figured so prominently in his account: the Bekuone in Ouessa had indeed immigrated from Memer.

There are certainly limits to the "invention" of history: the more recent genealogy is better known, important ancestors must necessarily be mentioned in all accounts, and the local credibility of any version hinges on the use of regionally widespread, plausible images and arguments. Within these limits, however, there is considerable latitude for improvisation and variation, even in ritual settings. I had expected that if not in my interviews, then at least during sacrifices at the earth shrine the founding ancestors and previous earth priests would be enumerated completely and in the "correct" order. However, I soon learned that this was not the case. Although some ancestors and places of spiritual power were always called upon, the order of enunciation could change, and further names, including forefathers who had not held earth-priestly office, could be added on one occasion and omitted on others. Unlike the more formalized recitation of clan history during the *bagr* initiation that had stabilized the Kusiele accounts of the foundation of Lawra, the Gane invocation of Ouessa's history during sacrifices was much more impromptu and makeshift.

Matters became even more complex, and contradictory stories multiplied, when I listened to the histories that members of the other Dagara patriclans of Ouessa narrated—the Kusiele, Kpiele, and Bekuone. Ouessa's unstable politics of memory may be an extreme case that reflects the particularly severe colonial discontinuities in the chain of transmission of historical knowledge. But it is certainly not untypical for the fragmented historical consciousness of segmentary societies, and I suspect that had I dug deeper into Lawra history, I would have discovered even more deviating accounts and controversies over the "true" history.

Buttressing the New Settlement, Recruiting Allies

Despite the many variations and contradictions in local memories, there are a few key "facts" on which nearly all informants agreed, such as that Ouessa was inhabited before the Gane arrived. That the previous inhabitants erected not only a bush camp, but a more permanent settlement is suggested by the local record of trees.[83] In Ouessa's oldest sections, Kontchire and Kyetiile, as well as in the neighboring Dagara villages of Dianlé, Sorguogang, Dalgang, and Kolinka, there are vestigial parks of acacia (*Faidherbia albida*). Acacias do not grow spontaneously, but are sown by animal dung and, once they have taken root, need to be cared for—something Phuo, Sisala, and some other groups do because they value acacia highly as convenient cattle fodder during the dry season. Dagara, on the other hand, generally accord no great importance to these trees, and we find no young growth of *Faidherbia albida* in Dagara villages. Old stands of acacia are therefore a clear indication of the existence of earlier settlements, although, of course, they cannot reveal to us the identity of these previous inhabitants, indicating only that they must have kept domestic animals. Since most oral traditions mention former "Pougouli" settlers, and since a number of Phuo informants themselves point to their origins in Ouessa, we may assume that Ouessa was, indeed, formerly inhabited by Phuo families, and that the Dagara, in one way or another, drove them away.

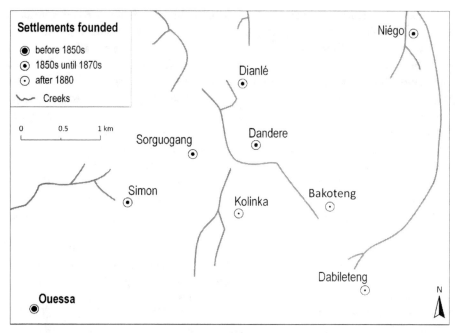

Map 1.4. Foundation of settlements east of Ouessa

All my interlocutors also agreed that Ouessa is the oldest Dagara village in the area, that it was founded by Gane hunters, and that most of the Dagara settlements to its east and northeast were established with the consent of the Ouessa earth priests. Collating the genealogical information that I collected from the Gane and in neighboring villages, whose founders are supposed to have passed through Ouessa, we can conclude that Ouessa must have come into existence by the 1830s or 1840s at the latest, if not already by the end of the eighteenth century.[84] However, even if a small settlement of Gane hunters existed by the early nineteenth century, perhaps in more or less peaceful coexistence with some earlier Phuo farmers and iron smelters, it was not until the 1840s that the Gane pioneers started to expand their village. From that period onward, they were able to attract immigrants from other Dagara patriclans to Ouessa who eventually helped them to fortify their settlement and push the frontiers of their earth-shrine territory farther eastward, into what were formerly Sisala and Phuo hamlets and hunting grounds.

The site of the new Gane settlement in Ouessa, near one of the few fords across the Black Volta, offered definite strategic advantages. The Gane were renowned hunters, and wildlife was abundant near the river, particularly during the dry season, when other bodies of water usually dried up. The ford was likely to be used by other Dagara migrants, providing opportunities to recruit more settlers, for Ouessa itself and for strategic outposts. The migration narratives that I collected in Dagara settlements east of Ouessa confirmed that the founders of these villages had indeed passed through this ford and moved on with the consent, or even at the request, of the Gane earth priests. Furthermore, if Ouessa's previous inhabitants had in fact been iron smelters, as Gompag and other informants believed, they would have cut down many trees in order to produce charcoal for their furnaces.[85] This would have made it easier to establish farms; and as long as population densities were generally low and large thickets left between settlements, wildlife could still be abundant. Finally, a tributary of the Black Volta runs through Ouessa, providing good drinking water and opportunities for fishing. Ouessa, then, was on all accounts an attractive site for settlement, and it was for these reasons, my Gane informants explained, that their forefathers baptized it "Ouessa," literally, *wa-sa*, "come and be better," because "no matter where you came from and who you were, if you arrived here and worked hard, you would be someone."

To protect their new settlement, organize large-scale hunting expeditions, conduct certain rituals, and, of course, find suitable marriage partners, the Gane pioneers needed to recruit allies. For most purposes it was necessary, or at least advantageous, for these followers and allies to belong to different patriclans. In fact, as some of my Gane informants explained, the Gane pioneers Kontchire and Sornuor had migrated jointly with members of the Bimbiile and Kpagnyaane patriclans, who were also prominent hunters and joking partners (*lonluore*) of the Gane.[86] When the Gane stayed in Petit Leo, the Bimbiile and Kpagnyaane who lived nearby served as their *tampeludem*, that is, "ashthrowers," who pacify intraclan conflicts, one of the functions that *lonluore* typically perform. When the Gane later continued to Ouessa, they invited the Bimbiile and Kpagnyaane to accompany them and settle in Bidomo,[87] a short distance north of Ouessa. Tamao, a famous hunter, was one of the first Kpagnyaane to cross the Volta and move to Bidomo. However, relations with the Gane soon turned sour, as one of Tamao's descendants related, because

> Tamao was welcomed by the Gane in Ouessa and built his hut in Bidomo, but he did not get sufficient support from the Gane in the hunting expeditions that he organized. The Gane could not imagine how he wanted to be organizing hunting expeditions without having a large following. They were mocking him, asking him how he could venture into the bush with so few people in his own house. It was this lack of patronage of his hunting expeditions by the Gane that made our ancestor leave Bidomo and continue to this place [Niégo].[88]

Mockery is part and parcel of *lonluore* relations, but in Tamao's eyes it obviously went beyond the tolerable. The conflict arose because the Gane expected Tamao to recognize their claim to lead all communal hunting expeditions, while he himself aspired to be on an equal footing with them. Tamao therefore left Bidomo, ventured eastward and eventually established himself in Niégo, where he was a first-comer and thus "owner" of the hunt (*wiesob*) in his own right. A similar quest for independence must have propelled the Bimbiile to depart from Bidomo, which they regarded as "too crowded," as one of their descendants put it, and to "search for space [*vuo*]" in the thick forests (*kar*) of Dianlé.[89]

Interestingly, however, these rival pioneers continued to accept the spiritual protection of the Gane earth shrine, at least initially, until Tamao in Niégo "bought" a shrine stone from the Sisala—a development that I discuss in the next chapter.

With the departure of the Kpagnyaane and Bimbiile from Bidomo, the Gane needed new allies and eventually recruited them from among the Kusiele, Bekuone, and Kpiele patriclans. Significantly, the lineages of these three clans who settled in Ouessa were not renowned as hunters and therefore would not challenge the Gane's prerogatives. The Bekuone, for instance, are regarded as hardworking farmers who usually migrated "behind" other groups,[90] the Kpiele are closely associated with rain making, and the Kusiele of Ouessa are believed to have been powerful warriors. In reality, of course, it was individual men, not lineages or clans who were hunters, hoe-farmers, rain makers, or warriors, but in the popular imagination, entire kin groups are associated with specific abilities that are reflected in praise names, epithets, and aetiological legends. Whether this typology reflects historical experience is an open question, but it probably informed the expectations of the Gane toward their new allies.

How exactly the Kusiele, Kpiele, and Bekuone came to settle in Ouessa is disputed, but my informants agreed that they were all Gane *arbile*, sister's sons. Initially, the newcomers settled close to the Gane in the section of Kontchire in order to assist their hosts and each other in case of attacks by animals or human enemies. After some time, however, the *arbile* recruited more settlers from among their own clan mates in the hinterland, and eventually founded their own sections—Kyetiile (Bekuone), Boyogang (Kusiele), and Nandale (Kpiele) (see map 1.2). An analysis of the relevant genealogies reveals that it was not the first Kpiele, Bekuone, and Kusiele immigrants themselves, but rather their sons, who founded these sections, probably in the 1860s or even later. For the Gane, the expansion of the settlement had two advantages: it allowed the earth priest to effectively control a larger territory and gradually open up the bush, and it helped reduce the tensions that developed between the Gane and their allies. As Ouessa earth priest Then Daniel related:

> Some of the Kusiele and Bekuone were actually misconducting themselves, demonstrating their strength because of [the protection by] their *madebr* [uncles, i.e., the Gane]. They could go, for example, from Kontchire to other places to shoot somebody. Our own grandfathers never engaged in fighting or any act of the sort, and the people whom these Bekuone and Kusiele attacked would never consider coming to fight our section because of their good relation with our fathers. Nobody fought a *tengansob*! But they [the Bekuone and Kusiele] could attack people while they were busy drinking sorghum beer or gambling. Kporo [a Bekuone], for instance, could go and shoot somebody dead and then run to this place, knowing very well that nobody would dare to come here![91]

My Bekuone and Kusiele interlocutors proudly confirmed that, indeed, some of their ancestors "were very notorious people" and that this was why they had to move out of Kontchire.[92] However, they continued to cooperate closely with the Gane, and the uncle-nephew configuration obviously was a solid framework in which both the seniority of the earth-priestly group and the strength and rights of the late-comers could be negotiated.

Refashioning Migration Routes and Genealogies, Creating a Sense of Community

By narrating their ancestors' routes of migration, villagers locate themselves and their current neighbors within a wider network of patriclans. Such narratives can emphasize parallels and similarities as well as differences between kin groups, as Beidelman has shown for the Kaguru in East Africa.[93] Among the Dagara, migration accounts create both a sense of community in the present settlement and an awareness of belonging to a supralocal network of kin. Because they are central to community building, narratives of migration routes can be refashioned in order to produce a better fit with those of one's new neighbors or, in the case of conflict, to emphasize distance. The geographical details of such narratives therefore have to be taken with a grain of salt.[94]

Particularly information on the place of origin can hardly be taken at face value. Many of my interlocutors claimed, for instance, that their ancestors originally set out for their journey from Cape Coast or Accra in Southern Ghana, and then mentioned a place around Lawra as their next stop—an assertion that we should probably not take too literally since the reported distance between stopovers on ancestral migrations is normally not more than a few dozen kilometers at the most. To claim such a distant starting point mainly aims at enhancing the group's prestige, and, even more important, it creates a common place of reference for different patriclans now settling alongside each other.[95] The generic *tengkor*, the "old country" or "old village," serves the same purpose. Comparing my own interview data with information recorded in the 1960s, it becomes clear that many families who formerly spoke of *tengkor* as their ancestors' place of origin now refer to Accra or Cape Coast—a development that may be due to the influence of educated relatives.[96]

The accounts of migration routes within North-Western Ghana and South-Western Burkina Faso, on the other hand, are fairly reliable, as far as the informants' fathers and grandfathers are concerned and as long as the family still returns to some of the stopovers for sacrifices and festivities. The routes of earlier migrations, however, are often remodeled in accordance with those of other lineages in the new area of residence. There may indeed have been brief periods of joint travels, but they have subsequently come to be reinterpreted as a long common journey. This trend toward homogenizing migration routes can be found not only between different patriclans, but also among the different lineages within the same clan. In an attempt to emphasize cohesion and commonality, current cohabitation is thus reinterpreted as joint migration.

A complementary way to strengthen ties among the new neighbors is to project current kin relations, joking partnerships, and institutionalized friendships into the past. In Ouessa, as in many other places, it is particularly the *madebr–arbili* relation, with the *madeb* playing the role of the senior and the *arbile* the junior, that is mobilized to this end. Strictly speaking, *madeb–arbile* ties are relations not between groups, but between individuals from different houses. Thus, if a man marries several women who come from different patrilineages and houses, these women's children will have different *madebr*. If men and women of two houses intermarry back and forth, the positions of *madebr* and *arbili* will, over the course of time, alternate back and forth, and various individuals could be regarded both as *madebr* or as *arbili*, depending on whether people wish to emphasize a junior or a senior position. However, when Dagara speak of an entire lineage as being the *madebr* (or *arbili*) of another lineage, this usually refers to real ties of marriage that were once established, but also entails a metaphorical meaning that expresses social and political hierarchies.[97]

That the Gane in Ouessa are regarded as the *madebr* of their Kusiele, Kpiele, and Bekuone followers is therefore first and foremost a declaration of their status as first-comers. By definition, so to speak, the earth-priestly lineage has to be genealogically senior to the other founding families. Significantly, the genealogies that my Gane informants remembered usually reached at least one generation deeper than those presented by their *arbili*.

In principle, the *arbili* accept their position as juniors, but the precise terms of their relations with their uncles are often controversial. For instance, some Kusiele elders claimed that their ancestors and not the Gane were the actual first-comers in Ouessa who had driven away the Pougouli and then invited their Gane uncles from Petit Leo to join them. Out of respect for their *madebr*, this version runs, the Kusiele let them assume the earth-priestly office, which, as true first-comers, they could have insisted on taking themselves. Because of this generous gesture and the fact that the Kusiele provided the cowrie shells and sacrificial animals necessary for the installation of the earth shrine, the Gane appointed them as *kumberdem*, assistants of the earth priests, and *suodem*, holders of the sacrificial knife. The Kpiele elders, for their part, insist that the Gane came first and offered the position of *kumberdem* not to the Kusiele, but the Kpiele, who only because they were already responsible for the powerful shrines controlling lightning and rain did not want to take on a further task.[98] The Bekuone, in turn, claimed that initially they shared the work of the *kumberdem* with the Kusiele, but then chose to withdraw from this office. The Gane themselves, finally, refute most of these claims along with the Kusiele's far-reaching interpretation of their historic entitlements, namely that they have the right to distribute Ouessa lands to strangers—competing claims that led to severe conflicts in the context of land titling that I discuss in chapter 5.

In any case, the *madebr–arbili* relations between the Gane and the Kusiele, Kpiele and Bekuone were probably created only in Ouessa itself, or at the most in Petit Leo, but then projected into the past in order to lend temporal depth and strength to the new ties of neighborhood. At the same time, the narratives about how these relations developed provide a suitable idiom for debating hierarchical relations and differences in rights and entitlements in current village affairs.

Pushing Back Frontiers, Reigning in Strong Men

Dagara immigrants who wanted to join the new settlement but could not be converted into joking partners or nephews constituted a potential challenge to the Gane earth priests' authority. The best strategy was to send them to the outer frontier, into territory that the Gane earth priests wanted to bring under their control, but that was still inhabited by Phuo and Sisala. A case in point is Charles Meda's grandfather Demaal Naab, who came from Nandom probably during the 1870s. As Hien Daniel explained: "Demaal Naab was known to be a very strong man [*gandaa*], and he captured a lot of slaves, Yeri, Bobo [Bwaba], Pougouli, and others. Originally, he wanted to establish himself in Kontchire, but our ancestors refused because they wanted to avoid all trouble. They preferred to send him to Dianlé, to take care of this outpost."[99] Placing strong men like Demaal Naab on the more distant frontier prevented competition for power in Ouessa itself and directed potentially destructive energies toward external adversaries.

These frontiersmen initially often established themselves more or less peacefully in the interstices between existing Phuo or Sisala settlements until they were able to mobilize more followers. The fact that Dianlé and Niégo, the first two Dagara villages founded after Ouessa, bear Phuo or Sisala names is evidence for such a period of cohabitation. And despite assertions that their ancestors conquered the territory with their "very powerful arrows," some of my Dagara interlocutors eventually revealed that the Phuo and Sisala had initially welcomed the Dagara newcomers. In the case of Dalgang, for instance, the Sisala allegedly even gave Dal, the Dagara pioneer, an earth-shrine stone, and open conflict broke out only much later.[100]

In other cases, there was no period of cohabitation, and the Dagara frontiersmen defiantly claimed the territory to which the Gane earth priests had sent them from the outset. As one informant explained, if the Dagara pioneers counted a minimum of "six strong young men" who were armed with bows and arrows, protective medicines, and "a spirit of combat and perseverance," they could impose themselves without further ado. An example is Gor and his numerous sons, who established their new settlement near Dalgang "by force," as one of Gor's descendants related: "Gor, in fact, had a lot of people! While he and his people still lived on the other side of the Volta, he sent his son Demale on a hunting expedition to explore the area across the river. Demale discovered this place [Gorgang] . . . and told his father that the place was very good, but that he had also seen some people who looked like Sisala or Pougouli." "They were Yeri," another elder present at the interview intervened, and the first speaker continued:

> Yes, they were Yeri. Anyway, Demale asked the Yeri leader who had settled them, and the Yeri man said that they had discovered the place by themselves. Demale then told

them that now he wanted to establish himself in this place and that the Yeri would have to leave. He went back to inform his father and proposed to drive these people away. Then he went to consult the Ouessa earth priests. They told him that if he and his people were able to drive the Yeri away, they would give them the land. So Demale and Gor alerted their men, and one day, early in the morning, they went to surprise the Yeri. They shot arrows at the people and the animals, and those who survived fled and abandoned the place. . . . Later, the Ouessa *tengandem* came to give Demale and his people a small stone so that they could conduct their own sacrifices.[101]

In Sorguogang, a small settlement a little south of Dianlé, I was told a similar story, only that Sorguo's conquest was said to have been successful not because of the number of warriors whose support he could enlist, but due to his personal courage and extraordinary magical powers.[102]

In each of the three settlements, Dalgang, Gorgang, and Sorguogang, my interlocutors claimed that their ancestors had been the very first Dagara in the area and their respective settlement the oldest one. They agreed, however, that their forefathers came with the consent of Ouessa earth priest Laazie and that the latter had promised them extensive rights over the land if they were able to effectively occupy it. The reference to Laazie suggests that this rather violent phase of Dagara expansion to the east of Ouessa must have taken place during the 1860s and 1870s. It was followed by the gradual colonization of the interstices between the new settlements and further expansion of the Dagara frontier southward, toward the Sisala villages of Hiela, Kierim, and Hamile. Simon, Kolinka, and Bakoteng were the last Dagara villages to be established on Ouessa territory before the colonial period (see maps 1.2 and 1.4).[103]

The Sisala tried to halt the Dagara advance, for instance, by pushing down the walls of the first Dagara houses in Bakoteng and Kolinka. In the long run, however, they were not able to prevent the Dagara encroachment into their territory. The village names bear witness to these conflicts, as my informants explained. Kolinka, for instance, is supposed to mean "to go around and keep watch," and Simon "the place for strong people."[104] My Dagara interlocutors disagreed occasionally on who exactly helped whom to overcome Sisala resistance, but their narratives left no doubt that, by the end of the nineteenth century, the Dagara were present in the area in sufficient numbers to recruit a large number of warriors at short notice. The incursions of the Zaberma warlords did not affect these Dagara settlements,[105] and it is even likely that some Dagara strong men, like Demaal Naab in Dianlé or Kporo, a Bekuone in Ouessa, who are said to have captured many slaves, cooperated with these warlords.

Subsequently, however, under the colonial regime, the balance of power changed, and the Sisala could now assert their land ownership more successfully. The Dagara, who continued to expand, had to negotiate the terms of their settlement rather than impose themselves. It took some time until colonial "pacification" became effective and the newly introduced institution of chieftaincy took root. However, from the 1920s onward, the Dagara who set out from Ouessa, Niégo, and their satellite settlements to push farther east, into Sisala land, were no longer able to create their own new earth shrines, but had to accept Sisala overlordship. The next section turns to the case of Laponé, a village about thirty kilometers from Ouessa, to explore how Dagara immigrants created new communities under these conditions.

New Dagara Settlements under Conditions of Restricted Autonomy (1980s and 1990s)

In Dagara settlements established during the colonial period on Sisala land, the newcomers were often granted rather generous conditions by their Sisala hosts, with respect to their economic as well as sociopolitical rights. In the past decades, however, Sisala landowners increasingly felt that the Dagara were taking undue advantage of their hospitality and illegitimately encroached upon their resources. They therefore attempted to control the immigrants more rigidly. Laponé is a case in point, and my Dagara interlocutors in this settlement often complained about the ways in which the Sisala landowners restricted their access to land and other resources on village territory.

Laponé is a typical example of Dagara settlements established on Sisala land after independence. The first Dagara family settled in Laponé in the mid-1980s, others followed suit, and by 2001, there were nineteen Dagara houses comprising members of seven different patriclans who had come from various Dagara villages in Burkina Faso and Ghana. Unlike in older Dagara hamlets on Sisala land, the Sisala of Laponé are not yet in the minority, but account for about two-thirds of the total population of approximately 1,500. They have settled not only Dagara, but also four Mossi and three Lyela families and sometimes play these "strangers," as they insist on calling them, off against each other.[106] However, while the Sisala attempt to place strict limits on the settlers' economic, social, and political autonomy, the latter try to carve out a space for making their own community and turning Laponé into their permanent home. In chapter 3, I discuss how the Dagara families of Laponé confront Sisala attempts to constrict their bundle of land rights ever more firmly. Here, my focus is on the dynamics of their migration into Sisala territory, and their strategies of building a new local community, even under conditions of restricted autonomy to manage their own affairs.

Mobility, Multilocality, and the Creation of a New House

"Lack of food," "hunger," or, metaphorically, "the belly" were the brief first answers that the Dagara immigrants gave when I asked them why they had decided to move to Laponé. In their original villages, prospects of setting up a viable farm of their own were bleak because there was no longer any "free" bush available and there were too many brothers competing for a share of the family fields. Laponé, by contrast, offered sufficient space and fertile land. In my informants' eyes, the high yields made up for the heavy work that the preparation of the new fields demanded and for the disadvantages of living "deep in the bush" (*muopuo*), in a village difficult to access, particularly during the rainy season, and far away from the familiar markets and other places of socializing.

Most Dagara heads of household in Laponé were in their forties, or older, when they arrived in the new village—the latest age at which a typical Dagara villager would want to build his own house, or at least a separate granary and rooms of his own in the family house. With few exceptions, the Laponé immigrants had worked for a number of years as seasonal migrants or semi-permanent plantation workers in Southern Ghana or in the Ivory Coast, and used part of their savings to establish their farms and houses in the new village. They were all married and came in the company of their adult sons or their brothers, thus being able to mobilize the workforce necessary to cope with the challenges of farming "in the bush." The only immigrant who came alone, accompanied only by his wife and young children, had to give up his new farm after a few years and return to his place of origin.

Setting up a farm on the expanding agricultural frontier is a family enterprise. In most cases, the migrants were sent to Laponé by their fathers or elder brothers in order to secure land not only for themselves, but for the entire lineage. However, the reasons why particular family members were chosen or volunteered to migrate into "the bush" were to be found in complex histories of competition and conflict in the family and the original village. Thus, while the lack of land and related economic issues provided the general motivation to move to the frontier, the selection of the actual migrant followed a social logic—a combination of different "push factors" that had also characterized earlier Dagara mobility. The pioneers usually went as a sort of vanguard, exploring the conditions under which the Sisala would assign land and testing the fertility of the fields as well as the general living conditions. When they found the latter acceptable, they asked the Sisala earth priest for land and later brought in further relatives and friends from their home villages.

A typical example is the late Mimirdem, a member of the Kusiele patriclan and the first Dagara man who came to Laponé. Mimirdem was born around the mid-1920s in Pina, a Sisala village not far from Laponé, shortly after his father had moved there, escaping from a Dagara settlement west of the Volta where the exactions of labor and produce by the local colonial chief were extremely harsh. As a young man, Mimirdem worked seasonally on pineapple plantations of the Ivory Coast and yams farms in Ghana's Brong Ahafo Region. When he voiced his plans to establish his own house back home, his senior brother, who had become the head of the family after the father's death, asked him to seek out land outside of Pina. The family farm was not large enough to accommodate all heirs, and the Sisala of Pina felt that their land reserves were not sufficient to allocate additional land to any Dagara family. Pina hosts a lively market that attracts Sisala and Dagara from many surrounding villages, and it was during market days that Mimirdem had become friends with Fawiera, the Sisala earth priest of Laponé. When Mimirdem explained his difficulty, Fawiera offered him land in Laponé to establish a "bush farm." For several years, Mimirdem and his family continued to live in Pina, but during the farming season often stayed in a temporary shelter on their farm in Laponé. Eventually Mimirdem felt that traveling between Pina and his farm in Laponé was too inconvenient and decided to build his own house in Laponé. His senior brother accompanied him to Fawiera in order to ask the earth priest for permission to settle in Laponé—a gesture underscoring that Mimirdem's move was a family decision.[107]

Mimirdem was then already in his late fifties, and his adult four sons who accompanied him—three of them married—provided more than the necessary labor force. Two sons were soon given their own shares of the farm, while the other two continued to farm with their father. Furthermore, Mimirdem invited the son of a friend in Kondon, one of his in-laws in Kelendou, a distantly related Kusiele man in Pina, and the son of a brother in Bozo to join him in Laponé, and he introduced all of them to Fawiera, who gave them land. By 2001, Mimirdem had adult grandsons who followed the customary pattern of seasonal migration to the Ivory Coast before establishing their own households. One or two of these grandsons will eventually take over their fathers' and Mimirdem's farms in Laponé. The others have already started to explore the land reserves in Sisala villages farther into the bush because in Laponé, too, the Sisala announced some time ago that they will no longer give additional land to Dagara farmers.

In the case of Der Somé, who belongs to the Bekuone patriclan and who in 1988 had come to Laponé from Tapumu, a village in Ghana, it was a group of brothers who moved to Laponé and assisted each other on the farm and in the construction of their houses. As in Mimirdem's case, Der Somé's father had migrated from an old village in the Dagara hinterland to a Dagara settlement established on Sisala land during the colonial period. Eventually, the land he had been given was no longer sufficient to accommodate all his sons. Listening to information that circulated on the regional markets and exploiting his networks of friends and kin, Der Somé eventually met a Sisala from Laponé who offered him land. Through the intervention of Mimirdem, whom the Sisala regarded as the Dagara spokesman and representative, Der was introduced to the Sisala earth priest and given permission to settle in Laponé. He came with his two wives and children, and two younger "brothers" (actually patrilineal cousins), and was later followed by one his senior brother's sons and a distantly related junior "brother." Unlike Mimirdem, however, whom the Sisala had given a single expanse of land that he then further subdivided himself, Der Somé and his brothers were each given smaller, separate fields and construction sites.

Most Dagara in Laponé came in one of these two constellations—a father with his adult sons, like Mimirdem's group, or a group of "brothers," as in Der Somé's case. The move to Laponé was, and continues to be, embedded in multilocal family networks that consist of farmhouses in different villages between which the men (usually patrikin), women, and children move back and forth, depending on their age, the demographic development of the respective nuclear families, and the available resources and labor

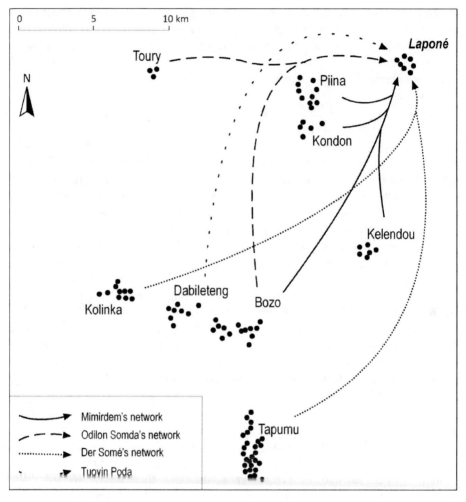

Map 1.5 Laponé: Dagara settlers' provenance

demands of the dispersed family farms. Seasonal migration and sometimes also longer periods of work in Southern Ghana or the Ivory Coast are part and parcel of this family enterprise, and often precede the move to the local agricultural frontier.[108]

Both Dagara settlers and their Sisala hosts regard the first year in a new village as a kind of test period. After the Dagara immigrants have asked for land, the Sisala landowners, together with the earth priest, sacrifice a number of fowl that the newcomers have to furnish in order to determine whether the immigrant is welcome by the ancestors of the land giver and the spirits of the earth, the bush, and the ponds. Normally, these fowl are "accepted"—indicated by their falling on their backs after their throats have been cut and they have been thrown into the air—and the migrant is assigned a piece of land that he will prepare for sowing, assisted by his wife, sons, and other supporters. During the first agricultural cycle, the newcomers lodge with a friend or relative in Laponé, or build a temporary shelter. Only after one or two successful harvests will they start to construct a regular adobe house. This is partly due to time constraints. To build a house requires at least a full month's work, in addition to the support from a substantial number of men and women, at least during some phases of the construction, who can be more easily recruited when the newcomers have familiarized themselves with their new covillagers. Furthermore, the immigrant and his wife need to "test" whether the new farm is conveniently located and sufficiently fertile and whether there are any social or—in the case of non-Christians—spiritual impediments to establishing themselves more firmly. Particularly the women who interact with the wives of the Sisala landowners and other Dagara immigrants, when fetching water or firewood or brewing sorghum beer, have to consider whether they can integrate into the new environment.

Even after the first year, the move to the new village is a gradual one. Initially, the migrants still bring from their original villages some foodstuffs as well as laborers for clearing the bush. In the course of time, they build up networks of mutual assistance in their new neighbourhood, and eventually, if all goes well, send parts of the harvest to needy family members "back home." They retain some rights in their original homes and may, in the event of a crisis in their new settlement, return. Yet how long, how much, and which form of assistance can be expected from one's "home" people (and, conversely, how much support the latter can expect from the emigrants) is a matter of negotiation and depends on the specific circumstances. Full brothers, for instance, feel under more pressure to help migrants in crisis (and vice versa) than more distantly related patrikin. Furthermore, claims to land in the original village weaken considerably after one generation has lapsed. While a request for support during an emergency could not be easily denied by a man's patrikin, he could hardly expect to be given farmland of sufficiently good quality in his grandfather's village. My interlocutors in Laponé indeed found the idea of returning to their "starting" point in the event of difficulties, instead of seeking additional land or social peace in new villages farther afield, rather absurd. "We will always move ahead," Der Somé declared; "we would not go backward, but we would be looking somewhere else for what we need!"

The decisive step toward a more permanent home, a true *yir*, in the new village is the ritual opening of the house by the earth priest that allows the owner to sacrifice to his ancestors, establish protective medicines, inter the placenta of a newborn, and bury the dead. Even Dagara Christians, who are generally critical of "pagan" sacrifices, grudgingly comply with the requests of the Sisala earth priest that the new house owners have to provide sacrificial animals in order to be granted these rights. Mimirdem was the first Dagara in Laponé to open his house. Others followed suit. And by the end of the 1990s, half of the Dagara houses in Laponé had undergone the prescribed rituals.

Those who have not done so have come to Laponé only recently, have not yet accumulated the necessary gifts, or are for one reason or another reluctant to satisfy Sisala demands. Some take recourse to pragmatic solutions, such as sending their pregnant women to deliver in their home village or the district hospital, asking the elderly or seriously ill to return "home" in order not to die in the new village, or request support from their fellow villagers with opened houses. Others just go ahead and inter the placenta or establish protective shrines and clan medicines in the house (*bese*) and on the fields (*puotiib*) without the official consent of the Sisala, and solve any resulting problems by paying a customary fine.

Even a ritually opened house in Laponé, however, is initially only a *yipaala*, a new house, that for many purposes remains intimately linked to the "old" or "big" house (*yikura* or *yikpee*) in the original village. Arrangements for paying the bride price, burials, major sacrifices to the ancestors, and many other affairs require consultation with, and often must be physically carried out in, the *yikpee*. Except for the intervention of, and potential restrictions by, the Sisala earth priest, the process of establishing a new house on the frontier is not fundamentally different from the way in which Dagara sons gradually gain autonomy from their fathers in all Dagara villages.[109] Again, much depends on the nature of the relations between the migrant and his extended family. However, in case of tensions, or if time is pressing and the original village is too far away, distantly related clan mates or joking partners who reside in the new village can be called in as substitutes for the relatives "back home." Usually, however, the new house cannot become a *yikpee* for the newcomer himself, but only for his sons who carve the ancestor shrine for their father in Laponé. So far, this has happened only in the houses of Mimirdem and two other families. One condition, however, is crucial for development into a *yikpee*, namely, the continuity of relatively peaceful relations with the Sisala hosts. "Wherever they threaten to chase you from the village," a recently arrived Dagara immigrant explained to me, "this place can never become your *yikpee*. So it will always take some time, until you know that you will be able to stay, and that your children will be allowed to stay to take care of your funeral, before the place can really become your new home."[110]

Building a New Dagara Community

For all intents and purposes, then, the Dagara settlers in Laponé are part of multilocal family networks and maintain various exit options in case of difficult times. In his study of the neighboring Dagara settlement in Pina, where Laponé's Dagara pioneer Mimirdem was born, Georges Savonnet argues that such strong supralocal family ties and the fact that the Sisala did not grant the Dagara "strangers" full ownership of the land prevented the immigrants from creating any true local community. Savonnet asserts that they remained an agglomeration of dispersed, economically autonomous individual houses without closer ties among each other and without any strong commitment to the locality.[111] Yet according to my own observations, this is not true for

Laponé, and certainly not for the much older Dagara settlement of Pina, where solid neighborly relations and a sense of local belonging have long since developed, just like in Dagara communities such as Lawra, Ouessa, and others that were founded in the eighteenth and nineteenth centuries. What is different from these older villages, however, is the fact that these neighborly relations are in important ways mediated by the Sisala landowners. The latter ultimately decide whether a Dagara newcomer is admitted to the village and where he is assigned land to farm and a plot for constructing a house. Furthermore, the Sisala exclude the Dagara and other immigrants from active participation in the sacrifices to the earth shrine—that is, from rituals that express, and regularly reaffirm, membership in the group of first-comers and their close allies. Nevertheless, even though the Sisala continue marking them as strangers, the Dagara immigrants establish neighborly relations and develop a sense of local belonging.

When I last visited Laponé in January 2001, I found the Dagara villagers happily celebrating the public final ceremony of the *bagr* initiation in the house of Der Somé. In order to attend the *bagr* festival in Der's new residence, some Bekuone relatives from Tapumu had traveled the whole morning on their bicycles; others had come on foot the day before. They were joined by clan mates and friends from nearby settlements and by representatives from all Dagara houses in Laponé. A sizeable delegation from the Sisala earth priests' and village chief's house also honored the occasion with their presence.

The *bagr* initiation in Der Somé's house was the first of its kind since the Dagara had come to Laponé, and a clear sign that the new Dagara community had come of age. Der Somé was among the Dagara houses that were ritually opened, and he was therefore also allowed to carry out the *bagr* rituals and sacrifices. The latter demonstrated publicly that he and his people considered their house in Laponé not simply a temporary farm settlement, but their new home. Der's house was thus on the way to becoming a *yikpee*, a ritually autonomous "big house," to which sons and grandsons will eventually have to return for certain sacrifices, even if they move farther afield on the expanding Dagara frontier. At the same time, the *bagr* festival helped to strengthen the Dagara immigrants' community in Laponé as a whole.

The nucleus of this new community is constituted by the very networks through which the Dagara settlers have been recruited and were introduced to the Sisala landowners. In the case of Laponé, there are three such networks. The first is centered on late Mimirdem and embraces five other Dagara houses whose members came to Laponé from Pina, Kondon, Kelendou, and Bozo, thanks to Mimirdem's support. One of Mimirdem's protégées was his brother's son, Odilon Somda. Odilon, in turn, organized the second network that comprises altogether eight houses (including his own) who belong to different patriclans, and, with one exception, immigrated from the same village, namely Bozo. And while Mimirdem and his clients were "traditional believers," as they sometimes call themselves, Odilon and his people are staunch Catholics. The third network consists of five houses that came to Laponé from Tapumu, thanks to Der Somé's intervention, and who all belong to the Bekuone patriclan.

There is only one Dagara house in Laponé that stands apart, namely that of Tuoyin Poda, a Muslim from a Dagara-Dafing house in Dabileteng, near Bozo. Tuoyin is a well-known *karamogo*, as the Muslim healers are usually called in the region, and was invited by a Fulbe herder to serve as the Imam of Laponé's small Muslim community. In spite of being a Bekuone, Tuoyin keeps his distance from the other Dagara in Laponé and relies instead on his religious networks. Otherwise, even before settling in Laponé, the members of the three Dagara networks of patrikin, in-laws, and friends were already assisting each other on their farms and with regard to certain ritual obligations, and they continued to do so in the new village.

In addition to these imported networks, the immigrants build new ties of mutual help and friendship. Men with adjoining farms set up *kotaa* arrangements (farming groups); and the women form teams when they search for firewood, carry water, or brew sorghum beer. Just like on the historical frontier, the patriclan system is a powerful instrument that allows the organization of assistance beyond one's closer kin relations for all social matters such as births, marriages, and funerals. Furthermore, mutual help can be recruited along the lines of the matriclan and, most important, through marriages among the newcomers. Der Somé, for instance, took his third wife in Laponé—a woman who had come from Pina and thus helped him establish ties to Mimirdem's network. Some of the younger Dagara men in Laponé are courting the daughters of earlier immigrants. For all important ceremonies, the Dagara settlers of course invite relatives and friends from their original villages, but like Der Somé's *bagr* festival, such festivities also strengthen ties in the new neighbourhood.

An important aspect of creating a new local community is the social appropriation of village space. The Sisala generally prefer to settle "strangers" at a distance from their own houses and retain the last word about the location of the newcomers' houses (and farms), but usually allow the immigrants to suggest a suitable place. The latter thus attempt to re-create the spatial arrangements that they customarily prefer. The Mossi of Laponé, for instance, came in two groups, from two different points of origin, and settled accordingly in two densely built-up nuclei (see map 1.6). The Dagara, on the other hand, have followed their custom to build dispersed houses, and live in two large separate sections, west and east of the village market, while the Sisala and Mossi houses comprise the village center. Patriclan relations and *kotaa* farmwork groups, however, bridge the separation between Dagara sections, and the children and young men and women who grow up in Laponé are quite familiar with all these locations.

The Sisala do not allow the immigrants to name their section, but insist that the entire place has only one correct name—Laponé.[112] However, as I soon discovered, the Dagara and Mossi unofficially gave their own names to their quarters and to many places in the bush. These names, in their own languages, allude to the pioneering settlers or to the patriclans dominant in a certain neighborhood, or to some outstanding natural

Table 1.2. Dagara Houses in Laponé and Their Networks (2001)

Network	Head of household (age in 2001) (original immigrant)	Patriclan	Original village	Relation to "network"	Arrival in Laponé
Mimirdem †	Gbele Poda (55)	Kusiele	Pina	Mimirdem's son	1987
Mimirdem	Odilon Somda (37)	Kusiele	Bozo	Mimirdem's brother's son	1988
Mimirdem	Kog Kambire (25) (father Nuor-eru †)	Kusiele	Pina	Clan mate	1989
Mimirdem	Yaaku Poda (29) (father Kpiin †)	Batane	Kelendou	Yaaku's father = Mimirdem's in-law	1989
Mimirdem	Zaade Somé (??) (Zaade's father †)	Berwuole	Kondon	Zaade's father = Mimirdem's friend	1990
Mimirdem	Lucien Meda (60)	Bekuone	Bozo	Mimirdem's friend	1994
Odilon Somda	Dieudonné Meda (55)	Meto Man	Bozo	Odilon's friend	1992
Odilon Somda	Tadam Somda (55)	Kpagnyaane	Toury	Tadam's brother = Odilon's friend	1993
Odilon Somda	Tobia Meda (46)	Kpiele	Bozo	regarded as Odilon's clan mate	1994
Odilon Somda	Simon Hien (35)	Bekuone	Bozo	friend of Odilon's friend Dieudonné Meda	1999
Odilon Somda	Valère Hien (36)	Kuseble	Bozo	regarded as Odilon's clan mate, close relations with Tobia Meda	1999
Odilon Somda	Valère Somda (30)	Meto Man	Bozo	clan mate of Odilon's friend Dieudonné Meda	2000
Odilon Somda	Appollo Meda (??)	Bekuone	Bozo	friend of Odilon's friend Dieudonné Meda	2000

Table 1.2. Dagara Houses in Laponé and Their Networks (2001) (continued)

Network	Head of household (age in 2001) (original immigrant)	Patriclan	Original village	Relation to "network"	Arrival in Laponé
Der Somé	Der Somé (60)	Bekuone	Tapumu		1989
Der Somé	Beyele Somé (50)	Bekuone	Tapumu	Der's patrilineal cousin	1989
Der Somé	Faakyie Hien (45)	Bekuone	Tapumu	Der's patrilineal cousin	1989
Der Somé	Bangnikuo Somda (40)	Bekuone	Tapumu	Der's clan mate and "son"	1990
Der Somé	Waayir Somda (40)	Bekuone	Kolinka	Der's clan mate and "brother's" son	1997
Tuoyin Poda	Tuoyin Poda (??)	Bekuone	Dabileteng		1994

feature, or to an event closely connected with a particular place. The names are not yet standardized, but are used like nicknames, depending on the speaker and the occasion. However, they clearly indicate that the Dagara (and Mossi) are developing their own collective mental map of the new village, and are thus transforming Laponé into their home. This social appropriation of space is supported by the installation of shrines by the non-Christians in and around their houses and on their fields—a development that is, more or less grudgingly, tolerated by the Sisala as long as the immigrants respect the taboos surrounding the earth shrine and other important Sisala places of power in Laponé territory.

Finally, the new local community is buttressed by the institution of a headman whom the Sisala expect the Dagara and other migrant communities to nominate and who is usually selected from among the first immigrants. In Laponé, it was Mimirdem whom his fellow migrants and the Sisala hosts alike acknowledged as the first-comer among the Dagara settlers and hence their legitimate representative. Mimirdem was expected to introduce all further Dagara immigrants to the Sisala earth priest, settle conflicts among the newcomers, and act as their spokesman vis-à-vis the Sisala villagers and the state administration. Although in fact some Dagara migrants came to Laponé without Mimirdem's assistance, they still emphasized that he had ultimately mediated their contact with the Sisala authorities and thus helped them to settle there. Even Odilon emphasized that he was Mimirdem's "son" and always consulted him before approaching the Laponé earth priest. There are indeed some indications that Mimirdem was not the first Dagara to come to Laponé. But whoever preceded him was not able to gain recognition

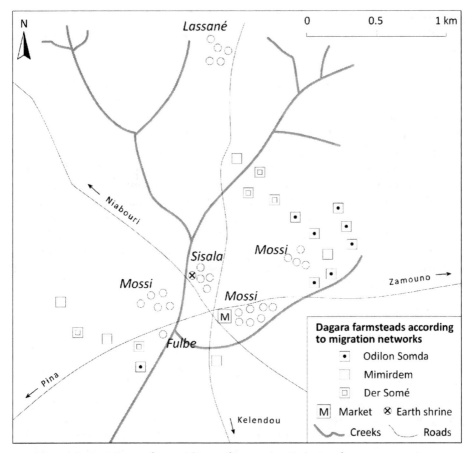

Map 1.6. Laponé: Dagara farmsteads according to migration networks

as a first-comer, either among the migrants or their hosts. The same processes are at work here as in older Dagara communities like Ouessa, namely, that the memory of past migrations is adapted to the needs of the new community, and that the most successful immigrant is redefined as first-comer, even if he was not physically the first.

Just as the office of the earth priest is vested not in the individual first-comer, but his entire lineage, the headmanship of the migrant community is regarded to be a heritable office. After Mimirdem's death, the Sisala therefore asked his senior son Gbele to take over. Many of the younger Dagara, however, and in particular the Christians, do not consider Gbele, a nonliterate "traditional believer," as the most effective advocate of their interests. Informally they turn to Odilon, who has gone to school and is much more outspoken than Gbele, as their advisor and supporter vis-à-vis the Sisala. Yet Odilon and his supporters do not publicly challenge the first-comer ideology or Gbele's position, but rather explain that Odilon merely assists his older "brother." In any case, the institution of the headman, even if the office is held by a relatively weak leader, provides an important organizational focus for the immigrant community.

In older Dagara settlements on Sisala land, second-generation immigrants have recently developed a discourse of local belonging and ownership that explicitly opposes the Sisala's insistence on their status as strangers, as I discuss in more detail in chapter 4. In Laponé, by contrast, the first generation of Dagara immigrants born in the new community is just coming of age, and the heads of household are still very much aware that they owe their presence in the village to their more or less friendly relations with the landowners. However, in Laponé, too, first signs of a much more self-assertive ethnic-cum-local discourse against Sisala "exploitation" could not be ignored in my interviews with younger immigrants. The bases of this growing self-confidence are to be found in the daily routines of mutual support and the symbolic construction of a new local community outlined above. Organizing mobility and building a local community, then, are not opposing aims, but can be reconciled, as the example of Laponé and other Dagara settlements show.

Conclusion

"Our people move because of manliness [*deblu*], because of agriculture [*kob*], and because of roaming around in the bush [*muo puo yob*]," said Dabire Der, one of those old Dagara men who took delight in telling me in vivid detail about their ancestors' travels and travails, succinctly summarizing the reasons for Dagara mobility. *Deblu*—which here means the quest for autonomy and refers to the ideal of physical and spiritual power as well as the violent confrontations that its realization often entailed—was perhaps a more important aspect of migration in the eighteenth and nineteenth centuries than in the colonial and postcolonial periods, when violence no longer played a central role in Dagara expansion. But even today, the ideal of setting up one's own farm and becoming a *yirsob,* the head of a house, is an important factor propelling young men to move to the agricultural frontier. *Kob*—which refers to the lack of fertile farming land—is a reason for mobility that has become ever more important since population densities have grown and soils in older villages have deteriorated. *Muo puo yob*—which means the spirit of adventure, the inclination to explore hitherto unknown regions—is, strictly speaking, not a reason for migration, but rather a paraphrase of the ideology of mobility and frontiersmanship that has been, and still is, typical of many Dagara men. This was, and continues to be, enhanced by the ability of the Dagara migrants to mobilize efficient, broad, and flexible networks of patri- and matrikin, joking relations, allied clans, and friends.

This chapter has discussed how since at least the mid-eighteenth century, Dagara-speaking groups have expanded the territory under their control in the Black Volta region at an impressive rate, often at the expense of neighboring societies. The reasons for Dagara mobility seem to have gradually shifted toward the increasing importance of the search for available farmland. During earlier periods, the imperatives of hunting expeditions as well as the dynamics of village conflicts and feuds within and between kin groups played a more prominent role. Whether the degree of mobility actually increased or decreased is difficult to assess. Colonial pacification made the move to the frontier less risky in many respects, and the frontiersmen no longer necessarily needed to be strong warriors or fearless hunters. On the other hand, they now had to accept Sisala overlordship in terms of land ownership as well as ritual and political authority. While this was precisely what some Dagara migrants sought when they wanted to escape from the harsh rule of their own chiefs—as I discuss in chapter 4—it may have discouraged others from moving to the frontier. Still, a remarkable number of Dagara settlements were founded on Sisala land in the 1930s and 1940s, both in the British and French colonies. They gradually expanded, demographically and spatially in terms of cultivated areas, until the 1970s and 1980s, when they saw a new wave of Dagara migrants moving into ever-remoter Sisala villages.

The historical experience of being a people on the move has crystallized in a pronounced ethos of mobility and a corresponding ideology of *muo puo yob*, "roaming in the bush," and frontiersmanship. One should beware, however, of essentializing Dagara mobility. Most frontiersmen in these recent settlements come from neighboring Dagara villages created during the colonial period, and only few are recruited from the more distant hinterland.[113] There are many houses in the older Dagara villages that have existed in the same place for successive generations and that do not export migrants to the agricultural frontiers. They cope with the increasing demographic pressure on the land by switching to a more intensive, semi-permanent, or permanent cultivation of their fields, borrowing additional land, wherever available, from neighbors and distant relatives, and increasing their participation in labor migration.

On the whole, however, the Dagara were, and continue to be, much more mobile and expansive than the Sisala or Phuo. This phenomenon is, to a great extent, due to the historical coincidences of the settlement process. The Dagara came "late" and found the best ecological niches for hunting and farming already occupied by the Sisala and others. In part, the Dagara were able to displace these other groups and thus gain access to sufficient natural resources of good quality. The two main precolonial Dagara strategies of land appropriation (and displacement of the previous inhabitants) were demographic pressure through the influx of new settlers, and open conflict. When colonial rule halted the more or less violent expansion, many Dagara once again found themselves on marginal soils. Mobility—albeit in new forms and under new circumstances with respect to land ownership—thus became even more imperative than before.

Beyond these ecological and economic factors, however, mobility was, and continues to be, promoted by the striking capability of the Dagara to mobilize efficient and broad networks of patri- and matrikin, joking relationships, allied clans, and friends, allowing them to recruit a relatively large number of new settlers within a short time. This was a crucial asset with respect to the security of newly founded settlements and to the strategies of territorial encroachment with which the Dagara frontiersmen used to occupy the new land. Even in villages that remained under Sisala control, their position was considerably stronger if they managed to increase their numbers. In a good number of settlements founded in the 1930s and 1940s, the Dagara have indeed reduced the Sisala to a minority. Thus, demographic pressure continues to operate as an important factor in the de facto appropriation of land, even though the de jure ownership remains in the hands of the Sisala "first-comers"—a conflict-ridden development that I discuss in chapter 4.

More generally, this chapter confirms what a number of recent studies have asserted, namely that mobility was, and continues to be, a vital element in the survival strategies of many African populations. At the same time, however, I have also shown how important it is to examine the history and micropolitics of mobility in order to add nuance to this general observation. As the case of the Black Volta region shows, different groups can and have, in the course of time, developed distinct patterns of mobility, and often these different modes are complementary and closely interrelated. In the case explored in this book, for example, early arrival in the region and the concomitant opportunities to appropriate the most favorable ecological niches have allowed a higher degree of sedentariness, while late-comers were often forced to stay more mobile and expand in search of better-quality land and other conditions more amenable for establishing their settlements. Such differences in degrees and patterns of mobility have been supported by different forms of social organization, and eventually crystallized into a different ethos of mobility. Just as research on labor migration has shown that the search for salaried work or other sources of income outside one's original village can become an important ritual of initiation into adulthood,[114] the impetus to leave one's original village in search of new rural homes can become an integral part of a way of life.

The various case studies of migration and the establishment of new settlements discussed in this chapter have also shown that no deterministic, monocausal explanation can do justice to the multilayered, complex dynamics of mobility that African populations experience. We observed an intriguing mix of "push" and "pull" factors that motivated temporary or more permanent migrations, and an intricate interplay of ecological and economic as well as social, political, and ideological factors that motivated people to move (or stay, as the case may be). Furthermore, establishing a new farmstead away from "home" generally proved to be a gradual, partially reversible process that was often preceded (as well as followed) by less dramatic forms of mobility such as, in the precolonial period, extended hunting expeditions or, in more recent times, visits to distant markets, pilgrimages to shrines or mission stations, marriage, and the like. Also, bouts of labor migration and wage labor often preceded, and financially supported, the move to the agricultural frontier, the risks of which continued to be mitigated by maintaining various exit options, both in the direction of the migrants' original homes as well as to open spaces farther afield. Combining different forms of mobility therefore serves to hedge the risks of particular livelihood strategies and promote personal well-being, a strategy that has only recently begun to be explored more systematically.[115]

At the same time, the insights gained from the case of Dagara and Sisala mobility corroborate the findings of most anthropological studies on migration: namely that, although it is important to understand the collective dimensions of a "culture of migration," as Michael Lambert has called it,[116] we should not ignore the relevance of individual decision making and agency.[117] Even in a general context of mobility, not everyone necessarily moves, and certainly not during all phases of his or her life. In the Black Volta region, for instance, historically only specially equipped individuals set out to explore new frontiers, and, currently, many families carefully decide who among its offspring will be the most suitable candidate to resettle elsewhere and who should keep the home fires burning. Hence, here again, we must beware of deterministic models.

Finally, the chapter has shown that organizing mobility does not preclude building a local community. *Pace* Kopytoff's argument that Africans were indifferent to rootedness in physical space,[118] the cases discussed in this chapter have shown that both frontiersmen and late-comers took great care to appropriate the new territories into which they moved, economically, socially, and ritually. The politics of place-names offered one indication of this interest in marking space, as did the elaborate migration-and-settlement narratives that connect the deeds of the immigrants' culture heroes to certain landmarks. In the same vein, lineage elders refashioned their group's migration narratives in order to symbolically bolster the new ties of neighborhood, further solidarity, and promote a sense of belonging in the new settlement. The next chapter shows in more detail why the conventional paradigm of precolonial Africa's free surplus land, indifference to territoriality, and absence of property, as well as the inalienability of land, needs to be reassessed. It explores how a stable ritual order and property rights over immobile resources were established, and contested, in the context of mobility.

2 Staking Claims

Earth Shrines, Ritual Power, and Property Rights

CREATING A PEACEFUL order on the frontier can be a bloody affair. In their attempt to establish new settlements, Dagara frontiersmen often resorted to violence toward previous inhabitants or competing immigrants. However, if their newly founded homes were to endure, prosper, and attract more settlers, they also needed to create a peaceful social order that ensured, among other things, that villagers could feel safe from human and spiritual hazards, and that provided a degree of material security by allowing them to enjoy the fruits of their labor. In the Black Volta region, as in many other parts of the West African savanna, such an order centered on the earth shrine and its custodian. Earth shrines were created from stones or other objects assumed to be potent, such as iron rods or clay pots, and usually taken care of by a member of the first-comers' lineage. The frontiersmen and their allies often established other shrines for the spirits of the bush, hills, and rivers, but generally the earth shrines were, and continue to be, regarded as more powerful. In exchange for sacrifices that the earth priest offered on behalf of the community, the earth god was believed to grant the local community permission to exploit the natural resources and guarantee its material and spiritual well-being.

Most important, however, earth shrines and their custodians not only provided for spiritual protection and fertility, but were, and still are, central to the definition of property rights regarding the land and related resources. Earth priests had no political authority and could not enforce their rules through violence or other secular means. But their control of the most important spiritual resource gave them a form of power, or at least substantial influence, in the regulation of access to the land and related resources and, more generally, in village affairs and relations with neighboring settlements.

Earth shrines thus simultaneously constitute territorial cults and economic, social, and political institutions. In a literal sense, they are containers for the earth deity and the spirits of the pioneers' ancestors that need to be regularly appealed to for blessing. And they are symbolic vessels that embody the local community's inextricable link with the land. "Shrines are," as Allan Dawson puts it, "physical manifestations of a group's claim to a particular piece of land and thus markers of identity. . . . [T]he shrine is autochthony made real."[1] In a context of mobility, however, autochthony is constantly challenged and redefined, and shrines are not locally fixed, but can travel with the pioneers or depart together with the previous inhabitants whom these pioneers displace. Shrines can be abandoned in one place and reestablished or created anew in another location; they can be destroyed, neglected, or revitalized, redefined or newly legitimized; in short: they can be adjusted to the needs and claims of the new inhabitants of the territory, and they can become objects of intense contestation.

That earth shrines are central to religion and land tenure in the Black Volta region was already noted by colonial administrators and anthropologists, but scholarly attention focused either on the earth cult as religious institution[2] or on the secular, economic system of land rights connected with it, not on the complex connections between these two aspects. A case in point for the latter perspective—that came to dominate "applied" research since the 1950s, often commissioned by governments with the aim of boosting agricultural productivity, are the perceptive descriptions of customary land rights by R. J. H. Pogucki on Northern Ghana and Jean Louis Boutillier on what was then Upper Volta. They highlighted the importance of earth shrines as embodiments of particularly strong property titles, but their rights-oriented view led them to overlook the importance of ritual politics for defending, challenging, or redefining land tenure. Such an overly structuralist perspective on indigenous land tenure continues to dominate much of the newer policy-oriented literature on land rights.[3] On the other hand, the overly romanticist image of the earth priest as a noble "high priest" or "priestly king,"[4] or as a religious "recluse" uninterested in wealth and worldly power[5] that colonial officers developed and that persists among some contemporary development experts and land planners is just as misleading.

In order to understand how first-comer claims, control over earth shrines, and property rights come together on the historical frontier as well as in current land conflicts, we need to get beyond these partial visions. This chapter shows how the office of the earth priest, and more generally ritual prerogatives, were, and continue to be, often mobilized (or contested) in order to legitimate (or challenge) economic interests and political privileges. It is only by taking the links between property rights and the ritual order into account that we can better grasp these dynamics.[6]

The chapter explores the changing role that earth shrines played in Dagara expansion and in the relations between the Dagara immigrants and their Sisala neighbors. It discusses how frontiersmen and late-comers established, expanded, or transmitted earth shrines, and how these practices arose in response to the challenges of securing or contesting property rights over immobile resources in a sociohistorical context of mobility. Which rights over resources resulted from the establishment of a shrine, and what did first-comers—and competing late-comers—believe regarding the transferability of some or all of these rights? What social (and spiritual) services were earth priests expected to deliver, and how could these services be translated into more mundane privileges? And in which ways were claims to first-comer status and control over an earth shrine mutually constitutive?

In all of these questions, narratives—or "good stories," as Jacob puts it[7]—that recount the migration of one's ancestors into the area, the foundation of the settlement and the establishment of an earth shrine as well as subsequent transactions of shrines and land, play a decisive role. They help to build consensus and define property claims, or articulate challenges to existing ownership rights and "define alternatives."[8] In addition to exploring the politics of establishing, extending, and transferring earth shrines, this chapter therefore also analyzes indigenous theories of property and the ways in which ritually enshrined property rights were, and continue to be, strengthened by narrative strategies of persuasion. Finally, it discusses how colonial ideas about indigenous land tenure interacted with local visions and interests concerning land, privileging notions that "allodial" property is inalienable and thus strengthening first-comer arguments.[9]

Constructing Ritual Protection on the Frontier

Just as ancestor shrines mark a proper house, the earth shrine signifies a proper village. The underlying concept of earth shrines shows some similarities among all societies in the Black Volta region and the West African savanna more generally. All land is believed to be under the ritual protection of an earth god with whom the first-comers concluded a kind of pact.[10] The territory under the protection of a particular earth shrine is called *tengan* (literally the "crust" or "skin of the earth") in Dagara, and *tebuo* in Sisale. It includes the settlement as well as different categories of uninhabited bush. Among the Dagara, the earth shrine itself usually consists of a stone (*tengan kuur*) and a tree (*tengan tie*) under which the stone is buried and where sacrifices are carried out. Among the Sisala, the earth shrine often also contains objects such as iron rods, mud bricks, or clay pots that are usually placed, together with some local stones, in or near the pit where the first-comer supposedly dug into the earth for the construction of his house.

During the early phases of settlement in the region, when land was not scarce, the earth-shrine "parish," to use Goody's term,[11] was probably understood not as a flat, homogeneous territory with separating linear boundaries, but as a field of ritual power, with a well-defined center (the earth shrine) in the inhabited and regularly cultivated space, and with concentric circles of influence that thinned out toward scattered bush fields and the uncultivated bush. In any case, the earth priest's control over activities in these latter areas was not as effective as in the inner domains. It was only when more and more bush was cultivated that the boundaries between neighboring earth-shrine parishes had to be defined more precisely—a conflict-ridden process that I discuss in the next chapter.

The custodians of the earth shrine were generally not regarded as the owners of the natural resources in a strictly economic sense, and the degree of control that they should exercise over land once allotted to other villagers is often hotly debated. But because of their privileged access to the earth gods, they were the only frontiersmen capable of ritually transforming "virgin'" bush into exploitable resources and surveying the proper order of all earth-related matters. From these indispensable tasks the earth priests derived, and continue to derive, their income (ritual gifts from covillagers and immigrants) and special rights to control all hunting, fishing, and gathering activities.[12] Both among the Sisala and the Dagara, the custodian of the shrine, the *tengansob* (Dagara) or *totina* (Sisala), is supposedly a descendant of the first settler. He is responsible for sacrifices to the earth, allocates land to new settlers, plays an important role in the ritual opening of new houses, and opens the annual fishing and hunting parties. In cases of suicide or other deaths deemed unnatural, the earth priest must intervene to repair the damage done to the earth before the corpse can be buried. However, the power of the earth-priestly office is restricted by numerous taboos. Although the earth priest benefits from the sacrificial meat and beer and is entitled to lost property and stray domestic animals, the office is generally regarded as dangerous and unrewarding. Yet while individuals may be reluctant to become *tengansob* or *totina*, their extended kin group within which the office hereditarily circulates will strongly affirm the right to choose the earth priest from the kin group's ranks.

While these basic concepts are shared by the Dagara and Sisala, each group has developed its own ideas about the installation and handling of an earth shrine and about who should be its custodian. These differences reflect, and at the same time reinforced, the various strategies of mobility discussed in the previous chapter.

Mobile Stones and Contested Earth-Shrine Hierarchies among the Dagara

The stone at the center of the Dagara earth shrine is a transportable object; it may be carried in a bag from one location to another. An earth shrine is believed to transfer its powers to any stone lying on the ground surrounding the *tengan*. This is how the "mother" shrine can produce "children" (*kubile*, small stones), which may be carried away by members of the earth-priestly lineage to be installed elsewhere.

If a new Dagara settlement is founded on land under the protection of an existing Dagara earth shrine with the consent and help of the shrine's custodian, the ritual dependence of the younger settlement is usually not disputed. Communal sacrifices at the beginning and the end of the farming season were thus initially performed at the older earth shrine, but eventually an elder of the new settlement would be given permission to carry out most of the sacrifices on behalf of the new neighborhood and to ritually open new houses and supervise the burial of the dead. This could lead to the establishment of an independent earth shrine whose custodians, in some cases, even denied its past affiliation with the mother shrine. The ritual dependence of a new settlement usually lasted for several generations, but in most cases the new village would strive to gain more autonomy. Independence means that serious offenses against the earth, even suicide, can be made good through sacrifice at the new village's *tengan* without having to refer to the mother shrine. But achieving independence generally was, and continues to be, a lengthy, tedious process that is usually not well received by the original village. In some cases, the founding lineages of new settlements therefore refused to ask the earth priest of a neighboring village for a *kubile*, turning instead to a more distant settlement where a closely related segment of their own patriclan held the office of the *tengansob* and was expected to make less onerous demands. Alternatively, the Dagara frontiersmen could also seek ritual protection by obtaining a shrine stone from a nearby Sisala settlement and avoid dependence from fellow Dagara altogether.

The Dagara pattern of fission of shrine parishes and of establishing "daughter shrines" transforms the territorial cult into a surprisingly mobile institution. In combination with the strategic advantages of the patriclan system, this was another factor that supported the territorial expansion of the Dagara. Moreover, the Dagara have few restrictions concerning the recruitment of the custodians of the shrine and few taboos on the admissible origins of the shrine stone. In ten of the thirty-one Dagara villages east of the Black Volta in which I collected information about the origins of the earth shrines, I was told that the shrine stone was given by, or purchased from, the previous inhabitants, namely Sisala, Phuo, or Nuni, and that these earth shrines were in no way regarded as less powerful than those using stones of Dagara origin.[13] In two villages, the Dagara frontiersmen were said to have carried the shrine stone along with them from their original settlements. In five cases, the earth shrine had evolved either out of what was once a *tengankubile*, a small shrine established for the new settlers by one of the older Dagara villages, or out of a *wiekuur*, a field shrine, or "bush shrine," that the newcomers had installed themselves. The remaining fourteen villages had only *tenganbile* (dependent earth shrines) and were still obliged to consult the *tengankpee* (major earth shrine) in the neighboring Dagara village for all serious problems.

As I went on interviewing Dagara earth priests and other informants about the history of the earth shrines, I was also confronted with many stories about a puzzling variety of medicinal, hunting, and field shrines, and was presented with competing views about whether or not these shrines could legitimately be transformed into *tenganbile* or even *tengankpee*. My interlocutors agreed neither on the terminology nor on the question of who was authorized to establish which shrines and whether the shrines protected only the lineages of their custodians or the entire community.

Some informants insisted that a *wiekuur* (literally, bush stone) was exclusively a hunting shrine that could never be transformed into an earth shrine because the latter accepts only domestic animals as sacrificial gifts while hunting shrines have to be "fed" with wild animals. Others explained that only particular patriclans, namely the Kpagnyaane and the Gane, could establish proper hunting shrines, and that members of these clans would always take some *wiekube* (bush stones) with them on their migrations and could, when they founded a new settlement, create an earth shrine from these stones. Still others used the terms *wiekuur* and *puotiib* (field medicine) interchangeably and held differing views on the question of whether lineages who did not hold earth-priestly office could establish such shrines on their own, or only with the consent of the earth priest, or not at all. And they disagreed whether a field shrine protected only the fields of a particular lineage or of an entire village section, and thus served as a *tengankubile* that could eventually be transformed into a *tengankpee*.[14]

Furthermore, although Dagara earth shrines are territorial cults for a circumscribed area, they can also develop into "deterritorialized" mobile healing cults whose ritual power extends far beyond the earth-shrine parish. Some earth shrines have become famous for their extraordinary power to grant fertility, health, and prosperity, and people come from near and far in order to sacrifice at the shrine for the solution of their personal problems. The clients can ask the earth priest for a small stone from the shrine that they would take along for their personal protection—traveling shrine stones that need to be kept effective by regularly "charging their battery," as my interlocutors put it, through sacrifices at the original shrine.[15] In the frontier process, these mobile stones could eventually be "reterritorialized" and help establish in a newly founded village a personal or lineage protective shrine or even an earth shrine, if the shrine custodian succeeded in claiming first-comer status vis-à-vis later immigrants. However, the nature of the new shrines—personal healing, lineage protective, or supralineage territorial cult—and their obligations toward the original earth shrine were, and continue to be, the subject of intense debate. In some cases, the custodians of the mother shrines attempted to translate their ritual authority into more secular privileges of property rights over land, or at least the right to regular gifts from the proceeds of the land under the protection of the daughter stones.[16]

In any case, the conflicting stories about the nature and "biographies" of healing, hunting, field and earth shrines reflect the fact that creating new villages and ritual protection on the frontier was a gradual process. When the frontiersmen "discovered" a suitable site and constructed their first provisional huts, they often did not see an immediate need to establish an earth shrine because the felt sufficiently protected by their mobile personal and clan medicines (*tii*) and various hunting and field shrines. An earth shrine became necessary only when the women and further settlers from different patriclans arrived. The earth cult regulated the social relations between the first-comers and these late-comers by instituting taboos against violence, bloodshed, and illicit sexual encounters ("in the bush"), and by ritually sanctioning the leading role of the earth-priestly lineage. The continued fertility of the land, the women, and the domestic animals, so the Dagara and their neighbors believed, could not be ensured without internally peaceful relations and the good offices of an earth priest. However, just as the settlement history, clan composition, and interaction between first-comers and late-comers varied from village to village, so did the specific circumstances of how an earth shrine was created and how it related to existing protective and medicinal shrines.

The negotiable rapport between the various shrines and cults allowed adaptation of the ritual landscape to changing constellations of power. In principle, the *tengansob* had to, and still has to, be informed about, and give his consent to, the installation of any other shrine or cult, be they part of a patriclan's ancestral traditions or newly imported "foreign" medicines against witchcraft or theft. However, the authority of the *tengan* over these other cults was, and still is, generally imposed only ex post facto. The illicit introduction of a new protective cult or the arrogation of *tengankpee* powers by a *tenganbile* is only "discovered" (and punished) when a diviner attributes specific incidences of death, infertility, illness, or other misfortunes to this transgression. However, depending on their influence and power, the transgressor and his followers may either make reparations at the *tengankpee* or decide to ignore the diviner's dictum and opt for ritual secession. If misfortune continues to trouble the new ritual community, they may eventually reorient themselves toward the original shrine, or they may turn to another powerful earth shrine farther afield. In any case, instead of seeking to condense the welter of shrine names and attributes into a well-ordered taxonomy, we should understand that the contradictory terminology and explanations that my interlocutors put forward are part and parcel of the ongoing negotiation of ritual hierarchies.

Negotiation as well as conflict also characterized the relations between the Dagara pioneers and the earth priests of older Sisala (and Phuo) villages. While the incoming Dagara were usually aware of their existence and sometimes sought their consent before settling, there was always an alternative, though confrontational strategy, namely to establish an earth shrine from their own mobile protective stones or hunting shrines, or through filiation with an existing Dagara earth shrine. The latter became a symbol around which local identities crystallized, and helped to transcend the latent antagonism between individual houses or patriclan segments. Some villages such as Ouessa thus ritually controlled more than a dozen villages and hamlets where they had established branches of their earth shrines (*tengankubile*), and although earth priests were never themselves military leaders, they may have played a considerable role in mobilizing military alliances—for instance against Sisala or Phuo resistance. The system of hierarchical earth shrines may thus be also seen as a cultural strategy capable of creating solidarity and military support beyond the immediate local community.

However, ritual dependency on senior Dagara villages did not exclude the possibility that the new Dagara settlers eventually also settled into friendly terms with their Sisala (or Phuo) neighbors. Indeed, they often did so, following initial conflict, by acquiring an additional earth shrine that could then be used to gain independence from the older Dagara settlements. In the eyes of the Sisala, the already established Dagara settlers were just as much late-comers as the more recent Dagara arrivals. For the latter, the hierarchical relationship with an older Dagara settlement sometimes implied heavier burdens than ritual dependency on another ethnic group. In any case, an earth shrine neither was nor is presently an ethnically bounded resource. Moreover, the Sisala were not merely passive victims of the Dagara expansion, but often seem to have actively asserted their rights. What kind of ritual protection the new Dagara settlement finally chose, whether from a senior Dagara village or from Sisala neighbors, depended on the specific local power relations.

Sisala Earth Shrines

The Sisala, on the other hand, have no concept of fission of earth-shrine areas or of ritual dependence between earth shrines, even though alliances between neighboring villages are in some cases reflected by the identical names that their earth shrines bear. Each Sisala village has its own major shrine at which the full range of rituals necessary for protection, fertility, and reparation after the violation of taboos can be carried out without referring to other settlements. In keeping with their ideology of having been the true first-comers in their new settlements, Sisala rarely report having met previous inhabitants, and usually claim that they created the earth shrines themselves in the new location. The origins of the stones or other objects at the center of the earth shrines, however, seem to be as diverse as among the Dagara, with one important exception—namely, that the Sisala would never admit to having received—and much less to having purchased—an earth-shrine stone from anyone outside their own ethnic group. In ten of the twenty-one Sisala villages[17] that I visited, I was told that the pioneering ancestor carried a stone from the earth shrine in his original settlement to the new place; in five cases, it was the earth priest of a neighboring Sisala village who established a shrine stone for the newcomers (apparently by taking some earth or a stone from his village); and in only six cases was the shrine for the new village said to have been created from local resources—from an "object" discovered in the bush, from one of the mud bricks used to build the first house, or from a hunting shrine transformed into an earth shrine.[18]

Regarding the recruitment of the custodians of Sisala earth shrines, some narratives reveal that it was sometimes not actually being first-comers, but ruse and trickery that determined who could impose himself as the legitimate founder of the earth shrine and thus owner of the land. Tensions between the successful earth-priestly lineage and the true first-comers who lost the contest[19] were usually resolved by allowing the latter to control the shrines to the spirits of the bush and/or the water. More generally, in Sisala villages created by immigrants from different places of origin, the offices of *totina* (earth priest), *bakabele* (guardian of the bush), and *fuotina* (guardian of the water) are distributed among the different kin groups, while in settlements of more homogeneous origins, the *totina* family also officiates as *fuotina* and *bakabele*.[20] In this respect, Sisala ritual organization seems to be less formalized than that of the Phuo, with whom the Sisala are linguistically and culturally closely related,[21] and more flexible, very much like the Dagara one, with the important difference, however, that ritual hierarchies exist only within, not between settlements.

However, while the Sisala deny any hierarchical relations among their own villages, Sisala earth priests do not hesitate to claim continued ritual authority (and property rights) over the settlements of Dagara late-comers to whom they once gave a shrine stone. They insist that their Dagara clients should continue to consult them in all serious affairs such as suicide or murder—expectations that Dagara usually vehemently reject. Sometimes, my Sisala interlocutors even denied that their forebears had ever given a shrine stone to the Dagara immigrants and claimed that such a transfer would have been completely "against custom" and thus impossible. However, these assertions are probably recent attempts to reinterpret, in the context of diminished exit options and the colonial freezing of property relations, what might have originally been more egalitarian and cooperative ritual relations with the Dagara immigrants.

Negotiating Ritual Independence: Why Some Villages Have Multiple Earth-Shrine Stones

The Niégo earth shrine comprises three different shrine stones: one given by the Ouessa earth priest, one acquired from the Sisala of Kelendou after violent conflict, and a third one purchased from the Sisala of Hiela. All three stones are said to have been placed together under the *tengan tie* (earth-shrine tree) in Niégo-Susulipuo. This section is the political and ritual center of Niégo, and the *tengan tie* stands near the house of Baabobr, one of the founders of Niégo and the great-grandfather of the late Somda Beyaa, who officiated as Niégo earth priest at the time of my research. Somda Beyaa himself admitted the existence of only two shrine stones, the one from Ouessa and the one from Hiela, but he asserted that all sacrifices at the shrine served to pacify both *tengankube*.[22] Informants from other sections of Niégo insisted that there was a third shrine stone. When I discussed my findings on the Niégo earth shrine with my Dagara friends from other villages, they regularly rejected the possibility that this could be true. Some denied that it was possible to combine different stones in a single earth shrine and said that my Niégo informants were telling me outright lies. Others insisted that if the founders of Niégo had indeed combined different stones, this was certainly against all taboos of the earth deity and extremely dangerous. It created a situation that would sooner or later "explode," as one interlocutor put it.[23] According to Somda Beyaa, however, who conceded that the history of the Niégo earth shrine was unusual, the combined earth shrine had not yet caused any calamity, and all Niégo informants had their own explanations of why this should be so.

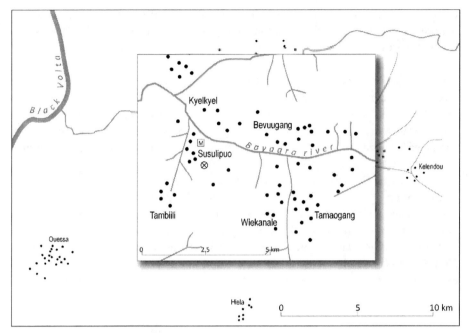

Map 2.1 Niégo and its sections

The task of reconstructing the complicated history of how Niégo and its earth shrine(s) were founded very much came to resemble detective's work. I had to compare and put together countless contradictory versions and partial perspectives that I collected in Niégo's various sections, namely, Tambiili, Wiekanale, Tamaogang, Kyelkyel, and Bevuugang, as well as in Ouessa, Hiela, and Kelendou (see map 2.1). The difficulties stem, at least in part, from the intense past and present conflicts over shrine hierarchies, property rights, political authority, and, more recently, administrative boundaries in which my informants were involved.

Three major fault lines affected the historical narratives and resulted in a proliferation of competing versions. The first concerns the competition between the two patriclans who assert to be the founders of Niégo, namely the Kpagnyaane and the Bimbiile—or Tambiile, as they are usually called by the Kpagnyaane. These clans claim that although they descend from a common ancestor, they were separated at some point during their joint migration. In order to facilitate intermarriage and mutual ritual assistance, they formed two distinct clans that both passed through Ouessa, but when moving farther eastward, ultimately settled in different sections, Dianlé and Niégo. Although they put up a united front before outsiders and continue to cooperate in ritual activities, they compete with each other over seniority and prestige as well as over more tangible assets such as rights over land and shares in sacrificial animals. These tensions result in competing claims regarding the order of settlement and the identity of the ancestors involved in opening the bush. The second line of conflict concerns Niégo's relations with the Gane earth priests of Ouessa, which were, from the very beginning, strained. While Ouessa claimed that Niégo should continue to pay allegiance to the senior earth shrine in Ouessa, the Niégo earth priests asserted their independence. Ouessa versions of Niégo history thus offered a useful corrective to the material collected in Niégo, but were also severely biased. Third, the Sisala from Kelendou and Hiela not only contradicted many Dagara statements and demanded that Niégo should still pay respect to them, but also competed between each other over seniority, land rights, and responsibility for, as well as income from, the Dagara "settlers."

All these tensions were compounded by the disputes sparked by the colonial introduction of new political hierarchies—which made Niégo-Susulipuo, at least for some time, the center of a paramount chiefdom—and by the recent redrawing of administrative boundaries that placed the Sisala villages of Hiela and Kelendou, on the one hand, and Niégo and its Dagara satellite settlements, on the other, in different provinces. However, it is precisely these multilayered conflicts and tensions that make Niégo an excellent case to study if one wants to understand the multiple links between ritual and secular politics, spiritual protection, and property rights. The case of Niégo illustrates that the ritual order established by the frontiersmen was, from the very beginning, dynamic, negotiable, and often intensely contested. Sisala and Dagara earth priests and their allies repeatedly attempted to take advantage of changing constellations of power in order to extend the territory under their ritual authority and augment the prestige and income that could be derived from controlling an earth shrine.

How Tamao and Baabobr Acquired a Shrine Stone from the Sisala of Hiela: The Niégo Earth-Priest's Story

In our first interview, Somda Beyaa, the Niégo earth priest, told me what can be regarded as the official version presented to outsiders.[24] He elaborated how his ancestors, who belonged to the Kpagnyaane patriclan, founded Niégo and acquired the land and an earth-shrine stone from the Sisala of Hiela:

> Our ancestors left Wuli and came to settle in Burutu, near Nandom. From there they went across to the other side of the Black Volta and settled on the Be'en *tengan*, near Memer.... From Be'en they came across [the Black Volta] to settle at Bidomo near Ouessa. While they still lived at Bidomo, they roamed up here [to Niégo] where they saw a lot of trees and water that animals could drink. Our ancestor was a hunter and discovered this place on a hunting expedition. When he got here, he saw the Bayagra, the Kyebagme, and the Ganyuu, three big water bodies [which made it an attractive place for hunters as well as for permanent settlement], and went back to Bidomo to inform his people. He then came to settle here [in Niégo] for about three years.
>
> He did not hear the sound of anybody. He proceeded to Kelendou to find out who was for this place, but they said they did not own the place. He went to Bouara, and the people there also said they did not own this place, but they directed him to

Hiel [Hiela]. He went to Hiel, they are Sisala [*langme*], and he met the elders Piino, Kponcho, Nawil, Balipuo, and Bentere . . . and told them that he was looking for a place. . . . They told him that . . . he should return home and farm millet and guinea-corn for two consecutive seasons before meeting them again. He farmed for three years and then went to meet them again. They [the elders of Hiela] asked him if he could settle at the place. He told them yes, he could settle. They then told him to go back and provide a bull and a cow, a ram, ten thousand cowries, a big basket full of malt plus some fowl. When he had acquired all these things, he informed them, and they fixed a date when they were going to come to his place. He brewed pito [sorghum beer], and when they came, they killed the bull and told him that the place [Niégo] that they were giving to him was like a daughter they were giving out in marriage. The things they collected from him were the dowries of the daughter [i.e., the Niégo *tengan*] who now belonged to him, whether bitter or cool [i.e., he was allowed to carry out all types of sacrifices and solve even serious problems at his own earth shrine]. My [great-]grandfather then appealed to all those before him [i.e., his Kpagnyaane clan mates], to the members of the Bimbiile clan and to other strangers to come and fill the place and assist him in his hunting expeditions. . . . And many people really came to fill the place.[25]

When I asked why his forefathers had left Bidomo, Beyaa briefly explained that the relations between the Kpagnyaane and Gane earth priests of Ouessa had been strained due to competition over hunting rights. Beyaa did not mention, however, that his forefathers had been given a protective stone by the Ouessa *tengandem*. On the contrary, he emphasized the dangers of putting two earth-shrine stones together:

It is true that in Burutu, our ancestors were the *tengandem*. But when they went across the Black Volta, they could not carry the *tengan* along to all these places. . . . That was why when they got here they had to look for the owners of the *tengan* as far as Hiel. Moreover, this place belongs to one particular *tengan*, and since two *tengame* cannot coexist we could not bring ours to this place. . . . Any person who tells you that this place was ever under the Ouessa *tengan*, is a liar! Ouessa never owned this place. It belonged to the *langme*, and we came to beg for the place, we begged it from our [Sisala] friends and they gave it to us and showed us the taboos [*kyiiru*] of the *tengan* and the boundary [*turbogr*].

Poda Yir-ieru, a Kpagnyaane elder in Tamaogang, a section on the eastern periphery of Niégo, added some interesting details to Beyaa's version. He explained how Tamao, the most renowned of the Kpagnyaane pioneers, organized the group's territorial expansion and looked for spiritual protection. "Tamao was a hunter," Yir-ieru related:

He did not cultivate. During his hunting expeditions, whenever he discovered a water course where the animals drank, he returned to inform his brothers who would then come to join him. . . . They would construct a hut, hunt together, and kill the animals, and he would then bring more people to establish themselves near this hut. As soon as the place became crowded, Tamao himself would leave again and continue to search for new hunting grounds.[26]

Tamao and his people thus gradually advanced from Bidomo to Dianlé, then to Niégo-Susulipuo and farther on to Tamaogang. Poda Yir-ieru agreed with Beyaa that Niégo was founded on territory belonging to the Sisala from Hiela. The latter cultivated the land only occasionally and had no qualms to grant Tamao permission to hunt. When Tamao's clan mates started to come in more significant numbers, wanting to establish permanent houses and farms, the Dagara frontiersmen found it necessary to create a proper earth shrine, and turned again to the Sisala of Hiela. Like Beyaa, Poda Yir-ieru related that the Sisala regarded the land and the shrine as "their daughter" who needed to be dowried, but added that it was not the hunter Tamao, but his own grandfather Baanibe, a successful, rich farmer, who provided the animals and cowries that the Sisala demanded.

From other informants I learned that Tamao had used a stone from the Ouessa *tengan* for protection before acquiring an earth-shrine stone from Hiela. Therefore I decided to go back to interview Somda Beyaa a second time.[27] Beyaa now confirmed that the Gane earth priests had actually given Tamao and his people a small stone to protect them from harm. They had used this stone while they settled at Bidomo and Dianlé (which still belongs to the Ouessa earth-shrine area) and took it along when they continued to Niégo. However, once settled in Niégo, the protection this stone offered was no longer sufficient, and Tamao had to acquire a proper earth shrine from Hiela. As Beyaa explained: "If you establish yourself on somebody's land, you cannot just declare yourself the owner; the *tengan* would never be with you and you would not prosper. You cannot take the *tengan* by force, you have to find the owner, and ask for permission, and only if it is granted, can things go well for you."

Because Tamao was a hunter and not interested in staying too long in any one place, Beyaa went on, he left the earth-shrine stone in the care of his junior brother Baabobr, a farmer, who had established himself in Niégo-Susulipuo, where our interview took place. While tending the Niégo earth shrine, Baabobr and his successors also continued to attend the great annual sacrifices at the Ouessa *tengan*, and regularly sent the head and the skin of some of the bigger animals slaughtered at the Niégo *tengan* to Ouessa, at least until quite recently. Furthermore, whenever a diviner told them to do so, they would ask the Ouessa earth priest to perform sacrifices for them in Bidomo or Dianlé. Beyaa left open whether this happened in acknowledgment of Ouessa's authority over part of the Niégo *tengan* or out of respect for vows that the Kpagnyaane ancestors had made at their old settlement sites. Beyaa was thus ambivalent whether, to use the customary Dagara terms, the regular gifts and sacrifices were for "matters of the land" (*tengan yele*) or for "matters of the forefathers" (*saakumine yele*)—a difference that has important consequences in terms of the extent to which Ouessa could still claim the right to interfere in Niégo ritual and secular affairs.

How Tengnibie Acquired a Shrine Stone from the Sisala of Kelendou: The Story of the Tambiile in Bevuugang

It was in Bevuugang, a section of Niégo founded by the Tambiile, that I was presented with an explicit story about the composite nature of the Niégo *tengan*. The Tambiile ancestor Tengnibie and his people had probably been invited by Tamao and his brother Baabobr to push the Dagara frontier farther northward into Sisala territory. Indeed, Tengnibie did eventually manage to create a new settlement, Bevuugang, that is separated from Susulipuo by a river. My informants in Bevuugang narrated vividly how Tengnibie initially experienced a period of relatively peaceful coexistence with the Sisala, but, as the Dagara immigrants became more numerous, violent exchanges ensued until the Sisala finally withdrew. Before displacing them altogether, however, Tengnibie requested an earth-shrine stone from them in order to protect the new Dagara settlement:

> When our ancestor Tengnibie arrived, the Sisala [*langme*] had already settled here, but he ... did not know that there were already people here. So when he built the walls of his house, the *langme* tore them down anytime he went back home [probably to Susulipuo]. This happened several times. Then he decided to sleep by the building in order to keep watch over it. [When he met the Sisala, they] told him that the land was theirs, but that he could go ahead and build his house. Over the course of time, however, Tengnibie killed many Sisala, and so eventually they said that it was better not to stay close to a person like Tengnibie and moved back to Kelendou.
>
> It was the *langme*, not the Dagara, who had named the place Niégo, "big water." The ruins of their houses and their acacia trees [*gur*] are still here. The people of Kelendou owned this place but gave it to Tengnibie. ... If our ancestors would have allowed the *langme* to leave without telling them about the *kyiiru* [taboos] of the place, it would not have been going well for us. So when the *langme* were about to go, they told our ancestors to give them ten thousand cowries plus a cow before they could let them know the *kyiiru* of the land. Instead of the ten thousand cowries and the cow, however, our ancestors gave them Tengnibie's sister, and they were then shown the boundaries of the *tengan*. It was like somebody marrying a wife.[28]

Bevuugang's earth-shrine politics thus differed from that of the Dagara pioneers in Dianlé, Dalgang, Dandere, and other settlements closer to Ouessa. The latter had either immediately placed the new lands under the protection of the Ouessa *tengan* or accepted a Sisala shrine stone only for an initial period and later replaced it with an Ouessa *tengankubile*. The Tambiile of Bevuugang, on the other hand, used the ritual protection that they acquired from the Sisala in order to become, and remain, independent from Ouessa.

My Tambiile informants then explained how Niégo's territory was created by combining land from Kelendou, Ouessa, and Hiela:

> One part of the Niégo land belonged to Hiela. This place [Bevuugang] belonged to Kelendou. The other side, Jaffien [toward Dianlé], which shares a boundary with Ouessa, belonged to the Yeri [Phuo]. ... These were three separate places, but when

the Dagara arrived in their numbers, one single *teng*, called Niégo, has been carved out from these three places.

At that time, Jaffien already belonged to Ouessa, . . . to the Gane. Baabobr was their sister's son [*arbile*] . . . , and so the Gane asked him to move up to this place [Susulipuo]. They carved out a small place from the Jaffien *tengan* and gave it to him so that he could have it together with his people, who had started to come in numbers. Baabobr settled at the boundary [*turbogr*] between Niégo and Hiela. . . . [When his brother Tamao] used to hunt in the area, the Sisala from Hiela were not happy with his activities. They told him that if he wanted, they would also give him the *tengan* for himself and his people. They collected ten thousand cowries and a cow before giving him the place of Hiela. . . .

Tengnibie was here [in Bevuugang], and when the *langme* [from Kelendou] gave up and moved away for the Dagara to settle, Tengnibie and Baabobr brought their two areas together. So Hiela, Niégo, and Jaffien are the three *tengame* that have all been brought together to constitute Niégo.[29]

My Tambiile interlocutors asserted that Tengnibie's stone was the original Niégo earth shrine and more powerful than the other stones because it was a *tanmigr tengan*—literally, a bowstring earth shrine—that had been acquired after waging war on the Sisala, and in exchange for a woman, not for cowries and animals like the stone from Hiela.[30] However, because Baabobr was a leper and could not easily move across the river that separates Susulipuo from Bevuugang, Tengnibie and his son Bevuu (after whom the settlement was named) agreed to conduct all sacrifices to the Niégo *tengan* jointly at the shrine tree in Susulipuo. This agreement lasted until the time of Kuumware, Baabobr's grandson, when the Kpagnyaane refused to give the Tambiile their due share of the sacrificial meat. The Tambiile therefore revived their own shrine stone, under a tree in Bevuugang, and ever since have conducted their *tengan yele* independently of Susulipuo. For some time, however, the Niégo earth shrine actually contained three different stones.

Somda Beyaa, of course, did not agree with this account and denied that the Tambiile ever acquired a shrine stone from Kelendou, let alone that such a stone was the true Niégo *tengan*. Clearly, accepting such a claim would have diminished his own ritual power. The Sisala elders from Kelendou, for their part, also rejected the Tambiile's assertion that the Sisala had given Tengnibie an earth-shrine stone. According to them, the Dagara immigrants and the Sisala, who cultivated bush farms on what later became Bevuugang lands, initially used to "solve problems together," that is, sacrificed jointly at the same earth shrine. However, as Ali Wiekanor from Kelendou explained, "when the *kielo* [literally, hawks, that is, the Dagara] killed one of our people, we went and brought the dead body to Kelendou, mourned and buried him here . . . and since that time we no longer do things [sacrifices] together with them."[31] The Sisala gave up their bush farms, withdrew to Kelendou, and left the land to the Dagara, who then, according to Wiekanor, established their own earth shrine. When I inquired about the alleged marriage of a Dagara woman with a Sisala from the Kelendou earth-priestly family, Wiekanor explained that his ancestors had indeed married some Dagara women from Bevuugang, yet not in exchange for an earth-shrine stone, but for food.[32] It is not surprising that my interlocutors in Kelendou denied that their ancestors gave the Dagara in Bevuugang a shrine stone. Acknowledging such a gift would amount to accepting that the Dagara had become the legitimate owners of the land. Denying it means emphasizing that Kelendou had never renounced its rights of ownership. And although the current chances that the Sisala could regain effective control over Bevuugang lands are slim, the situation might change and allow the Sisala to redress their past loss.

Yamba's Suicide, and How the Sisala of Hiela and the Ouessa Earth Priests See It

The Sisala from Hiela, for their part, confirmed that their ancestors established an earth shrine for the Kpagnyaane in Susulipuo, but insisted that the latter had remained clients and had not gained autonomy, either in terms of ritual or property rights. According to their story, one of the Hiela earth priest's forefathers, by name of Piina, used to cultivate a bush farm in Niégo and made friends with a Dagara hunter,[33] who occasionally came into the area on hunting expeditions and eventually asked for permission to settle. When the Dagara became more numerous, Piina decided to move back to Hiela, even though Dagara-Sisala relations generally remained peaceful. The Hiela earth priests eventually gave a small earth-shrine stone to the Dagara immigrants, "so that they could also take care of sacrifices around the settlement." However, the Sisala "never collected anything" in exchange for this stone, my informants in Hiela insisted. In their eyes, the Dagara thus never gained ritual independence, but still "refer all big cases and sometimes even the smaller ones to us."[34]

The Gane earth priests of Ouessa, for their part, denied that Niégo ever acquired ritual independence from Ouessa. Because Baabobr was a Gane *arbile,* the Ouessa earth priest had given him a *tengankubile* for protection on the frontier. Initially, Baabobr and his people honored their obligations toward Ouessa and brought all big animals to the Ouessa shrine. Eventually, however, they wanted to "eat" more, quarreled with their Gane uncles, and clandestinely acquired an earth-shrine stone from the Sisala.[35] Niégo's secession from Ouessa may have occurred as late as the 1940s, as some of my informants suggested.[36] In any case, the Gane earth priests are said to have exhorted the Kpagnyaane to return the Ouessa *tengankubile*, lest they experience serious misfortune. However, the Niégo secessionists did not heed the advice and were soon punished severely, at least so the Ouessa loyalists believe, by a series of suicides in the Kpagnyaane earth-priestly family.

The most spectacular incident was the suicide of Yamba, the junior brother of the Niégo earth priest Kuumware. Yamba is said to have gotten up in the middle of the night, probably in the year 1945, walked on the path toward Hiela, and hung himself at a tree near the Hiela earth shrine.[37] The Hiela earth priests refused to release Yamba's body, and it was only after the Kpagnyaane paid a heavy fine of 60,000 cowries plus several cows, rams, goats and countless fowl that they were finally allowed to bury the corpse at Niégo. It is not quite clear how this can be construed as a punishment by the Ouessa *tengan*, but this is how the Ouessa loyalists analyzed the event.

With the exception of Somda Beyaa, who avoided speaking about the issue altogether, all informants agreed that Yamba in fact committed suicide, and that the Niégo earth priests eventually paid the fine to Hiela. However, they differed in their interpretations of the underlying causes of the events. The Sisala in Hiela, of course, regarded the suicide as the Hiela earth shrine's prompt revenge for the Niégo earth priests' false claims that they were the full owners of Niégo lands and that they had once settled there with the permission and support of Ouessa, not Hiela.

An elder from Bakoteng who had recently experienced his own conflicts over farmland with the Sisala from Hiela and thought the latter were savvy opportunists who fought for their advantage by all possible means offered a more secular reading of the events. This informant related that for quite some time before Yamba's suicide, the Sisala of Hiela had complained that the Niégo earth priests disregarded their authority and paid allegiance to the Ouessa *tengan*. Whatever the reasons for Yamba's suicide, the event now provided the Sisala with the long-awaited opportunity to force Kuumware's family to comply with their obligations toward Hiela, and to break relations with Ouessa.[38]

Everyone thus interpreted the same event as a (supernatural) confirmation of their own version of the relations between Hiela, Ouessa, and Niégo. The fact that the Kpagnyaane did pay the fine to Hiela suggests that for the time being, Hiela was able to impose the terms of those relations. However, this does not necessarily mean that the Kpagnyaane earth priests also underwrote Hiela's interpretation of the events. The indeterminacy of events, such as a suicide, makes their interpretation a matter of politics and of who can rally more support for his version of the affair.

Niégo's Earth-Shrine Politics in Historical Context

Taking together all the bits of information that I was able to gather, the following tentative history of Niégo's earth-shrine politics emerges. To begin with, when the Kpagnyaane still lived at Bidomo, they received a *tengan kubile* from the Ouessa earth priests, which they eventually took along when they left Bidomo for good and settled first in Dianlé and later in Niégo-Susulipuo. Tamao, the Kpagnyaane pioneer who continued exploring potential settlement sites and erected only temporary huts must have felt sufficiently protected by his hunting medicine. However, when his clan mates joined him, an earth shrine needed to be established. It is likely that the Ouessa earth priests readily agreed that their *tengan kubile* traveled eastward because they were relieved to see their troublesome Kpagnyaane *arbili* establish themselves at a safe distance away, while the stone would guarantee that the newly opened territory came under the authority of the Ouessa *tengan*. However, the Gane and the Kpagnyaane probably had, from the very beginning, a different reading of Ouessa-Niégo relations. While the former insisted on a hierarchy between themselves as seniors and the Kpagnyaane as juniors and late-comers, the latter saw themselves as more or less equal partners. Gifts by the Kpagnyaane to the Ouessa earth shrine will thus have been interpreted as fulfillment of an obligation by one party and as voluntary offering by the other.

Susulipuo, the first Kpagnyaane settlement that Tamao and his brother Baabobr established in the Niégo area, was located on what was formerly the Jaffien earth-shrine territory controlled by the Phuo. Since earlier Dagara frontiersmen had already driven the few Phuo and Sisala out and placed the land under the Ouessa *tengan*, there was little resistance to Kpagnyaane settlement in this part of what later came to be called Niégo. During their hunting excursions, Tamao met the Sisala from Hiela, and his Tambiile hunting partner Tengnibie encountered the Sisala from Kelendou, and both probably established friendly relations. Meanwhile, the Kpagnyaane of Susulipuo recruited more clan mates and also called on Tengnibie and his Tambiile relations to help push the frontier of Dagara settlements northward and eastward, farther into Sisala territory. However, while the hunting expeditions seem to have been inoffensive, the construction of permanent Dagara settlements on what the Sisala earth priests of Hiela and Kelendou regarded as their territory caused alarm. Most likely, news about the violent encounters between Dagara and Sisala near Ouessa had spread,[39] and the Sisala of Kelendou and Hiela may have felt that it was preferable to conclude some kind of arrangement with the Dagara before the situation deteriorated. The Dagara, for their part, must have also become concerned, because crossing larger rivers such as those that separate Susulipuo from Hiela and Kelendou territory meant traversing a ritual boundary beyond which the Ouessa *tengan*'s powers may not reach. In any case, the Sisala decided to give up their bush farms on which the Dagara had started to encroach, but not without demanding substantial payments for the land that they ceded. These land transfers were marked by ritual offerings and, perhaps, the installation of earth-shrine stones for the Dagara. Again, the nature of the transfers was probably interpreted differently from the very beginning. The Dagara read it as a transmission of all ritual and economic rights, including the right to use all natural resources, control further immigrants, and enjoy the full income from the earth shrine. The Sisala, on the other hand, insisted that they never gave up their allodial title to the land and expected that the Dagara should still symbolically and materially honor the Sisala first-comers' privileges. It is possible, however, that the Sisala developed this interpretation only ex post facto, in the course of the colonial pacification, which suppressed violence and thus strengthened the Sisala position; perhaps they hoped that, with the right kind of stories, they could gain colonial support for their claims.

Despite the different origin of their earth-shrine stones, the Kpagnyaane and Tambiile decided to conduct all earth-shrine-related sacrifices together. Since Hiela and Kelendou were closely related, at least so my Dagara informants told me, there was no ritual danger in placing the stones together at Susulipuo. Nor did the Ouessa stone cause any problem because it could ultimately be traced back to the Phuo of Jaffien—another group closely related to the Sisala of Hiela. Over the course of time, however, tensions between the Kpagnyaane and Tambiile sections of Niégo developed, and this affected their ritual cooperation. Conflicts over land rights and bickering about how to divide the sacrificial meat were aggravated by the fact that under colonial rule the Kpagnyaane furnished the village chief, who redistributed obligations of tax and *corvée* labor among Niégo's different sections and patriclans rather unevenly. When many of Tengnibie's descendants fled to British territory in order to evade the colonial exactions, Bevuugang-Susulipuo relations further soured. In any case, the Tambiile earth priests withdrew from the joint earth-shrine sacrifices in Susulipuo, and apparently carried their Kelendou shrine stone back to Bevuugang, although some versions asserted that the stone was "abandoned" when so many Tambiile left for the British colony.

In the 1930s, the French transferred the paramount chieftaincy from the Kpagnyaane house in Susulipuo to Denyuu in Dianlé, one of the old Niégo chief's nephews who had received some formal education and fought in the French army and who promised to be an able administrator working in the interest of the French rulers. Furthermore, the colonial officers attempted to simplify their administration by amalgamating the paramount chiefdoms of Ouessa and Niégo and placing all Dagara east of the Volta under one single *chef de canton*.[40] Denyuu readily set about extending his sphere of influence and politicized earth-shrine affairs. According to what various informants told me, he insisted that the Ouessa *tengankubile* in Dianlé, which was now the headquarters of the paramountcy, be upgraded and treated as a *tengankpee*, where great earth-shrine sacrifices were conducted that had to be attended by all Dagara of the area, including the Niégo earth priests. Through this and other measures, Denyuu wanted to strengthen Dagara claims to full rights to the land and force the Dagara to sever whatever ritual ties they still maintained with their Sisala neighbors. These politics, in turn, exacerbated Sisala fears of Dagara dominance and led at least the Sisala of Hiela to exert more pressure on the Kpagnyaane in Niégo to honor their obligations toward the Hiela *tengan*. In the long run, Denyuu's attempts to weaken Sisala property rights did not succeed. On the contrary, because Denyuu established a rather authoritarian regime, many Dagara decided to flee to Sisala territory and readily acknowledged their hosts' ritual, economic, and political authority because the Sisala chiefs' exactions were less severe than those of Denyuu. Dagara villages like Niégo that had already asserted their own ritual authority and property rights would not relinquish these gains, but they came under increasing pressure from all sides. The Kpagnyaane earth priests thus had—and still have—to jockey between expectations from Ouessa and Hiela, as well as cope with the internal challenges from the Tambiile. And occasionally, as in the case of Yamba's suicide, they paid a very high price for jealously defending their autonomy. That the Niégo earth shrine contains two different shrine stones, and for some time even hosted three stones, is the material reflection of this complicated history.

What the Niégo example makes very clear is how fraught with issues of power are the establishment of an earth shrine and the definition of its position—as junior, senior, or equal—in the regional network of earth shrines. Changing power constellations, be they provoked by demographic developments or colonial politics, invite local actors to rearrange shrine hierarchies and, concomitantly, ritual and property rights. The historical narratives are sufficiently vague to allow for a reinterpretation of these rights, and even events such as suicides or other misfortunes are submitted to very different interpretations. Finally, even if one party manages to impose for a time its reading of the signs, and this results in practical action, the others may tacitly maintain their alternative versions in the hope of validating them when power relations shift in their favor.

Arguing Property Rights, Claiming First Possession

Earth shrines provide ritual protection, and the earth cult is a powerful instrument for organizing sociopolitical relations between first-comers and late-comers, by exclusion from or inclusion in the ritual community as well as by establishing or contesting shrine hierarchies. At the same time, earth shrines, and the associated landmarks that indicate *tengan* boundaries, are visible markers of property—similar to fences or boundary stones in European societies.[41] However, in order to successfully communicate property claims such symbols must be interpreted. Earth shrines and boundary marks are thus embedded in a web of narratives that spell out how the shrine came into existence and possibly how it was transferred, who controls it and why, and which area comes under its jurisdiction. In the absence of land registers or other property-related written evidence, these orally transmitted narratives play a decisive role in legitimating or, as the case may be, challenging property rights. In order to buttress their claims, contestants in conflicts over land and land-related resources, even when they meet in a modern law court, inevitably present different versions of how their ancestors settled in the area, and how land ownership or farming rights were subsequently transmitted. Such property narratives aim at persuading owners and nonowners alike, and thus building the consensus integral to property regimes. They enclose theories of "first possession," that is, theories about the origin of property and about the legitimate modes of transferring this original property from one group of owners to the next.

In order to elucidate local concepts of first possession that inform the debates and negotiations of the Dagara and their neighbors in the Black Volta region, I look at general normative statements that my informants put forward, as well as explore narratives that were elaborated in the context of concrete conflicts. It is in such situations of disagreement and contestation that the interested parties are forced to make explicit their underlying interpretations of legitimate ownership, first-comer status, and land transfers. The diagnostic event that I use here concerns recent conflicts over property rights in Baadaateng, a Dagara settlement in Burkina Faso, near the Black Volta, which had been abandoned for almost fifty years and was resettled by Dagara farmers in the

1980s. As this case shows, the Dagara, as notorious late-comers, employ a much wider range of arguments to sustain their property claims and are more flexible in their definition of the pivotal event that constituted first possession than are their Sisala (and, in the Baadaateng case, Nuni) neighbors.

Competing Property Claims: The Case of Baadaateng

Baadaateng is a Dagara village located on the eastern banks of the Black Volta that was probably founded toward the latter part of the nineteenth century.[42] Until the 1920s, Baadaateng and some neighboring settlements were quite densely populated. Gradually, however, colonial taxation and forced labor as well as military recruitment took their toll on the number of able-bodied men. In addition, many families fled from the French to the neighboring British colony. Fewer adult men in the village meant that less bush could be cleared, an important activity since thicket and bush are potential breeding grounds for the tsetse fly that transmits sleeping sickness. Thus, by the late 1920s, a series of vicious epidemics brought sleeping sickness, river blindness, and perhaps also meningitis to Baadaateng and the neighboring settlements, striking them so severely that the few remaining survivors resettled elsewhere in the region, away from the river. Among the victims were the old Baadaa, the Dagara frontiersman in the disputed area and hence the earth priest of the village named after him, as well as several of his sons. Other members of his family fled, and the earth shrine was abandoned.

Who was the legitimate owner of these lands? Answers to this question necessarily had to define the decisive property-constituting act: Was it the discovery and ritual pacification of the area, or the active clearing and working of the land? Which rights of usufruct and alienation were to be derived from any of these activities? And to whom and by which means were these rights transferred? Unsurprisingly, these questions became critical only when some enterprising peasants resumed farming the abandoned lands in the late 1970s.

Since the mid-1970s, the government of what was then Upper Volta, as part of its campaign to eradicate river blindness and other diseases, has sprayed pesticides in the valleys of the Black Volta and its tributaries. This made it possible for individual Dagara farmers from surrounding settlements to start clearing the bush and establish new farms in the vicinity of abandoned villages such as Baadaateng. The first group to farm on Baadaateng lands came in 1978–79, from Bakoteng (see map 2.2). These farmers belonged to the Berwuole patriclan, a clan closely related to the Gane, of which Baadaa was a member. The eldest of these Berwuole farmers had settled in Baadaateng as a child, before the epidemics broke out, and was now claiming that he and his group were resuming work only on what had once been family land, which meant that it was not necessary to ask permission from an earth priest to do so. Most of the group were Christians, and even the few non-Christians felt sufficiently protected against potential spiritual dangers by the fact that the land had once been tilled by their ancestors as well as by the circumstance that they were relatives of the earth priest's clan, albeit distant ones.

However, when a problem arose concerning stray animals, which are generally regarded as earth-shrine property, these Dagara farmers did not dare to handle the matter alone, but turned to the Dagara earth priest of Ouessa, the custodian of the oldest and most powerful Dagara earth shrine in the area east of the Black Volta and north of the 11th parallel. Furthermore, the Ouessa earth-priestly family belongs to the same Gane patriclan as Baadaa and therefore considered itself to be the legitimate custodian of Baadaateng land after Baadaa's death. In addition, Ouessa also ritually controls Bakoteng, the home village of the group of Berwuole who began farming in Baadaateng.

When these settlers consulted him, the Ouessa earth priest sacrificed some of the stray animals at the Ouessa earth shrine and returned some to the Berwuole family to be sacrificed at a *tengankubile* that he established for them in Baadaateng. The Berwuole therefore now act as earth priests in Baadaateng, conducting regular sacrifices at the shrine and taking care of the day-to-day affairs related to land, such as the allocation of farms to new settlers or the granting of permission to build houses. However, major problems, such as suicide or other exceptional disturbances of peace and fertility, still have to be brought before the Ouessa earth shrine.[43]

Nuni Claims to Allodial Title and Mossi Immigration

Not long after the Ouessa earth priest established their *tengankubile* in Baadaateng and thus asserted their property rights, the Nuni earth priests from nearby Bon questioned their authority over Baadaateng lands, and claimed that in fact the Nuni were the true owners of this land. Their ancestor, the Nuni elders asserted, had been a great hunter and the very first person to discover and subsequently settle in the entire area, long before the arrival of Baadaa. They insisted that Baadaa had indeed asked their ancestors for permission to settle in Bon. Baadaa eventually became a good friend of their grandfather, who therefore gave him some land and his own earth shrine, but also instructed him that serious matters still had to be taken to the major earth shrine in Bon. The Nuni were convinced that property rights had automatically returned to Bon when Baadaateng was abandoned. Comparing the land to a woman, they explained: "When a father gives his daughter in marriage to a person and that person dies and the girl does not have another man, doesn't he take the daughter back into his house?"[44] Consequently, the Dagara from Bakoteng should have asked the Nuni and not the Ouessa earth priest for permission to cultivate what had once been Baadaateng lands.

However, my various Dagara interlocutors presented a completely different story regarding the origins of the Baadaateng earth shrine, claiming that it was in fact the Nuni of Bon who had received the earth shrine from Baadaa and not the other way around. The eventful history of the Nuni earth shrine of Bon is too complex and controversial to be presented here in detail.[45] Suffice it to say that my Nuni informants were adamant in their claim that there were "no boundaries" between Ouessa and Bon, and that Bon owned all lands down to the Sompar hill, an important place of spiritual power on the eastern banks of the Black Volta, on the fringes of Baadaateng, which families from many different communities approach in order to carry out sacrifices and ask for well-being. In the eyes of the Nuni from Bon, decisive evidence that neither the Berwuole nor Ouessa had any rights over the disputed land was provided by the fact that the former Ouessa earth priest died a few weeks after a visit to Bon, after the Nuni elders had led him into the presence of their earth shrine. Of course, Hien Daniel, the Ouessa earth priest whom I interviewed on the matter, did not see any connection between this visit and his predecessor's death. In any case, claim stood against claim, but not much seems to have happened for the next few years. The Nuni stated their property claims, and the Dagara ignored them, continuing to farm and taking more serious matters to the earth priest of Ouessa—which the Nuni apparently tolerated.

Matters took on more urgency with the arrival of a new group of farmers looking for land, namely Mossi immigrants. Small groups of Mossi have been settling in South-Western Burkina Faso for many decades, but in the 1970s and 1980s their numbers increased considerably, due to pressure on land and droughts in their home areas. For many earth priests in the Black Volta region, the Mossi are interesting clients because they often give substantial gifts in order to overcome the wariness with which their massive immigration is generally regarded by the local population.

Since 1983, a few Mossi families came to Bon, and the Nuni earth priest gave them land bordering on the old Baadaateng lands and told them to farm in the direction of Baadaateng.[46] Evidently he used the Mossi to secure Nuni control over the disputed land—a typical strategy among those who claim to be first-comers to defend their property rights against their neighbors or incursions by strangers. The Dagara of Baadaateng clearly understood the message. The first confrontation developed when a Dagara farmer, settled by the Dagara earth priests of Baadaateng, and a Mossi, who had been given the land by the Nuni earth priests, literally met in the bush, when clearing their fields. They challenged the boundaries of each other's farms and called on their respective land givers to settle the matter. The encounter of the Berwuole of Baadaateng, the Ouessa earth priest, and the Nuni ended, after a heated exchange of harsh words, with the pragmatic drawing of a boundary between the two farms. But this did not, of course, solve the basic question of who was the legitimate owner of Baadaateng lands and was therefore authorized to allocate use rights to these lands.

The Mossi continued to pay allegiance to Bon and the Dagara to Ouessa because neither earth priest was able, or willing, to enforce his claims against the wishes of the new farmers. Apart from ritual-magic resources, such as the threat to invoke the earth god's wrath, the earth priests indeed have few means to compel others to adopt their interpretations of local boundaries and property rights. In principle, they can, and often do, also attempt to enlist local political support. At the time of the first open

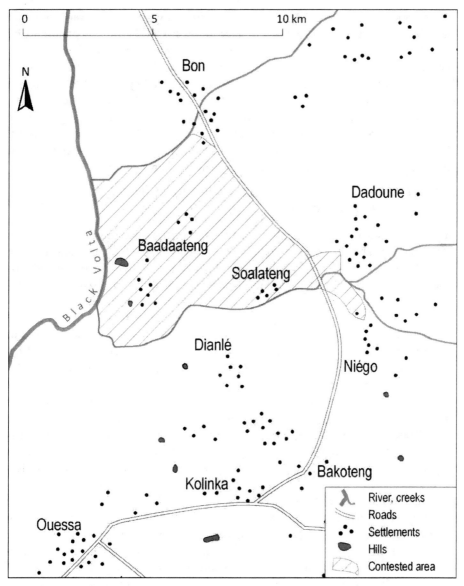

Map 2.2. Baadaateng and surrounding settlements

confrontation between the Dagara and the Nuni earth priests, however, it was not advisable for the holders of traditional office to involve local government authorities in land conflicts because the 1984 agrarian reform law, promulgated by the revolutionary regime of Thomas Sankara, had confirmed that all lands in Burkina Faso were "national estate." Although the government was unable to implement these legal prescriptions at the local level and had to more or less tolerate the continuation of traditional tenure arrangements, the revolutionary impetus of "the land belongs to those who work it" slogans was not lost on Mossi immigrants and other farmers in search of land. In a climate of political radicalization, no earth priest could hope for much outside support for traditionalist claims based on first-comer status.

A Rival Dagara Earth Priest, the Claims of Baadaa's Grandson, and the New District Boundary

In 1987, the Sankara regime was replaced by a reformist government. The agrarian reform law was amended twice, in 1991 and 1996, and although the new law held fast to the "national estate" principle, the general political climate became more accommodating of traditional authorities, such as earth priests and chiefs. In the Baadaateng case, this may have encouraged the involvement of a third player who raised claims to Baadaateng as well as neighboring Soalateng lands, namely the Dagara earth priest of Dadoune. He asserted that the land belonged neither to Ouessa nor to Bon, but to Dadoune, and started allotting land to newcomers in his own right. He derived his entitlement from his historical connections with Baadaa, who had been his grandfather's maternal uncle and allegedly established the Dadoune earth shrine, originally as a *tengankubile*, while the major sacrifices continued to take place in Baadaateng. After Baadaa's death, the Dadoune earth priest carried out all sacrifices concerning their own village, including the big ones, at the earth shrine in Dadoune, thereby transforming it into an autonomous major shrine (*tengankpee*). When the Baadaateng lands were eventually resettled, Dadoune's earth-priestly family attempted to appropriate the original shrine stones, presumably still lying in Baadaateng, in order to unequivocally establish itself as the legitimate heir of Baadaateng lands.

As was to be expected, Dadoune's actions provoked protest from various sides: the Nuni in Bon, the Berwuole in Baadaateng, as well as the Gane in Ouessa. The latter told me that they went, armed with bows and arrows, to confront the Dadoune earth priest. They argued that Dadoune was unlawfully usurping the rights of their uncles, namely the Ouessa earth priests. Allegedly, the earth priest of Dadoune responded meekly that Ouessa was right and that Dadoune had only "forgotten" to inform them of his intention to allocate land to strangers. If this conversation ever took place in this way, the Dadoune earth priests had obviously been caught in their own logic. They had claimed rights to Baadaa's property by invoking their status as sisters' sons, which allowed Baadaa's senior brothers in turn to assert that the rights of brothers were superior to those of nephews.

Dadoune's intervention ultimately brought a fourth contender into play, namely the only surviving direct descendant of Baadaa. This grandson, appropriately named Kuu-nume, "sweet death," after the massive toll the epidemics had once taken in the family, had first lived in Bon with his grandmother's family, which happened to also be closely related to the Nuni earth priests of Bon. Later he was brought to live with Gane relatives in Zoner, across the Black Volta. In 1999, when we interviewed him, Kuu-nume still considered himself too young and inexperienced in traditional matters to resettle in Baadaateng and assume the office of the earth priest as the legitimate heir of his grandfather. However, he left no doubt that he was unwilling to relinquish his right to the original shrine and ultimate ownership of the Baadaateng lands. "When somebody is the first to establish himself somewhere," he stated confidently, "those who come later can never become the owners of this land. It is always the first-comer who is the land owner and the earth priest."[47]

Of course, the Berwuole in Baadaateng told a different story. For them, the important matter was not the authenticity of the shrine as such—they did not insist that they were indeed sacrificing at Baadaa's old shrine—but the clan-based claims to property that were linked to it. Furthermore, they felt that once the Berwuole had invested their labor and ritual skills in the reestablishment of the abandoned village, the runaway grandson had no right to come and claim the fruits of these efforts as his own. And, while Baadaa's grandson insisted on the rights of his particular lineage, the Gane earth priests from Ouessa and the Berwuole emphasized the rights of the entire patriclan and even of related clans to Baadaa's old property.

Again, not much changed as a result of these competing claims to ownership—the different parties publicly stated their points of view, and the de facto exploitation of the disputed land by the Mossi, on the one hand, and by the Dagara from Bakoteng and Dianlé on the other, continued as before. As in many other cases, the contentious question was not the actual exploitation of the natural resources, but rather the right to allocate these to interested users, and the right to collect various "fees" for the ritual services that the earth priests provide, such as the opening of the land for the construction of houses and the burial of the deceased.

Recently, however, the conflict was politicized in the context of the delimitation of new administrative provinces. The districts of Ouessa and Niégo as well as that of Bourra, to which Bon belongs, had formed part of Sissili Province. But the new provinces set up in 1996 shifted Ouessa and Niégo to the predominately Dagara Ioba Province, while Bourra remained with the Sisala-dominated Sissili Province. Bon's Nuni earth-priest family always felt culturally and politically closer to the Sisala than to the Dagara, and managed to stay administratively linked to Bourra throughout the colonial and postcolonial periods despite the fact that, in terms of proximity, Niégo would have been a more convenient administrative center.

So, where did the newly resettled Baadaateng belong from an administrative point of view? In the 1920s, Baadaateng had been ruled by the Dagara *chef de canton* Denyuu, based in Dianlé, mainly for ethnic reasons. The new residents of Baadaateng took it for granted that they, too, politically belonged to Dianlé and hence Ouessa District. The Nuni, on the other hand, claimed that because they were the true allodial owners of Baadaateng lands, Baadaateng was naturally part of their district and hence of Sissili Province.

Matters came to a head when the young men from the Nuni earth priest's house uprooted a "Welcome to Ioba Province" signboard on the road between Niégo and Bon and replanted it three or four kilometers farther toward Niégo—at the small river that they considered to be the actual territorial boundary. The Dagara called in the district head, a public meeting was held, and the Nuni youths were eventually imprisoned until their family put the signboard back where it had originally been. For all practical administrative matters, Baadaateng continues to be treated as part of Ioba Province. For the time being, the Dagara were able to impose their reading of the local history, not least because they had better contacts with the local administration than did the Nuni, and more educated relations who could argue their case at the regional and national levels. Furthermore, the district and regional authorities argued that administrative boundaries had nothing to do with landed property, but were merely a matter of practicality and, perhaps, the local political history. Yet the Dagara interpreted the administrative decision as tacit support of their property rights. And the Nuni, of course, regard the underlying conflict as unresolved and await a future opportunity to redress the historical wrong that they believe they have suffered.

"Empty Territory" versus Labor Theory of Property

The indigenous terms for property used in the Baadaateng case and other debates on land ownership are inherently ambiguous. To begin with, all terms denoting property can refer to human beings as well as to objects, similar to the English word "belonging," which can relate to both things and persons. As was the case in many precolonial African societies, Dagara, Sisala, and Nuni did not distinguish between rights in things and rights in persons.[48] Furthermore, the meanings of the Dagara verb *so* (to own), and its associated noun *-sob* (owner), which are usually employed when speaking of property, range from full ownership, social and economic control, to mere custodianship. Depending on the context, the *tengansob* can thus be seen as the proprietor or merely the administrator of the land, or as the custodian of the earth shrine, responsible for communication with the earth god. Similar ambiguities characterize the respective Sisala and Nuni terms of "ownership." As Goody has succinctly pointed out, the same term *so* in relation to land can be used to refer to at least three different levels of rights: the right to farm and establish farm shrines; the right to control the lineage land and the ancestor cults; and the right to establish an earth shrine and make decisions concerning communal territory.[49] Thus, the extent of rights claimed needs to be further spelled out, and the same words can be interpreted differently by different interlocutors. These interpretations are intimately linked to conceptions of first possession and subsequent property transfers.

What can we learn from the Baadaateng case and similar disputes about these indigenous theories of the origin of property? What basic act of first possession was cited as the legitimate source of all subsequent transfers? What constitutes the "allodial title," as the most comprehensive property rights are called in Ghanaian legal parlance, or, in Francophone usage, the *droit éminent sur la terre*,[50] the "supreme right" over the land?

Generally, the Dagara and their Nuni and Sisala neighbors share the view that first-comer status confers the most comprehensive rights over land—that is, ultimate ownership—although there is considerable disagreement over whether this ownership includes the right, or even the capacity, to transfer the allodial title to another group. As I discussed in the previous section, first-comers are believed to have established a special relationship with the spirits of the land, setting up an earth shrine and thus playing a crucial role in opening up the wild bush or forest for human settlement, even if they did not themselves invest labor in agriculture. First-comers believe that in addition to the rights over land derived from active cultivation—a right that late-comers also enjoy—they are entitled to all benefits from natural resources and territorial control, including those that can be appropriated without investing agricultural labor, that is, fish, game, wild fruits, stray animals, and ownerless objects, as well as the income (usually in the form of sacrificial animals) they derive from the land-related ritual services they provide to others and from expiatory payments for violations against the laws of the earth god.[51]

Although all agree on the importance of first-comer status, local people are less in agreement on the question of who exactly is a true first-comer. In Baadaateng and other cases, we find two major argumentative strategies concerning the pivotal event that defines first-comer status. The first is similar to the *res nullium* argument that also helped legitimate European expansion in North America, according to which the new territory is defined as empty and possible traces of earlier inhabitation ignored, whereby the "discoverers" become the legitimate owners.[52] This is the argument that the Nuni of Bon presented. It is likely that historically their ancestors were indeed the first to discover the area around Baadaateng on one of their hunting expeditions along the Black Volta. They never claimed to have settled in Baadaateng or cultivated Baadaateng lands, but derived their property rights from the inclusion of Baadaateng in their old hunting territory established in a region that they claim to have found empty. In other cases, similar first-comer narratives do admit the presence of former inhabitants, but dehumanize the latter, claiming that they were human beings with ape-like tails, or not human at all, but *kontome*, bush spirits, which the first-comers overcame by ruse and force. Alternatively, former inhabitants are said to have left before the true first-comers settled.[53] As Igor Kopytoff put it in his succinct discussion of first-comer–late-comer relations, first-comers usually engage "in what one may call an 'accumulation of symptoms' of seniority."[54]

In the Baadaateng case, Nuni territorial control originally probably involved simply securing large territories for communal hunting expeditions and defining spheres of interest or zones beyond which wounded game would no longer be pursued. However, from these rights over hunting lands, the Nuni and other "first-coming" hunters and frontiersmen subsequently also derived property rights over agricultural land, when others entered into their territory. As Ruth Marshall-Fratani has noted in relation to a similar case in the Ivory Coast, it was only with the immigration of "strangers" that property rights needed to be more explicitly defined.[55] In the eyes of the Nuni of Bon, ultimate spiritual and administrative control over the entire area, including Baadaateng, has always rested with them, and they claimed that when Baadaa asked them for permission to settle and cultivate the land, he himself recognized these property rights. The Nuni thus presented a set of arguments that in some ways resembles a combination of the *res nullium* and consensus theories of property, introduced into European thinking by Hugo Grotius.[56]

The second line of argument concerning the pivotal event that defines first-comer status and property rights is very much reminiscent of John Locke's labor theory of property and the common-law idea of ownership derived from continued possession.[57] This is basically the argument used by the Dagara in Baadaateng and many other settlements, and it is an argument typically invoked by late-comers. The group that actually takes possession of a territory, by cutting down the bush, fighting wild animals, building houses, cultivating the earth, and finally also establishing an earth shrine, becomes by these very acts its legitimate owner.

Both lines of argument naturalize the property-constituting act. According to local thinking, property evolves not from "relations between and among persons with regard to things,"[58] but from a direct, unmediated relation of the first-comers with the "thing," that is, land and land-related resources. First possession is established by acquiring the land from its original suprahuman "owner," namely the earth god, through the exchange of ritual offerings, or by mingling one's labor with the formerly "ownerless" land, or by a combination of both acts. It is as if the property narratives make the social relations involved in any of these acts of first possession invisible in order to remove property from negotiation and questions of power, at least on the level of the ideological order.[59]

In local land conflicts, however, the two argumentative strategies—possession through discovery and subsequent pacification of the earth god, and possession through labor—often intertwine. In the Baadaateng case, for example, the Dagara emphasized their role in opening the bush, but at the same time also claimed that the Nuni had not yet arrived on the scene and that Baadaa originally settled in empty territory. In any event, Baadaa and his supporters (and today the peasants coming from Bakoteng) presented themselves as first-comers vis-à-vis all other late-comers in Baadaateng and thus as the legitimate owners of the entire territory. In doing so, they also claimed to control lands that they had themselves never actively cultivated.

This shows that the various arguments substantiating property claims—rights based on discovery and spiritual pact versus the right to ownership through labor—have nothing to do with the question of to which ethnic group their proponents belong, but rather emerge from the dynamics of settlement history. This is also evident from the manner in which the Dagara earth priests from Ouessa and Dadoune argued their case, since they, like the Nuni, regard Baadaa's settlement as part of their spiritual field of influence.

Obviously, then, late-comers such as the Dagara thus cannot rely on the labor argument alone when they want to claim land beyond that which they have physically worked themselves. When extending their territorial claims vis-à-vis what we could term "latest-comers"—more recent immigrants, be they Dagara or Mossi—they draw on the same repertoire of "discovery" arguments as the Sisala, Nuni, or Phuo. The latter's narratives, however, never resort to a "labor" argument in order to legitimate first possession. Thus, despite the mixture of arguments employed by all groups, the emphasis on what ultimately constitutes the decisive pivotal event differs between the first-comers and the late-comers.

Can Earth Shrines Be Sold? Debates on the (In)alienability of Land

In property theories derived from the European or North American experience, "first possession" is usually assumed to result in continuous occupation and use of the newly acquired object by those who have claimed first ownership.[60] However, in an African context where mobility and shifting cultivation were dominant realities, and a large amount of reserve land was often regarded as important for the future well-being of the group, land was sometimes left fallow for long periods. First possession thus did not necessarily involve the continuous cultivation of the entire area to which claims were laid. This brings in the factor of space and the spatial boundaries of property claims (see chapter 3), as well as the factor of time, both of which raise important questions: What ideas do the various groups in the Black Volta region hold regarding the duration of property rights? Can the whole range of entitlements established by first possession be transferred or are they in principle inalienable? Do they expire if not followed up by the investment of labor? Conversely, can the continuous working of a given expanse of land eventually establish property rights even if the land was held in first possession by a different group? Which transfers of the property rights are regarded as legitimate, and is there a right to reparation in case of illegitimate transfers?[61] The last question becomes particularly important when, as was often the case with precolonial land transfers between Sisala first-comers and Dagara late-comers, the transfer of earth shrines and property rights occurred in a context of violence and massive Dagara encroachment on Sisala land. Can these transfers, under new circumstances such as colonial pacification and the establishment of the colonial (and postcolonial) state, be reversed or otherwise challenged and reinterpreted?

As is to be expected, first-comers and late-comers provide different answers to these questions. Debates about the (in)alienability of land, and, more particularly, contested histories of how earth shrines were acquired, play an important role in past and current land conflicts in the Black Volta region. In what follows, I explore indigenous concepts of land transfers and discuss how African and European views on land tenure influenced each other and were instrumentalized by the contesting parties. Colonial officials developed, often in cooperation with African chiefs, a rather romantic view of precolonial land tenure, namely that land ownership was ultimately vested in the ancestors of the first-comer lineage and that Africans therefore regarded land as inalienable. These notions have been perpetuated not only by anthropologists but also by those local Africans whose position would be weakened by admitting the possibility of land "sales." African immigrant farmers, on the other hand, tend to emphasize that land transfers were a reality even in the precolonial period. And while competing conceptions of precolonial African land tenure have become a powerful reservoir of arguments in current land conflicts, such disputes over the (in)alienability of land are probably actually as old as the agricultural frontier itself.

Dowrying the Land: Indigenous Concepts of Land Transfers

First-comers tend to believe that only more or less comprehensive rights to use land can be ceded, but never full property rights, which would include the right to spiritually control and allocate the land to third parties. Like the Nuni earth priests in the Baadaateng case, they claim that they retain ultimate control over the land, even though their ancestors granted extensive rights to the Dagara immigrants by giving them an earth-shrine stone. They insist that although the land had not been cultivated or sacrificially propitiated for several decades, their original property rights cannot and did not expire.

Dagara immigrants, on the other hand, usually admit that their forefathers were, relatively speaking, late-comers who settled with the permission of the Sisala, Phuo, or Nuni already living in the area. But then they often insist that their ancestors had actually "bought" an earth shrine (using the word *da*, which is also applied to market transactions) and all its secrets from the previous inhabitants. Through this, they acquired the allodial title to the land, and any obligations toward the original owners that may have once existed ceased.[62] The Sisala (and Nuni) deny that this is even possible and claim that an earth shrine, and hence the land, is in principle inalienable. If they do concede that a transfer of an earth-shrine stone did take place, they deny that the stone was paid for and refuse to acknowledge that the original property rights have been ceded. To be sure, these debates also occur within and between Dagara settlements, but they become particularly pronounced when the difference between first-comers and late-comers coincides with ethno-linguistic boundaries.

All of my interlocutors agreed that the allodial title to land can be inherited within the group that has legitimately acquired such property rights through first possession.

There is debate, however, on how the boundaries of the property-holding group within which such transfers are acceptable should be defined. Can the allodial title be inherited only within the restricted lineage, or also within the entire patriclan, or even the ethnic group? In the Baadaateng case, for instance, we have seen that there were competing interpretations of who was the legitimate heir to the abandoned territory. The Berwuole from Bakoteng could not trace direct descent from Baadaa, but argued that they belonged to Baadaa's patriclan, and as such were his rightful successors. They further bolstered this argument, however, by claiming that they inherited fields that their own fathers had cultivated, and over which the latter had thus established property rights through the exertion of labor. The earth priest of Ouessa, for his part, invoked the same argument of shared membership in the patriclan, and, in addition, pointed to the seniority of the Ouessa earth shrine. Baadaa's land, so his argument ran, was a Gane, and since the Gane earth priests of Ouessa were senior and had once given Baadaa the permission to establish himself in Baadaateng, Baadaa's land ultimately belonged to the Ouessa earth shrine and its custodians. Baadaa's only surviving grandson, Kuu-nume, on the other hand, argued that Baadaa had never received a shrine stone from Ouessa, but had established himself as a first-comer in his own right. Furthermore, Kuu-nume defined the community of eligible heirs much more narrowly, and claimed that only Baadaa's direct descendants were the true owners of Baadaateng land.

We can find similar disagreements about the boundaries of the relevant property-holding group among the Sisala (and, for that matter, Nuni). Here, the boundaries of the first-comer group are sometimes even extended to embrace the entire ethnic group. Thus, when Sisala late-comers established themselves in existing Sisala villages, they were often included among the allodial titleholders, and their heirs would enjoy the same strong entitlements as the first-comers. In most cases, however, the immigrants would construct some sort of kin relation with the villagers in order to further support inclusion in the property-holding group. In any case, property transfers within one's own primordial group, however contested its boundaries may be, are regarded as perfectly legitimate.

Both Dagara and Sisala interviewees sometimes metaphorically compared land transfers between different groups, particularly those across ethnic boundaries, to marriage—thus extending the language of kinship and affinity to the relations between first-comers and immigrants. Because of its intimate association with fertility, land is regarded as female. The Dagara therefore interpret the cowries and cows that they claim to have exchanged with the Sisala for the allodial title as the "bride price" that they have paid to the bride's family—the landowners. In Ouessa, for instance, members of the earth-priestly family claimed that the earth shrine was given by the Phuo, or Sisala, for saving the life of one of the original earth priest's women, or for sparing the earth priest's wife when attacking the previous landowners. In other cases, for instance in Niégo-Bevuugang, the Dagara claim to have received the earth shrine not in exchange for cowries and cows, but directly for having given a marriageable woman.

Although the Sisala (and Nuni) nowadays deny that they ever received such a bride price, wife, or any other payment for the land, they often do concur with the notion of the land as woman.[63] Thus, while first possession of the land is naturalized by a narrative focus on the heroic deeds of a lonely hunter and his encounter with bush spirits or the earth deity, subsequent transfers of property rights are humanized.

However, Sisala (and Nuni) first-comers and Dagara late-comers tend to disagree about the practical consequences of the metaphorical equation of land transfers with marriage, particularly concerning the land/woman's relationship with her original family/owner. In the Baadaateng case, the Nuni argued that when their grandfathers had given a piece of land to Baadaa, it was like giving him a wife. However, they then claimed that when Baadaa and his people abandoned that land for some time, the wife had automatically returned to her original house, and insisted that if the Dagara family wanted her (the land) back, they needed to ask the Nuni owners once again. Thus, in the eyes of the land givers, the land transfer established a relationship that implicitly retained a strong bond to the original owners, much as a gift establishes a lasting bond between giver and recipient. In other words, although a woman is given to another group in marriage, she always remains a full member of her paternal house.

The Dagara land receivers, on the other hand, usually argue that, for all intents and purposes, once the bride price has been paid, the separation of the woman from her family is complete. My Dagara interlocutors in Niégo, for instance, asserted that after acquiring the earth-shrine stone from Hiela, they were autonomous and would never invoke any Sisala names during sacrifices but only those of their own ancestors. It was "like in marriage," Niégo earth priest Somda Beyaa explained, "when we marry, the woman no longer belongs to her family. From time to time she may write letters to them or visit them, but we [the husband's house] would have nothing to do with them."[64] Thus the transfer of an earth shrine can be talked about in different ways, either in terms of a purchase, implicating exchange and equality, or in terms of a gift, invoking the language of kinship and dependency.

These different interpretations of the metaphors of marriage and kinship in the context of debates on the legitimacy of transfers of property rights ultimately reflect the diverging interests of first-comers and late-comers. Significantly, attempts by the Dagara and other late-comers to claim an allodial title through purchase or with reference to a labor theory of property, asserting that property rights are created by virtue of the continuous cultivation of land alone, have not been very successful. Consequently, as we have seen in the Baadaateng case, late-comers, too, tend to present some appropriately adapted variant of a first-comer narrative. This narrative incorporates, and even privileges, the first clearing of the land (as against the mere "discovery" of an empty territory), thus transforming a labor-theory justification of property into a justification based on having been the first. Similarly, Dagara narratives about purchasing an earth shrine from the Sisala often invoke some additional argument of first-comership. This persuasive power of the first-comer ideology to which even late-comers subscribe has historical reasons that must be sought not only in the dynamics of the frontier process itself, but also in the feedback of colonial ideas on indigenous property into local discourse.

Colonial Concepts of African Land Ownership

Colonial debates on West African systems of land tenure began when European administrations needed to appropriate land for public use and guarantee security of tenure to European firms interested in concessions for mining or commercial agriculture. "One widely favored solution," writes Anne Phillips about British colonial land policies, "was for the state to . . . set itself up as landlord," by vesting in the Governor or the Crown all "waste lands . . . , a very flexible concept which could embrace vast territories."[65] However, British plans for a bill to put all "crown lands" of the Gold Coast Colony and the adjoining protectorates in the hands of the colonial power encountered vehement opposition from African lawyers and chiefs, and eventually had to be dropped. The Aborigines' Rights Protection Society in particular impressed upon the British that all land, whether occupied or not, belonged to African chiefs or families.[66] Although the British finally accepted these assertions, they initially saw this "communal system of land holding" as an "obstacle to progress,"[67] and recommended the gradual privatization of land ownership.

In the 1910s and 1920s, however, when hopes for the economic future of the colony were placed in African peasant production rather than capitalist transformation, British land policies shifted toward maintaining "native customary tenure" and strictly controlling the developing African land market. Most British officials were now convinced that individualized land ownership and, more important, outright land sales were "untraditional"—an idea that many chiefs who stood to gain from rights rooted in inalienable allodial ownership were only too happy to support, while tacitly redefining the contents of "custom." As Kathryn Firmin-Sellers's comparative study of the colonial transformation of customary tenure in two different settings in Southern Ghana has shown, questions of power and alliances, particularly of chiefs or other powerful figures with the colonial (and postcolonial) state, were central to the local playing out of new institutional configurations of land rights.[68]

French administrators, too, eventually admitted that land was nowhere "vacant and without owner," but always "the property of a corporation," be it a "people, tribe, clan or family," and that each "cell" of the property-holding corporation enjoyed merely "use rights" of the communal land.[69] While Maurice Delafosse acknowledged that "from the native point of view," the state domain set up by the French authorities was "illegal,"[70] Henri Labouret, drawing on his experience as district commissioner in the Black Volta region, questioned whether local land tenure should be understood in terms of European notions of property at all. According to local beliefs, he argued, land was under the influence of supernatural powers that needed to be propitiated by an earth priest recruited among the first-comers. And although the population recognized some form of exclusive, "monopolistic" control over certain expanses of land, it had no concept of "property" in any strict sense.[71] Immigrating "strangers" had to ask the original hunting communities for permission to settle, and land could never be sold or otherwise definitely alienated.[72] These insights, however, did not prevent the French colonial government from declaring all lands in Francophone West Africa "state domain," even though on the ground, outside urban areas and zones of intense cash-cropping, colonial administrators rarely interfered with local land-related practices.[73]

While the chiefs and educated African elite of the Gold Coast Colony and the Ashanti Protectorate successfully resisted British attempts to vest all lands in the crown, the colonial regime was able to impose, in 1927, the Land and Native Rights Ordinance for the Northern Territories that declared all territory, occupied as well as unoccupied, "public lands"—that is, land vested in and administered by the governor "for the use and common benefit . . . of the natives."[74] Several amendments clarified that the governor was not the "owner," but the "trustee" of the land, and the term "public lands" was eventually replaced by "native lands." Yet all titles of occupancy and leases had to be issued by the colonial authorities, with the explicit aim of protecting the "natives" from land speculation. Postcolonial legislation even compounded this de jure divestiture of Northern Ghanaian landowners' property rights, and only with the ratification of the 1979 constitution were Northern lands legally returned to their original owners.[75]

Just like their French counterparts, however, the British (and postindependence regimes in Ghana) did not, and still do not, command the necessary resources to enforce national land legislation in any systematic or comprehensive way. In both colonies, local ideas and strategies of constructing, contesting, and enforcing property claims have therefore remained immensely important, and earth priests, chiefs, and family heads de facto continued to administer all land-related matters. But this does not mean that "customary tenure" remained unchanged—on the contrary. As colonial pacification made the more or less violent Dagara encroachment on Sisala, Phuo, and Nuni lands ever more difficult, increasing emphasis was placed on peaceful exchange and persuasion. Furthermore, local actors actively sought to influence colonial officers' views on local land tenure in order to enlist potential allies for their cause. Colonial (re)interpretations and oversimplifications of local arguments, on the other hand, fed back into local discourses on land rights—particularly concerning the questions of who held allodial title and of whether land was indeed inalienable.

The British were generally much more concerned than the French about the compatibility of their policies with African "tradition," and they conducted systematic enquiries into, and explicitly discussed, local land tenure almost from the outset of colonial rule. This is why it is easier to find written traces of the impact of local African land debates on British concepts of land tenure (and vice versa) in British colonial archives, but we may assume that similar processes took place in the French colony. Already in the early 1910s, in preparation for (ultimately abandoned) plans to introduce a land tax, British administrators in the Northern Territories were asked to submit information on native "systems of land tenure." Provincial Commissioner Captain Moutray Read surmised that in the Black Volta region, as elsewhere in the Northern Territories, "land tenure does not exist in the form that it is understood in civilised countries. Land . . . is not regarded as an estate, or a possession of any value, it is regarded as part of the universe, just as the sun, moon and stars are."[76] Or, as Chief Commissioner C. H. Armitage put it, land stood "under the guardianship of Spirits."[77] Read's successor, Wheeler, on the other hand, admitted that in "the past, under pressure of a larger and denser population, the question of ownership was settled by resort to arms," and thus ultimately by power, not religion alone.[78] A. W. Cardinall, referring to the densely populated North-Eastern parts of the Northern Territories, explained that the earth priest was "the original owner of the land, and is so to this day," and that selling land was prohibited because this would "place the Earth-god . . . in servitude." But Cardinall also observed that "communal holding of land is no longer known" and that the "clearer of land becomes *ipso facto* the owner for all time," thus supporting a labor theory of property.[79] In a similar vein, Lawra-Tumu District Commissioner Michael Dasent insisted that "land belongs to the Earth God," that the earth priest "administers the land in trust for the people," and that "no native occupier or owner of land would be allowed by the Community to sell or alienate the land." But in other parts of his write-up, Dasent argued that land ownership had been acquired either by "peaceful occupation" or "by conquest," thus pointing to a history of land transfers that contradicted his previous assertions of the inalienability of land.[80]

One could interpret these contradictions in British descriptions of indigenous land tenure as further proof of the complete lack "of any rudimentary understanding" of local culture by the colonial authorities, as Sean Hawkins characterizes it in his study on the colonial encounter in Lawra District.[81] My own reading, however, suggests that these contradictions were not due to ignorance, but to profound ambiguities in local informants' representations to the British. They reflected ongoing conflicts over property rights. This becomes particularly clear in a debate that developed in the early 1930s between Lawra District Commissioner St. John Eyre-Smith and his successor, John Guinness, about whether the Dagara from Nandom had actually purchased an earth-shrine stone from the Sisala in Lambussie, thereby obtaining ritual independence and full property over their lands, or whether they still owed some form of allegiance to Lambussie.

Arguing the (In)alienability of land: The Case of the Nandom Earth Shrine

The case that I analyze in this next section concerns the ongoing controversies surrounding the transfer of land by the Sisala of Lambussie to the Dagara of Nandom, a transfer that the former interpreted in terms of a gift, invoking the language of kinship and dependency, while the latter saw it as a purchase, implicating exchange and equality. While there are no documents through which we could trace this debate to its very beginnings, we do have evidence of similar debates in the 1930s, when British colonial officials engaged in a heated exchange over the nature of the previous land (and shrine) transfer that must have echoed Dagara and Sisala positions as they existed at the time. Together with information from earlier British (and French) inquiries into local tenure systems, the Nandom-Lambussie case thus allows us to infuse some historical depth into the discussion of local property theories, and to analyze the interconnections between colonial and indigenous discourses on land ownership.

The British debate over the status of Nandom lands arose in the context of the introduction of indirect rule, which politicized the concept of an "allodial title" to land, rendering it the hallmark of native status and legitimate chiefly authority. In preparing for the administrative reforms, the political officers were instructed to research the traditional political structures in their districts.[82] John Guinness, Lawra-Tumu District Commissioner in 1932, interviewed, among others, the Nandom earth priest, "a descendant of Zenoo [Zenuo], the Dagara hunter of the Dikpiele clan, who is said to have founded Nandom."[83] Although Guinness claimed that his inquiries when addressed to the Sisala earth priest of Lambussie brought to light the same story, the version he recorded in writing was unmistakably biased in favor of the Dagara in that it emphasized the early autonomy of Nandom from Lambussie. According to this version, Zenuo encountered the Sisala of Lambussie on his first hunting expedition into the area that would become Nandom, but because he spoke a different language he could not communicate with them, and therefore built a hut without asking the Sisala for permission. Only when the people of Lambussie "kidnapped" his family and took them to their village while he was out hunting did he accept the Sisala's invitation to settle in Lambussie. However, because of constant squabbles over the theft of his goats, Zenuo soon reasserted his autonomy. For this, he was granted land by the Sisala, with their permission built a house near his first hut, and, in return for 60,000 cowries and several animals, was given his own earth shrine, with which he became earth priest of Nandom and rightful owner of Nandom land.[84]

All versions that my Sisala interlocutors related to me had Zenuo come directly to Lambussie on his hunting expedition, where he settled down at the invitation of the earth priest. The kidnapping episode was absent, and only the theft of the goats as the motive for the subsequent founding of Nandom with the permission of the Lambussie earth priest was told in a fashion similar to the version recounted by the Nandom earth priest. However, the Sisala insisted that the people of Nandom did not receive their own shrine stones until long after they had left Lambussie. Furthermore, they were said not to have paid for these, since the sale of an earth shrine was strictly forbidden. Even today, my Sisala informants insisted, the Nandom earth priests must consult the Lambussie earth priests when faced with serious matters. In fact, Lambussie and Nandom sacrifice to the same earth god, called Kabir, but in the eyes of the Lambussiele, their shrine to Kabir is not only older, but also more powerful than that of Nandom.[85]

We do not know exactly what Nansie, the Sisala earth priest at the time, told Guinness or whether his version resembled the one related to me a good fifty years later by his son Nansie Issifu Tomo. The fact that Guinness claimed that the Lambussie version was the same, word for word, as the Nandom version may well have been due to his reluctance to record variants that seemed basically similar to him. However, Eyre-Smith's severe criticism of Guinness's report indicates that even at that time, different interpretations of the relations between Nandom and Lambussie must have existed, and it seems likely that while Guinness's main informants on this matter were Dagara, Eyre-Smith relied more on Sisala opinions. His central objection to Guinness's report concerned the alleged payment of 60,000 cowries for the Nandom earth shrine. "This cannot be accepted at its face value and . . . such a procedure was unknown and is not supported by the facts," he insisted.[86] Guinness admitted that it was perhaps not the land itself, but "the privilege of the tingdanaship" that had been paid for,[87] but he did not budge from his assertion that with this transfer Nandom had received full control over the land.

Guinness thus postulated Nandom's independence from Lambussie and emphasized that the earth priests of Nandom and Lambussie would rarely visit one another. Only in the event of a drought would they meet near Lambussie in order to consult the earth deity and make offerings to it. "Apart from this the Tingdanaships have no other than a historical connexion, and the people of Nandom do not look to a spiritual authority beyond their own home."[88] Eyre-Smith, on the other hand, was convinced that Nandom, as well as Lambussie, continued to be *tengani-le* (small earth-shrine areas) that had to consult the superior shrine in many matters. If Guinness had only investigated further, Eyre-Smith insisted, he would have discovered this superior earth shrine in Katu, some three miles from Lambussie. He claimed to have obtained confirmation from both the Nandom Naa and the Lambussie Kuoro that "if any 'bad thing' happened to this country they would have to go to the Tengansobe of the Tengani of Katu."[89] The earth priests of Nandom and Lambussie had obviously concealed this fact from Guinness, Eyre-Smith argued, because their chiefs had forbidden them to speak about it for fear that the reference to their belonging to a single large *tengani* area would curtail their own power. And indeed, Eyre-Smith did suggest that the Nandom chiefdom be placed under the paramount chief of Lambussie.[90]

The disagreement between Eyre-Smith and Guinness over the status of the Nandom earth shrine was partly the result of the shifting political interests of the local chiefs and earth priests, who used settlement history, and related questions of land ownership, to legitimate their respective political projects. The British commissioners, who conducted their interviews at different moments in the local political power struggles during the mid-1920s (Eyre-Smith) and early 1930s (Guinness), were thus caught up in their African interlocutors' argumentative strategies. Eyre-Smith's purported

"Tengani of Katu," for instance, of which neither Guinness nor my informants had ever heard, probably refers to Keltu, an area in Lambussie where a family resides that plays a central role in the installation of a new earth priest and exercises the earth priest's duties during an interregnum.[91] Eyre-Smith must have interviewed this family during such an interregnum, which apparently used the opportunity to underscore its own importance, before the new Lambussie earth priest, Nansie, assumed office, the very earth priest that Guinness questioned subsequently.[92] Furthermore, Guinness and Eyre-Smith were probably drawn into conflicts over the chieftaincy in Lambussie, and listened to settlement and earth-shrine histories deployed to support competing claims to office. Finally, the competing historical narratives also reflected the changing relations between Nandom and Lambussie.

In the old Lambussie Kuoro's version of Nandom's continued spiritual dependence on Lambussie, Eyre-Smith may have found ammunition for his favorite plan to amalgamate the two chiefdoms under Lambussie's control. However, this plan did not find favor with Eyre-Smith's successors and superiors, who preferred separating Lambussie from the neighboring Dagara chiefdoms and including it in a great all-Sisala "native state."[93] Whether the Nandom Naa ever heard about Eyre-Smith's plans is unclear, but that administrative changes were forthcoming with the introduction of indirect rule was fairly obvious to all the chiefs in Lawra District. Most of them, especially the Nandom Naa, were interested in maintaining the status quo—as, incidentally, was Guinness, who accordingly was only too willing to adopt Nandom's historical arguments for its autonomy from Lambussie. The new Lambussie Kuoro, for his part, was opposed to the British "all-Sisala native state" project because it would have implied his submission to the Tumu Kuoro. Thus he, too, wanted to maintain the status quo of Lambussie's incorporation into Lawra District. For this, he needed the support of Nandom (as well as the other Dagara/Dagaba chiefdoms of Jirapa and Lawra), which he would not have received had he insisted on Nandom's dependency. It is therefore likely that at the time of Guinness's inquiry, he did agree that Nandom had received its own earth shrine, and thus achieved its independence, from Lambussie early on. However, this agreement was not to last. In the late 1940s, after a period during which Lambussie had for various reasons been politically subordinated to Nandom, the Lambussie chief and his earth priest strove to regain independence from Nandom and therefore not only reemphasized their ancient ownership of Nandom lands, but even claimed that they continued to be the legitimate owners of these lands.[94]

Eyre-Smith's and Guinness's views, however, were not shaped by their local informants' perspectives alone, but also by their own visions of African history and their ideas for political reform. For Eyre-Smith, the earth-shrine parishes, whose boundaries had supposedly remained unaltered for centuries, were the cornerstone of stability in that primitive society, which had occasionally been shaken by periodic invasions and migrations.[95] This is why he had felt it necessary to criticize so vehemently Guinness's thesis that the various Sisala and Dagara lineages had peacefully moved into

to their Dagara neighbors. The narratives concerning these expansions and (non) transfers are usually hotly contested and subject to ongoing reinterpretation. This makes it difficult to assess the extent to which full property rights during this time were still passed from Sisala into Dagara hands.

After the 1920s, during the third phase, the transfer of ritual authority—and shrine stones—to the Dagara ceased altogether, and the Dagara thus were no longer able to become full-fledged landowners, even when they continued to found new settlements. The *pax colonia*, which only really became effective in the Black Volta region from the 1910s onward, changed the balance of power in favor of the Sisala (and other first-comers): it eliminated the recourse to violence in the appropriation of new territories and prevented the forceful conversion of late-comers into first-comers. The Sisala refusal to cede earth shrines to the expanding Dagara suggests that the previous transfer of earth shrines had perhaps not been quite as voluntary as some narratives claim, or at least that such transfers had somehow been problematic for the Sisala. On the other hand, in the 1930s and 1940s, a good number of Dagara from the Ouessa and Niégo areas opted deliberately to settle outside the Dagara earth-shrine parishes on Sisala-controlled territory because they wanted to escape the particularly harsh rule of the Dagara paramount chief. Thus, if much of the current landscape of allodial titles is due to the colonial freezing of a previously more dynamic situation, this is only so because some local actors saw it in their interests to support colonial officials' ideas about the impossibility of "alienating" ancestral land and because others thought it better to live on "foreign" land.

More generally, the chapter has argued that contrary to Chanock's and others' claims that the colonial regime reified "custom" in the interests of chiefs and elders, "customary tenure" remained as contested and negotiable during the colonial period as before.[103] Moreover, colonial officials disagreed among themselves about the major characteristics of local tenure regimes and often were, usually somewhat unknowingly, drawn into ongoing local disputes, the outcomes of which they could rarely predict, much less dictate. That notwithstanding, colonial officers' ideas on inalienable communal land ownership as well as colonial land legislation certainly did influence local discourses on property rights and could tilt the balance of power in favor of first-comer claims. Analyzing the increasing opportunities of Asante chiefs to control land and appropriate surplus, Sara Berry has argued that "what changed under colonial rule was neither the interdependence of wealth, power, and belief nor the complexity of contestation, but the cast of contestants and the terms in which they framed and negotiated claims."[104] With regard to the Black Volta region, I would stress that not even the general terms in which assertions of property rights were formulated changed very much; first-comer narratives continued to provide the common idiom for struggles over ritual prerogatives and land rights, even though the emphasis certainly shifted further toward privileging claims grounded in "historical depth." Yet more important was the impact resulting from the eventual removal of opportunities to resort to violence, which made it necessary to rely more on the power of persuasion and the apt manipulation of social and political networks that supported specific narratives, as the analysis of contemporary land conflicts in chapter 5 shows. In any case, the colonial freezing of the transfer of allodial property rights in no way put an end to the contestation and reinterpretation of claims to ownership. Even today, particularly those allodial titles that were acquired in the turbulent last decades before colonial rule are closely scrutinized and, when changing power constellations provide room for maneuver, questioned.

Finally, although this chapter has focused on conflicts over earth shrines and property rights between Sisala first-comers and Dagara late-comers, its findings also apply to other contexts where later immigrants, who belong to the same ethno-linguistic group as the first-comers, have attempted to found new settlements and claim land ownership. However, frontier situations characterized by ethnic heterogeneity throw into particularly sharp relief the paradoxical intertwining of violence and consensus, and the competing indigenous ideas about the origins and transfer of property rights on which the different narratives about the earth shrine rest.

3 Setting Boundaries, Negotiating Entitlements

Contested Borders and Bundles of Rights

Property rights over land involve not only arguments about time, usually stated in the form of claims of first possession and its legitimate transfer, but also about their spatial scope. In the Black Volta region, as in many other areas of the West African savanna, the original definition of spatial boundaries of landed property was, and continues to be, closely tied to a mental map of spiritual territories under the guardianship of earth deities that are propitiated by the first-comers at the earth shrines. Originally, these boundaries were mainly concerned with the definition of hunting rights, and rarely patrolled. However, with increasing population densities and the growing importance of agriculture for local livelihoods, earth-shrine boundaries assumed new functions, namely, defining the extension of property rights over farmland. Concomitantly, earlier notions of fuzzy, open border zones were complemented by concepts of linear boundaries. Since the twentieth century, local mental maps have also become influenced by the new politico-territorial boundaries of chieftaincy and administrative districts, which some groups readily translated into boundaries of property rights. These rights, in turn, have recently developed into an important source of income from immigrants who are expected to pay some form of rent (under the guise of symbolic gifts) to the allodial titleholders—a development that has made the definition of property boundaries all the more important. These new understandings of boundaries, however, have not completely eclipsed older notions of spiritual territories, and in current land conflicts, the local population draws on a palimpsest of border concepts.

Furthermore, "property" is actually an umbrella term for a complex bundle of socially and politically embedded rights over land and land-related resources. Rights over land are nested, and pertain to different economic and ritual activities such as hunting and gathering, grazing animals, cultivating food crops or commercial plants, planting or felling trees, conducting sacrifices, building houses, or cutting the sod for burials. These rights cover different time spans and differ in territorial reach, ranging from allodial ownership of larger village territories under specific earth shrines, to long-standing heritable proprietorship of smaller portions of family lands, and finally to temporary-use rights to specific fields (or trees, etc.). On any given piece of land, several different persons or groups usually hold some kind of claim. Their respective rights may have different expiry dates, so to speak, and some resources are used by different right-holders at different times. Moreover, different types of spatial boundaries may be relevant for different rights. Mobility and common practices of multilocality—a family may build their house, for instance, in one village, but continue to cultivate fields and propitiate their ancestors in another settlement—further complicate the matter. Moreover, intricate histories of interaction between first-comers and late-comers, and the typical ambiguity of the composition of the "bundle of owners" as well as the bundle of rights that the latter acquired, provided and continues to provide potential for a plurality of (re)interpretations, debate, and sometimes conflicts.

This chapter explores how hunters and agriculturalists in the Black Volta region went about defining—or, as the case may be, challenging—boundaries between earth-shrine parishes, and how these ritual borders were eventually translated into legal boundaries that delimited property rights. It discusses what role conflict and peacemaking rituals historically played in the establishment of new earth-shrine territories, and how first-comers and late-comers drew, and continue to draw, on different notions and rival histories of boundaries in order to defend their competing claims. The chapter also investigates the impact of colonial and postcolonial politico-territorial boundaries on such debates, and examines how shrinking land reserves as well as new economic opportunities can provoke attempts to (re)define the contents of the bundle of rights that landowners have ceded to later immigrants. Finally, it will discuss how frontiersmen and late-comers attempted to transform various practices of "access"—that is, the de facto use of resources and "the ability to benefit from things"[1]—into legitimate property rights, or, conversely, tried to prevent precisely such a transformation and instead restrict and delegitimize certain forms of access.

Setting Boundaries: Changing Mental Maps and Contested Earth-Shrine Borders

Allen Abramson has recently argued that "mythical" and "jural" concepts of land are usually mutually exclusive. Economic rights over land, including comprehensive ownership, he claims, can only be "safely alienated" to "non-descendants" if the ancestral land has been emptied of its mythical connections and become "disenchanted."[2]

Mythical and jural lands, Abramson further maintains, imply different concepts of the past: "Whereas in ritual, the past is invoked to summon up ancestral powers in the interests of providing a continuous line of mediation with the present, the jural past is always invoked . . . as genealogy to establish the disconnections inherent in any particular current claim to ownership." Moreover, mythical lands have "sacred centers," but no "boundaries and measurable areas."[3]

The case of Black Volta region shows, however, that these uses of the past are not as neatly distinguishable as Abramson suggests, and that mythical lands may very well become the objects of rather mundane contestation. Sisala and Dagara generally agree that land has mythical properties, binding the purported owners to the first-comers and founders of the earth shrine, and ultimately to the earth deity. But they also tend to translate control over spiritual territories into secular economic privileges, and in conflicts over property or use rights they constantly switch between mythical and jural histories of the land. The demographic pressure on and the economic interests in land, of course, have changed over time, and new configurations of power have prompted projections of current linear boundary concepts into the past, as well as reinterpretations of formerly spiritual bonds as lucrative patron-client relations. However, conflicts over the nature and course of land boundaries, and over the privileges to be derived from "ownership" seem to be as old as the frontier itself. Despite the fact that land was, in principle, plentiful and exit options always available, settlements did fight over earth-shrine boundaries. And, when peaceful coexistence, for instance between established villages and later immigrants, gave way to increasing tensions and open conflict, establishing a boundary where previously there was none was often the means of last resort to solve the problems.

Mobility was, and continues to be, a challenge for the stability of boundaries. The immigration of new groups, often settling in the interstices between established earth shrines, could change the demography of any given area, thereby affecting the balance of power and making it difficult for an earth priest, for instance, to enforce the newcomers' respect for his authority and the earth-shrine parish's boundary. On the other hand, the spiritual services that an earth priest rendered to his followers were, and still are, often interpreted as proof that the area which the client cultivates or where he builds his house belongs to the earth priest's territory. This could mean that a migrant who maintained close relations with his original earth priest, despite moving into the neighboring bush, thereby surreptitiously expanded the boundaries of the area to which the earth priest claimed control. Moreover, any group could, in the course of time, turn to different earth priests for its different needs, thus creating a history of multiple allegiances that the respective authorities would, in case of land conflicts, play against one other. In short, the history of boundary making in the Black Volta region provides many examples of how spiritual boundaries may become resources in secular property conflicts, and of how changing secular interests and power configurations may result in the redefinition of the spiritual topography.

Hunting Territories, "Meeting Places," and Lineal Boundaries

In the early phases of the expanding settlement frontier, allodial property rights were mainly geared at securing large hunting territories. In the immediate vicinity of settlement nuclei, households would clear land and establish farms, and thus create some form of enduring rights over their fields by the exertion of labor. But the larger areas, or rather, spheres of interest, over which the first-comers to an area claimed control, were defined as the zones beyond which wounded game would no longer be pursued, zones with boundaries that were not linear and exclusive, but rather fuzzy and open, usually designated by ritually charged landmarks. The spatial connotations of these two modes of land tenure, the one regulating hunting and gathering activities, the other related to agriculture, were rather different. Hunters establish control over specific sites and routes; agriculturalists control plots of land, imagined as a two-dimensional mental map.[4] However, since in the Black Volta region hunting and farming were practiced by members of the same group, or even by the same persons, the concomitant mental maps coexisted and in some ways interlocked.

That hunting activities played an important role in the early spatial definition of earth-shrine areas is reflected in the fact that all larger rivers—particularly the Black Volta and its confluents—constitute earth-shrine boundaries. Virtually no earth priest regularly claims that the area under his control extends beyond the Black Volta or any of its confluents, and if, in the course of land conflicts, such a claim is occasionally raised, it encounters vehement opposition and is soon dropped. It was in the river valleys that wild animals roamed in the dry season, and where hunters who followed the animals were most likely to meet fellow hunters. At rivers, hunters from different groups had to negotiate, in consultation with the earth priests, to whom the hunters paid loyalty, their potential cooperation as well as rights over the prey. Furthermore, rivers were difficult to cross in the rainy season, and earth priests would have found it extremely cumbersome to render their services to people living on the other side, just as the latter would not have been able to attend sacrifices at the earth shrine for many months on end—another reason that earth-shrine areas usually ended at the banks of rivers. Finally, rivers that held abundant fish and water throughout the year were themselves important resources. Thus, as Niégo earth priest Somda Beyaa explained, "Everybody wants to have access to the river and that is why they declare it a boundary."[5]

The Bayagra River, separating the Dagara settlement of Niégo from the Sisala villages of Hiela and Kelendou, is an instructive example of this mode of boundary making. The Bayagra once had plenty of water and fish, Somda Beyaa related, and because all three villages wanted to own it, "they finally agreed to turn it into a boundary in order to make sure that it belonged to all of them." Originally, Beyaa explained, when their earth shrines were still closely linked, the Dagara and Sisala would open the annual communal fishing campaign toward the end of the dry season with joint sacrifices to the river spirits. However, after a time some Sisala as well as a few Dagara who defied the

Niégo earth priest's authority started fishing individually, and secretly, during the night. Serious conflicts between Niégo, Kelendou, and Hiela could only be avoided by establishing the river as a boundary between the earth-shrine areas, and assigning fishing rights on different stretches of the river to the different villages. The ritual importance of the Bayagra River and the past sharing of its natural wealth is still remembered in stories that are told by both Sisala and Dagara villagers. Nobody is allowed to point to the river and "show" the boundary, these stories assert. Whoever happens to come to the river for the first time will invariably meet some mythical creature singing, and before crossing the river, the traveler must close his eyes and dance to the tune, with his back facing the river, otherwise he will invariably get lost in the bush. People settled near the river are safe because during childhood their parents would have put mud from the riverbanks into their mouths in order to protect them from the capricious spirits of the place.[6] These stories and the history of interethnic encounters at the Bayagra River demonstrate that boundaries are highly ambivalent. They are places of encounter and joint exploitation of resources, but also sites that are potentially dangerous and divisive.

Two different indigenous terms for boundaries are currently in use, and there is no reason to doubt that both have been around for considerable time. In Dagara—and equivalent expressions exist in Sisala—people speak either of *turbogr*, literally, a series of holes (a ditch), or of *tuoritaa zie*, literally, meeting places. In his story of the Bayagra River, for instance, Somda Beyaa employed both terms, and explained how the concept of the river as a meeting place was eventually replaced by the idea of the water course as a *turbogr*. More generally, the term *turbogr* is always used when referring to linear boundaries between contiguous fields, which are often physically marked by paths, ditches, shrubs, or marks on trees. But my interlocutors sometimes also applied the expression *turbogr* to earth-shrine borders if they wanted to emphasize the ritual and economic autonomy of neighboring earth-shrine areas. More often, however, my informants insisted that there existed no "real" boundaries—*turbogr*—between contiguous earth shrines, but that the neighbors owned the border zone jointly (*langtaa*). Furthermore, these "open" borders were marked not by any imaginary dividing line, but by landmarks such as rocks, hills, rivers, or outstanding big trees that constituted *tuoritaa zie* and were regularly commemorated in sacrifices. The histories of these meeting places usually refer to the more or less peaceful encounter of two hunters, or, alternatively, to violent confrontations between neighboring groups that were ultimately settled by a peacemaking sacrifice at the *tuoritaa zie*. Sometimes these ritually charged *tuoritaa zie* were later (re)interpreted as markers of the *turbogr* between two earth-shrine areas. *Turbogr* and *tuoritaa zie* are thus not mutually exclusive concepts, but emphasize different aspects of boundary making. The first underlines separateness and is more closely associated with the idea of linear boundaries; the second refers to places of ritual power and commemorates a history of contact (sometimes including conflict) and mutual agreement.

In Tantuo, a village near Nandom where the Dagara immigrants eventually managed to drive out the former Sisala inhabitants who resettled farther eastward but continued to put up resistance against Dagara encroachment, I was presented with a particularly compelling story about the creation of a *tuoritaa zie*—in this case a battle-field rather than a place of peaceful encounter—that subsequently became part of a *turbogr*. As a member of the Tantuo earth-priestly family explained:

> When the Dagara and the Sisala were fond of fighting each other, there was something that looked like an animal which used to urge them to continue fighting whenever they stopped. This animal was wild and used to stand erect in the night and would shout in the direction of both the Sisala and the Dagara. The shouts usually invited the Sisala to come immediately to the rescue of their kinsmen who were about to be wiped out by the Dagara. A similar message was also sent in the direction of where the Dagara lived. As soon as this animal sounded what appeared to have been a signal cry for war, the two sides immediately would mobilize and begin to fight each other. But any time they got to the spot where the mysterious animal used to stand, it vanished.
>
> This continued until a time when both the Dagara and the Sisala chose one person from each of their sides. These men also were mysterious [*yibier*] [i.e., they had magical powers]. They went out to lay in ambush during the night. When the animal came up at its usual time, the two men quickly pounced on it. . . . It was the Sisala man who first shot at it, followed by the Dagara. When the animal was killed, they realized that it was a four-legged animal, but it used to stand on its feet. From that time onward, both the Dagara and the Sisala realized that it was a hoax that had brought about the fight between them. The animal was buried in a trench, together with all their weapons such as bows and arrows. This meant that their antagonism had come to an end, since the thing which was responsible for that had been buried.
>
> The spot [*zie*] at which the mysterious animal was buried became the boundary [*turbogr*] between the Sisala and the Dagara. None of the sides could cross over the grave of the animal to lay claim to any territory on the other side. It was also said that there is a tree on the *turbogr* which is not to be cut at all. These are the things I have heard but have not seen for myself.[7]

Not everywhere was a *tuoritaa zie* eventually transformed into a *turbogr*. In Ko, for instance, one of the oldest Dagara villages in the Nandom area, with a long history of interethnic encounters and marriages as well as joint exploitation of hunting grounds and water resources, the place where weapons were ritually buried did not become part of a *turbogr*. The founding families of Ko and the neighboring Sisala settlements of Lambussie and Konguol still acknowledge historical ties of kinship and the fact that they honor the same earth deity, namely Kabir. "Ko and Lambussie were one territory [*teng been*] without boundaries [*turbogr*]," James Bayuo, the chief of Ko, and his elders explained, because both villages continued to sacrifice to Kabir, although now at different shrines.

> Lambussie and Ko can be said to be like a woman who has given birth to twins. . . . Our fathers told us that under no circumstance should the young men of Ko and Bussie [Lambussie] engage in a fight. If they did, all the relatives [*yirdem*] of the side that was the aggressor would perish. In order to ensure the observance

of this pact, Ko and Lambussie met at a certain valley that appeared to have been their boundary [*tuoritaa zie*]. They provided a dog, which wakes people up, bow and arrows, which are used in fighting, and a cock, which shows people the way at dawn. All these objects were buried in a trench in that valley. My father showed me where all these things were buried.

Up to this day there has not been a major conflict between us and the people of Bussie. Let me add that there was a sort of line in that same valley which the people from Ko and Lambussie were told not to cross and farm without informing the other side. . . . Some time ago there was some misunderstanding over farmland between young men from Ko and Bussie that nearly led to a fight. Some of us made it clear to the Sisala young men that instead of resorting to fighting, we should rather come together and unearth what our fathers had buried. They then told us that they were going home to consult their old men, and that ended the conflict.[8]

When I asked whether this "line" was a *turbogr*, my interlocutors in Ko were adamant that it was not. They insisted that people from both villages were allowed to farm on either side of the boundary if they informed each other properly. The neighboring villages of Lissa, Varpuo, and parts of Tom, on the other hand, were separated from Ko by a *turbogr* because they sacrificed to the earth god Nyoor, not Kabir. In this case, thus, the *turbogr* marked the territorial reach of two different powerful earth shrines, each of which claimed control over the inhabitants and their sacrificial gifts, stray animals, lost objects, and so forth.[9]

"Imaginary Lines" versus "Spheres of Control":
A Debate among British Administrators

Considering the available evidence, it is likely that the sometimes complementary, sometimes competing notions of earth-shrine borders as *turbogr* and/or *tuoritaa zie* already coexisted in the region during the early phases of expanding frontiers. Which of the two concepts was emphasized depended on the concrete circumstances of the local settlement history and could be controversial. Such controversies were echoed in a debate about the nature of village and earth-shrine boundaries in which British administrators in the Northern Territories of the Gold Coast engaged in the early years of colonial rule. During one of his first tours of inspection through the area under his administration, the commissioner of the North-Western Province, Captain Moutray Read, complained that people were "living in compounds all over the country," not in compact settlements, and that this made it "very difficult to ascertain the boundaries of villages" and draw up a precise map, which was Read's aim.[10] Whether it was only difficult for an outsider to discover these boundaries, which nevertheless existed, or whether there simply were no boundaries in any strict sense of term, was a matter that provoked a lively exchange between Read and his successor, Wheeler. The latter reported that the local population regarded land "as the property of Villages, but not of tribes or Kingdoms." Land was controlled by earth priests who would "look after the fetish of the Rivers and Land, and . . . give land for farming to persons who desire the same, and receive a 'dash' in return."[11] Nobody could "make a farm even in the far away 'bush' without this permission," Wheeler argued, and concluded that some concept of a boundary separating neighboring earth priests' spheres of influence must have existed. Even if Read's observation was correct, and "tribal and village boundaries were not laid down or marked out before the British Government took over this Country," this did not prove, Wheeler asserted, "that no boundaries of any sort existed. They might have been formed by natural objects in the Landscape, or by imaginary lines as are 'fishing boundaries' off the Coasts of European Countries."[12]

Wheeler's account provoked Read to further explain his own findings. Land, Read argued, was "not regarded as an estate, or a possession of any value," and therefore people were originally not concerned with boundaries of village territories.

> Where one village might encroach upon the lands said to belong to another the matter was settled by mutual agreement, arbitration by another chief or by resort to arms. This absence of boundaries necessarily leading to many disputes, and, where uncultivated bush existed between villages, to that being considered common ground for the collection of natural produce and hunting. Later on boundaries were made and agreed upon by occupiers of farmlands.[13]

In his earlier report, Read had already discussed the complicated layers of rights to land—rights to hunt, gather natural produce, and cultivate a particular area—and pointed out the difficulties of spatially delimiting these different rights. One should therefore rather speak of different spheres of control, Read suggested, when, "for instance, the people of one village would not go to the outskirts of the next village to pick their sheabutter nuts."[14] But in Read's eyes it was misleading to use the term "imaginary lines," as Wheeler proposed, because the spatial scope of the different rights did not necessarily coincide and their boundaries were not always linear.

It is likely that Read's and Wheeler's different understandings of boundaries to some extent reflected competing, or, as the case may be, complementary, African perceptions of how rights over land and other natural resources should be spatially defined. While Wheeler's perspective probably drew more on local concepts of borders as *turbogr*, Read's views echoed indigenous notions of borders as meeting places. These perceptions were linked to the local population's livelihood strategies, which differed depending on the natural habitat and population density and could place more emphasis on hunting and gathering, shifting cultivation, or working farms more permanently. Moreover, British administrators must have been presented with different accounts by first-comers and late-comers.

In any case, Read and Wheeler as well as their African interlocutors asserted that boundary making was potentially conflict-ridden, but also that some form of agreement was necessary because violence (or the threat of violence) alone could not secure property rights. That consensus was both needed and fragile is also one of the reasons why boundaries were, and still are, surrounded by supernatural sanctions. "Showing" boundaries, particularly between earth-shrine areas, is generally regarded as danger-ous, and even fatal for anyone who is not spiritually equipped to do so.[15]

Defining Farm Boundaries: The Territorialization of Spiritual Services

As more and more bush was eventually brought under cultivation, agricultural prop-erty rights had to be defined in more detail, and boundaries with neighboring settle-ments delineated more precisely. Where the *turbogr* between earth-shrine areas was following the course of a river, the definition of the territory in which the earth priest had the right to allocate land was rather unambiguous. But in many cases, where earth-shrine parishes were "separated" by a jointly exploited border zone, marked by a few ritually charged meeting places, establishing an exact linear boundary was, and continues to be, a gradual and contested process.

The difficulties arise in part from the accustomed method of allocating bush farms, on which many of the West African savanna societies relied and still rely today. When someone asked the landowner or the earth priest for farmland, the latter would "show" him a rectangular strip of land in the bush by marking, with a cutlass, some trees or shrubs on both sides of the strip and pointing into the direction into which the new farm should be extended. But he would not demarcate any boundary at the far end of the piece of land. Usually such a bush farm adjoins a number of similar farms, each of them relatively narrow, but, depending on the workforce of the farmer and the num-ber of years of cultivation, extending deep into the uncultivated bush. Often, the farm's "bottom" is situated in a valley, and the neighboring farmers all eventually work their way up into the bush—an ecologically sound system that ensures that all farmers enjoy more or less the same variation of soils and microclimates.[16] Sooner or later, however, these farmers will literally "meet" their colleagues from neighboring settlements who have also been pushing their farms farther into the bush, in the opposite direction. It is at this point, in the context of competing property claims, that the boundary between the two settlements has to be defined more precisely.

Boundary making thus partly depended, and still depends, on the pace with which the neighboring settlements extend their farms outward, into the border zone. This is why earth priests, as soon as land was viewed as a potentially scarce resource, often deliberately invited "strangers" to start clearing the bush on the periphery of the earth-shrine area, thus physically demonstrating their hosts' property claims. In order to settle competing claims in the border zones, the land givers usually discuss the history of the respective farms (and villages) and trace precisely who has given whom the right to farm, and/or build, in the contested area. The contours of the earth-shrine area—and of the allodial title to land—therefore were, and continue to be, defined according to the question of which earth priest originally granted per-mission to cultivate or build. In other words, the social networks of these spiritual services are interpreted territorially. The history of granting access to resources is thus converted into a history of boundary making, and the various land grants are imagined as if connected by a line, a practice that often results in a meandering and zigzagging boundary.

However, because earth priests render a variety of services and allocate different rights to their clients (such as the right to farm, harvest fruits, build houses, and bury the dead) and because these rights and services are often contested, ambiguous, and changeable, the spatial allegiance of a specific house, or a field, is not always unequivocal. Depending on the context and interests at stake, people may refer to different services, which they may even have acquired from different earth priests, as evidence for their property rights.

In turn, earth priests may invoke a long and complicated history of rendering certain spiritual services to their clients in order to extend their territorial claims. An earth priest who resents that his neighbors, in his view, are encroaching upon his territory will, of course, contest these histories and their implications for the delimitation of the earth-shrine parish boundaries. In such a case, when competing earth priests cannot agree on who actually had the legitimate right to grant permission to farm the land, build a house, or bury the dead in a particular area, and thus where the boundary between earth-shrine areas runs, they sometimes employ a "test." The candidate who claims to be the legitimate earth priest is invited to eat the sacrificial meat from the compound in question, or to remove the ritually dangerous ebony peg that his competitor has placed in the ground of the farm in question in order to prevent the land from being cultivated. If the earth priest survives the test, his position as allodial titleholder is strengthened. But, as we have seen in the case of the conflict between Niégo and Hiela, discussed in the previous chapter, the attribution of misfortune, illness, or death to the breaking of an earth-related taboo is not self-evident. It depends on who is able to impose his interpretation of the course of events. Boundary making, therefore, is also a question of power and prowess.

How charged with issues of power defining a boundary can be becomes particularly clear from the story that Togbir Somé, the earth priest of Bevuugang, told about Bevuugang's relations with the neighboring Dagara settlement of Kondon. According to Togbir, it was his ancestors who had given some Dagara immigrants permission to settle in Kondon, on the periphery of the territory that the Sisala of Kelendou had ceded to Bevuugang. In the beginning, the newcomers referred all earth-shrine-related matters to the Bevuugang *tengan*. However, when they were joined by further kin and friends from across the Black Volta and the new settlement grew, relations with Bevuugang eventually soured. In order to gain independence from Bevuugang, the Dagara in Kondon turned to the Kelendou earth priests, the original owners of the territory, and in exchange for a substantial number of animals and cowries, the earth priests authorized the founders of Kondon to establish their own earth shrine. However, Bevuugang and Kondon were not separated by a *turbogr*, Togbir Somé insisted, because both villages were built on the same original earth-shrine territory and both had established their shrines with Kelendou's authorization. Over the course of time, the inhabitants from Kondon extended their farms into the valley between Kondon and Bevuugang. The Kondon farmers asserted that their earth priest had given them the go-ahead because the land was under the authority of the Kondon earth shrine. The Bevuugang earth priest, for his part, claimed that the land was part of what the Sisala had originally given to his ancestors. When the dispute escalated and the two villages nearly attacked each other with bows and arrows, both sides agreed that a boundary (*turbogr*) had to be set. His grandfather Bevuu, Togbir related, summoned the elders from the two settlements to meet in the contested valley,

> and even told the people to bring their bows and arrows to the meeting in order not to be surprised. They met, facing each other, Bevuu and his people sitting on one side, and the people from Kondon sitting on the other side. Bevuu told them to nominate a person . . . to come and show the *turbogr*, and then he would also send someone to show the *turbogr*. The Kondon people did not dare to come forward, but stayed there, sitting on their side. Bevuu then told Sienpiin, from the Nakyele house in Bevuugang [joking partners of the Kpagnyaane who could help settle conflicts] to come and show them the boundary. Sienpiin showed the Kondon people a place that was very close to their houses [*laughs*], and they had to accept this, this was now the *turbogr*! Sienpiin also showed where the people of Kondon should cultivate, and where our people have their farms. And it is at these places that we still farm.[17]

In the case of Kondon and Bevuugang, boundary making was a collective and public act, condensed in one decisive encounter. In many other cases, however, defining the territorial reach of earth shrines and allodial titles is a drawn-out, piecemeal process that consists of more individualized discussions of the ritual allegiance of particular compounds and farms.

Earth-Shrine Parishes and State-Made Borders

Since colonial times, local notions of farm, village, and earth-shrine boundaries have been increasingly influenced by the new concepts of space, and linear borders, that the introduction of chiefdoms and administrative units implied. In the Black Volta region, the political landscape as well as the spatial delimitation of property rights were also reordered by the new international border between British and French territories. The history of this border offers an instructive example of how local and European notions of boundary making interacted. It shows that the colonial (and postcolonial) state did not have the means to strictly enforce European concepts of lineally bounded sovereign territories but had to adapt to, or at least tolerate, local notions of spiritual territories and the more openly defined border zones this entailed. At the same time, the inhabitants of the border zone readily adopted the new border, and associated notions of linear boundaries (that merged with existing concepts of the *turbogr*) whenever it suited their interests. Such processes of adaptation as well as appropriation are also typical of the ways in which the local population dealt with internal administrative boundaries of districts and provinces.[18]

British and French attempts to expand their spheres of influence in the Black Volta region, in the wake of the Berlin Conference of 1884–85, resulted in a flurry of treaties that the aspiring colonial powers concluded with regional warlords, and kings and subchiefs of the Mossi, Wala, Gonja, and Dagomba states. However, determining the precise boundaries of the territories over which the African signatories of the treaties exercised some sort of control proved to be difficult.[19] The Fanti official and representative of the British crown, G. E. Ferguson, for instance, complained repeatedly that the political boundaries in the region were "unsatisfactory and ill-defined" because they depended on temporary and shifting alliances between local rulers and strongmen.[20] During the early phases of colonial expansion, therefore, European officials were forced to adapt to indigenous concepts of domains of power with shifting borders. At the same time, some European actors also saw advantages in these local concepts and used them to their own ends, namely, in order to expand their spheres of influence.[21]

The various treaties of protection fuelled competition between the British and the French, and in some cases even led to military confrontation. In an attempt to forestall further escalation, the first provisional boundary agreement was concluded in 1897. It defined the border between French and British territory along the Black Volta and along the "boundary of the States of Wa."[22] While the boundary along the river was unambiguous, the latter proved to be one of those "ill-defined" boundaries of which Ferguson had complained. As a result, the Anglo-French Convention of 1898, which laid the basis for today's international border between Ghana and Burkina Faso, maintained the riverine boundary, but fixed the northern border of British territory along an abstract geographical line, namely, the 11th parallel, running east of the Black Volta to Togoland.

In the following years, British and French troops withdrew to their respective sides of the new border. But until the 11th parallel had actually been surveyed, the border functioned as a buffer zone rather than a line, and a number of frontier villages were simply declared "neutral" territory, where neither the French nor the British were to station military forces or collect taxes.[23] Finally, in 1900, a British-French boundary commission worked for eight months on the basic cartography and delimitation of the 300-kilometer-long border along the 11th parallel and informed the local population to which colonial power they now belonged. A second commission in 1904 undertook the actual demarcation on the ground. Interestingly, for lack of more sophisticated infrastructure, the commissioners resorted to local boundary-setting practices, using footpaths and small streams wherever feasible, as well as setting up piles of stones and marking trees.[24]

Although the commission tried to avoid dividing villages in half, the international border did run through many earth-shrine parishes, the boundaries of which, of course, were invisible to European eyes.[25] The commissioners did observe, however,

that villagers used resources in a fairly wide zone around their farmsteads, including fields, pasture, and water on the other side of the border. They decided to allow
these practices to continue, but demanded that "villages"—that is, the built-up space
of settlements—should not extend physically across the border.[26] "Natives who are not
satisfied with the attribution of their village to any of the two powers [French or Brit-
ish]," the boundary agreement of April 1904 stipulated, "will have, during the period
of one year . . . , the possibility to emigrate to the other side of the border. After this
period, the authorities of a village close to the border will under no circumstances be
allowed to exercise their functions across the boundary line . . . and the inhabitants of
these villages will no longer be able to construct houses on the other side of the border."[27] This clause was designed to put an end to continued cross-border mobility, but
in the absence of sufficient personnel, it could hardly be enforced. In 1924–25, a third
boundary commission restored the many boundary markers along the 11th parallel
that had disappeared or been destroyed, and again decreed that compounds unsatis-
fied with their allocation to one or the other colony were free to move to the other
side of the border.[28] Yet attempts to consolidate the border as a dividing line between
sovereign national territories and property regimes never amounted to more than the
elaboration of a detailed census of the monetary value of the resources that "natives" of
the French colony used on British territory and vice versa. It is likely, however, that the
census exercise made the local population aware of potential future problems involved
in the extension of earth-shrine parishes across the border, and some Sisala landowners responded by giving this land to Dagara settlers—a development that I discuss in
the next chapter.

Legally, allodial ownership of lands in Northern Ghana and in the adjacent
regions of the French colony was vested in the colonial and, later, in the independent
governments that held the land in trust for the local population. In the eyes of government officials, land ownership obviously had to end at the borders of the respective
colonial territories. Even when the 1979 Ghanaian constitution eventually returned
all Northern lands to their original owners, this was not meant to officially sanction
revival of allodial titles extending across the border. Non-nationals remained excluded
from rights over land, no matter what their traditional entitlements may have been.[29]
However, with the exception of the years during the Second World War, the colonial
and postcolonial governments did not succeed in controlling movement or resource
use across the border. The first demarcation exercise after independence, in 1973, corrected the course of the border in several places and erected concrete pillars, at about
one-kilometer intervals. For a few years, Ghanaian border guards patrolled the area
more actively to suppress drug trafficking and other kinds of smuggling, and many
of my interlocutors spoke of this period as "the time when the border came." On the
whole, however, controls were and continue to be restricted to traffic at the border post
in Hamile, while the continued use of land, pasture, and water across the border rarely
attracts the attention of government authorities.

Because the state was unable to enforce the new border in a top-down fashion, much depended on how the borderlanders dealt with it from below. How did they perceive the border? During the first few decades following the demarcation by the colonial powers, it was probably not seen as a continuous line separating two sovereign territories but interpreted in terms of familiar local concepts of a buffer and contact zone between two different networks of power. From the very beginning, however, the borderlanders knew quite well to which of the two colonial powers they were subject, and quickly learned to use the border as a political resource, to avoid criminal prosecution, colonial taxation, and forced labor requirements. From the mid-1920s, if not earlier, the borderlanders also had relatively clear ideas of the linear course of the boundary. The British district commissioner who was responsible for the maintenance of the boundary markers along the 11th parallel between the Black Volta and Bourra remarked that although the meandering footpath connecting the markers did not neatly correspond to the official boundary, it was regarded as such by the "natives."[30]

The local appropriation of the border, however, remained selective. Although relevant to political questions, the border was largely ignored in land matters and ritual affairs. Although the border along the 11th parallel often cut through earth-shrine areas, the earth priests continued to exercise their rights and duties across the border, including the allocation of land to new immigrants. Until very recently, agricultural land was not regarded as "national" territory, and access to land was mediated not by citizenship in a nation-state, but by membership in a local community, as defined by kin relations and relations between first-comers and late-comers.[31]

The only early exception to this pattern involved the border-post village of Hamile, where the colonial authorities attempted to close the border when France and Britain became enemies during the Second World War. The paramount chief responsible for "British" Hamile felt that it was detrimental to the British cause for the residents of Hamile to continue to pay allegiance to the Sisala earth priest of Hamile, who was a French "native." The chief suggested that ritual allegiance be transferred to a related earth-priestly family in Happa, a neighboring Sisala village on British territory. Here, then, for the first time, the ritual earth-shrine territories were redefined according to criteria of national sovereignty, although the precise meaning of this transfer of ritual authority was contested.[32] Similar transfers of ritual authority took place after the last redemarcation exercise of 1973. The earth priests of Hiela in Burkina Faso, for example, delegated their right to ritually mark burial sites to their Sisala relatives in Bangwon, on the Ghanaian side of the border. While the Hiela earth priests insisted that their relatives in Bangwon send them part of the gifts that they received from settlers on formerly Hiela lands, Bangwon claimed that Hiela had actually transferred its allodial rights, including its rights to gifts. No matter how controversial, the basis of such transfers always lies in kinship and ethnic relationships between the givers and the receivers of ritual authority and property rights. This was also the case in Kyetuu, where ritual authority over land in Ghana was transferred only recently in the context of a long-standing land conflict and hardening ethnic boundaries, which I discuss in the next chapter.

More generally, in the last few decades the local population has increasingly come to understand the international boundary as a continuous dividing line, separating two contiguous territories. In turn, this new understanding seems to have transformed local perceptions of village and earth-shrine territories. In many villages in the region, the boundaries of earth-shrine areas are hardening, in contrast to the traditionally more subtle shading and interlocking of frontiers and qualitative notions of territoriality.[33] The strategic use of the international border in some land conflicts is only one of the factors underlying these developments; growing population densities and the decreasing availability of farmland are just as important. In any case, it is important to understand that the new perspective on boundaries is not a quasi-automatic modernization of older understandings of space, but the result of intense conflicts, often with strong ethnic overtones.

Shifting Allegiances, Redefining Boundaries

Varpuo is a large Dagara village in Burkina Faso, some ten kilometers north of Niégo. Although founded rather late, toward the end of the 1920s, it counted 1,250 inhabitants in 1996, and since the early 1980s it has had the status of an administrative entity, entitled to send its own representative, the *responsable administratif de village* (RAV), to all meetings of the district administration in Niégo. After my first visits to Varpuo, I was puzzled. The RAV explained to me that Varpuo did not have its own earth shrine, but took all land-related matters to the earth priest of Dadoune, who regarded Varpuo as part of the territory under his authority. Varpuo's founding families originally came from Dadoune, and even belonged to the same patriclan as the Dadoune earth priest, and therefore the allegiance seemed to be natural. From other informants, however, I soon learned that not all of Varpuo "followed" the Dadoune earth priest, but that some sections lived and farmed on land that the Nuni of Danfi claimed to own, and paid allegiance to the Danfi earth priest. Still others took their land matters to the Nuni earth priest of Bon, who also claimed to hold the allodial title to some of Varpuo's territory.[34]

My first interpretation was that despite the fact that Varpuo was socially and politically a single village, it was founded on lands belonging to three different earth-shrine parishes, namely Dadoune, Danfi, and Bon, and therefore the different sections of Varpuo took their land-related matters to three different earth priests. However, when I attempted to identify which part of the village exactly belonged to which *tengan,* I discovered that matters were more complicated. The ritual allegiance—and recognition of the allodial title—depended not only on the current location of the respective houses (and their farms), but also on the history of their movements to and within Varpuo. While it is not possible here to trace all of these individual histories or to discuss their social and spatial implications in detail, exploring the trajectory of one

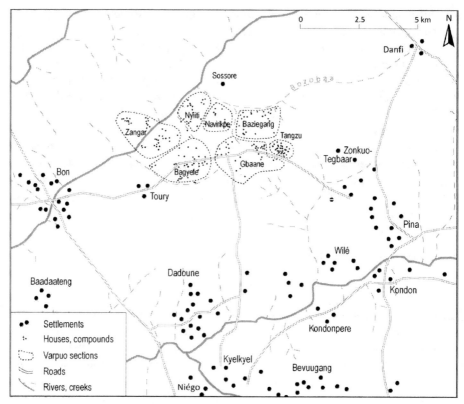

Map 3.1. Varpuo and neighboring settlements

family that remained loyal to the Danfi earth priest while its neighbors in Varpuo followed Dadoune can illustrate the issues at stake.

The case of Varpuo and this family offers an instructive example of boundary making as a contested process. Particularly when people begin to establish farms in formerly "open" border zones between earth-shrine areas, the expectations of neighboring holders of allodial titles that something is to be gained (or that they stand to lose something) rise, and they tend to assert their property rights more insistently. The example of Varpuo also shows that the drawing of boundaries between earth-shrine areas is difficult and fraught with conflict because of the tension between typical strategies of mobility and multilocality, and the (spatial) definition of property rights to an immobile resource, namely land.

In Search of Fertile Land: Somda Lokpag's Story

When I interviewed Somda Lokpag, the elder of a large family in Varpuo who belongs to the Meto-Man patriclan, he related that his ancestor Sansara was the first Dagara from Dadoune to venture into the thick bush in the environs of what later became Varpuo. Sansara was a courageous hunter and primarily attracted by the abundant wildlife in the area. However, during his hunting expeditions he also discovered that the land was excellent for farming, and that there was plenty of water. Toward the early 1920s, Sansara and his brothers therefore decided to establish themselves more permanently on this frontier, in the virgin bush northeast of Dadoune (see map 3.1). They learned that the Nuni earth priest of Danfi claimed to be the owner of this area and accordingly asked him for permission to build a house. They called their new settlement Zonkuo-Tegbaar, literally, "millet water—stretch out your legs," in reference to the abundant harvests that they were able to obtain.

Sansara's principal motive in moving to Zonkuo-Tegbaar was land. Dadoune, his original village, had been established toward the late nineteenth century by Dagara immigrants from across the Black Volta and eventually became "crowded," as Somda Lokpag explained. Furthermore, his ancestor's access to Dadoune's diminishing land reserves was limited because he belonged to the Meto-Man patriclan, not the Meto-Kaziile, who were the first-comers of Dadoune, furnished the earth priests, and set the best lands aside for themselves.[35] Finally, moving far into the bush helped Sansara to evade the onerous tax and *corvée* labor obligations exacted by the French colonial regime.

Sansara and his people were not the only ones in Dadoune to seek additional land, but they were the first to move away entirely. Others initially established only bush farms, with temporary sheds, returning to live in Dadoune during the dry season. Dadoune's houses are situated just north of the Kabarvaro, a Black Volta confluent that marks the village's boundary with Bevuugang. Bush farms could therefore be established only by pushing the agricultural frontier northward and northeastward, toward the next Volta tributary. As the distances between the bush farms and homes in Dadoune increased, some families eventually found it too cumbersome to always return to the village and thus decided to replace the farm sheds with regular adobe houses. And this is how the settlement of Varpuo—appropriately named "in the bush" or "in the leaves"—came into being.

Initially, the new settlers faced fierce resistance from the authoritarian Dagara *chef de canton* Denyuu, who feared that the migrants wanted to escape his control by hiding in the bush. Denyuu even sent his native policemen to tear down the first houses that the Varpuo pioneers had built. Effectively, many families from Dadoune had sent one or two men to establish themselves in Varpuo in order to cultivate the land and feed the extended family because in Dadoune, under the closer scrutiny of Denyuu, all able-bodied men were relentlessly recruited for *corvée* labor or military duty. However, the chief of Dadoune, whose own relatives were also among the villagers building houses in Varpuo, eventually managed to convince Denyuu that he was in full control of the movement and would ensure that the frontiersmen continued to pay allegiance to the paramount chief as well as honor their obligations concerning taxes and *corvée* labor.

A Contested Transfer of Property Rights:
How Dadoune Acquired Land from Danfi

When I wanted to know more about relations between Dadoune, Danfi, and Varpuo, Somé Gérard, Dadoune's chief and earth priest of the Meto-Kaziile patriclan, explained that his ancestors established Dadoune on land that originally belonged to the Nuni of Danfi. As in many other cases on the Dagara frontier, the immigrants first lived peacefully side by side with the Nuni as well as some Phuo established in the area, but, as soon as they became more numerous, encroached on their neighbors' land, which eventually led to violent conflicts. The very name Dadoune—which, according to my Dagara informants, means "buying" or "invoking hostility"—was chosen in commemoration of these conflicts. In order to put an end to the confrontations, the Dagara newcomers finally "bought" the land (*tengan*) from the Danfi earth priests in exchange for a substantial sum of cowries, a cow, and some rams and fowl. The Meto-Kaziile became the earth priests and, according to Somé Gérard, were allowed to handle all land-related affairs. They thus established a member of their family as "deputy" earth priest in Varpuo, and only very severe matters, such as suicide, still had to be taken to the Danfi earth priest.[36]

My Dagara informants in Dadoune and Varpuo did not quite agree on how relations between Danfi and Dadoune further developed, but they did concur that the Nuni had failed to clearly delineate the boundaries of their original land grant. This is why, when Dadoune became "crowded," the Dagara did not ask the Nuni for permission to establish their bush farms on the land that later developed into the new settlement of Varpuo. When the Nuni eventually noticed how far into the bush—which they perceived to be Danfi territory—the Dadoune-Varpuo settlers were pushing their farms, they felt "exploited," even "cheated." They demanded additional payments before they would allow the Dadoune earth priest to extend the area under his ritual authority to include Varpuo.

According to another version, the Dadoune *tengandem* had actually paid only a first installment when they acquired their land from Danfi. Now, as Varpuo had grown, the Nuni demanded the second part of the payment. Still others asserted that it was not the Nuni earth priests, but rather the Dagara paramount chief, Denyuu, who insisted on this second payment because he wanted to make sure that Varpuo was on territory fully owned by the Dagara, and therefore under his political command.[37] In any case, probably during the late 1930s or early 1940s, Dadoune did make a second payment to Danfi—consisting, according to some informants, of 100,000 cowries, plus a cow and other animals. The Varpuo lands were thus annexed to the area under the control of the Dadoune earth shrine.[38] Apparently, however, once again the transfer did not entail the drawing of an exact linear boundary between the two territories.

Joining the New Village, Honoring Old Obligations: Somda Lokpag's Story Continued

Meanwhile Sansara and his family grew weary of the challenges of living rather iso-lated in Zonkuo-Tegbaar, "in the bush," and decided to join their relatives and old friends from Dadoune who were moving into Varpuo. Sansara built a new house in that section of Varpuo that stretches toward Zonkuo-Tegbaar. This allowed the family to continue to cultivate their farms at Tegbaar while enjoying the sociability of living much closer than before to the other houses of Varpuo. Sansara's move to Varpuo must have occurred around the time, or even before, the land was officially transferred to the Dadoune earth priest by its former Nuni owners.

In any case, as Somda Lokpag explained, Sansara felt that the Danfi earth priests' original authorization to settle in Zonkuo-Tegbaar included the permission to relocate to Varpuo, also on Danfi territory, and that there was no need to consult with the Dadoune earth priest. When the Varpuo representative of the Dadoune earth priest came to his house to collect the customary gift of millet for the Dadoune *tengan*, San-sara refused to honor this demand. He insisted that he was "following" Danfi since it had been the Nuni of Danfi who had once given him the permission to settle in the area. One of the reasons behind Sansara's refusal to submit once again to the authority of Dadoune was, of course, the long-standing tensions between the Meto-Man and the Meto-Kaziile. When the Dadoune *tengandem* complained to the Danfi earth priests about Sansara's stubbornness, the latter explained that they had not forced Sansara and his people to continue paying their allegiance to Danfi, but that obviously they would not send them away if their loyal clients continued to come. There was little the Dadoune earth priest could do to oblige Sansara to recognize his authority, and thus Sansara's house and fields remained, and still remain, an island of Danfi property and ritual authority within Dadoune-Varpuo territory.

Another family in Varpuo that currently pays allegiance to, and recognizes an allodial title of, the Danfi earth priest had even originally received permission from the Dadoune earth priest to build its house. Later, however, they quarreled over his ritual services during a funeral that had been too slow in the eyes of his Varpuo clients. The Dadoune earth priest had insisted that the family must pay a past debt before he could give the go-ahead for the burial, but the family refused to pay and started mourning the corpse without him. In order to publicly express his disapproval of the family's com-portment, the earth priest threw shea-tree leaves into the open grave—an open threat to the family's well-being that could be removed only by substantial "debt" payments. Instead of appealing to the Dadoune earth priest, however, the mourners turned to the Danfi earth priest for spiritual protection (which the latter readily offered), and since then have "followed" Danfi.

Similar explanations were forwarded in other cases where Varpuo houses do not belong to the Dadoune *tengan*, but to Danfi or Bon. The Nuni earth priests of Danfi and Bon were not averse to receiving the dissatisfied Dagara clients. Sometimes they also actively helped things along by claiming, for instance, that the field that someone from Varpuo was cultivating, or the plot where he had built a house, was not part of Danfi's land grant to Dadoune but actually on Danfi (or Bon) earth-shrine territory. As a result, Varpuo is not a neatly bounded territorial unit under a single allodial title, namely, that of Dadoune, but rather an ensemble of houses and bush farms with some well-established and some highly contested boundaries, and a few scattered, island-like patches of land under different ritual jurisdictions and allodial titles.

Setting Boundaries in a Context of Mobility: Lessons from the Case of Varpuo

The case of Varpuo, with its complex patchwork of rights and claims, is an extreme case. But it clearly illustrates the potential for (re)interpretation and conflict that local practices of boundary making entail, and, more generally, the difficulties in delineating the boundaries of an immobile resource such as land in a context of mobility and multilocality. When moving from one location to another, or when accommodating immigrants, local actors basically have two options to define the spatial boundaries of allodial property. The first is to regard the boundaries of the relevant allodial title as dependent on the question of from whom one has received the land and spiritual services (the two do not always coincide). Or, from the perspective of the land givers, the borders of allodial property rights are to be defined along the land grants and spiritual services that the earth priests have accorded over time. Property spaces are thus defined flexibly, and boundaries can extend or shift, so to speak, in line with people's movements (or the expansion of their farms), as long as they stay loyal to the original service provider. This is much in line with Paul Bohannan's observation that the "folk geography" of the Tiv in Nigeria was premised not on a Western grid-type map, but on a flexible map of social relations that grew along with agricultural expansion.[39] However, I would disagree with Bohannan that this mental map prevented the evolution of property concepts. As the case above shows, local actors most certainly did adjust their definitions of rights to land to confront the challenges presented in a context of mobility, and I argue that these local understandings are indeed notions of property, in a broad sense.[40] Further, because the history of land transfers (and of spiritual services) between first-comers and late-comers in the Black Volta region is usually drawn-out and complicated, landowners and immigrants alike tend to invoke different time horizons in order to legitimate their respective claims. The price to be paid for the flexibility of this type of boundary-making is continued ambiguity, and often long-standing conflict, because the boundaries must continually be negotiated anew.

The second option is recourse to comprehensive public boundary-making ceremonies, like those that I described for Tantuo, Ko, and Kondon. Although these ceremonies may have originally defined not border lines, but only points and landmarks, the latter have, in the past decades, increasingly come to be interpreted as indicators of linear boundaries. Particularly where land reserves are shrinking and "virgin" bush has virtually disappeared, people are increasingly unwilling to tolerate pockets of "foreign" property rights, such as those of the Danfi earth priest and Sansara's family in Varpuo. Furthermore, when Dagara farmers in search of fertile land approach Sisala (and Nuni) landowners, the latter nowadays tend to clearly indicate at all four sides the extension of the farm that they allocate, thereby setting linear boundaries, instead of just "showing" the direction into which the Dagara should farm.[41]

In the case of Varpuo, however, matters were particularly intricate because there was a communal transfer of land (and ritual) rights, but not, at least according to most informants, a ritual showing of the new boundary. Furthermore, while the transfer of the allodial title should have reorganized the service relations for all members of the recipient community, shifting their allegiance to the Dadoune earth priest, not all villagers were willing to honor the latter. Sansara's family, for instance, was not willing to sever its former ties to Danfi; others were dissatisfied with the Dadoune earth priest's comportment and approached the former owners of their land, namely the earth priests of Danfi and Bon, for spiritual support. Since the latter, in their own view, had never really given up all ancestral connections to the land in question, they agreed to render these services. All these developments undermined, and continue to undermine the (re)definition of clear-cut boundaries to demarcate the allodial title.

Landed Property as a Bundle of Rights

Since the late 1940s, colonial administrators had begun to develop an increasingly nuanced understanding of African land tenure that acknowledged the complicated nature of land boundaries as well as the complex web of interlocking communal, family, and individual rights to land.[42] The Assistant Commissioner of Lands R. J. H. Pogucki, for instance, wrote a comprehensive report on "land tenure in native customary law" on the basis of more than six months of intensive inquiries in various areas of the Northern Territories of the Gold Coast, including the Black Volta region.[43] Roughly a decade later, in the context of government plans for a land tenure reform, his French colleague J.-L. Boutillier presented an equally detailed description of land rights in Upper Volta based on existing materials as well as fresh research.[44] These two studies carefully outlined that indigenous entitlements to land and other natural resources were multilayered and sometimes overlapping. Pogucki emphasized that it was important to differentiate between rights to the land used for building versus rights to the buildings themselves; rights to trees versus rights to water, pasture, and hunting grounds. And he distinguished between allodial rights in land, usually vested in the earth priests (or, in some parts of the Northern Territories, in chiefs); permanent, heritable farming rights held by families who were full members of a community; and temporary farming rights assigned to individuals and "strangers." In a similar vein, Boutillier summarized his findings as a hierarchy of rights, ranging from the most comprehensive property rights, namely, those derived from allodial title (*droit éminent*), and rights stemming from more or less permanent possession (*appropriation*) accorded qua first-comer status, conquest, long occupation, or some form of transfer, to rights of usufruct (*droit de culture*).[45] Both authors discussed in detail how these various rights were acquired and transmitted. And they suggested that the scope of the earth priests' rights vis-à-vis those of "ordinary" landholding families was diminishing as a result of increasing population density and shrinking land reserves.

These studies certainly represented a departure from the early colonial administrators' rather simplistic conception of African land tenure. But even Pogucki, Boutillier, and other administrators, geographers, and anthropologists of their time continued to think of traditional land tenure in terms of a coherent, homogeneous, and more or less stable system of rules and beliefs. Legal pluralism (a term not yet in use at the time) was not intrinsic to indigenous systems of tenure, these authors believed, but a consequence of the incorporation of traditional African societies into modern market economies and the colonial political order. That Africans could have debated, and held opposing views, about property rights even before the advent of colonial rule, did not enter the minds of these colonial officers and early scholars.

Even today, the dominant understanding of indigenous tenure systems among administrators and politicians as well as some researchers is still more or less colored by evolutionist and technocratic paradigms that conceive of legal systems as homogeneous, internally logical corpuses of rules.[46] However, past and current land conflicts provide abundant evidence that the composition of the "bundle of rights" and of the "bundle of owners," to use Geisler and Daneker's terms,[47] always was, and continues to be, contested and negotiable. Even if rights appear to have been defined consensually for a long time—and found their way into anthropological descriptions of "tenure systems"—we often find that, in the context of new legal stipulations or shifts in power relations, they are reinterpreted and renegotiated.[48]

Tying and Untying the Bundle of Rights, Negotiating the Bundle of Owners

In African agricultural societies, Shipton and Goheen argue, "unevenly distributed rights in land are adjusted by an infinity of arrangements, often *ad hoc* and sometimes unnamed, for seasonal or longer-term transfers that may include land loans, entrustments, or share contracts."[49] These arrangements often give rise to competing interpretations, particularly in the following generation. The heirs of right receivers may invoke a labor theory of property in order to strengthen their claims to a particular piece of land that they, or their fathers, have worked; while the heirs of the right givers may argue that village and lineage lands are indivisible and that individual use rights cannot be inherited. Who has the authority to transfer rights and over which parts of a given property? Who are the legitimate recipients of transferred rights? What is the nature of the rights transferred? And what is the temporal dimension of the transfer? All these questions must be settled. They become particularly acute when land transfers to "strangers" are on the increase.[50]

Among the Dagara and their neighbors, the earth priests claim to hold the allodial right—that is, the ultimate, superior title—to all natural resources, including farmland, water, wild animals, uncultivated bush, and wild fruit-bearing trees, gold, and other minerals as well as lost objects and stray cattle. They assign more or less comprehensive and long-term usufruct (and de facto property) rights to covillagers that may include the right to concede derived usufruct rights to third parties. This broadest outline of hierarchically layered land rights represents the minimal consensus among the local population; all further details were, and continue to be, contested and negotiable.

Debates on the extent of property rights, for instance, that the earth priests retain after having assigned land to the local "native families" were already recorded in the early 1920s when Lawra-Tumu District Commissioner Michael Dasent collected information for a questionnaire on land tenure that was to be used in preparing a new "Native Lands Ordinance." Dasent asserted that the earth priest "is all powerful" and remained the ultimate owner of all lands, but he also stated that the land was now the full "property" of the beneficiaries of the earth priests' land allocations.[51] These and further contradictory statements must have reflected local disputes, and it is likely that competing interpretations of property transfers and use rights are as old as the expanding agricultural frontier itself. They certainly continue today, with an ever-expanding argumentative arsenal now derived not only from local theories of legitimate ownership, but also from national land legislation and various informal written titles.

Disputes often concern the question of who belongs to the group of right holders. For example, it may be unclear as to who precisely is to be included in the earth priests' group, and who is entitled to take certain decisions on behalf of this group, decisions such as those pertaining to land transfers or ritual authorizations for immigrants. Is it only the ritually installed earth priest himself that may do so, or the entire patrilineage, or even all local members of his patriclan? What are the powers of the *suosob* (among the Dagara, the holder of the sacrificial knife), particularly if he does not belong to the same patriclan as the *tengansob*? Furthermore, it is a matter of debate as to who among a group of "owners" can claim a share in the proceeds from a given transfer of land rights. Similar questions may arise among those who were granted rights by the earth-priestly group. Land transactions were, and still are, usually sanctioned by the exchange of gifts and the performance of a sacrifice. But whom exactly do the participants in such rituals represent—only their immediate families, the extended patrilineage, or the entire patriclan? Are newly arriving sections of the same patriclan obliged to negotiate anew land grants and ritual authorization with the earth priests, or are they covered by the existing agreements of their clan mates? Such questions can become particularly contested when right givers and right recipients belong to different ethnic groups.

Such disputes often merge with controversies regarding the scope of rights that may vary depending on the resource in question. Are rights to nonagricultural resources, such as collecting firewood and fruits from wild trees, hunting, or fishing, tacitly included in the land transfers, or do they need to be negotiated separately and explicitly? And are they granted to the entire ethnic community or only to specific pioneering families? In many Dagara settlements on Sisala land, for instance, the Sisala landowners will allow the Dagara immigrants to grow annual crops on their allocated fields, but reserve for themselves the right to harvest whatever trees there are, and prohibit any cutting or planting of trees by the immigrants. Furthermore, earth priests usually claim that they retain certain rights over bodies of water, such as the right to initiate communal fishing campaigns and to perform sacrifices to the water spirits, even if they have granted to immigrants perennial rights to farm and build on the land around the water. Similarly, earth priests often assert that they have the right to allow itinerant herdsmen to drive their cattle not only through uninhabited bush, but also through fields cultivated by immigrants—an adamant demonstration of their claims to allodial title that easily provokes disputes if the cattle cause any damage.[52] Further cause for conflict is connected with the necessity of obtaining the earth priest's authorization concerning all rites associated with "blood," such as funerals or the burying of the placenta after the birth of children, and rites associated with the construction of a house and ancestral as well as field shrines. Even in an urban setting, where construction lots have been surveyed and registered, the earth priest formerly responsible for the land may still assert his responsibility for cleansing the earth after a suicide.

Competing interpretations also arise concerning the duration of transferred rights. People generally agree that the original earth-priestly land grant to a village's founding families is inherited by their descendants, who do not have to refer back to the earth-priestly family. However, there is disagreement on the question of whether the heirs of immigrants and ethnic strangers have to renegotiate their forefathers' land grants with the earth priest. Furthermore, what happens to farmland if an entire patrilineage died out or left the village? This question arose repeatedly in the former French colony, where flight to neighboring British territory was extremely common. Can the offspring of such families later return and claim their ancestors' land quasi-automatically, insofar as it has not been occupied by other villagers, or do they have to consult the earth priest, who will treat them like newcomers?

The list of potentially controversial issues could easily be expanded. Suffice it to emphasize here that first-comers and holders of the allodial title often disagree with late-comers about whether the latter's rights to resources and ritual authorization have been given as a kind of all-inclusive package, or whether these rights to resources have to be negotiated and paid for separately. Rights recipients often attempt to tacitly extend the rights that they have been granted initially, and sometimes try to redefine ritual rights that they were accorded into rights over economic resources, or vice versa. Ultimately, the relations of power, at the local as well as the wider regional and national levels, determine which interpretation of the composition of the bundle of rights and the bundle of owners carries the day. Demographic clout, the larger political context, but also questions of ritual power play a role here. The younger generation of Dagara

Christians, for instance, is sometimes less hesitant than their traditionalist forefathers to occupy Sisala resources since they are less fearful of supernatural sanctions. The cases of Bayagra, Buonbaa, and Laponé that I discuss in the last section of this chapter offer instructive examples of these developments.

Defining Property Rights in the Context of Monetization

Ambiguities and contested interpretations of how to define the bundle of rights and delineate the bundle of owners have characterized land transactions (both commercial and noncommercial) within extended families and patrilineages as well as between patriclans, frontiersmen, and late-comers, or earth priests and settlers since the very beginning of the frontier process. However, they are thrown into particularly sharp relief when such transactions become important sources of income because land reserves become more scarce or land becomes more valuable due to urbanization or the introduction of new cash crops. Although on the whole there seems to be no clear-cut trend toward an increasing monetization of land ownership in the Black Volta region, past decades have certainly seen changes in local understandings of property rights and practices of land transactions. In order to understand these changes, it is necessary, as Sara Berry suggests, to distinguish between the individualization of property rights, the commercialization (and monetization) of land transfers, and the formalization of land transactions by recourse to titles, *petits papiers* (small papers), or legal proceedings.[53] These three processes may, but need not always, occur jointly. On the contrary, the more frequently that quasi- or outright commercial land transactions with "outsiders" occur, the more often chiefs or earth priests activate dormant allodial rights to challenge the right of individual families to transfer land to third parties without referring to their "superior" authority.[54]

With respect to the individualization of land rights in Dagara and Sisala villages, my evidence suggests that for quite some time specific fields or building plots have indeed been clearly assigned to smaller lineage segments, or even individuals, and that such long-standing use rights have been considered to be heritable. However, this practice of granting rights to smaller bundles of owners is much less pronounced when it comes to the right to alienate these individualized holdings to outsiders. In this context, the land is still regarded as an integral part of the larger family territory, and individuals who transfer land without consulting the lineage heads or holders of the allodial title are often forcefully reprimanded, or even threatened with spiritual sanctions.[55]

The picture is similarly complex regarding the commoditization of land, that is, the exchange of rights to land for money. Land rights may be monetized even within families and lineages, where well-connected and well-endowed commercial farmers consolidate their holdings by buying land from poorer relatives. These internal transactions are usually less visible (and thus often less vulnerable to moral criticism) than exchanges with outsiders, and are often legitimized with reference to kinship solidarity. Transactions between landowners and land-seeking immigrants, too, have certainly become increasingly monetized in recent decades.[56] However, although the sums to be paid by those who receive land may be quite specific and substantial, the actual rights exchanged are often less precisely defined. The content of the contract may initially be self-evident to both parties, but as soon as the circumstances change—for instance, if the land receiver decides to use the plot for a purpose different from what was at first expected—it must often be renegotiated. Furthermore, even commercial land transfers are usually firmly embedded in social relations such as friendship or patron-client relations.

State-led attempts to standardize and formalize land transfers, through titling programs and the like, have generally not been successfully implemented. State land administrations are usually too distant, slow, and cumbersome, and the transaction costs of registration prohibitive. At the same time, attempts to translate the complex bundles of owners and bundles of rights to pieces of land that are often circumscribed by rather vague boundaries into clear-cut written titles are difficult and fraught with conflict. Furthermore, corruption and political networking often undermine the formal rules of land transactions, rendering state formalization rather "informal."[57] By contrast, complex means of "informal formalization"[58] have become increasingly popular, including contracts between individuals simply scribbled on sheets of notebook paper; contracts validated by the signature of a customary or administrative authority (in Burkina Faso: *certificats de palabre*, signed by the earth priest and the district head, alongside the buyer and seller of the land); or certificates of land allocation issued by the chief and the Town and Country Planning Authority or the Lands Commission (in Ghana).[59]

However, these informal forms of formalization rarely specify the nature of the rights transferred (the word "sale" is often not even mentioned) and, far from putting an end to debate, rather open a new arena of contestation.[60] In an oral context, land transfers are usually marked by ritual offerings made in the presence of the land giver, the land receiver and, in most cases, the holder of the allodial title, who would invoke the wrath of the earth deity against any wrongdoers. All of these rituals and landmarks are, as we have seen, polysemic and have to be elucidated by narratives, which may exist in competing variations and which, in the event of conflict, can be validated by invoking more than one authority. In principle, these ambiguities carry over into written procedures, be they state-backed or informal, so that these newer practices simply increase the number of validating authorities to which disputing parties may appeal.[61] In any case, taking conflicts over land transfers to court or to the district administration forces defendants and plaintiffs to translate their concepts of ownership of and interests in land into European terms (for example, allodial title, freehold, leasehold, etc.). To a certain extent, court procedure standardizes claims and legitimating arguments. Still, this standardization of customary tenure in the courtroom (or at the district head's office) does not put an end to debate; on the contrary, courts have become a convenient way of registering and, if initially unsuccessful, parking one's claims until sometime in the future when conditions for reopening the case look more promising.

On the whole, much of my evidence points to sustained efforts on the part of "autochthones" as well as immigrants to constrain the outright commercialization of land. Part of these efforts is the invocation of the spiritual dangers of selling land, considered detrimental to its fertility and to the community. If this belief is widely enough shared, it can be quite powerful. Similarly important is the introduction of subtle differences in land transfers depending on the use to which the land will be put. Most Dagara and Sisala are convinced that land may not be refused to a well-intentioned stranger who needs it to survive, but that sufficient land must be reserved for the following generation of one's family. Persons intending to cultivate the land, or plant trees, in order to earn money, fall into a different category. These considerations are complemented by debates over to what ends and by whom money from land transactions may be used.

Nevertheless, the inhabitants of the Black Volta region are certainly aware that in other parts of Burkina Faso and Ghana land transactions are increasingly commercialized: they have observed this as labor migrants, settler farmers in zones of intensive cash-cropping, or local villagers' educated relatives have alerted them to the opportunities, but also to the problems and dangers inherent in the sale of land rights. Furthermore, new state-led attempts at tenure reform, such as the *gestion des terroirs*, the registration of customary titles, or community-based natural resource management schemes have been followed attentively and have also impacted how people in the Black Volta region think about land transactions. In any case, awareness has spread of the necessity of arming oneself with powerful arguments, and of being able to bolster these with written local histories or similar documents. At the same time, as land has become scarcer and/or financially valuable, the rising stakes of any specific interpretation of what constitutes the bundle of rights that are being transferred have intensified local debates.

(Re)Negotiating the Bundle of Rights in Changing Configurations of Power

With few exceptions, since the early years of colonial rule Sisala (and Nuni) earth priests have ceased to give earth-shrine stones to immigrant Dagara settlers. In some cases, however, they continued to transfer full property rights over the land (at least so the Dagara claim) and authorized the newcomers to carry out the essential rituals themselves. The latter then usually incorporated the newly acquired territory into existing Dagara earth-shrine areas.[62] From about the 1940s onward, however, transfers of allodial titles, regardless of whether accompanied by the gift of an earth-shrine stone or not, ceased altogether. Sisala (and Nuni) landowners have merely granted more or less comprehensive use rights, and in recent decades have attempted to restrict the bundle of rights that they transferred.

The extent of the transferred rights was usually indicated by the nature of the gifts that the Sisala (and Nuni) demanded in exchange. Receiving the allodial title to land and full ritual rights, including the authority to ritually open houses, bury the dead, and propitiate the earth after bloodshed or a suicide, required the gift of one or more cows plus a substantial number of cowries—a ritual exchange that often invoked the rhetoric of a metaphorical "marriage" payment, as discussed in chapter 2. By contrast, the transfer of less comprehensive farming rights, be they temporary or even semi-permanent, was, and continues to be, devoid of such metaphors and is accompanied by offerings of smaller animals and/or fowl for sacrifices. In recent times, the number of animals and the amount of money that the Sisala (and Nuni) have demanded for such transactions have increased considerably, but the payment never includes cows, thus distinguishing these latter transactions clearly from the former more comprehensive transfers.

That more recent transfers never involve the allodial title is ultimately accepted by all parties, although the younger generation of Dagara "settlers" that was born on Sisala land strongly resents the implications of this "settled fact."[63] Both Sisala and Dagara, however, often reinterpret past transactions in order to widen the scope of their rights. They narrate stories that diminish (or, alternatively, aggrandize) the number of gifts their ancestors received, or even deny that any such exchange ever took place, thereby redefining the scope and precise content of the bundle of rights that has been transferred. Such reinterpretations typically occur at certain critical moments of "institutional uncertainty," to use Christian Lund's expression.[64] Moments such as the installation of a new earth priest,[65] the transfer of a deceased settler's farming rights to his heirs, or the arrival of a group of new immigrants offer opportunities to redefine past transactions and establish new conditions. Furthermore, changing local or regional power configurations, modifications in the national land legislation, the redrawing of district boundaries, or other wider political developments can also open spaces for the renegotiation of the bundle of rights.

The three examples that follow show how local actors reinterpret past land transactions and renegotiate their respective rights in situations of political change, availing themselves of new configurations of power. The related cases of the Dagara settlements of Bayagra and Buonbaa (in Burkina Faso) mainly concern developments during the colonial period that have important repercussions in disputes about the allodial title after the end of colonial rule. The case of Laponé, on the other hand, looks at the (re) negotiation of land rights in recent decades. It shows how Sisala landowners attempt to reduce the bundle of rights that they assign to newly arriving "settlers" and, whenever an opportunity presents itself, to renegotiate the more generous land grants they made to earlier immigrants.

Establishing and Abandoning an Allodial Title: Mwiensang's Story of Bayagra

Mwiensang Somda Kondon was a self-assured, outspoken man in his fifties, a well-known diviner and healer as well as, according to rumors among his neighbors, a

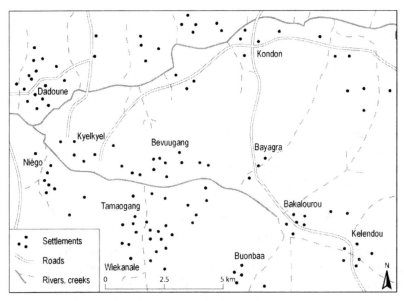

Map 3.2. Bayagra, Buonbaa, and neighboring settlements

fearsome sorcerer. When I conducted a group interview in Buonbaa, a Dagara village under the authority of the Sisala earth priest of Kelendou, Mwiensang was present and eager to put his version of Buonbaa's history on record as well. It soon became obvious, however, that his relations with the Buonbaa elders were strained, and because they did not allow him to speak out, Mwiensang later came up to me and offered to tell me the "truth" about Buonbaa's history if I could afford a visit to his house in Bayagra. Even from our short exchange it was clear that Mwiensang would have an interesting story to tell, and, some ten days later, I sat in his courtyard, next to the impressive mud figures at which he would offer sacrifices to the river and various bush spirits on behalf of his clients.

Mwiensang related how his grandfather Kaa, a powerful hunter and farmer who had moved around quite a bit, eventually settled in Gaaper, on the eastern frontier of the area under the authority of the Niégo earth shrine.[66] Still restless and looking for more fertile land, Kaa continued to explore the bush farther eastward, and finally decided to establish himself near the Bayagra River. The Niégo earth priest had granted him permission to put up a house, but one day Kaa found that the walls of the new building had been torn down overnight. He discovered that the perpetrators were the Sisala of Kelendou, who claimed to be the owners of the land where Kaa was building. Kaa threatened to kill them, but they pleaded for mercy and offered friendship. They would transfer the land, and all associated ritual rights, to Kaa if he paid a cow, several goats, fowl, and cowries. Kaa accepted the offer and thus became, as Mwiensang explained, the full owner of the land stretching between Gaaper and the Bayagra River.

As Kaa did not want to be bothered by the restrictions that surround the earth-priestly office, he suggested that the newly acquired land be placed under the spiritual authority of the Niégo earth shrine. As Mwiensang further related, in order to formalize the land transfer, the earth priests from Kelendou and Niégo met at the Bayagra River, and by ritually marking the trees and sacrificing to the river confirmed the new earth-shrine boundary. Moreover, Mwiensang insisted that Kaa and his people even policed the border in order to protect their property rights: whenever they would catch, for instance, a Sisala woman harvesting *dawa-dawa* trees on their territory, they confiscated the fruits she had gathered.

Neither my Sisala informants in Kelendou nor the Niégo earth priest Somda Beyaa agreed with Mwiensang's claims. Somda Beyaa insisted that the Niégo territory had been expanded by his own ancestor Tamao, not by Kaa, who belonged to a different patriclan. The Sisala, in turn, denied the property transfer altogether and asserted their uninterrupted ownership of Bayagra lands until present times.[67] In order to understand their assertion, we need to look at Bayagra's further development, and the history of the neighboring settlement of Buonbaa.

Kaa and his family must have come to Bayagra during the 1910s or 1920s. However, they were unable to attract a larger number of cosettlers and make the new settlement prosper. On the contrary, their labor force was soon diminished when the demands of the Dagara paramount chief Denyuu for taxes and *corvée labor* became unbearable, and Kaa decided to send two of his sons to resettle in nearby Fielmuo, on British territory. Soon afterward, Kaa died, and the remaining family left Bayagra, either joining their relatives in Fielmuo, or, as Mwiensang's father, Sô, did, moving to Kondon. But apparently, Mwiensang explained, life in Kondon proved difficult. First, Sô's wife died for no apparent reason, and then further misfortunes occurred. Sô consulted a diviner and learned that he should return to Bayagra to look after the house and land once so valiantly acquired by his father—which he did, taking along his son Mwiensang who had been born in Kondon (hence his name). When Sô died a few years later, his brothers from Fielmuo came to Bayagra for young Mwiensang. Mwiensang grew up in the British colony, became a *kontonbilesob* (owner of bush spirits, diviner-healer), and for a good thirty years practiced his trade successfully in various Ghanaian cities. Meanwhile, Kaa's house and land in Bayagra would remain deserted for many years to come.

Acknowledging Sisala Property Rights: The Establishment of Buonbaa

Sô's death must have occurred in the early 1930s. Toward the end of the decade, a group of Dagara farmers from Kondon established a new settlement near the remains of Kaa's house. The group's leaders even belonged to the same patriclan as Kaa, the Meto-Man, but neither mobilized this link in order to claim allodial title to the land on which they settled, nor did they continue to call the place Bayagra. On the contrary, they had asked the Kelendou earth priest for permission to settle, paying symbolic fees for the assignment of farmland and for the ritual opening of houses and the burial of their relatives. Why these Dagara farmers explicitly acknowledged Sisala ownership of the land is indicated by the name that they chose for the new settlement: Buonbaa, "place of rest" or "resting under the shadow."[68] As the elders explained in our interview, Buonbaa served as a place of refuge from Denyuu's harsh rule.[69]

The colonial regime tended to define the reach of a chief's authority according to the boundaries of land ownership. Kelendou formed part of the Sisala paramountcy of Bourra, and the Bourra chief—not least because he was eager to increase the number of his dependants vis-à-vis his prepotent Dagara rival Denyuu—was purportedly less harsh in the implementation of colonial demands than the latter. As several of my Dagara interlocutors explained, Denyuu sought to extend his influence, invoking ethnic criteria, to include even Dagara settling on Sisala land. However, the Sisala landowners and their new Dagara clients joined forces in convincing the colonial officers that not the ethnic identity between chief and subjects, but the customary loyalty of late-comers toward their landowning hosts should be the cornerstone of defining the boundaries of political domination.

The Dagara settlers themselves thus upheld and defended Kelendou's allodial title to Buonbaa-Bayagra land and were content with extensive use rights. As in the case of Varpuo, Denyuu sent his native policemen to force the Dagara headman of Buonbaa to acknowledge his authority. But, as the Buonbaa elders explained, the latter insisted that once the Sisala had given them the land to farm, they had to follow them, their subordination to any Dagara paramount chief thereby ceasing. This point was also successfully impressed upon the French authorities, particularly by the Bourra *chef de canton* Kama Nadie. Kama, a literate and well-connected ex-soldier, had been installed by his family precisely in order to forestall Denyuu's expansionist policies.[70] Against the alliance of this paramount chief, the Sisala landowners of Kelendou, and the Dagara settlers, Denyuu was powerless, and Buonbaa, including Kaa's former area of settlement, was reconverted into Sisala-controlled territory.

The settlement soon attracted Dagara settlers from different patriclans, who all sought Kelendou's permission before establishing themselves. Some families came from Kondon, others from Niégo, and still others, after the end of colonial rule, returned from the Fielmuo area in Ghana, where land was becoming scarce. Buonbaa thus became a crowded village of more than forty houses whose offspring now look for fresh farmland farther eastward, in less densely populated Sisala areas.

Reclaiming Former Rights: Mwiensang's Return to Bayagra

In the early 1980s, the tense political situation in Ghana after Rawlings's coup d'état, the severe food shortages in the wake of droughts, and difficulties in finding enough clients as a healer made Mwiensang decide to return to his old base in Bayagra. Furthermore, he related, his tutelary spirits informed him that if he wanted to prosper, he needed to look after his grandfather's and father's graves. In 1983, Mwiensang thus reestablished himself on his grandfather's lands in Bayagra.

However, he soon encountered serious resistance, both from the Dagara of Buonbaa and the Kelendou earth priest. The latter asserted that Bayagra had always been Kelendou property, and that Kaa had only acquired extensive use rights. Once Kaa had died, and Mwiensang's family abandoned the place, the land had automatically reverted to its Sisala owners. Mwiensang therefore was not entitled to any privileged treatment, but was like any newcomer asking for land. As the Kelendou earth priest saw it, the case was like that of a widow (i.e., the land) who, after her husband's death, returned to her paternal home because her in-laws were not taking care of her; should any of the latter later decide to (re)marry her, he would have to ask her parents for permission, just as any other suitor would. And, of course, the Sisala left no doubt that should Mwiensang decide to stay, the bundle of rights that they would assign him would not be as extensive as it had been for his grandfather.

Mwiensang was adamant that he was the legitimate heir to all property rights that his grandfather had acquired, and that he did not need to ask for anybody's permission to reconstruct the old house, recultivate his forebears' farms, or perform his ritual activities as a healer. He was convinced that the majority of Dagara in Buonbaa sided with the Sisala only because they were afraid that his "provocative" behavior might be detrimental to their relations with the Kelendou landowners and even endanger their access to land. Furthermore, they feared his spiritual power, Mwiensang believed, regarding him as a witch and hoping to enlist Sisala support to evict him from the area.

The Dagara front against Mwiensang, however, was by no means united. Some of the younger Catholic families in the area resented their Sisala hosts' imposition of heavy fees for burials and for the ritual opening of houses. As Christians, they rejected such "pagan" customs, but the Sisala insisted that they be performed. When one of the Catholics recently buried his father without informing the Kelendou earth priest and without paying the "customary" goat, fowl, millet, sorghum beer, salt, groundnuts, and 1,500 francs CFA, he was denied the right to continue cultivating his bush farm near Kelendou. Some non-Christian Dagara from Buonbaa, too, complained about the newly installed Kelendou earth priest. According to them, he had increased considerably the payments that the "strangers" needed to make if they wanted additional land to farm, and imposed conditions for the transfer of use rights within the Dagara community that were much stricter than those his predecessor had set. Although they would not openly support Mwiensang's bold claims to his old property, they admired his outspokenness and obstinacy vis-à-vis the Sisala.

When I last visited Bayagra and Buonbaa in the year 2000, an uneasy truce was in place. Mwiensang grumbled that his opponents had conspired to send a young man to kill him. But he continued to receive clients at his shrines and farm his grandfather's land without Sisala authorization. The Dagara in Buonbaa, for their part, were apprehensive of increasing "exploitation" by the Sisala. The latter, in turn, complained that the younger Dagara generation no longer respected the landowners' rights and encroached on communal resources such as firewood, grazing land, and tree fruits to which they were not entitled.

Restricting the Bundle of Rights: The Case of Laponé

Similar attempts to restrict the settlers' "mechanisms of access," to use Ribot and Peluso's term,[71] also characterized relations between the Sisala and the Dagara and Mossi immigrants in Laponé, whose settlement history was discussed in chapter 1. More specifically, the Sisala landowners attempted to prevent any de facto use of the land and other resources from being translated into legitimate property rights. Recall that a sizeable group of the Laponé Dagara settlers came from Bozo, which is a Sisala village. Here numerous Dagara families had settled in the 1930s and eventually undermined their Sisala hosts' property rights and political authority (developments that I discuss in chapter 4), thus setting a precedent that alarmed Sisala throughout the area. Not least because of what happened in Bozo, the Laponé earth priest and chief made quite clear, when I interviewed him, that they were in full control of their "visitors," as they insisted on calling the Dagara and Mossi farmers, and that the developments in Bozo would not be repeated in Laponé.[72] For one, once their land reserves started shrinking, the Laponé earth priest allowed no further immigrants to settle, except for very close relatives of the already established families. Furthermore, the Sisala of Laponé did not hesitate to tell any "stranger" who was "troublesome" that Laponé was not his home and that he should go back to where he came from. Although nobody was ever expelled from the village, many Dagara believed that should push come to shove, the Sisala would invoke their ancestors' wrath, or even resort to witchcraft in order to make the immigrants' life in the village unbearable.

On the whole, however, my Sisala interlocutors nevertheless felt that the "strangers" were an asset to the village rather than a burden. The immigrants contributed to the ranks of able-bodied men and women available for communal labor, and helped to defend the village against "enemies." Indeed, by assigning their "strangers" farmland in the village's border zones, Laponé landowners staked their claims to contested areas. When I visited the village, there were disagreements with the state forestry department, and any visible proof of land utilization was a tangible argument in the renegotiation of the boundary between the forest reserve and village lands. Furthermore—although my Sisala informants did not mention this explicitly—land-seeking "strangers" represented an attractive source of income. The Dagara and Mossi farmers' regular "gifts" (animals, money, shares in the harvest, just to name a few) given for permission to use the land and to be allowed to perform vital rituals constituted a substantial flow of resources, despite the restriction that sacrificial animals should be slaughtered and consumed jointly by the Sisala community.

My Dagara and Mossi informants, in any case, complained vociferously that the Sisala were "eating" at their expense without working hard on their own fields. Particularly farmers from older Dagara villages on Sisala land, like Bozo or Pina, complained that the Laponé landlords imposed much stricter conditions than those they were used to. Unlike in Pina, for instance, where the Sisala requested a single initial "payment" before assigning a field, in Laponé they demanded one *tine* (approximately 15 kg) of millet and several chickens after every harvest. The Dagara also complained that the "price" of a new field had increased considerably over the years.[73] The most expensive ritual was the "opening" of the house, involving the payment of a minimum of one sheep, one goat, four or more chickens, and several thousand francs CFA. This was why half of the Dagara houses had not yet been "opened," and their residents had to either send their afterbirth to be buried at the Sisala earth priest's house or secretly take it to a Dagara neighbor with an "opened" house. Funerals were another occasion calling for burdensome payments, and the Dagara deeply resented that the Sisala had, so far, denied all their pleas to give them their own cemetery. A cemetery would have involved a larger one-time collective payment, but would have diminished the cost of individual funerals and increased Dagara ritual autonomy. However, the Sisala argued that this would violate an irrevocable taboo of the Laponé earth god. Any violation of the earth shrine's prohibitions, ranging from having sex or delivering a child in the bush to catching fish or collecting néré (*dawa dawa*) or shea nuts, had to be atoned for by substantial gifts to the Sisala earth priest.[74]

Sisala attempts to restrict the immigrants' rights were particularly stringent with regard to communal resources such as wild fruit trees, firewood, fish, and so forth. As a young Dagara farmer explained:

> The Sisala do not allow us to collect *dawa dawa* [néré]. As for shea nuts, if our women get up early and find the nuts, they can get some, but if the Sisala women arrive first, they take everything. . . . They tell us that we have not come for harvesting *dawa dawa* or shea nut, but for farming and food. . . . They even come to harvest in our own fields, just before our doorsteps. . . . As for fishing, the fish is for them, they don't invite us for the communal fishing, and when they surprise a Dagara or a Mossi fishing secretly, they don't allow it! . . . Even our pigs, when they catch our pigs in the water, they say that the pigs are catching fish, and they won't allow it. They kill the pigs and share the meat among themselves, not giving any of the meat to the owner! . . . As for firewood, the wood on our fields actually should belong to us, but the *langme* often come to steal it. Last year, I have cut down trees in my new field, clearing it before sowing millet, but the Sisala women have stolen part of that

wood. . . . In any case, we do not live in freedom here, and whoever complains is told that he can just return to wherever he came from, because if they would attempt to change their earth shrine's taboos, they would die.[75]

These restrictions on the use of common resources clearly aimed to protect an important source of income for the Sisala villagers, namely the sale of néré, shea nuts, and firewood. But the tug-of-war concerning these collectible resources also has a symbolic dimension. In local understandings of property rights, only first-comers with allodial title to the land are entitled to resources that can be exploited without the investment of agricultural labor. If the Sisala were to allow later immigrants to freely use non-labor-related resources, this would symbolize their de facto inclusion in the ranks of first-comers and landowners.

Despite their complaints about these restrictions and their hosts' "greediness," the Dagara (and Mossi) in Laponé also acknowledge that the obligatory gifts offer some measure of security. Presenting the customary sacrificial chicken for the assignment of farmland is a public affair, and in the absence of a written contract, solemnly formalizes the agreement in which the landowner and "his" settler have entered by invoking the presence of the ancestors and guardian spirits of the area. As some Dagara farmers explained, they would be worried had the Sisala not demanded animals for the sacrifice. Even the Christian Dagara, who are less afraid of the earth god's wrath, accept that the sacrifice represents a binding agreement. Similarly, the annual gifts that the settlers present their hosts affirm that the immigrant farmers' loyalty to their hosts and serve as a reminder that they continue to use their fields, which the landowners should therefore not allocate to any other person.

In Laponé, the composition and scope of the bundle of rights is still largely a matter of negotiation between individual landowners and their clients.[76] However, there is a general trend toward reducing the size of the bundle and increasing the fee that is to be paid. As one of my Sisala interlocutors admitted, because of the recent "scramble for land"

> what used to be a very small symbolic gift has now really become a type of rent. Formerly, one would only ask a good friend to allow one to farm on his land, so there was a friendly link between a landowner and the settler-farmer. . . . But now, ever higher amounts of produce are demanded. . . . Up to five goats and some money can be requested by the field owner [*bagatina*] before the farm is given. . . . A very difficult *bagatina* in Billaw [Ghana], for instance, started demanding from his Dagara settlers that they come to renew their contracts every year and always come with two of their sons as witnesses. He wants the descendants of the settlers to know that the land is not theirs.[77]

In recent years, and particularly when tenancy arrangements are negotiated across ethnic boundaries, the individual settlements between landowners and land users have become increasingly permeated by collective agreements and group pressure.

Younger Dagara farmers who have traveled widely in search of work and come in contact with political parties or labor unions sometimes quote the revolutionary dictum of the 1980s that "land belongs to those who work it." They are well aware that, at least in Burkina Faso, Sisala claims to ultimate land ownership and gifts from land-seeking farmers run against state legislation. However, these Dagara farmers feel they must comply with the customary rules because local state representatives are unwilling to or incapable of enforcing the law. And they fear that if they "misbehave," the Sisala might refuse to grant access to land—not only to themselves, but also to their relatives, and not only in Laponé, but also in neighboring Sisala villages.

Such fears are not without grounds. The Sisala have developed effective intervillage networks of information on who are "good" clients and who should be avoided, and they assist each other in boycotting "troublesome" settlers. At the same time, however, if there is land available, it is generally regarded as going "against custom" to refuse someone access to a field where he could farm for subsistence. But there are other methods to turn undesirable settlers away. The landowners can, for instance, wait until an unwanted client goes on a stint of seasonal labor migration and assign his plot to another client, or settle a newcomer on the other end of the stretch of land assigned to an already settled client, thus restricting the latter's ability to extend his farm. Most important, however, the very mechanism by which the immigrants must organize access to fresh land through personal networks with individual Sisala landowners works as an as an instrument of social control. When a Dagara resident takes a Dagara newcomer to the Sisala authorities, the former is responsible for the latter's behavior, and any infraction of local rules by the new settler will be referred to his Dagara host. Even Christians, who do not fear the earth god's supernatural sanctions, are disciplined by the close-knit networks among the settlers.

The Dagara (and Mossi) farmers on Sisala land usually avoid open confrontation, and attempt to further their interests by investing in clientelist ties with their Sisala hosts and by encroaching upon local resources clandestinely (for instance, secretly fishing and hunting, collecting firewood in "forbidden" areas, clandestinely harvesting shea nuts, or pushing their farms a few meters deeper into the bush than officially permitted). Only occasionally does this subtle tug-of-war escalate into open conflict and take on overt ethnic overtones—developments that are closely related to the politicization of land rights that I discuss in the next chapter.

Conclusion

This chapter has explored the territorialization of property rights. It has shown how, in the Black Volta region, this involved drawn-out and conflict-ridden processes of defining the spatial boundaries of earth-shrine territories. As Thomas Sikor and Christian Lund have argued, the setting of territorial boundaries to property rights, by establishing signboards, fences, ditches, or other physical markers, also entails claims of territorial jurisdiction.[78] In other words, in a social order centered on earth shrines, where their custodians are the guardians of the most comprehensive property rights over land, the spiritual and mundane services provided by the earth priest (which implies assertions of his legitimate authority) and the territorial definition of the allodial title are mutually constitutive. These links between property and authority are particularly complicated in segmentary societies and contexts of pronounced mobility, such as the ones discussed in this book.

As the case studies in this and the preceding chapter indicate, all groups in the Black Volta region generally acknowledge the authority of earth priests as custodians of the most important shrines and providers of vital spiritual services. Likewise, they all more or less agree that first-comer status carries with it particularly strong rights to landed resources. However, what this means on the ground is often contested. Although the functions of property rights have gradually shifted from regulating hunting and gathering activities to organizing agriculture in an increasingly densely populated region, older layers of claims to ownership of large hunting territories have not disappeared but have often been translated into entitlements, even to territory that is now used for agriculture. Generally, when it comes to the translation of any general claims to first-comer status into concrete property rights with precise spatial boundaries, people often engaged, and continue to engage, in sheer endless reinterpretations and contestations of only apparently "settled facts." For instance, without challenging earth-priestly authority as such, they argue that in a particular case, a specific holder of office is not the relevant authority or a specific piece of land is "out of bounds" (that is, falls outside the jurisdiction of a particular authority).

Such contestations often play off, as we have seen, the factor of time, or history, as it were, against the attempt to fix spatial boundaries, arguing that changing circumstances necessitate corresponding changes to the definition of rights to the land. More generally, mobility and multiple practices of multilocality mean that the recognition of authority, enshrined in relations between people, can be transported along with their movements, and so be exploited to redefine the territorial extension of rights to resources in the new settlement. In principle, this is what happened when the inhabitants of an established village moved into the bush to clear further land and claimed that this land was "covered" by the protection of the original earth shrine, while a neigboring jurisdiction argued precisely the opposite. As a number of cases discussed in this chapter have shown, up until colonial pacification such opposing claims to the spatial extension of property and authority were often settled by small-scale warfare, which ended with a ritual of peacemaking that established, at least for some time, a new boundary. Landmarks that feature in narratives, and regular ritual activities at the places of power into which the former battlefields have often developed, serve to maintain these boundaries. However, this does not once and for all end contestation, not least because the colonial introduction of chieftaincy as well as postcolonial land legislation and the introduction of new institutions such as land departments or *comités de gestion de terroir* have further complicated the situation of long-standing legal pluralism. Far from ending ambiguity, they have created even more opportunities for negotiation, competition, and contestation. All these institutions, both "traditional" and "modern," claim to be the relevant authorities to validate property rights, and thus offer contestants numerous forums to seek recognition of their claims or gather support in their opposition to the claims of others.[79]

In addition to investigating the contested territorialization of property rights, this chapter has also explored the multiple openings for debate and conflict that result from typical fuzziness of the composition of the bundle of rights claimed by first-comers or transferred to later immigrants. Property is only "part of a larger picture of access to resources, whether legally recognized or not," as Sikor and Lund argue. Property is about "claims which are considered legitimate" while access "is about the ability to benefit."[80] This distinction between "access" and "property" helps to clarify the dynamics of interactions between landowners and immigrant farmers that I have discussed in the latter part of this chapter, in a broader framework.

Obviously, property rights, whether generally regarded as legitimate or not, do not automatically allow their holders to effectively benefit from access. However, they are better than no rights at all because even if they have no value at a particular moment due to specific power constellations, they may be successfully invoked when circumstances change. This was the case, for instance, with Sisala first-comers who had to tolerate Dagara occupation of what they regarded as their ancestral lands during the early decades of colonial rule, but subsequently were able to translate their claims into tangible benefits when later immigrants found it safer to recognize their ownership rights. Conversely, late-comers and immigrant farmers continually attempt to extend their de facto access to land and related resources and also try to stablize their "ability to benefit from things"[81] by claiming that these resource uses are included in the rights already granted to them. Alternatively, they may deny that there is any preexisting authority already in possession of rights to the land and argue that they themselves created property by taming the wilderness and regularly cultivating the land.

In any case, the "grey" area between "what people have rights to and what they merely have access to"[82] allows for pragmatic arrangements that are necessary to ensure that farming activities continue and families are able to survive despite so many unsettled property issues. The de facto access to resources that people are able to achieve can be interpreted in very different ways—as tangible proof of underlying property rights, or as incidences of illegitimate usurpation of such rights. Whose claims—beyond temporary pragmatic arrangements—are strengthened in the long run and whose legitimization strategies are more successful ultimately depends on shifting constellations of power and authority. At the local level, such shifts may take place upon the death of a well-connected officeholder or when the demographic clout of the immigrant farmers increases. At the same time, these small-scale dynamics may be cross-cut by changes at the regional or national level, such as new legislation or government policies. Some of the most important of these changes—particularly the introduction of chieftaincy and the concomitant ethnicization and politization of property rights that took place from the colonial on into the postcolonial period—are discussed in next chapter.

4 Ethnicity, Autochthony, and the Politics of Belonging

Property is "not about things . . . but about relationships between and among persons with regard to things," as Sally Falk Moore once succinctly observed.[1] Property rights over, and access to, land are mediated by membership in specific communities, ranging from the nuclear or extended family, the clan, first-comers, or the ethnic group, to, in modern property regimes, the nation-state. The boundaries of these property-holding groups were and continue to be notoriously ambiguous; membership is often contested and needs to be (re)negotiated and validated. Furthermore, just as land tenure is governed by multiple, often competing sets of rules, and various institutions claim authority over the allocation of rights, so is belonging complex and layered, as Jean-Pierre Jacob and Pierre-Yves Le Meur argue.[2] Currently, invoking shared national citizenship, for instance, is often not enough to guarantee effective access to, and durable rights over, landed resources outside one's "home" community. Yet how broadly or narrowly "home" is defined, and who is regarded as belonging to the local citizens who enjoy full economic and political rights, are contentious issues.

This chapter explores the politics of belonging and how they played out in different historical contexts—on the expanding settlement frontier before colonial rule, under the influence of colonial ideologies of ethnicity and autochthony, and in the framework of the postcolonial nation-state. I discuss how belonging was (and is) constructed in the context of agrarian mobility, and how membership in a community was (and is) translated into rights over land. Previous chapters have explored how frontiersmen and later immigrants have created bonds of patrilineage and clan, affinal ties, friendship as well as village solidarity on the frontier. Now, the focus shifts toward the construction of imagined communities beyond kin and village, and investigates ideologies of ethnicity and autochthony, and their complex interrelations. What role did ethnicity play before colonial rule? To what extent did the boundaries between first-comers and late-comers acquire ethnic connotations, and how did Sisala and Dagara frontiersmen negotiate rules of inclusion and exclusion? Colonial ideas about "tribes" generally privileged sedentary forms of belonging and reinterpreted older idioms of host-guest relations as configurations between autochthones, firmly rooted in a specific territory, and immigrant strangers. How did this affect the indigenous definitions of the bundles of owners and the landscape of property rights? And how did relations between local communities and landed property further develop in the context of the postcolonial nation-state?

If claims to land are linked to group membership, the reverse is also true: land ownership has been and is still used as a way of defining belonging. This chapter therefore also explores the dynamics of converting control over land into social and political capital. Landlessness may once have been a rewarding strategy, particularly for pastoralists or other migrant groups, but this is no longer the case. Since the colonial politicization of ideologies of autochthony, nonterritorial strategies of belonging have lost considerable ground.[3] This has also affected the ways in which relatively mobile farmers relate to the land. Colonial and postcolonial policies have generally strengthened the economic and political rights of first-comers. Immigrants or "strangers" now see themselves obliged to use all available avenues to gain access to land in order to become "sons of the soil," while locals try to exclude newcomers from fuller control over land. In Dagara and Sisala villages, as various case studies in this chapter show, these struggles have often crystallized in conflicts over the right to appoint the village chief or over chiefly hierarchies between villages as well as in competing claims to represent an area in modern political institutions.

Ethnicity in the Context of Agrarian Mobility

Ethnicity is an enigmatic notion. Like other key terms in the social sciences and history, it belongs not only to the theoretical repertoire of social scientists but also to the vocabulary of politicians, chiefs, peasants, local intellectuals, and social movements. Ethnic groups both encompass and transcend families and assert a collective identity, or are defined by outsiders as a group, or, as is most often the case, both. Contemporary ethnic ideologies generally claim that members of the we-group share their entire culture, ancestry, language, and history, and are rooted in a specific territory. Yet the criteria demarcating group boundaries are variable and refer only to a small part of the total cultural repertoire that a group often shares with its neighbors. Ethnicity is indeed a protean category that rests on no single essential trait. It may draw on traditions of origin or descent, possession of any number of cultural and social traits, language, region, membership in (or opposition to) a polity or religion, or any combination of these; but at the same time it need not involve any particular one of these bases. Thus, while ethnic discourses argue in an essentialist manner and natural-ize social relationships, the "contents" of any particular ethnicity are historically con-tingent, and the boundaries of "ethnic" communities are malleable and can be adapted to serve specific interests and contexts.[4]

In previous chapters, I have been referring to the "Dagara," the "Sisala," and other groups as if this terminology were unproblematic. It is therefore high time to ask what role ethnicity actually played in the precolonial history of the Black Volta region and how it was later transformed, particularly in relation to land ownership. To what extent did the ethnic identities and boundaries that characterize the current sociocultural landscape influence the thinking and actions of the local population in the eighteenth or nineteenth centuries? When my interlocutors described past violent encounters as "tribal wars," was this a projection of contemporary concepts onto the precolonial past, or did it indeed reflect a long-standing sense of belonging to an ethnic group?

It is difficult to answer these questions definitively because we have no contempo-rary sources from which to reconstruct, with any certainty, group names and identities that were prevalent during the eighteenth and nineteenth centuries. The colonial intro-duction of apparently clear-cut ethnic categories, which were reified through cartog-raphy and ethnographic description as well as administrative practice, certainly influ-enced local narratives of the past. However, the colonial ethnicization of indigenous forms of belonging did draw on existing group names and boundary-setting practices. And based on a careful interpretation of early colonial sources and of my interlocutors' narratives on clan histories and encounters with strangers, I would argue that even in precolonial times, the population of the Black Volta region did indeed espouse a sense of belonging to larger communities, beyond the narrow confines of the patriclan and the local village. And it seems that particularly on the settlement frontier, where groups speaking different languages and coming from distinct origins interacted, these community ideologies could develop ethnic overtones.

A Segmentary Sense of Unity: Precolonial Conceptions of Belonging

The dominant social reality of the Black Volta region in the eighteenth and nine-teenth centuries was shaped by relatively small, and often mobile groups of relatives, overlapping networks, and flexible boundaries. The "house" (a local kin group as well as a supralocal clan) and the earth-shrine area were the cornerstones of local societies. Taken together with ties built on matrilineal descent, they created inte-grative institutions that crossed, and still cross, cultural and linguistic boundaries. An earth-shrine area was capable of integrating a population that spoke different dialects or languages, as long as all shared a set of core beliefs, such as the recogni-tion of the earth deity and the rights of first settlers. Language and culture (in the narrow sense)—in European thought the conceptual pillars of ethnic and national community—played only a limited role in the organization of neighborly relations and supralocal social belonging.

However, because the region was never isolated from the greater political developments of the Niger Bend, there were also other types of social boundaries that extended beyond local community ideologies. Group labels like "Dagaba," "Grunshi," and "Lobi" were probably originally terms that Muslim scholars, merchants, and warriors coined for the non-Muslim population of the region.[5] When the British and French incorporated the Black Volta region into their empires and made their first tours of the area, they began to use these names as ethnic terms. And it is this process of embedding colonial ethnic terms in older nomenclatures that made it seem that the newly delimitated groups had historical depth; the continuity of names is thus easily (mis)taken for the continuity of communities themselves.[6]

These collective names, shaped or at least redefined by outsiders, probably did not correspond to a large-scale collective self-awareness as Sisala, Dagaba, or Dagara comparable to the identities with which these names are associated today. Yet in some cases, these external processes of labeling may have reinforced indigenous developments toward a sense of belonging to larger communities. Mobility with respect to settlement, but also marriage, ensured inter-"ethnic" encounters. Regional markets, burial rites, and initiation cults exposed people to linguistic and sociopolitical differences. And particularly in frontier areas, where new settlers competed with established first-comers over land ownership and ritual control, community ideologies could develop ethnic overtones if the boundary between first-comers and late-comers coincided with linguistic difference.

This is reflected in the collective names used locally to refer to neighbors. Sisala are usually called *langme* by the Dagara, literally "people who unite, huddle together, remain together." This was sometimes explained by my Dagara interlocutors as a nonjudgmental reference to the rather compact building style of Sisala villages that presents a stark contrast to the scattered settlements of the Dagara. On other occasions it was viewed as describing the "cowardice" of the Sisala, who were said to have withdrawn in fear from the onslaught of both the slave raiders and the Dagara frontiersmen. In turn, the Sisala often describe the Dagara as *kyielo*, "eagles," or "hawks." From the Sisala perspective, this is usually a reference to the mobility and restlessness of the Dagara, who are immigrants to their area; while from the Dagara perspective, it is a reference to their warlike qualities.[7]

In the first chapter, I discussed how Dagara and Sisala attitudes toward mobility and their ways of imagining group cohesion differed. While the Dagara frontiersmen clearly remembered the migratory routes of each patrilineage and maintained multiple links to their original communities as well as various stations en route, the Sisala placed more emphasis on the creation of new bonds of brotherhood in the new habitat and insisted that it was dangerous to return to one's place of origin. The Dagara cultural ideal for manliness was in line with their expansionism: becoming a *yirsob*, that is, heading one's own lineage. If it was necessary to migrate to the frontier in order to achieve this ideal, all the better. The Sisala, on the other hand, privileged sedentariness and staying together on one's own land, even if this entailed not becoming the head of the lineage. Migration, although viewed as sometimes unavoidable, was in principle an unwelcome response to external threats or unbearable internal conflicts. These different frontier strategies, arising in response to the contingencies of the regional settlement history of first-comers and late-comers, seem to have developed into different, even complementary, styles of community formation and ethnic consciousness. While the Dagara seem to have opted for ethnic exclusiveness and constructed images of ethnic unity around the experience of the joint movements of related patriclans, the Sisala emphasized ethnic inclusiveness, first-comership, and rootedness in their new habitat.[8]

As discussed in previous chapters, Dagara villagers have constructed a sense of unity around the notion of *tengkor* (the old place, the old land) or *teng peri* (at the bottom, or end, of all lands or villages) from which the frontiersmen are imagined to have set out. *Tengkor* usually functions as a generic term that provides a common origin to the different lineages that settled together in a new frontier village. Furthermore, although each patrilineage followed its own distinct migration route, this often intersected, and partly overlapped, with the itineraries of befriended or related clans. Migration-and-settlement narratives were often refashioned in order to produce such overlap and emphasize close ties with other Dagara lineages with whom the frontiersmen needed to cooperate in the new locale. None of the kin groups would have had a bird's-eye view of the entire group, but they did certainly have a sense of belonging to a larger group of clans and families who moved together and were linked by multiple ties of friendship, kinship, and marriage. Moreover, the frequent fission and fusion of kin groups, and the necessity of integrating newcomers and recruiting additional allies that went along with the frontier process must have contributed to a certain degree of cultural homogenization. Although each Dagara patriclan had, and still has, distinct "medicines" (such as arrow poison, etc.), forms of representing the ancestors, taboos, and praise formulas, moving together and intermarrying promoted the exchange of knowledge and clan histories as well as the creation of a core of interrelated practices and common norms. Taken together, these processes probably fostered a growing consciousness of "we, the Dagara" (even though we do not know whether such a self-designation was actually used).[9]

To have been the first-comers to the area where they settled neither was nor is part of what Dagara normally came to conceive as essential for their group identity, although frontiersmen and their descendants have argued along these lines when it became necessary to defend property claims. Instead, my elderly Dagara informants were invariably proud of the warlike qualities of their ancestors who had fearlessly conquered the wild bush. First-comership was thus usually redefined as a conquest of sorts rather than merely a first discovery. This is reflected in the opposition of "Sisala bush" (*Lang wie*) versus "Dagara land" (*Dagara teng*), that is, land protected by an earth shrine, a term some of my Dagara interlocutors employed when explaining the deeds of their forebears.[10] They regarded the frontier that was inhabited by Sisala as uncontrolled bush, and the Dagara as people who tamed the wild territory and thereby asserted claims over the land.

Significantly, only few Dagara lineages remember any non-Dagara origins of their ancestors. One of the rare exceptions to this pattern are the "Yeri," who were originally traders or artisans with a Mande-Dyula or a Dafing background. Despite assimilating to the language, practices, and worldviews of their Dagara hosts, they still commemorate their distinct identity by, for example, conducting certain funeral rituals.[11] Generally, however, such non-Dagara origins, if they ever existed, are forgotten or denied—a style of imagining ethnic unity that is typical of expansionist groups.

For Sisala notions of ethnic unity, the heterogeneous origins of the various lineages making up a new settlement constitute no problem; on the contrary, they regard their mixed origins as a strength.[12] Sisala often describe themselves as living in communities of "refugees" who have been strengthened by absorbing, and culturally assimilating, new immigrants. Various observers have recorded Sisala narratives on the diverse geographic and cultural roots of the villages' component patrilineages, who continue to remember their Dagaba, Kasena, Grunshi, Mossi, or Dagomba origins while also identifying as, and certainly speaking one of the dialects of, Sisala.[13] Sisala narratives use no generic term for their ancestors' place of origin, but usually refer to specific, named villages, and say little about the routes of migration and intermediate stops. In order to create a sense of unity, Sisala elders draw on first-comer images and stories of long-standing rootedness in, and full ownership of, a specific territory. Although narratives about great warriors and fearless hunters can also be found among the Sisala, they do not seem as prominent as among the Dagara and are usually complemented, if not contradicted, by images of peacefulness and hospitality toward well-intentioned newcomers. Furthermore, neighboring Sisala villages sometimes entered defensive alliances, reinforcing such bonds by swearing an oath at the earth shrines of the associated settlements and adopting common shrine names. However, such alliances rarely embraced more than a handful of villages, and it is unlikely that there was any broader sense of a greater Sisala identity.

More generally, and beyond the difference between Sisala and Dagara ways of imagining unity, we should probably think of precolonial ethnicity in the segmentary societies of the Black Volta region as a kind of decentralized sense of unity that was heightened in frontier areas. Marital ties between lineages that spoke different languages or dialects and followed different cultural practices (for instance, with respect to inheritance) were frequent. The descendants of these marital unions consequently had various options to identify with different groups, and they could draw on their various memberships according to the needs of their specific situations and life projects. However, such flexible identifications notwithstanding, this did not prevent people on the frontier from making ethnic distinctions and establishing ethnic boundaries that were mobilized, particularly during the latter part of the nineteenth century, in conflicts over the control of land and related resources.

At the same time, we should bear in mind that this ethnic consciousness did not at all preclude intraethnic feuds, which were as frequent, or even more frequent, than interethnic conflicts. Moreover, religion was probably more important than ethnicity when it came to drawing social and political boundaries in the larger regional context, particularly when Muslim founders of states and slave raiders declared *jihad* against "infidels" in the second half of the nineteenth century. But ultimately, for mundane questions of access to and ownership of land, neither religion nor ethnicity played any directly decisive role. The property-holding communities were defined along lines of descent and, to a certain extent, affinal ties, both of which could cut across ethnic and religious boundaries. Thus, in order to lay claim to natural resources, it was not sufficient to invoke a common ethnic identity. However, as I discuss below, under certain circumstances ethnic commonality helped to establish or strengthen the kin alliances that were necessary to "conquer" frontier territories.

(De)Emphasizing Difference: The Precolonial Negotiation of Ethnic Boundaries

On the whole, ethnic boundaries seem to have been much more permeable in precolonial times than they are today, and cultural exchange and assimilation, including linguistic flexibility, more important than the emphasis on difference. However, much depended on the dynamics of the settlement process. Kopytoff has argued that segmentary societies almost inescapably absorbed new arrivals into the existing networks, incorporating them as kin, clients, or slaves and assimilating them culturally.[14] As Kopytoff has also pointed out, however, this dynamic worked only as long as the immigrant group was not able to defy the host society. In the case of Dagara expansion, the frontier process seems to have undergone different phases, typically starting with the peaceful cohabitation of small groups of Sisala first-comers and Dagara frontiersmen that eventually gave way to competition and even violent conflict if the Dagara pioneers increased their numbers by recruiting additional followers from their original villages. While cohabitation often resulted in the downplaying of ethnic difference, or even ethnic "conversion," conflict was usually associated with the hardening of ethnic boundaries.

How did ethnic conversion work? Since the frontiersmen rarely traveled by themselves and often preferred to establish themselves near existing settlements, the first step must have been the arrival of a small group of "strangers" who were accepted into the local community and gradually learned its language as well as the relevant cultural practices without necessarily giving up membership in their original patriclan. A fuller conversion would occur as a result of adoption into existing clans or intermarriage, particularly if the latter worked in both directions, with immigrant women marrying men of the host community and vice versa. In the Black Volta region, ethnic belonging would usually be defined along the lines of the dominant, patrilineal pattern of inheritance, which also regulated ownership of land and the "house"; thus, the second generation, or, to be precise, the children of the immigrant women, would then be integral members of the host society.[15] However, matrilineal connections always remained important, and in many cases the "assimilated" children (and subsequent generations) could reactivate these connections should they continue their migration, or should further immigrants from their original group arrive and change the ethno-demographic balance.

An interesting case in point are the movements, and associated changes in the emphasis of ethno-linguistic identifications, of the ancestors of the late Ghanaian Archbishop Peter Dery, who belonged to the Berwiele patriclan (the clan's Dagara name is "Bawiele" in the dialect of the Dagaba from Jirapa). Dery saw himself as a man of "eclectic roots," "a Dagao with the Dagara, a Sisala with the Sisala."[16] The history of Dery's family illustrates how one patriclan could embrace people of various linguistic and cultural orientations, and how their members could strategically draw on both Dagara and Dagaba and Sisala networks, identifying alternatively as Dagara, Dagaba, or Sisala whenever this was useful for their specific life projects.

His ancestors, Dery explains in his memoirs, originally came from Dagbon, the Dagomba kingdom, and later moved to "Mossi country." Probably after some family disagreement, one branch of the family (to which Dery traces his descent) traveled southward and "came into contact with some Kasena and some Gurunshi," and later with the Sisala. They moved through Tumu, Gbal, Wiiro, Nabing, and Zoole, until they finally arrived, probably around the mid- or late eighteenth century, at Konguol, a Sisala village not far from Lambussie.[17] The interaction with the Sisala must have been "quite long" and "intensive," Dery reasons, for the group gradually adopted the Sisala language and came to regard Konguol as "their original homeland."[18] In Konguol, the group eventually divided up again. One section stayed in Konguol; another moved southward, eventually settling in Tizza and other Dagaba villages near Jirapa; a third migrated toward Wa and finally established itself in Sombo and Kaleo. While the Berwiele in Konguol continued to identify as Sisala, their clan mates in Sombo, Kaleo, and Tizza became Dagaba. However, all sections recognized their common origins and membership in one patriclan—a sense of unity that was also kept alive by regular visits as well as the residential mobility of some clan members.

Dery's great-grandfather was among those who stayed in Konguol. Drawing on the support of his widely dispersed patriclan, he worked as an itinerant dry-season trader, in addition to his regular farming activities, and was able to accumulate considerable wealth. Faced with a lack of space for his people and his cattle, he decided to move from Konguol to Ko, a neighboring Dagara village, and thus "became" Dagara. He married a Dagaba woman whom he had met during one of his visits to the Berwiele in Tizza, and probably around the 1830s, this woman gave birth to Dery's grandfather

Yaa. Yaa grew up in Ko, but later decided to settle close to his mother's brothers in Tizza. He was his mother's only son, had to compete with the numerous sons of Yaa's other wives for access to land and other resources, and thus expected to be better off with, and receive more support from, his maternal uncles in Tizza. Like his father, Yaa married a Dagaba woman, but he also kept in touch with his Sisala clan mates in Konguol and his Dagara relatives in Ko.

When Yaa died, his children inherited a large herd of cattle and other assets. Because this invited envy and animosity from fellow villagers, all but one of Yaa's sons decided to leave Tizza and return to Konguol. However, on their way to Konguol, they were stopped by one of the Berwiele elders in Ko, who invited them to settle near him instead of going to Konguol, because, as this elder supposedly argued, "you have become assimilated to the Dagara and lost your Sisala identity."[19] The migrants—among them Archbishop Dery's father, Porekuu—accepted the invitation and eventually founded a new section of Ko that later came to be known as Zimuopere. It was in Zimuopere that Archbishop Dery was born, around 1918, as he calculated. Despite living among, and identifying with, the Dagara of Ko and Zimuopere, Porekuu and his brothers often visited their Sisala clan mates in Konguol and participated in all important sacrifices at the ancestor shrines. As Dery, who often accompanied his father to Konguol when he was still a young boy, remembered, the ancestors were addressed in both Dagara and Sisala.[20] Thanks to such continuous investment in both Sisala and Dagara ancestral ties, Porekuu and his family were able to find refuge in Konguol during the 1930s, when Porekuu's prominent engagement as Catholic convert and catechist provoked intense conflicts with the chiefs of Zimuopere and Nandom. Porekuu's son Dery eventually became a priest. But who knows? Had he married a Sisala woman from Konguol, his family might eventually have reemphasized their Sisala identity.

During the latter part of the nineteenth century and certainly during the colonial period, stories of interethnic marriage and flexible identifications such as that of Archbishop Dery's ancestors became exceptional. During earlier periods, however, they were rather common. Among the founding ancestors of Lambussie (today clearly a Sisala settlement), for instance, was a group of Dagaba frontiersmen from around Wa, or more precisely, from Sankana and Bussie, from which my interlocutors also derived the name Lambussie, the Bussie of the "Lang" (that is, Sisala). The Lambussie earth priest and his elders claimed that their Dagaba ancestors eventually adopted a Sisala identity when they encountered, and intermarried with, other immigrants who had come to Lambussie from Kasena- and Sisala-speaking areas farther north.[21] Zenuo, the founder of Nandom, is said to have set out from the Dagara village of Tom and followed his sister when she married a Sisala from Lambussie. He is supposed to have lived for quite some time in Lambussie, where he may have assimilated to his Sisala hosts' language and cultural practices. However, conflicts over his growing herds made him decide to separate and establish his own settlement, namely Nandom, together with Dagara friends from Tom who were searching for new land—a process that was most likely accompanied by a reemphasis of Zenuo's Dagara roots.[22]

Significantly, most ethnic conversion stories that I was told referred to the villages of Lambussie, Billaw, Konguol, Dahile, Ko, and a few others, that is, along the current border "between" Sisala- and Dagara-owned earth-shrine territories. This zone was probably an ancient settlement frontier and contact zone where Dagara-speaking frontiersmen coming from the south and southwest encountered Sisala-speaking groups arriving from the north and northeast. While the first small groups of Dagara pioneers were absorbed into the Sisala-speaking frontier communities and "became" Sisala, later Dagara immigrants, if they came in greater numbers, maintained their own identity and constructed separate settlements at some distance from the Sisala dwellings. And during the earlier phases of the encounter, back-and-forth movements between Sisala and Dagara identifications, as in Archbishop Dery's ancestors' case, were still common.[23]

Toward the latter part of the nineteenth century, however, ethnic boundaries generally hardened. According to all available evidence, the major reason was that the Sisala increasingly resisted Dagara expansion and preferred to keep their ranks closed. The Muslim warlords' incursions into the Black Volta region eventually closed off the exit options to which the Sisala previously resorted if they could not control the Dagara advance by incorporating the Dagara intruders.[24] The Dagara, in turn, could now easily find spouses and mutual support among their own people. If intermarriage between Sisala and Dagara still occurred, it was now only Sisala men marrying Dagara women, not vice versa—a marriage pattern that remains in place today. Since ethnic belonging as well as land are inherited patrilineally, this may well have developed as a deliberate strategy of the Sisala to restrict further encroachment on their territory. In both groups, the mother's brothers are expected to support their nephews, and thus the sons whom a Sisala woman were to have with her Dagara husband would be regarded as Dagara, but could raise some legitimate claim to Sisala land.

The Dagara frontiersmen, for their part, now more frequently resorted to violence when attempting to expand the territory under their control at the expense of the existing Sisala settlements. Analyzing a similar case of expansion of a segmentary society in southern Ethiopia, David Turton argues that armed conflicts typically occurred toward the end of a longer period of more or less peaceful encroachment of Mursi groups upon non-Mursi territory.[25] The violent encounters provided the opportunity to eventually call for peacemaking ceremonies, which then marked the boundary between the Mursi and their neighbors, and thus established de jure property rights over what before had already become de facto Mursi lands. In the Black Volta region, a comparable dynamic seems to have characterized Dagara-Sisala relations during the last decades of the nineteenth century. Territorial gains supported by the systematic use of violence, and the increasing importance of being capable of waging war, contributed to the growing salience of ethnic identities. Long-standing kin relations and friendships across ethnic boundaries were still kept alive, and could be activated to mitigate conflicts.[26] However, the intensifying competition over land hardened ethnic boundaries. Property rights over land and the status as propertied first-comers became increasingly tied up with ethnic identity—a development that was to be propelled by colonial processes of ethnicization and ideologies of autochthony.

Grounding Ethnic Belonging: The Colonial Creation of Chiefdoms and "Tribes"

Colonial domination, and particularly the introduction of chieftaincy, had a profound influence on mobility, ethnic relations, and land tenure. The colonial administration, working through a hierarchy of local chiefs, endeavored to restrict residential mobility in order to improve their control over labor resources and, in the French colony, poll-tax collection. In addition, the gradual imposition of the *pax colonia* largely curbed the recourse to violence and thus changed the balance of power in favor of the Sisala (and other groups on whose territory the Dagara encroached). When the Dagara now established new settlements, they had to accept the ritual authority of the Sisala landowners and were no longer able to forcefully convert themselves into first-comers and thus acquire an allodial title. Furthermore, the colonial creation of chiefdoms and "tribes" contributed to the hardening of ethnic boundaries and the ethnicization of land rights.[27]

Early travelers and colonial administrators characterized the peoples north of the Wala kingdom by first of all pointing to the fact that they did not pay allegiance to any of the surrounding states.[28] British officers noted repeatedly that in much of the Black Volta District (later renamed North-Western Province), "each compound is practically a law unto itself,"[29] and complained about the "extremely independent nature" of the native(s) who "will owe no other authority beyond the head of his own family."[30] Their French counterparts west of the Black Volta, too, grumbled about the "complete anarchy" of the "Dagari."[31] Nonetheless, the colonial officers believed that every African belonged, from birth to death, to a particular "tribe" that was clearly distinct from all neighboring tribes in its physiological, linguistic, and cultural features. Particularly the British insisted that administrative boundaries should follow "tribal" boundaries as much as possible because the legitimacy of the chiefs, through whom the British (and French) wanted to administer their territories, was to be based on the ethnic identification that the chiefs shared with their subjects. In practice, however, the European administrators soon realized that both the unambiguous classification of the local population into clearly bounded ethnic categories and the creation of chiefdoms along ethnic lines were difficult tasks. Nonetheless, they remained convinced that mapping ethnic boundaries was not wholly impossible, and that, once the boundaries were discovered, they could eventually be transformed into the bases of the boundaries of the native states. Holding fast to this conviction, despite all evidence to the contrary, was part of the "working misunderstanding"[32] between local actors and colonial administrators that did finally produce a new political landscape of "tribes" and apparently ethnically defined chiefdoms.

The colonial ethnic map partly ignored and partly made strategic use of the ambiguities of overlapping identities and fuzzy boundaries. Toponyms were redefined as ethnonyms and vice versa; the mobility of the population was disregarded, or conceptually watered-down as "intermingling"; and multiethnic settlements were redefined as monoethnic. Once established and fixed in writing, the colonial ethnic nomenclature proved quite enduring. This resulted partly from the self-referentiality of colonial reporting, and partly from the central significance accorded to the tribe as a model of political order. What also permitted these categories to be retained, once they had been constructed, was the fact that despite the rigidity of the taxonomic terms, their geographic location as well as their specific content (that is, the attributes and value judgments ascribed to them) changed whenever new realities or new perspectives needed to be accommodated.[33]

A similar "working misunderstanding" characterized the introduction of chieftaincy. Interacting with local actors who were themselves interested in political centralization and power, the British and the French eventually succeeded in transforming the political landscape. In the British protectorate, a typical model appears to have been the recruitment of the first chiefs from the local "strong men"—renowned warriors, rich traders, or well-to-do farmers with large houses. However, not everywhere did these first chiefs also belong to the earth priest's patrilineage, and even where they did, the offices of earth priest and chief were from the very beginning separate. The extent of the new chiefdoms was therefore defined not according to the borders of the earth-shrine areas, but in terms of the size of the kinship, friendship, and clientele networks of the chiefs. By 1907, the British officers had divided the Lawra District into ten "native states," each under the authority of a "head chief," of which some encompassed up to thirty settlements, while others included only two or three. In the early 1930s, the smaller native states were allocated to the four largest ones (later called "divisions"), Lawra, Jirapa, Nandom, and Lambussie, as subdivisions. The Lawra Confederacy, which was created in this way, survived the administrative reforms of the 1950s and continues today to mark out the framework within which local political alliances and enmities are formed and the establishment of new districts and constituencies is disputed.[34]

French administrators first experimented with installing powerful "strangers" from surrounding chiefly societies as chiefs for the supposedly anarchic "Lobi" and "Dagari." However, they soon found that these chiefs' authority was extremely limited, and therefore also took to recruiting influential locals as chiefs, from among the earth-priestly families, precolonial "strong men," or, after World War I, returning soldiers.[35] The Dagara and Sisala settlements around Ouessa, Niégo, and Bourra became part of the Cercle de Léo and were first organized into two *cantons* (Ouessa and Niégo), with their respective *chefs de canton*, for the Dagara population, and several smaller units (Bourra, Niabouri, and others) for the Sisala. By the mid-1920s, in an attempt to implement William Ponty's doctrine of the "politique de race," these units were amalgamated into one single paramount chiefdom for the Dagara, and two for the Sisala population, which, however, actually comprised many multiethnic settlements.[36]

Neither in the British protectorate nor the French colony were the new chiefdoms congruent with earth-shrine areas or with ethnic groups, and all plans at further amalgamation failed in the face of the opposing interests of the smaller chiefs, who saw themselves as having been robbed of their influence. It was therefore not a matter of "tribes" being organized in chiefdoms; rather, chiefdoms, whose borders were influenced through quite different factors than ethnic ones, were provided belatedly with ethnic labels.

The chiefs, for their part, soon adopted the new ethnic ideologies in the interests of securing the continuity of their rule and extending the area under their control. They devised "tribal" histories for themselves that reinterpreted the older models of migration histories, which had focused on the patrilineage, in terms of the newly introduced ethnic categories. Where competition over land and other resources intersected with ethno-linguistic boundaries, colonial ethnic terminologies also offered a new idiom of expressing the fault lines between Dagara frontiersmen and Sisala first-comers and, potentially, for enlisting support both from one's "own" people and the European administrators. Indigenous processes of hardening ethnic boundaries and colonial ideas of tribal communities thus mutually influenced and reinforced each other.

At the same time, however, collective ethnic identifications continued to be subject to debate and negotiation, particularly in struggles over political overlordship and property of land. In the early 1930s, for instance, the British attempted to convince the Sisala chiefs from Lambussie to join their fellow Sisala in Tumu in order to create an all-Sisala native authority. But Yesibie, the Lambussie paramount chief, wanted to maintain the status quo of Lambussie's incorporation into Lawra District. Presenting Lambussie's "Dagarti" origins as an argument, he insisted that his people

> were not really Issalas [sic] and did not speak the proper Issalla language. . . . The Lambussie people originally came from around Lawra. . . . The Nandom people came from round about Babile, Burifoo, Lawra etc. and were given land by the Lambussie people [at that time Dagarti]. Lambussie people intermarried with Issalla women and eventually came to speak a kind of bastard Issalla, though they nearly all can still speak Dagarti. Lambussie therefore wishes to be incorporated with the Lobi-Dagarti district [i.e., Lawra] rather than with the Issalla district.[37]

Fifteen years later, Yesibie's successor was to claim precisely the opposite when he sought to convince the British that the Lambussie native authority needed autonomy from the Dagara chief of Nandom, under whose authority it had been placed for a number of years. He now stressed that the people of Lambussie were indeed Sisala and could not live according to their own customs if they were forced to follow a Dagara paramount chief.[38]

The most important argument for why Lambussie first wanted to remain with the Lawra Confederacy and later insisted on independence from Nandom was not, however, cultural propinquity to, or difference from, the "Dagarti," but the land question. Yesibie feared that he risked losing some of "his" land (and subjects) if he followed Tumu.[39] By the late 1920s, a substantial number of Dagara from Nandom had settled on Sisala land in the Lambussie Division. So far, they had respected Sisala property rights and political authority, but now Yesibie anticipated that once Lambussie joined an all-Sisala chiefdom on the grounds of shared ethnicity, the Dagara of Lambussie would not be allowed to follow him, but would rather fall back under the rule of their former Dagara paramount chief, namely the Nandom Naa (and with them the land that they occupied). As long as Lambussie belonged to the same confederacy as the Nandom division, Yesibie believed, it was easier for the Sisala to retain some measure of control over the land on which the Dagara immigrants settled. In other words, Yesibie feared that the extension of the political authority of the Nandom Naa would have consequences for the territorial boundaries of his own, or rather his various earth priests', property rights. Accepting Nandom overlordship, on the other hand, carried the same danger of losing the land, because in the long run, as Yesibie's successor feared, the Nandom chiefs would convert political authority into rights over land.

Yesibie's and other chiefs' claims to control "the lands" in their respective divisions were novel insofar as the paramount chiefdoms usually embraced more than one earth-shrine parish. Each Sisala village under the political authority of the Lambussie paramount chief continued to have its own independent earth shrines whose custodians regarded themselves as the traditional owners of their respective village territories. Yesibie's main interest, however, was not to establish any direct economic or ritual control over these "Lambussie lands," but to strengthen his political rule by invoking, in a traditionalizing fashion, his status as member of the group of first-comers and landowners. More generally, the newly established chiefs often attempted to validate their claims to political authority by bringing allodial property rights and settlement history into play. And precisely because Dagara and Sisala chiefs did not, in their own right, have any traditional control over land, they ingeniously extended the property-holding community from the earth-priestly lineage to the entire ethnic group.

This ethnicization of land rights was a subtle, gradual, and somewhat contradictory process. British and French administrators were aware that in the Black Volta region neither the "tribe" nor even the "village or local community" were legal entities that held property in common.[40] However, they believed that the local history was driven by tribal migrations, and thus tended to assign first-comer and late-comer positions to entire ethnic groups, rather than individual lineages—an assumption that was readily adopted, and further refined, by chiefs and other local actors. By asserting that they were members of the same ethnic group as the first-comers, people claimed, and were granted, privileged access to land, while ethnic strangers were denied full property rights, no matter how long they might have actually resided in a village. And although the day-to-day management of land tenure remained in the hands of earth priests and lineage heads, ethnicity, often mobilized by the chiefs, eventually became an ever more important ideological resource in land conflicts. As we shall see in the next section, this ethnicization of land rights was intricately connected with new discourses of autochthony.

Ideologies of Autochthony: Indigenous Host-Guest Relations, Colonial Natives, and the Legitimization of Chiefly Authority

Discourses of autochthony have, in recent years, become increasingly important in West African land conflicts as well as in competition for political power. They are similar to, and often intertwine with, ethnic ideologies. However, they are even more flexible than the latter since they do not necessarily invoke a common history or shared cultural practices, but merely erect a boundary between "autochthones," "natives," or "indigenous people" on the one hand, and "strangers," "foreigners," or "immigrants" on the other. The questions of who precisely is indigenous, and to where, have given rise to intense debate and negotiation. Sometimes autochthony becomes almost coterminous with national belonging, as in the Ivory Coast, where farmers of Burkinabé origins were labeled as foreigners and expelled. But in most cases, autochthony refers to social belonging and political rights within a given nation-state, and draws a boundary that excludes internal immigrants. The home territory and community, however, where one can claim "native" status can be as narrowly conceived as the village or even the first-comer lineage within the village, or as widely defined as the chiefdom or the entire ethnic group. The power of autochthony discourses rests precisely on the latitude they offer in redefining boundaries according to changing contexts and interests.[41]

Autochthony discourses, Geschiere and Nyamnjoh argue, developed out of the dialectics of the "liberation" of labor in African capitalism. Plantation and mine owners, in cooperation with colonial administrators, uprooted migrants from their traditional ways of life in order to recruit the necessary labor, while enforcing ethnic classifications and stabilizing home ties for purposes of tighter control.[42] Such connections between colonial *divide-et-impera* strategies and current identity politics are certainly relevant. In the Black Volta region and many other parts of West Africa, however, autochthony discourses are not entirely of colonial origin, but also arise out of (and transform) precolonial relations of hosts and strangers, or first-comers and late-comers. It is precisely these historical roots that make the colonial (and postcolonial) category of natives (versus strangers) such a powerful instrument for advancing economic and political claims.

Hosts and Guests: Indigenous Traditions

In the Black Volta region, boundaries between "us" and "them" reflected, and still reflect, the two basic, nonethnically defined principles of belonging—namely, the sacrificial community of an earth shrine and the kin group. Local and kinship criteria of belonging may reinforce each other, constituting a graded, flexible scale of otherness. The Dagara word *saan* (and the corresponding Sisala term *nihuara*), for instance, means both guest and outsider. Even a relative from another village is treated as a *saan* when he first arrives. If he stays, he may then gradually become integrated and join the people of the house (*yirdem*). A nonrelative remains a *saan* in the host's house, while in the village he gradually comes to be acknowledged as a member of the house and is no longer seen as an outsider. Many proverbs refer to the dangers as well as rewards involved in dealing with the *saan* and the fact that he does not have complete participatory rights in his new home. Anyone who is not a guest, relative, or friend of a particular household is referred to as *zagle*, meaning he is not allowed to interfere in local affairs. The same holds true for a *nuora* (literally, to push, stick something in), an adopted member of the family or a slave, who might nonetheless in due time be integrated into the household. Kin who have remained in the original home describe the family's labor migrants as *muopuo nibe*, or "bush people," a reference to the difference between the house (and earth-shrine parish) as domesticated nature and bush as wilderness. Strangers from outside the village, or neighboring groups, are also occasionally called *muopuo nibe*, and thus classified as belonging to the nondomesticated wilderness. In any case, *zagle, nuora*, and *muopuo nibe* describe social, not necessarily cultural or linguistic distance.

For property rights over land the most important distinction was whether a person belonged to the community who sacrificed at the earth shrine or not. This difference would be expressed by the Dagara terms *tengandem* (ritual custodians and "owners" of the land) or *tengbiir* (children of the earth/ village) versus *saame* (strangers, guests). Again, this distinction did not rest on language or culture. Although there were, and still are, no separate indigenous terms for the configuration of first-comers and late-comers or, as the British would later put it, natives and strangers, people were very much aware of the order of arrival of the different families in a village. They would use the terms *tengbiir* and *tengandem* (and corresponding terms in Sisala) to describe this order, but these terms were, and continue to be, relational and flexible. They can be used to include all first-comers, that is, all kin groups that helped establish the village, namely the earth-priestly lineage and its close allies. When people are interested in drawing further distinctions, however, they may reserve the term *tengandem* or *tengdem* (owners of the village) for only the earth-priestly lineage. Late-comers are often referred to as *saame*, guests, outsiders, or strangers, but can also be included in the category of *tengbiir* once they have been incorporated into the village's sacrificial community and when the latter wishes to distinguish itself from "latest-comers" with lesser rights. Such latest-comers, or settlers who do not take part in the sacrifices at the earth shrine, are always referred to as *saame*.

By and large, the host-stranger model was, in the past, geared toward the gradual inclusion of the stranger into the local society. He (or she) could be incorporated by marriage or by some form of adoption that would, among the Dagara, often use the patriclan system. Among the Sisala, it was more often the category of nephews (*tolbie*) that was used in order to integrate strangers. In both cases, those who began as strangers could end up as junior kin and thus become part of the *tengbiir*. In spite of the permeability of the boundary between hosts and strangers, there were, to be sure, also cases of disagreement about who was the legitimate first-comer and who a late-comer and stranger. As I have shown in previous chapters, in order to defend their privileged access to land and other resources, people could argue about what constituted the pivotal event defining first-comer status, and about the social inclusiveness of the first-comer group as well as the territorial reach of the area that the latter controlled. However, important for our context here is that many settlement histories report a remarkably rapid integration, or, as we could also call it, autochthonization, of newcomers into the local community, either by incorporating them into an existing settlement, or granting them permission to found their own small earth shrine—dynamics that could work both within and across ethnic boundaries.

From Hosts and Guests to Natives and Strangers: The Colonial Recruitment of Chiefs and the Redefinition of Autochthony

With colonial pacification and the freezing of property rights, this process of autochthonization came to a halt. Immigrants could no longer resort to violence in order to impose their autochthonous status, and now generally encountered more resistance by the first-comers if they wanted become part of the *tengbiir*, particularly when the distinction between autochthones and strangers coincided with ethnic boundaries. The host-stranger model continued to play an important role in organizing access to land, but strangers could no longer become natives if they belonged to a different ethnic group, no matter how many generations they had resided on the land.

The colonial redefinition of the permeable boundary between first-comers and late-comers into the more rigidly conceived difference between natives and strangers or immigrants was associated with two developments. The first had to do with new opportunities for cash-crop production and the concomitant increasing value of land. Particularly in the cocoa-producing areas of the forest belt of the British Gold Coast and the Ashanti Protectorate (as well as in the French lower Ivory Coast), the immigration of strangers took on unprecedented dimensions. The local chiefs and landowners were interested in planting cocoa, but often lacked the necessary labor force, and were usually quite willing to accommodate migrants as long as the latter respected their property rights and either offered labor services or were willing to pay some form of revenue for the use of the land. Depending on the availability of labor, landowners and chiefs could impose conditions in their own favor, or had to accept share-cropping arrangements that granted the immigrants more extensive rights to the piece of land they worked. Among the local population, in turn, chiefs at the various hierarchical levels and nonchiefly lineage elders often contended over the question of who had which rights to the land and thus to revenues from the immigrants. The British generally supported the chiefs' claims, especially those of the higher-ranking ones, to be the ultimate custodians of the land and thus entitled to revenues. However, much depended on the specific local configurations of power. In any case, the status as a "native" and thus a member of the landowning community became increasingly attractive. In some cases, chiefs even attempted to redefine not only recent immigrants, but even well established late-comers as strangers in order to increase the constituency of those who had to pay revenues for land use.[43] Although the Black Volta region lacked any extended cash-crop economy, these Southern disputes over the redefinition of the rights that natives enjoyed over strangers did have an impact on local conflicts over land because the new ideas traveled north, both with colonial officers and returning labor migrants.

The second development that transformed relations between first-comers and late-comers was their increasing politicization. The British "native authorities" model, and the French "politique de races," assumed that legitimate political authority was based on shared ethnicity. However, colonial administrators had to acknowledge that in reality many villages, and even more so some of the larger areas that they wanted to place under the authority of a single paramount chief, were ethnically mixed—a situation they explained by assuming that in the course of tribal migrations groups had intermingled. But who was then to become the chief of these multiethnic communities? In the case of precolonial chiefdoms, colonial officers usually respected the indigenous hierarchies, regardless of whether the African rulers defined themselves as autochthones or as prestigious conquerors who had immigrated as strangers. In segmentary societies, such as those in the Black Volta region, however, the chiefs were to be recruited among the true natives who had been the first to settle in the area. And in multiethnic settings, this presupposed defining which of the local ethnic groups were the autochthones, and which the immigrants and strangers who could, at best, be represented by subordinate headmen.

Yet, how to distinguish the autochthones from the strangers was a difficult task, particularly since local information on the settlement history was often contradictory. In Lawra District, for instance, a British commissioner mused, after speaking to a number of local elders, that only those who had lived in a locality for more than six generations should be considered true natives, but at the same time admitted that hardly any family in the district fulfilled this criterion.[44] In the absence of any reliable written history and in view of unending local disputes about the order of arrival of the various groups, the chief commissioner of the Northern Territories finally settled for a pragmatic definition: everybody whose parents belonged to one of the "indigenous tribes" of the Northern Territories was to be regarded as a "native."[45] This definition shifted the burden of historical argument from entangled, piecemeal lineage mobility to the grander picture of tribal migrations, but it seemed workable because it provided sufficient leeway for maneuver and interpretation. In a similar vein, French colonial officers distinguished between "autochthonous" and "conquering races." They conjectured that Dyan, Pougouli, and Sisala, among others, were "autochthones," while Dagara, Wiile, and Birifor had only more recently immigrated into the area as "conquerors."[46]

Colonial models of autochthony thus radically simplified the precolonial landscape of nuanced, flexible host-guest relations, and tended to conflate first- and latecomer status with ethnic boundaries. Colonial officials were content to attach the label "native" to an entire ethnic group in a given area, and left it to the chiefs and lineage heads to sort out the micropolitics of belonging. However, despite the unwillingness of colonial administrators to involve themselves in such local disputes, competing claimants who tried to enlist their support in struggles over political authority and access to resources confronted them with countless conflicting versions of the settlement history. Furthermore, temporarily defeated versions were kept alive and brought back into play when circumstances changed, for instance, when a new administrator took office or a powerful earth priest or chief died. Despite the conceptual simplification, therefore, the ascription of native and stranger status continued to be negotiable on the ground to a certain extent, and depended on local power relations.

Earth Priests versus Chiefs: Autochthony and Competing Claims to Authority

The colonial idea that chiefs should be recruited among the natives did not define in any detail how the new officeholders should relate to the earth priests, that is, the authority that embodied first-comer status and land ownership par excellence. In fact, from the very beginning, the relationship between chiefs and earth priests, and between the respective territories under their authority, was contentious. As already mentioned, the boundaries of the new chiefdoms did not corresponded with the earth-shrine parishes, and quite a few chiefs did not belong to earth-priestly families. The pragmatics of chiefly power politics rarely followed the contours of the landscape of property rights and spiritual authority. However, the idea that the chiefs' powers should flow from an allodial title to the land and that chiefdoms should match earth-shrine parishes soon became a powerful instrument in colonial and local debates about appointments to chiefly office and about the territorial delimitation of chiefdoms.

Conflicts often arose with regard to the question of which rights the earth priest held when it came to selecting and appointing the chief. Further, people disagreed about the extent to which chiefs could intervene in land matters. These questions were, unsurprisingly, hotly contested in places where the chief and the earth priest belonged to different patrilineages, but they could also arise if they were members of the same kin group. During one of the "native authorities conferences," that is, meetings of all chiefs of Lawra District, the Lawra Naa stated what could be regarded as the orthodox view. As the British district commissioner who had convened the meeting reported:

> The Lawra Na related, and the meeting agreed, that before the advent of Europeans, the head of each family was the ruler of each family, that leaders in war would

be regarded as men whose opinion must be listened to (for obvious reasons), and that the Tingansobs [earth priests], as descendants of the first settlers, held power in the adjudication of land and imposed sanctions in matters where the land had been defiled. . . . It was recognised that chiefship was a modern innovation. . . . It transpired that the first chiefs appointed on the European arrival were nominated to the first Commissioners by the Tingansobs, and that in this action lay the only "Custom" that could be said to pertain.[47]

On the basis of this "custom," the Lawra Naa concluded, the candidates for a vacant chiefship were to be selected from among the deceased chief's "patrilineal family," but had to be "approved by the Tingansob of the area concerned."[48] The assembled chiefs, however, did not clarify what was to happen should the earth priest refuse to endorse a candidate presented by the chiefly family. In Nandom, for instance, where the chief and the earth priest belonged to different patriclans, several such disagreements occurred and gave rise to long-standing conflicts over chiefly succession. The faction that did not want to bow to the Nandom earth priest's preference for a particular candidate argued that the very office of the chief originated from precolonial positions of power quite distinct from authority derived from the control over land; hence the earth priest should have no say in the appointment of the chief.[49] However, in most cases, the orthodox view that demanded the earth-priestly endorsement of the chief's appointment was officially upheld, even if it was not followed to the letter.

The orthodox view with regard to the chief's role in land matters was, and still is, often summarized in the dictum that "the chief rules the people, while the earth priest rules the land." Ideally, this meant that the chiefs were not entitled to interfere in local land disputes that did not concern their own families, nor were they authorized to establish new markets, settle immigrants, or collect gifts or fees for the use of the land under their jurisdiction, at least not without previously consulting the earth priests and sharing some of the revenue with them. In reality, however, chiefs would rarely hesitate to intervene in land affairs whenever they felt it was opportune. They would argue that the earth priests' duties concerned only "religious" aspects of the land, while the native authorities should attend to its secular administration, particularly when it came to dealing with strangers—a view that the colonial officials, for reasons of administrative expediency, usually endorsed.

On the whole, chiefs gained increasing influence over land affairs, and earth priests tended to be sidelined.[50] Here again, however, much depended on the specific local power relations—for instance, the degree to which the earth-priestly lineage was connected with the chiefly family, and whether it could rally the support of educated relatives in order to defend its rights vis-à-vis the chiefs and the colonial administration. In any case, in all these conflicts, local settlement history and arguments about the identity and prerogatives of first-comers, intermingled with colonial ideas about autochthony, were intensely debated.

Earth Shrines and "Native States": The Controversial Territorialization of Chiefly Rule

With regard to the spatial demarcation of the chiefdoms in relation to earth-shrine boundaries, chiefs and colonial officers often invoked traditionalist arguments that political authority should arise from land ownership and control over an earth shrine. However, just as often, such ideological principles were superseded by the pragmatics of chiefly power politics—a development that made the situation of legal pluralism even more complex because pragmatic decisions were later reinterpreted as normative precedents, as we shall see in the next chapter.

In the case of the Lawra paramount chiefdom, for instance, the chiefs reinterpreted the local settlement history in ways that suited their political interests. When interviewed by the British district commissioner in 1908, Gari, the incumbent Lawra Naa and a member of the earth-priestly family, narrated a version of the story of Kontol, the settlement's founding ancestor, that supported extensive claims to political control over neighboring settlements and legitimated the position of Lawra as the center of a large paramount chiefdom.[51] In the same vein, Gari's successor put on record that Lawra was "one of the biggest" earth-shrine territories, "with about 150 square miles,"[52] and described how Kontol, upon arrival in Lawra, had "proceeded to mark out his domain . . . by marking trees." Thus, the British commissioner concluded, Kontol and his descendants, including the Lawra chiefs, owned all lands around Lawra and the entire territory up to "the present villages of Furu, Yagtori, Zambano, along the Kanba River to a point beyond Gengempwe and then back down to the Volta river."[53] More recently, Lawra Naa Abayifaa Karbo insisted that the area under the authority of the Lawra earth shrine even reached well beyond Nandom, into present-day Burkina Faso, and that it was only out of the present generation's general "lack of respect" for tradition that these distant villages no longer honored their duties toward their parental shrine.[54] All these claims exploited the ambiguities of local histories of earth shrines and their territorial reach.[55] In the case of Lawra, the chiefs obviously attempted to reclaim older layers of property rights over hunting territories and spheres of spiritual influence as a legitimate basis for extending their political control. However, the Lawra chiefs' policies themselves were not always consistent with such principled arguments. They were unwilling, for instance, to relinquish control over villages whose land admittedly never belonged to the Lawra earth shrine but had been included in the paramount chiefdom for reasons of administrative convenience.

Neither local actors nor colonial administrators agreed on the question of whether a close correspondence between earth shrine areas and chiefdoms was really practicable or even desirable. District Commissioner St. John Eyre-Smith, for instance, proposed that the 1930s reform of the "native authorities" should be used to correct the errors of the early colonial administrators who had established the chiefdoms without regard for earth-shrine boundaries. Only if chiefdoms were defined according to the earth shrines' spheres of influence, and thus the chiefs firmly placed under the control of the earth gods, Eyre-Smith believed, could the chiefs' tendency to exploit their subjects be kept in check.[56] Eyre-Smith's colleague John Guinness, on the other hand, campaigned for the continuance of the existing chiefdoms and emphasized that the chiefly office had local roots that were quite independent from the earth priests, namely in powerful war leaders and other "self-made men."[57] Guinness admitted that conflicts of authority could arise when the boundaries of chiefdoms and earth-shrine parishes did not coincide, but insisted that the local population had usually come up with pragmatic solutions to this problem. The Gegenkpe subchief, for instance, politically followed the Nandom Naa, but lived on land that belonged to the Lawra earth shrine and did not find it "unnatural," Guinness argued, "to go to the Lawra Tingdana when he wishes to make a sacrifice, and to the Chief of Nandom when he has a civil complaint."[58] Any reorganization along earth-shrine boundaries, Guinness concluded, would create new problems, particularly if, as was sometimes the case, they ran through the middle of a settlement.[59]

What carried the day was the position of Guinness and many of his colleagues, who wanted to stabilize the system of chiefdoms introduced thirty years earlier and argued that the earth-shrine organization was too complex to serve as the basis for an effective administrative order. However, Eyre-Smith's arguments for a close correspondence of earth-shrine parishes and chiefdoms were, and continue to be, rehearsed in many local conflicts about the (re)demarcation of political allegiance. The long-standing conflicts over the political allegiance of Hamile, an increasingly prosperous border town originally under the authority of the Nandom paramount chief, are a prominent case in point. Here, the Sisala earth priests and chiefs of the neighboring settlement of Happa, a village in the Sisala-ruled Lambussie paramount chiefdom, claimed that they were the legitimate political authorities of Hamile because the town was built on land that they owned. The case was particularly intricate because Hamile is divided by the international border, and the Hamile Sisala earth priests lived in the French colony, while what came to be the British section of Hamile was founded shortly before the onset of colonial rule by some Dagara families, with the consent of the Sisala earth priests. However, due to the difficulties of managing their earth-priestly duties across the border, the latter delegated some of their powers to their Sisala relatives on British territory, namely the earth priests of Happa. These new owners soon started arguing that the true natives of Hamile were Sisala, not Dagara, and that the town should therefore be placed under the Lambussie Native Authority (and eventually Lambussie Local Council). The British initially opposed these attempts, but after a long and embittered dispute the chiefs of Happa and Lambussie finally agreed to Hamile's placement under the authority of the Lambussie Local Council.[60]

More generally, the colonial concept of "native authorities" was based on a territorial definition of political rule that assumed sedentariness and unambiguous boundaries. The chiefs should rule over all persons who resided in a specific territory—natives, strangers, and settlers alike. Local practices of mobility and multilocality, however, with farmers sometimes having their houses in one, but their farms in another chiefdom, or with people moving back and forth between several farmsteads, made the definition of residence and the distinction between natives and settlers thorny questions. On the ground, the delineation of the chiefdoms was therefore a piecemeal and contested process. The area of rule of the divisional chiefs and *chefs de canton* was defined through lists of subchiefs and villages owing them *corvée* labor. When the British introduced a poll tax in 1934, taxation lists were drawn up that fixed the membership of all men to a compound, all compounds to a village, and all villages to a division—an exercise that the French colonial officers had undertaken already much earlier and that made great strides toward a territorial definition of political belonging. However, in both colonies, the assumption of linear boundaries between the chiefdoms remained problematic, and in fact such boundaries were conspicuously absent from all colonial maps. Instead, the colonial officers continued to rely on lists containing the names of the villages and village headmen who were subordinate to a given native authority.

The paramount chiefs, for their part, attempted to extend their sphere of control by drawing on whatever arguments best fit their case. They would invoke the landscape of earth shrines and allodial property rights if this went in their favor, as in the case of Lawra and Hamile. But they could also argue along lines of personalized relations of domination and political loyalty. In the British protectorate, for instance, when increasing numbers of Dagara farmers from the Nandom Division moved in search of fertile farmland into the Sisala-ruled Lambussie and Tumu chiefdoms, the Nandom Naa first tried to prevent them from migrating altogether. When he did not succeed in this attempt, not least because colonial officers supported the cause of the land-seeking migrants, he still insisted that because the latter maintained close family ties to their true native home, they should continue to pay their taxes to Nandom.[61] Eventually, however, his claim was successfully countered by the Sisala chiefs' assertion that anyone wanting to farm their land should pay taxes and accept political subordination to their chiefdom. Similarly, in the French colony, the Dagara paramount chief Denyuu, who reigned from the 1930s to the end of the colonial period, took the French "politique de race" concept rather literally and claimed authority over all Dagara east of the Black Volta River. But, as we saw in the last chapter, when he tried to govern even those Dagara who had settled on Sisala land, this was resisted by the Sisala chiefs—and eventually the French—who insisted on the territoriality of rule. Consequently, ever more Dagara who wanted to escape his despotic command moved onto land, the Sisala ownership of which they deliberately recognized, placing themselves under the Sisala chiefs' authority (and protection).

As these examples show, the colonial politicization of autochthony and the territorialization of political rule eventually transformed the local mental map(s) and set the stage for new conflicts over land and belonging. This was not, however, the automatic result of colonial policies. Even though the colonial administration exerted considerable influence on local relations of power, much depended on the particular local configurations. An instructive example of such processes in which the meaning of land ownership and belonging was redefined is the history of the Dagara in Bozo, to which I now turn.

(Re)Negotiating the Relations between "Natives" and "Settlers"

Bozo is a large village just outside the Ouessa earth-shrine area that was founded by the Sisala, but since the 1930s has also attracted many Dagara farmers. At least 90 percent of Bozo's current population of about 1,500 inhabitants are Dagara.[62] Only three Sisala farmsteads remain, one of them being that of the Sisala earth priest and chief.[63] In many respects, Bozo is a special case because the conditions for the allocation of land to the immigrant Dagara were not dictated by their Sisala hosts alone, but resulted from complicated negotiations between Dagara settlers, missionaries, colonial authorities, and Sisala chiefs and landowners. Yet precisely because of this intricate and contested history of Sisala-Dagara relations, the case of Bozo sheds light on the ways in which local as well as supralocal configurations of power shaped the dynamics of mobility, land rights, and belonging under colonial rule, and set the stage for current disputes between Sisala first-comers and Dagara settlers over property rights, political representation, and the question of who is autochthonous.

An Oppressive Chief and His Fugitive Subjects: The Dagara Settlement of Bozo

The settlement of Dagara farmers in Bozo during the 1930s and early 1940s was part of the massive exodus provoked by the harsh rule of Denyuu, the Dagara *chef de canton*. Issa Nadie, the current chief of the Sisala *canton* of Bourra, to which many of the disaffected Dagara fled, remembered that it was only after his father, Kama Nadie, became chief in 1941 that Denyuu's attempts to encroach on Sisala villages could finally be restrained.[64] Kama's predecessor Nyengu was illiterate and had great difficulties in countering Denyuu's skillful combination of persuasion and violence and, most important, his ability to secure French support for his undertakings. Denyuu had been to school, was employed as interpreter in Ouagadougou, and fought in the French army during the First World War. But Nyengu eventually called on his cousin Kama, who, like Denyuu, spoke French and worked as an interpreter for the French, and could therefore establish direct contacts with the colonial authorities in Léo in order to represent Bourra's interests. As a result, the French authorities placed a good number of additional Sisala and Nuni villages under the Bourra Kuoro's control, and, as Issa Nadie put it, Kama was effectively able to "protect" the Dagara refugees against Denyuu's incursions.

This protection, however, came at a price for the Dagara, namely that they had to recognize the Sisala as landowners (notwithstanding the formal state domain) and political overlords. But many Dagara were obviously willing to pay this price because they regarded the Sisala chiefs' requisitions of tax and *corvée* labor as considerably lighter than Denyuu's. For similar reasons, large numbers of Dagara villagers from the *cantons* of Niégo and Ouessa, controlled by Denyuu, fled into British territory and settled close to the border, near Sisala villages such as Nimoro, Koro, and Piina.

That many Dagara refugees were content with a position as settlers who were not expected, or even allowed, to sacrifice at the earth shrine is explained by not only political but also religious factors. In 1929, the White Fathers established a new mission station in Jirapa, on British territory, and within a few years attracted thousands of converts from among the Dagara of Lawra District as well as the neighboring French colony.[65] The missionaries' teachings that the converts should abandon sinful "heathen'"practices, such as sacrifices at ancestor and earth shrines, and that they should not perform *corvée* labor on Sundays, soon created tensions between the new Christians and the chiefs (and earth priests). When the latter turned to the colonial officers for assistance, these often agreed that the chiefs' authority was endangered. However, initial open conflict between converts and chiefs, missionaries and colonial officers, eventually gave way to compromise, and the chief commissioner of the Northern Territories finally agreed that the Christians were entitled to "complete liberty of conscience and worship," but should also not forget that they "remained under the authority of the chiefs."[66] The details of how to bring about the peaceful coexistence of Christians and non-Christians were largely left to the local authorities, and many minutiae of the rights and duties of Christians and "traditionalists" continued to be a matter of dispute, the outcome of which depended on local power relations.

One way how the new Dagara Christians attempted to evade objectionable ritual obligations vis-à-vis ancestors and earth shrines, particularly if they were young and under much pressure from their elders and chiefs, was to migrate into Sisala territory and thus become settlers. This did not solve all problems because the Sisala earth priests generally insisted on payments for the construction of houses, the burial of the placenta of newborn babies, and the performance of funerals. But my interlocutors left no doubt that their Christian fathers or grandfathers had definitely preferred such routine payments to a personal involvement in sacrifices at the earth shrine, as was expected of them in their home villages. Such considerations were also one of the driving forces behind the Dagara settlement in Bozo, a Sisala village just outside the Ouessa earth-shrine area.

From Guests to Settlers: The French Establishment of a Christian Dagara Refuge in Bozo

By the early 1930s, the movement toward the new faith had taken on mass dimensions, and often more than ten thousand converts and onlookers gathered in Jirapa. The number of Dagara who traveled from Upper Volta to Jirapa took on such proportions that the French authorities became concerned that a good many pilgrims might eventually become emigrants, resulting in an undesirable drain of taxpayers and labor power. In early 1933, therefore, the French governor called a meeting in Ouessa with the colonial officers responsible for the *cercles* of Ouagadougou, Diébougou, and Gaoua, and the relevant authorities of the Catholic mission, including the White Fathers stationed in Ouagadougou and in Jirapa. Since it seemed impossible to control border crossings more rigidly, it was finally decided that the missionaries should open new stations on French territory, thus making the pilgrims' journey to Jirapa unnecessary. The choice fell on Dissin and Dano (and, to be opened later, Gaoua), villages west of the Black Volta that were deemed to be in the middle of areas with large numbers of Dagara converts. In turn, the White Fathers had to promise to send all Upper Volta converts in Jirapa back to these new stations on French territory.[67]

In the summer of 1933, the French commander of the Léo subdivision and his superior in Ouagadougou tried to convince the White Fathers that they should establish a third mission station, east of the Volta. The colonial authorities were concerned about the increasing number of Dagara from around Ouessa, Niégo, and Dianlé who fled into the British protectorate, threatening to leave the region seriously depopulated. Apparently, Denyuu was particularly onerous toward Christians and kept tormenting the numerous converts who regularly met in Kolinka, where the White Fathers had stationed two Mossi catechists—at least this was what these catechists reported to the missionaries in Ouagadougou and what an investigation by the colonial officer in charge confirmed. In order to prevent the Kolinka Christians from also taking off for greener pastures in the British protectorate and to convince some of the refugees who had already settled across the border to return, the French officers proposed to establish a model village for Dagara Christians on a suitable stretch of "empty" land, not far from Kolinka, but independent of Denyuu. The settlers were to be given sufficient land, and they would be exempted from tax payments and forced labor for a period of three years while they helped to construct the mission station. The French commander in Léo was to choose a convenient place for the Christian settlers and organize the labor necessary for clearing land, digging wells, and constructing a road, while the colonial headquarters in Ouagadougou was to provide the money and materials required to build the new mission. "You are the only ones to hold them back," the administrator of Ouagadougou implored the missionaries—at least according to the latter's minutes of the meeting—"I want to create a village independent of Daniou [Denyuu] . . . and if 8 or 10,000, or even the whole world came to you: a Christian district. I would love that."[68]

The apostolic vicar in Ouagadougou was skeptical, but did not entirely oppose the project. His regional superior, Blin, however, was much more critical, mainly because the White Fathers did not have sufficient personnel to operate an additional station, but also because the project was motivated by "administrative maneuvers." "If it is true that the exodus [toward British territory] is caused by the behavior of a *chef de canton*," Père Blin wrote to the superior general in Algiers, "it is not difficult for the administration to replace him. We should not interfere in these political affairs without very good reasons."[69] The administrator in Léo, however, obviously took the White Fathers' approval for granted, and toward the end of 1933 had already effectively settled the first ten Dagara families on Bozo land.

The site was apparently chosen in consultation with Bourra Kuoro Nyengu because Bozo seemed to have more than sufficient space to accommodate the Christian refugees. The settlement plan was announced in Kolinka, and those Christian families interested in moving to Bozo were invited to witness how the colonial policemen, in the presence of the Bourra Kuoro and the French commander of Léo, surveyed the land along the road from Ouessa to Léo and assigned contiguous parcels of one hundred meters width each to the new settlers. Earlier on, the commander had already ordered the Sisala chiefs of the surrounding villages to send their subjects to clear the bush along the road and thus prepare the settlement of the Dagara newcomers. "We were given the land south of the road," Somda Eloi, one of the early Christian settlers remembered; "the telephone poles marked the boundaries between the plots, and we were told to farm towards the south."[70] Because the French state regarded itself as the paramount owner of all land, a government-initiated settlement project, such as the one in Bozo, did not require an earth priest's approval. Bourra Kuoro Nyengu had apparently simply informed the Bozo earth priest that the Dagara Christians would be given some village land. "Those days, our elders were afraid," explained the Sisala chief of Bozo, "there used to be very heavy beatings if they disobeyed colonial orders."[71]

However, the balance of power soon changed. With the 1934 "revolt" of the Christianized Bwa, a group living not far north of Dano, the relationship between the colonial administration and the mission deteriorated,[72] and the White Fathers decided that they would not construct a mission station east of the Volta for some time to come. The French authorities, for their part, became increasingly wary of Christian zealots and returned to their policy of a more or less unconditional support for the native chiefs. The Dagara settlers in Bozo thus could no longer expect any immediate protection of their interests from either the missionaries or the colonial administrators, but had to negotiate the conditions of their settlement directly with their Sisala hosts and the Bourra Kuoro, under whose authority they fell.

From Settlers Back to Guests: Sisala Attempts to Reinstate Patron-Client Relations and the Tug-of-War over Land Rights

From what different informants recounted about the subsequent history of the Dagara in Bozo, it is clear that the Sisala aimed at reinstating the model of patron-client relations that governed the relationship between Sisala first-comers and Dagara settlers in other villages. In any case, they tried to get the immigrants to recognize their status as the only true natives and landowners. Obviously, they could not take back the parcels of land that had already been allotted, but they certainly could and did attempt to prevent any further encroachment.

The plots that the converts had been given proved to be quite fertile and produced good harvests. This, together with the relative peace the Christians enjoyed with regard

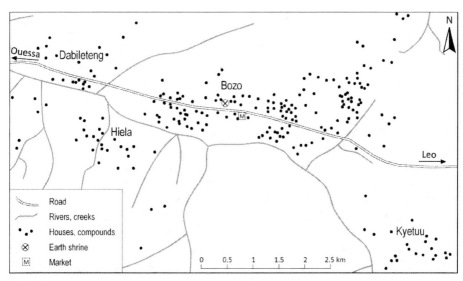

Map 4.1. Bozo

to their religious activities, attracted numerous relatives from Kolinka and other Dagara villages to join the first ten families, with the result that the original copious land grants no longer sufficed in face of the increasing demand. Inevitably, with the increasing number of farm hands, some of the Bozo Christians soon reached the "bottom" of their parcels, where they encountered Dagara immigrants who had been settled by the earth priest of Kyetuu and who were farming in the opposite direction toward Bozo. "A serious fight developed," Somda Eloi remembered,[73] but eventually, the French commander and the Bourra Kuoro intervened and firmly instructed the Bozo Dagara not to farm south of the small river that separates Bozo and Kyetuu (see map 4.1).

Any further expansion of land cultivated by the Dagara thus had to take place north of the Ouessa-Léo road, that is, on territory on which the Sisala had their own compounds and which they managed to supervise much more closely than the southern parts of Bozo. Before assigning any land north of the road and giving permission to farm, the Sisala landlords demanded gifts, such as fowl, cowrie shells, flour, and sorghum beer, as sacrifices to the earth god and to the spirits of the bush and the water. These gifts were a symbolic recognition of Sisala property rights and, to some extent, the acceptance of a host-stranger relationship, as well as, by implication, nonautochthonous status. Furthermore, the Sisala preferred to settle non-Christian Dagara newcomers who shared the Sisala's respect for the earth god, rather than to allow the already established Christian settlers to extend their fields. When the latter brought in additional relatives, the Sisala attempted to impose the same conditions on them as on other newcomers. In any case, relations between the Sisala's non-Christian Dagara clients and the first group of Christian settlers were somewhat tense. It seems, thus, that the Sisala made use of these intra-Dagara tensions to serve their own interests, pursuing a sort of divide-and-rule strategy to regain control over their land.

Moreover, the Sisala attempted to redefine the early Christian settlers—who regarded themselves as full owners of the land—as strangers by demanding, for instance, ritual payments for "opening" their houses and the right to bury the dead. Whether the Dagara Christians really refused such ritual payments from the very beginning, as my Dagara interlocutors in Bozo insisted, or rather initially gave in to some of the Sisala demands, resisting only much later, remains unclear. One of my Dagara informants from Ouessa remembered witnessing, as a boy in the early 1960s, during one of his visits to his relatives in Bozo, Sisala and Dagara young men seriously attacking each other after an exchange of insults. He could not remember the precise reason for the clash, but asserted that Dagara-Sisala relations had already been very tense and that after this event the Dagara Christians in Bozo stopped all further payments to the Sisala.[74]

Be that as it may, the history of Dagara-Sisala relations in Bozo was, and continues to be, a lengthy tug-of-war. This concerns ritual obligations as well as land tenure and other economic rights, such as fishing in the village pond, collecting firewood on village territory, or harvesting *dawa-dawa* and shea-nut trees—rights that the first-comers usually claim as their exclusive privilege. One source of leverage with which the Sisala in Bozo attempted to impose their conditions was land: they were reluctant to allot additional farmland to disobedient Dagara. They also asked the Bourra Kuoro for support, but apparently he did not discipline the Dagara to the extent they would have liked, because he did not want to jeopardize his Dagara subjects' willingness to contribute tax payments and *corvée* labor—an important asset in his relations with the colonial administration.

The major resources that helped the Dagara Christians quite successfully defend their ritual autonomy and economic rights were their demographic weight and their fearlessness with regard to supernatural sanctions. The Bozo Kuoro, for his part, deplored the fact that the Sisala minority barely stood a chance in face of Dagara encroachment because of the Dagara's numbers and because they could rely on the support of quite a few educated relatives. He was adamant, however, that the use of the land was ultimately sanctioned not by any secular law, but by the spiritual authority of the earth god and his human representatives.[75] Moreover, the Sisala have not relinquished their claims to allodial ownership of all village lands, including the plots once allocated to the early Christians. And in recent chieftaincy conflicts, they have vociferously defended their status as the only autochthonous inhabitants of Bozo and their exclusive right to furnish the village chief.

Autochthony, Chieftaincy, and Dagara Demands for Political Representation

The Sisala in Bozo repeatedly insisted that the Dagara settlers may only nominate a headman who remains subordinate to the Bozo Kuoro. In the same vein, they challenged Dagara aspirations to nominate the village *délégué* during the Sankara régime in the 1980s, and, in recent times, the *responsable administratif du village* who represents village interests vis-à-vis the district administration. Competing versions of the settlement history and arguments about autochthony were, and continue to be, major weapons in these contentions. The Dagara emphasize that they were settled not by the Sisala landlords, but by "white power," that is, the combined effort of the missionaries and the French authorities. Some of my Dagara interlocutors even insinuated that the whites had bought the land from the Sisala earth priests and transferred full property rights to the Dagara Christians. Further, in an attempt to present themselves as the true first-comers, they pointed out that there were only few Sisala houses when the Dagara arrived and that it was effectively the brave Dagara newcomers who cleared the bush and tamed the land. The Sisala, on the other hand, minimized the colonial administrators' and missionaries' role in the settlement of the Dagara. They insisted that their ancestors, when asked for assistance by the Bourra Kuoro, freely and in the spirit of customary hospitality offered land and protection to the Dagara "strangers" in need, without ever transferring any property rights.

These rival interpretations of the settlement history are reflected in competing narratives about the installation of a Dagara chief. According to my Dagara informants, the Christian settlers chose their representative without any Sisala intervention. Their first spokesman was Louis Gyerku, a much-respected catechist. After Louis's death, his former assistant Somé Jean took over, and from Jean the chiefly office went to his younger brother, Jean Paul. Because the Dagara chief's rank was equal to that of the Bozo Kuoro, the latter had no right to interfere in the succession, Jean Paul explained, going on to assert that since the large majority of inhabitants of Bozo were Dagara, the Dagara Naa was actually the chief not only of the Dagara, but the entire village.[76]

The Sisala, for their part, claimed that Louis had been appointed by the Bozo Kuoro and that Jean had succeeded Louis only after the Sisala had given their consent. Jean Paul, however, had not consulted the Sisala and thus arrogated the office. They would therefore not recognize him, not as the Dagara representative and much less as chief of the whole of Bozo. "We don't want to give this our village to strangers," Bozo Kuoro Banuosin argued. "We own the village, and we should take care of the people under us. . . . To own a place which has shade and a stranger tells you to leave the shade and sit in the sun, will you agree?!"[77] Expanding this argument, Bourra Kuoro Issa Nadie insisted that anyone coming to a village at which others had already previously arrived was automatically a stranger: "He cannot stand up one day and claim to be a full villager."[78] Consequently, the Bozo Dagara had no right to appoint a chief.

Issa Nadie, in turn, explained that his father, Kama, had asked Jean to accompany the Bozo Kuoro to all administrative meetings in Bourra and Léo and later convey all relevant messages to the Dagara in Bozo because Jean was fluent in both Dagara and Sisala, while the Bozo Kuoro only spoke Sisala. However, this never implied that Jean (or Louis, for that matter) was a chief in his own right. In the course of time, the Sisala in Bozo learned to speak Dagara (and French), but unfortunately, Issa Nadie explained, his father forgot to annul the former arrangement. Jean, and later Jean-Paul, thus continued to be invited to meetings in Bourra—a fact that the Dagara wrongly interpreted as recognition of their right to have a chief of their own. "And because today they are more numerous than the autochthones . . . and have sent many children to school," Issa Nadie complained, "they tell us that they cannot follow any minority, that they are going to rule the village. But the natives told them 'no, even if you would be one million, we are still the masters of the village!'"

Such disputes became particularly acute after Bourra Kuoro Kama's death in 1984. It is likely that this was also due to changes in the political environment. The Sankarist régime then in power initially did not recognize chieftaincy, but rather promoted a populist discourse of grassroots democracy. In 1995, however, when Issa Nadie assumed chiefly office after a long interregnum, the political climate had shifted toward a certain acceptance of the important role that chiefs (and earth priests) could play in local development. And after a nearly violent confrontation between the Sisala and Dagara in Bozo, mainly over questions of land rights, the Bourra Kuoro's defense of the Sisala in Bozo was apparently tacitly supported by the state administration. During a reconciliatory meeting in Bozo that he attended together with the Bourra district head and the *haut commissaire* from Léo, "the Dagara finally recognized that they had behaved wrongly."[79] My Dagara interlocutors, for their part, never mentioned this meeting or any such public declaration of their status as strangers, but rather reported that conflicts with the Sisala over questions of land ownership continued.

Not only in Laponé, as mentioned in the last chapter, but throughout the region, the Dagara generally see the Bozo case as an example of the absurdity and injustice of traditional land rights that associate land ownership with first-comer status and autochthony, and link political representation to the contingencies of settlement history at the expense of respect for the demographic majority and educational qualifications. The Sisala, on the other hand, regard the Bozo case as an alarming example of how the Dagara unscrupulously exploit any rights they were once accorded as guests and start to present themselves as masters—an example that should warn all Sisala villages to control their Dagara immigrants much more tightly from the outset.

The Bozo case has taken us well beyond colonial times. This *longue durée* perspective makes particularly clear how local struggles over native-stranger and patron-client relations were, and continue to be, shaped by wider power configurations. Colonial ideologies of autochthony and the territorialization of political authority supported first-comers in their attempts to resist the forceful autochthonization of late-comers that had characterized precolonial mobility. Late-comers, on the other hand, assented to the first-comers' economic and political privileges and their own status as strangers when it suited them (as in the case of the flight from Denyuu's rule) or when they were forced to do so because they lacked powerful external allies. However, it was only after independence, when the chieftaincy was eventually freed from its stigma as an instrument of colonial exploitation, that many younger Dagara aspired to fuller political participation in village affairs and started to regret the price their fathers had paid for settling on Sisala land, namely, accepting a status as settlers.

Ethnicity and Autochthony in the Postcolonial Nation-State: Negotiating Land Rights, Belonging, and Political Representation

During decolonization and after independence, ideologies of autochthony, closely intertwined with idioms of ethnic belonging, lost nothing of their force. On the one hand, the economic stakes connected with land have steadily risen. Increasing land shortage as well as new opportunities of cash-cropping or deriving income from the parceling out of land for construction purposes have increased competition over access to, and control over, land. Claims of being first-comers, and thus autochthones, have been, and still are, translated into assertions of allodial property rights. They serve as powerful idioms to exclude late-comers and settlers from ever-larger portions of the bundle of rights over land, or to insist that they must pay some form of compensation for whatever rights are temporarily transferred to them.

The introduction of local councils and national parliaments, on the other hand, has intensified debates over belonging and the right to represent local communities in the larger political arena. In principle, in the new nation-states colonial subjects were transformed into citizens of equal rights, without regard of ethnicity or regional origins, and without reference to local distinctions between first-comers and late-comers. However, Burkina Faso and Ghana, like many other African states, have, in their legal definitions of citizenship, combined principles of *ius soli*, that is, belonging based on residence, with elements of *ius sanguini*, that is, belonging based on descent, and thus opened the door to ideologies of autochthony.[80] Autochthony could now be invoked for demarcating not only local, but also national belonging. This became particularly relevant in borderlands such as the Black Volta region, where mobility across the international boundary was increasingly reinterpreted, at least by some actors, as indications of foreign origins and doubtful loyalties. Furthermore, independent Ghana inherited the colonial model of the nation as a sort of federation of "native states." To be fully Ghanaian therefore presupposes, in the minds of most Ghanaians, being a proper member, or in colonial parlance, "native," in an ethnic-cum-local community. Similar concepts influence images of the nation in Burkina Faso.[81]

Arguments about autochthony were projected onto the new secular representative institutions such as local and district councils and are even mobilized when choosing parliamentary candidates. The old disputes about how to circumscribe local administrative boundaries, identify natives and strangers, and define political allegiances thus resurfaced and even intensified, particularly during phases of democratization when "autochthonous" minorities feared to be dominated by more numerous "settlers."

Like under colonial rule, however, none of these developments was, or is, automatic. How rigidly the boundary between natives and strangers is drawn depends on the specific interests at stake and the existing balance of power. The very same persons can define the first-comer group more narrowly in one context, and more inclusively in another, vis-à-vis, for instance, a third, still more distant group. Furthermore, it is important to keep in mind that disputes about the relations between first-comers and late-comers can occur in any village, or between villages, regardless of their ethnic composition. However, when the dividing line is reinforced by ethnic boundaries, conflicts often take on larger dimensions because the adversaries tend to mobilize allies along ethnic lines, well beyond the immediate opponents in the initial disagreement.

Finally, local conflicts over land and belonging are increasingly informed by national legislation as well as by models of land tenure and native-stranger relations that are imported from other parts of the country. In Ghana, for instance, the 1979 constitution restituted all Northern Ghanaian "public lands" to their previous "owners," that is, to those persons or the "appropriate skin" (that is, chiefdom) in whom the lands were vested before they were entrusted to the (colonial) government.[82] This legal stipulation set off a series of attempts by chiefs and earth priests to reassert their control over land that they had previously allotted either to individual families or government agencies. They demanded that ultimate property rights should return to them or, in case of land on which administrative structures had been built, that they be paid adequate compensation. Particularly when paramount chiefs in the precolonially chiefless societies of the Upper West Region voiced such demands, they often argued along the lines of customary land tenure in the traditional kingdoms of the Ashanti and Northern regions, where land was, and continues to be, vested in "stools," or "skins," and controlled by the chiefs, not an earth priest.[83]

Such extralocal influences do not necessarily work only to the benefit of those who claim first-comer status and an allodial title. During the revolutionary regimes of Sankara and Rawlings, for instance, it was settlers and domestic migrants who received implicit, and sometimes even explicit, government support for their claims to land. Sankara's and Rawlings's dictum that the land should be distributed according to the farmers' needs and belong to those who work it encouraged many migrants to denounce the gifts exacted by autochthonous landowners as exploitation, and to demand free access to land as well as state support in securing their de facto property rights. The actual success of such attempts, however, depended very much on local power configurations, such as the relations between the *delegué* or the representative in the Committee for the Defence of the Revolution and the family of the local earth priest or chief.[84] Even after the demise of the revolutionary regimes, the argument that national citizens should have unencumbered access to land throughout the country, regardless of their ethnic identity, is still invoked by many migrants. They are sometimes supported by local government institutions if the latter are "shopping" for clients[85] and want to assert their own role against chiefs and earth priests. On the whole, however, Ghanaian and Burkinabé government officials have shifted back toward recognizing the important role of earth priests and chiefs in land administration. More generally, we can conclude that although African states are often too weak to enforce national land legislation down to the grassroots level, the knowledge that such legislation exists, as well as the possibility of resorting to state authorities or courts for enforcement, can influence local tenure conflicts and have an impact on the relations between "autochthones" and immigrants.

"This Is Ghanaian Territory": Land Rights, National Sovereignty, and Challenges to Autochthony's Privileges

The conflicts that surrounded the use of a fish pond in Kyetuu, a village that straddles the border between Ghana and Burkina Faso, offer an instructive example of disputes over the legitimacy of autochthony's privileges, and of the strategic use of national legislation and state authorities in such local struggles.[86] They also illustrate how autochthony is ethnicized, and how such primordially defined loyalties intersect with politico-administrative boundaries.

Kyetuu is inhabited by a small group of Sisala farmers whose ancestors founded the village and a large group of Dagara farmers who settled on Kyetuu land in colonial times.[87] The last border demarcation of 1973 defined the contested pond as lying on Ghanaian territory, but the Sisala earth priests, who live on the Burkina Faso side of the border, still regard the pond as well as the rest of the village territory as part of their ancestral lands. Before 1973, the small stream that broadens into the pond marked the international border, and so the pond belonged to both Burkina Faso and Ghana. In an attempt to correct its deviation from the 11th parallel, the last border demarcation altered the course of the boundary, and the pond now lies wholly on Ghanaian territory. This is an issue, however, only for those who challenge the traditional foundations of land and fishing rights and insist that land ownership is ultimately determined by national citizenship.[88]

For the Sisala, in addition to providing fish and being a source of water for people and animals, the pond has ritual importance. It had once moved the Sisala earth priests' ancestor, a powerful hunter, to settle in Kyetuu. The crocodiles that used to inhabit it were regarded as holy animals whose presence was both proof and assurance of the pond's, and, by implication, the village's, well-being. Eventually, however, the crocodiles disappeared, and for a long time the pond no longer held water year-round, as it had before. Around 1990, the Kyetuu earth priests finally decided to invest not only ritually, but also materially, in the improvement of the pond. They paid a contractor to come with heavy equipment and dredge the pond. As a result, the pond once more contained water and plenty of fish throughout the year.[89]

Traditionally, fishing was a communal activity, undertaken, with rather cumbersome baskets, toward the end of the dry season, after the earth priests had performed the necessary sacrifices to the spirits of the pond. The catch was divided into three portions, one belonging to the earth priests, the other two to the participants, including

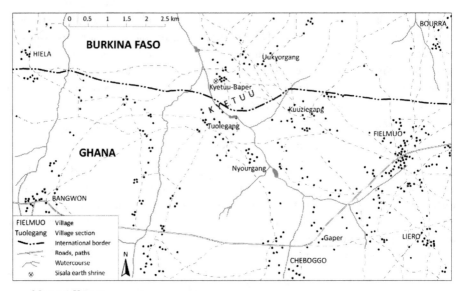

Map 4.2. Kyetuu

the Sisala living in Burkina Faso and the Dagara families who have their farmsteads near the pond. Beyond this communal basket-fishing event, fishing by individuals using rod and line was tolerated as long as the catch was small. However, in response to the pond's improvement, a number of young Dagara men from Kyetuu and neighboring Dagara settlements on the Ghanaian side of the border bought large modern, fine-meshed fishing nets and turned fishing into a year-round, profitable individual enterprise. The technical know-how and equipment were imported from Southern Ghana, where many of the young men had worked as seasonal labor migrants. Nets are much more efficient than the traditional baskets, but the Sisala objected to their use—because of a taboo, some said, or because the Sisala themselves could not afford the expensive nets, others explained. Moreover, the Sisala feared that the new, efficient nets would quickly deplete the number of fish and disrupt their reproductive cycle. The earth priests pleaded with the Dagara headman to exhort the fishermen to cease such intensive fishing, but the headman and other Dagara elders complained that the young men defied their authority. Tensions erupted when a young Dagara challenged the earth priests' messenger to a fight and, after a fierce exchange of insults, injured him badly. When the Sisala young men arrived at the pond to take revenge, the Dagara young men purportedly threatened to gun them down, yelling that they were defending Ghanaian territory, on which Burkinabé citizens such as the earth priest and his supporters had no right to trespass for fishing.

After the violent clash, the Burkinabé Sisala earth priests and the Ghanaian Dagara headman of Kyetuu turned to the Sisala chief of Bangwon, a neighboring village in Ghana, to mediate the conflict. The latter, in turn, felt that the issues at stake were of such a serious nature that he had to involve his superior, the paramount chief of Lambussie. Incidentally, a close relative of the Lambussie chief had been the Ghanaian chairman of the 1970s Ghana–Upper Volta Boundary Commission. On his tours of inspection, he had sensitized the borderland villagers to the territorial and political problems involved in establishing a state border, and it may have been because of his efforts that some of the Sisala earth-shrine areas across the border were reorganized. By the time of the fish-pond conflict, he had died, but exactly as he would have done, the Lambussie Kuoro made very clear to all involved that even though the pond was undoubtedly on Ghanaian territory, nobody had the right to take matters concerning the international border into his own hands. The Lambussie Kuoro suggested, however, that, in order to avoid future trouble, the Kyetuu earth priests from Burkina Faso should transfer all of their traditional rights over land in Ghana to the Sisala earth priest of Bangwon, the village that already controlled Tuolegang and Nyourgang, two of the three Dagara sections of Kyetuu on Ghanaian territory, in chieftaincy matters. This transfer was formally effected at a large meeting in the summer of 1998, during which the responsible Dagara and Sisala authorities diplomatically agreed that the pond was a communal resource to be used conscientiously by all and that nobody should start fishing before the Bangwon Kuoro had given the go-ahead. Thus, while the earth priests based their claims on the notion of an undivided spiritual domain that happened to straddle the international border, the Ghanaian chiefs reframed the matter in terms of modern political divisions.

Shortly after the 1998 meeting, the Lambussie Kuoro died. The chief of Bangwon, then an employee of the Tumu District administration, was absent from his home village most of the time and more than once postponed his visit to Kyetuu that should have clarified the details of the new arrangement. By the beginning of 1999, the Dagara young men had resumed their fishing activities. They argued that the Kyetuu earth-priest family's sons had started to fish again as well and that the pond would be empty, were the Dagara to wait for the official go-ahead. The Dagara elders, in turn, complained that they were unable to control their recalcitrant young men, who were evidently not about to forego an attractive source of income. Two years later, the Kyetuu earth priests, apparently frustrated by the Bangwon Kuoro's laissez-faire attitude, renewed their attempts to reassert control over what they still regarded as their pond. Once again, they addressed their complaint to the Dagara headman of Tuolegang, who, in turn, again referred the matter to the Bangwon Kuoro. This time, however, the Bangwon chief decided to act and called in the Ghanaian police, who arrested two of the Dagara fishermen, releasing them only after their families paid considerable bail. Whether the young men were actually brought to court remains a moot point, but according to rumors, no sooner were they released from the police detention than they resumed their profitable fishing activities. When I last visited the area in 2006, I was told that the Kyetuu earth priests had finally given up crossing into Ghana and that, because of the constant harassment they suffered at the hands of the Dagara young men, they no longer sacrificed at the pond. The Bangwon Kuoro, on the other hand, had apparently decided to tolerate the Dagara young men's net fishing in exchange for a generous share in the catch.[90]

The fish-pond conflict reveals a complex interplay of land-related discourses and strategies, drawing on traditionalist, Christian, colonial, and modern nationalist arguments. The Kyetuu earth priests were most forward in their traditionalist line of argument, insisting that as first-comers and spiritual authorities they have the right to control all land-related issues, even across the border. The older generation of Dagara settlers, on the other hand, argued partly in keeping with this traditionalist conception of land rights, but also evoked discourses of mutual respect, hospitality, and even friendship, while at the same time claiming that their fathers received the land and certain ritual rights from the Sisala in exchange for substantial gifts.

The younger Dagara, however, were born in the village and felt that they were *tengbiir*, "children of the land," and therefore full citizens of the village, on a par with their Sisala peers. Most of them were no longer willing to accept that, more than seventy years after their grandfathers' arrival, the historical configuration of first-comers and late-comers still justified distinctions in terms of land rights and political participation. These young Dagara were more aware than their parents of the existing legislation that limits the privileges to be drawn from autochthony, and they often emphasized shared nationality as a basis of their rights. They believed that as Ghanaians (or Burkinabé) they should enjoy the right to settle freely anywhere on national territory. They insisted that the pond was on Ghanaian territory and that the earth priests, because they were Burkinabé citizens, had no rights over it. In addition, they fused Christian arguments and the revolutionary discourse of the Rawlings regime, claiming that the land and related resources such as the pond should belong fully to those who need and cultivate them.

The Lambussie chief and the Sisala from Bangwon partly supported the earth priests' traditionalist line of argument, but also sought to come to terms with the international border. For them, the question of land was, and continues to be, closely intertwined with ethnicity and political power, and they looked for solutions that would strengthen the position of the Sisala as a whole vis-à-vis the Dagara. In their eyes, the Kyetuu land conflict was symptomatic of a larger ethnic struggle between the marginalized Sisala and the dominant Dagara. The Dagara not only constitute the demographic majority in many of the Sisala villages of the region, but because of their massive conversion to Christianity also had earlier access to formal education than did the Sisala. Dagara therefore outnumber Sisala in the regional administration and public services on both sides of the border, and many Sisala see their group as the historical loser, always in danger of being overruled by the Dagara—a view that also impacted the conflict over district boundaries that I discuss in the next chapter. They cling all the more strongly to their position as landowners and use it to retain political control at least at the local level. The Dagara, on the other hand, who are increasingly resentful of being denied full citizenship in village and district politics, attempt to consolidate their land rights and gain more political influence.

The Dagara fishermen and the Sisala chiefs and earth priests both made use of state authorities and national land legislation, but in different ways, exploiting the ambiguities of Ghanaian land laws. On the one hand, the 1992 Ghanaian constitution leaves no doubt that bodies of water are state property, under the supervision of the district assemblies and other relevant government authorities, and that the integrity of Ghanaian territory, particularly in border areas, needs to be protected at all times.[91] It was along these lines, and with Rawlings's earlier populist pro-use-rights discourse in mind, that the fishermen and their supporters insisted that the Burkinabé earth priests could not expect, and much less enforce, customary obligations across the border. On the other hand, the same constitution and, even more explicitly, the *Land Policy* published in 1999, guarantee the security of traditional "land ownership . . . based on an absolute 'allodial' or permanent title."[92] To "protect the rights of land owners and their descendants from becoming landless or tenants on their own land" is stated as one of the primary objectives of government land policies. Government should also help to "facilitate equitable access to . . . land," the authors of the policy document write, but insist that the land seeker "agrees with the landowner to adhere to the covenants and other customary practices governing the disposal of the land."[93] Regarding land conflicts along the international boundary, the document stipulates, somewhat ambiguously, that "initiatives in resolving issues, problems and disputes arising from cross-border activities . . . lie with the traditional authorities and District Assemblies."[94] The Lambussie Kuoro, and later the Bangwon chief, could thus count on the official support for their course of action, although, strictly speaking, they were not the allodial landowners of the disputed area according to the local settlement history. Nevertheless, they were the recognized "traditional authorities," and that was what counted.

Negotiating Belonging: Autochthony and Disputes over the Symbols of Ownership

With regard to the everyday use of the land, the question of allodial ownership may not be immediately relevant, particularly if the settlers have acquired, over time, extensive and inheritable customary use rights, as is the case in most older Dagara settlements on Sisala land. The Sisala landowners tend to complain about Dagara encroachment on their resources, while the Dagara grumble about Sisala expectations of gifts in recognition of their property rights. But both sides usually leave matters at that and tolerate whatever arrangement has been worked out over the years. Such a laissez-faire attitude, however, does not apply to the most important symbolic validation of social belonging at the family level, namely, funerals, or to the chief collective symbol of ownership, that is, place-names.

For the Dagara immigrants, burying their relatives in the new settlement instead of their original village is the crucial ritual that transforms a temporary farm shelter into a true house and thus creates a new home. The Sisala generally do not allow the Dagara to establish their own burial grounds, and insist that they must be consulted, and presented with substantial gifts, before they will grant permission for the burial. For both sides, this is a strong reminder of the distinction between autochthones and strangers. The Sisala often expressed fears that loosening control over such essential rituals as funerals is spiritually dangerous and might encourage their "guests" to regard themselves as overlords. My Dagara interlocutors, on the other hand, complained bitterly that they were made to feel like second-class villagers, but felt that there was not much they could do with regard to the funerals, except exploit, wherever possible, the competition between neighboring earth priests interested in securing additional clients.[95]

The Sisala put up similar, or even stronger, resistance with respect to place-names that publicly symbolize ownership and belonging. Interestingly, in quite a few Dagara villages, which were originally inhabited by Sisala first-comers who had then been displaced by Dagara frontiersmen, the original Sisala place-names were retained. But, my interlocutors would often explain them with Dagara folk etymologies and even deny that they were Sisala names.[96] Most villages on Dagara-owned land, however, have straightforward Dagara names that usually refer to characteristics of the natural environment or some aspect of the settlement process, as, for instance, "to squat for some time" (Nandom); "come and improve" (Ouessa); or "to bring about hostility" (Dadoune). In Dagara settlements established on Sisala land after the 1920s, however, the Sisala strongly opposed any "Dagarafication" of place-names. This often led to the existence of dual designations, with one set of names used by the Sisala landowners, the other by the Dagara villagers. The important question then was, and continues to be, which of the names would be used in official documents and for administrative purposes.

For instance, in the case of Buonbaa, which was discussed in the last chapter, the Dagara farmers recognized the Kelendou earth priest's property rights, but still preferred to call their new settlement by their own Dagara name, Buonbaa, literally, "place of peace." This name expressed, as my Dagara interlocutors explained, that the settlement had been founded as a refuge and new home following their ancestors' flight from Denyuu's tyranny. The Kelendou chief, however, protested that the correct name was not Buonbaa, but Bakzing, the Sisala term for "big bush farm." The Dagara, in turn, resented this name because it implied that their settlement was like a temporary dwelling in a not quite civilized place. And they complained that the Sisala even actually treated their village like a "bush" settlement, preventing regional development projects from arriving in Buonbaa. My Dagara interlocutors insisted that I write down the name Buonbaa, but on official maps this name does not appear, and despite the large number of houses in Buonbaa, the population census simply includes the inhabitants in the population of Kelendou.[97] However, it is possible that, thanks to its demographic weight and the influence of educated Dagara migrants working in the administration, Buonbaa may one day figure in official documents.

In a similar case, the Sisala paramount chief of Bourra adamantly opposed the name that the Dagara had originally given their new section, namely Navirikpe, meaning "to settle against all resistance," a name that referred to the current chief's father's resistance against the Dagara installation. But when the Dagara eventually came up with a new proposal, Zelkpe, literally "to beg to enter," he accepted that they use this Dagara name—not least because it adequately reflects, as the Bourra chief felt, the relationship between the landowners and the settlers.[98] Again, however, this name does not figure in official documents, and the section is treated as part of Bourra.

Place-names also served as symbolic weapons in the long-standing dispute between the Nandom Naa and the Lambussie Kuoro over the political allegiance of the border town Hamile. The Sisala name Hamile, which most inhabitants and government authorities used and continue to use, bears witness to the settlement history, namely, the town's establishment by the Sisala earth priests who now reside in French Hamile. It also confirms that historically, the international border notwithstanding, Hamile was one single village. However, when the Sisala chiefs of Happa and Lambussie petitioned that British Hamile should secede from Nandom and come under the authority of Lambussie Division and its local council, they took to speaking (and writing) of Hamile as Zongo, a Hausa word normally used to designate the quarters of Muslim urban migrants. In the case of Hamile, this designation was intended to emphasize that the settlement was mainly inhabited by "non-native" traders and thus undermine the legitimacy of the Dagara farmers' claims to furnish its headman.[99] The Nandom Naa, for his part, started to use the name Muoteng, "Muo's village," in reference to the Dagara founder of the British section of Hamile, and insisted that Muoteng was in fact not part of French Hamile, but of the neighboring "British" Dagara village of Kokoligu that belonged to the Nandom paramountcy.[100] As mentioned earlier, the Minister of Local Government eventually granted the Happa chief's petition and in 1952 attached Hamile to the Lambussie Local Council, and Hamile remained the official name. Recently, however, the Happa authorities sent a petition to the Upper West Regional Minister that Hamile be renamed and referred to by its allegedly true original name, New Hapaa (*sic*). Apparently they feared that Hamile, which has many more inhabitants and greater economic clout than Happa, could eventually strive to dominate them politically as well.[101] The new name (which the regional administration eventually rejected) would enshrine their claims to anteriority, allodial title, and political authority, present Hamile as an appendix of Happa, and thus deny "autochthonous" status to Hamile's multiethnic community of farmers and traders.

Negotiating Political Representation: Autochthony, Ethnicity,
and the Legitimacy of Chiefs, Councilors, and Members of Parliament

As the examples of Buonbaa and Hamile show, contention over place-names and their official recognition is closely connected with conflict about politico-territorial boundaries, or, more precisely, chiefly and administrative hierarchies. The latter, in turn, have important consequences for the question of who should legitimately represent a particular village or group of villages in larger political institutions, such as traditional councils, local councils, regional boards, or even the national parliament. In Ghana in particular, but to some extent also in Burkina Faso, claims to political representation are fought not only in the domain of modern institutions of local government and national politics, but also in the field of the chieftaincy. In fact, these two fields are so intertwined that a settlement's demands to be represented by its own local councilor or assemblyman, for instance, are often prefaced, or accompanied, by requests to be upgraded in the hierarchy of chiefs from, say, village headman to subchief. And petitions for political recognition are regularly addressed to the relevant traditional council of chiefs as well as the district assembly and state executive authorities, such as the district and regional administrations.

The backdrop to this entanglement of political spheres is the colonial heritage that still molds local government structures. Although the constitutions of Ghana and Upper Volta (and later Burkina Faso) all but eliminated the political role of chiefs, the colonial geography of the native authorities and *chefferies de canton* was carried over into the local government structures established in the 1950s and 1960s. Orientation along chiefdom boundaries was to ensure that the local councils, as a Gold Coast commission of inquiry into electoral reform put it, constituted "units of co-operation and common interest."[102] Population densities and economic factors were also taken into consideration, but contestants would often argue that historical loyalties, rooted in the time-honored institutions of chieftaincy, weighed more heavily than sheer demography. Thus, in many areas, the colonial geography of chiefdoms shaped, and continues to shape, the contours of secular local government, even up until the latest decentralization reforms—the creation of district assemblies in the late 1980s in Ghana and the introduction of a new system of *collectivités territoriales* in 2004 in Burkina Faso. As a result, the language of autochthony and rights derived from land ownership regularly resurfaces in struggles over political representation.[103]

A recent example of such struggles is the case of Fielmuo, a populous Ghanaian Dagara settlement with a large market, a multiethnic community of resident traders, shopkeepers, and craftsmen, several schools, a clinic, and a mission station. The Dagara started their campaign for more political representation by insisting that the Fielmuo headman be upgraded to a full subdivisional chief, on par with the Sisala chief of Nimoro, the Sisala village on whose lands Fielmuo was founded around 1918 or 1920. While Fielmuo attracted ever more immigrants and economic activities,

Nimoro lagged behind. But in the eyes of the Sisala chiefs and politicians, the Fielmuo Dagara headman always remained subservient to the Nimoro Kuoro, who, in turn, followed the divisional chief of Zini in what was formerly Tumu, and is now Sissala West District. The Dagara argue that their ancestors have in fact acquired their own earth shrine from the Nimoro earth priests and thus become landowners in their own right—a claim that the Sisala vehemently deny. The Sisala also reject Dagara claims that the Fielmuo chief had once been installed directly by the colonial authorities, not by the Nimoro Kuoro, and therefore should now follow the Zini Kuoro directly, not through the Nimoro chief.

The (so far unsuccessful) petitions to upgrade the Fielmuo chief were written, and followed through all corridors of power, by members of the Fielmuo Citizens Association, recently renamed Fielmuo Area Development Association. The association was formed in the 1960s by the first educated villagers, and, despite some temporary lapses, has remained active. It constitutes an important forum through which the increasing number of school and university graduates from Fielmuo who work as teachers, public servants, and professionals all over the country attempt to promote the development of their hometown and increase its political clout. In the long run, the association would like to see Fielmuo as the headquarters of a new administrative district. This proposed district would regroup a number of Dagara settlements around Fielmuo that were all founded on Sisala land and currently belong to various Sisala chiefdoms (and districts). And because the Sisala landowners fear that this move would ultimately endanger their property rights, they vehemently oppose all moves to upgrade Fielmuo, including the move to install a Fielmuo chief.[104] Because of its large population, Fielmuo is, of course, represented by its own assemblyman, a Dagara, in the Sissala West District Assembly. However, there is a tacit understanding that the Fielmuo representative could not rise to become, for instance, the presiding member of the assembly or propose a Dagara man or woman as district chief executive—positions that the "autochthonous" Sisala wish to preserve for themselves.

More generally, the Sisala chiefs, politicians, and educated elite were, and still are, adamant that only autochthones are full, true citizens of a given locality—and the argument is easily extended to larger areas—who have a quasi-natural right to furnish the chief as well as to fill modern elected positions, regardless of whether they constitute a minority or majority. Dagara requests for (more) political representation, on the other hand, tend to invoke the democratic principle of constituting a sizeable majority of the local population, no matter whether autochthone or immigrant. When pressed by such appeals, the Sisala chiefs and modern political elite often argue that the Dagara farmers have such a migratory lifestyle that they cannot assume full responsibility for the development of the land and village where they temporarily settle and that they should therefore not be given any decisive role in local decision-making processes.

Interestingly, this argument echoes a long tradition of European thinking about landed property as the basis of political community. "For centuries," Andrew Reeve notes, "the idea that only landowners had a sufficient interest to be entitled to share in political power was dominant."[105] Adam Smith, for instance, and other property theorists of the time contrasted the sound interest of stable, sedentary landowners working for the "common good" of their local community with the potential irresponsibility of the trader, who could always leave when more profitable opportunities beckoned. Until the end of the nineteenth century, British voting rights were indeed restricted to land- and house-owners.[106] The British colonial concept of native authorities certainly drew on this intellectual and political heritage, and it was, and continues to be, readily appropriated by African landowners. And no matter how reluctant some of the independent governments of Ghana (or Burkina Faso) were to support "traditional authorities," they hardly tried to actively further the aspirations of "non-natives" to chiefly positions.

Even with regard to secular representatives in local government bodies, government officials often were, and continue to be, hesitant to oppose claims to autochthonous prerogatives.[107] Ideologies of autochthony were, and still are, often pronounced when it comes to the choice of candidates for parliamentary elections. On the ground, they are not always effective, not least in view of the multiethnic composition of many constituencies and the necessity to score a majority of votes. However, when local party organizers discuss the selection of candidates, Sisala landowners often attempt to dissuade Dagara settlers from running for office because they feel that their constituency should be represented by a true "son of the soil," no matter how long the Dagara candidate and his family may have lived in the constituency. And often enough, this sentiment is respected by the higher ranks of the political parties that need to capture the autochthonous vote. If a nonautochthonous candidate is nominated, his loyalty toward the native landowners will certainly be questioned during the campaign, and there are cases in which Sisala landowners attempt to use their control over land as a political tool.

During the Ghanaian parliamentary elections of 2004, for instance, the New Patriotic Party's (NPP) candidate for the Lambussie constituency came from one of the two Dagara founding families of Hamile. The candidate of the then oppositional National Democratic Congress (NDC), on the other hand, was a Dagaba teacher, but she was married to a Sisala lawyer and former district commissioner. The NDC candidate cultivated a campaign image of being a champion of Sisala interests, and apparently tried to win over Dagara farmers living on Sisala land by suggesting that a victory for the NPP candidate could provoke reprisals from Sisala landowners. The NPP candidate, for his part, had to exert enormous effort to undo the damage done by the rumor that he would use his victory to consolidate Dagara dominance by establishing a Nandom-Lambussie district and "taking away" Sisala land. His opponents not only questioned his legitimacy to represent, as an immigrant offspring, a "Sisala" constituency, but also accused him of being "not really Ghanaian" since some of his siblings live and work in Burkina Faso—an attempt to extend the local autochthony argument to matters of national citizenship. Ultimately, the NDC candidate won the elections, not least due to the massive support from Dagara farmers who believed that she would better be able to defend their interests and also deliver development to the constituency. To a certain extent, thus, the ethnic card, which some observers expected to work in favor of the Dagara candidate, at least in settlements with a strong Dagara majority, failed to trump. And to make matters even more complex, the paramount chief of Lambussie supported the NPP rather than the NDC candidate because of his long-standing party-political loyalties, which went in favor of the NPP.

More generally, then, the relevance of autochthony in secular politics is contested and ambiguous. Particularly when it comes to representing a constituency's interests in the national arena, it is not always autochthony and ethnicity that prevail because voters also believe that the candidate's integrity and his or her qualifications and political experience are of just as much, if not more, importance. Furthermore, in the larger political arena, the very scope of autochthony may be redefined. There are instances in which my interlocutors would emphasize what is common to Dagara, Dagaba, and Sisala, pointing to the strong ties created by marriage and friendship that bridge the boundaries of language, dialect, and ethnic identity, and evoking a past shaped by a shared history of mobility and successful adaptation to a difficult natural environment. However, depending on the issues and interests at stake, these inclusivist leanings can always be overshadowed by more exclusivist autochthony rhetoric and an interpretation of "tradition" that privileges first-comer status and land ownership.

Conclusion

The ethnicization of property rights and the politicization of autochthony are the most important, and problematic, colonial legacy, a legacy that has informed many postindependence land-related disputes. Colonial distinctions between natives and strangers or settlers and the identification of entire ethnic groups as first-comers or late-comers drastically simplified the multitude of local categories of identification within and between villages over who came first and which rights this entailed. Yet while these large-scale dichotomies have become part of the ideological arsenal mobilized in conflicts over land and political authority, colonial (and, for that matter, postcolonial) governments rarely engaged themselves in sorting out the micropolitics of belonging on the ground. These politics were left in the hands of the colonial officials' local intermediaries, namely, the chiefs. These, in turn, needed to secure the cooperation of the earth priests and other local stakeholders in order to manufacture a minimum of local legitimacy for any differential treatment of natives and settlers. The practical implications of the new ideologies of autochthony, therefore, have been varied and complex.

In the economic domain, chiefs and earth priests have usually found it difficult to enforce any collective agreement regarding the treatment of land-seeking strangers. Even when land is used as a weapon in political conflicts, their regulatory authority has been disputed not only by the strangers but also internally, by the co-owners of land in their own communities where subtle differences among the autochthones themselves, between first-, late-, and latest-comers, have been, and continue to be, controversial. In the Black Volta region, the decision to transfer land and the extent of use rights ceded to strangers have remained largely an affair between individual landowners and immigrant farmers, except for collectively enforced restrictions concerning the strangers' access to nonagricultural resources such as firewood, wild fruit-bearing trees, or medicinal plants that are regarded as the earth priests' and first-comers' prerogatives. The rapport between landowners and immigrant farmers is usually institutionalized in a type of patron-client relationship that Jean-Pierre Chauveau has aptly called *tutorat*, "guardianship."[108] The *tutorat* is anchored in a moral economy that obliges landowners to grant those who need it access to the essential means of subsistence. At the same time, it can facilitate, in the cloak of a customary exchange of land use rights for gifts and loyalty, the increasing commercialization of land rights. In any case, the individual bundles of rights that different immigrant farmers hold may vary considerably, which makes it rather unlikely that they form a united front to assert their interests vis-à-vis the landowners. More generally, then, it seems difficult to make out clear-cut fault lines between competing interest groups. At least in Northern Ghana (and Burkina Faso), "rising tensions over land and fear of dispossession" have not, as Sara Berry points out in regard to Ghana's cocoa-producing areas, "pitted ordinary citizens against 'traditional' rulers," but rather produced a landscape of frequently shifting alliances as well as small-scale disputes over the definition of who came first and should thus enjoy stronger rights.[109] The state, in any case, has rarely attempted to assert itself as an arbiter in such disputes, but rather has left the sorting out of land conflicts to a variety of institutions, ranging from informal councils of village elders or neotraditional chiefs to formal courts, district heads, employees of the regional ministries of agriculture, or *gestion de terroir* committees that sometimes are advised by international development experts.

In the political domain, however, the boundary between autochthones and strangers has become a collective reality, particularly when it coincides with ethnic distinctions. It would certainly be exaggerated to speak of a development from precolonial mobility and flexible constructions of social belonging toward sedentariness and rigidly defined ethnic categories during the colonial and postcolonial periods. Even before the colonial creation of "tribes," there was a sense of ethnic difference that could become more acute when late-comers competed with previous inhabitants for fertile land and ritual authority. Furthermore, colonial tribal constructs did not end the negotiability of ethnic boundaries, nor would the political privileges associated with autochthony terminate agricultural mobility or prevent strangers from founding new settlements. To a certain extent, however, colonial rule did harden the boundary between natives and strangers and increase the rigidity of ethnic categories. In any case, the intricate processes of ethnic conversion and autochthonization, often by violent means, that were commonplace in earlier periods, gradually subsided. Postcolonial regimes in Ghana and Burkina Faso did not fundamentally challenge these boundaries and the associated conviction that sedentariness, long-standing local roots, and property constitute the legitimate basis for a responsible exercise of political authority, at least at the local level. The late-comers themselves have contributed to the success of first-comer discourses by downplaying, in their own settlement narratives and political petitions, their ancestors' mobility, and instead emphasizing their role in "civilizing" the bush through hard work. In other words, if they cannot credibly produce a full-fledged first-comer story to support their claims to land and political representation, they argue in terms of a labor theory of property, and thus attempt to redefine the criteria of what constitutes true first-comers.

In her discussion of recent land tenure reforms in Africa, Catherine Boone has emphasized that property rights are intimately connected to, and have important consequences for, the constitutional order and state- and nation-building projects at large.[110] In "communal regimes" of tenure, Boone argues, people enjoy access to land as members of allegedly natural communities, and neotraditional authorities are expected to regulate land issues; their political counterparts are "indirect rule" systems that envision the nation-state as a federation or mosaic of local states. "User rights regimes," on the other hand, correspond to political systems based on "direct rule" that do not recognize "ancestral entitlements to, and political authority over the land," but insist on the state as the sole source and arbiter of property rights and on a universalist model of citizenship.[111] This typology is somewhat schematic because, in reality, the two property regimes and types of political constitution can coexist and be interlaced, as Boone herself concedes. But it is useful in drawing attention to the close association of concepts of property with notions of citizenship.

Currently, both Burkina Faso and Ghana have, by and large, subscribed to the "communal regimes" model of tenure that Boone describes, at least as far as the connections between rural land tenure and political participation is concerned. At the same time, however, "direct rule" models dominate other domains of state activity. Moreover, previous periods of "user rights regimes" have left their institutional and ideological imprints. Local disputes over land, property, and belonging thus take place in a political environment characterized by legal and institutional pluralism, or, to use Thomas Bierschenk and Olivier de Sardan's terms, by "polycéphalie" and "empilement,"[112] that is, the coexistence of multiple authorities and various layers or sediments of institutional and ideological forms. As a result, despite the dominance of ideologies of autochthony in public discourse, there is no automatic trend toward defining ever-larger groups as strangers and increasingly excluding them from political representation. Much depends on specific configurations of power, and the abilities of and opportunities for the different parties to build networks of support and construct their cause as legitimate—dynamics that the next chapter explores by discussing three recent conflicts over land that developed in the context of new economic opportunities and decentralization policies.

5 History versus history

Contemporary Land Conflicts
in a Context of Legal
and Institutional Pluralism

LAND IS A special substance: immobile, nonincreasable, and nonrenewable. In the Black Volta region, it is central to material livelihoods and spiritual well-being as well as to the politics of belonging and citizenship. With increasing pressure on land and rising economic, social, and political stakes, debates over property rights have multiplied—debates over who the rightful owners of a piece of land are, how far back in time property histories need to be traced, and where and how to draw the spatial boundaries of property. Because "property and public authority are mutually constitutive and contingent,"[1] conflicts over land rights invariably entail disputes about which institutions are competent to arbitrate between competing claims. As neither the Ghanaian nor the Burkinabé state commands the necessary resources to enforce national land legislation comprehensively, local ways of constructing, contesting, and enforcing property claims have remained important. What is more, at least in Ghana, recent land policies have strengthened customary land rights without, however, doing away with entitlements that stem from modern land legislation. Contemporary land conflicts thus evolve in a context of legal and institutional pluralism, and the various actors draw on multiple resources, both conceptual and political, to (re)define, assert, defend, or recover property rights.

History therefore matters immensely. On the one hand, the dynamics of land conflicts and the ways in which people understand their rights to land are informed by the regional history of migration, settlement, and first possession. On the other hand, people invoke their specific versions of this history when making their claims. Analyzing three recent land disputes, this chapter elucidates how the developments discussed in the preceding chapters, namely the changing strategies of mobility, the ambiguities of property rights, and the politics of belonging, interconnect. The first case concerns the right to allocate land to immigrant farmers interested in planting cashew trees. The second relates to state intervention into property rights in Burkina Faso, namely, a *lotissement* project that surveyed, parceled, and allocated building land. The third case arose during the redemarcation of district boundaries in the context of Ghanaian decentralization policies.

Studying land disputes in a similar setting of legal and institutional pluralism in the Moluccas, Franz von Benda-Beckmann observed that conflicts typically arise when new land-seeking parties come on the scene and demand that landowners clarify formerly ambiguous property rights; when new land uses such as planting commercial trees invest the issue of stable, long-term access to land with unprecedented importance; when previously "oral" land rights, subject to multiple interpretations, are fixed in writing and therefore need to be defined unambiguously; and when issues of citizenship and political rights are connected to landed property.[2] The cases discussed in this chapter correspond quite neatly to this typology, with the exception perhaps of conflicts connected with the codification of customary tenure for which the land reform in the Ivory Coast would be a case in point.[3]

For each case discussed in this chapter, I explore how first-comer claims were raised, or contested, and how historical narratives were reworked as the conflicts moved through different arenas. I will also discuss the conflicts' processual dynamics: how and where the struggles evolved, which allies were mobilized, and which institutions became involved. The first two conflicts are set in Burkina Faso, the third in Ghana, but the issues at stake are not specific to either country. With the exception of the *lotissement* scheme discussed in the second case, each conflict could have occurred, and indeed in similar form does occur, in the neighboring country as well. What differs, however, at least to a certain extent, is the processual dynamics; here, the specific legal and institutional framework of each country has some bearing on how people forge alliances or frame their arguments. Wherever necessary, I explain these state-specific configurations. Furthermore, each of the conflicts analyzed in this chapter contains some element of confrontation between Sisala and Dagara farmers. It is important to note that this is merely a result of the fact that I have done much of my fieldwork along this ethnic frontier and among Dagara farmers cultivating Sisala-owned land. Interethnic struggles over land are no more frequent than intraethnic ones, and indeed, as will become evident in the case analyses, Dagara-Sisala conflicts are often interconnected with disputes within each of the groups as well as with other "strangers" such as the Mossi.

Finally, that conflicts take center stage does not mean that Dagara or Sisala farmers are constantly fighting about land; on the contrary, although the ambiguity of property rights could give rise to competing claims about nearly every single piece of land, open conflicts are surprisingly rare. But I use conflicts as diagnostic events that render otherwise implicit norms and strategies visible. Moreover, exploring under which circumstances open confrontations arise also allows us to appraise the "limits of negotiability."[4] The chapter concludes by arguing that as long as the state is not capable of reliably guaranteeing property rights and as long as control over land plays a central role in the definition of local belonging and national citizenship, property conflicts will remain inconclusive and embittered debates about first-comer claims will continue to thrive.

Cashews, Cash Crops, and Competing First-Comer Claims

Across the entire West African savanna, planting (and felling) trees, particularly trees with commercial value, is considered a serious affair, as a number of case studies of conflicts surrounding tree tenure in Burkina Faso and Niger have shown.[5] Planting trees signals long-term interest in the land, and, in principle, only the landowner is allowed to do so. Conversely, whoever plants, harvests, or fells trees without being challenged tends to interpret this as a tacit recognition of his claims to own the land on which they stand. Any attempt by an immigrant farmer to plant trees is therefore carefully observed and often challenged. The following case concerned trees and property rights over land in the border zone between the Sisala settlement of Kierim and the Dagara village of Kolinka, whose earth priest pays allegiance to the senior earth shrine of Ouessa. After having been farmed by a Kolinka Dagara family, the disputed field lay fallow for many years, but was recently (re)claimed by a Sisala farmer from Kierim who wanted to lease it to a Mossi trader interested in planting lucrative cashew trees.

A Series of Confrontations

In mid-1997, the elders of Nuuzuo-yir, the Kolinka earth-priestly house, were alerted by neighboring farmers that a Mossi trader living in the nearby border town of Hamile had begun to plant neat rows of cashew seedlings on their fallow field. When the Nuuzuo-yir elders confronted the Mossi planter, he explained that he had been given the land and the go-ahead to plant trees by a Sisala farmer from Kierim. The Nuuzuo-yir elders insisted that the field had once been given to their grandfather by the earth priest of Ouessa, and that it was part of the land reserve they were keeping for their sons and grandsons. They told the Mossi in no uncertain terms to stop planting trees, and called on Ouessa earth priest Hien Daniel for support. The latter indeed confirmed that the field was part of his ancestors' land grant to Nuuzuo-yir and, as some of my informants reported, even placed an ebony stick in the ground, a powerful symbol of earth-priestly authority that bans all further use of the land. According to local beliefs shared across ethnic boundaries, nobody except the rightful earth priest dares to remove such an ebony stick lest he be killed by the earth god. That the Kierim earth priest did not touch it, my informants explained, clearly proved that the land was not under the Kierim earth shrine's authority, and thus no Kierim villager had the right

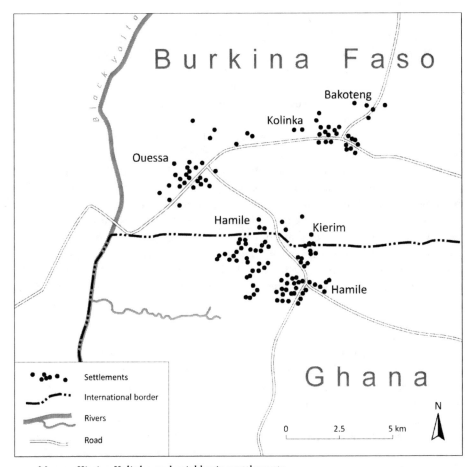

Map 5.1. Kierim, Kolinka, and neighboring settlements

to allocate it to any third party. Other informants denied that the Ouessa earth priest took recourse to such a dangerous spiritual sanction, but were no less sanguine about the Nuuzuo-yir elders' property rights.

The Mossi planter, for his part, turned to his landlord in Kierim, who, in turn, informed the Kierim Kuoro, the village chief, and also a member of the Kierim earth priest's family who claimed the allodial title over all Kierim village land. When a first encounter between the Nuuzuo-yir elders and the Kierim Kuoro resulted in an exchange of harsh words, the latter decided to take the matter to the Ouessa *préfet*, the district head. Kierim had recently joined Ouessa District for practical reasons of proximity, but relations with the Dagara majority in the district had been tense, not least because of what the Sisala regarded as Dagara encroachment on their land. In any case, the Kierim Kuoro must have felt the chances of striking a compromise with the Nuuzuo-yir elders or the Ouessa earth priest on his own to be so slight that he preferred to take recourse to a state agent.

The *préfet* summoned the state forestry agent, the Sisala landlord, the Kierim Kuoro, the Nuuzuo-yir elders, and the Ouessa earth priest for a meeting in his office.[6] In his defense of Kierim's claims to the disputed land, the Kierim Kuoro went far back in time, narrating how his ancestors had arrived in the area long before the Dagara of Ouessa and how the latter had actually received their land, and an earth-shrine stone, from the Kierim earth priest, whom they still had to consult in serious matters such as suicide. As tangible proof of Kierim's allodial rights over Ouessa territory, the Kierim Kuoro cited the problems into which the Dagara had lately run at the Ouessa pond when they had fished there without Kierim's permission, causing the pond to "rebel" by allowing some of the Dagara young men to be bitten by snakes. Since Kolinka was a satellite settlement of Ouessa, it also ultimately fell under Kierim's ritual overlordship. However, as the Kierim Kuoro categorically insisted, the contested cashew plantation-to-be was not even part of the land granted to Ouessa, but belonged to the Kierim land reserve over which the Nuuzuo-yir family had no rights whatsoever. Unfortunately, he further complained, this was not the first time that the Dagara had violated the property rights of the Sisala who out of friendship had once invited them to settle alongside them.

Ouessa earth priest Hien Daniel was furious at having to listen to these "outrageous lies" and countered that his ancestor Kontchire, who then still lived on the western banks of the Black Volta, had, on one of his hunting expeditions, discovered the territory that was later to become Ouessa. He soon realized, however, that the area was not empty, as he had hoped, but inhabited by Yeri or Phuo iron smelters whose scattered descendants currently still lived west of the Volta. As Kontchire wanted to settle on the newly discovered territory, he invited some of his nephews of the Kusiele patriclan, who were known as strong warriors, to help him kill or at least drive away these smelters. Eventually, only the wife of the Phuo earth priest survived; pleading for her life, she promised to reveal to Kontchire the secrets of the earth shrine. Kontchire accepted her offer and even took her into his house. The Sisala of Kierim played no role in any of this, Hien Daniel asserted; on the contrary, the Kusiele warriors eventually took to raiding nearby Sisala settlements, capturing slaves, and selling them to the regional slave markets, meaning that no Sisala would have dared to come near Ouessa, let alone offer them an earth-shrine stone. Hien Daniel also insisted that the Kierim Kuoro's claims regarding the pond were a blatant lie: the earth priests of Ouessa were the legitimate owners of the land and the pond, but had some time back invited ritual specialists from Kierim who knew how to prevent the fish from escaping into the Volta River. The pond had indeed "rebelled" lately, but not because of any disrespect toward its alleged Kierim owners, but because the Dagara themselves had failed to perform the necessary sacrifices.[7] As for Nuuzuo-yir and other houses of Kolinka, Hien Daniel concluded, it was the Ouessa earth priest who once gave them their lands, including the contested field, and the Sisala had no right to claim ownership to, let alone to sell this land to strangers.

Somewhat overwhelmed by these contradictory stories, the *préfet* allegedly told the litigants that, being a stranger to the area and a relatively young man, he could not possibly judge a case of disagreement among "his parents." They should go back to their respective villages and continue to consult the elders. When I asked the different parties about the subsequent course of events, the Kierim Kuoro insisted that the Ouessa earth priest finally accepted his assertion that Kierim had originally given them the land and that therefore no boundary existed between Ouessa, Kolinka, and Kierim. To cool matters down, however, he asked the Mossi to leave the disputed land and offered him a different plot. Some of my Dagara informants, on the other hand, attributed the Mossi planter's retreat to Hien Daniel's ebony stick and related that the cashew seedlings had mysteriously fallen victim to a bush fire. Subsequently, the young men of Nuuzuo-yir house started to farm the land because, as the Nuuzuo-yir elders explained, this was the best way to nip future false claims in the bud. When I asked them to comment on the Kierim Kuoro's statement that there was no boundary between Kierim and Kolinka, they explained that, in fact, when the Ouessa earth priest had given their grandfather land, he had not demarcated a linear boundary between Ouessa and Kierim, but only indicated a suitable location for the house and shown the direction into which they should farm. Since the Dagara had more people than the Sisala to clear the bush, they soon extended their farms quite far in the direction of Kierim, and when they met the Sisala from Kierim, who also pushed their farms toward Kolinka, a boundary was pragmatically agreed upon.

Both sides thus saw their claims validated. The Kierim Kuoro could not prevent the Dagara from reworking the disputed land, but insisted that they did so only because he permitted it and that they actually recognized his property claims. The Nuuzuo-yir elders interpreted the outcome of the dispute rather differently, namely, as a confirmation of their ownership. The case never reached final settlement and may be reopened in the future, if the balance of power changes.

The Issues at Stake

Boundaries of village and earth-shrine territories are crucial for defining property rights and often a core issue in contemporary land conflicts in the Black Volta region. As we have seen in earlier chapters, and as the Nuuzuo-yir elders explained, exact linear boundaries between neighboring settlements were never drawn at any explicit moment, but resulted from agreements between farmers who gradually pushed their fields farther into the bush and usually declared the land they had managed to cultivate as part of the area under control of the earth priest who had given them the go-ahead. Uninterrupted active cultivation thus was, and continues to be, tangible proof of ownership, but land left fallow is usually respected as property of the group that originally farmed it. However, particularly in border zones, fallow land often invites competing claims.[8] In the Kierim-Kolinka conflict, the parties did not even agree whether their ancestors had ever established a boundary. The Kierim Kuoro regarded not only the field in question but the entire Kolinka area as part of Kierim's earth-shrine territory, while the Nuuzuo-yir elders insisted on the existence of a boundary and the location of the contested land on Kolinka's side. In the absence of any written evidence, it is difficult to know whether this disagreement existed from the beginning or arose only recently. The Sisala landowner, in any case, claimed that his ancestors had once given the Nuuzuo-yir farmers permission to cultivate the land temporarily, but had never relinquished his property rights, and that the fallow land had therefore reverted to its original owners, who could dispose of it as they saw fit. The claimants thus disagreed both on the allodial title and subsequent transfers of farming rights.

As is typical for many disagreements over ownership, matters came to a head only when the economic stakes rose. In recent years, cashew trees have become an attractive source of income in the region, and it is often immigrant Mossi entrepreneurs rather than local farmers who have the necessary capital and know-how to start a plantation. The Mossi usually agree to pay substantial sums of money to gain access to land, and the professed Kierim landowner obviously wanted to seize this opportunity. At the same time, to allow a more or less dependent client to establish an enduring tree plantation was a sensible strategy to prove his property rights in no uncertain terms and forestall any advances of farmers from Kolinka.[9] Although the rights over the commercial trees and their proceeds could possibly—and in other cases have indeed—become the source of conflicts between the Mossi planter and his landlord, most Sisala believe that the Mossi rarely challenge their property rights as openly as their Dagara neighbors.

That the uses to which the contested field was to be put mattered is also typical for many contemporary land conflicts in the region. Had the Sisala farmer wanted only to cultivate the fallow land to feed his own family, the Dagara claimants would have certainly found it more difficult to refuse his demands. They would have probably allowed him to farm the land while insisting that they, and not he, were the rightful owners. In keeping with the locally dominant moral-economy discourse that criticizes the increasing commercialization of land, the Nuuzuo-yir farmers asserted that they needed the field for their own subsistence and thus added moral legitimacy to their case. To summarize, it was the combination of a complicated history of boundary making and the intention of one party to convert the land in question into a new source of revenue by selling it to cash-cropping strangers that resulted in an open quarrel over competing property claims.

Making a Good Case: The Anatomy of Convincing First-Comer Narratives

In order to advance or defend property claims, it is not enough to cultivate the land or contest claims of possession by, for instance, burning trees—assuming that, indeed, the fire on the cashew farm was not accidental. Such actions must be supported by property narratives that resonate with local theories of ownership. Once earth priests or village chiefs are called upon for support or mediation, the issues at stake shift from the content of a particular decision regarding a piece of land to the question of who holds the allodial title and therefore has the authority to decide on the use or allocation of land. Typically, thus, even when struggling over small pieces of land, disputing parties link the latter's history to that of the wider earth-shrine area and invoke the time of settlement and first possession. As the Ghanaian lawyer Ben Kunbuor points out, as long as Sisala and Dagara claimants insist that an allodial title cannot be acquired by "outright purchase," they must "struggle to fit their claim of ownership under the category of first-comers in a timeless history."[10] By invoking first-comer narratives, parties asserting competing claims define themselves as members of larger communities. This is why the Kierim-Kolinka case and similar land conflicts often acquire ethnic overtones, and are regarded by many as incidents in a long history of competition between "the Sisala first-comers," "the Dagara late-comers," and "the Mossi traders." However, when property narratives are presented in local arenas, as they were in the Kierim-Kolinka case, they usually do not refer to entire ethnic groups, but focus on the migration of specific ancestors and lineages, and events that took place at specific locations with which the speakers and the audience are familiar.

The Ouessa and Kierim earth priests' narratives demonstrate the efforts invested to frame the respective group's history as a story of first-comers, even when the accounts soon reveal that matters are much more complicated. Hien Daniel insisted that Kontchire discovered an empty territory, only to admit later that Kontchire eventually had to come to terms with some previous inhabitants. The Kierim Kuoro was adamant that his ancestors were the true first-comers to the area, but in our interview he also disclosed that they had fled from attacks by Dagara warriors and actually settled on the land of a Sisala group that had been decimated by an epidemic or for want of descendants. As I have shown in previous chapters, establishing a new settlement was in fact always a collective enterprise, and frontiersmen often preferred to settle where others had already cleared part of the bush. But most property narratives construct episodes of the founding ancestor as a lonely hunter arriving in an empty territory.

Hien Daniel's and the Kierim Kuoro's narratives are also typical examples of how parties attempt to advance their claims by maneuvering the openings that the first-comer idiom contains. With regard to the decisive event that determines who is recognized as first-comer, the Kierim Kuoro relied mainly on the lonely-hunter motif, while the Ouessa earth priest added the notion of conquest and superiority. The Nuuzuo-yir elders, in turn, focused on their ancestors being the first to effectively cultivate the land in question. The claimants also differed in how they defined the territorial and social reach of the group they identified as the first-comers. The Kierim Kuoro declared that Ouessa lands were originally part of Kierim's hunting territory, and that although Kontchire and his group had been given an earth-shrine stone that allowed them to distribute land to latest-comers, this did not transform them into true first-comers—an assertion that was aimed at weakening Hien Daniel's claims to full allodial ownership. Hien Daniel, on the other hand, denied that Kierim's rights ever covered Ouessa lands, and declared that his ancestor had acquired an earth shrine, without any further qualifications, from former inhabitants who had vanished. The Nuuzuo-yir elders, for their part, asserted first-comer status only for their own farms, but otherwise supported the Ouessa earth priest's claim to allodial title over the entire territory of Ouessa, including Kolinka. However, they probably would have told a different story had Hien Daniel invoked this title not to defend them against Kierim, but to request a share—in the form of sacrificial gifts—in any revenue they might receive by leasing land to strangers.

Finding a Friendly Jury: The Importance of Local Networks and Arenas

As important as "good stories"[11] are, they alone do not suffice, but must also be validated. It is at this point that sustained investment in social networks and considerations of political power become relevant, as Sara Berry has convincingly shown.[12] In land conflicts in traditionally segmentary societies, the first authority invoked to decide between competing claims is usually that of the lineage elders. In many cases, however, these elders will eventually bring the earth priest, as the holder—or at least guarantor—of the allodial title, into play, particularly if the conflict is between different lineages or, as in the Kierim-Kolinka case, between different villages and between local landowners and immigrant farmers. Although the authority of chiefs to intervene in land matters is strongly contested in Sisala and Dagara villages, in Ghana as much as in Burkina Faso, they are usually also called upon for mediation and support, not least because, at least in Ghana, state officials often regard them to be competent local interlocutors.

In Kierim, the earth priest and the chief belong to the same house and intervened jointly. In Kolinka, too, the Nuuzuo-yir house for many years furnished both the earth priest and the village chief; but the old chief died in the early 1980s, just when the revolutionary régime under Sankara all but banned the chieftaincy. While other villages still held on to their chiefs and continued to appoint successors, in Kolinka people decided to abandon the chieftaincy and instead elected the deceased chief's son first as *délégué* and later as *responsable administratif du village* (RAV). Since the Kolinka RAV and the earth priest were parties to the conflict with Kierim, they turned to the Ouessa earth priest for support. The chief of Ouessa, himself illiterate and with no educated relative in the house to support him, was not much respected. People therefore preferred to take their problems to the self-assertive and vocal earth priest and to the Ouessa RAV, an educated man from the same patriclan as the chief and well-connected with the earth-priestly house as well as state authorities.

More generally, claimants engage in "forum shopping," to use Benda-Beck-mann's term.[13] On whose support they call depends not only on the person's office and institutional role, but also on his or her personality, knowledgeability, connections, and influence. At the same time, earth priests, chiefs, and RAVs, for their part, also actively shop for conflicts in order to enhance their authority and revenues. This did not happen in the Kierim-Kolinka case, but it does in many other land conflicts. Had the Nuuzuo-yir elders decided to handle the case on their own, the Ouessa earth priest would have certainly intervened.

None of these local forums is impartial. They usually have their own interests at stake, not least to establish themselves as the relevant authorities. If the contestants cannot agree on which story is better, there are no arbitrators who could decide between competing versions. Earth priests may invite the spirits of the land to judge the case through the acceptance or refusal of a sacrifice (indicated by the way in which the sacrificial chicken dies, on its back or otherwise) or through an oath, accompanied by swallowing crumbs of soil, an act that is believed to invoke the wrath of the earth god in case of a lie. However, the gods' decision, which is conveyed by death, illness, or misfortune for the trespassers, is contingent on human interpretation and, unsurprisingly, not all parties agree on how to interpret the signs. Hence, though much depends on the networks each party can enlist to support his claims, the defeated litigants will still cling to their own version.

Matters are further complicated because even at the local level there may be more than one arena in which claimants have to manufacture the persuasion necessary to secure their property rights. In the Kierim-Kolinka case, for instance, the offstage comments on Hien Daniel's ritual sanctions were just as important as the public controversy over settlement history. People were divided on the question of whether the earth priest had actually planted an ebony stick; even if the Kierim landowner or the Mossi planter had felt threatened by this action, they would not have openly admitted it. While the Ghanaian and Burkinabé state institutions categorize narratives about first possession as legitimate parts of customary land tenure, these institutions would regard traditional spiritual sanctions as illegal and bordering on witchcraft. Thus, rumors of such sanctions are kept from reaching official ears and probably also from the curious anthropologist. However, this does not make them less effective, particularly when they are fuelled by the widespread belief that it is morally questionable and even dangerous to sell land for profit to strangers. Similarly, the local population's general dislike of Mossi entrepreneurs is probably responsible for the fact that the burning of the cashew seedlings obviously went unchallenged; nobody reported any perpetrator or initiated an official investigation.[14] To be sure, Mossi farmers have planted trees in Hamile, Kierim, and Ouessa with the consent of the landowners, but in this particular case, the planter's host must have found the property claims too difficult to defend and the risks of losing the investment too high.

To sum up, while settlement-and-first-possession narratives operate in the public arena and could potentially be brought to court, offstage rumors, spiritual threats, and silent resistance such as crop burning or invoking a moral-economy-of-subsistence discourse play an equally important role in defending or contesting property claims— phenomena that James Scott has identified as "weapons of the weak."[15] Such weapons may also work, I would argue, to the advantage of the not-so-weak. Information and judgments in both arenas, public encounters and informal rumors, are interrelated and can feed into each other. Disputing parties therefore attempt to manufacture consent, or at least acquiescence, on all levels, not least by long-term investment in broad social networks.

In Search of a Verdict: Bringing in the State

In the late 1990s, the official institutions pertinent to dealing with the Kierim-Kolinka case were the *commissions villageoises de gestion de terroir*, village committees responsible for planning local land use and settling disputes. In an attempt to undermine customary land tenure, the 1984 Burkina Faso land reform law set up these committees that were to include only members of the popularly elected *comités de défense de la révolution* and to exclude earth priests and chiefs. However, in most villages the committees were either never set up or unable to operate successfully. Eventually, the government was forced to invite back in the *autorités coutûmiers*, that is, the traditional authorities. Yet the 1996 revision of the land reform law left basic ambiguities of the older legislation unresolved, such as, the committees' relation with state authorities and the issue of how to handle intervillage disputes.[16] At the time of the Kierim-Kolinka conflict, Kierim had not yet established its own committee. The Ouessa committee was formally set up—with the earth priest, the *suosob* (the holder of the sacrificial knife), the RAV, and representatives from among local traders and public servants as members—but hardly ever met. The situation in most neighboring villages was not much different. The 2004 law on the creation of rural and urban communities charged these new territorial structures, that is, the local councils and elected mayors, with the administration of their respective portions of the "national estate," but it is unlikely that they will be much more effective than the old *commissions villageoises*.[17]

While in Ghana land conflicts involving higher economic stakes are often taken to the courts,[18] this does not seem to be the case in Burkina Faso, at least not in rural settings like the one discussed here. Here, the *préfet* was, and continues to be, the most accessible state institution to arbitrate in a land conflict. He would have to be informed anyway if a conflict escalated. However, though "neutral," the *préfet* is usually unable to assess the credibility of claimants' narratives because he lacks the requisite highly localized knowledge of the settlement history. Like a judge in court, he may, at best, be attuned to the stories' internal contradictions or their probability in terms of generally held beliefs about how customary tenure works. Ultimately he will rule according to his impression of how authoritatively these stories are presented. In the Kierim-Kolinka case, however, the *préfet* did not even inspect the disputed field or call in further witnesses, and avoided making any statement on the substance of the matter. Asking the claimants to address the matter to supposedly knowledgeable elders, he did not invoke his official authority, but employed a language of kinship and respect of seniority.

For the district head to refrain from taking a more active stance is typical for many land conflicts. It is partly due, as Hagberg and Lund have convincingly argued, to the fact that a *préfet* must always beware that some of the local actors, whom he usually does not know well because of being frequently relocated to new district stations, could be well connected with regional or national power holders.[19] If his actions were to go against their interests, they may use these connections to the detriment of his career. In the Kierim-Kolinka case, for instance, the fact that one of the Nuuzuo-yir relatives was a Member of Parliament certainly contributed to the *préfet*'s reluctance to take a more decisive stance.

Even if state institutions—local committees, district heads, mayors, or courts—were to intervene more actively and reach a decision, the defeated party may still cling to its version of the case. The inconclusiveness of the dispute settlement due to the plurality of property legitimizations and mediating institutions is the most notorious feature of the Kierim-Kolinka and many other land cases. While pragmatic solutions, informed by the current configuration of power and influence, regulate the immediate use of land, competing claims concerning more comprehensive property rights remain unresolved. The "losers" at any given moment will preserve their version of the story until a new opportunity to right past wrongs arises; political fortunes may shift, and a better-connected Kierim Kuoro, or a less belligerent Ouessa earth priest, may turn the tables.

Lotissement or *quartiers des autochtones*?
Contested Land Titling in Small Towns

The Burkina Faso land reform law prescribes a *lotissement*, a housing development scheme, for larger cities that surveys, parcels and demarcates, attributes, and finally taxes urban building land. Smaller towns also can, if they so wish, demand that their building land be surveyed and divided into plots, and the government strongly recommended that all district headquarters undertake *lotissement* projects.[20] In Ouessa District, the lead was taken by the border town of Hamile in the mid-1990s; Ouessa itself followed a few years later. In both cases, the *lotissement* gave rise to a proliferation of customary claims and intense debate about property rights.

Lotissement projects constitute dense, potentially disruptive moments of transition from a traditionalist order of property, based on claims to first-comer status and first possession and administered by earth priests or chiefs, to a modern ownership regime imposed, regulated, and legitimated by the nation-state. De jure, of course, all land in Burkina Faso for which no private title has been registered is part of the national domain, but, as mentioned earlier, the de facto administration of rural lands was, and continues to be, largely left in the hands of the traditional owners.[21] In Ouessa and other small rural towns, *lotissement* projects are therefore experienced by many as a form of expropriation or, as Tribillion puts it, "land rights imperialism" by the state.[22]

The *lotissement* is usually carried out on already built-up land, and the local population often refuses to understand why they should suddenly go through costly administrative procedures so that they may continue to live on the land that their families have occupied for generations. Moreover, *lotissement* projects differentiate between residents and nonresidents, but anyone who has erected a building on the land to be parceled at least six months prior to the *lotissement* is counted as a resident, including recently immigrated traders or public servants.[23] Autochthony thus no longer confers any special rights. Residents can apply for a building plot earlier and at a lower price than nonresidents, whose demands are addressed only after all residents' demands have been satisfied. The *commission d'attribution* usually encourages all adult residents of old, large family houses to apply for a plot and thus reconstitute their family holdings, and although nobody can request a specific plot, the committee normally attempts to respect the existing residential patterns as much as possible. However, despite such adjustments, the legal stipulations still depart radically from the customary distinction between first-comers and late-comers.

Spatial boundaries of properties are now lineally defined and physically demarcated; the size of properties is measured in abstract square meters; traditional names of town quarters, even though in further use in daily life, are replaced for administrative purposes by letters and numbers; in short, land is emptied of its spiritual and historical connections and converted into a homogeneous entity that can be evenly parceled and distributed. Property is assigned to named individuals, not corporate groups, and access to land is, in principle, no longer gained through membership in a kin group or patron-client relationship, but instead through national citizenship and participation in an open land market. The relevant body that legitimates and governs property rights is not the earth priest and the group of first-comers but the nation-state, even if the latter's powers are devolved to decentralized *communes*.

On the ground, however, the very procedures of transition from the old to the new order reveal that the state does not operate on a tabula rasa. Indeed, attempts to impose a modern property regime have intensified local debates about ancient settlement histories and the customary rights that follow from them. On the one hand, the anticipation of a *lotissement* scheme creates a demand for building plots, which immigrants who want to qualify as future residents acquire from local proprietors according to traditional procedures. This thriving new market for nonsurveyed land has multiplied conflicts between, but also within, local lineages about who the legitimate owners (and sellers) of the land are, whether the land should be alienated at all, and, if so, how to share the proceeds of land sales—conflicts that have become ubiquitous in and around many towns in Burkina Faso.[24] On the other hand, some local groups, namely the Sisala in Hamile and the Kusiele patriclan in Ouessa, petitioned that their quarters be defined as *quartiers des autochtones* or *quartiers traditionels*, which are exempted from parcellation, individual registration, and taxation. The law itself provides for such exceptions, which may also be applied to *lieux sacrés*, sacred places such as the earth shrine or important sacrificial or burial sites.[25] Any such adjustment of the new order, however, involves, as Le Meur has succinctly argued, difficult processes of translating traditional local knowledge guarded by elders and ritual specialists into publicly accessible and administratively functional data,[26] and it gives rise to competing interpretations of first-comer status. It was no coincidence that in Ouessa and Hamile I was confronted with a larger number of contradictory historical narratives than nearly anywhere else.[27]

Who Needs a lotissement?

Ouessa was originally a Dagara peasant village, but its status as district headquarters, with various schools, a police station, and primary health-care services, and its location near the Burkina Faso–Ghana border attracted an ever-increasing number of immigrants—teachers and administrators, as well as traders, shopkeepers, and operators of bars and small restaurants. Ouessa also hosts customs offices and the *gendarmerie*, responsible for the border, and has become an important stopover for trucks carrying goods between Ghana and Burkina Faso, the northern Ivory Coast, and Mali. In 1996, Ouessa counted only slightly more than two thousand inhabitants, but fewer than half of the heads of household were Dagara, roughly one-third were Mossi, and the rest were a mixture of different origins.[28]

When I came to Ouessa on one of my regular visits in February 2000, people were intensely debating the advantages and problems connected with the *lotissement*. Many were apprehensive that a few months earlier a team of surveyors from the urban-planning institute in Bobo-Dioulasso had arrived and, without much explanation, started to measure plots, draw up cadastral maps, place border markers, and tear down some of the adobe structures that stood in the way of planned streets. Earth priest Hien Daniel and his ritual assistant Nifaakang, a vocal Kusiele elder responsible for sacrifices at the earth shrine (*suosob*), were especially opposed to the *lotissement*, not least because it undermined their property claims and threatened to deprive them of money obtained from land-seeking immigrants. For poorer farmers the stipulated costs of the *lotissement* seemed out of reach—3,500 Francs CFA for the application (*demande*) for a plot, another 3,000 for its attribution (*indication*), and an occupancy tax (*taxe de jouissance*) of 100 CFA per square meter, adding up to some 56,500 CFA (roughly US$110) for a plot of five hundred square meters on which the applicants had been living for years.

Most of my local informants believed that the driving force behind the *lotissement* were the *ressortissants* (migrants) and their association, formed by educated Dagara from Ouessa District who worked in various ministries and businesses in Ouagadougou and Bobo-Dioulasso. The *ressortissants* themselves, however, insisted that they, too, had been taken by surprise. They suspected that the initiative had come from the former district head, who never had bothered to inform the population of Ouessa and was transferred to another district before the surveyors arrived. However, once the initiative was under way, the *ressortissants* wanted to make sure that it was conducted in an orderly, accountable, and acceptable manner. They themselves were interested in securing a building plot in their home district in order to put up a solid house for retirement and perhaps a small business that could profit from the increasing long-distance traffic. The so-called *permis urbain d'habiter*, an official usufructuary title to the land obtained in the course of the *lotissement*,[29] could protect them both from encroachment by rural relatives or competing traditional property claims, and future state-initiated infrastructure projects as well as further *lotissement* initiatives. Burkina Faso was seeing a wave of *lotissements*, my interlocutors explained, and Ouessa's lands would soon be parceled anyway, certainly no later than the reconstruction of the road. Whoever had erected a building beforehand risked seeing it demolished without compensation, so it was better to act early. Furthermore, the taxes on the plots would help finance the future *commune rurale* and develop Ouessa's infrastructure.[30]

The second group that supported the *lotissement* were the better-off immigrant traders and shopkeepers, and public servants who had built a house and sometimes also set up a business in Ouessa. Previously, the security of their investments had relied mainly on their personal relationships with the local landowners. Although customary land transfers had, in the recent past, usually been documented by a so-called *certificat de palabre*, signed by the landowner, the recipient of the land, and witnesses, including the earth priest, these papers rarely specified the boundaries of the land in question and the extent of the rights that were transferred.[31] A surveyed, clearly demarcated, and registered plot with a government-issued *permis urbain d'habiter* that could eventually be transformed into a formal ownership title seemed to offer better protection.

Why a quartier des autochtones? Hamile Sets a Precedent

It was not in Ouessa itself, however, but in Hamile, the actual border post, where the immigrant traders, particularly the Mossi, lobbied for a *lotissement*. Mossi migrants had started to settle in Hamile as early as the 1910s, but their numbers increased only in the 1970s due to the drought in central Burkina Faso. By the mid-1990s, Mossi households made up more than 70 percent of Hamile's more than three thousand inhabitants, while the Sisala, the autochthonous group, were reduced to a mere 7 percent.[32] Many Sisala landowners were initially happy to earn some extra income by renting out land to Mossi immigrants who were willing to pay substantial sums, but the initially cordial relations between hosts and strangers then soured.[33] Younger Sisala men in particular began to criticize their fathers for giving away land too easily instead of reserving some for them. The Mossi traders, on the other hand, complained about increasing Sisala demands for loans and presents. Tension also built up regarding some customary Sisala practices, particularly that of letting pigs roam about freely—an important source of income for Sisala families, but a nuisance for Muslim Mossi traders and vegetable gardeners.[34] When the Mossi asked the district head to implement government decrees and order the animals to be contained by their owners, many Sisala felt that their rights as authochthonous inhabitants were impinged upon. They claimed to be unable to control the pigs, and accused the Mossi of poisoning the animals. The Mossi, for their part, insisted that the pig conflict was actually an expression of Sisala resentment against the fact that a Mossi, and not a Sisala, had recently been elected as the RAV—a position the Sisala felt should be reserved for autochthones. Against this background, the *lotissement* offered the Mossi a welcome opportunity to secure at least their urban investments, allowing them to inherit or sell their houses and shops freely, without depending on the Sisala's cooperation or having to fear they might be evicted.

The Hamile *commission d'attribution* that was responsible for the pre-*lotissement* census, the compilation of the applications and the distribution of the plots, was comprised of two Mossi and one Sisala member, in addition to the presiding district head and the technical staff. However, it was only when the surveyors' work actually began that the Sisala realized how dramatically the *lotissement* was going to impinge on their control over Hamile lands. Expecting no support for their concerns from the *préfet* or the Mossi RAV, they turned to their Member of Parliament. The latter suggested that the Sisala be allowed to demarcate a *quartier des autochtones*, and after negotiations with the district head and the *haut commissaire* of Léo, the provincial governor, on whom the parliamentarian had called for assistance, such a quarter was indeed established. In this section that takes up roughly one-third of the entire parceled land and embraces the earth-shrine and other important places of spiritual power as well as most of the older Sisala compounds, plots were demarcated but not individually assigned, and the inhabitants pay no taxes. The zone is treated as communal property that the autochthones are allowed to administer without state intervention. The few Mossi houses in this sector continue to depend on the goodwill of their Sisala hosts, and it is likely that they will eventually relocate to the parceled area outside the *quartier*. According to some of my Sisala informants, it is even possible that the Sisala themselves will eventually decide to attribute and register their plots in the name of individual owners in order to moderate property conflicts among themselves and to be able to sell plots to outsiders, if they so wish—a development that has taken place in many other *quartiers traditionels* in Burkina Faso.[35] For the time being, however, the Sisala are content that they have succeeded in safeguarding at least some of their traditional rights from interference by the Mossi and state authorities.

Who Are Ouessa's Autochthones?

When the district head embarked upon the Ouessa *lotissement* project, he wanted to avoid the "mistakes" committed in Hamile, and from the very start proposed to create a *quartier des autochtones*. As mentioned above, he was transferred before the initiative began—according to rumors, his removal was a consequence of his altercations with the Sisala in Hamile and the Member of Parliament—but his plans were eagerly taken up by some of Ouessa's family heads, particularly the Kusiele sacrificial assistant Nifaakang. The Dagara *ressortissants* argued that a special sector for the autochthones was not feasible in Ouessa because, unlike the Sisala minority in Hamile, the Dagara constituted almost half of Ouessa's population and were not concentrated in a single section that could be demarcated as a *quartier des autochtones*. Nifaakang and other advocates of such a quarter, however, defined autochthony in much narrower terms, based on the role that the different Dagara patriclans played in Ouessa's settlement history. Their claims sparked embittered debates about which clan or lineage came first, who accommodated strangers, and whether all this should play any role in present village affairs and land management.[36]

The obvious candidate for autochthonous status in Nifaakang's sense would have been the earth-priestly lineage of the Gane patriclan, but the earth priest and most other Gane families lived in Kontchire, a sector of Ouessa outside the zone that was to be parceled (see map 1.2). This encouraged Nifaakang to declare that his ancestors and other Kusiele clan mates were actually the true first-comers in Ouessa and that their section, lying within the *lotissement* scheme, should therefore be defined as an autochthonous quarter. He asserted that his ancestors had arrived earlier than the Gane, purchased the Ouessa earth shrine from the Sisala of Kierim, and only ceded the earth-priestly office to the Gane because the latter were their much-respected maternal uncles. The first Ouessa earth shrine, Nifaakang declared, had actually been established in the Kusiele section, and the spiritual power emanating from this ancient sacred place prevented strangers from putting up buildings in this part of town, making it a true *quartier des autochtones*. Nifaakang even insisted that he had the right to perform all earth-priestly duties and to allocate land to strangers in the entire urbanized zone of Ouessa, while the Gane commanded only the land in and around Kontchire. Indeed, after Hien Daniel died in 1999, and while the new, relatively young Gane earth priest Gompag was still settling into office, Nifaakang presented himself as the Ouessa earth priest whenever state officials or representatives of nongovernmental organizations asked for the local traditional authorities.

Members of other Dagara patriclans in Ouessa, and particularly earth priest Gompag, vehemently rejected these claims to Kusiele superiority. Gompag was not fundamentally opposed to a *quartier des autochtones*, but accused Nifaakang of distorting the settlement history to suit his personal interests, namely to continue selling land to strangers on his own account. The original earth shrine, Gompag insisted, had been established by the Gane in Kontchire. Only during the colonial regime, when many Gane fled to the British colony, was the shrine temporarily sheltered in the more populous Kusiele section. After independence, however, it was immediately returned to Kontchire. Other informants explained that the fact that strangers preferred to settle not in the Kusiele, but in the Bekuone section, across the road, had no spiritual motivation at all. It was simply because the Bekuone elder Yelkepki, an *ancien combattant*, a veteran, who had traveled widely and felt at ease interacting with non-Dagara, was the only one in Ouessa willing to accommodate the Mossi when they first arrived in the 1950s, and because subsequent Mossi immigrants preferred to establish themselves near their relations. Furthermore, as these critics pointed out, Nifaakang obviously saw no spiritual dangers in giving out land to strangers, and thus his arguments against the *lotissement* were contradictory.

Nifaakang and his supporters continued their opposition to the *lotissement*, but the *commission d'attribution* refused to delineate a proper *quartier des autochtones*. It did, however, reserve some forty plots in the Kusiele sector, twenty for the Kusiele under Nifaakang and twenty for the Gane under Gompag, that were not assigned to individual owners and not taxed, and so were de facto treated as a traditional section. By mid-2008, finally, the Kusiele and Gane elders decided that it was to their own advantage, after all, to officially register these reserved plots under individual names and obtain their *permis urbain d'habiter*. The Commune de Ouessa, which had been formally established in the meantime and was now responsible for the administration of building land, therefore invited Ouessa residents who had not yet been awarded land in the first round to apply for a plot. Like other lineage heads previously, Nifaakang and Gompag instructed their relatives to submit as many applications as possible in order to reconstitute family holdings, but had to accept that members of other patriclans, and even non-Dagara, also successfully submitted applications and therefore qualified to build in their sector.[37] Thus, the ethnic mixture characteristic of other neighborhoods in Ouessa now also reached this more traditional quarter. The competition between Gompag and Nifaakang over the office of the earth priest, however, has not abated, and Nifaakang continues to claim ownership of land outside the parceled zone.

Traditional Rights and the Commoditization of Land

By April 2001, the Ouessa *commission d'attribution* had distributed 1,108 individual plots, and held only few pieces of parceled land in reserve. Over 45 percent of the plots were assigned to Dagara, 25 percent to Mossi, about 9 percent to Bobo, and the rest to Gurunsi, Samo, Bisa, and other ethnic groups mainly, but not exclusively, from South-Western Burkina Faso (see map 5.2). These percentages reflect roughly the ethnic composition of Ouessa's inhabitants, and most land went to residents. In terms of professions, some 30 percent of the beneficiaries were peasants and "housewives," more than 34 percent public servants, teachers, and nurses, 11 percent traders and businessmen, and the rest students, employees, catechists, and others.[38]

Since 2001, some original beneficiaries have sold or otherwise transferred their land—or, to be precise, their provisional occupancy permits—because they could not afford the taxes or, more often, because they had never intended to keep the land for themselves. To assess the magnitude of this land market is difficult because, contrary to legal stipulations, most transfers are not reported to the *commune*, particularly not when they take place within the family. But I was reliably told that some well-to-do traders and public servants were accumulating quite a number of plots, and that it was possible to obtain up to 350,000 Francs CFA or more (roughly US$700) for a piece of land that had originally cost less than one-fifth of this sum. Yet despite this thriving

Map 5.2. Ouessa *lotissement*: ethnic distribution

land market, so far no residents have been evicted from the parceled zone, not least because the *commune* hesitates to enforce the legally prescribed three-year period after which a plot can be withdrawn if the occupant has not paid the taxes and put up a building. Judging from the experience of comparable cases of small-town *lotissements*, it is unlikely that withdrawals will be effected in the near future because the local councilors interested in being reelected would avoid such a highly unpopular measure.

The modern land market thus remains, in many ways, embedded in the local web of long-standing social and political relations. Significantly, in Ouessa and other small-town *lotissements*, the earth priests also continue to claim spiritual control over all land, including the parceled zone, and in many cases, in fact, still are consulted and asked to perform sacrifices in the event of a suicide or other misfortune. This may also serve as a subtle reminder of the old property regime and of who the autochthones are. However, if immigrants like the Muslims in Hamile simply refuse to recognize the earth priest's spiritual authority, there is little the latter can do.

On the fringes of the formally managed housing schemes, however, earth-priestly authority remains important and ownership claims based on customary tenure have multiplied. Because of the advantages of resident status in new *lotissements*, the demand for plots in areas that are expected to be surveyed and parceled in the near future has risen dramatically. Land in these zones is acquired according to "traditional" proce- dures, that is, by approaching the allodial title holder with substantial presents and payments in order to obtain a *certificat de palabre*. In Ouessa District, as soon as word of plans for a second *lotissement* leaked out, more than 150 heads of household acquired building plots and put up temporary sheds in an area along the Ouessa-Hamile road that has been uninhabited until very recently. Unsurprisingly, this new scramble for land has intensified the long-standing conflicts between Nifaakang and other Dagara families as well as between Ouessa and Kierim over traditional boundaries, and it has prompted a new round of debate on the settlement history.

That debates on customary rights and settlement histories intensify when peri-urban land markets expand is also a common feature in Ghana. Here, however, the legislation never even attempted to depart from traditional tenure as radically as the Burkina Faso land reform did, but accommodated the chiefs' and other traditional property claims from the very beginning. Conflicts in Northern Ghana often revolve around the ques- tion of which traditional authority—family elders, earth priests, or chiefs—should have a say at which stage in the process of land transfers.[39] Despite the fact that this is not a legal requirement, paramount chiefs like the Nandom Naa and the late Lawra Naa, for instance, usually insist that their signatures as witnesses—for which they charge con- siderable sums of money—are needed before any land transfer can be recognized and registered by the District Town and Country Planning Department and the Regional Lands Commission. Interestingly, the competent state authority, namely Regional Lands Officer Rafael Hokey, was convinced that in most of the Upper West Region the chiefs were certainly not the true customary authorities in land affairs, but felt that there was little he could do against their impositions, particularly if they were tolerated on the ground. The "customary land secretariats" that the Lands Commission was charged to set up were, according to Hokey, even more unlikely to curb the chiefs' influence on land transfers, despite the latter's untraditionality.[40] In a way, then, in Ghana even in the modern property schemes in urban and peri-urban areas, the state not only accepts the legitimacy of allodial titles whose justification lies beyond its sphere, but also leaves their administration mainly in the hands of nonstate authorities.

Unraveling First-Comer Claims

In both Burkina Faso and Ghana, attempts to modernize land tenure in build- ing schemes have resulted not in the elimination, but rather the proliferation of traditionalist claims. The dynamics of the associated debates and conflicts differ from those discussed in the Kierim-Kolinka case insofar as legal regulations are immediately relevant and state authorities play a more active role. The relevant actors embrace a broader range, including, in the Hamile and Ouessa cases, the district head (and later the mayor and communal council) and the provincial governor, the resident traders, and public servants from other parts of the country, the urban educated migrants, and the Member of Parliament. This cast of actors has important consequences for the ways in which first-comer claims have to be framed in order to convince.

The Sisala strategy was to shield all internal struggles over ownership and authority from external scrutiny, and present themselves as a victimized ethnic minority in danger of losing its home in a place that it originally built up. The fact that the Sisala have indeed been reduced to only 10 percent of the small town's population and that their collective status as first-comers was undisputed certainly helped to make their cause stronger. In addition, their plight resonated with regionally widespread anti-Mossi sentiments and, moreover, with international discourses on the protection of minority rights. In the Ouessa case, on the other hand, nobody mobilized a Mossi-Dagara opposition, and first-comer claims were raised not on behalf of an entire ethnic group, but on behalf of a specific patriclan, or even of only a specific lineage. Such intricate local quarrels over the settlement history could not be easily transformed into a morally convincing collective cause. Furthermore, the Dagara late-comer families themselves were opposed to the creation of a *quartier des autochtones*, and even though the "reserve" solution was not what Nifaakang and his allies had aspired for, they would have found it very difficult to rally any outside support for further claims.

In his study of Ghanaian land conflicts, both in rural and urban contexts, Kojo Amanor has argued that the invocation of customary tenure and claims to allodial titles serves the interests of powerful chiefs and elders, who are often aligned with urban business elites, and effectively expropriates and alienates weaker groups.[41] These observations certainly apply to a good number of cases in Southern Ghana, but are less pertinent for the Upper West Region, where the economic stakes in land are usually lower and appeals to customary tenure do not always buttress the interests of the powerful alone. Considering the Ouessa and Hamile *lotissement* cases, Amanor's assessment surely is too one-sided. Although Nifaakang's quest to continue profiting from the local land market may be seen in this light, he is economically and politically much less powerful than some of the immigrants who have the necessary means to pursue their business under all tenure regimes, whether traditional or modern. One could, however, contend that Nifaakang's maneuvers did alienate the young men and less astute members of his own extended family, who indeed began to complain that he had sold lineage land without prior consultation. In Hamile, on the other hand, their campaign for a *quartier des autochtones* effectively protected the Sisala against rather powerful business interests and potential dislodgment from their long-standing residential quarter. Thus, claims to first-comer status and traditional property rights do not per se intensify socioeconomic differentiation, but can also be invoked by the less powerful in support of their interests. When first-comer arguments are connected with a collective cause and not just individual or family interests, they can become morally compelling beyond mere utilitarian considerations. What role this can play in political struggles is a question to which I now turn with the example of land conflicts in the context of the redemarcation of district boundaries in Ghana.

Land as Political Leverage: Landowner-Settler Conflicts and Contested Administrative Boundaries

The series of protracted and massive conflicts between Sisala landowners and Dagara tenant farmers that developed in the former Lawra District in North-Western Ghana toward the end of the 1980s is an example of the complex ways in which property rights, chieftaincy, and modern political representation are enmeshed, and how access to land, or its denial, can be instrumentalized in political struggles.[42] On the surface, most conflicts concerned the obligations of Dagara tenant farmers in the Lambussie chiefdom toward their Sisala landlords; other conflicts related to the controversial boundary between the Nandom and the Lambussie earth-shrine areas. The second type of conflict was similar to the Kolinka-Kierim dispute discussed above: the parties disagreed about which earth priest had given them the permission to build a house and set up their farms and about who thus held the allodial title to the disputed land. Issues at stake in the first type of conflict involved complaints by Sisala landowners that Dagara living as settlers on their land, having sometimes done so for several decades, put up buildings without their hosts' prior permission, farmed outside the boundaries of the land assigned to them, and showed a general lack of respect for Sisala property rights. Sisala landlords also objected to the behavior of Dagara tenant farmers who had set up bush farms on Sisala-owned land, but continued to live in and pay political allegiance to the Nandom chiefdom. It was demanded that these farmers either settle in Lambussie or abandon their farms on Lambussie lands. In all cases, Sisala landowners exerted pressure by not allowing their Dagara tenants to cultivate their bush farms for three consecutive seasons. Nandom-based farmers were denied access to Sisala-owned land altogether; Dagara living in the Lambussie area were allowed to cultivate a few plots around their houses but had their bush farms taken away. These dramatic measures were revoked only after extensive rounds of negotiation involving an ever-widening circle of individuals and institutions—earth priests, village and paramount chiefs, members of the educated elite, youth associations, and politicians at the district, regional, and even national levels.

As we have seen in the two previous chapters, the specific conditions of tenancy arrangements are normally negotiated between the individual landlords and their clients, and can differ greatly according to the parties' relative bargaining power and the specific history of their relationship. Moreover, the boundary conflicts between Lambussie and Nandom involved competing claims to an allodial title, but were not directly connected to the disputes between Sisala landowners and Dagara settlers. The latter generally acknowledge the Sisala's allodial property rights, even when they endeavor to extend their own entitlements. Everybody in the area therefore knew that the massive scale and collective dimension of the land conflicts were only to be explained by the fact that beneath the surface of the publicly declared reasons for the farm seizures was a political agenda connected to the ongoing redemarcation of administrative districts. Indeed, had the Lambussie Kuoro, the paramount chief, not exerted considerable pressure on the landowners in his area to act collectively—a fact that was officially denied but admitted in many informal conversations—the farm seizures would probably not have occurred on the scale they did, and they would not have been linked to the controversies about the new districts. The Nandom Naa, in turn, exhorted his Dagara subjects to stop working as seasonal laborers on Sisala farms and attempted to deny Sisala vendors access to the Nandom market.[43] These chiefs, then, became major players in the conflicts for reasons connected to their own agendas of power politics.

However, there were also broadly shared ethnic sentiments at work, and many Sisala were indeed opposed to the joint Nandom-Lambussie district that the educated elite of Nandom proposed. Furthermore, the district redemarcation constituted one of the "strategic moments" that arise from time to time, with changes of government, the adoption of new legislation, or new government policies, and that "create[d] openings for rearrangements of . . . rights and positions."[44] For the Sisala landowners, the district dispute offered an opportunity to strengthen their allodial title to the land and renegotiate landowner-settler relations in terms more favorable to their interests.

Claims to first-comer status played an important role at all levels of the conflicts. As the latter moved from the local to the regional and national political arenas, lineage and village narratives were reformulated in terms of stories about tribal movements. However, before analyzing this transformation, it is necessary to take a brief look at one of the land disputes that took center stage during the complicated negotiations to revoke the farm seizures, namely the Taalipuo conflict, and to outline the major developments with regard to the controversial district redemarcation.

The Taalipuo Conflict

Taalipuo is a small Dagara settlement located on the border between the Nandom and Lambussie paramount chiefdoms. Initially, Taalipuo—literally, "among the shea nut trees"—was just the Dagara name for an area northeast of Nandom where a few Dagara farmers from the village of Nandomkpee, home of the Nandom earth priest, had set up bush farms. Eventually, the farmers found it too cumbersome to walk the long distance to their fields, and, during the early 1940s, they decided to construct houses and take up residence in Taalipuo. Politically, the new hamlet followed the chief of Nandomkpee, who in turn paid allegiance to the Nandom Naa. This was unproblematic at the time because the Lambussie chiefdom, for reasons of internal succession disputes, had been placed under the supervision of the Nandom chief.[45] The question of land ownership, however, seems to have been contested from the very beginning.

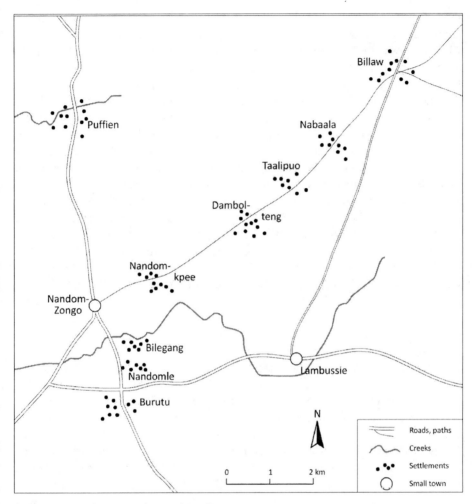

Map 5.3. Taalipuo, Nandom, and Lambussie

Some of my Dagara informants in Taalipuo asserted that their grandfathers, then still living in Nandomkpee, asked the Sisala of Nabaala, a neighboring village in the Lambussie chiefdom, for permission to set up their bush farms. They thus admitted that Taalipuo territory was indeed Sisala property, as the Nabaala authorities fervently claimed in the recent conflict. However, the same informants insisted that when it came to building houses, their grandfathers turned not to Nabaala, but to the Nandom earth priest. The latter gave the go-ahead and also instructed them to tell the Sisala, should the latter ever complain, that there was no boundary between Nandom and the Sisala lands. Subsequently, the Nabaala earth priest demanded that the Taalipuo farmers give the customary fowl, sorghum beer, and cowrie shells for the sacrifices that are necessary to ritually open a new house. But the Dagara refused because they were Christians who could not support such "heathen" practices, and the Sisala allegedly left without insisting their demands be met. Other Dagara informants in Taalipuo, however, did not mention this episode of early Sisala complaints, nor did they admit that the first Dagara farmers ever asked the Sisala for permission to set up their farms. According to their version, everything was authorized by the Nandom earth priest, and thus Taalipuo lands—the built-up space and the surrounding fields—were Dagara property. All informants agreed, however, that the land farther afield, toward Nabaala, on which the Taalipuo families eventually established additional bush farms, belonged to the Sisala and could only be cultivated with the latter's approval.[46]

The most recent dispute arose when two Dagara families in Taalipuo decided to erect new houses. The Nabaala earth priest, supported by the Nabaala chief, protested that he had not been asked for permission before construction work commenced. The Dagara builders countered that the houses were located within the area that the Nandomkpee earth priest had once shown them and that they needed no further authorization. This time, however, the Nabaala authorities were not willing to relinquish their claims. They insisted that it was their fathers who had once allowed the Dagara to establish farms and build houses on land that was and always remained Sisala property. It was only due to their fathers' leniency, "because the natives of Nabaala did not know that a time would come when these people would struggle to be the landowners,"[47] they explained, that the Dagara settlers' expansionist drive had not been confronted more firmly. In view of the increasing scarcity of land and in the interest of their own children, however, they could no longer allow the Dagara to flout Sisala property rights. Moreover, the Nabaala chief argued, it was not right that the Dagara in Taalipuo paid political allegiance to the Nandom Naa, because allegiance to a chieftaincy should follow the lines of land ownership. Until all inhabitants of Taalipuo acknowledged that he, the Nabaala Kuoro, was their rightful chief and that they thus belonged to the Lambussie paramountcy, they would not be allowed to cultivate their bush farms.

On his own authority, the Nabaala chief, a simple village chief without influential political connections, would probably not have dared to take such a drastic measure to redress what he regarded as past wrongs. He must have been encouraged to do so by the Lambussie Kuoro, for whom the question of the boundaries of property rights and chiefly authority assumed crucial importance in the discussions of the redemarcation of district boundaries. The Taalipuo conflict therefore became intricately linked to the dispute between Nandom and Lambussie over the new administrative districts.

District Reform and the Problem of Settling District Boundaries

The demarcation of new districts, propagated by the Rawlings government in order to "bring the government closer to the people," was officially conducted in accordance with three criteria: population, economic viability, and existing infrastructure. Local demands for new districts, however, were usually also based on existing chiefdoms (or ethnic groups) that formed part of larger districts but should, in the eyes of the petitioners, be awarded their own administrative unit. The population of the former Lawra District, with its four paramount chiefdoms of Lawra, Jirapa, Nandom, and Lambussie, was sufficient to create two or even three new districts, but neither Nandom nor Lambussie alone had the required fifty thousand inhabitants and therefore needed a partner if they were to break away from Lawra.[48] The Nandom Dagara educated elite, organized in the Nandom Youth and Development Association (NYDA), petitioned for a joint Nandom-Lambussie district because of its infrastructural advantages, but also because the association hoped that this would help protect the interests of the Dagara who had migrated from Nandom into Sisala-controlled Lambussie lands.[49] However, most Sisala politicians still remembered the bitter disputes between Nandom and Lambussie over the political allegiance of Hamile and related issues in the 1950s and 1960s, and preferred the creation of a joint district with Jirapa, despite the greater physical distance to the new district headquarters and other inconveniences. They feared that should Dagara and Sisala participate in a single common district, it would further bolster Nandom's dominance because the sizeable group of Dagara settlers living in the Lambussie Traditional Area could join with their "brothers," the Dagara of Nandom, to gang up against the Sisala and use their political influence to undermine the latter's property rights.[50]

At the heart of these concerns were tensions arising from the unequal development of Nandom and Lambussie. Due to extensive conversion to Catholicism, the Dagara of Nandom enjoyed earlier and more widespread access to education than the Sisala. They have therefore had access to a greater variety of employment opportunities and have secured more infrastructure for their villages and Nandom. Sisala politicians also viewed the Dagara as being more skillful lobbyists. NYDA activists, on the other hand, saw the emphasis on ethnic difference as a political strategy initiated by a small Sisala elite, and insisted that after more than sixty years of settlement it was simply unjust to continue to classify the Dagara farmers as settlers, effectively excluding them from full political participation.

To the dismay of the NYDA petitioners, however, the government decided in favor of a Jirapa-Lambussie and a Lawra-Nandom district. The new administrative boundary between Nandom and Lambussie was to follow the boundaries of the chiefdoms, and in March 1987, the Lawra District secretary went on a tour of inspection in order to explain the boundary changes to the village chiefs and the local population. At a meeting in Hamile, the Nandom Naa declared that only the territory east of the Nandom-Hamile road was part of the Lambussie Traditional Area and thus the new Jirapa-Lambussie District, while the territory west of the road, where the market and most shops are located, was under the jurisdiction of Nandom. This announcement provoked outcries from various segments of Hamile's population,[51] and was almost immediately followed by the above-mentioned mass seizure of Dagara farms. The Lawra

District secretary confirmed that all of Hamile belonged to Lambussie, and exhorted the Nandom Naa and his chiefs to respect this fact while the Lambussie Kuoro, for his part, should allow the Dagara farmers to continue cultivating Sisala land. After further "peace talks" between Sisala chiefs and landowners and Dagara farmers, the administrators felt that the matter had been resolved.[52]

However, NYDA was not yet willing to give up on the district question, and tensions were fuelled anew by further petitions and counterpetitions, including letters to politicians in Accra, and by confidential meetings of youth association activists with the regional secretary in Wa. The latter refused to rescind the original decision with regard to the district, but although the district dispute was officially settled, the land conflicts continued. Again at the start of the agricultural season in 1988, many Dagara farmers cultivating Sisala land were not allowed to work their fields, and it was during this season that the Taalipuo conflict became the focus of attention. The District Security Committee organized a series of meetings in Taalipuo with the aggrieved Dagara farmers and the Sisala landowners, as well as the earth priests from Nandom, Nabaala, and Lambussie. However, the resulting agreements were never implemented, since rival local dignitaries disputed the authority of those at the meeting. As the earth priests could not resolve the matter, other institutions were brought into play: the paramount chiefs, the political authorities at the district, regional, and national levels, and the youth associations, which stood as the legitimate spokesmen of the aggrieved farmers, as well as individual members of the Dagara and Sisala educated elite. However, none of these could resolve the conflict, and, during the 1989 agricultural season, the Taalipuo and other Dagara farmers cultivating Sisala land were yet again barred from the fields.

The Gordian knot was finally cut by the late Archbishop Peter Dery, a man of mixed Dagara and Sisala ancestry who commanded much respect throughout the region.[53] After preliminary talks with both sides, he managed to summon the Nandom and Lambussie paramount chiefs and earth priests, representatives from Nabaala and Taalipuo, and individual members of the Sisala and Dagara educated elite to a meeting. Dery greatly simplified matters by concentrating on the Taalipuo issue and treating the district matter as closed. He avoided going into the complexities of settlement history and ethnic relations, and reminded the chiefs and others present that "land is the creation of God for the use of human beings." Eventually, the chiefs agreed that three of the disputed Taalipuo compounds should be placed under the jurisdiction of the Jirapa-Lambussie District, while the rest of Taalipuo was to remain under Nandom. In return, "the Lambussie Traditional Area will revoke all existing seizures of farm lands of immigrant and settler farmers."[54] The agreement was implemented, and since then no overt conflicts have erupted in the disputed area. However, the sociopolitical status of long-term Dagara settlers, particularly the immigrants' children and grandchildren, continues to be a source of tension and has sparked innumerable squabbles.

The Face-Off between Sisala Landowners and Dagara Settlers

Many NYDA activists complained that Archbishop Dery not only betrayed Nandom's cause for a district of its own, but also left the Dagara farmers in Lambussie at the mercy of their Sisala landlords. Indeed, the agreement recognized Sisala property rights and stipulated that anyone who wanted to farm or build in the Lambussie Traditional Area "should approach the Traditional land owners in accordance with Custom to be granted the same."[55] My NYDA interlocutors admitted that a general agreement could not homogenize the existing variety of tenancy arrangements, but feared that this vague appeal to custom allowed the Sisala landowners to further commercialize land leases and exploit immigrant farmers. However, the archbishop himself believed that the invocation of custom instead helped constrain exploitative redefinitions of land leases and repeatedly exhorted the Sisala landowners that customary tenure obliged them to grant access to land to those who needed it to feed their families. At the same time, he took seriously Sisala fears of becoming landless in their own villages, and advised landowners to forestall future disputes with immigrant farmers by stipulating unequivocal boundaries on all sides of the land to be granted (instead of indicating, as is customarily done, just the lateral boundaries), defining the number of years after which the contract needed to be renewed, and putting the agreement into writing.[56]

That the land conflicts ended with a clear-cut endorsement of Sisala property rights owes much to wider political developments. NYDA arguments that the Dagara immigrants from Nandom had helped to "tame" the "wild bush" in Lambussie and should therefore be accorded more rights than "mere settlers,"[57] invoked not only a specific interpretation of the first-comer idiom, but also the revolutionary rhetoric of the early Rawlings regime, namely that the land should belong to those who work it. By the late 1980s, however, government policies had returned to support traditional property rights, and the 1992 constitution reendorsed the constitutional provision of 1979 that all Northern lands once held in trust by government were to be restored to "any person who was the owner of the land before the vesting" of the land in the president.[58] Indicative of the shift in official attitudes toward land rights was the address that the regional secretary delivered to the newly established Jirapa-Lambussie District Assembly in 1989. The secretary exhorted Sisala landowners to ensure "maximum agricultural production" by returning to "traditional land tenure practices," instead of following the "alien practices" they had recently adopted. In the past, he insisted, "the relationship between immigrant farmers and the landowners was never one of servant and overlord," and land was "never used as a means of subjugating the landless . . . , no fees were charged, no percentage of produce was exacted and no act of allegiance to the landowner was required."[59] The secretary thus acknowledged that control over land could be turned into an instrument of economic and political exploitation, but refrained from questioning land ownership as such and rather sanctioned traditional practices that include, of course, ideas about first-comer status and allodial titles.

On the ground, these and similar exhortations did not arrest the overall trend toward an increasing commercialization of tenancy arrangements. Moreover, the bundle of rights that landowners transfer to immigrant farmers, particularly when the latter are newcomers, or when older immigrants desire to establish additional farms, has become ever more restricted, and is more closely monitored than before, as we have seen in the previous chapters. And although the state has not intervened directly in these tenancy agreements, the outcome of the Taalipuo conflict has made sufficiently clear to both landowners and Dagara settlers that the latter can expect no official support for any attempt to claim more comprehensive property rights, at least not under the current political regime.

Making a Good Case: First-Comers, Land Gods, and Tribal Migrations

Throughout the conflict, first-comer narratives played an important role, but their scope and emphasis changed as the conflict traveled through different political arenas. At the village level, the Taalipuo farmers and Nabaala landowners, for instance, discussed the settlement history and first-comer claims of specific local lineages. At stake were questions such as under which chief's rule someone's grandfather moved to exactly which location in the new settlement, from whom he had received land, and how, where, and with whose permission his sons had later built their houses and expanded their fields.

When the District Security Committee summoned a meeting with the earth priests, the custodian of the Nabaala shrine was soon sidelined by the earth priest of Lambussie, who claimed that the disputed land originally belonged to the Lambussie earth-shrine area and that he was therefore the rightful authority to be consulted for any conflict resolution. He interpreted the Nabaala-Taalipuo conflict immediately in the framework of the ancient settlement history of Nandom and Lambussie, and discussed with his Nandom counterpart whether there were any traditional boundaries between these two earth-shrine areas, and, if not, what this meant for the current conflict. The document that the two earth priests eventually thumb-printed confirmed that both parishes "worshiped" the same "land god" Kabir, and therefore "never shared any common boundaries." As the document further explained, "the Lambussie people who were . . . the first settlers released part of their land to Zenuo who was the first Nandom Dagarti settler on their land." The signatories agreed that the Lambussie Kabir was "senior to that of Nandom," thus implying that the Nandom earth shrine, built with stones that the Sisala earth priest once gave to Zenuo, never gained full autonomy. And, as some of my Sisala interlocutors explained, the insistence on seniority and "no boundaries" was actually meant to claim that Lambussie continued to hold an allodial title over all Nandom lands. For all practical purposes, however, the Sisala did not intend to interfere with Nandom land affairs, but wanted to remind the Dagara of these historical truths and to warn them that no "Nandom settler" should ever "lay claim to any portion of land belonging to the Lambussie people." The "land in dispute" in the Taalipuo case, the document concluded, "belongs to the Nabaala people."[60] Another member of the Nandom earth-priestly patriclan who claimed to be the rightful custodian of the shrine later argued that his uninformed rival's surrender to Lambussie's hegemonic claims was unwarranted because Nandom's earth shrine had been independent from the very beginning.[61]

In any case, all these historical narratives invoked a bigger picture of first possession and land transfers, and lumped different lineages together under labels such as the "Lambussie people" vis-à-vis the "Nandom people." This notwithstanding, they still closely followed the genre of village and lineage settlement histories. Christian Lund's observation that earth priests and chiefs invoke "two different forms of *past*" when formulating their arguments in land conflicts, the former referring to "*tradition* as a timeless past," the latter to "significant *historical events*,"[62] does not apply to the Sisala and Dagara cases that I have investigated (and does not entirely seem to fit with Lund's Bolgatanga case, either). In the Lambussie-Nandom conflict, earth priests and chiefs would disagree on some historical "facts," but fundamentally relied on the same type of narratives; the different scale of histories (of lineages, local groups, or tribes) that they invoked had more to do with in which forum they were presented than with who told them.

Tribes made their appearance in petitions addressed to regional and national politicians. In a letter to the Upper West regional secretary, for instance, the Issah West Development Union protested against NYDA's district plans and complained that "the Lobi settlers in the Lambussie Traditional Area" had only recently immigrated from Burkina Faso into Ghana and failed to respect the property rights of the Sisala "natives."[63] Categorizing the Dagara as Lobi—a group that is often regarded as the most anarchic and primitive people in the Black Volta region—was clearly intended to discredit NYDA's cause.[64] Asserting they were in fact of non-Ghanaian origins and recent immigrants into the area also insinuated that they were not rightful citizens and should therefore not be allowed to speak up in district affairs. To refute these allegations, Benedict Der, a Dagara professor of history at the University of Cape Coast, placed Dagara migrations firmly in the ancient history of West African kingdoms. He asserted that according to their oral traditions the Dagara were "a Dagomba people" whose "ancestors . . . split off from the Dagomba in the time of Na Nyagse (1476–1492) and moved westwards into what is now the Wa District," and eventually continued to Nandom, where they arrived "during the 1660s." In subsequent centuries, some Dagara from Nandom crossed the Black Volta westward, settling in what was to become French territory. In order to escape "forced labor and the imposition of taxation by the French colonial authorities," some of these emigrants later "returned home" to Nandom and, for lack of land, to Lambussie. Moreover, because of their deep historical roots in Ghana, Der insisted, "the Dagara in the Lambussie Traditional Area cannot . . . appropriately be called immigrant settlers from Burkina Faso."[65]

Recounting the early small-scale movements of different Dagara-speaking kin groups as a massive tribal exodus from the Dagomba kingdom asserted Dagara ethnic unity. It transformed them into one of the typical Ghanaian tribes that constitute the main actors in the dominant schoolbook and university-textbook versions of West African history. Firmly establishing Dagara origins in present-day Ghana lent legitimacy to their current political cause. And, finally, attaching a concrete date, and one as early as the seventeenth century, to the Dagara arrival in their present area of settlement conveyed a strong claim to first-comer status, at least with respect to the Nandom area itself. That Sisala and Dagara youth association activists found it necessary to present such claims in the genre of tribal migration accounts is ultimately a result of the colonial ethnicization and politicization of land tenure that still dominates the public debate on property rights and traditional authority in Northern Ghana.[66] Furthermore, that a group interested in strengthening its position vis-à-vis government attempts to define local or regional competitors as outsiders (the Lobi argument), or as an "internal other against which a 'pure' national identity is cast," is a typical strategy in many postcolonial political conflicts, as Sara Dorman and others have convincingly argued.[67] First-comer narratives are transformed into claims to autochthony, and the latter is associated with being good citizens.

Challenging First-Comer Claims

Presenting first-comer claims for entire ethnic groups instead of specific ancestors involved strategic slippages with regard to the territory for which these claims were actually raised. For all practical purposes, the Dagara accept that the earth shrines and thus the allodial titles in the Lambussie Traditional Area are controlled by the Sisala. Despite questioning the legitimacy of ancient shrine transfers, the Sisala, in turn, recognize that the Dagara have established earth shrines and allodial titles in the Nandom Traditional Area. In the ideological warfare during the land conflicts, however, both sides extended their property claims beyond these boundaries and deliberately confounded past and current Dagara migrations.

In a letter to the government information bureau, for instance, the NYDA chairman acknowledged that the Sisala were the first to arrive in the area, but redefined the pivotal event that identified true first-comers. Without further specifying whether he referred to the precolonial or more recent phase of Dagara migration, the chairman argued that "the pioneer Sissaala [sic] settlers could not have tamed and put under cultivation the wild bush that the area was without the Dagaabas. Descendants of these intrepid conquerors of the land cannot now be dismissed . . . as mere settlers."[68] If the decisive act of first possession was to cultivate and conquer the land, then, the letter seemed to suggest, the Dagara should be accorded full rights to land ownership and equal political participation—demands that obviously referred to the situation of the more recent Dagara immigrants into the Lambussie Traditional Area. At the same time, the letter invoked a long shared history of interethnic marriage, friendship, and economic as well as political cooperation, beyond distinctions between ethnic groups or first-comers and late-comers, and appealed that this history be garnered to promote development in a joint district.

In offstage discussions, Sisala and Dagara youth association activists were more belligerent in their quest to establish the historical legitimacy of their group's plight. Some of my Dagara interlocutors challenged Sisala first-comer claims as impossible to prove. In the once-impenetrable bush, they asserted, immigrants could hardly "determine which land they have settled on and how many other people were there." And they explained that before colonial pacification the Dagara newcomers had often imposed themselves violently, driving the Sisala "farther and farther away." If the latter now claimed that even the Nandom lands were actually theirs, this was as unjustified as "the story with the Israelites and the Arabs: you conquer, you fight somebody and get his land, and then later on he comes back and says that because there is peace now, just give me back my land."[69] Or, as another discussant suggested, the situation was like that in North America: "If the Indians . . . would get up and say that all these [immigrant] guys have to get out because that land doesn't belong to them, do you think that would be fair?! Where would they go?" The land should be used for farming and feeding all people, my interlocutors concluded in our increasingly emotional discussion of the ongoing farm seizures, asserting that "the land doesn't belong to you, because no human being has created the land!"

My Sisala informants, on the other hand, insisted that their people felt threatened by the massive presence of Dagara farmers in the Lambussie area who were "really taking too much of our land." Interpreting the current immigration in the light of the precolonial history of Dagara expansion, Banu Vito, chairman of the Issah West Development Union, complained that the Dagara "just let you feel that you don't matter anymore, that land has no owner, so everybody can jump in." Land-seeking Dagara should, of course, be allowed to farm in order to feed themselves, Banu Vito conceded—"We don't want to starve them to death, we are all Ghanaians"—but only if they respected their Sisala hosts' property rights. These rights, based on the group's status as first-comers in the entire area, were at the heart of Sisala identity and needed to be defended against all Dagara attempts to bring "the sheer fact of numbers and the present trend of modernization" into play. If the current conflicts were not fundamentally about these historical rights, Banu Vito concluded evocatively, "why would a minority ethnic group like the Sisala want to pit its mind against a whole vast Dagarti people if we didn't have something true to stand and fight for?"[70]

My Dagara and Sisala interlocutors obviously disagreed about how far back in time the legitimization of property rights should reach. The Sisala evoked the period of first arrivals and laid claim to a vast territory, including present-day Nandom Traditional Area. It is indeed possible that Sisala pioneers once regarded this large area up to the Black Volta as part of their hunting grounds, and the existence of early Sisala settlements on land that is now controlled by Dagara-owned earth shrines was confirmed by many interlocutors, both Sisala and Dagara. However, as the Issah West activists and others were well aware, the Sisala cannot possibly recuperate this ancient property. But by presenting themselves as a vulnerable ethnic minority and framing their cause in terms of time-honored rights, they lent their plight moral legitimacy—a strategy that also resonated with the return of official land policies toward privileging custom and autochthony. In this environment—or, to use Li's terms,[71] a "conjuncture" that rewarded the indigenous or autochthonous "slot"—the Dagara, as notorious late-comers, had more difficulty arguing their case consistently. In offstage comments, they insisted that property rights acquired through conquest were as definitive and valid as rights acquired by more peaceful methods. In onstage discussions, they foregrounded the legitimacy of rights acquired through labor and long-term occupancy, the moral right to subsistence regardless of the history of property transfers, and the claim to political recognition stemming from the basic equality as citizens of a nation-state. Both Dagara and Sisala, then, shared the grammar of first-comer claims, but differed in their interpretations of what exactly constituted the decisive act of coming first and how past events should relate to present circumstances. This fundamental difference in perspective has not been settled by the agreement that Archbishop Dery was able to bring about, and it is likely to remain unresolved.

Conclusion

In their comparative analysis of the agrarian roots of the recent civil wars in the Ivory Coast and Sierra Leone, Jean-Pierre Chauveau and Paul Richards argue that the insurgencies' dynamics were informed not only by state failure and political competition in the national arena, but also by long-standing fault lines of local conflict inherent in distinct versions of the "lineage mode of production."[72] Accumulation among Gola cash-crop producers in Sierra Leone was based on the exploitation of unpaid labor performed by young commoners for chiefs and rich traders in what Chauveau and Richards characterize as a "trade-linked, slave-based ranked lineage" system that has increasingly developed toward a class society.[73] As a result, when the young men's exit options in the urban economy and the diamond fields came under pressure and local exploitation by cash-strapped chiefs intensified, the youths' protest took on the character of "anger at class oppression rather than ethnic hatred."[74] Gban cocoa producers in the Ivory Coast, on the other hand, lived in more "egalitarian communities characterized by the labor of 'free youth' at the core,"[75] and accumulated wealth on the basis of labor and payments from immigrant tenant farmers, while their own young men worked in the cities. When the economic crisis forced these youth to return, they found their future jeopardized by their elders' massive transfer of land to the strangers. Gban youth therefore "fight to protect tradition against 'lax' elders and scapegoat migrant foreigners." Among the Gola, by contrast, "class conflict between ranked lineages and underclass interests . . . results in attacks on the symbols and personnel of the ranked lineage system itself."[76] In a third, expansive type of lineage society among Akan groups in the Ivory Coast, young men are expected to obey their chiefs as in the Sierra Leonean ranked lineage system, but are also encouraged to accumulate wealth on their own by moving to the agricultural frontier. Here, "migrant youths from the expansive communities . . . clash with local youth on the forest frontier in episodes of inter-ethnic violence."[77]

The Dagara and Sisala cases discussed in this book do not easily fit into any of these three types of lineage societies—if at all, they merge elements of the second, egalitarian, and the third, expansive, type, but without the latter's precolonial traditions of stratification. One could, perhaps, claim that Dagara and Sisala social organization constitutes a fourth type of a lineage society, characterized by the centrality of the earth shrines for the definition of social hierarchies, property rights, and ritual authority that is sometimes, but by no means always, transformed into economic privilege. However, operating in a context of pronounced mobility, relatively low economic stakes in the absence of large-scale cash-cropping opportunities, and the continued viability of exit options, such as seeking urban employment or moving to the agricultural frontier, these earth-shrine-centered lineage societies seem to have developed no clear-cut cleavages that would inevitably result in potentially violent confrontations. The conflicts analyzed in this and previous chapters, in any case, do not reveal any single major fault line, but involve variable sets of actors, interests, and coalitions. Complex lines of conflict and cross-cutting alliances prevented the emergence of organized ethnic or class-based blocs. This explains, in part, why land-related conflicts in the area under study have so far remained relatively nonviolent, unlike the cases analyzed by Chauveau and Richards. There were, and continue to be, occasional incidences of violence—when, for instance, newly planted trees considered illegitimate are secretly burned, an earth priest's young men tear down a house that is allegedly being constructed without permission, or Sisala and Dagara young men confront each other in vehement verbal attacks over fishing rights or a perceived lack of mutual respect. However, these aggressive acts do not coalesce into systematic violence, not least because there are no entrepreneurs who would benefit from organizing the youth of any adversary into militarized fighting factions—an important element of all sustained collective violence, as Derman, Odgaard and Sjaastad's overview of recent land-related conflicts in Africa emphasizes.[78]

Moreover, the issues at stake in the conflicts discussed above and in many other struggles over land could hardly be resolved by violent means. The conflicts concern not primarily access to land or use rights, but above all the allodial title, that is, the right to allocate use rights and alienate land or some rights over it to third parties. These property rights have a temporal depth that strongly discourages violence; if they are to become effective and last, they must be built on some form of consensus. As we have seen in the precolonial history of Dagara expansion, even where violence did play a role in the appropriation of new lands, the territorial gains had to be secured by ritual means, namely, the acquisition of an earth shrine, and by the construction of some kind of first-comer narrative. That these strategies of legitimization are not always fully successful and can be challenged retrospectively when the balance of power shifts has become evident in the Nandom-Lambussie case where Sisala contested property rights that the Dagara claim to have acquired more than two centuries ago. However, none of the claimants believed that any past illegitimate appropriation of land could be set right by violent reprisal.

The allodial title is of crucial importance not only because of the potential economic benefits it may entail. In fact, although by local standards earth priests and other allodial titleholders can derive considerable income from renting out or selling land, enterprising and well-connected immigrant farmers may establish much more profitable agricultural ventures on the basis of tenancy arrangements, as various Ghanaian and Burkinabé case studies have shown.[79] But allodial property rights are also central to the definition of belonging and securing a home that embodies the bonds to one's ancestors and from which one cannot be easily evicted in the event of, for instance, ethnic conflict. And as long as even membership in the modern nation-state is mediated by this kind of "primary patriotism,"[80] as is the case in Ghana and Burkina Faso as well as other West African countries, people will go to any length to defend or reclaim such strong property rights. This is also one of the reasons why disputes over allodial titles tend to be enduring and inconclusive.

It is symptomatic that all disputes discussed in this chapter had a long prehistory of conflict, and were instances in a sequence of confrontations that could reach far back into the precolonial period. Conversely, because even in struggles over use rights claimants usually refer to the allodial title, rather trivial land disputes can turn into debates about ancient histories of first possession. There is no impartial institution that can decide on the veracity of competing versions of local history. Since claimants disagree on when a break is to be made with the past beyond which past wrongs should no longer be redressed, conflicts about the allodial title remain basically irresolvable. In most cases, therefore, conflicts are merely suspended. Pragmatic solutions, informed by the current configuration of power and influence, regulate the immediate use of the land, but competing claims concerning the allodial title continue to simmer. Claimants may resort to the local administration or the courts and enlist the support of their educated urban relatives to frame their claims in ways that make them more convincing in state controlled arenas. However, even when state institutions intervene and reach a decision, the defeated party may still cling to its version of the case and merely await a new opportunity to pursue its claims once again. As Christian Lund observed: "Claims to land and property are not necessarily extinct merely because the rights [redefined by state legislation on land tenure] are. . . . Land claims have an extended shelf life and store well. . . . It seems that for every opportunity occurring there is an ample stock of pent up competing claims to be put forth."[81]

The question we may still ask is whether beneath the continuous ambiguities and reinterpretations of land rights, and the reversibility of conflict resolutions, there is a dominant trend toward increasing exclusion of the less powerful. Pauline Peters has forcefully criticized the exaggerated emphasis of recent work on African land tenure that has emphasized the flexibility of customary tenure and the negotiability and indeterminacy of land rights.[82] Her point is well taken: questions of power need indeed to be taken as seriously as the discussion of rights. But as Peters herself concedes, rural inequality in West Africa stems not from an increasing differentiation between landless laborers and large landowners, but rather from increasingly exclusive boundaries between natives and strangers, particularly if the latter have few assets to offer to their hosts,[83] and from the manipulation of customary tenure by urban political elites investing in commercial agriculture[84] or by enterprising chiefs who attempt to transform traditional custodianship of land into private property.[85] Peters is certainly right to remind us that "the stories so well told about inclusionary practices of land-use and about the ability of 'small acts' and small people to outmaneuver the powerful must be complemented and modified by stories of differentiation, displacement and exclusion."[86] I am less convinced, however, that much is gained by identifying all instances of exploitation and the "deepening rifts between and within kin-based, ethnic and regional groups"[87] as building blocks of "class formation," as Peters and Bernstein[88] propose without defining exactly which classes are supposedly in the making. I would contend that a focus on class formation is unable to capture the complex ways in which people perceive their own positions and pursue their interests, and lends an aura of unwarranted inevitability and homogeneity to processes that are politically mutable and regionally diverse. As Derek Hall, Philip Hirsch and Tania Murray Li have argued with regard to "land dilemmas" in Southeast Asia, we need to keep in mind that all forms of property and land rights, whether broadly distributed or monopolized by a powerful few, contain elements of "exclusion," that is, they exclude some categories of people from the land and deny some forms of land use. Instead of merely asking whether the current situation is characterized by a trend toward "more" exclusion, we should "focus on the changing ways in which people are excluded from access to land,"[89] and explore how new forms of regulating land rights, uses of force, market dynamics, and legitimatory discourses (for instance, on indigeneity or national development) transform people's entitlements to and ability to make a living off the land.

In any case, the playing field is certainly not level, and the historical conjunctures of "negotiation in inequality," as Lund puts it,[90] have shifted considerably over the past decades. The overall trends that Toulmin and Cotula identify in their summaries of findings from case studies on access to land in various West African countries also characterize, to a certain extent, developments in the Black Volta region: increasing scarcity of land in view of continued demographic growth and the expansion, albeit uneven, of cash crops; rising commercialization of access to land, with landowners demanding significant flows of cash from migrant farmers in exchange for secondary rights; growing difficulties for young men and women to gain access to land for farming, particularly when landowners decide to reallocate land to more affluent migrants; and, finally, the increasing importance of ethnicity in defining the boundaries between allodial title holders and strangers.[91]

Underlying these more recent trends is the basic change brought about in the early decades of the colonial regime, namely, the freezing of the landscape of allodial titles—they can be challenged, renegotiated, or reclaimed, but no longer newly created, because even land on the uncultivated frontier is imagined as someone's property. This closure of unpossessed territory is reinforced by the cessation of former processes of ethnic conversion and autochthonization, once aided by the use of force, and by the politicization of autochthonous status. These developments create specific challenges for migrants and others relying on multilocal, mobile strategies of livelihood, but they can also intensify competition within landowning communities, pitting earth priests against late-comers, and the latter against latest-comers. And sometimes, migrants gain room for maneuver because they are courted as important allies in these internal disputes, as I have shown in some cases discussed in this book.[92]

First-comer narratives are the dominant idiom in which these struggles and claims to allodial property and belonging are expressed, but they are so malleable that they do not necessarily support the interests of the more powerful alone. As the examples in this chapter demonstrate, they can mask individual strategies of enrichment, but also defend a moral economy of subsistence farming against powerful interests of commercialization. They can be told in ways that shore up xenophobic sentiment or allude to human-rights discourses in the defense of indigenous minorities, but they can also buttress a labor theory of property. And they can operate at various levels of inclusion and exclusion, within and between villages as well as between entire ethnic groups.

The inconclusiveness of property claims owes much to the vicissitudes of state legislation on land tenure, as Lund has convincingly argued, and to the fact that "no single institution has been able to enforce and sustain hegemony over rule making. The ambiguous policies by the colonial government and the political rent seeking of later governments undoing previous policies have engendered expectations of future gratification of presently denied claims."[93] Beyond these conjunctures of the larger political and legal history, however, there is a reason intrinsic to first-comer ideologies that accounts for irresolvable ambiguity: they locate the origin of legitimate property not in any social contract, but in the encounter of man and nature, or, to be precise, man and the earth deities or bush spirits. And they do not establish any human institution that could legitimately arbitrate competing claims concerning this encounter. The foundational act of allodial property, so to speak, is removed from the social sphere and the volatility of power and prowess.

The reasons why this was attractive for people in the Black Volta region and other areas of West Africa have been discussed in various chapters of this book. As we have seen, the narratives do reflect important elements of the frontier process and the ways in which first possession occurred. Defining first-comers as endowed with some form of control over the distribution and use of landed resources and with ritual authority as earth priests helped to order the social reproduction of the frontier communities. Late-comers had little choice but to either accept this basic order, chose an exit option, or overthrow it by force, but only to impose themselves as first-comers vis-à-vis further newcomers. Once this earth-shrine-centered order was in place, there was no way to return to any concept of unowned, open-access space. Second, first-comer justifications of property were flexible enough to allow for significant changes in the nature and scope of property rights while upholding the basic principles of an order based on precedence. Third, locating the "pivotal event," no matter whether it was imagined in terms of discovery or first cultivation, in an encounter between man and nature was particularly suited to a segmentary society that recognized no centralized political authority. It naturalized property and the origins of earth-priestly authority, and all legitimate claims to the allodial title had to, and still have to, relate back to an act of first possession in a chain of transmission that tends to systematically downplay the role of violence and social convention.

Obviously, first-comer ideologies that once helped to establish a flexible and effective social order on the frontier contain substantial potential for conflict in view of the developments outlined above, with gradually closing exit options and no means of creating new allodial titles. If disputing parties do not agree on a temporal base line—after the foundational act—beyond which restitution of an allegedly arrogated allodial title can no longer be reasonably demanded, all land conflicts may potentially turn into an irresolvable *regress ad infinitum*. Any such line, however, can only be politically defined, and thus refers us back to the question of which institutions ratify or invalidate property claims. In societies with precolonial chiefdoms, this authority, together with the allodial title, was vested in the chiefs. And although this does not preclude multiple contestations, as Berry, Amanor, and other scholars have amply shown, the basic institutional location where property conflicts should traditionally be mediated is fairly clear-cut.[94] Among segmentary, noncentralized societies, on the other hand, it was the colonial state that established itself as the first sovereign power, and this was how the landscape of allodial property rights was frozen. But this did not, of course, prevent people from challenging colonial authority, and continuing to mobilize first-comer stories in support of their claims. Moreover, the colonial state itself—the British to a greater extent than the French—invoked custom as a legitimating principle and thus helped to maintain the currency of first-comer claims in property debates. Brief periods of postcolonial regimes supportive of user-rights that relied on the idea of the nation-state as the ultimate owner, or at least custodian, of the national territory have boosted the late-comers' labor-theory approaches to property. But these were soon supplanted when the state began once again to accord greater weight to customary tenure. And as long as the modern state's imagery of citizenship and nation draws on older idioms of quasi-natural communities, the conundrum of first-comer ideologies will continue. The only way ahead seems to be the depoliticization of property, undoing its intimate connections with autochthony, belonging, and political representation. Ultimately, this requires the strengthening of institutions that can successfully mediate property conflicts by virtue of the fact that their legitimacy derives from a social contract and is not tied up with the irresolvable ambiguities of first-comer narratives.

Notes

Introduction

1. Peter Geschiere and Joseph Gugler, eds., "The Politics of Primary Patriotism," special issue, *Africa* 68 (1998).

2. The earth priest is usually assumed to be a descendant of the first settlers who concluded a spiritual pact with the earth deities and thereby obtained permission to found a village and distribute the land—arrangements that I explain in more detail below. That place-names and names of the alleged founder of a settlement are often identical is a mnemonic device that is sometimes confusing for the uninitiated researcher (and reader), but typical of the area's migration-and-settlement stories.

3. This is a verbatim, but condensed, excerpt from what was a much longer narrative in my interview with Tantuoyir, Soyeru Buolu, and others, 27 November 1989, Tantuo.

4. That property rights are held qua membership in a group even holds true for individual private ownership and other rights granted by state land legislation, because an individual holds these rights only as a citizen of a specific nation-state. On the connections between property rights and citizenship, see chapter 4 in this book and Christian Lund, "Landrights and Citizenship in Africa," Discussion Paper 65 (Uppsala: Nordiska Afrikainstitutet, 2011).

5. Carol M. Rose, *Property and Persuasion: Essays on the History, Theory and Rhetoric of Ownership* (Boulder: Westview Press, 1994), 297.

6. For an insightful discussion of the importance of the first-comer/late-comer configuration on the African frontier, see Igor Kopytoff, "The Internal African Frontier: The Making of African Political Culture," in *The African Frontier: The Reproduction of Traditional African Societies*, ed. Kopytoff, 3–84 (Bloomington: Indiana University Press, 1987). However, Kopytoff does not discuss the frontier process in terms of the establishment of property rights.

7. Arjun Appadurai, "The Past as a Scarce Resource," *Man* 16 (1981): 201–19.

8. For a history of ethnicity and political conflict in the Ghanaian part of the Black Volta region, see Carola Lentz, *Ethnicity and the Making of History in Northern Ghana* (Edinburgh: Edinburgh University Press, 2006).

9. "We are managing" is an expression that farmers from Ghana's Upper West Region often use to describe their efforts to make ends meet in the face of difficult circumstances; it has provided the title of Kees van der Geest's insightful study of rural livelihood strategies in Northwestern Ghana, *"We're Managing!": Climate Change and Livelihood Vulnerability in Northwest Ghana*, Research Report 74 (Leiden: African Studies Centre, 2004).

10. The figure is culled from CEDEAO-CSAO/OCDE, *L'atlas web de l'intégration régionale en Afrique de l'Ouest*, 2006, www.atlas-ouestafrique.org/spip.php?article168.

11. This figure is taken from Camilla Toulmin, "Negotiating Access to Land in West Africa: Who Is Losing Out?" in *Conflicts over Land and Water in Africa*, ed. Bill Derman, Rie Odgaard, and Espen Sjaastad (Oxford: James Currey, 2007), 96. According to Kasim Kasanga and N. A. Kotey (*Land Management in Ghana: Building on Tradition and Modernity* [London: IIED, 2001]), 80 percent of all land in Ghana is held under "customary arrangements."

12. For a comprehensive discussion of this concept and related recent research, see Franz von Benda-Beckmann and Keebet von Benda-Beckmann, "The Dynamics of Change and Continuity in Plural Legal Orders," *Journal of Legal Pluralism and Unofficial Law* 53/54 (2006): 1–44.

13. Sara Berry, "Debating the Land Question in Africa," *Comparative Studies in Society and History* 44 (2002): 648.

14. See, for instance, Gershon Feder and R. Noronha, "Land Rights Systems and Agricultural Development in Sub-Saharan Africa," *World Bank Research Observer* 2 (1987): 143–89; and Gershon Feder and David Feeny, "Land Tenure and Property Rights: Theory and Implications for Development Policy," *World Bank Economic Review* 5 (1991): 135–53. For a critical discussion of the "freehold-mortgage doctrine" and the Kenyan land titling program, see Parker Shipton, *Mortgaging the Ancestors: Ideologies of Attachment in Africa* (New Haven: Yale University Press, 2009).

15. Jean-Philippe Platteau, "The Evolutionary Theory of Land Rights as Applied to Sub-Saharan Africa: A Critical Assessment," *Development and Change* 27 (1996): 29–86.

16. On these policy-related debates, see, for instance, Richard Barrows and Michael Roth, "Land Tenure and Investment in African Agriculture: Theory and Evidence," *Journal of Modern African Studies* 28 (1990): 265–97; John W. Bruce, "Do Indigenous Tenure Systems Constrain Agricultural Development?" in *Land in African Agrarian Systems*, ed. Thomas J. Bassett and Donald E. Crummey (Madison: University of Wisconsin Press, 1993), 35–56; John W. Bruce and Shem Migot-Adholla, eds., *Searching for Land Tenure Security in Africa* (Washington D.C.: World Bank and Kendall Hunt, 1994); and Volker Stamm, *Zur Dynamik der westafrikanischen Bodenverfassung. Eine ökonomische Analyse am Beispiel Burkina Fasos* (Hamburg: Institut für Afrika-Kunde, 1996); Volker Stamm, "Endogene Konfliktregeln und staatliches Recht bei Auseinandersetzungen um Bodenressourcen," *Afrika Spectrum* 32 (1997): 297–310; Philippe Lavigne Delville, ed., *Quelles politiques foncières en Afrique? Réconcilier pratiques, légitimité et légalité* (Paris: Karthala, 1998); Camilla Toulmin and Julian Quan, eds., *Evolving Land Rights, Policy and Tenure in Africa*, Department for International Development Issues Series, London, 2000; Camilla Toulmin, Philippe Lavigne Delville, and S. Traoré, eds., *The Dynamics of Resource Tenure in West Africa* (Oxford: James Currey, 2002); and Lorenzo Cotula, ed., *Changes in "Customary" Land Tenure Systems in Africa* (London: International Institute for Environment and Development [IIED], 2007). For a critical overview of these debates and policy changes, see Sara Berry, "Privatization and the Politics of Belonging in West Africa," in *Land and the Politics of Belonging in West Africa*, ed. Richard Kuba and Carola Lentz, 241–63 (Leiden: Brill, 2006); and Kojo S. Amanor and Janine Ubink, "Contesting Land and Custom in Ghana: Introduction," in *Contesting Land and Custom in Ghana: State, Chief and Citizen*, ed. Ubink and Amanor, 9–26 (Leiden: Leiden University Press, 2009).

17. On how classical anthropological views of African social organization continue to shape contemporary policy discourses, see Pierre-Yves Le Meur, "Une petite entreprise de réassamblage du monde. Ethnographie et gouvernance des ressources foncières en Afrique de l'Ouest," *Ethnologie française* 41, no. 3 (2011): 331–42.

18. Jack Goody, *Technology, Tradition and the State in Africa* (London: Oxford University Press, 1971), 29–30.

19. See Kopytoff, "The Internal African Frontier," 22, 41.

20. Elizabeth Colson, "The Impact of the Colonial Period on the Definition of Land rights," in *Colonialism in Africa, 1870–1960*, ed. Victor Turner, vol. 3, *Profiles of Change: African Society and Colonial Rule* (Cambridge: Cambridge University Press, 1971), 202.

21. Paul Bohannan, "Africa's Land," in *Tribal and Peasant Economies*, ed. George Dalton (New York: Natural History Press, 1967), 51–60; see also Paul Bohannan, "'Land,' 'Tenure' and 'Land-Tenure,'" in *African Agrarian Systems*, ed. Daniel Biebuyck, 101–15 (London: Oxford University Press, 1963).

22. For a discussion on early land markets and the colonial freezing of property transfers in Ghana and West Africa, see Gareth Austin, *Labour, Land and Capital in Ghana: From Slavery to Free Labour in Asante, 1807–1956* (Rochester: University of Rochester Press, 2005); Kojo Amanor,

"Customary Land, Mobile Labor and Alienation in the Eastern Region of Ghana," in *Land*, ed. Kuba and Lentz, 137–59; and Stefano Boni, "Indigenous Blood and Foreign Labor: The Ancestralization of Land Rights in Sefwi (Ghana)," in *Land*, ed. Kuba and Lentz, 161–85. For an insightful discussion of territorial attachment, property rights and land "sales" in Kenya, see Shipton, *Mortgaging the Ancestors*. An early critique of the "abundant land" paradigm was formulated by Thomas J. Bassett, "Introduction: The Land Question and Agricultural Transformation in Sub-Saharan Africa," in *Land in African Agrarian Systems*, ed. Thomas J. Bassett and Donald E. Crummey, 3–31 (Madison: University of Wisconsin Press, 1993).

23. For further examples, see, for instance, the case studies in Claude-Hélène Perrot, ed., *Lignages et territoire en Afrique aux XVIIIe et XIXe siècles. Stratégies, compétition, intégration* (Paris: Karthala, 2000).

24. Duran Bell, "The Social Relations of Property and Efficiency," in *Property in Economic Context*, ed. Robert C. Hunt and Antonio Gilman, 29–45 (Lanham: University Press of America, 1998).

25. On the transcultural usefulness of such a broad notion of property, see Chris M. Hann, "Introduction: The Embeddedness of Property," in *Property Relations: Renewing the Anthropological Tradition*, ed. Hann, 1–47 (Cambridge: Cambridge University Press, 1998); Franz von Benda-Beckmann and Keebet von Benda-Beckmann, "A Functional Analysis of Property Rights with Special Reference to Indonesia," in *Property Rights and Economic Development: Land and Natural Resources in Southeast Asia and Oceania*, ed. T. van Meijl and Franz von Benda-Beckmann, 15–56 (London: Kegan Paul, 1999); and Christian Lund, "Negotiating Property Institutions: On the Symbiosis of Property and Authority in Africa," in *Negotiating Property in Africa*, ed. Kristine Juul and Lund, 11–43 (Portsmouth, N.H.: Heinemann, 2002).

26. Leonard T. Hobhouse, *Property, Its Duties and Rights* (London: Macmillan, 1915), quoted in Tim Ingold, *The Appropriation of Nature: Essays on Human Ecology and Social Relations* (Manchester: Manchester University Press, 1986), 229.

27. I am aware of the difficulties of applying the term "allodial," which is steeped in British notions of feudal land rights, to Francophone West Africa with its different legal traditions around concepts of "eminent domain" or "national domain." However, if we understand "allodial" simply as reference to the most comprehensive set of rights, including the rights of *usus, fructus,* and *abusus* of the land in question, this transposition may be permissible. For a Francophone legal discussion of customary land rights, see the relevant entries of Etienne Le Roy in *Encyclopédie juridique de l'Afrique* (Abidjan: Les nouvelles éditions africaines 1982), 5: 39–47, 71–81.

28. For instance, in their recent overview of processes of deagrarianization and dispossession in South East Asia, Derek Hall, Philip Hirsch, and Tania Murray Li do not hesitate to employ notions of "property" and ownership for all regions they study, including land held under "customary" arrangements, and argue that "exclusion" should not be stigmatized as a problematic feature of capitalist regimes, but as necessary element in all concepts of property and land rights (*Powers of Exclusion: Land Dilemmas in Southeast Asia* [Honolulu: University of Hawai'i Press, 2011]).

29. On the general history of property concepts and the debates around John Locke's "labor theory" of property, see Jean-Philippe Lévy, *Histoire de la propriété* (Paris: Presses Universitaires de France 1972); James Tully, *A Discourse on Property: John Locke and His Adversaries* (Cambridge: Cambridge University Press, 1980); Andrew Reeve, *Property* (Atlantic Highlands, N.J.: Humanities Press International, 1986); Alan Ryan, *Property* (Minneapolis: University of Minnesota Press, 1987); and John Brewer and Susan Staves, eds., *Early Modern Conceptions of Property* (London: Routledge, 1995). For an overview of anthropological debates on property, see Hann, *Property Relations*.

30. Rose, *Property and Persuasion*, 25–44. See also Louise Fortman's example of narrative contestations of property in Zimbabwe, "Talking Claims: Discursive Strategies in Contesting Property," *World Development* 23, no. 6 (1995): 1053–63.

31. On contested definitions of the "pivotal event," see William P. Murphy and Caroline H. Bledsoe, "Kinship and Territory in the History of a Kpelle Chiefdom (Liberia)," in *The African Frontier*, ed. Kopytoff, 121–47.

32. Charles C. Geisler and Gail Daneker, eds., *Property and Values: Alternatives to Public and Private Ownership* (Washington: Island Press, 2000), xiii.

33. C. K. Meek, *Land, Law and Custom in the Colonies* (Oxford: Oxford University Press, 1946), 1.

34. See, for instance, ibid.; R. J. H. Pogucki, *Report on Land Tenure in Native Customary Law of the Protectorate of the Northern Territories of the Gold Coast, Part II* (Accra: Lands Department, 1951); Daniel Biebuyck, *African Agrarian Systems* (London: Oxford University Press, 1963); Jean-Louis Boutillier, *Les structures foncières en Haute-Volta*, vol. 5, *Études voltaïques*, Mémoires (Ouagadougou: IFAN-ORSTOM, 1964); and William Allan, *The African Husbandman* (Edinburgh: Oliver and Boyd, 1965). For an informative historical overview of both land policies and research on "the land question" in Africa, see Berry, "Debating"; for comprehensive summaries of more recent debates, see Platteau, "The Evolutionary Theory"; and Pauline Peters, "Inequality and Social Conflict over Land in Africa," *Journal of Agrarian Change* 4, no. 3 (2004): 269–314.

35. Examples of this interest are Émile Le Bris, Étienne Le Roy, and François Leimdorfer, eds., *Enjeux fonciers en Afrique noire* (Paris: Karthala, 1982); Bernard Crousse, Émile Le Bris, and Étienne Le Roy, eds., *Espaces disputés en Afrique noire. Pratiques foncières locales* (Paris: Karthala, 1986); Piet Konings, *The State and Rural Class Formation in Ghana* (London: KPI, 1986); R. E. Downs and S. P. Reyna, eds., *Land and Society in Contemporary Africa* (Hanover, N.H.: University Press of New England, 1988); and Thomas J. Bassett and Donald E. Crummey, eds., *Land in African Agrarian Systems* (Madison: University of Wisconsin Press, 1993).

36. See, for instance, Cathérine Coquéry-Vidrovitch, "Le régime foncier rural en Afrique noire," in Émile Le Bris et al., eds., *Enjeux fonciers*, 65–84; Martin Chanock, *Law, Custom and Social Order: The Colonial Experience in Malawi and Zambia* (Cambridge: Cambridge University Press, 1985); and Martin Chanock, "Paradigms, Policies and Property: A Review of the Customary Law of Land Tenure," in *Law in Colonial Africa*, ed. Kristin Mann and Richard Roberts, 61–84 (Portsmouth, N.H.: Heinemann, 1991). Of course there are exceptions to these general trends, for instance, Colson's "The Impact of the Colonial Period," a perceptive early article on the precolonial dynamics of land rights connected with shifting cultivation and their colonial transformation; and Sally Falk Moore's seminal study of the history of Chagga customary law and land litigation in Tansania (*Social Facts and Fabrications: "Customary Law" on Kilimanjaro, 1880–1980* [Cambridge: Cambridge University Press, 1986]).

37. Terence Ranger, "The Invention of Tradition in Colonial Africa," in *The Invention of Tradition*, ed. Eric Hobsbawm and Ranger, 211–62 (Cambridge: Cambridge University Press, 1983); see also Leroy Vail, ed., *The Creation of Tribalism in Southern Africa* (London: James Currey, 1989).

38. Tania Murray Li, "Indigeneity, Capitalism, and the Management of Dispossession," *Current Anthropology* 51, no. 3 (2010): 397. Li argues that from the 1990s, many World Bank policy makers continued colonial paradigms of distinguishing between a small sector of modernizing capitalist farmers and a vast majority of "traditional" small-holders, who needed to be protected, by strengthening (and in reality inventing) communal tenure, from dispossession by market mechanisms.

39. Berry, "Debating," 639–40; see also "Hegemony on a Shoestring: Indirect Rule and Access to Agricultural Land," *Africa* 62, no. 3 (1992): 327–55; Sara Berry, *No Condition Is Permanent: The Social Dynamics of Agrarian Change in Sub-Saharan Africa* (Madison: University of Wisconsin Press, 1993); Sara Berry, *Chiefs Know Their Boundaries: Essays on Property, Power and the Past in Asante, 1896–1996* (Oxford: James Currey, 2001); and Berry, "Privatization." For a similarly nuanced perspective on the manifold meanings of land, see also the overview articles by Parker Shipton and Mitzi Goheen, "Understanding African Land-holding: Power, Wealth and Meaning," *Africa* 62, no. 3 (1992): 307–25; and Parker Shipton, "Land and Culture in Tropical Africa: Soils, Symbols, and the Metaphysics of

the Mundane," *Annual Review of Anthropology* 23 (1994): 347–77, which also address the religious dimensions of land, an aspect that is largely absent from Berry's work.

40. Kathryn Firmin-Sellers's comparative study (*The Transformation of Property Rights in the Gold Coast* [Cambridge: Cambridge University Press, 1996]) of the colonial transformation of "customary tenure" in two different settings in Southern Ghana has likewise shown how central questions of power and alliances, particularly with the colonial (and postcolonial) state, were to the local playing out of new institutional configurations of land rights.

41. See Christian Lund, *Law, Power and Politics in Niger: Land Struggles and the Rural Code* (Hamburg: Lit-Verlag, 1998); Christian Lund, "Struggles for Land and Political Power: On the Politicization of Land Tenure and Dispute in Niger," *Journal of Legal Pluralism* 40 (1998): 1–22; Christian Lund, "A Question of Honour: Property Disputes and Brokerage in Burkina Faso," *Africa* 69 (1999): 575–94; and Kristine Juul and Christian Lund, eds., *Negotiating Property in Africa* (Portsmouth, N.H.: Heinemann, 2002).

42. Christian Lund, *Local Politics and the Dynamics of Property in Africa* (Cambridge: Cambridge University Press, 2008).

43. Henry Bernstein, "Rural Land and Land Conflicts in Sub-Saharan Africa," in *Reclaiming the Land: The Resurgence of Rural Movements in Africa, Asia and Latin America*, ed. Sam Moyo and Paris Yeros, 67–101 (London: Zed Books, 2005).

44. Peters, 'Inequality," 269; see also Pauline Peters, "The Limits of Negotiability: Security, Equity and Class Formation in Africa's Land Systems," in *Negotiating Property*, ed. Juul and Lund, 45–66.

45. Kojo Amanor, "Conflicts and the Reinterpretation of Customary Tenure in Ghana," in *Conflicts over Land and Water in Africa*, ed. Bill Derman, Rie Odgaard, and Espen Sjaastad, 56 (Oxford: James Currey, 2007).

46. Janine M. Ubink and Kojo S. Amanor, eds., *Contesting Land and Custom in Ghana: State, Chief and Citizen* (Leiden: Leiden University Press, 2009).

47. Thomas Spear, "Neo-traditionalism and the Limits of Invention in British Colonial Africa," *Journal of African History* 44 (2003): 3–27.

48. Jacob Metzer and Stanley L. Engerman, "Some Considerations of Ethno-nationality (and Other Distinctions), Property Rights in Land, and Territorial Sovereignty," in *Land Rights, Ethno-Nationality, and Sovereignty in History*, ed. Engerman and Metzer, 7 (London: Routledge, 2004).

49. See ibid. for a summary of these debates; the rise of ideologies of "absolute" private ownership rights in early European thought is discussed by John Brewer and Susan Staves (in their introduction to *Early Modern Conceptions*, 1–18), who also show that in practice, property rights in land remained politicized and tied to numerous older use-rights.

50. Catherine Boone, "Property and Constitutional Order: Land Tenure Reform and the Future of the African State," *African Affairs* 106, no. 425 (2007): 557. On the conflicts in the Ivory Coast, see Jean-Pierre Chauveau, "Question foncière et construction national en Côte d'Ivoire," *Politique Africaine* 78 (2000): 94–125; Ruth Marshall-Fratani, "The War of 'Who Is Who': Autochthony, Nationalism, and Citizenship in the Ivoirian Crisis," *African Studies Review* 49, no. 2 (2006): 9–43; and Catherine Boone, "Africa's New Territorial Politics: Regionalism and the Open Economy in Côte d'Ivoire," *African Studies Review* 50 (2007): 59–81. For an overview of further case studies and a general discussion of the political ramifications of African land conflicts, see Bill Derman, Rie Odgaard, and Espen Sjaastad, "Introduction," in *Conflicts over Land and Water in Africa*, ed. Derman, Odgaard and Sjaastad, 1–30 (Oxford: James Currey, 2007). On the nexus between property and citizenship, see Jean-Pierre Jacob and Pierre-Yves Le Meur, "Introduction. Citoyenneté locale, foncier, appartenance et reconnaissance dans les socitétés du Sud," in *Politique de la terre et de l'appartenance. Droits fonciers et citoyenneté locale dans les socitétés du Sud*, ed. Jacob and Le Meur, 5–57 (Paris: Karthala, 2010). See also the overview of recent literature in Lund, "Landrights and Citizenship."

51. See, for instance, the work of Stephen Jackson on Eastern Congo, "Sons of Which Soil? The Language and Politics of Autochthony in Eastern D. R. Congo," *African Studies Review* 49, no. 2 (2006): 95–123.

52. Peter Geschiere and Francis Nyamnjoh, "Capitalism and Autochthony: The Seesaw of Mobility and Belonging," *Public Culture* 12 (2000): 423–52.

53. Peter Geschiere and Stephen Jackson, "Autochthony and the Crisis of Citizenship: Democratization, Decentralization, and the Politics of Belonging," *African Studies Review* 49, no. 2 (2006): 1.

54. The term "conjuncture" in this context has been usefully introduced by Tania Murray Li, "Articulating Indigenous Identity in Indonesia: Resource Politics and the Tribal Slot," *Comparative Studies in Society and History* 42 (2000): 149–68.

55. Bambi Ceuppens and Peter Geschiere, "Autochthony: Local or Global? New Modes in the Struggle over Citizenship and Belonging in Africa and Europe," *Annual Review of Anthropology* 34 (2005): 387.

56. See, for instance, Antoine Scopa, "Bailleurs autochtones et locataires allogènes. Enjeu foncier et participation au Cameroun," *African Studies Review* 49, no. 2 (2006): 45–67; Alec Leonhardt, "Baka and the Magic of the State: Between Autochthony and Citizenship," *African Studies Review* 49, no. 2 (2006): 69–94, on Cameroon; and Jackson, "Sons," on Eastern Congo. For a comprehensive discussion of recent studies on autochthony in the Ivory Coast, Cameroon, the Great Lakes Region, as well as, by way of comparison, Belgium, see Ceuppens and Geschiere, "Autochthony"; and Peter Geschiere, *The Perils of Belonging* (Chicago: University of Chicago Press, 2009).

57. For a classical discussion of earth priests and earth shrines in the Black Volta region, see St. John Eyre-Smith, *A Brief Review of the History and Social Organisation of the Peoples of the Northern Territories of the Gold Coast* (Accra: Government Printer, 1933); Jack Goody, "Fields of Social Control among the LoDagaba," *Journal of the Royal Anthropological Institute of Great Britain and Ireland* 87 (1957): 75–104; for a broader comparative perspective, see Jürgen Zwernemann, *Die Erde in Vorstellungswelt und Kulturpraktiken der sudanischen Völker* (Berlin: Reimer, 1968).

58. For a discussion of the different roles of earth priests in various regions of Burkina Faso, see Richard Kuba, Andrea Reikat, Andrea Wenzek, and Katja Werthmann, "Erdherren und Einwanderer. Bodenrecht in Burkina Faso," in *Mensch und Natur in Westafrika*, ed. Klaus-Dieter Albert et al., 373–99. *Ergebnisse aus dem Sonderforschungsbereich 268* (Weinheim: Wiley-VCH, 2004).

59. For more details on the "allodial" title, a term commonly used in Ghanaian legal parlance, but also in everyday conversations, see Gordon R. Woodman, *Customary Land Law in the Ghanaian Courts* (Accra: Ghana Universities Press, 1996).

60. Christian Lund's work on the Bolgatanga earth priests' association provides a compelling example (see "Who Owns Bolgatanga? A Story of Inconclusive Encounters," in *Land*, ed. Kuba and Lentz, 77–98).

61. See Ingold, *The Appropriation of Nature*, 154–58. While Ingold (222–42) discusses the control that hunters and gatherers exercise over land in terms of "custodianship" rather than property, Barnard and Woodburn, whom I would follow here, do not hesitate to apply a minimalist conception of property— socially recognized control, in combination with "some restriction on other people's control of the same 'thing'"—to hunter-gatherers' relations to "land and ungarnered resources" ("Property, Power and Ideology in Hunter-Gatherer Societies: An Introduction," in *Hunters and Gatherers*, ed. Ingold et al., 13–16 [Oxford: Berg, 1997]). For a discussion of "territoriality," "tenure," and "property" in hunter-gatherer societies and among early agriculturalists, see also Maurice Godelier, "Territory and Property in Primitive Society," in *Human Ethology*, ed. Mario von Cranach, et al., 133–55 (Cambridge: Cambridge University Press, 1979); and Michael J. Casimir, "The Dimensions of Territoriality: An Introduction," in *Mobility and Territoriality: Social and Spatial Boundaries among Foragers, Fishers, Pastoralists and Peripatetics*, ed. Casimir and Aparna Rao, 1–26 (Oxford: Berg, 1992).

62. John Peel, "The Cultural Work of Yoruba Ethnogenesis," in *History and Ethnicity*, ed. Elizabeth Tonkin et al., 200 (London: Routledge, 1989).

63. Sally Falk Moore, "Changing African Land Tenure: Reflections on the Capacities of the State," *European Journal of Development Research* 10 (1998): 33.

64. Catherine Boone, *Political Topographies of the African State: Territorial Authority and Institutional Choice* (Cambridge: Cambridge University Press, 2003): 3, 8.

65. For a comprehensive history of the colonial introduction of chieftaincy in the area, see Carola Lentz, "'Chieftaincy Has Come to Stay.' La chefferie dans les sociétés acéphales du Nord-Ouest Ghana," *Cahiers d'Etudes Africaines* 159 (2000): 593–613; and Lentz, *Ethnicity*, 33–71, 104–37.

66. Kathryn Firmin-Sellers, "Institutions, Context and Outcomes: Explaining French and British Rule in West Africa," *Comparative Politics* 33 (2000): 253–72; Boone, *Political Topographies*.

67. On these policies, see Raymond B. Bening, "Land Policy and Administration in Northern Ghana," *Transactions of the Historical Society of Ghana* 16 (1995): 227–66; and Lund, *Local Politics*, 25–37.

68. Lund, *Local Politics*, 37–46.

69. Since Robin Horton's discussion ("Stateless Societies in the History of West Africa," in *History of West Africa*, ed. J. F. A. Ajyayi and Michael Crowder [1975; London: Longman, 1985], 1: 87–128) of the methodological problems of writing the history of noncentralized societies in West Africa, these questions have hardly been addressed, except in a book on "lineage histories" edited by Claude-Hélène Perrot, *Lignages et territoire* (2000); and an article by Martin Klein on reconstructing the history of the slave trade ("The Slave Trade and Decentralised Societies," *Journal of African History* 42 [2001], esp. 50–51).

70. For some examples, see Carola Lentz, "Colonial Ethnography and Political Reform: The Works of A. C. Duncan-Johnstone, R. S. Rattray, J. Eyre-Smith and J. Guinness on Northern Ghana," *Ghana Studies* 2 (1999): 119–69; and Carola Lentz, "Of Hunters, Goats and Earth-Shrines: Settlement Histories and the Politics of Oral Tradition in Northern Ghana," *History in Africa* 27 (2000): 193–214.

71. Henri Labouret, *Les tribus du rameau Lobi* (Paris: L'Institut d'Ethnologie, 1931), 15–43.

72. Mathieu Hilgers has made a similar observation in his analysis of conflicting historical narratives on the founding of Koudougou (Burkina Faso) ("Les conflits autour de l'histoire de Koudougou [Burkina Faso]," *Cahiers d'Études africaines* 47, no. 86 [2007]: 313–44). For an illuminating example of local debates on conflicting migration narratives from Tanzania, see Jamie Monson, "Memory, Migration and the Authority of History in Southern Tanzania, 1860–1960," *Journal of African History* 41 (2000): 347–72. For a more general discussion on the "production of history" and different understandings of historical "truth," see David William Cohen, "The Undefining of Oral Tradition," *Ethnohistory* 36 (1989): 9–17; David William Cohen, "La Fontaine and Wamimbi: The Anthropology of 'Time-Present' as the Substructure of Historical Oration," in *Chronotypes: The Construction of Time*, ed. John Bender and David E. Wellbery, 205–25 (Stanford: Stanford University Press, 1991); Elizabeth Tonkin, *Narrating our Pasts: The Social Construction of Oral History* (Cambridge: Cambridge University Press, 1992); Henri Moniot, "Profile of a Historiography: Oral Tradition and Historical Research in Africa," in *African Historiographies: Which History for Which Africa?* ed. Bogumil Jewsiewicki und David Newbury, 50–58 (Beverly Hills: Sage, 1986); Henri Moniot, "L'histoire à l'épreuve de l'Afrique," *Cahiers d'Etudes Africaines* 138–39 (1995): 647–56; as well as David Berliner's overview of the discussion on memory ("The Abuses of Memory: Reflections on the Memory Boom in Anthropology," *Anthropological Quarterly* 78, no. 1 [2005]: 197–211).

73. Interview with Buu Kuoro Mahama Baanuomake et al., 10 December 1997.

74. Joseph C. Miller, ed., *The African Past Speaks* (Folkestone: Dawson, 1980), 5–21; Jan Vansina, *Oral Tradition as History* (Madison: University of Wisconsin Press, 1985), 160–73.

75. My own material is complemented by the findings of other members of a research team with whom I worked between 1997 and 2002 in the context of a larger interdisciplinary research project on

the West African savanna at the University of Frankfurt/Main (SFB 268), financed by the Deutsche Forschungsgemeinschaft. See Kuba, Lentz, and Werthmann, eds., *Les Dagara*; and Richard Kuba, Carola Lentz, and Claude N. Somda, eds., *Histoire du peuplement et relations interethniques au Burkina Faso* (Paris: Karthala, 2003) for some results of our collective research. My colleagues' studies covered the dynamics of Dagara expansion on the western frontier (see, for instance, Richard Kuba and Carola Lentz, "Arrows and Earth Shrines: Towards a History of Dagara Expansion in Southern Burkina Faso," *Journal of African History* 43 [2002]: 377–406; and Richard Kuba, "Comment devenir Pougouli? Stratégies d'inclusion au sud-ouest du Burkina Faso," in *Histoire du peuplement*, ed. Kuba, Lentz, and Somda, 137–65); interethnic relations between Dyan, Phuo, and Lobi (Michaela Oberhofer, "Un village dyan au sud-ouest du Burkina Faso. Relations interethniques en mutation," in *Les Dagara*, ed. Kuba, Lentz and Werthmann, 141–58; and Michaela Oberhofer, *Fremde Nachbarn. Ethnizität im bäuerlichen Alltag in Burkina Faso* [Cologne: Köppe Verlag 2008]), as well as Mossi immigration into South-Western Burkina Faso (see, for instance, Andrea Wilhelmi, "Die Konstruktion von Autochthonie. Fallstudie zur dörflichen Gemeinschaftsbildung in einem staatlichen Umsiedlungsprojekt im Südwesten von Burkina Faso," master's thesis, Department of Historical Anthropology, Goethe University, Frankfurt/Main, 2000; and Katja Werthmann, Modeste Somé, and Andrea Wilhelmi, "Il y a l'entente comme il y a la mésentente. Vingt ans de cohabitation entre Dagara et Mossi dans les anciens villages A.V.V.," in *Les Dagara*, ed. Kuba, Lentz, and Werthmann159–78) and more recent migrations in the context of state-led settlement projects and the discovery of gold deposits (see, for instance, Katja Werthmann, "Gold Diggers, Earth Priests, and District Heads: Land Rights and Gold Mining in Southwestern Burkina Faso," in *Land*, ed. Kuba and Lentz, 119–36). Altogether, we conducted several hundred interviews and documented oral traditions from more than 150 villages, mainly in Burkina Faso's Ioba and Sissili Provinces, and Ghana's Lawra-Nandom and Jirapa-Lambussie Districts. Nearly all interviews have been translated into English or French. Copies of these transcriptions and their translations are available for consultation at the Department of Anthropology and African Studies, Mainz University; Frobenius Institute, Goethe University, Frankfurt/Main; the Melville Herskovits Library, Northwestern University, Evanston; the National Archives of Burkina Faso, Ouagadougou; and the library of the Institute of African Studies, University of Ghana, Legon.

76. Vansina, *Oral Tradition*, 137–46, 152–60.

77. For more details on this method, see Carola Lentz and Hans-Jürgen Sturm, "Of Trees and Earth Shrines: An Interdisciplinary Approach to Settlement Histories in the West African Savannah," *History in Africa* 28 (2001): 139–68.

78. For a recent excellent reflection on how to combine multiple sources and oral recollections in the reconstruction of the history of a particular "landscape" that achieves even greater historical depth than what is attempted in this volume, see Jan Bender Shetler, *Imagining Serengeti: A History of Landscape Memory in Tanzania from Earliest Times to the Present* (Athens: Ohio University Press, 2007).

79. This pertains particularly to developments in the British colony, while the French colonial regime formally established state ownership of all territories.

Chapter 1

1. "Mobile Africa: An Introduction," in *Mobile Africa: Changing Patterns of Movement in Africa and Beyond*, ed. Mirjam de Bruijn et al. (Leiden: Brill, 2001), 1.

2. Ibid., 2. For an overview of historical and contemporary aspects of mobility in Africa, see Han van Dijk, Dick Foeken, and Kiky van Til, "Population Mobility in Africa: An Overview," in *Mobile Africa*, ed. de Bruijn et al., 9–27. See also Aderanti Adepoju, "Migration in Africa: An Overview," in *The Migration Experience in Africa*, ed. Jonathan Baker and Tade Akin Aina (Uppsala: Nordiska Afrika Institutet, 1995), 87–108.

3. Kopytoff, "The Internal African Frontier," 7, 18.

4. For a brief overview of migrations in West Africa, see Dennis D. Cordell, Joel W. Gregory, and Victor Piché, *Hoe and Wage: A Social History of a Circular Migration System in West Africa* (Boulder: Westview Press, 1996), 20–31.

5. Considerable controversy has surrounded "Dagara" ethnic names. British colonial administrators introduced the terms "Dagarti" and "Lobi," which some Ghanaians continue to use; French district commissioners employed the term "Dagari," which is still used by many Burkinabé. Jack Goody (*The Social Organisation of the LoWiili* [London: H. M. Stationery Office, 1956], 16–26), who wrote the first major ethnography on the Dagara, introduced the term "LoDagaa," which he subdivided further into the LoDagaba and the LoWiili. Most of those so labeled reject all of these names as incorrect or even pejorative, but there is much discussion of what term to use instead. Some believe that the people living around Wa, Nadawli, and Jirapa (in Ghana) form a distinct group, the "Dagaba," speaking their own dialect, "Dagaare," and that the term "Dagara" should be reserved for the speakers of the "Lobr" dialect, that is, the population of Lawra, Nandom, and parts of South-Western Burkina Faso. Others hold that "Dagara" is the only correct unitary term for both the language and the entire ethnic group. For more details on the controversies on ethnic names, see Carola Lentz, "Colonial Constructions and African Initiatives: The History of Ethnicity in Northwestern Ghana," *Ethnos* 65 (2000): 120–24; and Sebastian Bemile, "Promotion of Ghanaian Languages and Its Impact on National Unity: The Dagara Language Case," in *Ethnicity in Ghana: The Limits of Invention*, ed. Carola Lentz and Paul Nugent, 204–25 (London: Macmillan, 2000). For simplicity's sake, and because much of my discussion indeed refers to the speakers of the "Lobr" dialect, I use the term "Dagara" throughout this book.

6. Since the 1960s, population censuses in Ghana and Burkina Faso no longer record ethnic identities, and due to high rates of mobility, it is difficult to estimate the demographic strength of any ethnic group on the basis of general census data. The numbers provided here are taken from various sociolinguistic reports, summarized in the most recent SIL *Ethnologue* report, available on the Internet (see www.ethnologue.com/show_country.asp?name=ghana; and www.ethnologue.com/show_ country.asp?name=BF).

7. For Ghana, see www.ghanadistricts.com, with data from 2000 and later; for Burkina Faso, the figures come from www.citypopulation.de and are based on the 1996 census .

8. Ladis K. J. Kristof, "The Nature of Frontiers and Boundaries," *Annals of the Association of American Geographers* 49 (1959): 270–71.

9. On the territorial strategies of patriclans and lineages, see also the case studies in Claude-Hélène Perrot, ed., *Lignages et territoire en Afrique aux XVIIIe et XIXe siècles* (Paris: Karthala, 2000).

10. Marshall D. Sahlins, "The Segmentary Lineage: An Organization of Predatory Expansion," *American Anthropologist* 63 (1961): 342, 336.

11. See, for instance, David Turton, "A Journey Made Them: Territorial Segmentation and Ethnic Identity among the Mursi," in *Segmentary Lineage Systems Reconsidered*, ed. Ladislav Holy (Belfast: Queen's University, 1979), 119, 132. Turton made this point in a study of armed conflict between two noncentralized southern Ethiopian societies. See also Henri Labouret, "La guerre dans ses rapports avec les croyances religieuses chez les populations du cercle de Gaoua," *Bulletin du comité d'études historiques et scientifiques de l'AOF* (1916): 289–304; Günther Wagner, "Political Organization of the Bantu of Kavirondo," in *African Political Systems*, ed. Meyer Fortes and E. E. Evans-Pritchard (London: KPI, 1940), 229; Paul Bohannan, "The Migration and Expansion of the Tiv," *Africa* 24 (1954): 7–9; Pierre Bonnafé, Michèle Fiéloux, and Jeanne-Marie Kambou P. Bonnafé, "Un vent de folie? Le conflit armé dans une population sans État. Les Lobi de Haute-Volta," in *Guerres de lignages et guerres d'États en Afrique*, ed. Jean Bazin and Emmanuel Terray (Paris: Karthala, 1982), 95.

12. Bohannan, "The Migration," 7; Wagner, "Political Organization," 227; Turton, "A Journey," 142.

13. This chain-reaction model was certainly popular among colonial officers, and it is not impossible that the folk model is partly the result of feedback. For a particularly elaborate and speculative

version of the wave model in colonial historiography, see Eyre-Smith, *A Brief Review*, 12; a discussion of Eyre-Smith's and other colonial officers' approaches to regional history can be found in Lentz, "Colonial Ethnography," 148–65.

14. On the philosophical roots of this model, see László Vajda, "Zur Frage der Völkerwanderungen," *Paideuma* 19–20 (1973–74): 5–52.

15. Wa sources state that wars were waged from Wa against the Dagara. According to the Arabic manuscript *Al-akhbar Saltanat Bilad Wa*, "Lobi" (which may refer to certain Dagara groups) threatened Wa until they were defeated by the Mamprusi prince Saliah. The *Ta'rikh Ahl Wala*, written in 1922 but based on older oral traditions, refers to the same event, but states that Saliah was fighting against "Dagati," "Wiili," and "Birfu." Saliah is a figure of the late seventeenth or early eighteenth century and apical ancestor of the rulers of Wa (see Ivor Wilks, *Wa and the Wala: Islam and Polity in Northwestern Ghana* [Cambridge: Cambridge University Press, 1989], 51–52, 88). However, according to all oral evidence I collected, it is unlikely that the power of Wa ever extended as far north as Lawra and Nandom. More generally on slave raids in what is today Northern Ghana, see Benedict Der, *The Slave Trade in Northern Ghana* (Accra: Woeli, 1998).

16. In the following section as well as in the first section of chapter 2, I adapt passages from Kuba and Lentz, "Arrows." Richard Kuba has kindly agreed to allow my use of sections of our coauthored article here.

17. Interviews with Tigwii S. Amoah, 12 December 1997; 20 January 1998; 10 February 1999; and 26 February 2000, Hamile. On the static ideal model of the lineage among the Sisala, see also Eugene Mendonsa, "Economic, Residential and Ritual Fission of Sisala Domestic Groups," *Africa* 49 (1979): 388–407; on the spiritual power of Sisala elders and the role of divination and the ancestor cult in controlling the migration of dependent juniors, see Eugene Mendonsa, *The Politics of Divination: A Processual View of Reactions to Illness and Deviance among the Sisala of Northern Ghana* (Berkeley: University of California Press 1982), 50–53, 149–210; and Eugene L. Mendonsa, *Continuity and Change in a West African Society: Globalization's Impact on the Sisala of Ghana* (Durham: Carolina Academic Press, 2001), 185–218.

18. Interviews with Laponé Kuoro (chief) Kumasi et al., 22 February 2000; Mahama Baanuomake et al., 10 December 1997, Buu; Zankor Bahiise et al., 10 December 1997, Dahile; Happa Kuoro Hilleh Babrimatoh et al., 30 November 1994.

19. Interviews with Bozo Kuoro Banuosin Kel-le et al., 17 December 1997; Bourra Kuoro Issa Nadie et al., 27 November 2001; Bouara Kuoro Nawie Zogyir et al., 19 December 1997. On the "pregnant-woman-slit-open" motif, see also Rüdiger Schott, "'La femme enceinte éventrée.' Variabilité et contexte socio-culturel d'un type de conte ouest-africain," in *D'un conte à l'autre. La variabilité dans la littérature orale*, ed. Veronika Görög-Karady, 327–39 (Paris: Éditions CNRS, 1990).

20. Interviews with Topulwy Bukari et al., 26 January 1998, Pina (Burkina Faso); Hiela Kuoro Emoho Yelgie, Baagyawii Yelgie et al., 18 December 1997, 22 February 1999, Hiela; Hamile Kuoro Puli Nagie, Bewaar Bei et al., 29 December 1996, Hamile; Tigwii S. Amoah, 13 December 1997, Hamile; Kierim Kuoro Bombie Naagyie, Buuyor Naagie et al., 19 December 1997, Kierim; Mahama Baanuomake et al., 10 December 1997, Buu.

21. The only exception seems to be a legend reported by Edward Tengan (*The Social Structure of the Dagara: The House and the Matriclan as Axes of Dagara Social Organisation* [Tamale: St Victor's Major Seminary 1994], 15), which explains the separation of the Kuwere patriclan from the original Kpiele house with a "pregnant-woman-slit-open" story.

22. On this, see also Sahlins, "The Segmentary Lineage," 341. Similarly, Raymond Kelly's discussion of Nuer "tribal imperialism" (*The Nuer Conquest: The Structure and Development of an Expansionist System* [Ann Arbor: University of Michigan Press, 1985]) concludes that the reasons for their impressive territorial expansion throughout the nineteenth century, at the expense of their Dinka

neighbors, are to be sought in "cultural rather than biological imperatives" (ibid., 241), especially in their brideprice system, which necessitated the production of more animals and hence access to larger pastures.

23. Jack Goody, "The Mother's Brother and the Sister's Son in West Africa," *Journal of the Royal Anthropological Institute* 89 (1959): 61–88.

24. Similar attitudes toward and strategies of mobility are typical of the Lobi (Michèle Fiéloux, *Les sentiers de la nuit. Les migrations rurales lobi de la Haute-Volta vers la Côte d'Ivoire* [Paris: ORSTOM 1980], 111–12) as well as of the Mossi. In the latter case, however, mobility was also intimately linked to a project of political hegemony; see Michel Benoit (*Oiseaux de mil. Les Mossi du Bwamu (Haute-Volta)* [Paris: ORSTOM, 1982]) for a critical view and Mark Breusers (*On the Move: Mobility, Land Use and Livelihood Practices on the Central Plateau in Burkina Faso* [Münster: Lit, 1999]) for a more sympathetic perspective of Mossi mobility; see also Pierre-Joseph Laurent et al., *Migrations et accès à la terre au Burkina Faso* (Paris: Harmattan 1994), 92. There are also many parallels between the Dagara ethos of the *yirsob* and the Kikuyu ideal of the *mûramati*, the lineage head, in control of sufficient land to accommodate himself and his followers autonomously; among both groups, these ideals result in a strong culture of mobility; on Kikuyu cultural ideals and migrations, see Yves Droz, *Migrations kikuyus. Des pratiques sociales à l'imaginaire* (Neuchâtel: Editions de l'Institut d'Ethnologie, 1999), 233–92.

25. For an early description of the technology, social organization and ritual practices of Lobi, Dyan, Birifor, and Dagara hunting, see Henri Labouret, "La chasse et la pêche—dans leurs rapports avec les croyances religieuses parmi les populations du Lobi," *Annuaire et mémoires du comité d'études historiques et scientifiques de l'AOF* (1917): 244–76.

26. Some interlocutors believed that Tokuri was a village near Wallembele, in present-day North-West Ghana, others located it in Burkina Faso, and still others around Samoa, a Ghanaian Sisala village east of Lambussie.

27. Interview with Bozo Kuoro Banuosin Kel-le, Bozo, 17 December 1997. The act of naming expressed the ritual relationship with the local spirits and, at the same time, established the earth shrine ("under a tree").

28. Interview with Aansokang Daanikuu, Faata Biku et al., 14 January 1998, Fielmuo. Significantly, the Sisala earth priest responsible for Fielmuo claimed that the events had occurred the other way around, that is, that one of their ancestors used to hunt in the area of Niégo, became a regular guest of a fellow Dagara hunter, and finally, when French colonial rule became unbearable, invited the latter to cross the border and settle near his home in the British protectorate; interview with Suleiman Balesemule et al., Nimoro, 14 December 1997.

29. Population densities above 35 persons per square kilometer and clearing of the bush between homesteads reduce the risk of infection. For details and discussion of various hypotheses, see J. P. Hervouët, "Modes d'utilisation de l'espace et onchocercose," Abidjan: ORSTOM, unpublished manuscript, 1985; J. M. Hunter, "River Blindness in Nangodi, Northern Ghana: A Hypothesis of Cyclical Advance and Retreat," *Geographical Review* 56 (1966): 389–416; Fréderic Paris, "Système d'occupation de l'espace et onchocercose. Foyer de la Bougouriba—Volta Noire (Burkina Faso)," in *Table ronde. Tropiques et santé. De l'épidémologie à la géographie humaine*, ed. Centre d'Étude de Géographie Tropicale [Talence/Paris [Travaux et Documents de la Géographie Tropicale], 1982), 259–70; and J. Remme and J. B. Zongo, "Demographic Aspects of the Epidemiology and Control of Onchocerciasis in West Africa," in *Demography and Vector-Borne Diseases*, ed. Michael Service (Boca Raton: CRC Press, 1989), 367–86.

30. See, for instance, the figures in Fabre, "Circonscription de Diébougou, dénombrement de la population indigène," 1904, Archives Nationales de Mali (ANM), 5D33; and Quégneaux, "Circonscription de Diébougou, récensement," *Annexe au rapport politique Mai 1912*, Archives Nationales de la Côte d'Ivoire (ANI), 5EE11, 2/3. A comparison of early colonial maps with more recent

ones clearly shows that the valleys along the Black Volta and its bigger tributaries, which had been relatively densely settled around the turn of the century, were virtually depopulated by the 1960s; see, for instance, the maps prepared by the Anglo-French Boundary Commission traveling along the 11th parallel in 1900 and along the Black Volta in 1902 (Public Record Office [PRO], London, MPG 915; PRO, CO 1047, Gold Coast 425), and the relevant sheets of the Survey of Ghana maps of 1967. For the Dagara and Sisala villages in the British protectorate, detailed village-level census figures are only available from 1921 onward; see The Gold Coast, *Census Report and Returns* (Accra Government Press 1929–33); The Gold Coast, *The Gold Coast in 1931, Appendices* (Accra Government Press 1933). The impact of epidemics on Northern Ghanaian population densities is discussed in T. E. Hilton, "Depopulation and Population Movement in the Upper Region of Ghana," *Bulletin of the Ghana Geographical Association* 11, no. 1 (1966): 27–47; for a case study of the demographic effects of onchocercosis in the valleys of the Red and White Volta, see Jean-Paul Lahuec, "Contraintes historiques et onchocercose. Une explication des faits de peuplement dans la sous-préfecture de Garango, nord pays Bissa—Haute Volta," in *Table ronde. Tropiques et santé. De l'épidémologie à la géographie humaine*, ed. Centre d'Étude de Géographie Tropicale (Talence/Paris [Travaux et Documents de la Géographie Tropicale], 1982), 253–58.

31. Kopytoff, "The Internal African Frontier," 40–48.

32. On the heterogeneous ethno-linguistic backgrounds of Sisala lineages, see Rattray, *The Tribes of Ashanti Hinterland* (Oxford: Clarendon Press, 1932), 465–96.

33. A house was (and continues to be) inhabited by a segment of a larger patriclan and, in the precolonial period, could have well over one hundred inhabitants. As considerations of security became less imperative after colonial pacification, smaller units could (and indeed did) settle on their own. The residents of the house are referred to as *yirdem*, literally, "the owners of the house," while the *yirsob* is the authority-wielding head of the house (literally, "owner of the house"), usually the eldest male of the agnatic kin group. The *yirdem* include affinal relatives and can also incorporate non-kin (guests, clients) and, formerly, slaves. For a fuller discussion of Dagara kinship and indigenous terminology, see Goody, *Social Organisation*; Lentz, *Ethnicity*, 16–18; Alexis Tengan, *Hoe-Farming and Social Relations among the Dagara of Northwestern Ghana and Southwestern Burkina Faso* (Frankfurt/Main: Peter Lang, 2000); and Alexis Tengan, "Space, Bonds and Social Order: Dagara House-Based Social System," in *Bonds and Boundaries*, ed. Hagberg and Tengan, 87–103.

34. Some patriclans are so closely related that they consider themselves to be one, in certain contexts, while others have numerous subdivisions. Since it depends on the occasion whether they emphasize unity or differentiation, it is difficult to establish the precise number of patriclans. For different lists of Dagara patriclans, see Père Jean Hébert, *Esquisse d'une monographie historique du pays Dagara. Par un groupe de Dagara en collaboration avec le père Hébert* (Diébougou: Diocèse de Diébougou 1976); Rattray, *The Tribes*, 426–8; E. Tengan, *Social Structure*, 47–52; and A. Tengan, *Hoe-Farming*, 166–67.

35. A patrilineage usually consists of more than one domestic group (a unit mainly defined in terms of joint agricultural exploitation). For a classical discussion of the fission of Dagara domestic groups, and the role of uterine relations for the fission, see Jack Goody, "The Fission of Domestic Groups among the Lodagaba," in *The Developmental Cycle in Domestic Groups*, ed. Goody (Cambridge: Cambridge University Press, 1958), 53–91.

36. For some examples, see E. Tengan, *Social Structure*; and A. Tengan, *Hoe-Farming*, 161–98.

37. Depending on the specific circumstances of the migration, ancestor shrines may also have been taken along from the very beginning. The form that this transfer takes varies from patriclan to patriclan and depends on the precise genealogical position of the migrant(s). Of the clans whose ancestors are represented by carved wooden sticks, some clans take all shrines along, others only the one shrine of the most important recent ancestor; still other clans use stones to represent ancestors.

38. On the importance of this relation, see also Nurukyor Claude Somda, "Espace et mobilité lignagère dans le sud-ouest du Burkina Faso," *Berichte des Sonderforschungsbereichs 268* (Frankfurt/Main), no. 14 (2001): 449–53.

39. Some Dagara patriclans trace their ancestors' migrations back to what is currently North-Eastern Ivory Coast and the area around Batié (Nord) in Burkina Faso; others claim to have set out from the present-day Wa District and the environs of Nadawli. Many elders narrate that their forebears settled for a while in the area around Babile, Tugu, Konyuokuo, and Zakpe. This micro-region seems to have been something like a hub from which some moved in a northerly direction and then turned westward, across the Black Volta, into present-day South-Western Burkina Faso; others remained east of the Volta and continued north- and northeastward; and still others crossed the river more than once. For some examples of migration routes that our research group was able to document, see the contributions in Richard Kuba, Carola Lentz, and Katja Werthmann, eds., *Les Dagara et leurs voisins. Histoire de peuplement et relations interethniques au sud-ouest du Burkina Faso, Berichte des Sonderforschungsbereichs 268* (Frankfurt/Main), no.15 (2001).

40. For similar strategies and the subsequent development of relations between the Dagara pioneers and the existing Phuo population on the western frontier of Dagara expansion, see Richard Kuba, "Marking Boundaries and Identities: The Precolonial Expansion of Segmentary Societies in Southwestern Burkina Faso," in *Berichte des Sonderforschungbereichs 268* (Frankfurt/Main), no. 14 (2001): 415–26; Kuba, "Comment devenir Pougouli"; Kuba and Lentz, "Arrows"; Georges Savonnet, *Pina—étude d'un terroir de front pionnier en pays Dagari (Haute Volta)* (Paris: Mouton, 1970), 15–21, offers some information on Dagara-Sisala-Nuni interaction on the settlement frontiers of Niégo and Bourra districts (Burkina Faso), but his pre-twentieth-century chronology is highly speculative.

41. Andrew P. Vayda, "Expansion and Warfare among Swidden Agriculturalists," *American Anthropologist* 63 (1969): 205, 214–15.

42. Examples of these processes will be provided in chapter 4.

43. Domestic slavery is a controversial topic, among intellectuals as well as the local population, both Sisala and Dagara. For a history of slavery among the Sisala, see Swanepoel, "'Too Much Power Is Not Good': War and Trade in Nineteenth Century Sisalaland, Northern Ghana" (Ph.D. diss., Syracuse University, 2004), 84–128. On a recent debate among Dagara intellectuals about the role of the Dagara not only as victims, but also as beneficiaries of slave raids and slave trade, see Der, *The Slave Trade*; Nurukyor Claude Somda, "L'esclavage. Un paradoxe dans une société égalitaire," *Cahiers du CERLERSH* 17 (2000): 267–90; and Valère Nacièle Somé, "Le dagara sous le sol de l'esclavage," *Cahiers du CERLERSH*, special issue 1 (2001): 57–97. More generally on slavery in West African segmentary societies, see Andrew Hubbell, "A View of the Slave Trade from the Margin: Souroudougou in the Late Nineteenth-Century Slave Trade of the Niger Bend," *Journal of African History* 42 (2001): 25–47; and Klein, "The Slave Trade," 49–65. Many of my Dagara and Sisala informants readily admitted that some members of their own and other villagers' families were of slave descent, but would firmly refuse to disclose details because slave ancestry can become an important weapon in local disputes over property and authority.

44. In any case, however, as other studies on segmentary societies in West Africa have shown, there seems to be no direct link between demographic pressure and migration rates. Bohannan stated for the Tiv that it is precisely in those areas in which "land shortage [and hence population density] is least severe that the rate of migration appears to be most rapid" ("The Migration," 2).

45. On the Zaberma raids east of the Black Volta, see J. J. Holden, "The Zaberima Conquest of North-West Ghana," *Transactions of the Historical Society of Ghana* 8 (1965): 60–86; Lentz, *Ethnicity*, 24–32; and Natalie J. Swanepoel, "Every Periphery Is Its Own Center: Sociopolitical and Economic Interactions in Nineteenth-Century Northwestern Ghana," *International Journal of African Historical Studies* 42, no. 3 (2009): 411–32. On Karantao and other slavers in the Niger Bend, see Nehemia Levtzion, *Muslims and Chiefs in West Africa: A Study of Islam in the Middle Volta Basin in*

the Pre-Colonial Period (Oxford: Clarendon Press 1968), 147–54; on the demographic advantage, see Hilton, "Depopulation," 28.

46. For examples of Dagara settlements in the Gonja area, see A. Tengan, *Hoe-farming*, 283–94; on Dagara communities in the Brong Ahafo Region, see various articles by Isidore Lobnibe: "Forbidden Fruits in the Compound: A Case Study of Migration, Spousal Separation and Group-Wife Adultery in Northwest Ghana," *Africa* 75 (2005): 559–81; "Legitimating a Contested Boundary: Northern Ghanaian Immigrants and the Historicity of Land Conflict in Ahyiayem, Brong Ahafo," *Ghana Studies* 9 (2006): 61–90; and "Between Aspirations and Realities: Northern Ghanaian Women and the Dilemma of Household (Re)production in Southern Ghana," *Africa Today* 55 (2009): 53–74.

47. See, for instance, the maps on population densities and different agro-ecological regimes in North-Western Ghana in Jacob Songsore, "Population Growth and Ecological Degradation in Northern Ghana: Myths and Realities," *Research Review* (N.S.), Legon (Ghana), 12 (1996): 56–59; and Jacob Songsore, "The Decline of the Rural Commons in Sub-Saharan Africa: The Case of the Upper West Region of Ghana," in *Regionalism and Public Policy in Northern Ghana*, ed. Yakubu Saaka, 153–76 (Frankfurt/Main: Peter Lang, 2001). The soil maps and other pertinent information compiled in an environmental database for Ghana ("Ghana—Country at a Glance"; www.grida.no/eis-ssa/eisnews; www.unep.org/unep.netafrica/ pdf/Ghana), as well as data available for Burkina Faso, suggest that the territory occupied by the Sisala is generally characterized by soils that are deeper, better watered, and hence more fertile than the ones on which Dagara settlements are located; however, local variation can be considerable, and in view of the dearth of more fine-meshed pedological data, we should be wary of constructing overly deterministic models. On Burkina Faso, see BUNASOL, ed., *Caracterisation des sols du centre-sud de la province de la Sissili et esquisse pedologique*, Rapport technique 69 (Ouagadougou, 1990); and various contributions in *Landnutzung in der westafrikanischen Savanne*, ed. Andrea Reikat, *Berichte des Sonderforschungsbereichs 268* (Frankfurt/Main), no. 9 (1997).

48. On aetiological legends about the Kusiele, see E. Tengan, *Social Structure*, 14–15; and A. Tengan, *Hoe-farming*, 179–81; on migration routes of the Kusiele in villages west of the Black Volta, see Hébert, *Esquisse*, 90–101.

49. For details on the history of chieftaincy in Lawra District, see Lentz, *Ethnicity*, 33–71, 104–37.

50. PRO, CO 96/493, Gold Coast No. 41, Governor Robertson to Colonial Office, 19 January 1910, enclosure 7. This version was apparently "coauthored" by the Lawra chief, his Muslim interpreter, and the district commissioner (see Lentz, *Ethnicity*, 88–90). For later colonial versions of the Kusiele migrations, see Lawra District Commissioner John Guinness, *Interim Report on the Peoples of Nandom and Lambussie*, 1932, NAG, ADM 11/1/824; Lawra District Commissioner J.A. Armstrong, *Report on the Peoples of the Lambussie and Nandom Divisions*, 1931/34, ibid. For the schoolbook version, see Donald St. John-Parsons, *Legends of Northern Ghana* (London: Longman, 1958), 46–48. On the connection between power and memory, see Laura Bohannan's work on Tiv genealogies, "A Genealogical Charter," *Africa* 22 (1952): 307.

51. See the version of the Kusiele recitations published by Goody and Gandah, *The Third Bagre: A Myth Revisited* (Durham: Carolina Academic Press 2002), 201–62, 337–80. To my knowledge, no other Dagara patriclan refers to details of its migration history in the *bagr*; for an example of the *bagr* of the Berwuole patriclan, see Alexis Tengan, "Dagara Bagr: Ritualising Myth of Social Foundation," *Africa* 69 (1999): 595–633.

52. Interviews with Lawra Naa Abeyifaa Karbo, 23 December 1994 and 4 January 1998, Lawra. The large sacrifices in Babile were also mentioned in Guinness, *Interim Report*, 21. Concerning Kusiele settlements founded later than Lawra, I conducted interviews in Piiri, Hamile, Kokoligu, and Fielmuo in Ghana, as well as in Ouessa, Pina, Buonbaa, and Laponé in Burkina Faso.

53. For more details on Karbo's biography, see Carola Lentz, *Die Konstruktion von Ethnizität. Eine politische Geschichte Nord-West Ghanas* (Cologne: Köppe, 1998), 423–34, 656.

54. See Goody and Gandah, *The Third Bagre*, xxii.

55. Interview with Yobo Kiebang, Kuuzin et al., 24 December 1994, Yirkpee. Ture and many other places mentioned in Kiebang's narrative cannot be found on any current map, but my informants sometimes made references to modern villages near these historical places.

56. Lawra Naa Abayifaa Karbo explained that Zegnaa also continued to Wa, founding the section of Sokparyiri, and that the Kusiele became the *tendambas* (earth priests) of Wa; on this see also Wilks, *Wa and the Wala*, 25–26, 32–33, 50.

57. Interview of 4 January 1998.

58. Interview of Sebastian Bemile with Naalukuu, Kakri Vitus Dapilah, and Yirkye Derzu, 22 August 2003, Babile.

59. Kpagnyaane informants asserted that their ancestors had also migrated from Batié, west of the Black Volta, settled jointly with the Kusiele in Kusele and later established themselves as hoe-farmers in Zakpe, Tolibri, and Kuol after the Kusiele had continued to Lawra. It is likely that the two patriclans intermarried; in any case, such close family links did not preclude armed conflict (interview of Sebastian Bemile with Nuo-ire, Yangsuo, and Tengan (all Kpagnyaane), 22 August 2003, Kuol).

60. Michèle Cros and Daniel Dory, "Pour une approche écologique des guerres Lobi," *Cultures et Développement* 19 (1984): 465–84.

61. The French colonial officer Henri Labouret (*Les tribus*, 24–25) and also Madeleine Père (*Les Lobi. Tradition et changement. Burkina Faso* [Laval: Ed. Siloë 1988], 93–96) report that Dyan informants indicated that their ancestors once lived in Lawra. Assuming the time span of each generation to be thirty years, Labouret calculated that the Dyan must have crossed the Black Volta westward around 1770. However, he did not rely solely on oral traditions, but was influenced by the "findings" of his British colleague, Lawra District Commissioner Eyre-Smith, with whom he conversed from time to time. Eyre-Smith, a passionate amateur historian, interpreted local history in the light of the Hamitic theory as a long chain of conquests and expulsions and conjectured that the "Janni" or "Jenné" people (Eyre-Smith's spelling of the Dyan) were related to the Songhay town of Jenné (on this, see Lentz, "Colonial Ethnography," 146–58). It is possible that the identification of Lawra's original inhabitants as "Dyan" was Eyre-Smith's invention, which was adopted by other British commissioners as well as members of the local chiefly family who closely cooperated with these officers.

62. "The Internal African Frontier," 56–57.

63. I am aware that British paramount chiefs and French *chefs de canton* represent somewhat distinct trajectories of power. While British colonial officers were usually concerned to recruit the paramount chiefs from among earth-priestly lineages or, in the case of precolonial centralized polities, attempted to respect the established hierarchies, French *chefs de canton* were often less ensconced in locally powerful and respected lineages, often coming from "foreign" groups of Muslim traders or former soldiers. However, I would argue that in the case of the Black Volta region, the parallels between the two colonial powers' approach to establish chiefs among the "stateless" peoples outweigh the differences. For more details, see chapter 4.

64. *Les frontières de la Côte d'Ivoire, de la Côte d'Or et du Soudan* (Paris: Masson, 1908), 200, 202.

65. Interview with Hien Daniel, 5 March 1997, Ouessa.

66. Interview of 8 January 1998.

67. Although many Dagara and Sisala narratives use the terms Yeri and Phuo (popularly called Pougouli) synonymously, research among these groups suggests differences in origin, migration routes, and often language; see Hébert, *Esquisse*, 150–61; Kuba, "Marking Boundaries"; and Kuba, "Comment devenir Pougouli"; Ursula Bürger, "Installation pacifique ou appropriation violente de terre? Réflexions sur l'histoire de l'installation des Phuo à Bonzan," in *Les Dagara*, ed. Kuba, Lentz, and Werthmann, 131–40; Thorsten Bär, "'On a trouvé une forêt vierge'. Légitimation des revendications foncières dans les traditions orales de Fafo," in *Les Dagara*, ed. Kuba, Lentz, and

Werthmann, 115–123; and Didier Knösel, "Migration, identité ethnique et pouvoir politique. Les Kufule d'Oronkua," in *Les Dagara*, ed. Kuba, Lentz and Werthmann, 87–95.

68. Interviews with Charles Meda, 20 November and 30 December 1997, Ouessa. Hien Daniel's assertion that Ouessa's earlier inhabitants were Phuo, not Sisala, is confirmed by Labouret (*Les tribus*, 30). However, according to Labouret, the Phuo left Ouessa ("Wasso") as early as 1740 of their own accord due to the infertility of the land. The oral traditions recorded by Père Hébert (*Esquisse*, 43–44, 173), on the other hand, assert that the Phuo were forcibly displaced by the Dagara immigrants. Some of the Phuo whom Richard Kuba interviewed between 1997 and 2000 did indeed mention Ouessa as one of their ancestors' earlier settlements, but were ambivalent on the question of whether they were evicted by the Dagara or left voluntarily (personal communication from Richard Kuba).

69. Interview with Samson Gompag, 3 January 2001, Ouessa. Other informants in Ouessa spoke not of Dyan, but Gan or Game who allegedly produced iron and left the area when the Dagara arrived (interviews with Boy-i-Der, Ouessa, 10 June 1999 [interview conducted by Grégoire Somé], and Ouessa Naa Nandi Meda, 22 November 1997).

70. Interviews with Casimir Meda, 24 February 1999 and 5 June 2000, Ouessa.

71. Interviews of 8 and 30 January 1998. The Gane in Mebar, however, do not confirm Hien Daniel's claim, but assert that some of their ancestors once immigrated from Memer (see Eveline Rudolf, "L'unité par la parenté? Du sense de l'appartenance clanique pour la vie sociale et politique à Mébar," in *Les Dagara*, ed. Kuba, Lentz and Werthmann, 63–69).

72. Interview of 3 January 2001.

73. Interview of 18 February 2000.

74. Interview of 24 February 1999.

75. Interview with More Somé, John-Bosco Dabiré et al., 1 March 1999, Memer; for an earlier version of Gane history from Memer, see Hébert, *Esquisse*, 102–3.

76. "A Genealogical Charter," 303.

77. On this, see Vansina, *Oral Tradition*, 116–20, 165–76; and Jack Goody, "Oral Tradition and the Reconstruction of the Past in Northern Ghana," in *Fonti orali—Oral Sources—Sources orales*, ed. Bernado Bernardi, Carlo Poni, and Alessandro Triulzi (Milan: Angeli, 1978).

78. Goody and Gandah, *The Third Bagre*, xiv–xx.

79. Louis Tauxier, *Le noir du Soudan: Pays Mossi et Gourounsi* (Paris: E. Larose, 1912), 372.

80. A comparison of settlements marked on the map that the Anglo-French boundary commission drew up in 1900 (PRO, MPG 915) with the situation fifty years later shows the severe depopulation around Ouessa.

81. Interview with Basima Babui et al., 25 November 1997, Ouessa. Babui, one of the first strangers to resettle in the depopulated village in the early 1950s, remembered that there were only six houses when he arrived.

82. Interview with Deboru's son Hien Kuukyampuor, 10 Februrary 1999, Ouessa.

83. On trees as historical sources, see Lentz and Sturm, "Of Trees and Earth Shrines."

84. On these calculations, see also Hébert, *Esquisse*, 94, 104. Père Hébert conducted his interviews in Ouessa in 1966; copies of the typescripts of his interviews were in the possession of the late Claude Nurukyor Somda, Département d'Histoire et Archéologie, Université de Ouagadougou, who kindly allowed me to peruse them.

85. On the history and techniques of iron smelting in North-Western Ghana among the Sisala and Dagara, see Leonard M. Pole, "Account of an Iron-Smelting Operation at Lawra," *Ghana Journal of Science* 14 (1974): 127–36, and "Iron-Working Apparatus and Techniques: Upper Region of Ghana," *West African Journal of Archaeology* 5 (1975): 11–39. More generally on the social organization and ritual implications of iron working in Africa, see Eugenia W. Herbert, *Iron, Gender and Power: Rituals of Transformation in African Societies* (Bloomington: Indiana University Press, 1993).

86. On the Dagara concept of "joking partners" who perform certain ritual and practical tasks for each other, see Goody, *The Social Organisation*, 79–82. With respect to the Bimbiile and Kpagnyaane, there is some disagreement on the history of their names and interrelation. Some of my informants believed that the Bimbiile were the original group that later subdivided into the Tambiile and Kpagnyaane clans in order to be able to intermarry and perform certain ritual services for each other. Others asserted that the founder of the Tambiile was the illegitimate son of a Kpagnyaane (alternatively, Bimbiile) girl who was forced to build his own house under the shea nut trees (*taam; tambiile* = children of the shea nut tree). Probably due to this association with an illegitimate union, none of my interlocutors identified himself as Tambiile, but used this name only to refer to others who, in turn, would refer to themselves as Kpagnyaane. On the Bimbiile and related clans, see also E. Tengan, *Social Structure*, 12–13; and A. Tengan, *Hoe-farming*, 169–71.

87. Bidomo was one of the villages abandoned in the 1920s; it is still marked—as "Bedama"— on the Anglo-French Boundary Commission's map of 1900 (PRO, MPG 915), but its actual position must have been nearer to the Black Volta than indicated on the map, at least according to my Ouessa informants.

88. Interviews with Niégo Naa Somda Beyaa et al., 28 November 1997; 23 February 1999, Niégo.

89. Interview with Yeleyire Somé et al., 15 February 1999, Dianlé.

90. The Bekuone are joking partners (*lonluore*) of the Kpagnyaane and Bimbiile, and various stories explain how the Kpagnyaane and Bimbiile enjoyed the millet porridge that the Bekuone farmers prepared, while the former furnished iron implements such as hoes and arrows that the Bekuone needed for farming and defending themselves, and how each group eventually taught the other its special skills. These and similar stories about the characteristics of different patriclans were presented with great relish by many of my informants. For examples, see also E. Tengan, *Social Structure*, 12–21; and A. Tengan, *Hoe-farmers*, 168–98.

91. Interview of 8 January 1998.

92. Interviews with Gaston Hien, Polé Paul Somé, Grégoire Somé et al., 24 November 1997, Ouessa; with Nifaakang Somé et al., 21 November 1997, Ouessa.

93. Thomas Beidelman, "Myth, Legend and Oral History: A Kaguru Traditional Text," *Anthropos* 65 (1970): 74–97.

94. The multifarious and often contradictory migration narratives of the different patriclans and lineages make it extremely difficult to sketch a general picture of the regional settlement history. By the 1930s, the British District Commissioner John Guinness had already noted, with some despair, that the Dagara and Sisala chiefs, earth priests, and elders of the Lawra-Tumu District narrated "badly beheaded" stories about the history of their villages that reached back only few generations and presented a "hopeless tangle of sectional migrations and settlements" (Guinness, *Interim Report*, ADM 11/1/824, § 1, 11, 41). For more details on Guinness's report and the harsh criticism it provoked among other colonial officers, see Lentz, "Colonial Ethnography."

For more recent attempts to compile Dagara patriclan migration routes, see Hébert, *Esquisse*. A number of Ghanaian B.A. theses document the oral traditions of specific settlements (see, for instance, Paul Kantunye Abdul-Korah, "History of the Dagaaba with Special Reference to the Manlaala," B.A. thesis, University of Ghana, Department of History, 1980; Salvius Anthony Claret Abobo, "A History of the Jirapa Traditional Area from the Early Settlement to 1980," B.A. thesis, , University of Cape Coast, Department of History, 1994; John Nobabaare Bonekang, "The History of the Dagaba: A Case Study of the People of Tizza," B.A. thesis, University of Ghana, Department of History, 1978; James Dasah, "Ulo: The History of a Dagaba Kingdom," B.A. thesis, University of Ghana, Department of History, 1974; Isidore Lobnibe, "A Short History of Hamile from the Earliest Times to 1950," B.A. thesis, University of Cape Coast, Department of History, 1994; and G. B. L. Siilo, "The History of Nandom from the Time of Settlement to 1908," B.A. thesis, University of Ghana, Department of History, 1973.

The few more comprehensive accounts of Dagara expansion are based on a rather limited corpus of interviews and, like the microstudies, tend to take oral traditions at face value without systematically comparing contradictary versions (if they ever collected more than one version). See, for instance, Benedict Der, "The Origins of the Dagara-Dagaba," *Papers in Dagara Studies* 1, no. 1 (1989): 1–25; Jack Goody, "Peuplement. Études comparatives, Nord-Ghana et Burkina Faso," in *Images d'Afrique et sciences sociales*, ed. Michèle Fiéloux et al., 51–55 (Paris: Karthala, 1993); Pierre-Claver Hien, "Frontières et conflits chez les Dagara et leurs voisins au sud-ouest du Burkina Faso (XVIIIème–XIXème siécle)," *Berichte des Sonderforschungsbereichs 268* (Frankfurt/Main), no. 14 (2001): 427–40; Nurukyor Claude Somda, "Les origines des Dagara," *Papers in Dagara Studies* 1, no. 1 (1989); and Nurukyor Claude Somda, "Espace." Methodological naiveté also characterizes most of the writings on the settlement history of the Dagara's neighbors, the Dyan, Lobi, Phuo, and Birifor currently living west of the Black Volta; see, for instance, Kunz Dittmer, "Die Obervolta-Provinz," in *Die Völker Afrikas und ihre traditionellen Kulturen*, ed. Hermann Baumann, pt. 2 (Wiesbaden: Franz Steiner, 1979), 495–542; Labouret, *Les tribus*; Henri Labouret, *Nouvelles notes sur les tribus du rameau Lobi. Leurs migrations, leurs évolution, leurs parlers et ceux de leurs voisins* (Dakar: IFAN 1958); Père, *Les Lobi*, 73–105; Madeleine Père, "Chronique des villages de la province du Poni en contribution à l'histoire du peuplement au Burkina Faso," in *Images d'Afrique et sciences sociales*, ed. Michèle Fiéloux et al. (Paris: Karthala, 1993), 57–73; Madeleine Père, "Contribution à l'histoire du peuplement de la province du Poni au Burkina Faso," in *Bonds and Boundaries in Northern Ghana and Southern Burkina Faso*, ed. Sten Hagberg and Alexis B. Tengan (Uppsala: Uppsala Studies in Cultural Anthropology, 2000), 41–52; Georges Savonnet, "La colonisation du pays Koulango (Haute Côte d'Ivoire) par les Lobi de Haute Volta," *Cahiers d'Outre Mer* 15 (1962): 25–46; Georges Savonnet, "Quelques notes sur l'histoire des Dyan (cercles de Diébougou et de Léo, Haute Volta)," *Bulletin de l'I.F.A.N.*, T. 37, ser. B, 3 (1975): 619–45. Very little has been written on the history of the Sisala; for some information, see Anne-Marie Duperray, *Les Gourounsi de Haute-Volta* (Wiesbaden: Franz Steiner, 1984), 13–61; Mendonsa, *Continuity and Change*, 20–56; and Rattray, *The Tribes*, 435–48. An excellent case study of the history of Dolbizan and surrounding villages, based on a methodologically sound use of archaeological sources and oral tradition, has recently been presented by Swanepoel, "Too Much Power."

95. For Ghanaian Dagara, reference to Accra or Cape Coast (or the Dagomba kingdom) may be an attempt to inscribe one's origins within the current nation-state, thus emphasising Ghanaianness; see chapter 5 for examples of conflicts in which proving one's citizenship became important. However, numerous Dagara elders in Burkina Faso make the same reference, perhaps because it fits well with the northerly direction of their ancestors' travels. On the Dagara intellectuals' debate on their group's origins, see Carola Lentz, "A Dagara Rebellion against Dagomba Rule? Contested Stories of Origin in North-Western Ghana," *Journal of African History* 35 (1994): 457–92.

96. When Père Hébert interviewed Dagara elders in the 1960s, both in Ghana and Burkina Faso, very few of his interlocutors mentioned Yendi in Dagbon, or Accra and Cape Coast as places of origin (*Esquisse*, 33–40). In my own interviews, Accra and Cape Coast (but not Yendi) were mentioned by lineage elders or their descendants who had referred to *tengkor* or a specific village in North-Western Ghana vis-à-vis Hébert. On the *tengkor* motif, see also A. Tengan (*Hoe-farming*, 57–58, 262–63 n. 1), one of the few Dagara intellectuals who does not take his interviewees' indications of their origins literally, but as a symbolic expression of the Dagara "migratory way of life."

97. See the classical analysis of Jack Goody, "The Mother's Brother," 67–71; and the instructive example from Liberia, discussed by Murphy and Bledsoe in "Kinship and Territory."

98. Interviews with Bapule Der Somé, 22 November 1997; Jean de Dieu Somé, 2 March 1999; and Boy-i-der Somda, 10 June 2000, Ouessa.

99. Interview of 5 March 1997. It is also possible that Demaal Naab was invited by his Bimbiile uncles (*madebr*) in Dianlé to protect them against their Sisala neighbors and Muslim slave raiders

who began to operate in the area. This was suggested in the interviews with Yeleyire Somé et al., 15 February 1999, Dianlé; and with Meda Charles, 20 November and 13 December 1997, Ouessa.

100. Interview with Kpieru Somda und Kuunzane Somé, 16 February 1999, Dalgang-Dandere. My Dagara interlocutors in Dalgang suggested that the Sisala initially welcomed the Dagara immigrants, and that the Dagara first accepted the Sisala village name of Jaffien, which supposedly means "stay and rest." Later, the Dagara founding ancestor Dal supposedly drove the Sisala away, who fled southward, to Nimoro, Mo, and other places in present-day Ghana—which was confirmed by Sisala informants (e.g., in an interview with Suleiman Balesemule et al., 14 December 1997, Nimoro). In Simon, a few kilometers south of Dalgang, there is a hill called Jaffien, with remains of walls and a stand of old acacias that indicate the existence of previous non-Dagara settlers. Jaffien may either have been the name of a dispersed settlement, covering Dalgang and this hill, or the place-name moved together with the displaced inhabitants, until they finally resettled in the Sisala villages of Bangwon, Happa, and Hamile, where a small hill with an important shrine also carries the name Jaffien. On the Boundary Commission map of 1900 (PRO, MPG 915) "Diafian" (Jeffian) still figures as an alternative name for "Bakutinga" (Bakoteng). This is an indication that it was only toward the end of the nineteenth century that the Sisala were ultimately displaced from this area.

101. Interview with Der Somda, Anfare Somé et al., 18 December 1999, Gorgang.

102. Interview with Der Somé (Dekulo) and Jacob Somé, 14 September 1999, Sorguogang.

103. Simon was founded by Bore, one of Laazie's *arbili* and thus a reliable client of the Gane earth priests. Bore later recruited further settlers from Dagara villages around Nandom and from across the Black Volta, and Simon quickly developed into a multiclan settlement (interview with Dieudonné Dabire, Adrien Somda, Bernard Poda et al., Kolinka-Simon, 4 December 1997). Kolinka was started by Baapare, one of Demaal Naab's "sons" from Dianlé, who had accumulated so many cows that he needed more grazing space than Dianlé could offer him (interviews with Baapare's grandsons Delle Hien, Yelezu Somda, We André Hien et al., 10 January 1998 and 23 November 2001, Kolinka). Bakoteng, finally, was founded by Bako, a Bekuone clan mate and junior brother of Dal, or, as a competing version has it, by Mori, a Berwuole from Dianlé who was closely related to the Ouessa earth priests (interviews with Anatole Somé, 5 December 1997, Ouessa; Der Dabire et al., 24 April 1999, Bakoteng; Adama Somé et al., 19 February 1999, Dabileteng; and Dominique Somda, Jacques Hien et al., 29 November 1997, 29 January 1998, Bakoteng). On the competing versions of Bakoteng history, see the controversy reported in the interviews conducted by Père Hébert and his collaborators in 1966 and 1967 (copies held in the personal archives of Claude Nurukyor Somda, Ouagadougou, were made available to me).

104. Interview with Adrien Somda, Dieudonné Dabire et al., 4 December 1997, Simon.

105. This was different in the Dagara settlements around Jirapa and Nandom (see Lentz, *Ethnicity*, 28–32).

106. Interviews with the Laponé *totina* (earth priest) Fawiera, the *kuoro* Kumasi et al., 22 February 2000; and the Mossi representative Sankara Issiaka, Dem Issiaka et al., 9 May 2000, Laponé.

107. Interviews with Mimirdem's son Naagbele Poda and his neighbors, 23 February 2000; the Dagara representative in Pina, Somda Bekodiong et al., 26 January 1998; and the representative of the Pina Sisala earth priest, Topulwy Bukari et al., 26 January 1998, Pina. On the history of Dagara migration into Pina, see also Savonnet, *Pina.*

108. For an extensive analysis of a similar case of complementarity of different forms of mobility, among the Mossi, see Breusers, *On the Move.*

109. On the physical and spiritual aspects of building a Dagara *yir*, see Honoré Poyouor Somé, "Habitations et occupation du sol. Le *yir* et le village dagara. L'exemple de Tobo," *Cahiers d'Outre-Mer* 43, no. 169 (1990): 77–95; E. Tengan, *Social Structure*, 5–11; and A. Tengan, "Space, Bonds and Social Order."

110. Interview with Valère Somda, Lucie Somé et al., 24 February 2000, Laponé.

111. Savonnet, *Pina*, 26–27.

112. Laponé, according to the earth priest Fawiera, means "to swallow entirely," a name that recalls the conflict between two brothers that led to the emigration of the founder of Laponé (interview with the Laponé earth priest Fawiera, the village chief Kumasi, and other Sisala elders, 22 February 2000).

113. In 1998, with the support of Grégoire Somé, I carried out a survey of twenty-six Dagara settlements created since the 1920s on Sisala land in the Bourra and Niabouri Districts in Burkina Faso, gathering information about the number of Dagara houses in each village, the original village of the house owner, the date of installation on Sisala land, and so forth. In Ghana, my survey was less exhaustive, but I conducted a few more in-depth case studies, namely in Fielmuo, Pina, Samoa, and Suke, where I also obtained information about the other Dagara settlements on Sisala land.

114. That (labor) migration can develop into an initiation ritual of sorts has been observed already in early studies on the Rhodesian Copper Belt; see, for instance, Clyde Mitchell, "The Causes of Labour Migration," *Bulletin of the Inter-African Labour Institute* 6 (1959): 12–47, and J. van Velsen, "Labor Migration as a Positive Factor in the Continuity of Tonga Tribal Society," *Economic Development and Cultural Change* 8 (1960): 265–78.

115. See, for instance, the literature discussed in an introduction to a special issue on mobility in Africa, edited by Katja Werthmann, Tilo Grätz, and Hans Peter Hahn ("Mobilität in Afrika. Multilokale Forschungen," special issue, *Afrika Spectrum* 39, no. 3 [2004]: 325–33).

116. Michael C. Lambert, *Longing for Exile: Migration and the Making of a Translocal Community in Senegal, West Africa* (London: Heinemann, 2002), xxvii.

117. For an overview on anthropological approaches to migration, see Andreas Ackermann, "Ethnologische Migrationsforschung. Ein Überblick," *Kea—Zeitschrift für Kulturwissenschaften* 10 (1997): 1–28; Caroline B. Brettell, "Theorizing Migration in Anthropology: The Social Construction of Networks, Identities, Communities, and Global Scapes," in *Migration Theory: Talking Across Disciplines*, ed. Caroline B. Brettell and James F. Hollifield, 97–135 (London: Routledge, 2000).

118. "The Internal African Frontier," 22, 41.

Chapter 2

1. Allan Charles Dawson, introduction to *Shrines in Africa: History, Politics, and Society*, ed. Dawson (Calgary: Calgary University Press, 2009), vii, ix.

2. Most of the early colonial literature focused on religious aspects of the earth cult; see, for instance, Tauxier, *Le noir du Soudan*; Henri Labouret, "La guerre dans ses rapports avec les croyances religieuses chez les populations du cercle de Gaoua," *Annuaire et mémoires du comité d'études historiques et scientifiques de l'A.O.F.* (1916): 305–16; A. W. Cardinall, *The Natives of the Northern Territories of the Gold Coast* (London: Routledge, 1920); A. W. Cardinall, *The Gold Coast 1931* (Accra: Government Printer, 1931); Rattray, *The Tribes*; and Eyre-Smith, *A Brief Review*. For more recent examples of a focus on the religious dimension of earth shrines, see, for instance, Zwernemann, *Die Erde*; Jean-François Vincent et al., eds., *La construction religieuse du territoire* (Paris: Harmattan, 1995); Michèle Dacher, "Organisation politique d'une société acéphale. Les Gouin du Burkina Faso," *L'Homme* 144 (1997): 7–29; and Danouta Liberski-Bagnoud, *Les dieux du territoire. Penser autrement la généalogie* (Paris: Éditions de la Maison des Sciences de l'Homme, 2002). For a more general discussion of territorial cults, and comparative examples from Central Africa, see J. M. Schoffeleers, ed., *Guardians of the Land: Essays on Central African Territorial Cults* (Gwelo: Mambo Press, 1979); and Richard P. Werbner, *Ritual Passage—Sacred Journey: The Process and Organization of Religious Movement* (Manchester: Manchester University Press, 1989).

3. Pogucki, *Report on Land Tenure*; Boutillier, *Les structures foncières*. For recent examples of a rather structuralist approach, see the contributions on Northern Ghana in Konrad-Adenauer-Stiftung, ed., *Decentralisation, Land Tenure and Land Administration in Northern Ghana* (Accra:

Konrad-Adenauer-Stiftung, 1996); and Kasanga and Kotey, *Land Management*; on Burkina Faso, see, for example, Stamm, *Zur Dynamik*.

4. Rattray, *The Tribes*, xii–xvi.

5. Eyre-Smith to the Secretary for Native Affairs, 2 March 1933, NAG, ADM 11/1/824, § 4.

6. For some recent studies that address these linkages, see, for instance, Jean-Pierre Chauveau, Jean-Pierre Jacob, and Pierre-Yves Le Meur, "L'organisation de la mobilité dans les sociétés rurales du Sud," *Autrepart* 30 (2004): 3–23; Jean-Pierre Jacob, *La tradition du pluralisme institutionnel dans les conflits fonciers entre autochtones. Le cas du Gwendégué (centre Burkina Faso)*, Document de travail de l'Unité de Recherche 095, 3 (Montpellier: IRD/GRET, 2002); Jean-Pierre Jacob, "Gouvernement de la nature et gouvernement des hommes dans le Gwendégué (centre-ouest du Burkina Faso)," *Autrepart* 30 (2004): 25–43; Richard Kuba, "La grammaire rituelle des hiérarchies. Migrations et chefs de terre dans une société segmentaire (Burkina Faso)," *Autrepart* 30 (2004): 63–76; Richard Kuba, "Spiritual Hierarchies and Unholy Alliances: Competing Earth Priests in a Context of Migration in Southwestern Burkina Faso," in *Land*, ed. Kuba and Lentz, 57–76; and the contributions in Dawson, ed., *Shrines in Africa*. Concerning the connections between the spiritual, economic, and political dimensions of first-comer cults and their relevance to the definition of property rights, there are interesting parallels with founders' cults in Asia; see Nicole Tannenbaum and Cornelia Ann Kemmerer, eds., *Founders' Cults in Southeast Asia: Ancestors, Polity, and Identity* (New Haven: Yale University Press, 2003).

7. Jacob, *La tradition du pluralisme*, 19–20.

8. Fortmann, "Talking Claims," 1054.

9. The first section of this chapter has adapted material from my article "Constructing Ritual Protection on an Expanding Settlement Frontier: Earth Shrines in the Black Volta Region," in *Shrines in Africa*, ed. Dawson, 121–52; the third section draws on my "First-Comers and Late-Comers: Indigenous Theories of Land Ownership in the West African Savanna," in *Land*, ed. Kuba and Lentz, 35–56; and the last section adapts parts of my "Is Land Inalienable? Historical and Current Debates on Land Transfers in Northern Ghana," *Africa* 80, no. 1 (2010): 56–80.

10. For information on the earth cult among neighboring societies, see Dacher, "Organisation politique" on the Gouin; see Liberski-Bagnoud, *Les dieux du territoire* on the Kasena; on the Birifor, see Georges Savonnet, *Les Birifor de Diépla et sa région insulaire du rameau Lobi (Haute-Volta)* (Paris: Mouton, 1976); on the Sisala, see Edward Tengan, *The Land as Being and Cosmos: The Institution of the Earth Cult among the Sisala of Northwestern Ghana* (Frankfurt: Peter Lang, 1991); on the Konkomba, see Allan Charles Dawson, "Earth Shrines and Autochthony among the Konkomba of Northern Ghana," in *Shrines in Africa*, ed. Dawson, 71–94; on the Tallensi, see Timothy Insoll et al., "The Archeology of Shrines among the Tallensi of Northern Ghana: Materiality and Interpretive Relevance," in *Shrines in Africa*, ed. Dawson, 41–70. On Dagara earth shrines, see Goody, "Fields of Social Control." For an overview, see Zwernemann, *Die Erde*; and Kuba et al., "Erdherren und Einwanderer."

11. Goody, *The Social Organisation*, 91.

12. For similar concepts among the Winye, see Jacob, *La tradition du pluralisme institutionnel*; Jacob, "Gouvernement de la nature"; for the Mossi, see Sabine Luning, "Ritual Territories as Local Heritage? Discourse on Disruptions in Society and Nature in Maane, Burkina Faso," *Africa* 77, no. 1 (2007): 86–103.

13. These villages were Lawra, Goziir, Nandom, Burutu, Ko, Kokoligu, Ouessa, Niégo, Dadoune, and Kondon. However, in Lawra, Burutu, Ko, Ouessa, and Kondon there were competing versions that denied a foreign origin of the earth shrine.

14. Similar ambiguities surround many landmarks that serve as "places of power," to use Elizabeth Colson's term ("Places of Power and Shrines of the Land," *Paideuma* 43 [1997]: 47–57). Some hills, for instance, are clearly regarded as the property of a specific patriclan, even though sacrifices

appeal to the spirits of the hill, and not necessarily only to the clan's ancestors; "strangers" who want to sacrifice at these places have to ask clan members or their *arbili* for permission, and are usually accompanied by the latter during their visit to the hill. Other hills, however, or, for that matter, the Black Volta are considered to be public places of power where everyone can sacrifice without previously consulting anyone. Whether these hills and the river are public because historically they have been evoked by members of so many different patriclans that no one could, or even tried to, establish any custodianship, or whether their power is regarded as too great to be contained by any single group, remains an open question. In any case, Colson's distinction between naturally "found" places of power that are always public and man-made shrines that are controlled by specific families does not quite hold for the Black Volta region.

15. For an instructive analysis of the nationwide ritual networks around such a mobile medicinal-cum-territorial cult, namely the Tongnaab in Ghana's Upper East Region, see Jean Allman and John Parker, *Tongnaab: The History of a West African God* (Bloomington: Indiana University Press, 2005). See also the discussion of territorial-cum-healing cults by Richard P. Werbner, "Safe Passage for Well-Being: Substances, Sacrifice and Oracle Supplicants," *Cambridge Anthropology* 29, no. 3 (2009): 46–68.

16. In the former Lawra District of North-Western Ghana, two contiguous territorial-cum-healing cults have been of particular importance and apparently even entered into competition: "Nyoor," with its ritual center in Eremon, and "Kabir," which originated in Lambussie and even crossed ethnic boundaries. On Nyoor, see also Goody, "Fields of Social Control," 70–83. Understanding Nyoor exclusively as a territorial cult, Goody interprets the spatial distribution of Nyoor stones as an indication of the original boundaries of the earth-shrine parish that was subsequently subdivided—an interpretation that is suggested by, among others, the Eremon earth priest, but that is contested by other villages whose loyalty Eremon claims (interviews with Kporkar, Dome Tang et al., 22 December 1994, Eremon; Panyaan Naa Edward Yirbekyaa et al., 23 December 1996; Tom Naa Severio Termaghre, 26 December 1996, Nandom; and the earth priest of Varpuo, Damian Bognye et al., 22 November 1989 [interview by Barbara Habig]). For more details on Nyoor and Kabir, see Lentz, "Constructing Ritual Protection," 139–41.

17. I conducted interviews in Bangwon, Happa, Nimoro, Lambussie, Billaw, Dahile, Buu, Nabaala, Pina, Samoa, and Suke in Ghana; and in Hamile, Kierim, Hiela, Bozo, Kyetuu, Bouara, Bourra, Kelendou, Pina, and Laponé in Burkina Faso. For more details on Sisala settlement histories and the ages of these various villages, see Lentz, "Constructing Ritual Protection," 129–36.

18. On this, see also E. Tengan, *The Land*, 84–88. Tengan's informants apparently made no mention of ancestors who carried stones along on their journey, but unfortunately Tengan does not specify his analysis according to the different villages where he gathered information. However, in Pina (Ghana), where one of Tengan's main informants lived, I was told by the earth priest that their shrine stone had been imported from Tokuri.

19. The typical story here is that two Sisala hunters, one of whom is the "true" first-comer while the other only pretends to be the pioneer, meet in the bush, disagree about who came first and decide to determine the truth of their respective claims through a "test." Upon his arrival in the new habitat, each hunter had placed an object in the pond—the true first-comer a broken brick, the late-comer a stone, both as proof of their presence in the area. The "test" shows that the unfortunate first-comer's object has dissolved while his competitor's stone "proves" his seniority. I collected such narratives in Hiela, Lambussie, Bourra, and Bouara; see also E. Tengan, *The Land*, 81–84; and Rüdiger Schott, "Le caillou et la boue. Les traditions orales en tant que légitimation des autorités traditionelles chez les Bulsa (Ghana) et les Lyela (Burkina Faso)," *Paideuma* 39 (1993): 145–62.

20. Interviews with Tigwii S. Amoah, 9 December 1997, 20 January 1998, and 10 February 1999, Hamile.

21. Among the Phuo, it is not necessarily the first-comers who establish an earth shrine, but specific lineages that specialize in performing the office of the earth priest. Other lineages perform functions such as the master of the bush and the master of rivers and ponds. If a village is founded by first-comers from a "bush-owning" lineage, they must first induce members of an "earth-owning" lineage to settle in the village so that they may install the shrine and become the earth priests. For the Phuo, it is completely unthinkable that earth-shrine stones may be carried along; in their eyes, earth shrines cannot be moved. On the organization of the Phuo earth shrines, see Kuba, "La grammaire rituelle," and "Spiritual Hierarchies."

22. Interviews with Somda Beyaa et al., 28 November 1997 and 23 February 1999, Niégo.

23. Interview with Meda Charles, 13 December 1997, Ouessa.

24. This version was similar to the one Somda Beyaa's father, Kuumware, narrated in an interview with the French White Father Père Hébert in 1966. According to Hébert, Kuumware was born around 1880, and Kuumware's father Mwinzume around 1860, and both were already born in Niégo. Mwinzume, in turn, was a son of the founding ancestor Baabobr, and thus Niégo must have been established at the latest by the 1850s. A copy of Père Hébert's notes on his interview with Kuumware, 22 June 1966, was in the possession of the late Claude Nurukyor Somda, Ouagadougou, who kindly made this material available to me. See also Hébert, *Esquisse*, 72–75.

25. Interview of 28 November 1997, Niégo-Susulipuo.

26. Interview with Poda Yir-ieru, Somda Daazebr et al., 17 February 1999, Tamaogang. Similar accounts were presented in interviews with the Bimbiile in Tambiili (near Susulipuo) (Somé Gabriel et al., 23 February 1999), and the Kpagnyaane in Wiekanale (Somda Mwaanyine et al., 17 February 1999).

27. Interview with Somda Beyaa et al., 23 February 1999, Niégo-Susulipuo.

28. Interview with Bevuugang Naa Somda Martin, earth priest Somé Togbir et al., 10 January 1998, Bevuugang.

29. Interview with Bevuugang Naa Somda Martin, earth priest Somé Togbir et al., 10 January 1998, Bevuugang.

30. Interviews with Bevuugang earth priest Somé Togbir et al., 27 April 1999; and with Mwiesang Kondon, 4 March 1999, Bayagra.

31. Interview with Ali Wiekanor Basawule, Nalah Yelgie et al., 21 January 1998, Kelendou.

32. Marriages with Sisala landowners in order to gain access to more land (and food) were part of Dagara strategies of territorial expansion, and also reported in other villages on the Dagara-Sisala frontier, for instance in Buu and Bapula (Ghana); interviews with Buu Kuoro Mahama Baanuomake et al., 10 December 1997, Lang-Buu; David Maasang et al., 11 January 1998, Dagara-Buu; Bapula Naa Bonihe Yozagr, Kuube Kyeyir et al., 16 January 1998, Bapula.

33. My interviewees in Hiela gave the hunter's name as "Belzume," which may be the same as Mwinsome, Baabobr's son and Niégo's first paramount chief under colonial rule. If Belzume and Mwinsome are indeed one and the same person, then my Sisala informants had either telescoped the genealogy and ascribed to the well-known figure of Mwinsome the deeds of one of his ancestors, or Dagara expansion into Sisala territory around Niégo had indeed occurred much later than my Kpagnyaane and Tambiile informants suggested.

34. Interviews with Baagyawii Yelgie, Balitor Naagie et al., 18 December 1997, Hiela,; and with Hiela Kuoro Emoho Yelgie and Kunyoko Yelgie, 22 February 1999, Hamile.

35. Interviews with Hien Daniel, 5 March 1997 and 8 January 1998; and with Gompag Samson, 22 November 2001, Ouessa.

36. Interviews with Somda Polé, 24 February 1999, Ouessa; Meda Charles, 13 December 1997, Ouessa; Dabire Zumetege, 27 November 1997, Dandere; Somda Dominique, 29 November 1997, Bakoteng; Hien Be-irnibe, 14 September 1999 Sorguogang.

37. The date was provided by Somda Dominique from Bakoteng, who remembered that the event took place exactly one year before he returned home from Kumasi in 1946 (interview of 29 November 1997).

38. Interview with Somda Dominique, 29 November 1997, Bakoteng.

39. For more details on these encounters, see chapter 1, 65–67.

40. French and British ethnic and chieftaincy policies are discussed in more detail in chapter 4. On the *cantons* and chiefdoms in the Cercle de Léo, to which Ouessa and Niégo belonged, see Tauxier, *Le Noir du Soudan*, 342–43, 348, 372; and Duperray, *Les Gourounsi*, 277.

41. On the "visible" communication of property rights, see Rose, *Property and Persuasion*, 267–304.

42. The Baadaateng case has been analyzed in more detail in Carola Lentz, "First-Comers and Late-Comers: Indigenous Theories of Land Ownership in West Africa," in *Land*, ed. Kuba and Lentz, 35–56.

43. Interviews with Somda Dominique, Hien Emile et al., 29 November 1997, Bakoteng; Hien Jacques, 27 November 2001, Bakoteng; Hien Daniel et al., 8 December 1998, 10 February 1999, Ouessa; Meda Casimir, Meda Be-yiire bere, 24 February 1999, 5 June 2000, Ouessa; Gompag Samson, 22 November 2001, Ouessa.

44. Interviews with earth priest Nabie Danlo, Nabie Bamo, Nabie Sibone, Nabie Niégo et al., 22 November 2001, Bon. See also interview with Nyiboro, Lure-ier et al., 9 January 1998, Bon; and with Wiekog Nabia, Bon Pio Danlo Nabia et al., 9 January 1998, Bon.

45. Interviews with Dadoune Naa Somé Gerard, Dabiré Tuoni Moru et al., 28 November 1997, and 28 February 1999, Dadoune; Somé Yelnang, Somda Sienatiin, Somé Guy et al., 25April 1999 and 23 November 2001, Dianlé-Soalateng; Somé Tieryuor, 29 April 1999, Sossoré; Somé Mwinbom, Somé Alphonse et al., 2 December 1997, Toury.

46. Interviews with the Nuni elders, 9 January 1998 and 22 November 2001, Bon; and with the Mossi representative Boureima Ouedraogo, 22 November 2001, Bon.

47. Interview with Kuunume Kpoda and Hien Vure, 26 April 1999, Zoner.

48. On European developments, where the distinction between ownership of people and of things only evolved in the course of the abolition of slavery and feudal serfdom, see Carol Blum, "Of Women and Land: Legitimizing Husbandry," in *Early Modern Conceptions*, ed. Brewer and Staves, 161–69.

49. Goody, *The Social Organisation*, 33–37.

50. Boutillier, *Les structures foncières*, 13.

51. On this, see also Boutillier, *Les structures foncières*, 39–53; and Jacob, *La tradition du pluralisme*.

52. On the debate over the *res nullium* argument for North America, see Anthony Pagden, *Lords of All the World: Ideologies of Empire in Spain, Britain and France, c. 1500–c. 1800* (New Haven: Yale University Press, 1995), chap. 3.

53. That the Kusiele, a Dagara patriclan, originally had "tails like monkeys" was claimed in an interview conducted by Lawra District Commissioner John Guinness with "Yare-Grunshi" informants in Lawra, in 1932 (Interim Report on the Peoples of Nandom and Lambussie, National Archives of Ghana, ADM 11/1/824, 25–26). On reports about potsherds or ruins of houses left by the former inhabitants, see the examples in chapter 1 of this book, 51–52, 54–56.

54. Kopytoff, "The Internal African Frontier," 60.

55. Marshall-Fratani, "The War of 'Who Is Who,'" 16.

56. On the consensus and the *res nullium* theory of property, see Richard Schlatter, *Private Property: The History of an Idea* (New Brunswick, N.J.: Rutgers University Press, 1951), chaps. 5 and 6; Tully, *A Discourse on Property*, 69ff.; and Rose, *Property and Persuasion*, 11–23.

57. See John Locke, *The Second Treatise of Government and A Letter Concerning Toleration* (1690; Mineola: Dover, 2002), chap. 5; Tully, *A Discourse on Propery*; and Reeve, *Property*, chap. 5.

58. Moore, "Changing African Land Tenure," 33.

59. See also Rose, *Property and Persuasion*, 282–83.

60. See, for instance, Rose, *Property and Persuasion*, 11–23; and Lévy, *Histoire*.

61. For a discussion of the findings of Ghanaian courts on these questions with regard to customary law, see Woodman, *Customary Land Law*, 55–115. For an overview of recent research on the history and current dynamcis of African land markets, see the contributions to a special issue of *Africa* 80, no. 1 (2010); and the introductory essay of Jean-Philippe Colin and Philip Woodhouse, "Introduction: Interpreting Land Markets in Africa," *Africa* 80, no. 1 (2010): 1–13.

62. For similar statements on land transfers in Dagara villages west of the Black Volta, see Hébert, *Esquisse*, 6–8.

63. On Dagara concepts of land as a female being, see also Goody, *The Social Organisation*, 32. E. Tengan's (*The Land*, 37–40) discussion of Sisala cosmological concepts does not explicitly mention that land is a gendered creature, but my Sisala and Nuni informants in Hiela, Bon, and other villages did compare land to a woman. On the broad dissemination, particularly in the Volta region, but also beyond, of the idea that the earth is the sky's wife, see Zwernemann, *Die Erde*, 30–33, 49–61, 89–97. The metaphorical comparison of land transfers to marriage, which establishes a lasting relationship between land givers and land receivers, is also reported in a study of the Kikuyu of East Africa, who have engaged intensively in precolonial land "sales" (Droz, *Migrations kikuyus*, 242–52, 255; see also Parker Shipton, *Bitter Money: Cultural Economy and Some African Meanings of Forbidden Commodities* [Washington: American Ethnological Society Monograph Series 1, 1989]). On early European debates on the "husbandry" of women and land, see Carol Blum, "Of Women and Land: Legitimizing Husbandry," in *Early Modern Conceptions*, ed. Brewer and Staves, 161–69.

64. Interview with Somda Beyaa et el., 23 February 1999, Niégo.

65. Anne Phillips, *The Enigma of Colonialism: British Policy in West Africa* (London: James Currey, 1989), 60.

66. On the Aborigines' Rights Protection Society's ideas and policies with regard to land tenure, see David Kimble, *A Political History of Ghana* (Oxford: Clarendon, 1963), 330–57.

67. Phillips, *The Enigma*, 61–62. On the failure to pass the public lands bill, see also ibid., 75–79, 118–32.

68. Firmin-Sellers, *The Transformation of Property Rights*. On the policy shifts and colonial debates on land tenure in British West Africa, see Phillips, *The Enigma*, 66–79, 111–32; with particular reference to the Ashanti Protectorate, see Berry, *Chiefs Know Their Boundaries*, 1–27. More generally, on the colonial "invention" of customary tenure, see Colson, "The Impact of the Colonial Period"; Chanock, *Law, Custom and Social Order*; and Chanock, "Paradigms, Policies and Property." On the precolonial and early colonial land market in the Gold Coast and Ashanti and its colonial suppression, see Amanor, "Customary Land, Mobile Labor and Alienation"; Gareth Austin, "The Political Economy of the Natural Environment in West African History: Asante and Its Savanna Neighbors in the Nineteenth and Twentieth Centuries," in *Land*, ed. Kuba and Lentz, 187–212; Boni, "Indigenous Blood"; and Kojo Sebastian Amanor, "Family Values, Land Sales and Agricultural Commodification in South-Eastern Ghana," *Africa* 80, no. 1 (2010): 104–25. For a discussion of the colonial "invention" of the "communal fix" in Asia, see Li, "Indigeneity."

69. Labouret, "La guerre," 305–6 (my translation).

70. Quoted ibid., 306.

71. Ibid., 307–10.

72. Ibid., 313–16.

73. On French colonial land policies, see Coquéry-Vidrovitch, "Le régime foncier"; Étienne Le Roy, "Les objectifs de la colonisation française ou belge," in *Encyclopédie juridique de l'Afrique*, (Abidjan: Les nouvelles éditions africaines, 1982), 5: 85–95; and Firmin-Sellers, "Institutions, Context and Outcomes." On French ideas about the inalienability of African land, see, for instance, Boutillier, *Les structures*

foncières, 13–15, 47–48, with reference to Upper Volta; and, more generally, Guy-Adjeté Kouassigan, "La nature juridique des droits fonciers coutumiers," in *Encyclopédie juridique de l'Afrique*, 5: 49–58; and Etienne Le Roy, "Caractères des droits fonciers coûtumiers" and "Les modes d'acquisition et les preuves des droits fonciers coûtumiers," in *Encyclopédie juridique de l'Afrique*, 5:39–47, 71–81.

74. Quoted in Bening, "Land Policy," 239. See also Lund, *Local Politics*, 28–37.

75. Constitution of the Republic of Ghana, 1979, § 188 (4). The 1992 constitution perpetuated this regulation. For more details on the history of colonial and postcolonial land policies in Northern Ghana, see Benedict Der, "Colonial Land Policy in the Northern Territories of the Gold Coast, 1900–1957," *Universitas* 4 (1975): 127–42; Kwame Ninsin, "The Land Question since the 1950s," in *The State: Development and Politics in Ghana*, ed. Emmanuel Hansen and Ninsin, 165–83 (London: Codesria Book Series, 1989); R. I. Alhassan et al., "Report by the Committee on Ownership of Lands and Position of Tenants in the Northern and Upper Regions," unpublished report (Accra,1978); and Bening, "Land Policy." Lund, *Local Politics*, provides various examples of the consequences of the legal changes for local power relations and property claims.

76. Read to Chief Commissioner, 5 December 1914; NAG, ADM 56/1/105, Land Tenure.

77. Armitage, Report on Land Tenure in the Northern Territories, 3 August 1914, Enclosure 1 in No. 42088 (Northern Territories Land Revenues and Taxes), NAG, CO 96/548: 8.

78. Land Tenure in the North-Western Province Northern Territories; Wheeler to Chief Commissioner, 20 September 1911; NAG, ADM 56/1/105.

79. Cardinall, *The Natives*, 16, 62, 65.

80. Dasent to Chief Commissioner, 9 November 1924; NAG, ADM 56/1/375.

81. Sean Hawkins, *Writing and Colonialism in Northern Ghana: The Encounter between the LoDagaa and "The World on Paper"* (Toronto: University of Toronto Press, 2002), 113.

82. For more details on the political background and methodology of these investigations and the research carried out by the government anthropologist R. S. Rattray a few years earlier, see Lentz, *Ethnicity*, 94–102, 112–19.

83. "Interim Report on the Peoples of Nandom and Lambussie," § 25, NAG, ADM 11/1/824. On the origins of the report, see Lawra-Tumu District, Informal Diary, 11–17 October 1932, Regional Archives Tamale (RAT), NRG 8/4/62.

84. Ibid.: § 22–25. The full verbatim version of this story, as well as a detailed discussion of present-day versions of the settlement history of Nandom that I recorded among various Sisala and Dagara families, can be found in Lentz, "Of Hunters."

85. Interview with Lambussie Kuoro K.Y. Baloro, 28 November 1989, Lambussie; interview with Nansie Issifu Tomo and his elders, 29 November 1994, Lambussie; interview with Darte Bason Boyuo, Ali Tumarah, Edmund Ebito et al., 2 December 1994, Lambussie; see also Raymond Bening, "Land Tenure System and Traditional Agriculture of the Sissala," *Bulletin of the Ghana Geographical Association* 18 (1976): 18.

86. Eyre-Smith to the Secretary for Native Affairs, 2 March 1933, § 17; NAG, ADM 11/1/824, cited hereafter as Eyre-Smith, *Comments*. On the polemical critique of Eyre-Smith, see also the exchange of letters between the Chief Commisioner of the Northern Territories and the secretary for native affairs, as well as H. A. Blair's commentary in NAG, ADM 11/1/824.

87. Guinness, *Interim Report*, § 33, 39.

88. Ibid., § 40.

89. Eyre-Smith, *Comments*, § 17–18.

90. Ibid., § 20, 35.

91. Interview with Lambussie Kuoro K.Y. Baloro, 24 November 1994; on this, see also E. Tengan, *The Land*, 92–105.

92. The earth priest of Lambussie whom I interviewed, Issifu Nansie Tomo, mentioned a longer interregnum period before the term of office of his father (interview, 29 November 1994, Lambussie).

93. On these plans and Lambussie's vacillating policies, see Lentz, *Ethnicity*, 107–9, 119–26.

94. See, for instance, the early letter of Tekowah Grunshie to the Chief Commissioner, 31 January 1938, NAG, ADM 56/1/301; for Lambussie's attempts to regain independence from Nandom and subsequent land conflicts between Dagara farmers from Nandom and Lambussie landowners, see Lentz, *Ethnicity*, 121–26, 209–12.

95. Eyre-Smith, *A Brief Review*, 26.

96. Ibid., 18, 22–3.

97. Eyre-Smith, *Comments*, § 36.

98. Guinness, *Interim Report*, § 4.

99. Ibid., § 6.

100. Eyre-Smith, *Comments*, § 4.

101. Generally on recent land policies in Ghana, supported by a World Bank titling program, that strengthen the role of "customary authorities" and particularly chiefs, see Julian Quan, Janine Ubink, and Adarkwah Antwi, "Risks and Opportunities of State Intervention in Customary Management: Emergent Findings from the Land Administration Project Ghana," in *Contesting Land*, ed. Ubink and Amanor, 183–208. For the increasing influence in Northern Ghanaian land dispute cases of arguments originating in Southern Ghanaian customary land tenure, see Benjamin Kunbuor, "'Traditional' and State Law in Land Conflicts: Case Studies from the Upper West Region of Ghana," *Working Papers on African Studies* (Berlin) 43 (2000); and "Multiple Layers of Land Rights and Multiple Owners: The Case of Land Disputes in the Upper West Region of Ghana," in *Ghana's North: Research on Culture, Religion and Politics in Northern Ghanaian Societies*, ed. Franz Kröger and Barbara Meier (Frankfurt: Peter Lang, 2003).

102. In the *Report of the Committee on Ownership of Lands and Position of Tenants in the Northern and Upper Regions*, the so-called Alhassan Report, which prepared the 1979 constitutional restitution of Northern "public lands" to their traditional owners, the "Lawra Traditional Area" (i.e., the chiefdoms of Lawra, Jirapa, Nandom, and Lambussie) was represented by Lambussie Kuoro K. Y. Baloro. Interestingly, the report stipulates that because "the office of the chief [has] in course of time become so important that the 'tindana' had to deal with the land in consultation with him," the "allodial title" now "vests jointly in the 'tindanas' and the chiefs" (Alhassan et al., *Report*, 37). Furthermore, the report states that "no sale of land is permitted . . . , neither by the chief nor the clan or family heads" and, most important, the land "can always be re-claimed after due notice" (ibid., 38). This latter proviso is clearly intended to permit the reopening of debate on all past land transfers, such as, for instance, the Lambussie-Nandom land grants.

103. See, for instance, Chanock, *Law*, and "Paradigms"; and Coquéry-Vidrovitch, "Le régime foncier."

104. Berry, *Chiefs Know Their Boundaries*, 26.

Chapter 3

1. Jesse C. Ribot and Nancy Lee Peluso, "A Theory of Access," *Rural Sociology* 68, no. 2 (2003): 153.

2. Allen Abramson, "Mythical Land, Legal Boundaries: Wondering about Landscape and Other Tracts," in *Land, Law and Environment: Mythical Land, Legal Boundaries*, ed. Abramson and Dimitrios Theodossopoulos (London: Pluto Press, 2000), 8–14.

3. Ibid., 15, 11.

4. On these different conceptions, see Ingold, *The Appropriation of Nature*, 154–58.

5. Interview with Niégo Naa Somda Beyaa et al., 23 February 1999. For an early discussion of the importance of rivers and other landmarks for boundary making as well as the transition from hunting to agriculture and its repercussions in land tenure in the Black Volta region, see Labouret, "La terre." On indigenous mental maps of village and earth-shrine territories, see also Père (*Les*

Lobi, 157–62) on the Lobi; Raymond Bening, "Indigenous Concepts of Boundaries and Significance of Administrative Stations and Boundaries in Northern Ghana," *Bulletin of the Ghana Geographical Association* 15 (1973): 7–20; and E. Tengan, *The Land*, 57–61, 80, 197–98, on the Sisala; and on the Winye (and immigrant Mossi), see Jean-Pierre Jacob, "Imposer son tutorat foncier. Usages autochthones de l'immigration et tradition pluraliste dans le Gwendégué (centre-ouest Burkina Faso), in *Histoire du peuplement*, ed. Kuba, Lentz, and Somda, 75–96. For a more general reflection on borders as "zones" or "lines" in the Black Volta region, see Hagberg and Tengan, eds., *Bonds and Boundaries*.

6. These and similar stories were narrated by Somda Beyaa, 23 February 1999; and related in interviews with Kelendou Kuoro Ali Wiekanor Basawule, 21 January 1998; Mwiensang Somda Kondon, 4 March 1999, Bayagra; and members of Yela-yir, 20 April 2000, Kelendou-Bayagra.

7. Interview with Tantuo *tengansob* Siengang Naaisine, Aasogr Nibaalieru et al., 18 December 1994. Similar stories about peace rituals that established boundaries were narrated in Buu and Kokoligu in Ghana as well as Ouessa and Hiela/Bevuugang in Burkina Faso.

8. Interview with Ko Naa James Bayuo and Ko *tengansob* Gabriel Tangsege, 18 December 1994. The burial of a cock, a dog, and bows and arrows in order to mark the end of an armed conflict between Ko and Lambussie is also reported in Jack Goody's account of Ko's history ("Fields of Social Control," 81–83) as well as in a group interview with informants from the Ko chief's house, conducted by Sebastian Bemile in Nandom, February 2001.

9. According to Lawra District Commissioner Eyre-Smith's (*A Brief Review*) pet theory of a centuries-old territorial order of earth shrines, Nyoor and Kabir were originally large hunting territories that were later, in the course of the expansion of agriculture, subdivided into smaller earth-shrine parishes whose custodians continued to remember their historical connections through joint sacrifices—an assumption that also informed Jack Goody's concept of maximal, major, and minor earth-shrine parishes (*The Social Organisation*, 91–99; "Fields of Social Control"). Such assumptions of straightforward territorial subdivision, however, miss the complicated shifts in, and local controversies about, the nature of the boundaries in question.

10. Report on Lobi mission, April 1905, NAG, ADM 56/1/50.

11. Land Tenure in the North-Western Province, Northern Territories; Wheeler to Chief Commissioner, 20 September 1911, NAG, ADM 56/1/105.

12. Ibid.

13. Read to Chief Commissioner, 5 Dec. 1914, NAG, ADM 56/1/105. See also the various letters and enclosures in Northern Territories Land Revenue and Taxes, PRO, CO 96/548, No. 42088.

14. Read to Chief Commissioner, 22 November 1908; enclosure 3 in Gold Coast No. 41 of 19 January 1910, PRO, CO 96/493, pt . II, sec. VI.

15. However, in case of conflict, earth priests may, of course, physically "show" the boundaries, and there are few restrictions on speaking, albeit rather vaguely, on the nature of boundaries. On taboos regarding boundaries, see also Rüdiger Schott, "Limits on the Access to Land, Cattle and Women among Some West African Peoples," in *Frontiers and Borderlands: Anthropological Perspectives*, ed. Michael Rösler and Tobias Wendl, 170–77 (Frankfurt: Lang, 1999).

16. For a detailed case study of the spatial dynamics of farming in Pina, a Dagara village on Nuni land in Burkina Faso, see Savonnet, *Pina*. The practice of marking trees in order to stake claims to land is also reported by Jean-Philippe Colin for the lower Ivory Coast ("Outside the Autochthon-Migrant Configuration: Access to Land, Land Conflicts and Interethnic Relationships in a Former Pioneer Area [lower Côte d'Ivoire]," *IRD Réfo, Document de travail de l'unité de recherche 095*, 10 [2004]: 6–8; "Lorsque le Far East n'était pas le Far West. La dynamique d l'appropriation foncière dans un ancien 'no-man's land' de basse Côte d'Ivoire," *Autrepart* 30 [2004]: 45–62). Interesting case studies from Ghana and Burkina Faso are also presented in D. Andrew Wardell et al., eds., *Negotiated Frontiers in Sudano-Sahelian Landscapes*, Sahel-Sudan Environmental Research Initiative, Occasional Paper 16 (2003).

17. Interview with Togbir Somé et al., 27 April 1999, Bevuugang. Informants in Kondon were not quite as explicit, but on the whole confirmed the information from Bevuugang; interviews with Kondon earth priest Kuube-ire Somda, Kondon Naa Dian Meda et al., 21 January 1998; Kuukyara Somda and Kondon Naa Dian Meda, 28 April 1999; Siedong Piina, Kondon Naa Dian Meda et al., 28 April 1999; Kuube-ire Somda, 28 April 1999. The chief of Kelendou, however, denied that Kondon had its own earth shrine and insisted that the village still depended on Kelendou for all earth-shrine-related matters (interview with Kelendou Kuoro Ali Wiekanor et al., 21 January 1998).

18. This section adapts arguments and material presented in Carola Lentz, "This Is Ghanaian Territory: Land Conflicts on a West African Border," *American Ethnologist* 30 (2003): 273–89.

19. See Wilks, *Wa and the Wala*, 103–40; and Jeanne-Marie Kambou-Ferrand, *Peuples voltaïques et conquête coloniale 1885–1914. Burkina-Faso* (Paris: L'Harmattan, 1993), for details of the treaties. The first, but rather defective, map of the Black Volta region was provided by the French captain Louis Binger in 1888–89; on the geographic and ethnographic mapping of the region by Binger and subsequent British missions, see Lentz, *Ethnicity*, 75–79.

20. Report of G. E. Ferguson on his travels through the "hinterland of the Gold Coast," in 1892 and 1894, quoted in Kwame Arhin, ed., *The Papers of George Ekem Ferguson, a Fanti Official of the Government of the Gold Coast, 1890–1897* (Leiden: African Studies Centre, 1974), 74, 116.

21. More generally on the interaction between African and European notions of (international) boundaries, see A. I. Asiwaju, "The Concept of Frontier in the Setting of States in Pre-colonial Africa," *Présence Africaine* 127–28 (1983): 43–49; A. I. Asiwaju, ed., *Partitioned Africans: Ethnic Relations across Africa's International Boundaries, 1884–1984* (London: Hurst, 1985); A. I. Asiwaju and P. O. Adenyi, eds., *Borderlands in Africa: A Multidisciplinary and Comparative Focus on Nigeria and West Africa* (Lagos: University of Lagos Press, 1989); and Paul Nugent and A. I. Asiwaju, eds., *African Boundaries: Barriers, Conduits, Opportunities* (London: Pinter, 1996).

22. On the 1897 agreement, see the "Historique (1890–1904) de délimitation Soudan-Gold Coast," Léo, 6 December 1924, Archives de la Délégation Générale du CNRST, Ouagadougou (CNRST), Délimitation des Frontières de Haute-Volta, Série B, III/1. The French original of the agreement uses the term *limite* for the British-French border and *frontière* for the political border of the "états de Oua [Wa]."

23. On the ad hoc agreements before 1900, see CNRST, Délimitation des Frontières de Haute-Volta, Série B, I/4 and 5.

24. See ibid., Série B, I/6, and Série B, II/1, "Mission d'abornement avec la Gold Coast, 1904"; see also "Rapport sur les marques frontiers," 31 August 1928, CNRST, Série B, III/4, préambule, § 5–7. For a discussion of the various phases of boundary demarcation, see also Pierre Claver Hien, "Le jeu des frontières en Afrique occidentale. Cent ans de situations conflictuelles au Burkina Faso actuel (1886–1986)" (Ph.D. diss., Université de Paris I, 1996).

25. On the importance of "seeing" property and the fact that all visual markers of property rights need to be explained by narratives or texts, see Rose, *Property and Persuasion*, 267–304.

26. CNRST, Série B, I/6, "Projet de délimitation," 22 November 1900, Articles III and IV; "Mission d'abornement avec la Gold Coast, 1904," ibid., Série B, II/1.

27. Quoted in the "Historique (1890–1904) de délimitation Soudan-Gold Coast," Léo, 6 December 1924, CNRST, Délimitation des Frontières de Haute-Volta, Série B, III/1. The English translation is mine.

28. On the 1924–25 boundary mission, see CNRST, Série B, II/2; and Hien, *Le jeu des frontières*, 337–40.

29. On the relevant current legal stipulations, see the constitution of the Republic of Ghana, 1992, § 266.

30. District Commissioner Lawra-Tumu, "Rapport sur les marques frontières," 31 August 1928, CNRST, Série B, III/4, conservation, § 2–4; populations locales, § 1–3. The European administrators

regularly took the local chiefs along on their tours of inspection of the boundary, walking with them on this footpath and instructing them about their task to survey cross-border mobility. For more details on the history of the international border and local perceptions, see Lentz, "This Is Ghanaian Territory."

31. For a highly instructive case study of the selective appropriation of the international border, see Paul Nugent, *Secessionists, Smugglers and Loyal Citizens on the Ghana-Togo Frontier* (Oxford: James Currey, 2002).

32. The history of this transfer is traced in a letter of Nandom Naa Imoru to the Minister of Local Government, 26 March 1952, Regional Archives, Tamale, NRG 8/2/73, and in the Intelligence Reports, July–August 1962, ibid., NRG 7/3/5. For details of the conflicts in the wake of this transfer, see Lentz, *Ethnicity*, 188–98, 221–27.

33. For an instructive case study of a similar development of indigenous border concepts in the borderland of Angola and Namibia, see Gregor Dobler, "Boundary Drawing and the Notion of Territoriality in Pre-colonial and Early Colonial Ovamboland," *Journal of Namibian Studies* 3 (2008): 7–30.

34. Interviews in Varpuo were conducted with Somé Kpiidong (RAV), Somda Lokpag, Meda Mwingyim et al., 28 January 1998; Somé Ezekyel, Hien Mwiedanmonon et al., 29 April 1999; Somé Théophile, 29 April 1999; Hien Besegni Ansolomy, Somé Kuukyale et al., 14 April 2000; and Meda Mwingyim et al., 15 April 2000. In addition, I interviewed the Nuni chief and earth priest of Danfi, Pio Wadogo, Wabuli et al., 29 January 1998; in Dadoune, Somé Gérard et al., 28 November 1997 and 28 February 1999; and in Bon, Nabie Danlo, Nabie Wiekog, Nabie Bamo et al., 9 January 1998 and 22 November 2001.

35. The relationship between the Meto-Man and Meto-Kaziile patriclans is similar to the one between Bimbiile and Kpagnyaane discussed in the previous chapter. Some informants explained that the Kaziile are the descendants of offspring who came out of an illegitimate liaison with a Meto-Man woman; others related that the original patriclan, the Meto-Man, was deliberately divided into two in order to increase the number of marriageable women. In any case, the two clans intermarry and regard themselves as closely related, but also compete over seniority and access to resources.

36. Interviews with Dadoune Naa Somé Gérard, Buonab et al., 28 November 1997 and 28 February 1999; further information on Dadoune history was collected in interviews with the Danfi earth priests, Pio Wadogo, Wabuli et al., 29 January 1998; and the *chef de canton* Denyuu's son Meda Charles, 3 February 1998. See also Hébert, *Esquisse*, 84–85.

37. The politicization of allodial property under the colonial regime is discussed in the next chapter.

38. The earth priest of Danfi acknowledged the payment, but reported that only 30,000 cowries were paid (interview with earth priest Wabuli and the Danh Chief Wadogo, 29 January 1998).

39. Bohannan, "Africa's Land," 55–56.

40. See the discussion of Hobhouse's early concept of property in the introduction.

41. This was highlighted, for instance, in the aftermath of a protracted land conflict between Nandom and Lambussie that I discuss in chapter 5.

42. See, for instance, Meek's comprehensive report that draws on anthropological expertise from various colonies (*Land*, 11–31).

43. See Pogucki, *Report*, published in 1951.

44. See Boutillier, *Les structures*, published in 1964.

45. *Les structures*, 14–5, 39–51.

46. See, for instance, Kasanga and Kotey, *Land Management*; and Kasim Kasanga, "Land Tenure and Regional Investment Prospects: The Case of the Tenurial Systems of Northern Ghana," *Property Management* 13 (1995): 21–31. See also Platteau, "An Evolutionary Theory."

47. *Property and Values*, xiii.

48. For instance, the devolution of Northern lands by the Ghanaian state to their previous "owners" in 1979 gave rise to renewed debates over who holds the allodial title and what prerogatives this title actually entails; see Lund, *Local Politics*, for instructive case studies of such debates in Ghana's Upper East Region.

49. Shipton and Goheen, "Understanding African Land-Holding," 311–12.

50. For a more general discussion of derived rights, and the transfer of such rights, see Philippe Lavigne Delville et al., *Negotiating Access to Land in West Africa: A Synthesis of Findings from Research on Derived Rights to Land* (London: International Institute for Environment and Development, 2002); and Camilla Toulmin, "Negotiating Access to Land in West Africa: Who Is Losing Out?" in *Conflicts over Land and Water in Africa*, ed. Bill Derman et al. (Oxford: James Currey, 2007), 95–115.

51. DC Lawra-Tumu, 9 November 1924; NAG ADM 56/1/375. On competing interpretations of the earth priests' rights, see also Zwernemann, *Die Erde*, 100–127; and Kuba et al., "Erdherren und Einwanderer."

52. For pertinent examples of disputes in which local chiefs, who claimed allodial title, allocated pasture rights to rich herders, see Steven Tonah, "Migration and Farmer-Herder Conflicts in Ghana's Volta Basin," *Canadian Journal of African Studies* 40, no. 1 (2006): 152–78.

53. Berry, "Privatization."

54. For pertinent examples, see Berry, *Chiefs Know Their Boundaries*, chap. 4; and Lund, "Who Owns Bolgatanga?" For a critical view of an "evolutionary" conception of recent changes in land tenure, see Mahir Saul, "Money and Land Tenure as Factors in Farm Size Differentiation in Burkina Faso," in *Land and Society in Contemporary Africa*, ed. R. E. Downs and S. P. Reyna, 243–79 (Hanover: University Press of New England, 1988); and Platteau, "An Evolutionary Theory."

55. For an instructive case study of conflicts within an earth-priestly family over land "sales," see Sten Hagberg, "Money, Ritual and the Politics of Belonging in Land Transactions in Western Burkina Faso, in *Land*, ed. Kuba and Lentz, 99–118.

56. For a more general discussion of the commercialization of land transactions, and the development of African land markets, see Jean Ensminger, "Changing Property Rights: Reconciling Formal and Informal Rights to Land in Africa," in *The Frontiers of the New Institutional Economics*, ed. J. N. Drobak and J. V. C. Nye, 170–75 (New York: Academic Press, 1997); Lavigne Delville, ed., *Quelles politiques*, 119–22; and the contributions in Tor A. Benjaminsen and Christian Lund, eds., *Securing Land Rights in Africa* (London: Frank Cass, 2003).

57. Benjaminsen and Lund, eds., *Securing Land Rights*, 3. More generally on state-led attempts at formal titling, see Bruce, "Do Indigenous Tenure Systems Constrain"; Ensminger, "Changing Property Rights"; Lavigne Delville, ed., *Quelles politiques*; and Toulmin et al., *The Dynamics*. On the most recent attempt in Ghana to register customary ownership, see Quan, Ubink, and Antwi, "Risks and Opportunities."

58. Benjaminsen and Lund, eds., *Securing Land Rights*, 3.

59. For examples and further details, see Philippe Lavigne Delville, "When Farmers Use 'Pieces of Papers' to Record Their Land Transactions in Francophone Rural Africa: Insights into the Dynamics of Institutional Innovation," in *Securing Land Rights*, ed. Benjaminsen and Lund, 89–108; and Paul Mathieu, Mahmadou Zongo, and Lacinan Paré, "Monetary Land Transactions in Western Burkina Faso: Commoditisation, Papers and Ambiguities," in *Securing Land Rights*, ed. Benjaminsen and Lund, 109–28.

60. For a more detailed discussion and some examples, see Benjamin Kunbuor, "'Traditional' and State Law."

61. On this, see the contributions in Lund, ed., *Negotiating Property*. For an interesting early discussion of the effect of writing on customary law and land tenure in Ghana, see A. N. Allott, *Essays in African Law, with Special Reference to the Law of Ghana* (London: Butterworth, 1960), 242–82.

62. Cases in point are, for instance, Varpuo, Toury, Kondon, Dabileteng, and Bayagra.

63. Lund, *Local Politics*, 90. "Settled Facts or Facts to Settle" is the fitting title of one of the chapters in Lund's book, which explores how people attempt to "curb the negotiability" of some aspects of their land rights while insisting on the "renegotiability" of others (ibid.).

64. Ibid.

65. Among the Sisala, a new earth priest publicly announces the earth shrine's rules and taboos during his ritual outdooring and can use this opportunity to tacitly innovate his predecessor's regulations (see E. Tengan, *The Land*, 101–3).

66. Interview with Mwiensang Somda Kondon, 4 March 1999, Bayagra.

67. Interviews with Kelendou Kuoro Ali Wiekanor Basawule, 21 January 1998; and Niégo Naa Somda Beyaa, 23 Febraury 1999.

68. Although Buonbaa is certainly a Dagara name, this local etymology cannot be easily corroborated by sound linguistic evidence.

69. Interviews with various representatives of the Meto-Kaziile, Kuwere, and Nakyele patriclans settling in Buonbaa, 19 February 1999, and with Konurudem Somda, the son of the first Meto-Man settler, 20 April 2000.

70. Interview with Naoulé Siyil, Amadou Foye Nadie, and Bourra Kuoro Issa Nadie, 27 November 2001.

71. Ribot and Peluso, "A Theory of Access," 160–61.

72. Interview with Laponé earth priest Fawiera, Laponé Kuoro Kumasi et al., 22 February 2000.

73. The first Dagara settlers in Laponé had presented 1,000 francs CFA, a gallon of sorghum beer, and four chickens—one for the sacrifice to the sacred pond (*fuo*), one for the ancestors of the landowner (*lele*), one for the bush spirits (*baka*), and one for the earth shrine (*tor zime*). The most recent arrivals had to give a minimum of 3,000 CFA and up to eight chickens. While the Sisala denied ever having raised the "customary" fee, my Dagara informants explained that the number of chickens required had increased because the earth priest now often declared that a sacrifice had failed—because the slaughtered chicken did not fall on its back—and demanded the ritual be repeated with a new fowl.

74. Interviews with Valère Somda, 15 February 2000 and 24 February 2000; Lucien Meda, 23 February 2000; Tobie Meda, 8 May 2000; Tadam Somda, 7 May 2000; and Yaaku Poda, 7 May 2000.

75. Interview with Dieudonné Meda, 2 January 2001.

76. For a general discussion and case studies of these clientelistic ties, referred to as *tutorat* in the francophone literature, see Jean-Pierre Chauveau, "Jeu foncier, institutions d'accès à la ressource et usage de la ressource. Une étude de cas dans le centre-ouest ivoirien," in *Le modèle ivoirien en question. Crises, ajustements, recompositions*, ed. Bernard Contamin and Harris Memel-Fôté, 325–60 (Paris: Karthala, 1997); and Jean-Pierre Chauveau, "How Does an Institution Evolve? Land, Politics, Intergenerational Relations and the Institution of the *Tutorat* amongst Autochthones and Immigrants (Gban Region, Côte d'Ivoire)," in *Land*, ed. Kuba and Lentz, 213–40. For an overview of the variety of institutional arrangements for "derived rights to land" in West Africa, see Lavigne Delville et al., *Negotiating Access to Land*.

77. Explanations by Gregory Sullibie Basing on occasion of an interview with Billaw Kuoro Forkoh Manoh et al., 3 December 1994. Similar explanations were offered in an interview with my Sisala interpreter Tigwii S. Amaoah and his friend Thomas F. B. Keting, 25 December 2000.

78. For a discussion of the importance of "territorializing" property claims, see Thomas Sikor and Christian Lund, "Access and Property: A Question of Power and Authority," in *The Politics of Possession: Property, Authority, and Access to Natural Resources*, ed. Sikor and Lund, 13–14 (Oxford: Blackwell, 2009).

79. More generally on legal pluralism and "forum shopping," see Keebet von Benda-Beckmann, "Forum Shopping and Shopping Forums: Dispute Processing in a Minang Kaban Village in West Sumatra," *Journal of Legal Pluralism* 19 (1981): 117–59.

80. Sikor and Lund, "Access and Property," 1, 5.
81. Ribot and Peluso, "A Theory of Access," 160–61.
82. Sikor and Lund, "Access and Property," 1.

Chapter 4

1. Moore, "Changing African Land Tenure," 33.
2. Jacob and Le Meur, "Introduction."
3. On the challenges that these shifts have entailed for pastoralists, see Han van Dijk, "Land Tenure, Territoriality and Ecological Instability: A Sahelian Case Study," in *The Role of Law in Natural Resource Management*, ed. Joep Spiertz and Melanie Wiber, 17–45 (The Hague: VUGA, 1996); Thomas Bierschenk, *Die Fulbe Nordbénins. Geschichte, soziale Organisation, Wirtschaftsweise* (Hamburg: Lit, 1997, 29–109); Youssouf Diallo, "Processes and Types of Pastoral Migration in Northern Côte d'Ivoire," in *Mobile Africa: Changing Patterns of Movement in Africa and Beyond*, ed. Mirjam de Bruijn and Dick Foeken, 153–68 (Leiden: Brill, 2001); and Samba Traoré, "Straying Fields: Tenure Problems for Pastoralists in the Ferlo, Senegal," in *The Dynamics of Resource Tenure in West Africa*, ed. Camilla P. Toulmin, Philippe Lavigne Delville, and Samba Traoré, 145–56 (Oxford: James Currey, 2002).
4. For more details, see Lentz, *Ethnicity*, 3–4, 6–10. The literature on ethnicity (in Africa) is vast; for some overviews of past research and debates, see, for instance, Crawford M. Young, "Nationalism, Ethnicity and Class in Africa: A Retrospective," *Cahiers d'Études Africaines* 103 (1986): 421–95; Terence Ranger, "The Invention of Tradition in Colonial Africa," in *The Invention of Tradition*, ed. Eric Hobsbawm and Terence Ranger, 211–62 (Cambridge: Cambridge University Press, 1983); Carola Lentz, "'Tribalism' and Ethnicity in Africa: A Review of Four Decades of Anglophone Research," *Cahiers des Sciences Humaines* 31 (1995): 303–28; Bruce Berman, "Ethnicity, Patronage and the African State: The Politics of Uncivil Nationalism," *African Affairs* 97 (1998): 305–41; Carola Lentz and Paul Nugent, "Ethnicity in Ghana: A Comparative Perspective," in *Ethnicity in Ghana: The Limits of Invention*, ed. Carola Lentz and Paul Nugent, 1–28 (London: Macmillan, 2000); Rogers Brubaker and Frederick Cooper, "Beyond 'Identity,'" *Theory and Society* 29 (2000): 1–47; and, particularly with respect to precolonial "ethnicity," see Thomas Spear, "Neo-traditionalism and the Limits of Invention in British Colonial Africa," *Journal of African History* 44 (2003): 3–27; as well as Paul Nugent, "Putting the History Back into Ethnicity: Enslavement, Religion, and Cultural Brokerage in the Construction of Mandinka/Jola and Ewe/Agotime Identities in West Africa, c. 1650–1930," *Contemporary Studies in Society and History* 50 (2008): 920–48.
5. See, for instance, the comments of the British administrator Captain Moutray Read on the origin of "Grunshi" (often used for the Sisala) as the name that Zaberma troops raiding the area for slaves had introduced, a derivative of the Sonrai word *grunga*, "fetish" (PRO, CO 96/493, enclosure 3 in Gold Coast no. 41 of 19 January 1910). District Commissioner Blair, however, traced "Grunshi" back to "Girousi," a Mossi and Dagomba term supposedly meaning "wearers of leaves" (Rhodes House Library [RHL], Mss. Afr. P. 626, Papers of Harold Blair, a 22-page manuscript on the Northern Territories, without title or date). Similarly, the name "Lobi" probably arose as a term used by the ruler of Kong and by the Dyula merchants for those gold-mining populations along the Black Volta that they never succeeded in controlling. See also the comments of the French administrator Ruelle that such names, given by outsiders, were often "imaginary" and the categorizations arbitrary (E. Ruelle, "Notes ethnographiques et sociologiques sur quelques populations noires du 2e Territoire Militaire de l'Afrique Occidentale Française," *Anthropologie* 15 [1904]: 668). The term "Dagaba," as opposed to "Wala," also connoted the dichotomies bush-civilization and infidel-Muslim, marking a religious and political boundary between Wa, as a center of Islamic learning and state power, and the "heathen," acephalous population of the surrounding area (see Wilks, *Wa and*

the Wala, 16–17, 51–2; and Mona Fikry, "Wa: A Case Study of Social Values and Social Tensions as Reflected in the Oral Testimonies of the Wala of Northern Ghana" [Ph.D. diss., Indiana University,1969], 223, 238, 270–73).

6. For a fuller discussion of these processes, see Lentz, *Ethnicity*, chaps. 1–3.

7. On this, see also E. Tengan, *The Land*, 18–20. That the Dagara were indeed an expansionist group seems to be supported by linguistic evidence. Gabriel Manessy argues that the linguistic simplifications that characterize Dagara are typical of the language of an expanding group that is later acquired by others as "second" language. Manessy also suggests that the Dagara probably expanded slowly and more peacefully than, for instance, the Mossi (who belong to the same linguistic family) ("Linguistique historique et traditions ethniques. Les peuples voltaïques dans l'est de la boucle du Niger," in *Zur Sprachgeschichte und Ethnohistorie in Afrika. Neue Beiträge afrikanistischer Forschungen*, ed. Wilhelm J. H. Möhlig et al., 160–62 [Berlin: Reimer, 1977]; and Gabriel Manessy, "Materiaux linguistiques pour servir à l'histoire des populations du sud-ouest de l'Haute Volta," *Sprache und Geschichte in Afrika* 4 [1982]: 152). I owe thanks to Klaus Beyer for drawing my attention to these otherwise profoundly "linguistic" texts that are quite impenetrable for the nonspecialist.

8. For an interesting discussion of a very similar case of distinct forms of imagining ethnic cohesion and different relations to the land among the Nuer and the Anywaa in Ethiopia, see Dereje Feyissa, "Land and the Politics of Identity: The Case of Anywaa-Nuer Relations in the Gambella Region," in *Competing Jurisdictions: Settling Land Claims in Africa*, ed. Sandra Evers et al., 203–22 (Leiden: Brill, 2005).

9. For the relation between Dagara ethnic identity and the patriclan system, see also A. Tengan, *Hoe-Farming*, 127–35, 161–98, who argues that the latter arises in response to the challenges of mobility and agrarian expansion.

10. This differs from the findings of A. Tengan (*Hoe-Farming*, 134–35), who cites his informants as opposing *Dagawiè* for the area around Nadawli (where the Dagara/Dagaba were probably indeed first-comers in the sense of first inhabitants) and *Langwiè* for the area around Lawra and Nandom, which has been originally inhabited by Sisala-speaking groups, according to Tengan's informants.

11. The name *yeri* is probably derived from a Mande word literally meaning "scattered, dispersed." On the Yeri and Mande immigration to Jirapa and Wa, see the Wala traditions mentioned by Wilks, *Wa and the Wala*, 35–36, 57–59; and Abobo, *A History of the Jirapa Traditional Area*. On Dagara-Yeri in Burkina Faso, see Hébert, *Esquisse*, 150–61; and Knösel, "Migration."

12. On similar images and narratives among the Phuo, see Kuba and Lentz, "Arrows," 398–99; and Kuba, "Comment devenir Pougouli."

13. See, for instance, the early ethnographic reports by various colonial officers, e.g., Captain B. Moutray Read, 1908, enclosure 3 in Gold Coast no. 41, Governor Robertson to Colonial Office, 19 January 1910 (PRO, CO 96/493); John Guinness, *Interim Report*; John Armstrong, *Report on the Peoples*; and Rattray, *The Tribes*, 465–96. See also Mendonsa, *The Politics of Divination*, 36–40; Duperray, *Les Gourounsi*, 14–33; and Swanepoel, "Too Much Power," 85–128, who complements oral sources with archaeological evidence.

14. "The Internal African Frontier," 30–32.

15. Among the Phuo, "strangers" were often absorbed by adopting them as "slaves"; on this, see Kuba and Lentz, "Arrows," 398–99; and Kuba, "Comment devenir Pougouli," 154–57. More generally on marriage policy and incorporation in Northern Ghana, see Jack Goody, "Marriage Policy and Incorporation in Northern Ghana," in *From Tribe to Nation in Africa*, ed. Ronald Cohen and John Middleton, 114–49 (Scranton: Chandler, 1970).

16. Peter Porekuu Dery, *Memoirs of the Most Rev. Peter Porekuu Dery, Archbishop Emeritus of Tamale* (Tamale: GILLBT Press, 2001), 15.

17. Ibid. At variance with the enumeration of place-names in his memoirs, in one of my interviews with Archbishop Dery (7 January 1995, Tamale), he mentioned Nabing (near Léo in what is today Burkina Faso) as the most important place of origin, and Tumu, Wiiro, Zoole, and other settlements as later stations on his ancestors' journeys. This fits better with information from other Berwiele interlocutors, like the earth priest and the chief of Ko, Gabriel Tangsege, and James Bayuo, who also mentioned Nabing as their ancestors' original village (interview, 18 December 1995, Ko). The approximate date of the Berwiele's arrival in Konguol has been calculated on the basis of the genealogy that Dery provided.

18. Dery, *Memoirs*, 18.

19. Ibid.

20. Interview with Archbishop Peter Dery, 7 January 1995, Tamale.

21. Interviews with Nansie Issifu Tomo et al., 29 November 1994, and Darte Bason Boyuo et al., 2 December 1994. One of my Dagara interlocutors who had himself conducted a number of interviews among his clan mates identified the Lambussie Dagaba immigrants as members of the Gane patriclan who recognize their constituent Sisala, Dagaba, Dagara, and even Phuo branches by the common taboo of the leopard (interview with Suuribatari-biin Soyiri, Bolgatanga, 24 December 2004). The ethnic "conversion" of some of the Lambussie founders was also reported by the British District Commissioners John Guinness and John Armstrong, who conducted interviews about the local settlement history in Lambussie and surrounding Sisala villages in the early 1930s. Their informants explained that their forebears were "originally Dagarti," but became Sisala through intermarriage with the "Jaffing people . . . to the North" and, after some initial clashes, also with the "Soro people to the East" (Armstrong, *Report on the Peoples*). The "Soro people" could, according to my interviews, refer to people from "Sor-re," an ancient Sisala settlement that my informants located in the surroundings of Tumu. Two brothers are supposed to have left Sor-re on a hunting expedition, in the direction of Lambussie, one eventually founding Pina, the other Samoa; later on, the Samoa group had a violent conflict with Lambussie over the abduction of a Samoa woman by a Lambussie man—perhaps the clashes to which Armstrong's informants referred (interview with the Samoa Kuoro, Shaku Tigwii et al., 28 November 2001). Guinness asserted Dagaba/Dagara origins for the Sisala of Lambussie, Happa, Nabaala, Dahile, and Billaw (*Interim Report*). For more details of these investigations, and the political project that inspired them, see Lentz, "Colonial Ethnography."

22. This is the gist of the story presented by Meda Charles, descendant of a lineage that regards Zenuo as their ancestor, but had already moved on to Burkina Faso sometime before the onset of colonial rule (interview, 20 November 1997, Ouessa). I found Meda's account particularly interesting because his family never became embroiled in the long-standing conflicts between Nandom and Lambussie that strongly influenced all the other versions that I collected among Zenuo's and his Sisala hosts' descendants. It is even possible that Zenuo's stay in Lambussie and the subsequent establishment of Nandom was in reality a drawn-out process, spanning two or more generations, but has been telescoped and ascribed to one heroic founding ancestor. For more details on the controversies about the establishment of Nandom and its earth shrine, see the respective section in chapter 2, 117–22; and Lentz, "Of Hunters, Goats and Earth Shrines."

23. Archaeological findings seem to support this scenario of mobility and fluid ethnic "boundaries." The furnaces for iron smelting that were found in Billaw (now a Sisala village near Lambussie) are very similar to the ones found in Dagaba-speaking villages around Jirapa and Tuopari, but differ from those Sisala settlements farther east, at Jefisi. For further details, see Pole, "Iron-Working Apparatus," 28–29, 34–35.

24. For a discussion of these exit strategies, see chapter 1, 39–42.

25. Turton, "A Journey."

26. For some examples, see Lentz, *Die Konstruktion*, 102–9.

27. For an in-depth analysis of these processes, see Lentz, *Ethnicity*, chaps. 2–4.

28. See, for instance, the reports by the Fanti representative of the British Crown, George Ekem Ferguson, who complained about the "wild tribes, naked, living in independent family communities" (quoted in Arhin, *The Papers*, 99, 109, 117). For an early French description of the "Gourounsi," whose linguistically and culturally heterogeneous peoples were supposedly constantly feuding among themselves, see the report by Captain Louis Binger, *Du Niger au Golfe de Guinée* (Paris: Librairie Hachette, 1892), 2: 34–35.

29. Monthly Reports, Black Volta District, May 1901, NAG, ADM 56/1/416.

30. Captain Moutray Read in a report on tours of inspection, March–May 1905, NAG, ADM 56/1/50.

31. Lt. Fabre, Monographie de la Conscription de Diébougou, Jan. 1904, Archives Outre Mer (Aix-en-Provence) (AOM) AOF, 16304, 14 Mi 686, p. 6; my translation.

32. D. C. Dorward, "Ethnography and Administration: A Study of Anglo-Tiv 'Working Misunderstanding,'" *Journal of African History* 15 (1974): 457–77.

33. Read, for instance, classified the Nandom and Lawra areas as "Lobi," and Jirapa as "Dagarti" (Report on districts traveled through on tours of inspection during March and May 1905, NAG, ADM 56/1/50). His successors, on the other hand, classified Jirapa as "Lobi-Dagarti" (see, for instance, *Gold Coast Civil Service List of 1910–11* [Accra: Government Press, 1910], 353). In 1918, Jirapa was then classified, together with Nandom and Lawra, as a "Lobi Division" (NAG, ADM 56/1/453, 18, 26), but afterward was regarded as Lobi-Dagarti once again, and from the mid-1930s finally as Dagarti, while Nandom now counted as Lobi-Dagarti.

34. For more details, see Lentz, *Ethnicity*, chaps. 2 and 4.

35. On changing French chieftaincy policies in South-Western Burkina Faso, see Henri Labouret, *Monographie du Cercle de Gaoua* (ca. 1924), typescript of 71 pages; consulted in the archives of the Diocese of Diébougou.

36. On Ponty's ideas, see, generally, Jacques Lombard, *Autorités traditionelles et pouvoirs européens en Afrique noire* (Paris: Armand Colin, 1967), 106–23; on the *cantons* and chiefdoms in the Cercle de Léo, see Tauxier, *Le Noir du Soudan*, 342–43, 348, 372; and Duperray, *Les Gourounsi*, 277. A detailed history of the politico-administrative organization of the colonial Cercle de Léo, including the organization of chieftaincy, is still lacking.

37. DC Lawra-Tumu to the Commissioner of the Northern Province, 21 April 1931, NAG, ADM 56/1/309.

38. See DC Lawra-Tumu to DC Wa, 1 October 1947, RAT, NRG 8/2/101: 2–3. For more details on these events and the relations between Nandom and Lambussie, see Lentz, *Ethnicity*, 112–26.

39. This was confirmed by Yesibie's son, Lambussie Kuoro K. Y. Baloro (interview, 28 November 1989).

40. See, for instance, Captain Read, in a supplement to responses to a questionnaire from the British Colonial Ministry on the "laws and customs of West African native communities," 1907–8, part II, section 7; NAG, ADM 56/1/91.

41. See Geschiere and Nyamnjoh, "Capitalism and Autochthony"; see also the discussion of the recent literature on autochthony in the introduction of this book, 14–15.

42. Ibid.

43. For more details and some examples, see Boni, "Indigenous Blood"; Austin, *Land, Labour and Capital*; and Amanor, "Customary Land, Mobile Labor."

44. Native Land Tenure, 1924; NAG, ADM 56/1/375, 12.

45. Northern Territories Land and Native Rights Ordinance, 1931; PRO, CO 96/702/7187.

46. See, for instance, Monographie de la Circonscription de Diébougou, 1904; AOM, AOF, 1 G 304 (14 Mi 686); and Mémoire de la Circonscription de Diébougou, 1906; AOM, AOF 1 G 327 (14 Mi 690); see also Tauxier, *Le Noir du Soudan*.

47. Lawra Confederacy Native Administration, Minutes of Conference 10–12 September 1940, RAT, NRG 8/5/17.

48. Ibid.

49. For a fuller discussion of these arguments and conflicts over chiefly succession, see Lentz, *Ethnicity*, 43–50, 129–32, 211–17.

50. More generally on the increasing tension between chiefs and earth priests in British territory, see Lund, *Local Politics*, 48–50; for examples from Lawra District, see Lentz, *Ethnicity*, 100–103, 130–31, 211–12. Although this development was particularly pronounced in the British protectorates, it also characterized the French colony. My interlocutors from earth-priestly families in Burkina Faso often complained in a similar fashion that once their ancestors had "given out" the chieftaincy to another family, the latter had arrogated all authority and no longer referred back to them.

51. See chapter 1, 42–52, for an extensive discussion of Kusiele migrations and Lawra's settlement history. Gari's narrative was recorded in the Lawra District Record Book (NAG, ADM 61/5/11, 251). For a discussion of this instance of a coproduction of history by local elders and British officials, see Lentz, *Ethnicity*, 88–90.

52. DC Michael Dasent, 9 November 1924, Native Land Tenure, NAG, ADM 56/1/375: 13.

53. Ibid., 11.

54. Interviews with Lawra Naa Abayifaa Karbo, 22 December 1989, 23 December 1993, 23 December 1994 and 4 January 1998. This version is, of course, adamantly contested by my informants in Nandom, who claim that their earth shrine as well as the shrines of villages under Nandom's paramountcy are independent from Lawra. For an account of the history of competitive political relations between Lawra and Nandom, see Lentz, *Ethnicity*, 55–59, 108–9, 180–82, 209–21.

55. For details, see, in chapter 2, 85–89, and chapter 3, 130–33.

56. Eyre-Smith, *Comments*, § 22. For a detailed discussion of Eyre-Smith's rather romantic view of the regional tradition of earth shrines, see Lentz, "Colonial Ethnography"; and Lentz, *Ethnicity*, 97–103.

57. Guinness, *Interim Report*, 2–3.

58. Ibid., 31.

59. Ibid., 30. In fact, most British officers were aware that earth-shrine boundaries were not as clearly defined as Eyre-Smith's model suggested. In 1928, Provincial Commissioner Whittall had ordered that a "Tindana map" with exact boundaries of earth-shrine parishes be drawn, but this plan never materialized (see Commissioner Northern Province to DCs, 29 December 1928, 30 October 1929, RAT, NRG, 8/2/27).

60. For a fuller discussion of the Hamile case, see Lentz, *Ethnicity*, 188–98, 221–27.

61. Interview with Michael Naateryel, 24 November 1989, Kulkya. For instructive examples of such conflicts, see Lentz, *Ethnicity*, 110–12; and Lawra District, Informal Diary, 20 November 1937, NAG, ADM 61/5/16; Lawra District Informal Diary, 11 February 1938, RAT, NRG 8/4/83; Handing-over Report, DC Lawra-Tumu, 7 November 1938, 19, RHL, Mss.Afr.s. 626, papers of H. A. Blair; Lawra-Tumu District, Informal Diary, 22 and 24 June 1939, RAT, NRG 8/4/83.

62. Population census of 1996. According to the information culled from the enumeration lists kept in the office of the Bourra District administration, Bozo's inhabitants in 1996 numbered 1,479 (694 men, 785 women), living in 203 households (but there are usually several households in one compound). Parts of the discussion of the Bozo case have been adapted from Carola Lentz, "'Natives' and 'Settlers': Negotiating Land Tenure in the Black Volta Region (Burkina Faso), 1930s–1990s," in *Une anthropologie entre pouvoirs et histoire. Conversations autour de l'œuvre de Jean-Pierre Chauveau*, ed. E. Jul-Larsen et al., 325–43 (Paris: Karthala 2011).

63. An Anglo-French Boundary Commission map dating from 1900 lists six farmsteads for Bozo (PRO, MPG 915); the census of 1908/9, however, does not even mention Bozo as an independent settlement (Tauxier, *Le Noir du Soudan*, 342–43). The settlement history of Bozo is controversial, but there was agreement that Bozo was not among the older, more powerful and populous Sisala villages

in the region (interviews with Somda Eloi et al., 22 March 2000, Bozo; Bozo Kuoro Banuosin Kel-le et al., 17 December 1997; Hiela Kuoro Emoho Yelgie, Kunyoko Yelgie et al., 22 February 1999; and Niepor Kombui et al., 16 December 1997, Kyetuu.

64. Interview with Bourra Kuoro Issa Nadie, Amadou Foye Nadie et al., 27 November 2001, Bourra.

65. On the reasons for the mission's great success, and a more detailed history of its further development, particularly its relations with the chiefs and colonial officers, see Lentz, *Ethnicity*, 153–74.

66. Chief Commissioner Northern Territories to Colonial Secretary, 9 March 1937, Regional Archives Tamale (RAT), NRG 8/19/7.

67. On the so-called Ouessa conference, see Diaire de Ouagadougou, 17 and 14 January 1933, Archives Générales des Missionaires d'Afrique, Rom (A.G.M.Afr.); R.P. Jean Lesourd, *Un peuple en marche vers la lumière. Les Dagaris* (Soisson: Imp. de l'Argue, 1938); Remigius F. McCoy, *Great Things Happen: Personal Memoir of the First Christian Missionary among the Dagaabas and Sissalas of Northwest Ghana* (Montreal: Society of the Missionaries of Africa, 1988), 125–28; and Magloire Somé, *La christianisation de l'ouest-volta. Action missionaire et réactions africaines, 1927–1960* (Paris: Harmattan, 2004), 113–17.

68. "Visite du Père Durrieu et du Père Mandrin à M Teyssier, Administrateur Maire du Cercle de Ouagadougou, en présence de l'administrateur Commandant de la Subdivision de Léo," 14 August 1933; enclosure in Mgr Thévénoud to Superior Voillard, 14 September 1933 (my translation); A.G.M.Afr, Doss. 195/3.

69. Supérieur Régional P. Blin to Supérieur Général, Maison Carrée, 29 August 1933 (my translation); A.G.M.Afr, Doss. 196/2. Unfortunately, this handwritten letter was barely legible; it could have been a draft that was not sent, but it certainly reflected the missionaries' reservations.

70. Interview with Somda Eloi, Somda Abel et al., 22 March 2000, Bozo.

71. Interview with Bozo Kuoro Banuosin Kel-le et al., 17 December 1997.

72. On these developments, see also Magloire Somé, *La christianisation*, 153–94.

73. Interview with Somda Eloi, Somda Abel et al., 22 March 2000, Bozo.

74. Interviews with Somé Grégoire, 23 January 1998 and 2 January 2001, Ouessa.

75. Interview with Bozo Kuoro Banuosin Kel-le et al., 17 December 1997.

76. Interviews with Bozo Naa Somé Jean Paul et al., 4 December 1997, and Somda Eloi et al., 22 March 2000.

77. Interview with Bozo Kuoro Banuosin Kel-le et al., 17 December 1997.

78. Interview with Bourra Kuoro Issa Nadie, 27 November 2001.

79. Ibid.

80. For the relevant laws, see the Ghana Citizenship Act of 2000 (Act 591), which continues most of the stipulations of the Ghana Nationality Act of 1971 (Act 361); and, for Burkina Faso, the Code des personnes et de la famille of 16 November 1989, Art. 134 and 140.

81. The "politics of primary patriotism" (Geschiere and Gugler, "The Politics") in Ghana is also evident in the stipulations of how Ghanaian citizenship can be acquired other than by birth: one of the qualifications for naturalization is that the person must be able to speak and understand "an indigenous Ghanaian language" (which does not include English); see Art. 14 (1) of the Ghana Citizenship Act of 2000 (Act 591). More generally on the Ghanaian nation-state model, see Lentz and Nugent, "Ethnicity in Ghana." For Burkina Faso, see the discussion in Claudette Savonnet-Guyot, *Etat et sociétés en Burkina Faso. Essai sur le politique africain* (Paris: Karthala, 1986), 193–203; and Svenja Haberecht, "'Gemeinsam bauen wir eine neue Nation!' Das Cinquantenaire in Burkina Faso," in *Staatsinszenierung, Erinnerungsmarathon und Volksfest. Afrika feiert 50 Jahre Unabhängigkeit*, ed. Carola Lentz and Godwin Kornes, 194–210 (Frankfurt/Main: Brandes and Apsel, 2011).

82. See chapter 21 of the Ghanaian constitution of 1979, which is deliberately ambiguous in its definition of the exact identity of the original owners.

83. The attempts of the late Lawra Naa Abayifaa Karbo to reassert control over "Lawra lands" offer a case in point. Karbo was a member of the so-called Alhassan Committee, a group of Northern lawyers and chiefs whose report eventually informed the constitutional changes in Northern land ownership. He made sure to record for the Lawra District that the allodial title was traditionally "jointly vested in tindanas and chiefs," and land sales were not possible ("land can always be re-claimed")—formulations that are highly debatable and clearly aimed at strengthening the chiefs' control over land (Alhassan, *Report*). When I interviewed him, Karbo claimed that the Lawra chiefly house held the allodial title over a vast territory allegedly once controlled by the Lawra earth shrine, including Nandom lands. He hoped for future benefits from a major irrigation scheme along the Kambah River (which forms the boundary between the Lawra and Nandom chiefdoms) for which North-Western politicians had been petitioning government for decades. And he wanted to make sure that Lawra collected royalties if the ongoing prospection for gold by an Australian company was successful. "I don't want the people," Karbo declared, "I just want the lands . . . so that in future all royalties and other benefits will come to us, not to the Nandom Traditional Council" (interviews with Lawra Naa Abayifaa Karbo, 23 December 1994 and 4 January 1998, Lawra). For examples of conflicts between chiefs and earth priests in Ghana's Upper East Region in the wake of the 1979 divestiture of public lands, see Lund, *Local Politics*, 47–67.

84. For examples from Burkina Faso, see Pierre Joseph Laurent et al., "Migrations"; and Sten Hagberg, *Between Peace and Justice: Dispute Settlement between Karaboro Agriculturalists and Fulbe Agro-Pastoralists in Burkina Faso* (Uppsala: Acta Universitatis Upsaliensis, 1998), 97–101, 197–200.

85. Von Benda-Beckmann, "Forum Shopping."

86. A detailed analysis of this conflict has been published in Lentz, "This Is Ghanaian Territory."

87. There are only 5 Sisala houses in Kyetuu-Baper, while the Dagara section Uukyorgang counts 21 houses, Kuuziegang 28, and Tuolegang 26. These numbers were given by various villagers in 1999. According to the population census of 1996, Kyetuu (officially written "Kiétou") in Burkina Faso had a total of 684 inhabitants; Kuuziegang had 352, according to the 1984 census of Ghana; and roughly the same number probably live in Tuolegang (which the census did not list separately).

88. My reconstruction of Kyetuu's history and the development of the conflict is based on interviews with Tuolegang Naa Kpiele Maasangyir et al., 14 January 1998, 26 February 1999 and 17 February 2000, Kyetuu-Tuolegang (Ghana); Kuuziegang Naa Kpagnyaane Gyile Bagwa, Kosi Debole et al., 25 February 1999, Kyetuu-Kuuziegang (Ghana); Tambiile Ralio Tengdong et al., 26 February 1999, Kyetuu-Nyourgang (Ghana); Suleiman Balesemule, Bombieh Nalbe, George Bentor et al., 14 December 1997, Nimoro (Ghana); Fielmuo Naa (Regent) Annsokang Daanikuu, Kyekole Daanikuu et al., 14 January 1998, Fielmuo (Ghana); Leke Sinu, Bangwon Kuoro Yinuroh Wiyor et al., 11 December 1997, Bangwon; Niepor Kombui et al., 16 December 1997 and 22 February 1999, Kyetuu (Burkina Faso); Kpiele Hien Yelkou, Bekuone Poda Der et al., 25 February 1999 and 17 February 2000, Kyetuu-Uukyorgang (Burkina Faso); Baagyawii Yelgie, Balitor Nagie et al., 18 December 1997; Hiela Kuoro Enoho Yelgie, Kunyoko Yelgie, 22 February 1999, Hiela (Burkina Faso).

89. The catfish (or barble) found in the pond can survive for several months in mud and multiply quickly with rising water levels.

90. Interviews with Cyril Naawmintuo, 24 November 2001 and 26 December 2006, Kyetuu-Uukyorgang (Burkina Faso); and Tigwii Amoah, 27 December 2004, Hamile (Ghana).

91. See § 257, 6 of the 1992 constitution of the Republic of Ghana; details are specified in the Water Resources Commission Act of 1996.

92. Ministry of Lands and Forestry (Republic of Ghana), *National Land Policy* (Accra: Sonlite Press, 1999), 2.

93. Ibid., 7–8.

94. Ibid., 15.

95. For examples, see chapter 3, 141–47.

96. Roughly one-third of the more than thirty Dagara villages in the Nandom and Ouessa areas with their own earth shrines bear such names with Sisala origins. Place-names are often called out during sacrifices to the earth god, and it is possible that the Dagara pioneers learned them from the earlier Sisala inhabitants and felt obliged to adopt them.

97. Population census of 1996, Bourra District; interviews with Kelendou Kuoro Ali Wiekanor Basawule et al., 21 January 1998; Dabire Kavar, Somé Betaar et al., 19 February 1999, Buonbaa; and Konurudem Somda et al., 20 April 2000, Buonbaa.

98. Interviews with Bourra Kuoro Issa Nadie et al., 27 November 2001; and Nicolas Tandia, 18 December 1997, Hamile.

99. See, for instance, the minutes of the emergency meeting of the Lawra Confederacy Council Finance and Staff Committee, 6 January 1962, NRG 7/4/8.

100. See, for instance, the Nandom Naa's letter to the Delimitation Commission, Accra, 8 December 1964, RAT, NRG 7/2/5.

101. Hapaa Traditional Council to the Minister of Local Government and Rural Development, 10 May 2005; and Hapaa Traditional Council to the Presiding Member of the Jirapa-Lambussie District Assembly, 10 July 2005. The Dagara, Mossi, and Grunshi communities of Hamile protested against the petition, and in their letter to the Regional Minister revived the name "Hamile-Muoteng" (Andrews Yirdong, Assembly Member, to the Upper West Regional Minister, Wa, et al., 8 February 2006). The letters were kindly made available to me by the regional administration in Wa.

102. Report of the Commission of Enquiry into Representational and Electoral Reform (Van Lare Commission) (Accra: Government Printing Department, 1953), 17.

103. For examples of such disputes in the 1960s, see Lentz, *Ethnicity*, 112–26.

104. Interviews with Suleiman Balesemule et al., 14 December 1997, Nimoro; Aansokang Dagnikuu, Faata Biku et al., 14 January 1998, Fielmuo; Bawa S. Dy-Yakah, 21 August 1994, Berlin; Lambussie Kuoro K. Y. Baloro, 15 January 1998, Lambussie; Ambrose Kokoro, 15 November 1989 and 9 December 2006, Wa; and Valentine Kuuzume, 10 February 2007, Accra.

105. Reeve, *Property*, 83.

106. See Reeve, *Property*; and Brewer and Staves, *Early Modern Conceptions*.

107. On the ambiguous policies of Nkrumah toward chieftaincy, see Richard Rathbone, *Nkrumah and the Chiefs: The Politics of Chieftaincy in Ghana 1951–60* (Oxford: James Currey, 2000); for Rawlings' policies vis-à-vis "traditional authorities," see the contributions in Irene K. Odotei and Albert K. Awedoba, eds., *Chieftaincy in Ghana: Culture, Governance and Development* (Accra: Sub-Saharan Publishers, 2006); and *Contesting Land*, ed. Ubink and Amanor. For the Burkina Faso government's relations with the chieftaincy, see Jean-Baptiste Ouedraogo, "The Articulation of the Moose Traditional Chieftaincies, the Modern Political System, and the Economic Development of Kaya Region, Burkina Faso," *Journal of Legal Pluralism and Unofficial Law* 37/38 (1996): 249–61; and Sten Hagberg, "Traditional Chieftaincy, Party Politics, and Political Violence in Burkina Faso," in *State Recognition and Democratization in Sub-Saharan Africa: A New Dawn for Traditional Authorities?*, ed. Lars Buur and Helen-Maria Kyed, 131–53 (New York: Palgrave Macmillan, 2007).

108. Chauveau, "How Does an Institution Evolve?"

109. Sara Berry, "Property, Authority and Citizenship: Land Claims, Politics and the Dynamics of Social Division," in *The Politics of Possession: Property, Authority, and Access to Natural Resources*, ed. Thomas Sikor and Christian Lund (Oxford: Wiley Blackwell, 2009), 40. The Black Volta region rather corresponds to the type of a "polyvalent political landscape" that Berry identifies in Bénin (ibid).

110. Boone, "Property and Constitutional Order."

111. Ibid., 584.

112. Thomas Bierschenk and Jean-Pierre Olivier de Sardan, "Les arènes locales face à la décentralisation et à la démocratization," in *Les pouvoirs au village. Le Bénin rural entre démocratisation et décentralisation,* ed. Bierschenk and Olivier de Sardan, 11–51 (Paris: Karthala, 1998).

Chapter 5

1. Lund, *Local Politics,* 174.

2. Franz von Benda-Beckmann, "Multiple Legal Constructions of Socio-economic Spaces: Resource Management and Conflict in the Central Moluccas," in *Frontiers and Borderlands: Anthropological Perspectives,* ed. Michael Rösler and Tobias Wendl, 131–58 (Frankfurt/Main: Lang 1999).

3. See Jean-Pierre Chauveau, "The Land Question in Côte d'Ivoire: A Lesson in History," International Institute for Environment and Development, Issue Papers 95, August 2000; and Jean-Pierre Chauveau, "La loi de 1998 sur les droits fonciers coutûmiers dans l'histoire des politiques foncières en Côte d'Ivoire. Une économie politique des transferts de droits entre 'autochtones' et 'étrangers' en zone forestière," paper presented at the LASDEL, Niamey, 2007.

4. Peters, "The Limits of Negotiability"; see also Peters, "Inequality."

5. For a history of the use of wild trees and the increasing popularity of tree plantations in Western Burkina Faso, see Mahir Saul, Jean-Marie Ouadba, and Ouettan Bognouou, "The Wild Vegetation Cover of Western Burkina Faso: Colonial Policy and Post-Colonial Development," in *African Savannas: Global Narratives and Local Knowledge of Environmental Change,* ed. Thomas J. Bassett and Donald E. Crummey, 121–60 (Oxford: James Currey 2003). On conflicts about trees, see also Pierre-Joseph Laurent and Paul Mathieu, "Authority and Conflict in Management of Natural Resources: A Story about Trees and Immigrants in Southern Burkina Faso," *Forests, Trees and People Newsletter* 25 (1994): 37–44; Christian Lund, "Struggles for Land and Political Power: On the Politicization of Land Tenure and Dispute in Niger," *Journal of Legal Pluralism* 40 (1998): 1–22; and Quentin Gausset, "L'aspect foncier dans les conflits entre autochtones et migrants au sud-ouest du Burkina Faso," *Politique africaine* 112 (2008): 52–66.

6. I could not obtain the minutes of this meeting (if any exist) but rely on information that the litigants presented to me shortly afterward. To reconstruct the conflict history, I spoke with the district head (who was, however, reluctant to comment on the conflict) and conducted interviews with Kierim Kuoro Bombieh Naagyie et al., 19 December 1997; Ouessa earth priest Hien Daniel, 8 January 1998; Ouessa responsible administratif du village Somda Denis, 11 January 1998, Ouessa; and Nuuzuo-yir elders Hien Delle, Somda Yelezaar et al., Kolinka, 10 January 1998 and 23 November 2001.

7. For more details on Hien Daniel's version of the establishment of Ouessa and its earth shrine and competing narratives, see chapter 1 of this book, 52–67.

8. See, for instance, Leslie C. Gray, "Investing in Soil Quality: Farmer Responses to Land Scarcity in Southwestern Burkina Faso," in *African Savannas,* ed. Bassett and Crummey, 72–90.

9. See also the settlement of Mossi in Baadaateng discussed in chapter 2, 103–6. For further examples of the strategic placement of "strangers" along contested borders of earth-shrine parishes, see Pierre-Joseph Laurent, Paul Mathieu, and Marc Totté, *Migrations et accès à la terre au Burkina Faso* (Paris: Harmattan 1994), 24–25; and Jean-Pierre Jacob, *La tradition du pluralisme institutionnel dans les conflits fonciers entre autochtones. Le cas du Gwendégué (Centre Burkina Faso),* Document de travail de l'Unité de Recherche 095, 3, Montpellier: IRD/GRET, 2002.

10. Benjamin Kunbuor, "Multiple Layers of Land Rights and Multiple Owners: The Case of Land Disputes in the Upper West Region of Ghana," in *Ghana's North: Research on Culture, Religion and Politics in Northern Ghanaian Societies,* ed. Franz Kröger and Barbara Meier (Frankfurt: Peter Lang, 2003), 125.

11. Jacob, *La tradition.*

12. Berry, *No Condition,* 160–66.

13. Benda-Beckmann, "Forum Shopping."

14. Similar acts of sabotage have been reported by Jack Goody ("Rice Burning and the Green Revolution in Northern Ghana," *Journal of Development Studies* 16 [1980]: 136–55) with respect to Northern Ghanaian rice farms run by military and political elites that were regarded as illegitimate by the local population; and by Kojo Amanor ("Night Harvesters, Forest Hoods, and Saboteurs: Struggles over Land Expropriation in Ghana," in *Reclaiming the Land: The Resurgence of Rural Movements in Africa, Asia and Latin America*, ed. Sam Moyo and Paris Yeros, 102–17 [London: Zed Books, 2005]), with regard to timber concessions in forest reserves in Southern Ghana, where local farmers felt expropriated by a coalition of urban business men, expatriate companies, and political authorities.

15. James C. Scott, *Weapons of the Weak: Everyday Forms of Peasant Resistance* (New Haven: Yale University Press, 1985).

16. The Agrarian Reform Law of 1984 (Ordonnance No. 84–050/CNR/PRES du 4 août 1984, portant réorganisation agraire et foncière) has been modified severally, most importantly in 1996 (Loi No. 014/96/ADP du 23 mai 1996, portant réorganisation agraire et foncière) and 1997 (Décret 97–54/PRES/PM/MEF du 6 février 1997, portant conditions et modalités d'application de la loi sur la réorganisation agraire et foncière). For a critical discussion of the *commissions villageoises*, see Armelle Faure, "Délimitation des terroirs. Bilan synthétique à partir des exemples burkinabé," in *Quelles politiques*, ed. Lavigne Delville, 497–503; Bernard Tallet, "Au Burkina Faso, les CVGT ont-elles été des instances locales de gestion foncière?" in *Quelles politiques*, ed. Lavigne Delville 390–402; and Lars Engberg-Pedersen, *Endangering Development: Politics, Projects, and Environment in Burkina Faso* (London: Praeger, 2003). For a discussion of the institutional insecurity created by the Burkina Faso land reform, and the latitude this leaves for skillful individual strategizing, see Christian Lund, "Les réformes foncières dans un contexte de pluralism juridique et institutionel: Burkina Faso et Niger," in *Inégalités et politiques publiques en Afrique. Pluralité des normes et enjeux d'acteurs*, ed. Gérard Winter, 195–207 (Paris: Karthala, 2001). For a similar example from Ghana, see Wolfram Laube (*Changing Natural Resource Regimes in Northern Ghana: Actors, Structures and Institutions* [Berlin: Lit, 2007], 309–41), who discusses how the weak implementation of legal stipulations in an irrigation scheme creates room for maneuver for powerful individuals whose actions then further destabilize the institutional framework.

17. For legal details, see Loi No. 055–2004 AN, du 21 déc. 2004, portant Code général des collectivités territoriales au Burkina Faso et textes d'application, articles 80–90; for an overview on the history of decentralization policies in Burkina Faso, see Raogo Antoine Sawadogo and Pamphile Sebahara, "Historique de la décentralisation au Burkina Faso," in *Décentralisation et citoyenneté au Burkina Faso. Le cas de Ziniaré*, ed. Pierre-Joseph Laurent et al., 59–78 (Paris: L'Harmattan, 2005); and Pierre-Joseph Laurent, "Développement local, stabilité politique et décentralisation. Aperçu sur la réforme en cours au Burkina Faso," in *Dezentralisierung, Demokratisierung und die lokale Repräsentation des Staates*, ed. Jakob Rösel and Trutz von Trotha, 101–17 (Cologne: Köppe, 1999). For a case study of local politics and land administration under the new legislation, see Pamphile Sebahara, "Pluralism institutionel et politiques de développement communal," in *Décentralisation*, ed. Laurent et al., 223–55.

18. See Richard Crook, "Access to Justice and Land Disputes in Ghana's State Courts: The Litigants' Perspective," *Journal of Legal Pluralism and Unofficial Law* 50 (2004): 1–28; and Richard Crook et al., *The Law, Legal Institutions and the Protection of Land Rights in Ghana and Côte d'Ivoire: Developing a More Effective and Equitable System*, Institute of Development Studies, Research Reports 58 (Brighton: University of Sussex, 2007).

19. See Sten Hagberg, *Between Peace and Justice*, 155–70; and Lund, "Les réformes foncières."

20. For legal details, see Décret 97–54/PRES/PM/MEF du 6 février 1997, portant conditions et modalités d'application de la loi sur la réorganisation agraire et foncière, article 61.

21. This is even acknowledged in the respective decree: all occupiers of the "domaine foncier national" must hold some form of state-authorized written title certifying his or her rights of

ownership or usufruct, but this obligation does not apply to "nonmanaged" rural land ("terres rurales non aménagées") cultivated for subsistence needs (see Décret 97–54/PRES/PM/MEF, 6 février 1997, art. 141 and 142).

22. Jean-François Tribillion, *Villes africaines. Nouveau manuel d'aménagement foncier* (Paris: ADEF 1993), 25. For a case study of the *lotissement* in Diébougou in South-Western Burkina Faso, where building land has been parcelled since the mid-1950s, see Marlis Gensler, "'Une foi loti . . .': Bodenrecht und Siedlungsgeschichte in einer westafrikanischen Kleinstadt (Diébougou, Burkina Faso)," *Working Papers of the Department of Anthropology and African Studies of the Johannes Gutenberg University of Mainz* 14 (2002); see also Bernard Ganne and Moussa Ouedraogo on Ouahigouya ("'Local,' 'politique' et 'territoire': Essai d'économie politique autour d'une ville moyenne. L'évolution de Ouahigouya au Burkina Faso," in *Petites et moyennes villes d'Afrique noire*, ed. Monique Bertrand and Alain Dubresson, 223–40 [Paris: Karthala, 1997]), and on Banfora, see Cathérine Goislard ("Esquisse d'une gestion foncière plurale. Banfora [Burkina Faso]," in *Petites et moyennes villes*, ed. Bertrand and Dubresson 163–77). On the contested legitimacy of *lotissement* projects, see also the classical study on Zinguichor (Senegal) by Gerti Hesseling (*Pratiques foncières à l'ombre du droit. L'application du droit foncièr urbain à Zinguichor* [Leiden: African Studies Centre, 1992]); on contested land sales and autochthone-immigrant conflicts in nonmanaged quarters in Yaoundé (Cameroon), see Antoine Scopa, "Bailleurs autochtones et locataires allogènes. Enjeu foncier et participation au Cameroun," *African Studies Review* 49, no. 2 (2006): 45–67.

23. For the legal details, see art. 154, 155 and 156 of the Décret 97–54/PRES/PM/MEF du 6 février 1997.

24. See, for instance, Paul Mathieu, M. Zongo, and L. Paré, "Monetary Land Transactions in Western Burkina Faso: Commoditisation, Papers and Ambiguities," in *Securing Land Rights in Africa*, ed. Tor A. Benjaminsen and Christian Lund, 109–28 (London: Frank Cass, 2003); and Sten Hagberg, "Money."

25. See esp. art. 157 of the Décret 97–54/PRES/PM/MEF du 6 février 1997. The terms *quartier des autochtones* and *quartier traditionel* are used interchangeably.

26. Pierre-Yves Le Meur, *Information foncière, bien commun et ressource stratégique*, Dossier 146, (London: International Institute for Environment and Development, 2008).

27. Similar cases of fierce debates on settlement history in the course of *lotissement* projects have been reported by Gensler for Diébougou ("Une fois loti"), and Mathieu Hilgers for Koudougou ("Les conflits autour de l'histoire de Koudougou [Burkina Faso]," *Cahiers d'études africaines* 186 [2007]: 313–44).

28. In 1996, the Département Ouessa counted 10,205 inhabitants, and Ouessa itself 2,155, with 353 head of households (Cahiers de récensement, Préfecture de Ouessa).

29. A successful applicant is "shown" the plot that the *commission d'attribution* assigned to him and, after having paid the obligatory fees, receives a document stating his name and the number, location, and size of his plot. This provisional usufructuary title can be turned into a definitive one, the *permis urbain d'habiter*, after paying the *taxe de jouissance* and erecting a permanent building and walls around the plot. Particularly in smaller towns, most urban residents on parcelled and registered land are content with this definitive usufructuary title and eschew the expensive and elaborate procedure to transform it into full private ownership, a *titre de propriété* or *titre foncier*. For the legal details, see Loi No. 014/96/ADP du 23 mai 1996, art. 67, 70, 245; and Loi No. 20/96/ADP du 10 juillet 1996, esp. art. 231.

30. Conversations with Simon Hien, Député Hien Moutan, Evariste Poda, Sylvain Somé, Bertin Somda et al., 16 and 19 Febraury 2000, Ouessa; interview with Stanislas Meda, 20 December 2000, Ouagadougou.

31. More generally, on these practices of informal formalization, see Carola Lentz, "Land Rights and the Politics of Belonging in Africa: An Introduction," in *Land*, ed. Kuba and Lentz, 22–29; Paul

Mathieu, "Transactions informelles et marchés fonciers émergents en Afrique," in *Politics, Property and Production in the West African Sahel: Understanding Natural Resources Management*, ed. Tor A. Benjaminsen and Christian Lund, 22–39 (Uppsala: Nordic Africa Institute, 2001); Sita Zougouri and Paul Mathieu, "Nouvelles transactions et formalisation des transactions foncières dans l'ouest de Burkina Faso. Le cas d'un village de la province de Houët," in *Gouvernance foncière au quotidien en Afrique*, ed. Pierre-Yves Le Meur and Christian Lund, Bulletin APAD 22 (Münster: Lit, 2002), 95–116; Benjaminsen and Lund, eds., *Securing Land Rights*; and Hagberg, "Money."

32. According to the 1996 census, Hamile had 3,176 inhabitants and 546 households, of which only 40 were Sisala (Cahiers de récensement, Préfecture de Ouessa).

33. Interviews with Tigwii Amoah, Hamile, 20 January 1998 and 10 February 1999.

34. Interviews with Salifu Ouedraogo et al., 24 January 1998, Hamile, and with Idrissa Sana and Zongo Braimah, 16 February 2000, Hamile.

35. See, for instance, Gensler, "Une foi loti," 39–44, 56–62.

36. In addition to listening in to numerous informal discussions, I conducted interviews with Somé Nifaakang, 22 November 1997, Ouessa; Ouessa RAV Somda Denis, 11 January 1998; Ouessa earth priest Gompag Samson, 18 February 2000, 3 January and 22 November 2001; Stanislas Meda, 20 December 2000, Ouagadougou; Somé Grégoire, 1 July 2008, Mainz.

37. Interview with the Ouessa deputy mayor Grégoire Somé, 1 July 2008, Mainz.

38. See Commune de Ouessa, Liste des attributaires de parcelle à usage d'habitation dans le département de Ouessa, 2 April 2001. With the support of several interlocutors, I have inferred ethnic identities from the beneficiaries' family names; the professions were registered in the list and grouped by me into larger categories.

39. See, for instance, the case studies on Bolgatanga by Lund (*Local Politics*, 76–88, 90–100). For cases in Southern Ghana, see Berry (*Chiefs*, 63–137); Janine Ubink, "Negotiated or Negated? The Rhetoric and Reality of Customary Tenure in an Ashanti Village in Ghana," *Africa* 78, no. 2 (2008): 264–87; and K. V. Gough and P. W. K. Yankson, "Land Markets in African Cities: The Case of Peri-urban Accra, Ghana," *Urban Studies* 37 (2000): 2485–500. For a more general discussion of the proliferation of customary claims in the context of Ghana's recent Land Administration Project, see Ubink and Amanor, *Contesting Land*.

40. Interviews with Rafael Hokey, Upper West Regional Lands Officer, 8 December 2006, Wa; E. S. Dam, Chairman of the Regional Lands Commission, 8 December 2006, Wa; and Antonio Carrillo, technical advisor for the Lands Administration Project, Ministry of Lands, Forestry and Mines, Accra, 23 February 2007. On the ambiguous role of chiefs in land transactions in the Upper West, see also Kunbuor, "'Traditional' and State Law," 18–19; more generally on practices and perceptions of corruption in the urban and peri-urban land market, see the results of a comprehensive survey, Center for Democracy and Development, Ghana, *Corruption and Other Constraints on the Land Market and Land Administration in Ghana: A Preliminary Investigation*, CDD-Ghana Research Paper 4, 2000; on the land secretariats, see also Quan et al., "Risks and Opportunities."

41. See Amanor, "Customary Land"; and Amanor, "Conflicts."

42. In the following section, I have adapted sections from Carola Lentz, "Decentralization, the State and Conflicts over Local Boundaries in Northern Ghana," *Development and Change* 37, no. 4 (2006): 909–19.

43. On this, see also Kunbuor, "Multiple Layers."

44. Lund, *Local Politics*, 88.

45. For more details on the history of Lambussie-Nandom relations, see Lentz, *Ethnicity*, 112–26.

46. Interviews with the Taalipuo Dagara headman Benjamin Kpiimogle, 17 December 1994; David Nowe et al., 17 December 1994, Taalipuo. Further interviews were conducted with Gaamuo Mwinpuo Le-ib et al., 11 December 1989, Nandomkpee; Soglikuu Saakum, Kuur Der et al., 17 December 1994, Nandom-Bilegang; W. K. Dibaar, 29 November 1994; Nandom Naa Dr Charles P. Imoro, 4

December 1989; Jirapa-Lambussie District Secretary Jacob Boon, 23 November 1989; executive members of the Nandom Youth and Development Association, 15 November 1989, Wa; and Archbishop Peter Dery, 17 November 1990, Tamale.

47. Interview with Nabaala Kuoro Kanii Kambang et al., 4 December 1994.

48. The 1984 population census of the old Lawra District recorded 67,721 inhabitants in the Nandom-Lambussie Local Council and 88,453 in the Lawra-Jirapa Local Council. For the history of the Lawra Confederacy Native Authority that was formed out of the Lawra, Jirapa, Nandom, and Lambussie chiefdoms in 1935 and became the basis of all local and district councils, see Lentz, *Ethnicity*, 107–12, 183–87, 219–21.

49. NYDA, Petition for the creation of a district for the Nandom Traditional Area, presented during the NYDA national delegates' conference, December 1986, 6.

50. Interviews with Jirapa-Lambussie District Secretary Jacob Boon, 23 November 1989; Lambussie Kuoro K. Y. Baloro, 28 November 1989 and 2 December 1994; and Bawa Salifu Dy-Yakah 2 December 1992, Tamale, and 31 August 1993, Berlin.

51. See, for instance, the letter signed by the "tribal Heads of the Dagarti, Moshi, Wala, Wangara, Grunshi, Kantosi, Zambrama and Fulani" to District Secretary Lawra, 31 March 1987. On the history of conflicts over Hamile's political allegiance, see Lentz, *Ethnicity*, 188–98, 221–27.

52. Lawra District Secretary to Lambussie Kuoro, Nandom Naa, and others, 5 May 1987; on the "peace agreement," see also *People's Daily Graphic*, 11 July 1987.

53. On the migration history of his family, see chapter 4, 173–75.

54. Summary of decisions taken at a meeting of Lambussie Kuoro, Nandom Naa, and their respective Tindanas with His Grace Archbishop P. P. Dery, Hamile, 23 January 1990. See also the report in *People's Daily Graphic*, 27 January 1990.

55. Summary of decisions, 23 January 1990.

56. Interview with Archbishop Peter Dery, 17 November 1990, Tamale.

57. NYDA National Chairman to Ag Director Castle Information Bureau, Accra, 25 May 1989.

58. Constitution of the Republic of Ghana, 1992, § 257.

59. Quoted in *People's Daily Graphic*, 27 May 1989.

60. Nansie Issifu Tomo and Soglikuu Saakum to Lawra District Security Committee, 26 September 1988.

61. Gaamuo Mwinpuo Le-ib et al. to Lawra District Security Committee, 19 October 1988.

62. *Local Politics*, 68–70, emphasis in original.

63. I could not obtain a copy of this letter written late 1987 or early 1988, but I reconstruct its contents from quotations presented in letters by the NYDA chairman and Prof. Benedict Der, University of Cape Coast, to the Upper West Regional Secretary, 8 February and 20 April 1988 respectively.

64. On the long-standing debate on whether the Dagara are actually "Lobi," see Lentz, *Ethnicity*, 79–86, 259–63.

65. Prof. Benedict Der, University of Cape Coast, to the Upper West Regional Secretary, 20 April 1988. For a fuller discussion of the "Dagomba"-origin hypothesis, see Lentz, "A Dagara Rebellion."

66. On the colonial creation of ethnic boundaries in North-Western Ghana, see Lentz, *Ethnicity*; on Ghana's foundational idea of the nation as a federation of native states, see Lentz and Nugent, eds., *Ethnicity in Ghana*, 6–10, 17–24.

67. Sara Dorman, Daniel Hammett, and Paul Nugent, "Introduction: Citizenship and Its Casualties in Africa," in *Making Nations, Creating Strangers: States and Citizenship in Africa*, eds. Dorman, Hammett, and Nugent (Leiden: Brill, 2007), 10.

68. NYDA National Chairman to Ag Director Castle Information Bureau, Accra, 26 May 1989. The use of the term "Dagaaba"—instead of Dagara—in this letter draws on the ethnic

terminology dominant in the public sphere and reflects NYDA's desire to mobilize the widest possible ethnic front for their cause. In other contexts, NYDA insisted that Dagara is the only correct term for the entire ethnic group, including the Dagaba of Jirapa. For more details, see Lentz, *Ethnicity*, 259–63.

69. Group discussion with Peter Der, Dr Edward Gyader et al., 15 Nov. 1989, Wa.

70. Interview with Vito Banu, 30 January 1990, Accra. Similar arguments were voiced in interviews with Jirapa-Lambussie District Secretary Jacob Boon, 23 November 1989; Lambussie Kuoro K. Y. Baloro, 28 November 1989 and 2 December 1994; and Bawa Salifu Dy-Yakah 2 December 1992, Tamale, and 31 August 1993, Berlin.

71. Tania Murray Li, "Articulating Indigenous Identity in Indonesia: Resource Politics and the Tribal Slot," *Comparative Studies in Society and History* 42 (2000): 149–68.

72. Jean-Pierre Chauveau and Paul Richards, "West African Insurgencies in Agrarian Perspective: Côte d'Ivoire and Sierra Leone Compared," *Journal of Agrarian Change* 8, no. 4 (2008): 515–52.

73. Ibid., 517.

74. Ibid., 545.

75. Ibid., 517.

76. Ibid., 522.

77. Ibid.

78. Derman, Odgaard, and Sjaastad, eds., *Conflicts over Land*. For Ghana, see the example discussed by Amanor ("Night Harvesters") of violent youth gangs attacking forest guards who were organized by urban businessmen in order to protect their economic stakes; for violence related to the politicization of land rights in Ghana's Northern Region, see on the Dagomba-Konkomba wars Artur Bogner, "The 1994 Civil War in Northern Ghana: The Genesis and Escalation of a 'Tribal' Conflict," in *Ethnicity in Ghana*, eds. Lentz and Nugent, 183–203; Hippolyte A. S. Pul, "Citizenship, Exclusion and Ethnic Conflict in the Post-colonial State," *African Anthropologist* 12, no. 1 (2005): 65–99; and Benjamin Talton, *Politics of Social Change in Ghana: The Konkomba Struggle for Political Equality* (New York: Palgrave Macmillan, 2010).

79. See, for instance, Konings, *The State*; Mahir Saul, "Money and Land Tenure as Factors in Farm Size Differentiation in Burkina Faso," in *Land and Society in Contemporary Africa*, eds. Richard E. Downs and Stephen P. Reyna, 243–79 (Hanover: University Press of New England 1988); Berry, *Chiefs*; Laube, *Changing Natural Resource Regimes*; and Lund, *Local Politics*.

80. Geschiere and Gugler, "The Politics of Primary Patriotism."

81. Lund, *Local Politics*, 179.

82. Peters, "The Limits of Negotiability"; Peters, "Inequality."

83. See Chauveau, "Question foncière"; Chauveau, "How Does an Institution Evolve?"; and Toulmin, "Negotiating Access to Land."

84. For examples, see Konings, *The State*; Saul, "Money and Land Tenure"; the contributions in Downs and Reyna, eds., *Land and Society*; Mitzi Goheen, "Chiefs, Sub-Chiefs and Local Control: Negotiations over Land, Struggles over Meaning," *Africa* 62 (1992): 389–412; and Laube, *Changing Natural Resource Regimes*, 321–28.

85. See, for instance, Amanor, "Night Harvesters"; Amanor, "Customary Land"; Amanor, "Conflicts"; Ubink, "Negotiated or Negated?"; and Ubink and Amanor, eds., *Contesting Land*.

86. Peters, "Inequality," 306.

87. Ibid., 270.

88. Bernstein, "Rural Land."

89. Hall, Hirsch, and Li, *Powers of Exclusion*, 4.

90. Lund, *Local Politics*, 9.

91. Toulmin, "Negotiating Access to Land"; Cotula, *Changes*.

92. See also Lobnibe's case study of Dagara farmers' involvement in boundary disputes in the Brong Ahafo Region ("Legitimating a Contested Boundary"), and Jacob's account of the role of Mossi immigrants among the Winye in Burkina Faso (Jacob, *La tradition*; and Jean-Pierre Jacob, "Imposer son tutorat foncier."

93. Lund, *Local Politics*, 179.

94. Berry, *Chiefs*; Amanor, "Customary Land."

References

Abdul-Korah and Paul Kantunye. "History of the Dagaaba with Special Reference to the Man-laala." B.A. thesis, University of Ghana, Department of History, 1980.

Abobo, Salvius Anthony Claret. "A History of the Jirapa Traditional Area from the Early Settlement to 1980." B.A. thesis, University of Cape Coast, Department of History, 1994.

Abramson, Allen. "Mythical Land, Legal Boundaries: Wondering about Landscape and Other Tracts." In *Land, Law and Environment: Mythical Land, Legal Boundaries*, edited by Allen Abramson and Dimitrios Theodossopoulos, 8–14. London: Pluto Press, 2000.

Ackermann, Andreas. "Ethnologische Migrationsforschung: Ein Überblick." *Kea–Zeitschrift für Kulturwissenschaften* 10 (1997): 1–28.

Adepoju, Aderanti. "Migration in Africa: An Overview." In *The Migration Experience in Africa*, edited by Jonathan Baker and Tade Akin Aina, 87–108. Uppsala: Nordiska Afri-kainstitutet, 1995.

Alhassan et al. "Report by the Committee on Ownership of Lands and Position of Tenants in the Northern and Upper Regions." Unpublished report. Accra, 1978.

Allan, William. *The African Husbandman*. Edinburgh: Oliver and Boyd, 1965.

Allman, Jean, and John Parker. *Tongnaab: The History of a West African God*. Bloomington: Indiana University Press, 2005.

Allott, Antony N. *Essays in African Law, with Special Reference to the Law of Ghana*. London: Butterworth, 1960.

Amanor, Kojo. "Night Harvesters, Forest Hoods, and Saboteurs: Struggles over Land Expro-priation in Ghana." In *Reclaiming the Land: The Resurgence of Rural Movements in Africa, Asia and Latin America*, edited by Sam Moyo and Paris Yeros, 102–17. London: Zed Books, 2005.

——. "Customary Land, Mobile Labor and Alienation in the Eastern Region of Ghana." In *Land and the Politics of Belonging in West Africa*, edited by Richard Kuba and Carola Lentz, 137–60. Leiden: Brill, 2006.

——. "Conflicts and the Reinterpretation of Customary Tenure in Ghana." In *Conflicts over Land and Water in Africa*, edited by Bill Derman, Rie Odgaard and Espen Sjaastad, 33–59. Oxford: James Currey, 2007.

——. "Family Values, Land Sales and Agricultural Commodification in South-eastern Ghana." *Africa* 80, no. 1 (2010): 104–25.

Amanor, Kojo S., and Janine Ubink. "Contesting Land and Custom in Ghana: Introduction." In *Contesting Land and Custom in Ghana: State, Chief and Citizen*, edited by Janine M. Ubink and Kojo S. Amanor, 9–26. Leiden: Leiden University Press, 2009.

Appadurai, Arju. "The Past as a Scarce Resource." *Man* 16 (1981): 201–19.

Arhin, Kwame, ed. *The Papers of George Ekem Ferguson, a Fanti Official of the Government of the Gold Coast, 1890–1897*. Leiden: African Studies Centre, 1974.

Asiwaju, A. I. "The Concept of Frontier in the Setting of States in Pre-colonial Africa." *Présence Africaine* 127–28 (1983): 43–49.

———, ed. *Partitioned Africans: Ethnic Relations across Africa's International Boundaries, 1884–1984.* London: Hurst, 1985.

Asiwaju, A. I., and P. O. Adenyi, eds. *Borderlands in Africa: A Multidisciplinary and Comparative Focus on Nigeria and West Africa.* Lagos: University of Lagos Press, 1989.

Austin, Gareth. *Labour, Land and Capital in Ghana: From Slavery to Free Labour in Asante, 1807–1956.* Rochester: University of Rochester Press, 2005.

———. "The Political Economy of the Natural Environment in West African History: Asante and Its Savanna Neighbors in the Nineteenth and Twentieth Centuries." In *Land and the Politics of Belonging in West Africa*, edited by Richard Kuba and Carola Lentz, 187–212. Leiden: Brill, 2006.

Bär, Thorsten. "'On a trouvé une forêt vierge'. Légitimation des revendications foncières dans les traditions orales de Fafo." In *Les Dagara et leurs voisins. Histoire de peuplement et relations interethniques au sud-ouest du Burkina Faso*, edited by Richard Kuba, Carola Lentz, and Katja Werthmann, 115–23. Frankfurt/Main: *Berichte des Sonderforschungsbereichs 268*, no. 15 (2001).

Barnard, Alan, and James Woodburn. "Property, Power and Ideology in Hunter-Gatherer Societies: An Introduction." In *Hunters and Gatherers*, vol. 2, edited by Tim Ingold, David Riches, and James Woodburn, 4–31. Oxford: Berg, 1997.

Barrows, Richard, and Michael Roth. "Land Tenure and Investment in African Agriculture: Theory and Evidence." *Journal of Modern African Studies* 28 (1990): 265–97.

Bassett, Thomas J. "Introduction: The Land Question and Agricultural Transformation in Sub-Saharan Africa." In *Land in African Agrarian Systems*, edited by Bassett and Donald E. Crummey, 3–31. Madison: University of Wisconsin Press, 1993.

Bassett, Thomas J., and Donald E. Crummey, eds. *Land in African Agrarian Systems.* Madison: University of Wisconsin Press, 1993.

Beidelman, Thomas O. "Myth, Legend and Oral History: A Kaguru Traditional Text." *Anthropos* 65 (1970): 74–97.

Bell, Duran. "The Social Relations of Property and Efficiency." In *Property in Economic Context,* edited by Robert C. Hunt and Antonio Gilman, 29–45. Lanham, Md.: University Press of America, 1998.

Bemile, Sebastian. "Promotion of Ghanaian Languages and Its Impact on National Unity: The Dagara Language Case." In *Ethnicity in Ghana: The Limits of Invention*, edited by Carola Lentz and Paul Nugent, 204–25. London: Macmillan, 2000.

Benda-Beckmann, Franz von. "Multiple Legal Constructions of Socio-Economic Spaces: Resource Management and Conflict in the Central Moluccas." In *Frontiers and Borderlands: Anthroplogical Perspectives*, edited by Michael Rösler and Tobias Wendl, 131–58. Frankfurt/Main: Peter Lang, 1999.

Benda-Beckmann, Keebet von. "Forum Shopping and Shopping Forums: Dispute Processing in a Minang Kaban Village in West Sumatra." *Journal of Legal Pluralism* 19 (1981): 117–59.

Benda-Beckmann, Franz, and Keebet von Benda-Beckman. "A Functional Analysis of Property Rights with Special Reference to Indonesia." In *Property Rights and Economic Development: Land and Natural Resources in Southeast Asia and Oceania*, edited by Toon van Meijl and Franz von Benda-Beckmann, 15–56. London: Kegan Paul, 1999.

———. "The Dynamics of Change and Continuity in Plural Legal Orders." *Journal of Legal Pluralism and Unofficial Law* 53/54 (2006): 1–44.

Bening, Raymond B. "Indigenous Concepts of Boundaries and Significance of Administrative Stations and Boundaries in Northern Ghana." *Bulletin of the Ghana Geographical Association* 15 (1973): 7–20.

———. "Land Tenure System and Traditional Agriculture of the Sissala." *Bulletin of the Ghana Geographical Association* 18 (1976): 15–34.

———. "Land Policy and Administration in Northern Ghana." *Transactions of the Historical Society of Ghana* 16 (1995): 227–66.

Benjaminsen, Tor A., and Christian Lund, eds. *Securing Land Rights in Africa*. London: Frank Cass, 2003.

Benoit, Michel. *Oiseaux de mil. Les Mossi du Bwamu (Haute-Volta)*. Paris: ORSTOM, 1982.

Berliner, David. "The Abuses of Memory: Reflections on the Memory Boom in Anthropology." *Anthropological Quarterly* 78, no. 1 (2005): 197–211.

Berman, Bruce. "Ethnicity, Patronage and the African State: The Politics of Uncivil Nationalism." *African Affairs* 97 (1998): 305–41.

Bernstein, Henry. "Rural Land and Land Conflicts in Sub-Saharan Africa." In *Reclaiming the Land: The Resurgence of Rural Movements in Africa, Asia and Latin America*, edited by Sam Moyo and Paris Yeros, 67–101. London: Zed Books, 2005.

Berry, Sara. "Hegemony on a Shoestring: Indirected Rule and Access to Agricultural Land." *Africa* 62, no. 3 (1992): 327–55.

———. *No Condition Is Permanent: The Social Dynamics of Agrarian Change in Sub-Saharan Africa*. Madison: University of Wisconsin Press, 1993.

———. *Chiefs Know Their Boundaries: Essays on Property, Power and the Past in Asante, 1896–1996*. Oxford: James Currey, 2001.

———. "Debating the Land Question in Africa." *Comparative Studies in Society and History* 44 (2002): 638–68.

———. "Privatization and the Politics of Belonging in West Africa." In *Land and the Politics of Belonging in West Africa*, edited by Richard Kuba and Carola Lentz, 241–63. Leiden: Brill, 2006.

———. "Property, Authority and Citizenship: Land Claims, Politics and the Dynamics of Social Division." In *The Politics of Possession: Property, Authority, and Access to Natural Resources*, edited by Thomas Sikor and Christian Lund, 23–45. Oxford: Wiley Blackwell, 2009.

Biebuyck, Daniel, ed. *African Agrarian Systems*. London: Oxford University Press, 1963.

Bierschenk, Thomas. *Die Fulbe Nordbenins. Geschichte, soziale Organisation, Wirtschaftsweise*. Hamburg: Lit, 1997.

Bierschenk, Thomas, and Jean-Pierre Olivier de Sardan. "Les arènes locales face à la décentralisation et à la démocratisation." In *Les pouvoirs au village. Le Bénin rural entre démocratisation et décentralisation*, edited by Bierschenk and Olivier de Sardan, 11–51. Paris: Karthala, 1998.

Binger, Captain Louis. *Du Niger au Golfe de Guinée*. Vol. 2. Paris: Librairie Hachette, 1892.

Blum, Carol. "Of Women and Land: Legitimizing Husbandry." In *Early Modern Conceptions of Property*, edited by John Brewer and Susan Staves, 161–69. London: Routledge, 1995.

Bogner, Artur. "The 1994 Civil War in Northern Ghana: The Genesis and Escalation of a 'Tribal' Conflict.'" In *Ethnicity in Ghana: The Limits of Invention*, edited by Carola Lentz and Paul Nugent: 183–203. London: Macmillan, 2000.

Bohannan, Laura. "A Genealogical Charter." *Africa* 22 (1952): 301–15.

Bohannan, Paul. "The Migration and Expansion of the Tiv." *Africa* 24 (1954): 2–16.

———. "'Land,' 'Tenure' and Land-Tenure." In *African Agrarian Systems*, edited by Daniel Biebuyck, 101–15. London: Oxford University Press, 1963.

———. "Africa's Land." In *Tribal and Peasant Economies*, edited by George Dalton, 51–60. Austin: University of Texas Press, 1967.

Bonekang, John Nobabaare. "The History of the Dagaba: A Case Study of the People of Tizza." B.A. thesis, University of Ghana, Department of History, 1978.

Boni, Stefano. "Indigenous Blood and Foreign Labor: The Ancestralization of Land Rights in Sefwi (Ghana)." In *Land and the Politics of Belonging in West Africa*, edited by Richard Kuba and Carola Lentz, 161–86. Leiden: Brill, 2006.

Bonnafé, Pierre, Michèle Fiéloux, and Jeanne-Marie Kambou. "Un vent de folie? Le conflit armé dans une population sans état. Les Lobi de Haute-Volta." In *Guerres de lignages et guerres d'états en Afrique*, edited by Jean Bazin and Emmanuel Terray, 73–141. Paris: Karthala, 1982.

Boone, Catherine. *Political Topographies of the African State: Territorial Authority and Institutional Choice*. Cambridge: Cambridge University Press, 2003.

———. "Africa's New Territorial Politics: Regionalism and the Open Economy in Côte d'Ivoire." *African Studies Review* 50 (2007): 59–81.

———. "Property and Constitutional Order: Land Tenure Reform and the Future of the African State." *African Affairs* 106, no. 425 (2007): 557–86.

Boutillier, Jean Louis. *Les structures foncières en Haute-Volta*. Vol. 5, *Études voltaïques*, Mémoires. Ouagadougou: IFAN-ORSTOM, 1964.

Brettell, Caroline B. "Theorizing Migration in Anthropology: The Social Construction of Networks, Identities, Communities, and Global Scapes." In *Migration Theory: Talking across Disciplines*, edited by Brettell and James F. Hollifield, 97–135, London: Routledge, 2000.

Breusers, Mark. *On the Move: Mobility, Land Use and Livelihood Practices on the Central Plateau in Burkina Faso*. Münster: Lit, 1999.

Brewer, John, and Susan Staves, eds. *Early Modern Conceptions of Property*. London: Routledge, 1995.

———. Introduction to *Early Modern Conceptions of Poperty*, edited by Brewer and Staves, 1–18. London: Routledge, 1995.

Brubaker, Rogers, and Frederick Cooper. "Beyond 'Identity.'" *Theory and Society* 29 (2000): 1–47.

Bruce, John W. "Do Indigenous Tenure Systems Constrain Agricultural Development?" In *Land in African Agrarian Systems*, edited by Thomas J. Bassett and Donald E. Crummey, 35–56. Madison: University of Wisconsin Press, 1993.

Bruce, John W., and Shem Migot-Adholla, eds. *Searching for Land Tenure Security in Africa*. Washington D.C.: World Bank and Kendall Hunt, 1994.

BUNASOL, ed. *Caractérisation des sols du centre-sud de la province de la Sissili et esquisse pédologique*. Rapport technique No. 69. Ouagadougou, 1990.

Bürger, Ursula. "Installation pacifique ou appropriation violente de terre? Réflexions sur l'histoire de l'installation des Phuo à Bonzan." In *Les Dagara et leurs voisins. Histoire de peuplement et relations interethniques au sud-ouest du Burkina Faso*, edited by Richard Kuba, Carola Lentz and Katja Werthmann, 131–40. Frankfurt/Main: *Berichte des Sonderforschungsbereichs 268*, no. 15 (2001).

Cardinall, A. W. *The Natives of the Northern Territories of the Gold Coast*. London: Routledge, 1920.

———. *The Gold Coast 1931*. Accra: Government Printer, 1931.

Casimir, Michael J. "The Dimensions of Territoriality: An Introduction." In *Mobility and Territoriality: Social and Spatial Boundaries among Foragers, Fishers, Pastoralists and Peripatetics*, edited by Casimir and Aparna Rao, 1–26. Oxford: Berg, 1992.

Center for Democracy and Development, Ghana. *Corruption and Other Constraints on the Land Market and Land Administration in Ghana: A Preliminary Investigation*. CDD–Ghana Research Paper 4. Accra, 2000.

Ceuppens, Bambi, and Peter Geschiere. "Autochthony: Local or Global? New Modes in the Struggle over Citizenship and Belonging in Africa and Europe." *Annual Review of Anthropology* 34 (2005): 385–407.

Chanock, Martin. *Law, Custom and Social Order: The Colonial Experience in Malawi and Zambia*. Cambridge: Cambridge University Press, 1985.

———. "Paradigms, Policies and Property: A Review of the Customary Law of Land Tenure." In *Law in Colonial Africa*, edited by Kristin Mann and Richard Roberts, 61–84. Portsmouth, N.H.: Heinemann, 1991.

Chauveau, Jean-Pierre. "Jeu foncier, institutions d'accès à la ressource et usage de la ressource. Une étude de cas dans le centre-ouest ivoirien.' In *Le modèle ivoirien en question. Crises, ajustements, recompositions*, edited by Bernard Contamin and Harris Memel-Fôté, 325–60. Paris: Karthala, 1997.

———. "The Land Question in Côte d'Ivoire: A Lesson in History." International Institute for Environment and Development: *Issue Papers* 95 (2000).

———. "Question foncière et construction nationale en Côte d'Ivoire." *Politique Africaine* 78 (2000): 94–125.

———. "How Does an Institution Evolve? Land, Politics, Intergenerational Relations and the Institution of the *Tutorat* amongst Autochthones and Immigrants (Gban Region, Côte d'Ivoire)." In *Land and the Politics of Belonging in West Africa*, edited by Richard Kuba and Carola Lentz, 213–40. Leiden: Brill, 2006.

———. "La loi de 1998 sur les droits fonciers coutûmiers dans l'histoire des politiques foncières en Côte d'Ivoire. Une économie politique des transferts de droits entre 'autochtones' et 'étrangers' en zone forestière." Paper presented at the LASDEL, Niamey, 2007.

Chauveau, Jean-Pierre, Jean-Pierre Jacob, and Pierre-Yves Le Meur. "L'organisation de la mobilité dans les sociétés rurales du Sud." *Autrepart* 30 (2004): 3–23.

Chauveau, Jean-Pierre, and Paul Richards. "West African Insurgencies in Agrarian Perspective: Côte d'Ivoire and Sierra Leone Compared." *Journal of Agrarian Change* 8, no. 4 (2008): 515–52.

Cohen, David William. "The Undefining of Oral Tradition." *Ethnohistory* 36 (1989): 9–17.

———. "La Fontaine and Wamimbi: The Anthropology of 'Time-Present' as the Substructure of Historical Oration." In *Chronotypes: The Construction of Time*, edited by John Bender and David E. Wellbery, 205–25. Stanford: Stanford University Press, 1991.

Colin, Jean-Philippe. "Lorsque le Far East n'était pas le Far West. La dynamique de l'appropriation foncière dans un ancien 'no man's land' de basse Côte d'Ivoire." *Autrepart* 30 (2004): 45–62.

Colin, Jean-Philippe et al. "Outside the Autochthon-Migrant Configuration: Access to Land, Land Conflicts and Interethnic Relationships in a Former Pioneer Area (Lower Côte d'Ivoire)." *IRD Réfo, Document de travail de l'Unité de Recherche 095* 10 (2004).

Colin, Jean-Philippe, and Philip Woodhouse. "Introduction: Interpreting Land Markets in Africa." *Africa* 80, no. 1 (2010): 1–13.

Colson, Elizabeth. "The Impact of the Colonial Period on the Definition of Land Rights." In *Colonialism in Africa, 1870–1960*, vol. 3 of *Profiles of Change: African Society and Colonial Rule*, edited by Victor Turner, 193–215. Cambridge: Cambridge University Press, 1971.

———. "Places of Power and Shrines of the Land." *Paideuma* 43 (1997): 47–57.

Coquéry-Vidrovitch, Catherine. "Le régime foncier rural en Afrique noire." In *Enjeux fonciers en Afrique noire*, edited by Émile Le Bris et al., 65–84. Paris: Karthala, 1982.

Cordell, Dennis D., Joel W. Gregory, and Victor Piché. *Hoe and Wage: A Social History of a Circular Migration System in West Africa*. Boulder: Westview Press, 1996.

Cotula, Lorenzo, ed. *Changes in "Customary" Land Tenure Systems in Africa*. London: International Institute for Environment and Development (IIED), 2007.

Crook, Richard. "Access to Justice and Land Disputes in Ghana's State Courts: The Litigants' Perspective." *Journal of Legal Pluralism and Unofficial Law* 50 (2004): 1–28.

Crook, Richard et al. *The Law, Legal Institutions and the Protection of Land Rights in Ghana and Côte d'Ivoire: Developing a More Effective and Equitable System*. Institute of Development Studies, Research Report 58. Brighton: University of Sussex, 2007.

Cros, Michèle, and Daniel Dory. "Pour une approche écologique des guerres Lobi." *Cultures et Développement* 19 (1984): 465–84.

Crousse, Bernard, Émile Le Bris, and Étienne le Roy, eds. *Espaces disputés en Afrique noire. Pratiques foncières locales*. Paris: Karthala, 1986.

Dacher, Michèle. "Organisation politique d'une sociéte acéphale. Les Gouin du Burkina Faso." *L'Homme* 144 (1997): 7–29.

Dasah, James. "Ulo: The History of a Dagaba Kingdom." B.A. thesis, University of Ghana, Department of History, 1974.

Dawson, Allan Charles. "Earth Shrines and Autochthony among the Konkomba of Northern Ghana." In *Shrines in Africa: History, Politics, and Society*, edited by Dawson, 71–94. Calgary: Calgary University Press, 2009.

———. Introduction to *Shrines in Africa: History, Politics, and Society*, edited by Dawson, vii–xvii. Calgary: Calgary University Press, 2009.

De Bruijn, Mirjam, Rijk van Dijk, and Dick Foeken. "Mobile Africa: An Introduction." In *Mobile Africa: Changing Patterns of Movement in Africa and Beyond*, edited by de Bruijn et al., 1–7. Leiden: Brill, 2001.

Delafosse, Maurice. *Les frontières de la Côte d'Ivoire, de la Côte d'Or et du Soudan*. Paris: Masson, 1908.

Der, Benedict. "Colonial Land Policy in the Northern Territories of the Gold Coast, 1900–1957." *Universitas* 4 (1975): 127–42.

———. "The Origins of the Dagara–Dagaba." *Papers in Dagara Studies* 1, no. 1 (1989).

———. *The Slave Trade in Northern Ghana*. Accra: Woeli Publishing, 1998.

Derman, Bill, Rie Odgaard, and Espen Sjaastad. Introduction to *Conflicts over Land and Water in Africa*, edited by Derman, Odgaard, and Sjaastad, 1–30. Oxford: James Currey, 2007.

Diallo, Youssouf. "Processes and Types of Pastoral Migration in Northern Côte d'Ivoire." In *Mobile Africa: Changing Patterns of Movement in Africa and Beyond*, edited by Mirjam de Bruijn et al., 153–68. Leiden: Brill, 2001.

Dittmer, Kunz. "Die Obervolta-Provinz." In *Die Völker Afrikas und ihre traditionellen Kulturen*, pt. 2, edited by Hermann Baumann, 495–542. Wiesbaden: Franz Steiner, 1979.

Dobler, Gregor. "Boundary Drawing and the Notion of Territoriality in Pre-Colonial and Early Colonial Ovamboland." *Journal of Namibian Studies* 3 (2008): 7–30.

Dorman, Sara, Daniel Hammett, and Paul Nugent. "Introduction: Citizenship and Its Casualties in Africa." In *Making Nations, Creating Strangers: States and Citizenship in Africa*, edited by Dorman, Hammett, and Nugent, 3–26. Leiden: Brill, 2007.

Dorward, David C. "Ethnography and Administration: A Study of Anglo-Tiv 'Working Misunderstanding.'" *Journal of African History* 15 (1974): 457–77.

Downs, R. E., and S. P. Reyna, eds. *Land and Society in Contemporary Africa.* Hanover: University Press of New England, 1988.

Droz, Yvan. *Migrations kikuyus. Des pratiques sociales à l'imaginaire.* Neuchâtel: Editions de l'Institut d'ethnologie, 1999.

Duperray, Anne-Marie. *Les Gourounsi de Haute-Volta.* Wiesbaden: Franz Steiner, 1984.

Engberg-Pedersen, Lars. *Endangering Development: Politics, Projects, and Environment in Burkina Faso.* London: Praeger, 2003.

Ensminger, Jean. "Changing Property Rights: Reconciling Formal and Informal Rights to Land in Africa." In *The Frontiers of the New Institutional Economics*, edited by John N. Drobak and John V. C. Nye, 170–75. New York: Academic Press, 1997.

Eyre-Smith, R. St. John. *A Brief Review of the History and Social Organisation of the Peoples of the Northern Territories of the Gold Coast.* Accra: Government Printer, 1933.

Faure, Armelle. "Délimitation des terroirs. Bilan synthétique à partir des exemples burkinabé." In *Quelles politiques foncières en Afrique? Réconcilier pratiques, légitimité et légalité*, edited by Philippe Lavigne Delville, 497–503. Paris: Karthala, 1998.

Feder, Gershon, and David Feeny. "Land Tenure and Property Rights: Theory and Implications for Development Policy." *World Bank Economic Review* 5 (1991): 135–53.

Feder, Gershon, and R. Noronha. "Land Rights Systems and Agricultural Development in Sub-Saharan Africa." *World Bank Research Observer* 2 (1987): 143–89.

Feyissa, Dereje. "Land and the Politics of Identity: The Case of Anywaa-Nuer Relations in the Gambella Region." In *Competing Jurisdictions: Settling Land Claims in Africa*, edited by Sandra Evers, M. Spierenburg, and H. Wels, 203–22. Leiden: Brill, 2005.

Fiéloux, Michèle. *Les sentiers de la nuit. Les migrations rurales Lobi de la Haute-Volta vers la Côte d'Ivoire.* Paris: ORSTOM, 1980.

Fikry, Mona. "Wa: A Case Study of Social Values and Social Tensions as Reflected in the Oral Testimonies of the Wala of Northern Ghana." Ph.D. diss., Indiana University, 1969.

Firmin-Seller, Kathryn. *The Transformation of Property Rights in the Gold Coast.* Cambridge: Cambridge University Press, 1996.

———. "Institutions, Context and Outcomes: Explaining French and British Rule in West Africa." *Comparative Politics* 33 (2000): 253–72.

Fortman, Louise. "Talking Claims: Discursive Strategies in Contesting Property." *World Development* 23 (1995): 1053–63.

Ganne, Bernard, and Moussa Ouedraogo. "'Local,' 'politique' et 'territoire'. Essai d'économie politique autour d'une ville moyenne. L'évolution de Ouahigouya au Burkina Faso." In *Petites et moyennes villes d'Afrique noire*, edited by Monique Bertrand and Alain Dubresson, 223–40. Paris: Karthala, 1997.

Gausset, Quentin. "L'aspect foncier dans les conflits entre autochtones et migrants au sud-ouest du Burkina Faso." *Politique africaine* 112 (2008): 52–66.

Geisler, Charles C., and Gail Daneker, eds. *Property and Values: Alternatives to Public and Private Ownership.* Washington: Island Press, 2000.

Gensler, Marlis. "'Une foi loti . . .'. Bodenrecht und Siedlungsgeschichte in einer westafrikanischen Kleinstadt (Diébougou, Burkina Faso)." *Working Papers of the Department of Anthropology and African Studies of the Johannes Gutenberg University of Mainz* 14 (2002).

Geschiere, Peter. *The Perils of Belonging*. Chicago: University of Chicago Press, 2009.

Geschiere, Peter, and Joseph Gugler. "The Politics of Primary Patriotism." Special issue, *Africa* 68 (1998): 309–19.

Geschiere, Peter, and Stephen Jackson. "Autochthony and the Crisis of Citizenship: Democratization, Decentralization, and the Politics of Belonging." *African Studies Review* 49, no. 2 (2006): 1–14.

Geschiere, Peter, and Francis Nyamnjoh. "Capitalism and Autochthony: The Seesaw of Mobility and Belonging." *Public Culture* 12 (2000): 423–52.

Godelier, Maurice. "Territory and Property in Primitive Society." In *Human Ethology*, edited by Mario von Cranach et al., 133–55. Cambridge: Cambridge University Press, 1979.

Goheen, Mitzi. "Chiefs, Sub-chiefs and Local Control: Negotiations over Land, Struggles over Meaning." *Africa* 62 (1992): 389–412.

Goislard, Cathérine. "Esquisse d'une gestion foncière plurale. Banfora (Burkina Faso)." In *Petites et moyennes villes d'Afrique noire*, edited by Monique Bertrand and Alain Dubresson, 163–77. Paris: Karthala, 1997.

Goody, Jack. *The Social Organisation of the LoWiili*. London: H. M. Stationery Office, 1956.

———. "Fields of Social Control among the LoDagaba." *Journal of the Royal Anthropological Institute of Great Britain and Ireland* 87 (1957): 75–104.

———. "The Fission of Domestic Groups among the LoDagaba." In *The Developmental Cycle in Domestic Groups*, edited by Goody, 53–91. Cambridge: Cambridge University Press, 1958.

———. "The Mother's Brother and the Sister's Son in West Africa." *Journal of the Royal Anthropological Institute* 89 (1959): 61–88.

———. "Marriage Policy and Incorporation in Northern Ghana." In *From Tribe to Nation in Africa*, edited by Ronald Cohen and John Middleton, 114–49. Scranton: Chandler, 1970.

———. *Technology, Tradition and the State in Africa*. London: Oxford University Press, 1971.

———. "Oral Tradition and the Reconstruction of the Past in Northern Ghana." In *Fonti orali—Oral Sources—Sources orales*, edited by Bernado Bernardi, Carlo Poni, and Alessandro Triulzi, 285–95. Mailand: Angeli, 1978.

———. "Rice Burning and the Green Revolution in Northern Ghana." *Journal of Development Studies* 16 (1980): 136–55.

———. "Peuplement. Études comparatives, Nord-Ghana et Burkina Faso." In *Images d'Afrique et sciences sociales. Les pays lobi, birifor et dagara*, edited by Michèle Fiéloux, Jacques Lombard and Jeanne-Marie Kambou-Ferrand, 51–55. Paris: Karthala, 1993.

Goody, Jack, and S. W. D. K. Gandah. *The Third Bagre: A Myth Revisited*. Durham: Carolina Academic Press, 2002.

Gough, Katherine V., and Paul W. K. Yankson. "Land Markets in African Cities: The Case of Peri-urban Accra, Ghana." *Urban Studies* 37 (2000): 2485–500.

Gray, Leslie C. "Investing in Soil Quality: Farmer Responses to Land Scarcity in Southwestern Burkina Faso." In *African Savannas: Global Narratives and Local Knowledge of Environmental Change*, edited by Thomas J. Bassett and Donald Crummey, 72–90. Oxford: James Currey, 2003.

Haberecht, Svenja. "'Gemeinsam bauen wir eine neue Nation!' Das Cinquantenaire in Burkina Faso." In *Staatsinszenierung, Erinnerungsmarathon und Volksfest. Afrika feiert 50 Jahre*

Unabhängigkeit, edited by Carola Lentz and Godwin Kornes, 194–210. Frankfurt/Main: Brandes and Apsel, 2011.

Hagberg, Sten. *Between Peace and Justice: Dispute Settlement between Karaboro Agriculturalists and Fulbe Agro-Pastoralists in Burkina Faso*. Uppsala: Acta Universitatis Upsaliensis, 1998.

———. "Money, Ritual and the Politics of Belonging in Land Transactions in Western Burkina Faso." In *Land and the Politics of Belonging in West Africa*, edited by Richard Kuba and Carola Lentz, 99–118. Leiden: Brill, 2006.

———. "Traditional Chieftaincy, Party Politics, and Political Violence in Burkina Faso." In *State Recognition and Democratization in Sub-Saharan Africa: A New Dawn for Traditional Authorities?* edited by Lars Buur and Helen-Maria Kyed, 131–53. New York: Palgrave Macmillan, 2007.

Hagberg, Sten, and Alexis B. Tengan. *Bonds and Boundaries in Northern Ghana and Southern Burkina Faso*. Uppsala: Acta Universitatis Upsaliensis, 2000.

Hall, Derek, Philip Hirsch, and Tania Murray Li. *Powers of Exclusion: Land Dilemmas in Southeast Asia*. Honolulu: University of Hawai'i Press, 2011.

Hann, Chris M. "Introduction: The Embeddedness of Property." In *Property Relations: Renewing the Anthropological Tradition*, edited by Hann, 1–47. Cambridge: Cambridge University Press, 1998.

———. *Property Relations*. Cambridge: Cambridge University Press, 1998.

Hawkins, Sean. *Writing and Colonialism in Northern Ghana: The Encounter between the LoDagaa and "the World on Paper."* Toronto: University of Toronto Press, 2002.

Hébert, Père Jean. *Esquisse d'une monographie historique du pays Dagara. Par un groupe de Dagara en collaboration avec le père Hébert*. Diébougou: Diocèse de Diébougou, 1976.

Herbert, Eugenia W. *Iron, Gender and Power: Rituals of Transformation in African Societies*. Bloomington: Indiana University Press, 1993.

Hervouët, J. P. "Modes d'utilisation de l'espace et onchocercose." Unpublished document. Abidjan: ORSTOM, 1985.

Hesseling, Gerti. *Pratiques foncières à l'ombre du droit. L'application du droit foncier urbain à Zinguichor*. Leiden: African Studies Centre, 1992.

Hien, Pierre Claver. "Le jeu des frontières en Afrique occidentale. Cent ans de situations conflictuelles au Burkina Faso actuel (1886–1986)." Ph.D. diss., Université de Paris I, 1996.

———. "Frontières et conflits chez les Dagara et leurs voisins au sud-ouest du Burkina Faso (XVIIIème–XIXème siécle)." Frankfurt/Main: *Berichte des Sonderforschungsbereichs 268*, no. 14 (2001): 427–40.

Hilgers, Mathieu. "Les conflits autour de l'histoire de Koudougou (Burkina Faso)." *Cahiers d'études africaines* 47, no. 186 (2007): 313–44.

Hilton, T. E. "Depopulation and Population Movement in the Upper Region of Ghana." *Bulletin of the Ghana Geographical Association* 11, no. 1 (1966): 27–47.

Hobhouse, Leonard T. *Property, Its Duties and Rights*. London: Macmillan, 1915.

Holden, J. J. "The Zaberima Conquest of North-West Ghana." *Transactions of the Historical Society of Ghana* 8 (1965): 60–86.

Horton, Robin. "Stateless Societies in the History of West Africa." In *History of West Africa*, vol. 1, edited by J. F. A. Ajyayi and Michael Crowder, 87–128. London: Longman, 1985.

Hubbell, Andrew. "A View of the Slave Trade from the Margin: Souroudougou in the Late Nineteenth-Century Slave Trade of the Niger Bend." *Journal of African History* 42 (2001): 25–47.

Hunter, J. M. "River Blindness in Nangodi, Northern Ghana: A Hypothesis of Cyclical Advance and Retreat." *Geographical Review* 56 (1966): 389–416.

Ingold, Tim. *The Appropriation of Nature: Essays on Human Ecology and Social Relations.* Manchester: Manchester University Press, 1986.

Insoll, Timothy, Benjamin Kankpeyeng, and Rachel MacLean. "The Archeology of Shrines among the Tallensi of Northern Ghana: Materiality and Interpretive Relevance." In *Shrines in Africa: History, Politics, and Society,* edited by Allan Charles Dawson, 41–70. Calgary: Calgary University Press, 2009.

Jackson, Stephen. "Sons of Which Soil? The Language and Politics of Autochthony in Eastern D. R Congo." *African Studies Review* 49, no. 2 (2006): 95–123.

Jacob, Jean-Pierre. *La tradition du pluralisme institutionnel dans les conflits fonciers entre autochtones. Le cas du Gwendégué (centre Burkina Faso).* Document de travail de l'Unité de Recherche 095, 3. Montpellier: IRD/GRET, 2002.

———. "Imposer son tutorat foncier. Usages autochtones de l'immigration et tradition pluraliste dans le Gwendégué (centre-ouest Burkina Faso)." In *Histoire du peuplement et relations interethniques au Burkina Faso,* edited by Richard Kuba, Carola Lentz, and Claude N. Somda, 75–96. Paris: Karthala, 2003.

———. "Gouvernement de la nature et gouvernement des hommes dans le Gwendégué (centre-ouest du Burkina Faso)." *Autrepart* 30 (2004): 25–43.

Jacob, Jean-Pierre, and Pierre-Yves Le Meur. "Introduction. Citoyenneté locale, foncier, appartenance et reconnaissance dans les sociétés du Sud." In *Politique de la terre et de l'appartenance. Droits fonciers et citoyenneté locale dans les sociétés du Sud,* edited by Jacob and Le Meur, 5–57. Paris: Karthala (2010).

Juul, Kristine, and Christian Lund, eds. *Negotiating Property in Africa.* Portsmouth, N.H.: Heinemann, 2002.

Kambou-Ferrand, Jeanne-Marie. *Peuples voltaïques et conquête coloniale 1885–1914. Burkina-Faso.* Paris: L'Harmattan, 1993.

Kasanga, Kasim. "Land Tenure and Regional Investment Prospects: The Case of the Tenurial Systems of Northern Ghana." *Property Management* 13 (1995): 21–31.

Kasanga, Kasim, and N. A. Kotey. *Land Management in Ghana: Building on Tradition and Modernity.* London: IIED, 2001.

Kemmerer, Cornelia Ann, and Nicole Tannenbaum, eds. *Founders' Cults in Southeast Asia: Ancestors, Polity, and Identity.* New Haven: Yale University Press, 2003.

Kelly, Raymond. *The Nuer Conquest: The Structure and Development of an Expansionist System.* Ann Arbor: University of Michigan Press, 1985.

Kimble, David. *A Political History of Ghana.* Oxford: Clarendon, 1963.

Klein, Martin. "The Slave Trade and Decentralised Societies." *Journal of African History* 42 (2001): 49–65.

Knösel, Didier. "Migration, identité ethnique et pouvoir politique. Les Kufule d'Oronkua." In *Les Dagara et leurs voisins. Histoire de peuplement et relations interethniques au sud-ouest du Burkina Faso,* edited by Richard Kuba, Carola Lentz, and Katja Werthmann, 87–95. Frankfurt/Main: *Berichte des Sonderforschungsbereichs 268,* no. 15 (2001).

Konings, Piet. *The State and Rural Class Formation in Ghana.* London: KPI, 1986.

Konrad-Adenauer-Stiftung, ed. *Decentralisation, Land Tenure and Land Administration in the Northern Region of Ghana.* Seminar Report. Accra: Konrad-Adenauer-Stiftung, 1996.

Kopytoff, Igor. "The Internal African Frontier: The Making of African Political Culture." In *The African Frontier: The Reproduction of Traditional African Societies*, edited by Kopytoff, 3–84. Bloomington: Indiana University Press, 1987.

Kouassigan, Guy-Adjeté. "La nature juridique des droits fonciers coutûmiers." In *Encyclopédie juridique de l'Afrique*, 5: 49–58. Abidjan: Les nouvelles éditions africaines, 1982.

Kristof, Ladis K. J. "The Nature of Frontiers and Boundaries." *Annals of the Association of American Geographers* 49 (1959): 269–82.

Kuba, Richard. "Marking Boundaries and Identities: The Precolonial Expansion of Segmentary Societies in Southwestern Burkina Faso." In *Proceedings of the International Symposium 1999*, 415–26. Frankfurt/Main: *Berichte des Sonderforschungsbereichs 268*, no. 14 (2001).

———. "Comment devenir Pougouli? Stratégies d'inclusion au sud-ouest du Burkina Faso." In *Histoire du peuplement et relations interethniques au Burkina Faso*, edited by Kuba, Carola Lentz, and Claude N. Somda, 137–67. Paris: Karthala, 2003.

———. "La grammaire rituelle des hiérarchies. Migrations et chefs de terre dans une société segmentaire (Burkina Faso)." *Autrepart* 30 (2004): 63–76.

———. "Spiritual Hierarchies and Unholy Alliances: Competing Earth Priests in a Context of Migration in Southwestern Burkina Faso." In *Land and the Politics of Belonging in West Africa*, edited by Kuba and Carola Lentz, 57–76. Leiden: Brill, 2006.

Kuba, Richard, and Carola Lentz. "Arrows and Earth Shrines: Towards a History of Dagara Expansion in Southern Burkina Faso." *Journal of African History* 43 (2002): 377–406.

———, eds. *Land and the Politics of Belonging in West Africa*. Leiden: Brill, 2006.

Kuba, Richard, Carola Lentz, and Katja Werthmann, eds. *Les Dagara et leurs voisins. Histoire de peuplement et relations interethniques au sud-ouest du Burkina Faso*. Frankfurt/Main: *Berichte des Sonderforschungsbereichs 268*, no. 15 (2001).

Kuba, Richard, Carola Lentz, and Claude N. Somda, eds. *Histoire du peuplement et relations interethniques au Burkina Faso*. Paris: Karthala, 2003.

Kuba, Richard, Andrea Reikat, Andrea Wenzek, and Katja Werthmann. "Erdherren und Einwanderer. Bodenrecht in Burkina Faso." In *Mensch und Natur in Westafrika. Ergebnisse aus dem Sonderforschungsbereich 268*, edited by Klaus-Dieter Albert, Doris Löhr, and Katharina Neumann, 373–99. Weinheim: Wiley-VCH, 2004.

Kunbuor, Benjamin. "'Traditional' and State Law in Land Conflicts: Case Studies from the Upper West Region of Ghana." *Working Papers on African Societies* 43 (2000).

———. "Multiple Layers of Land Rights and Multiple Owners: The Case of Land Disputes in the Upper West Region of Ghana." In *Ghana's North: Research on Culture, Religion and Politics in Northern Ghanaian Societies*, edited by Franz Kröger and Barbara Meier, 101–28. Frankfurt/Main: Peter Lang, 2003.

Labouret, Henri. "La guerre dans ses rapports avec les croyances religieuses chez les populations du cercle de Gaoua." *Bulletin du comité d'études historiques et scientifiques de l'AOF* (1916): 289–304.

———. "La chasse et la pêche dans leurs rapports avec les croyances religieuses parmi les populations du Lobi." *Annuaire et mémoires du comité d'études historiques et scientifiques de l'AOF* (1917): 244–76.

———. *Les tribus du rameau Lobi*. Paris: L'Institut d'Ethnologie, 1931.

———. *Nouvelles notes sur les tribus du rameau lobi, leurs migrations, leur évolution, leurs parlers et ceux de leurs voisins*. Dakar: IFAN, 1958.

Lahuec, Jean-Paul. "Contraintes historiques et onchocercose. Une explication des faits de peuplement dans la sous-préfecture de Garango, nord pays Bissa—Haute Volta." In *Table *ronde. Tropiques et santé. De l'épidémologie à la géographie humaine*, edited by Centre d'Étude de Géographie Tropicale, 253–58. Talence/Paris (Travaux et Documents de la Géographie Tropicale), 1982.

Lambert, Michael C. *Longing for Exile: Migration and the Making of a Translocal Community in Senegal, West Africa.* London: Heineman, 2002.

Laube, Wolfram. *Changing Natural Resource Regimes in Northern Ghana: Actors, Structures and Institutions.* Hamburg: Lit, 2007.

Laurent, Pierre-Joseph. "Développement local, stabilité politique et décentralisation. Aperçu sur la réforme en cours au Burkina Faso." In *Dezentralisierung, Demokratisierung und die lokale Repräsentation des Staates*, edited by Jakob Rösel and Trutz von Trotha, 101–17. Köln: Köppe, 1999.

Laurent, Pierre-Joseph, and Paul Mathieu. "Authority and Conflict in Management of Natural Resources: A Story about Trees and Immigrants in Southern Burkina Faso." *Forests, Trees and People Newsletter* 25 (1994): 37–44.

Laurent, Pierre Joseph, Paul Mathieu, and Marc Totté. *Migrations et accès a la terre au Burkina Faso.* Louvain-la-Neuve: CIDEP, 1994.

Lavigne Delville, Philippe, ed. *Quelles politiques foncières en Afrique? Réconcilier pratiques, légitimité et légalité.* Paris: Karthala, 1998.

———. "When Farmers Use 'Pieces of Papers' to Record Their Land Transactions in Francophone Rural Africa: Insights into the Dynamics of Institutional Innovation." In *Securing Land Rights in Africa*, edited by Tor A. Benjaminsen and Christian Lund, 89–108. London: Frank Cass, 2003.

Lavigne Delville, Philippe, et al. *Negotiating Access to Land in West Africa: A Synthesis of Findings from Research on Derived Rights to Land.* London: International Institute for Environment and Development, 2002.

Le Bris, Émile, Étienne Le Roy, and François Leimdorfer, eds. *Enjeux fonciers en Afrique noire.* Paris: Karthala, 1982.

Le Meur, Pierre-Yves. *Information foncière, bien commun et ressource stratégique.* London: International Institute for Environment and Development, Dossier 146, 2008.

———. "Une petite entreprise de réassamblage du monde. Ethnographie et gouvernance des ressources foncières en Afrique de l'Ouest." *Ethnologie française* 61, no. 3 (2011): 331–42.

Lentz, Carola. "A Dagara Rebellion against Dagomba Rule? Contested Stories of Origin in North-Western Ghana." *Journal of African History* 35 (1994): 457–92.

———. "'Tribalism' and Ethnicity in Africa: A Review of Four Decades of Anglophone Research." *Cahiers des Sciences Humaines* 31 (1995): 303–28.

———. *Die Konstruktion von Ethnizität. Eine politische Geschichte Nord-West Ghanas.* Cologne: Köppe, 1998.

———. "Colonial Ethnography and Political Reform: The Works of A. C. Duncan-Johnstone, R. S. Rattray, J. Eyre-Smith and J. Guinness on Northern Ghana." *Ghana Studies* 2 (1999): 119–69.

———. "'Chieftaincy Has Come to Stay'. La chefferie dans les sociétés acéphales du nord-ouest Ghana." *Cahiers d'études africaines* 159 (2000): 593–613.

———. "Colonial Constructions and African Initiatives: The History of Ethnicity in Northwestern Ghana." *Ethnos* 65 (2000): 120–24.

———. "Of Hunters, Goats and Earth-Shrines: Settlement Histories and the Politics of Oral Tradition in Northern Ghana." *History in Africa* 27 (2000): 193–214.

———. "Ouessa. Débats sur l'histoire du peuplement." In *Les Dagara et leurs voisins. Histoire de peuplement et relations interethniques au sud-ouest du Burkina Faso*, edited by Richard Kuba, Lentz, and Katja Werthmann, 29–61. Frankfurt/Main: *Berichte des Sonderforschungsbereichs 268*, no. 15 (2001).

———. "This Is Ghanaian Territory: Land Conflicts on a West African Border." *American Ethnologist* 30 (2003): 273–89.

———. "Decentralization, the State and Conflicts over Local Boundaries in Northern Ghana." *Development and Change* 37, no. 4 (2006): 909–19.

———. *Ethnicity and the Making of History in Northern Ghana*. Edinburgh: Edinburgh University Press, 2006.

———. "First-Comers and Late-Comers: Indigenous Theories of Land Ownership in the West African Savanna." In *Land and the Politics of Belonging in West Africa*, edited by Richard Kuba and Lentz, 35–56. Leiden: Brill, 2006.

———. "First-Comers and Late-Comers: The Role of Narratives in Land Claims." In *Competing Jurisdictions: Settling Land Claims in Africa*, edited by Sandra Evers, Marja Spierenburg and Harry Wels, 157–80. Leiden: Brill, 2006.

———. "Land Rights and the Politics of Belonging in Africa: An Introduction." In *Land and the Politics of Belonging in West Africa*, edited by Richard Kuba and Lentz, 1–34. Leiden: Brill, 2006.

———. "Constructing Ritual Protection on an Expanding Settlement Frontier: Earth Shrines in the Black Volta Region." In *Shrines in Africa: History, Politics, and Society*, edited by Allan Charles Dawson, 121–52. Calgary: Calgary University Press, 2009.

———. "Is Land Inalienable? Historical and Current Debates on Land Transfers in Northern Ghana." *Africa* 80, no. 1 (2010): 56–80.

———. "'Natives' and 'Settlers': Negotiating Land Tenure in the Black Volta Region (Burkina Faso), 1930s–1990s." In *Une anthropologie entre pouvoirs et histoire. Conversations autour de l'œuvre de Jean-Pierre Chauveau*, edited by E. Jul-Larsen et al., 325–43. Paris: Karthala, 2011.

Lentz, Carola, and Paul Nugent. "Ethnicity in Ghana: A Comparative Perspective." In *Ethnicity in Ghana: The Limits of Invention*, edited by Lentz and Nugent, 1–28. London: Macmillan, 2000.

Lentz, Carola, and Hans-Jürgen Sturm. "Of Trees and Earth Shrines: An Interdisciplinary Approach to Settlement Histories in the West African Savannah." *History in Africa* 28 (2001): 139–68.

Leonhardt, Alec. "Baka and the Magic of the State: Between Autochthony and Citizenship." *African Studies Review* 49, no. 2 (2006): 69–94.

Le Roy, Étienne. "Caractères des droits fonciers coûtumiers." In *Encyclopédie juridique de l'Afrique* 5: 39–47. Abidjan: Les nouvelles éditions africaines, 1982.

———. "Les modes d'acquisition et les preuves des droits fonciers coûtumiers." In *Encyclopédie juridique de l'Afrique*, 5: 71–81. Abidjan: Les nouvelles éditions africaines, 1982.

———. "Les objectifs de la colonisation française ou belge." In *Encyclopédie juridique de l'Afrique*, 5: 85–93. Abidjan: Les nouvelles éditions africaines, 1982.

Lesourd, R. P. Jean. *Un peuple en marche vers la lumière. Les Dagaris*. Soisson: Imp. de l'Argue, 1938.

Levtzion, Nehemia. *Muslims and Chiefs in West Africa: A Study of Islam in the Middle Volta Basin in the Pre-colonial Period*. Oxford: Clarendon Press 1968.

Lévy, Jean-Philippe. *Histoire de la propriété*. Paris: Presses Universitaires de France, 1972.

Li, Tania Murray. "Articulating Indigenous Identity in Indonesia: Resource Politics and the Tribal Slot." *Comparative Studies in Society and History* 42 (2000): 149–68.

———. "Indigeneity, Capitalism, and the Management of Dispossession." *Current Anthropology* 51, no. 3 (2010): 385–414.

Liberski-Bagnoud, Danouta. *Les dieux du territoire. Penser autrement la généalogie*. Paris: CNRS Éditions, 2002.

Lobnibe, Isidore. "A Short History of Hamile from the Earliest Times to 1950." B.A. thesis, University of Cape Coast, Department of History, 1994.

———. "Forbidden Fruits in the Compound: A Case Study of Migration, Spousal Separation and Group-Wife Adultery in Northwest Ghana." *Africa* 75 (2005): 559–81.

———. "Legitimating a Contested Boundary: Northern Ghanaian Immigrants and the Historicity of Land Conflict in Ahyiayem, Brong Ahafo." *Ghana Studies* 9 (2006): 61–90.

———. "Between Aspirations and Realities: Northern Ghanaian Women and the Dilemma of Household (Re)production in Southern Ghana." *Africa Today* 55 (2009): 53–74.

Locke, John. *The Second Treatise of Government and A Letter Concerning Toleration*. 1690. Mineola: Dover, 2002.

Lombard, Jacques. *Autorités traditionelles et pouvoirs européens en Afrique noire*. Paris: Armand Colin, 1967.

Lund, Christian. *Law, Power and Politics in Niger: Land Struggles and the Rural Code*. Hamburg: Lit, 1998.

———. "Struggles for Land and Political Power: On the Politicization of Land Tenure and Dispute in Niger." *Journal of Legal Pluralism* 40 (1998): 1–22.

———. "A Question of Honour: Property Disputes and Brokerage in Burkina Faso." *Africa* 69 (1999): 575–94.

———. "Les réformes foncières dans un contexte de pluralism juridique et institutionel. Burkina Faso et Niger." In *Inégalités et politiques publiques en Afrique. Pluralité des normes et enjeux d'acteurs*, edited by Gérard Winter, 195–207. Paris: Karthala, 2001.

———. "Negotiating Property Institutions: On the Symbiosis of Property and Authority in Africa." In *Negotiating Property in Africa*, edited by Kristine Juul and Lund, 11–43. Portsmouth, N.H.: Heinemann, 2002.

———. "Who Owns Bolgatanga? A Story of Inconclusive Encounters." In *Land and the Politics of Belonging in West Africa*, edited by Richard Kuba and Carola Lentz, 77–98. Leiden: Brill, 2006.

———. *Local Politics and the Dynamics of Property in Africa*. Cambridge: Cambridge University Press, 2008.

———. "Landrights and Citizenship in Africa." Discussion Paper 65. Uppsala: Nordiska Afrikainstitutet, 2011.

Luning, Sabine. "Ritual Territories as Local Heritage? Discourse on Disruptions in Society and Nature in Maane, Burkina Faso," *Africa* 77, no. 1 (2007): 86–103.

Manessy, Gabriel. "Linguistique historique et traditions ethniques. Les peuples voltaïques dans l'est de la boucle du Niger." In *Zur Sprachgeschichte und Ethnohistorie in Afrika. Neue Beiträge afrikanistischer Forschungen*, edited by Wilhelm J. H. Möhlig et al., 152–65. Berlin: Reimer, 1977.

———. "Matériaux linguistiques pour servir à l'histoire des populations du sud-ouest de l'Haute Volta." *Sprache und Geschichte in Afrika* 4 (1982): 95–164.

Marshall-Fratani, Ruth. "The War of 'Who Is Who': Autochthony, Nationalism, and Citizenship in the Ivoirian Crisis." *African Studies Review* 49, no. 2 (2006): 9–43.

Mathieu, Paul. "Transactions informelles et marchés fonciers émergents en Afrique." In *Politics, Property and Production in the West African Sahel: Understanding Natural*

Resources Management, edited by Tor A. Benjaminsen and Christian Lund, 22–39. Uppsala: Nordic Africa Institute, 2001.

Mathieu, Paul, Mahmadou Zongo, and Lacinan Paré. "Monetary Land Transactions in Western Burkina Faso: Commoditisation, Papers and Ambiguities." In *Securing Land Rights in Africa,* edited by Tor A. Benjaminsen and Christian Lund, 109–28. London: Frank Cass, 2003.

McCoy, Remigius F. *Great Things Happen: Personal Memoir of the First Christian Missionary among the Dagaabas and Sissalas of Northwest Ghana.* Montreal: Society of the Missionaries of Africa, 1988.

Meek, Charles K. *Land, Law and Custom in the Colonies.* Oxford: Oxford University Press, 1946.

Mendonsa, Eugene. "Economic, Residential and Ritual Fission of Sisala Domestic Groups." *Africa* 49 (1979): 388–407.

———. *The Politics of Divination: A Processual View of Reactions to Illness and Deviance among the Sisala of Northern Ghana.* Berkeley: University of California Press, 1982.

———. *Continuity and Change in a West African Society: Globalization's Impact on the Sisala of Ghana.* Durham: Carolina Academic Press, 2001.

Metzer, Jacob, and Stanley L. Engerman. "Some Considerations of Ethno-Nationality (and Other Distinctions), Property Rights in Land, and Territorial Sovereignty." In *Land Rights, Ethno-Nationality, and Sovereignity in History,* edited by Stanley L. Engerman and Metzer, 7–28. London: Routledge, 2004.

Miller, Joseph C., ed. *The African Past Speaks.* Folkestone: Dawson, 1980.

Ministry of Lands and Forestry (Republic of Ghana). *National Land Policy.* Accra: Sonlite Press, 1999.

Mitchell, Clyde. "The Causes of Labour Migration." *Bulletin of the Inter-African Labour Institute* 6 (1959): 12–47.

Moniot, Henri. "Profile of a Historiography: Oral Tradition and Historical Research in Africa." In *African Historiographies: Which History for Which Africa?,* edited by Bogumil Jewsiewicki und David Newbury, 50–58. Beverly Hills: Sage, 1986.

———. "L'histoire à l'épreuve de l'Afrique." *Cahiers d'études africaines* 138–39 (1995): 647–56.

Monson, Jamie. "Memory, Migration and the Authority of History in Southern Tanzania, 1860–1960." *Journal of African History* 41 (2000): 347–72.

Moore, Sally Falk. *Social Facts and Fabrications: Customary Law on Kilimanjaro, 1880–1980.* Cambridge: Cambridge University Press, 1986.

———. "Changing African Land Tenure: Reflections on the Capacities of the State." *European Journal of Development Research* 10 (1998): 33–49.

Murphy, William P., and Caroline H. Bledsoe. "Kinship and Territory in the History of a Kpelle Chiefdom (Liberia)." In *The African Frontier: The Reproduction of Traditional African Societies,* edited by Igor Kopytoff, 121–47. Bloomington: Indiana University Press, 1987.

Ninsin, Kwame. "The Land Question since the 1950s." In *The State: Development and Politics in Ghana,* edited by Emmanuel Hansen and Ninsin, 165–83. London: Codesria Book Series, 1989.

Nugent, Paul. *Secessionists, Smugglers and Loyal Citizens on the Ghana-Togo Frontier.* Oxford: James Currey, 2002.

———. "Putting the History Back into Ethnicity: Enslavement, Religion, and Cultural Brokerage in the Construction of Mandinka/Jola and Ewe/Agotime Identities in West Africa, c. 1650–1930." *Contemporary Studies in Society and History* 50 (2008): 920–48.

Nugent, Paul, and A. I. Asiwaju, eds. *African Boundaries: Barriers, Conduits, Opportunities.* London: Pinter, 1996.

Oberhofer, Michaela. "Un village dyan au sud-ouest du Burkina Faso. Relations interethniques en mutation." In *Les Dagara et leurs voisins. Histoire de peuplement et relations interethniques au sud-ouest du Burkina Faso,* edited by Richard Kuba, Carola Lentz, and Katja Werthmann, 141–58. Frankfurt/Main: *Berichte des Sonderforschungsbereichs 268,* no. 15 (2001).

———. *Fremde Nachbarn. Ethnizität im bäuerlichen Alltag in Burkina Faso.* Cologne: Köppe, 2008.

Odotei, Irene K., and Albert K. Awedoba, eds. *Chieftaincy in Ghana: Culture, Governance and Development.* Accra: Sub-Saharan Publishers, 2006.

Ouedraogo, Jean-Baptiste. "The Articulation of the Moose Traditional Chieftaincies, the Modern Political System, and the Economic Development of Kaya Region, Burkina Faso." *Journal of Legal Pluralism and Unofficial Law* 37/38 (1996): 249–61.

Pagden, Anthony. *Lords of All the World: Ideologies of Empire in Spain, Britain and France, c. 1500–c. 1800.* New Haven: Yale University Press, 1995.

Paris, Fréderic. "Système d'occupation de l'espace et onchocercose. Foyer de la Bougouriba—Volta Noire (Burkina Faso)." In *Table ronde. Tropiques et santé. De l'épidémologie à la géographie humaine,* edited by Centre d'Étude de Géographie Tropicale, 259–70. Talence/Paris (Travaux et Documents de la Géographie Tropicale), 1982.

Peel, John. "The Cultural Work of Yoruba Ethnogenesis." In *History and Ethnicity,* edited by Elizabeth Tonkin et al., 198–215. London: Routledge, 1989.

Père, Madeleine. *Les Lobi. Tradition et changement. Burkina Faso.* Laval: Ed. Siloë, 1988.

———. "Chronique des villages de la province du Poni, en contribution à l'histoire du peuplement au Burkina Faso." In *Images d'Afrique et sciences sociales. Les pays lobi, birifor et dagara,* edited by Michèle Fiéloux, Jacques Lombard, and Jeanne-Marie Kambou-Ferrand, 56–73. Paris: Karthala, 1993.

———. "Contribution à l'histoire du peuplement de la province du Poni au Burkina Faso." In *Bonds and Boundaries in Northern Ghana and Southern Burkina Faso,* edited by Sten Hagberg and Alexis B. Tengan, 41–52. Uppsala: Uppsala Studies in Cultural Anthropology, 2000.

Perrot, Claude-Hélène, ed. *Lignages et territoire en Afrique aux XVIIIe et XIXe siècles. Stratégies, compétition, intégration.* Paris: Karthala, 2000.

Peters, Pauline. "The Limits of Negotiability: Security, Equity and Class Formation in Africa's Land Systems." In *Negotiating Property in Africa,* edited by Kristine Juul and Christian Lund, 45–66. Portsmouth, N.H.: Heinemann, 2002.

———. "Inequality and Social Conflict over Land in Africa." *Journal of Agrarian Change* 4, no. 3 (2004): 269–314.

Phillips, Anne. *The Enigma of Colonialism: British Policy in West Africa.* London: James Currey, 1989.

Platteau, Jean-Philippe. "The Evolutionary Theory of Land Rights as Applied to Sub-Saharan Africa: A Critical Assessment." *Development and Change* 27 (1996): 29–86.

Pogucki, R. J. H. *Report on Land Tenure in Native Customary Law of the Protectorate of the Northern Territories of the Gold Coast, Part II.* Accra: Lands Department, 1951.

Pole, Leonard M. "Account of an Iron-Smelting Operation at Lawra." *Ghana Journal of Science* 14 (1974): 127–36.

———. "Iron-Working Apparatus and Techniques: Upper Region of Ghana." *West African Journal of Archaeology* 5 (1975): 11–39.

Pul, Hippolyte A. S. "Citizenship, Exclusion and Ethnic Conflict in the Post-colonial State." *African Anthropologist* 12, no. 1 (2005): 65–99.

Quan, Julian, Janine Ubink, and Adarkwah Antwi. "Risks and Opportunities of State Intervention in Customary Management: Emergent Findings from the Land Administration Project Ghana." In *Contesting Land and Custom in Ghana: State, Chief and Citizen*, edited by Ubink and Kojo S. Amanor, 183–208. Leiden: Leiden University Press, 2009.

Ranger, Terence. "The Invention of Tradition in Colonial Africa." In *The Invention of Tradition*, edited by Eric Hobsbawm and Ranger, 211–62. Cambridge: Cambridge University Press, 1983.

Rathbone, Richard. *Nkrumah and the Chiefs: The Politics of Chieftaincy in Ghana 1951–60*. Oxford: James Currey, 2000.

Rattray, Robert S. *The Tribes of Ashanti Hinterland*. Oxford: Clarendon Press, 1932.

Reeve, Andrew. *Property*. Atlantic Highlands N.J.: Humanities Press International, 1986.

Reikat, Andrea, ed. *Landnutzung in der westafrikanischen Savanne*. Frankfurt/Main: *Berichte des Sonderforschungsbereichs 268*, no. 9 (1997).

Remme, J., and J. B. Zongo. "Demographic Aspects of the Epidemiology and Control of Onchocerciasis in West Africa." In *Demography and Vector-Borne Diseases*, edited by Michael Service, 367–86. Boca Raton: CRC Press, 1989.

Rey, Pierre-Philippe. "Guerres et politique lignagères." In *Guerres de lignages et guerres d'états en Afrique*, edited by Jean Bazin and Emmanuel Terray, 33–72. Paris: Édition des Archives Contemporaines, 1982.

Ribot, Jesse C., and Nancy Lee Peluso. "A Theory of Access." *Rural Sociology* 68, no. 2 (2003): 153–81.

Rose, Carol M. *Property and Persuasion: Essays on the History, Theory and Rhetoric of Ownership*. Boulder: Westview Press, 1994.

Rudolf, Eveline. "L'unité par la parenté? Du sense de l'appartenance clanique pour la vie sociale et politique à Mébar." In *Les Dagara et leurs voisins. Histoire de peuplement et relations interethniques au sud-ouest du Burkina Faso*, edited by Richard Kuba, Carola Lentz, and Katja Werthmann, 63–69. Frankfurt/Main: *Berichte des Sonderforschungsbereichs 268*, no. 15 (2001).

Ruelle, E. "Notes ethnographiques et sociologiques sur quelques populations noires du 2e Territoire Militaire de l'Afrique Occidentale Française." *Anthropologie* 15 (1904): 657–74.

Ryan, Alan. *Property*. Minneapolis: University of Minnesota Press, 1987.

Sahlins, Marshall D. "The Segmentary Lineage: An Organization of Predatory Expansion." *American Anthropologist* 63 (1961): 322–45.

Saul, Mahir. "Money and Land Tenure as Factors in Farm Size Differentiation in Burkina Faso." In *Land and Society in Contemporary Africa*, edited by R. E. Downs and S. P. Reyna, 243–79. Hanover: University Press of New England, 1988.

Saul, Mahir, Jean-Marie Ouadba, and Ouettan Bognounou. "The Wild Vegetation Cover of Western Burkina Faso: Colonial Policy and Post-colonial Development." In *African Savannas: Global Narratives and Local Knowledge of Environmental Change*, edited by Thomas J. Bassett and Donald Crummey, 121–60. Oxford: James Currey, 2003.

Savonnet, Georges. "La colonisation du pays Koulango (Haute Côte d'Ivoire) par les Lobi de Haute Volta." *Cahiers d'Outre Mer* 15 (1962): 25–46.

———. *Pina, étude d'un terroir du front pionnier en pays dagari (Haute-Volta)*. Atlas des structures agraires au sud du Sahara, 4. Paris: Mouton, 1970.

———. "Quelques notes sur l'histoire des Dyan (cercles de Diébougou et de Léo, Haute Volta)." *Bulletin de l'I.F.A.N.*, T. 37, série B, 3 (1975): 619–45.

———. *Les Birifor de Diépla et sa région insulaire du rameau Lobi (Haut-Volta)*. Atlas des structures agraires au sud du Sahara, 12. Paris: Mouton, 1976.

Savonnet-Guyot, Claudette. *Etat et sociétés en Burkina Faso. Essai sur le politique africain.* Paris: Karthala, 1986.

Sawadogo, Raogo Antoine, and Pamphile Sebahara. "Historique de la décentralisation au Burkina Faso." In *Décentralisation et citoyenneté au Burkina Faso. Le cas de Ziniaré*, edited by Pierre-Joseph Laurent et al., 59–78. Paris: L'Harmattan, 2005.

Schlatter, Richard. *Private Property: The History of an Idea*. New Brunswick, N.J.: Rutgers University Press, 1951.

Schoffeleers, J. Matthew, ed. *Guardians of the Land: Essays on Central African Territorial Cults*. Gwelo: Mambo Press, 1979.

Schott, Rüdiger. "'La femme enceinte éventrée'. Variabilité et contexte socio-culturel d'un type de conte ouest-africain." In *D'un conte à l'autre. La variabilité dans la littérature orale*, edited by Veronika Görög-Karady, 327–39. Paris: Éditions CNRS, 1990.

———. "Le caillou et la boue. Les traditions orales en tant que légitimation des autorités traditionelles chez les Bulsa (Ghana) et les Lyela (Burkina Faso)." *Paideuma* 39 (1993): 145–62.

———. "Limits on the Access to Land, Cattle and Women among Some West African Peoples." In *Frontiers and Borderlands: Anthropological Perspectives*, edited by Michael Rösler and Tobias Wendl, 159–86. Frankfurt/Main: Peter Lang, 1999.

Scopa, Antoine. "Bailleurs autochtones et locataires allogènes. Enjeu foncier et participation au Cameroun." *African Studies Review* 49, no. 2 (2006): 45–67.

Scott, James C. *Weapons of the Weak: Everyday Forms of Peasant Resistance*. New Haven: Yale University Press, 1985.

Sebahara, Pamphile. "Pluralism institutionel et politiques de développement communal." In *Décentralisation et citoyenneté au Burkina Faso. Le cas de Ziniaré*, edited by Pierre-Joseph Laurent et al., 223–55. Paris: L'Harmattan, 2005.

Shetler, Jan Bender. *Imagining Serengeti: A History of Landscape Memory in Tanzania from Earliest Times to the Present*. Athens: Ohio University Press, 2007.

Shipton, Parker. *Bitter Money: Cultural Economy and Some African Meanings of Forbidden Commodities*. American Ethnological Society Monograph Series 1. Washington, 1989.

———. "Land and Culture in Tropical Africa: Soils, Symbols, and the Metaphysics of the Mundane." *Annual Review of Anthropology* 23 (1994): 347–77.

———. *Mortgaging the Ancestors: Ideologies of Attachment in Africa*. New Haven: Yale University Press, 2009.

Shipton, Parker, and Mitzi Goheen. "Understanding African Land-Holding: Power, Wealth and Meaning." *Africa* 62, no. 3 (1992): 307–25.

Siilo, B. L. "The History of Nandom from the Time of Settlement to 1908." B.A. thesis, University of Ghana, Department of History, 1973.

Sikor, Thomas, and Christian Lund. "Access and Property: A Question of Power and Authority." In *The Politics of Possession: Property, Authority, and Access to Natural Resources*, edited by Sikor and Lund, 1–22. Oxford: Blackwell, 2009.

Somda, Nurukyor Claude. "Les origines des Dagara." *Papers in Dagara Studies* 1, no. 1 (1989).

———. "L'esclavage. Un paradoxe dans une société égalitaire." *Cahiers du CERLERSH* 17 (2000): 267–90.

——. "Espace et mobilité lignagère dans le sud-ouest du Burkina Faso." Frankfurt/Main: *Berichte des Sonderforschungsbereichs 268*, no. 14 (2001): 449–53.

Somé, Honoré Poyouor. "Habitations et occupation du sol. Le *yir* et le village dagara. L'exemple de Tobo." *Cahiers d'Outre-Mer* 169 (1990): 77–95.

Somé, Magloire. *La christianisation de l'Ouest-Volta. Action missionnaire et réactions africaines, 1927–1960.* Paris: L'Harmattan, 2004.

Somé, Valère. "Le dagara sous le sol de l'esclavage." *Cahiers du CERLERSH*, special no. 1 (2001): 57–97.

Songsore, Jacob. "Population Growth and Ecological Degradation in Northern Ghana: Myths and Realities." *Research Review* (N.S.), Legon (Ghana), 12 (1996): 56–59.

——. "The Decline of the Rural Commons in Sub-saharan Africa: The Case of the Upper West Region of Ghana." In *Regionalism and Public Policy in Northern Ghana*, edited by Yakubu Saaka, 153–76. Frankfurt/Main: Peter Lang, 2001.

Spear, Thomas. "Neo-traditionalism and the Limits of Invention in British Colonial Africa.' *Journal of African History* 44 (2003): 3–27.

Stamm, Volker. *Zur Dynamik der westafrikanischen Bodenverfassung. Eine ökonomische Analyse am Beispiel Burkina Fasos.* Hamburg: Institut für Afrika-Kunde, 1996.

——. "Endogene Konfliktregeln und staatliches Recht bei Auseinandersetzungen um Boden-ressourcen." *Afrika Spectrum* 32 (1997): 297–310.

St. John-Parsons, Donald. *Legends of Northern Ghana.* London: Longman 1958.

Strassoldo, Raimondo. "Border Studies: The State of the Art in Europe." In *Borderlands in Africa: A Multidisciplinary and Comparative Focus on Nigeria and West Africa*, edited by A. I. Asiwaju and P. O. Adenyi, 383–95. Lagos: University of Lagos Press, 1989.

Swanepoel, Natalie J. "'Too Much Power Is Not Good': War and Trade in Nineteenth-Century Sisalaland, Northern Ghana." Ph.D. diss., Syracuse University, 2004.

——. "Every Periphery Is Its Own Center: Sociopolitical and Economic Interactions in Nineteenth-Century Northwestern Ghana." *International Journal of African Historical Studies* 42, no. 3 (2009): 411–32.

Tallet, Bernard. "Au Burkina Faso, les CVGT ont-elles été des instances locales de gestion foncière?" In *Quelles politiques foncières en Afrique? Réconcilier pratiques, légitimité et légalité*, edited by Philippe Lavigne Delville, 390–402. Paris: Karthala, 1998.

Talton, Benjamin. *Politics of Social Change in Ghana: The Konkomba Struggle for Political Equality.* New York: Palgrave Macmillan, 2010.

Tauxier, Louis. *Le noir du Soudan. Pays Mossi et Gourounsi.* Paris: E. Larousse, 1912.

Tengan, Alexis. "Dagara Bagr: Ritualising Myth of Social Foundation." *Africa* 69 (1999): 595–633.

——. *Hoe-farming and Social Relations among the Dagara of Northwestern Ghana and Southwestern Burkina Faso.* Frankfurt/Main: Peter Lang, 2000.

——. "Space, Bonds and Social Order: Dagara House-Based Social System." In *Bonds and Boundaries in Northern Ghana and Southern Burkina Faso*, edited by Sten Hagberg and Tengan, 87–103. Uppsala: AUU, 2000.

Tengan, Edward. *The Land as Cosmos and Being: The Institution of the Earth Cult among the Sisala of Northwestern Ghana.* Frankfurt/Main: Peter Lang, 1991.

——. *The Social Structure of the Dagara: The House and the Matriclan as Axes of Dagara Social Organisation.* Tamale: St Victor's Major Seminary, 1994.

Tonah, Steven. "Migration and Farmer-Herder Conflicts in Ghana's Volta Basin." *Canadian Journal of African Studies* 40, no. 1 (2006): 152–78.

Tonkin, Elizabeth. *Narrating Our Pasts: The Social Construction of Oral History*. Cambridge: Cambridge University Press, 1992.

Toulmin, Camilla. "Negotiating Access to Land in West Africa: Who Is Losing Out?" In *Conflicts over Land and Water in Africa*, edited by Bill Derman, Rie Odgaard and Espen Sjaastad, 95–115. Oxford: James Curry, 2007.

Toulmin, Camilla, and Julian Quan, eds. *Evolving Land Rights, Policy and Tenure in Africa*. London: Department for International Development Issues Series, 2000.

Toulmin, Camilla, Philippe Lavigne Delville, and Samba Traoré, eds. *The Dynamics of Resource Tenure in West Africa*. Oxford: James Currey, 2002.

Traoré, Samba. "Straying Fields: Tenure Problems for Pastoralists in the Ferlo, Senegal." In *The Dynamics of Resource Tenure in West Africa*, edited by Camilla P. Toulmin, Philippe Lavigne Delville, and Traoré, 145–56. Oxford: James Currey, 2002.

Tribillion, Jean-François. *Villes africaines. Nouveau manuel d'aménagement foncier*. Paris: ADEF, 1993.

Tully, James. *A Discourse on Property: John Locke and his Adversaries*. Cambridge: Cambridge University Press, 1980.

Turton, David. "A Journey Made Them: Territorial Segmentation and Ethnic Identity among the Mursi." In *Segmentary Lineage Systems Reconsidered*, edited by Ladislav Holy, 119–144. Queen's University Papers in Social Anthropology 4. Belfast: Queen's University, 1979.

Ubink, Janine M. "Negotiated or Negated? The Rhetoric and Reality of Customary Tenure in an Ashanti Village in Ghana." *Africa* 78, no. 2 (2008): 264–87.

Ubink, Janine M., and Kojo S. Amanor, eds. *Contesting Land and Custom in Ghana: State, Chief and Citizen*. Leiden: Leiden University Press, 2009.

Vail, Leroy, ed. *The Creation of Tribalism in Southern Africa*. London: James Currey, 1989.

Vajda, László. "Zur Frage der Völkerwanderungen." *Paideuma* 19/20 (1973–74): 5–52.

Van der Geest, Kees."We're Managing!" Climate Change and Livelihood Vulnerability in Northwest Ghana*. African Studies Centre, Research Report 74. Leiden, 2004.

Van Dijk, Han. "Land Tenure, Territoriality and Ecological Instability: A Sahelian Case Study." In *The Role of Law in Natural Resource Management*, edited by Joep Spiertz and Melanie Wiber, 17–45. The Hague: VUGA, 1996.

Van Dijk, Han, Dick Foeken, and Kiky van Til. "Population Mobility in Africa: An Overview." In *Mobile Africa: Changing Patterns of Movement in Africa and Beyond*, edited by Mirjam de Bruijn et al., 9–27. Leiden: Brill, 2001.

Van Velsen, J. "Labor Migration as a Positive Factor in the Continuity of Tonga Tribal Society." *Economic Development and Cultural Change* 8 (1960): 265–78.

Vansina, Jan. *Oral Tradition as History*. Madison: University of Wisconsin Press, 1985.

Vayda, Andrew P. "Expansion and Warfare among Swidden Agriculturalists." *American Anthropologist* 63 (1969): 346–58.

Vincent, Jean-Françoise, Daniel Dory, and Raymond Verdier, eds. *La construction religieuse du territoire*. Paris: Harmattan, 1995.

Wagner, Günter. "Political Organization of the Bantu of Kavirondo." In *African Political Systems*, edited by Meyer Fortes and Edward E.Evans-Pritchard, 197–238. London: KPI, 1940.

Wardell, D. Andrew, A. Reenberg, H. Olsen, and R. Harpøth, eds. *Negotiated Frontiers in Sudano-Sahelian Landscapes*. Sahel-Sudan Environmental Research Initiative, Occasional Paper 16, 2003.

Werbner, Richard P. *Ritual Passage—Sacred Journey: The Process and Organization of Religious Movement*. Manchester: Manchester University Press, 1989.

———. "Safe Passage for Well-Being: Substances, Sacrifice and Oracle Supplicants." *Cambridge Anthropology* 29, no. 3 (2009): 46–68.

Werthmann, Katja. "Gold Diggers, Earth Priests, and District Heads: Land Rights and Gold Mining in Southwestern Burkina Faso." In *Land and the Politics of Belonging in West Africa*, edited by Richard Kuba and Carola Lentz, 119–36. Leiden: Brill, 2006.

Werthmann, Katja, Tilo Grätz, and Hans Peter Hahn. "Mobilität in Afrika. Multilokale Forschungen." *Afrika Spectrum* 39, no. 3 (2004): 325–33.

Werthmann, Katja, Modeste Somé, and Andrea Wilhelmi. "'Il y a l'entente comme il y a la mésentente'. Vingt ans de cohabitation entre Dagara et Mossi dans les anciens villages A.V.V." In *Les Dagara et leurs voisins. Histoire de peuplement et relations interethniques au sud-ouest du Burkina Faso*, edited by Richard Kuba, Carola Lentz, and Werthmann, 159–78. Frankfurt/Main: *Berichte des Sonderforschungsbereichs 268*, no. 15 (2001).

Wilhelmi, Andrea. "Die Konstruktion von Autochthonie. Fallstudie zur dörflichen Gemeinschaftsbildung in einem staatlichen Umsiedlungsprojekt im Südwesten von Burkina Faso." MA thesis, Department of Historical Anthropology, 2000. University of Frankfurt/Main.

Wilks, Ivor. *Wa and the Wala: Islam and Polity in Northwestern Ghana*. Cambridge: Cambridge University Press, 1989.

Woodman, Gordon R. *Customary Land Law in the Ghanaian Courts*. Accra: Ghana Universities Press, 1996.

Young, Crawford M. "Nationalism, Ethnicity and Class in Africa: A Retrospective." *Cahiers d'études africaines* 103 (1986): 421–95.

Zougouri, Sita, and Paul Mathieu. "Nouvelles transactions et formalisation des transactions foncières dans l'ouest de Burkina Faso. Le cas d'un village de la province de Houët. In *Gouvernance foncière au quotidien en Afrique* (Bulletin APAD 22), edited by Pierre-Yves Le Meur and Christian Lund, 95–116. Münster: Lit, 2001.

Zwernemann, Jürgen. *Die Erde in Vorstellungswelt und Kulturpraktiken der sudanischen Völker*. Berlin: Reimer, 1968.

Index

Maps and tables are indicated by page numbers in *italics* followed by m or t.

districts, district head. *See* boundaries (and administrative boundaries); *préfet*
Djikologo, 55t1.1, 56, 57m1.3
Dorman, Daniel Hammett, 242
Duori, 50
Dyan, 23, 30, 48, 51, 54–55, 55, 55t1.1, 60–61, 184, 261n25, 265n61, 265n61, 267–68n94
Dyula, 131, 283n5

earth gods. *See* Kabir; Nyoor; sacrifices and sacrificial gifts
earth priests (*tengansob* [Dagara] or *totina* [Sisala]), 15–17, 21, 42, 53, 64, 77, 82–83, 84–85, 88, 102–3, 143–46, 150, 157, 233, 236, 251n2; ebony pegs of, 136, 214–15, 217, 221; as frontiersmen, 15, 18, 62, 84–85, 87, 109; and land conflicts, 7, 15–17, 21, 179–80, 184–85, 228, 233, 245, 287n50; and memory, 24, 56–59, 241; and modern property schemes, 13, 106, 223–24, 230–31, 242, 244, 245; multiple allegiances to, 86, 129, 136–37; ritual opening of houses (*yir*) by, 71, 73, 86, 136, 154, 160, 194, 233; romantic views of, 9, 83, 121. *See also* allodial ownership; first-comers
earth-shrine stone(s): acquisition/transmission of, 41, 62, 92–94, 95–97, 98, 121, 124, 273n21; origins of, 55t1.1, 56, 84, 87, 88–90, 99–100, 118, 121; and property rights, 17, 99, 101–2, 106, 112–14, 117
earth shrines (*tengan* (Dagara), *tebuo* (Sisala)): and the act of naming, 261n26; areas lying between domains of, 85, 134–35; and Dagara Christians, 190; elemental forms of, 16, 82, 84; and the establishment of new Dagara settlements, 30, 85–86, 123n2.3; and ethnicity, 73, 86–89; and hunting shrines, 16, 85–89, 98; multiple allegiances to, 129, 146–47, 171; and *pax colonia*, 26–27, 41–42, 116, 125; and property rights, 15, 30, 82–84, 117–22; ritual hierarchies of, 25, 85–89; and the spatial definition of property rights, 84–85, 127–28, 130; *tenganbile* (dependent earth shrines), 86–89, 94; three phases of earth-shrine-related politics, 124–25. *See also* earth-shrine stones; sacrifices to earth shrines and ancestor shrines
ebony pegs, 136, 214–15, 217, 221
elections and elected officials, 43, 197, 206–9, 220, 222, 223, 227, 230, 232
Eremon, 50, 272n16
ethnicity, 13, 168, 170–71, 179–80, 246, 259n6, 295–296n68; and agricultural expansion, 172, 176; and boundaries of political domination, 27, 138–41, 157, 169–72, 183–84, 247; and colonial mapping of "tribes", 23, 27, 176–77, 182–84, 210; and competition over land, 176, 230m5.2; and earth shrines,

73, 86–89; and ethnic conversion, 40, 172–75, 285n21; and inheritance, 173–75; mistakenly identified as an issue, 9, 17, 213, 219, 233–34; "politique de race", 178, 183, 188. *See also* autochthony; natives; Nuni; Phuo (Pougouli)
expansionist movements. *See* agricultural expansion
Eyre-Smith, St. John (Lawra District Commissioner), 117–22, 186–87, 265n61, 278n9. *See also* colonial rule; Great Britain

farming and farm land, 16, 42, 134, 143, 160, 164, 243, 247, 248; active cultivation as proof of ownership, 103–6, 217–18; and cattle driven across land by itinerant herdsmen, 150; hoe-farmer preference for second-growth land, 39–40, 48, 51; hoe-farming associated with kin groups, 51, 62; and intra-clan cooperation, 42–43, 48–50, 68–74; sabotage of, 221, 292n14; seizures of, 233–34, 243; spatial dynamics of, 135–37, 149, 193, 217–18, 278n16; surveying of farm plots, 192, 225–26. *See also* agricultural expansion; bush; land tenure
Ferguson, G. E., 138
Fielmuo, 22m1, 35–36, 156, 157, 200m4.2, 206–7, 261n28, 264n52, 270n113
Firmin-Sellers, Kathryn, 21, 115, 255n40
first-comer narratives, 44–50, 51–52, 109, 129, 241; malleability of, 4, 8, 18–20, 53–56, 225, 248; and the politics of belonging, 5, 18–20, 213, 214, 232–33; and property rights, 18–20, 36, 109–10, 118, 211, 218–20, 234. *See also* autochthony; first-comers; history; memory and remembrance; narratives of migration and settlement
first-comers: and burial grounds, 15, 71, 128, 154, 160, 194, 203–4; and colonial rule, 5, 17, 19–21, 26, 66–67, 125, 176–80, 249; contested nature of, 17, 109, 141–42, 248–49; and earth shrines, 16–17, 26–27, 86–89, 186–87, 273n21; and non-labor-related resources, 156, 160–61, 194; recruitment of relations and allies, 36, 37–40, 171; and territorial politics, 3, 17–19, 21, 69, 94, 97–98, 102–3, 110–13, 116, 128, 133–34, 155–57, 233; testing of, 272n19. *See also* ancestors; autochthony; earth-priests; first-comer narratives; late-comers; Phuo; settlers; Sisala; strangers
fishing: and earth-priests, 15, 85, 109; and first-comer claims, 4, 15, 109, 149–50, 160, 162, 194, 199–203, 216, 245; and river access, 130–31
flight (across borders), 20–21, 29, 46–47, 55t1.1, 58, 138–140, 190, 191, 261n28, 279–80n30. *See also* migration; mobility
Foeken, Dick, 28

189, 190, 191, 192, 193, 204, 214–17, 215m5.1, 219–32, 230m5.2, 264n52, 266nn68–70, 81, 269n103, 271n13, 273nn23, 274nn40, 43, 278n7, 288n67, 290n96, 291n7, 293n28, 294n38

pacification: *pax colonia*, 17, 23, 26–27, 41, 66–67, 79, 99, 111, 116, 163, 176, 182, 243, 262n33; ritual pacification, 15, 84–85, 102, 109, 110

paramount chiefs and paramountcies: and British Hamile, 140; and *chefs de canton*, 52, 100, 177–78, 265n63; and colonial rule, 176–80, 178, 183–84, 186–89, 287n50; Lambussie, 119, 178–79, 209, 234–36; Nandom, 119, 179, 187, 205, 231, 233–36, 287n54; Niégo, 92, 273n33; and territoriality, 204–9. *See also* Baloro, K.Y.; Bourra; Karbo, Abeyifaa, Lawra Naa (paramount chief of Lawra)

parties, party politics. *See* elections

patriclans, 31, 37–39, 40, 42–43, 48–50, 51, 58, 60–62, 63, 73–74, 87, 91, 151, 170, 185, 228–29, 262n34, 263n39, 267n90, 267n94, 271–72n14. *See also arbili*; clans; *madebr*; matriclans; narratives of migration and settlement; networks

patron-client relations, 4, 6, 28, 73, 87, 90, 97, 104, 129, 136, 145, 152, 161, 162, 172, 177, 192–94, 196, 204, 210, 218, 224, 233, 262n33. *See also tutorat*

Peters, Pauline, 13, 246–47

Petit Leo, 53, 54m1.2, 55t1.1, 56, 57m1.3, 61, 64

Phillips, Anne, 115

Phuo (Pougouli), 15, 23, 26, 30, 32, 53, 59–60, 55t1.1, 64, 65, 90, 99–100, 116, 184, 263n39, 263n40, 265–66n67, 266n68, 267–68n94, 273n21, 284nn12

Piina, 70m1.5, 190

Piiri, 45m1.1, 49, 264n52

Pina, 41, 68–69, 72–73, 74, 75t1.2, 142m3.1, 160, 264n52, 269n107, 270n113, 272n17, 278n16, 285n21

pioneers. *See* first comers; frontiersmen; mobility; settlers

place-names. *See* naming and place-names

Pogucki, R.J.H., 83, 147–48

political authority: distinguished from material and ritual control over the land, 15–16, 30, 82, 87, 183; and first-comer status, 5, 202–3, 206–7, 218–20; and property rights, x, 5, 10, 11, 12, 19, 43, 79, 87, 90, 91, 100, 118, 124, 148, 152, 157, 159, 166, 179, 185, 186–89, 196, 205, 209, 212–14, 231. *See also* chieftaincy, earth priests, local power

political representation, 206–7

politics of belonging. *See* belonging; home

population density. *See* demography

Pougouli. *See* Phuo

power: of chiefs, 119–21, 140, 143, 176, 179–80, 183–89, 206–9, 234–36; of earth priests, 15–17, 83, 109, 121,

198–99; of ebony pegs, 136, 214–15, 217, 221; landmarks as places of power, 16, 131–33, 163, 271–72n14; power objects, 38; of the *suodem* (holders of the sacrificial knife), 64, 149, 222. *See also* local power; political authority

préfet (district head): and land disputes, 108, 152, 215–17, 222–23, 226–27, 232

property rights: African concepts of property, 9–10, 18–20, 147–48; and citizenship, 14, 27, 211; colonial concepts of property and land tenure, 9–10, 12, 13, 17, 19, 21, 83, 84, 112, 115–17, 118, 122, 125, 139, 147–48; and constitutional order, 14, 17, 121–22; earth shrines as central to the definition of, 30, 82–84; and individualization, 115, 147, 151–152, 161–62; and the insufficiency of violence, 4–5, 82, 134–35, 245–46; local tenure regimes and state-control, 7–8, 199–203, 210–11; and *lotissement*, 213, 223–31, 230m5.2, 232, 293n29; property as a bundle of rights, 127–28, 147–48; and property transfers, 108–9, 110–12; and rights of *usufruct* (*droit de culture*), 102, 104, 115, 148, 149, 157, 160–61, 203, 226, 293–94n21, 293n29; and romanticist views of, 8–9, 83, 112, 120–22; spatial definition of, 84–85, 127–28, 130, 224. *See also* access to land; allodial ownership, title, rights; boundaries; bundles of rights; commercialization/commoditization of land; land transactions; political authority

Rattray, R.S., 121

Rawlings, Jerry, 158; district reform propagated by, 236–37; revolutionary user-rights supportive regime, 21, 122, 198, 202–3, 239

Read (British commissioner of the North-Western Province), 117, 133–35, 283n5, 286n33

Reeve, Andrew, 207–8

religion, 83, 117, 167–68; and social and political boundaries, 135–37, 172, 174, 283–84n5. *See also* Christians; earth gods; earth priests; earth shrines; Muslims; sacrifices and sacrificial gifts

responsable administratif du village, 141, 220, 222, 227

Richards, Paul, 210, 244

rivers, 130–31, 156; as boundaries, 38, 46–47, 91m2.1, 130–31, 143, 156; and earth shrines, 92–93, 130, 186, 277–78n5; as places of power, 38, 130–31, 271–72n14. *See also* Black Volta River

Rose, Carol, 5, 10–11

sacrifices and sacrificial gifts: and armed conflict, 41, 133, 278n8; and *bagr*, 38, 43–44, 50, 59, 73, 74; fowl sacrificed by newcomers to determine acceptance, 70–71, 154, 160, 161, 221, 282n73; and land transfers between different groups, 93, 94, 112–15, 154; to

CAROLA LENTZ is Professor of Social Anthropology at the Department of Anthropology and African Studies of Johannes Gutenberg University, Mainz. Since 1987, she has been conducting research on labor migration, ethnicity, the history of chieftaincy, land rights, and the politics of belonging in Northern Ghana and Burkina Faso. She is author of *Ethnicity and the Making of History in Northern Ghana* (2006), as well as other monographs and numerous journal publications, and she has edited, among other works, *Land and the Politics of Belonging in West Africa* (2006). Since fall 2011, she has been president of the German Anthropological Association.

CPSIA information can be obtained at www.ICGtesting.com
Printed in the USA
LVOW130352110613

337951LV00002B/4/P

"virgin-bush," and to search for "aboriginal" inhabitants. Like Labouret, Eyre-Smith believed that the earth-shrine parishes had been established in the course of the first human settlement of the territory, and that the earth priests mediated between the "primitive people" and the earth deity. Eyre-Smith was well aware that his thesis of the stability of the original "tengani areas" was difficult to reconcile with the mobility and population growth that undeniably had shaped the region. But he insisted that the *tengani-le*, the dependent shrines of later settlers, would always unquestioningly recognize the "Chief Priest" of the ancient earth shrine, which remained the decisive religious-territorial unit. Since land rights were "spiritual" rather than "material" and "the conception of land as property in the sense we understand it was unknown," land could not be sold nor otherwise alienated, but only "deputed" to new settlers who remained subordinate to the original earth priests.[96]

The assumption that the existence of earth-shrine parishes went back centuries was intimately bound up with Eyre-Smith's search for a traditional form of legitimization for future political centralization, with plans to introduce a central native authority in Wa that would administer all the *tengani* areas of the North-West.[97] The subordination of the Nandom shrine area to its original shrine-givers in Lambussie was part of this project of centralization that supposedly wedded the advantages of administrative rationality to the legitimacy of indigenous structures of authority. Guinness, on the other hand, campaigned for the continuance of the existing chiefdoms and stressed the precolonial roots of the chiefly office in the prosperous, influential "self-made men" who had existed in many places.[98] In Guinness's eyes, the *tingdana*, the earth priest, was also a type of self-made man, the difference simply being that the title of *tingdana* was inherited, "and the Tingdanas would therefore tend to become keepers of the traditions, and gather to themselves all the spiritual power that attaches to secret knowledge."[99] Nowhere did Guinness claim explicitly that the earth priests had been rich men, but he listed their revenues quite meticulously, including their rights to stray cattle, homeless children, lost objects, and fines for breaking a taboo of the earth god. Guinness's view of the office was rather pragmatic and allowed for the influence of power politics. Eyre-Smith, on the other hand, was appalled at the insinuation that the earth priests were interested in wealth and worldly power, and insisted that they lived like hermits and sacrificed all the gifts they received for the good of the community.[100] It is evident that in Eyre-Smith's vision of traditional land tenure, there was no place for the sale of an earth shrine, no matter what his African informants may have claimed, while Guinness did not hesitate to report his interlocutors' assertions that their ancestors exchanged cowries for a shrine stone and property rights.

Politically, the romanticized picture that Eyre-Smith (and before him R. S. Rattray) painted of the Black Volta region's past had little effect on the shape of the native authorities that were introduced in the 1930s and that laid the basis for even present-day political and administrative boundaries. Here what carried the day was the position of Guinness and many of his colleagues who wanted to stabilize the system of chiefdoms introduced thirty years earlier and who assumed that the earth-shrine organization was too complex and controversial to serve as the basis for an effective administrative order. However, with respect to the question of how far rights to political representation should be tied to allodial title, and whether the allodial title was at all transferable, Eyre-Smith's position echoed the dominant colonial discourse on the communal nature of traditional tenure and the inalienability of land. This discourse that reflected and, at the same time, reinforced the arguments of African chiefs and others claiming allodial title continues to shape present-day discussions on land rights and political representation.[101]

In Lawra District, the old debates on the inalienability of land have intensified, particularly since the 1970s, in the face of shrinking land reserves, the development of a new market for urban construction sites, and disputes about the delimitation of new administrative boundaries—disputes that I explore in chapter 5. In these debates, the inalienability argument continues to be the ideologically dominant position,[102] although the labor theory of property was and still is also regularly brought into play and occasionally even politically privileged, as during the brief intermezzos of Rawlings's and Sankara's "revolutionary regimes," which preached that access to land should follow the socialist principle of "to each according to his needs" and ultimately rests on the idea that land should be granted to those who cultivate it.

Conclusion

This chapter has discussed the politics surrounding the construction of ritual protection and a peaceful social order on the frontier. It has shown that in the Black Volta region, as in many other areas of the West African savanna, earth shrines stood, and continue to stand, at the center of territorial as well as mobile healing cults. At the same time, earth shrines were, and still are, essential to the definition and legitimization of property rights over landed resources. They constitute religious, economic, social, and political institutions, and the case studies presented in this chapter have demonstrated how important it is to study the intricate links between these dimensions if we want to fully understand the dynamics of the frontier process as well as past and current disputes over property rights. Most important, these case studies have revealed that "customary tenure" has never been a coherent and stable system of rules and beliefs, as many colonial officers and postcolonial policy makers wish to believe. Instead the term describes a repertoire of historically grounded arguments about ritual authority and property rights that is continually redefined and often contested. "Legal pluralism" is not exclusively the result of the colonial state's having introduced new ideas regarding land ownership. It also a product of the complex, longer-term dynamics of the frontier process and has characterized indigenous tenure from the very beginning. First-comer lineages, or individuals specialized in hunting, and late-comers who were more oriented toward agriculture, for instance, tended to hold different views on what

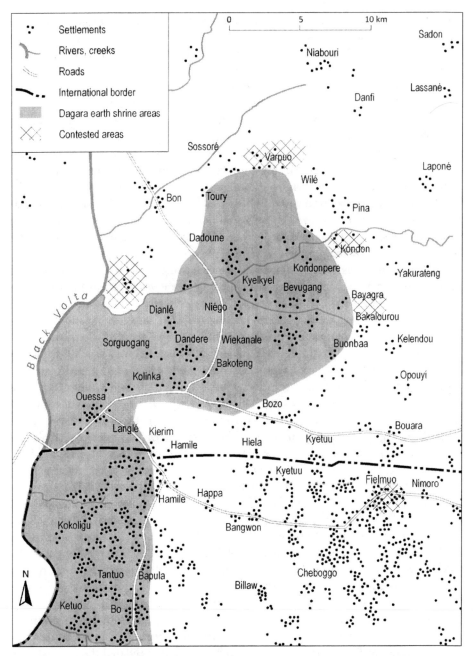

Map 2.3. Land east of the Black Volta under control of Dagara earth shrines

constituted the legitimate act of first possession from which property rights and ritual prerogatives were derived.

In the precolonial period, the segmentary societies of the Black Volta region had no overarching, generally recognized institutions that could successfully mediate between competing claims. Earth priests commanded some spiritual power, but there was always a way to challenge or circumvent their assertions of authority. Therefore, violence (or, in response, recourse to exit options and the search for "empty" territory) played an important role in establishing de facto control over land and other natural resources. However, in order to strengthen one's claims, creating consensus through persuasive narratives about first possession played an equally important role—not vis-à-vis violently displaced previous inhabitants, but vis-à-vis new immigrants and the latest-comers. Because of the absence of a superior political authority that could sanction such claims, these migration-and-settlement narratives rarely invoke any social contract (although they do mention human encounters and agreements), but rather locate the origin of property in the first-comers' pact with nature and the spiritual realm.

With regard to the eastern frontier of Dagara expansion that is the empirical focus of this book, a careful analysis of these competing narratives allows us to distinguish three phases of earth-shrine-related politics. The first covered the time until the beginning of the colonial regime, and was characterized by the "autochthonization" of newcomers, who managed to acquire full ritual authority and property rights over their new habitat—even though the previous inhabitants sometimes may have subsequently attempted to reclaim their original property. There were several ways in which an allodial title could be established. In some cases, the Dagara frontiersmen did in fact move into uninhabited territory, or successfully drove the previous inhabitants away and established their own earth shrine, often around a stone that they had carried along from their original village. In many cases, however, the Dagara pioneers established themselves alongside the previous (Sisala) inhabitants. Sometimes, they received the allodial title to the land together with an earth-shrine stone from the Sisala, usually in exchange for some substantial gifts (although the previous owners tended to later deny that this exchange ever took place). In other cases, they acquired only the land and placed it under the protection of an existing Dagara earth shrine. In a few cases, however, mounting tensions with the custodians of this older earth shrine, or unexpected problems such as inexplicable deaths, lack of drinking water, or drought, impelled the new settlers to acquire from their Sisala neighbors an additional shrine stone, replacing—or complementing—the Dagara earth shrine.

These strategies of extending existing earth-shrine areas or, when confronted with competing property claims, negotiating with the Sisala for an allodial title, continued into the second, intermediate phase, lasting approximately until the 1920s. During this second phase, the Sisala sometimes seem to have ritually validated the expansion of Dagara property claims by accepting substantial gifts in exchange for the additional land put under Dagara authority, but generally they no longer gave earth-shrine stones